Date   Due

LYNDON B. JOHNSON: THE EXERCISE OF POWER

LYNDON B. JOHNSON: THE EXERCISE OF POWER

A POLITICAL BIOGRAPHY BY

Rowland Evans & Robert Novak

 THE NEW AMERICAN LIBRARY

GC

GC

C11182

TABLE
OF CONTENTS

★★★★★★★★★★
INTRODUCTION
★★★★★★★★★★

To chronicle in definitive fashion Lyndon Johnson's long career would require many volumes. A definitive study of even so short a period as the first three turbulent years of his presidency could not be contained within the covers of a single book.

Nor have we attempted a personal biography. We have purposely omitted all but the briefest mention of his family background, his youth, and his young manhood. We scarcely touch upon the six years he served in the House of Representatives, a period deserving detailed study. We are not concerned here with his personal fortune, his private life, his living habits, or, except for its impingement on public affairs, his personality.

What we deal with in this book is the Public Person as contrasted to the Private Person. Specifically, we have attempted to show how the Public Person sought, achieved, and dispensed power, particularly after he became Senate Democratic Leader in January, 1953. This, then, is both a study of political power and a political biography.

We have counted heavily on primary source material. This being in no sense an authorized biography, we have had no privileged access to the Johnson files. Instead, we have relied on two major sources of primary material.

The first is our own personal observation as political reporters in Washington during all but a fragment of the period covered by this book. Our tenure as Capitol Hill correspondents—Evans from 1953 to 1963 and Novak from 1957 to 1963—embraces Johnson's entire tenure as Democratic Leader in the Senate. Those were the years during which we watched every maneuver of the Majority Leader with fascination and no little admiration, and talked to him regularly on the Senate floor, in his ever more splendid Senate offices, and at the LBJ Ranch in Texas, where we enjoyed the rich experience of his and Mrs. Johnson's hospitality.

Our second primary source consists of more than two hundred separate interviews we conducted from January, 1965, to the spring of

1966 specifically for this book. Those interviewed—political allies and political enemies, present aides and former aides, government officials high and low, political leaders and close friends—are our anonymous collaborators. They were indispensable and, although many, perhaps most of them, would prefer not to be listed here, we are in their debt. To them we give our grateful and sincere thanks.

We shall, however, list our generous colleagues in the Washington press corps who helped fill in the gaps of our information and provided fresh insights: Douglas Kiker and Andrew J. Glass of the *New York Herald Tribune*, Philip Geyelin of the *Wall Street Journal*, Alvin Spivak of United Press International, Joe Hall of the Associated Press, Philip Potter of the *Baltimore Sun*, and Hugh Sidey and Loye Miller of *Time*. We are also indebted to Michael C. Janeway of the *Atlantic Monthly*, who made available to us his unpublished paper, "Lyndon Johnson and the Rise of Conservatism in Texas," which proved most helpful in understanding Johnson's pre-Senate period.

Mary Jo Pyles, our assistant, did a painstaking professional job of research on varied aspects of this book, as well as devoting weary hours at all times of the day and night to type our manuscript. Geraldine Williams Novak meticulously researched and catalogued secondary sources dealing with Johnson's Senate career. Other essential research of secondary sources was performed for us by Sophie Burnham, Eugene Meyer, and Rima Meyer.

Our special appreciation goes to Robert A. Gutwillig of The New American Library, an editor whose discriminating pencil, resourcefulness, and encouragement were invaluable to us. We are indebted to him for his suggestions, his enthusiasm, and his willingness to travel from New York to Washington on a moment's notice to give us his assistance.

Finally, for their infinite patience and fortitude during our nighttime and weekend work on this book, we thank our wives, Katherine and Geraldine.

Rowland Evans
Robert Novak

September, 1966

LYNDON B. JOHNSON:
THE
EXERCISE OF POWER

Chapter I

★★★★★★★★★★

THE
PRESIDENT

> To make the most of power for himself, a President must know
> what it is made of.
> —Richard E. Neustadt in *Presidential Power*

Unique among American statesmen and political leaders, Lyndon Baines Johnson has been near or at the center of power in Washington for all the great political events of our epoch. He arrived in the Capital in 1931, more than a year before Franklin D. Roosevelt, as a twenty-three-year-old secretary to a right-wing millionaire Congressman from Texas. Increasingly, as the years went by and his power grew, he placed his own distinctive touch on each of those events. Among the truly powerful legislative leaders in our history, he is the only one since James Madison who has become the Chief Executive. He succeeded where Henry Clay, Thomas Brackett Reed, and Robert A. Taft failed.

No man in American history became President with a greater relish for power or with more experience in its exercise than did Johnson. Nor did any President assume the office with a prospect so spectacular in its opportunities and so difficult by the very nature of his assumption.

"Men . . . love their martyrs," Dostoevsky wrote, "and honor those whom they have slain." On November 22, 1963, Johnson became President, but it was the martyred John F. Kennedy and the Kennedy legend that men loved. Kennedy left Johnson a plan in domestic affairs that was only partially completed, and this plan, energized by a national longing to atone for Kennedy's assassination, gave Johnson his matchless opportunity. With the same grasp of political genius that marked his earlier years as the Senate's Majority Leader, Johnson completed Kennedy's plan. Then, in unprecedented partnership with Congress, he carried it far forward with a plan of his own, the Great

Society, a social and economic blueprint for a unified, prosperous America that excited and impressed the American people not only because of its audacious sweep but because so much of it became law.

The difficulty was the memory of Kennedy that still haunted Lyndon Johnson many months after he had been elected President in his own right. Thus, in the late spring of 1966, fully two and a half years after Kennedy's assassination, Johnson called several Senators to the White House to discuss a political matter. The business concluded, Johnson set off on a long monologue about the war in Vietnam. He quoted Senator Wayne Morse of Oregon, his most vitriolic Democratic critic on the war, as having said that "the Great Society is dead." When he heard about that verdict of Morse's, said Johnson, he ordered the Budget Bureau to give him a lengthy memorandum showing the spectacular increases in federal spending for education, health, poverty, and other Great Society programs above the Kennedy years.

The President reached on his desk for the Budget Bureau memorandum, read the statistics to the Senators, and then said: "They say Jack Kennedy had style, but I'm the one who's got the bills passed."

That was a typical Johnson reaction to criticism and it contained a flash of self-revelation, exposing several truths about Lyndon Johnson: his ego, his hypersensitivity, his intensely personal reaction to his critics, his lack of taste in slighting the dead President, and his fierce sense of competition with everybody—including John Kennedy.

But there was another, far different Lyndon Johnson. In February, 1965, the new President dropped in unexpectedly on a birthday luncheon at the Capitol for Senator George Aiken of Vermont, the much-beloved senior Republican of the Senate. All the Senate leaders were there, and for Johnson it was a triumphal homecoming.

"A few months ago," he told his colleagues, "we lost our beloved leader and colleague of many years, Jack Kennedy, in a terrible tragedy. He left partially finished many things he thought were in the best interests of our country. I happened to be called upon to pick up the torch that he had to leave. I want on behalf of this country, and on his behalf—watching us from Heaven—to thank every member here for your help in carrying on some of the things he was leading us toward, especially the leaders at this table. I know he thanks you."

There was nothing contrived in those words. They were, in fact, an essence of the sentiment that marks the other Lyndon Johnson, spoken in the direct and unsophisticated idiom of the Texas hill country. Johnson was *both* men: the detractor of Kennedy and the keeper of Kennedy's memory, and herein lies part of the secret of his command of power. Johnson has shed many tears for himself and he has shed tears for others. Johnson has cursed his friends behind their backs and showered them with presents. Johnson has unmercifully berated his closest White House aides in the presence of others, and has shown infinite tenderness when the occasion fit his mood.

Johnson is bigger than life—bigger in both the good and the bad. It is part of the contradiction that conceals the inner man. He hungers for affection, but his ego constantly intrudes. He preaches humility, but often subverts it with his own exuberant arrogance. In a deliberate exaggeration, one of his admiring counselors says: "90 percent of what he does is right, and 90 percent of the way he does it is wrong."

The conflict between objective and performance, between the public posture of the President and the private manipulations of the politician, is the essence of the Johnson paradox. The lofty goal and the hard use of power to achieve it are essential components for any successful presidency, but Johnson often overstates the goal and overuses his power to achieve it. Sometimes these characteristics have been self-defeating for him; sometimes they have produced greater accomplishments than he had any right to expect.

But the road to those accomplishments has been a jagged one, twisting and turning to fit the shape of his shifting goals and objectives. In the spring of 1966, a friend gently chided Senator Richard B. Russell, the conservative Southern patriarch, about Lyndon Johnson. Why was it, asked the friend, that Lyndon Johnson, the President was so different from the Lyndon Johnson who had been Russell's protégé in the Senate. "I asked him that," Russell replied softly, "and he told me, 'Dick, I'm an older and a wiser man than I was then.'"

As one of the many political patrons of Johnson during his long career, Russell has had an enduring relationship with Johnson sustained by few other men and stretching over nearly two decades. But even Russell has felt the thrust and parry of Johnson's nature, receiving kindness and his scorn almost at the same time. The President telephoned Russell almost every day during Russell's long illness in 1965. But when Russell publicly predicted that Ho Chi Minh, the Communist leader of North Vietnam, would win any honest election in Vietnam, Johnson ridiculed him behind his back in the White House. With heavy sarcasm, Johnson asked: "Since when did Dick Russell become an expert on elections in Southeast Asia?"

Yet, it was not surprising that Johnson would react harshly, even to an old and enduring friend and patron, on the subject of Vietnam. For the war in Vietnam had confounded his presidency. It was the worst of all crises ever faced by Johnson. It was natural that Johnson instinctively lashed out at Russell's remarks in a personal fashion, for always, Johnson has placed himself at the center, with the world revolving around him. In 1964, he remarked to a Texas politician that "the trouble with de Gaulle is that he's got the biggest ego in the world." Johnson saw nothing inconsistent between this verdict and his words at a White House state dinner for a visiting prime minister. He introduced a member of the United States Supreme Court to his foreign guest this way: "Mr. Prime Minister, I want you to meet a member of *my* Supreme Court."

But a different Johnson went unexpectedly to the Indian Embassy in the spring of 1966 during the visit of Mrs. Indira Gandhi, the Indian Prime Minister, and stayed for dinner. He moved one guest, the wife of a Senator, close to tears with an unrehearsed after-dinner toast. In words both noble and awkward, he described his aspirations for the world. The contrast between the two leaders was vivid: Mrs. Gandhi, diminutive, patrician, the leader of a powerful, patriarchal Kashmiri family who spoke polished sentences in precise, Oxford English; and Johnson, ungainly in his vast bulk, a man from the stock of farmers in the remote back country of Texas. With simple dignity, Johnson drew the contrast between himself and Mrs. Gandhi. Here, the crass exhibitionism of a President boasting about "my" Supreme Court was nowhere to be seen. In its place was an unpretentious tenderness.

That tenderness connotes but one of the many Johnsons, through all of which there runs a common theme: the theme of power, unifying all his disparate sides. Whether exhibitionist or unpretentious, whether considerate or insensitive, the single thrust of his long career has been the acquisition and the use of power. Johnson was born with the instinct of power, and long before he reached the White House he knew exactly where it rested, how to obtain it, and, most important, how to exercise it—sometimes with restraint, sometimes without. This ponderous, protean Texan, with the forbidding look of a chain-gang boss, knows more about the sources of power in the political world of Washington than any President in this century. He can be as gentle and solicitous as a nurse, but as ruthless and deceptive as a riverboat gambler, with the veiled threat in his half-closed eyes. He has come a long way to the White House, and there is no harder road to travel anywhere in the world.

Chapter II

★★★★★★★★★★

THE
ROAD TO
THE SENATE

The people who are going to be crushed by this are the little guys—the little guy down in my district, say, who makes $21.50 a week driving a truck and has a decent house to live in now, cheap, because of Mr. Roosevelt. . . .

> —Lyndon B. Johnson, as quoted in the *New York Times* of April 12, 1945, on the death of Franklin D. Roosevelt

My feelings are well known in my district and in Washington. And Harry Truman knows I am against him on this program. I just don't think Congress should try to cram his program down the throats of Southern states. . . .

> —Lyndon B. Johnson in a 1948 campaign statement on the Truman civil rights program

Economist John Kenneth Galbraith, then the young deputy administrator of the Office of Price Administration, first met young Congressman Lyndon B. Johnson in Washington in 1941 and quickly identified him—along with California's Jerry Voorhis*—as one of the two young liberal Democrats in the House, now that "Old Dr. New Deal" had given way to "Dr. Win the War," in Franklin Roosevelt's phrase.

Johnson's dependability as a Roosevelt man was vividly demonstrated on December 13, 1943, when the House passed a bill that had the effect of raising the wartime price ceiling on petroleum by thirty-five cents a barrel. From oil-rich Texas, only two Congressmen—Johnson and Wright Patman, an old-fashioned Populist—voted against the bill. All fifteen other members of the Texas delegation recorded on the

---

* Voorhis was defeated for reelection to Congress in 1946 by Richard M. Nixon.

roll call voted "aye." Many years later Johnson was to describe that vote as the most difficult—and the most politically damaging back in Texas—in his whole career as a legislator.

Thus in the early 1940s Johnson's was one sure vote for FDR in Congress at a time when Roosevelt's hold on Capitol Hill had slipped badly. He was on intimate terms with a coterie of top-level and middle-level New Dealers. Back in Texas, the Tory Democrats excoriated him as Roosevelt's pinup boy. But was he really the fully committed liberal Galbraith thought him to be? The answer is as complex and contradictory as Lyndon Johnson himself.

Johnson's Texas was the rugged, poor hill country near Austin, not the rich Texas of oil wells, the ambitious Texas of great cities, or the old Texas of black farmhands working the sprawling plantations. Johnson's political heritage was from the Populist, not the Tory Democratic tradition (his grandfather was elected to the legislature as a Populist). Through his father (also a state legislator), he was befriended as a young man by Representative Sam Rayburn, a leader of the Texas Democratic party's liberal wing. Blessed with Rayburn's sponsorship, he spent two years in the mid thirties as state director of the National Youth Administration (NYA), under the tutelage of Aubrey Williams, a militant left-winger. The portrait of Johnson that emerges is of a typical Southern radical—a twentieth-century version of James Stephen Hogg, the great Populist Governor of Texas in the 1890s.

But there was another side to the early Johnson. In 1931, twenty-three-year-old Lyndon Johnson came to Washington (preceding Franklin Roosevelt by well over a year) as secretary to newly elected Congressman Richard Kleberg, part-owner of the fabulous King Ranch. Kleberg was an archetypal Texas plutocrat with political views to match. Yet, Johnson spent four apparently happy years working for reactionary Kleberg before returning to Texas to work for radical Williams in the NYA.

This was no hill-country boy hewing to doctrinaire Populist defiance of the moneyed classes. For although Sam Johnson had his lean years (including years when Lyndon had to work his way through Southwest Texas State Teachers College at San Marcos), the Johnson family never missed a meal. A hard existence, yes, but never unrelieved poverty. On the contrary, Sam Ealy Johnson was a member of an easily identified gentry in the Texas hill country. During World War I and the period preceding it, he was in the state legislature, whose membership was limited to those who could afford to live in Austin during the biennial sessions. Sam Johnson's seat was at one time held by his father-in-law, Joseph Baines. Variously a school-teacher, farmer-rancher, and businessman, Sam Johnson made and lost good-sized fortunes by Blanco County standards in agriculture, insurance, and real estate before his financial condition began a steady decline in the agricultural depression of 1921. Those lean years for the Johnson family were Lyndon Johnson's formative years, but the Johnsons were still gentry in Blanco County. Accordingly the Lyndon Johnson who grew up and came to Washington did not seethe with the class struggle or a scorn of wealth—but he did harbor a fierce ambition to achieve the financial security his father had lost. His philosophy was more out of Horatio Alger than Jim Hogg.

The Texas-style Populism that influenced Johnson so deeply derived not from any theory of class struggle but from a dollars-and-cents economic struggle with Wall Street. Texas then was still Cotton Texas. And Cotton Texas was under the financial control of the powerful Eastern money centers for its banking, its insurance, and its export financing. Here was a debtor state at war with Wall Street in a never-ending—and, in truth, never-successful—battle to whittle away Eastern financial control and bring down interest rates.

From this economic struggle stemmed political consequences. In the early New Deal, a major function of Sam Rayburn, the chairman of the House Commerce Committee, in establishing the Securities and Exchange Commission was to fire broadsides for Cotton Texas against Wall Street. Indeed, for the first forty years of the century, the struggle against the New York financial interests was a unifying political force in Texas. Jesse Jones was a Houston cotton millionaire and a conservative at heart. But he allied himself with the destitute small ranchers of Lyndon Johnson's hill country, to be the spokesman for debtor Texas. In this spirit, he could join Franklin Roosevelt's New Deal, become his Secretary of Commerce, and remain a Roosevelt man until the late 1930s.

There was then an ideological ambivalence in Johnson from the start. And thus his quick emergence as a New Deal Congressman must be described in political, not ideological, terms. The heart of it was shrewd electoral tactics. Resigning his NYA job, Johnson, at twenty-eight, was one of seven candidates who entered a special election on April 10, 1937, to fill the seat from the 10th Congressional District left vacant by the death of Representative James P. Buchanan. The leading vote-getter on April 10 would be the winner, with no necessity for a runoff. All the other candidates were anti-New Deal. And yet a district encompassing the University of Texas at Austin together with farms and ranches in need of water and electrical power that only the federal government could supply was not by nature totally hostile to the New Deal. Testing here and there, Johnson quickly found that the more he praised Roosevelt, the deeper he buried his opponents.

Had Johnson been among the horde of young Democratic candidates elected in the 1936 landslide just four months earlier, his victory would have attracted scant attention in the White House. But now, the New Deal was in decline. A Johnson triumph now would be a national political event. The reason, of course, was Roosevelt's sudden fall.

Overconfident following the 1936 election, in which he carried forty-six out of forty-eight states, and angered by the Supreme Court's nullification of so much New Deal legislation, Roosevelt committed the great political blunder of his career on February 5, 1937, by calling on Congress to enlarge the Supreme Court so that he could pack it with New Dealers. Within one week, Roosevelt's political instincts—functioning again, but too late—knew that the Court-packing plan was doomed to defeat in Congress and certain to erode his prestige. Nowhere was opposition harsher than in Texas. The state's two most famous Democrats, Senator Tom Connally and Vice-President John Nance Garner, were against the Court plan. Even loyal Sam Rayburn refused to support it.

Johnson, an unknown candidate in a special Texas election, unexpectedly embraced the Court plan without reservations (or request from the White House) at a time when most of the President's friends were racing for the lifeboats. Not realizing just how dead the Court plan was in Washington, Johnson in Texas was solidifying his New Deal support against his six anti-New Deal opponents. It carried him to victory. Roosevelt was more than gratified. He interrupted a vacation cruise in the Gulf of Mexico to meet Johnson in Galveston the day after the special election.

From this special election, and the beginning of his unique relationship with Roosevelt, flowed a cornucopia of political goodies. The electric power and water needed for his dry, resource-starved district came from the New Deal. Through Roosevelt's help, Johnson landed a seat on the House Naval Affairs Committee. In 1937 he formed political alliances in Washington that were to last a decade.

Alvin Wirtz, a liberal lawyer from Austin, Texas, twenty years Johnson's senior and fast becoming his closest political adviser, showed him how to translate Washington influence into political dividends back home. Wirtz's law firm was assigned principal control over part of Samuel Insull's wide-ranging public utilities empire after Insull's fall—including a half-built Colorado River dam in Johnson's district.

Wirtz encouraged Johnson to obtain federal funds to finish the dam. Johnson succeeded. Moreover, Wirtz and Johnson saw to it that the contract for the dam went to a rising team of Texas contractors—the brothers George and Herman Brown.

But most important, the doors were opened to the great and near-great—to the Princes of the New Deal who usually didn't come within miles of a freshman Congressman. In separate conversations, Roosevelt remarked to those two feuding chieftains of the New Deal, Harold Ickes and Harry Hopkins, that here was a young man Franklin Roosevelt might have been—if he hadn't been saddled with a Harvard education! Further, the President added, young Johnson could well become the first President from the South since the Civil War. Ickes and Hopkins got the message and began introducing Johnson around and doing him little favors.

Slowly, Johnson began to assemble a stable of non-Texas advisers— some to last a generation, some to be shucked off quickly. Hopkins introduced him to a shrewd Wall Street lawyer named Edwin Weisl, who was deeply impressed by Johnson. Secretary of the Interior Ickes put him in touch with two brilliant men in their late twenties—a young lawyer from Memphis named Abe Fortas, then working his way up the ladder in the Interior Department, and Eliot Janeway, then business editor of *Time* and an unofficial economic adviser to Ickes. Weisl, Fortas, Janeway—all were called upon by the young Congressman for advice, as were FDR's Young Guard from the White House and the new Securities and Exchange Commission (through Johnson's interlocking relationships with both Rayburn and Roosevelt).

Apart from the fact that Sam Johnson had served with Sam Rayburn in the Texas legislature and backed Rayburn for Speaker in 1909, Lyndon Johnson had been attentive to Rayburn during his stint as Kleberg's secretary in the House. As chairman of the House Commerce Committee during Roosevelt's Hundred Days of 1933, Rayburn was midwife at the birth of the SEC. Thus the Rayburn link, together with Roosevelt's own sponsorship, put Johnson in close touch with SEC Chairman William O. Douglas and the young White House aides of the later New Deal—Ben Cohen, Thomas (Tommy the Cork) Corcoran, James Rowe.

The Johnson these powerful men came to know and admire was a tall, lanky, black-haired young man with a thin, straight-line mouth between two unforgettable features—a chin that jutted far out and slightly up from the lower jaw, with a deep cleft in the middle, and a large overhanging nose with wide nostrils. The face was long and thin

in those early days, and it was flanked by two very large ears with
long, hanging lobes. Entirely dominating this angular landscape were
the eyes: dark, intense, and slightly menacing. To those he courted,
such as Roosevelt's bright young men, Johnson was ingratiating, gay,
cocksure, and, on occasion, hilariously funny. To the rest of the world,
his manner changed with his mood and his mood was frequently
overbearing. He chain-smoked, he combed his glistening hair straight
back, and he fancied gabardine suits a cut too big for him, with the
trousers worn long. He wore shirts with extra-long collars and exotic
ties with small, hard knots.

Above all, Johnson loved to talk—but his only topic was politics, the
affairs of government and power. Exuberantly self-confident in dealing with the mightiest of the New Deal, the freshman Congressman
betrayed his nervous energy by his inability to sit still and his insistence on doing something, going someplace, seeing someone. Soon
much of Washington was hearing from him. At Christmastime, government officials who scarcely knew the young couple from Texas
were amazed when fat holiday turkeys arrived from Lyndon and
Lady Bird Johnson.

This fast-moving, gabby young Texan fascinated the White House
inner staff. But Roosevelt's men had no illusion about his ideological
commitment. They knew very well that Johnson's proximity to Roosevelt and his consistent support for New Deal programs were pragmatic, not ideological. Johnson, they suspected, was a young man of
infinite practicality, unencumbered with theory. His admiration for
Roosevelt—as viewed by Roosevelt's staff—was regard for action and
power, more than for ideology. Roosevelt was Johnson's idol. Johnson
consciously began to imitate the President's imperious manner and colorful speech patterns. He studied with fascination how FDR played
off subordinates, one against the other. Quite apart from Roosevelt,
Johnson was even then developing the changing series of father-
son relationships that marked his early political career—relationships
tinged with a characteristically Southern respect for elders but almost
always related to the nature of political power. What Congressman
Johnson did was to find the font of power in each of his undertakings
and then set out on a deliberate courtship: Roosevelt, as his President
and party leader; Rayburn, as House Majority Leader; Georgia's
crusty Representative Carl Vinson, chairman of the House Naval
Affairs Committee on which Roosevelt had wangled a seat for Johnson. In each of these relationships (particularly the Vinson one),
Johnson was the aggressive partner.

How much attention Johnson paid to the details of these father-son relationships is suggested by the birthday surprise he planned for Rayburn in the late 1930s. Johnson convinced his friends on the White House staff, Corcoran and Rowe, that it would be politically profitable for Roosevelt—and a mighty nice thing for Rayburn—if Roosevelt gave Rayburn a surprise new hat for his birthday. Where? In the President's Oval Office, of course. Rowe drafted a memo to the President, and he and Corcoran persuaded him on the idea. Johnson purchased the hat and invited the major committee chairmen in the House and a few Texas Congressmen. According to plan, Roosevelt telephoned Rayburn, fibbing that he was in a frightful jam and needed help at once. That drew Rayburn into the Oval Office for the surprise party.

The net gain for the young Congressman from Texas: a front-page newspaper picture showing him in the Oval Office with Rayburn and Roosevelt; a debt of gratitude from Rayburn; a pocketful of political IOUs from the Congressmen Johnson had slipped into the White House; and a growing conviction among the Washington power structure that here was an operator.

Johnson was Roosevelt's man in those early years—with a clear priority for Roosevelt over Rayburn and Vinson. Occasionally his father-son relationships competed with each other, as when Roosevelt used Johnson to run political errands. Just before World War II, high naval officers, angered by the fact that syndicated columnist Walter Winchell seemed to be exploiting his lieutenant commander's commission in the U.S. Naval Reserve, encouraged Vinson to launch a congressional investigation. No friend of Winchell, and usually attentive to the naval brass on such a question, Vinson was willing. But Roosevelt wanted no congressional manhandling of one of the few columnists supporting his interventionist policies toward the European war. "Daddy" Roosevelt used Johnson to quash the investigation, requiring Johnson to differ with "Daddy" Vinson. There was no investigation.

Johnson found himself in a more serious conflict of father-son relationships during the maneuvering over Vice-President Garner in 1940. John Nance Garner, representing the Tory wing of the Texas Democratic party, had been drifting ever further from the New Deal. He was out of the question as running mate in 1940, should Roosevelt try for a third term. More to the point in 1939, since few expected Roosevelt to run again, Garner—with Jesse Jones supplying money and advice—was building up steam as the anti-New Deal candidate for the Democratic presidential nomination.

That was the background in July, 1939, when labor leader John L. Lewis gave reporters his celebrated description of Garner as a "poker-playing, whiskey-drinking, evil old man." Garner immediately asked

Rayburn, the House Majority Leader, to repudiate this statement with a resolution by the Texas congressional delegation supporting him, thus rebuking Lewis. New Dealer Rayburn had grown a world apart from Garner since managing his campaign for President at the 1932 convention. Still, Rayburn knew that to be elected Speaker* he might need help from Garner, a former Speaker of the House who was still close to conservative Democratic Congressmen. Carefully calculating the impact on his own fortunes, Rayburn called the Texas delegation together and asked each Texan to sign a resolution supporting Garner and rebuking Lewis.

What Rayburn didn't know was that Roosevelt didn't want the resolution passed. But instead of confiding in Rayburn, Roosevelt murmured into the ear of Lyndon B. Johnson. Thus, it was Johnson who spoiled the careful Garner-Rayburn plot by refusing, in front of all the Texas Democrats, to sign. Later, he held his ground during a heated private argument with Rayburn. When "Daddy" Roosevelt and "Daddy" Rayburn collided, Johnson picked the White House. That's where the power was.

The battle between Johnson and Rayburn continued. In 1940 the Garner and Jones right-wing forces back in Texas proposed a serious plan to stop Roosevelt at the Chicago convention. Rayburn came up with a compromise: split the Texas delegation in thirds—one-third for Roosevelt, one-third for Garner, and one-third neutral. That wasn't good enough for Roosevelt. Calling signals for the President were Tommy Corcoran in the White House and Harold Ickes at Interior. The receivers: Lyndon Johnson and Johnson's closest political confidant, Alvin Wirtz, who had been brought to Washington as Ickes' Under Secretary of the Interior at Johnson's behest.

According to the White House plan, the Texas delegation would issue a statement pledging not to engage in a Stop Roosevelt movement. The statement would be issued at the White House jointly by Rayburn and Johnson. Unwilling to be coupled with a very junior Congressman, Majority Leader Rayburn balked. Johnson, backed by the prestige of the White House, insisted. Rayburn succumbed. Ickes described the finale in his diaries:

> When Johnson and Rayburn appeared in the President's office that afternoon, he told them benignly that they had been good little boys and that they had "papa's blessing." He treated them as political equals with the malicious intent of disturbing Sam Rayburn's state of mind. I think that he succeeded.

* Rayburn was elected Speaker on September 16, 1940, upon the death of William Bankhead of Alabama.

It is understandable, then, that while Roosevelt was singing Johnson's praises all over Washington, Rayburn was a bit more reticent about his old friend's son—White House birthday party or not. Old associates in the House do not remember Rayburn touting Johnson as a comer in that era. Nor does anyone remember that Rayburn performed many special favors for Johnson. On the contrary, when Johnson wanted a Texas vacancy on the powerful House Appropriations Committee, Rayburn made no move to intercede for him. As a result, strict seniority was followed, and the Texas delegation backed Representative Albert Thomas. The father-son relationship between Johnson and Rayburn was not to mature fully for another decade.

But why did Johnson turn to the White House rather than to his fellow Texan, the most important man in the House? Simply because Johnson's future, as he already had it measured and mapped, did not lie in the House. The tortuous climb up the seniority ladder, some twenty years' apprenticeship at Sam Rayburn's knee, were not for Johnson. The Senate was his goal—and, for a statewide race, Roosevelt's political charisma was worth more than Sam Rayburn's congressional patronage.

So it was that the young Congressman who basked in the bright light of Harold Ickes, Harry Hopkins, and William Douglas was a shadowy, unmemorable figure in the House itself, known well only to his fellow Texans, to members of the Naval Affairs Committee, and to a few others. Preoccupied with his luminous new friends in FDR's Young Guard, Johnson wasted no time hanging around the lobby outside the House chamber. To his fellow Congressmen of late New Deal days, he is but a dim memory.

His few friends in the House knew from the beginning he was waiting for his chance at the Senate, and that chance came when Senator Morris Sheppard of Texas died on April 9, 1941. A special election to pick his successor was set for June 28. The White House was militantly behind Johnson, the President himself discussing the election with Johnson. Tommy Corcoran, looking forward to a Texas Democratic party more friendly to Roosevelt, regarded Johnson as the way to get it. And, despite his tiff with Johnson a year earlier, Rayburn urged him on. Rayburn detested the Texas Tories. The New Deal tone of the campaign was reinforced when Johnson announced his candidacy from the very steps of the White House—where Roosevelt gave him a tacit endorsement.

But by accepting the President's blessing, Johnson was also accepting the cramped position that always hampers a pro-administration candidate. While his opponents could swing wildly, Johnson was confined within the limits of the Roosevelt policy. His speeches took on a somber, preachy tone, with the young Congressman admonishing both labor and business to stand behind Roosevelt in a time of national emergency. Johnson's lack of fire contrasted sharply with the brassy campaign of his principal opponent: demagogic, isolationist Governor W. Lee (Pass the Biscuits Pappy) O'Daniel, an under-educated grain salesman from Kansas who had been elected Governor eight months earlier on a lurid program of pension promises. Now, campaigning from a flatbed truck with a country band whooping it up behind him, Pappy O'Daniel played to the rising conservatism of Texas. He flayed the New Deal as a "gang of back-slapping, pie-eating, pussy-footing professional politicians who couldn't run a peanut stand." In response to O'Daniel's attacks, Johnson wrapped about himself the great names of the day. ". . . that Roosevelt-Rayburn program that I'm called a Nazi dupe, a CIO lawyer and . . . a yes-man . . . for following. I can say 'yes' to Roosevelt and Rayburn and Hull and Willkie on that program."

Although Johnson led by 5,000 votes the day after election, the margin steadily shrank as "corrected" returns poured in from rural counties. Four days later, O'Daniel was declared the winner over Johnson by a margin of 1,311 votes (out of more than 600,000 cast). When Johnson returned to Washington, Roosevelt needled him. The first thing *he* had learned in New York politics, he said, was to sit on the ballot boxes until the ballots were counted. Johnson learned that lesson himself from his 1941 defeat—but he also learned a deeper lesson: to run in Texas as an unwashed Roosevelt New Dealer was becoming less and less a political asset. That he had learned that lesson he kept to himself.

Shortly before Johnson's defeat in 1941, Abe Fortas, now a rising New Deal bureaucrat, invited guests to his apartment to meet his friend Lyndon Johnson. Talking incessantly and striding back and forth across the apartment floor, Congressman Johnson was consumed with one subject: defense preparedness. With Hitler on the march, he argued, it was essential for the U.S. to cast aside neutralism and prepare for war.

Although that was the approved Roosevelt line, Lyndon Johnson happened to believe it deeply himself. As a member of the Naval Affairs Committee, defense was his specialty. But beyond that, the preparedness issue was the obvious solution for the political problem that had now begun to torment Lyndon Johnson and that was not to be subdued for almost a generation. The problem, in a word, was **Texas.**

It was easy enough for Johnson to speak for his hill-country Texas as a hard-line New Dealer. But Oil Texas, Urban Texas, and Cotton Texas—the Texas of political power and financial ambition—had moved far beyond the New Deal's influence. The onetime land of the Populists was becoming the land of the oil buccaneers, who were battling government restraints and were wedded to a new laissez-faire. Texas was moving to the right. New Deal Congressman Maury Maverick of San Antonio, who, like Johnson, had supported Roosevelt's Court-packing scheme, was unseated in the 1938 elections.

As FDR's protégé, Johnson was not prepared to slip entirely out from under the New Deal. But how then could he have any chance at all as a statewide candidate for the Senate? The answer was—or seemed to be—the preparedness issue. Johnson had tried to avoid the domestic issues that divided liberals from conservatives in his 1941 Senate race and, from the vantage point of his seat on the Naval Affairs Committee, had concentrated on preparedness, claiming that his defense expertise was needed in the Senate. A month before that election day, Johnson and Roosevelt went through an elaborate charade to dramatize the darkening storm in Europe. In a well-publicized telegram to the President, Johnson asked whether the international crisis required his presence back in Washington. Roosevelt replied that the Texas Senate campaign—and, by implication, Johnson's part in it—was a "convincing demonstration of our democratic processes at work." The meaning was clear: Johnson should continue his campaign.*

As it turned out, the preparedness issue wasn't quite enough to overcome both the rising tide of Texas conservatism and O'Daniel's quick-fingered ballot-counters. Johnson had lost his first race for the Senate, the place that was to make him such a formidable political figure. After a five-month leave from Congress as a U.S. Naval Reserve officer immediately following Pearl Harbor, Johnson was reelected to the House in 1942, his fourth straight victory, and, returning there in 1943, sounded the preparedness issue harder than ever. That meant new prominence for Carl Vinson, chairman of the Naval Affairs Committee, in Johnson's constantly shifting relationships with Washington's men of power. Vinson now became Johnson's vital patron.

The Naval Affairs Committee had its own permanent investigating subcommittee run by a member with far more seniority than Johnson's. Nevertheless, Johnson persuaded Vinson to set up a special in-

---

* During the campaign, O'Daniel applied his own brand of corn to the preparedness issue by proposing that a separate Army, Air Force, and Navy be established by the State of Texas to guard its borders against invasion from Mexico. At Johnson's request, Roosevelt dispatched a telegram calling O'Daniel's proposal "preposterous."

vestigating subcommittee on the progress of the war. Its chairman?
None other than Lyndon B. Johnson. Johnson knew that the success or
failure of any investigation depends on the committee's chief counsel,
and he knew that the counsel for his committee must have two special
qualifications: he would have to be nonpolitical, and because of notorious Navy prejudices in the early 1940s, he would have to be non-
Jewish. Johnson telephoned his old friend William Douglas, who had
left the SEC to become an Associate Justice of the Supreme Court,
to ask for the loan of the best lawyer he could think of. In a fortuitous choice, Douglas sent over a thirty-three-year-old SEC utilities
analyst named Donald C. Cook—a coldly analytical lawyer from
Michigan who at that time had no interest at all in party politics.

Johnson gave Cook a free hand, with results that extended far beyond the work of the special investigating subcommittee. The Johnson-
Cook partnership flowered periodically over the next twenty years.
Moreover, the objectivity and thoroughness of the Johnson subcommittee's investigation, even though overshadowed in publicity by Senator Harry Truman's defense investigation, established Johnson as an
authority in the realm of defense.* The investigation put Johnson in
day-to-day contact with the highest officers in the Navy, a contact that
often transforms Congressmen who specialize in defense matters into
apologists for the military. The impact on Johnson was quite the opposite. His acute awareness of anti-Semitism in the Navy officer class
revealed his lack of illusion about the admirals, and what few illusions
he might have had were soon abandoned. He came to feel that naval
officers were unimaginative, often disorganized and misinformed, and
never to be solely relied upon in a time of national peril. That lack of
confidence in the upper military echelons was never to leave Johnson.

Later, during the postwar battling over the size of the military
force, Johnson found himself in a paradoxical situation. Despite his
well-concealed distaste for the military, he became a noisy advocate,
in sharp opposition to President Truman, of high military budgets
and, most particularly, of a big seventy-group Air Force. One reason
for this lay in the weapons revolution that accompanied World War
II. Almost overnight, a vast new industry—the aircraft industry—
sprang up, with unlimited demands on the federal dollar. Because of
successive engineering advances, the new aircraft industry promised
to become one of the most important and profitable in the country.
Ferocious competition for military contracts quickly built up political

* One of the Johnson subcommittee's reports was critical of the terms obtained
by the Navy in leasing some of its oil reserves to Standard Oil Company of California. The Navy official in charge was Adlai E. Stevenson, then an assistant to

pressures of explosive potential, and in the center of this competition was the State of Texas.

Apart from his identification as a New Dealer, Johnson's main problem in Texas during the 1940s was the lack of political and financial support from the oil and gas industry. Now, in the postwar years, Texas oil was on the march—supplanting cotton as the state's most politically potent industry, an almost unlimited source of campaign dollars to its political friends and a terror to its political enemies.

Tight government regulation preventing high profits to any single operator had reduced the political influence of oil during World War II. But with war's end came the oil and gas boom. Cotton Texas was overwhelmed by Oil Texas, and the historic debtor mentality was replaced by a wheeler-dealer mentality, backed by millions of oil dollars. The new-rich oil men needed reliable politicians. They acquired them by wholesale buying of the state's captive Mexican and Negro vote. The oil interests not only paid the voters' poll taxes but subsidized their leaders as well.

Even the leading political figures of Cotton Texas were in jeopardy at the hands of the oil buccaneers. Sam Rayburn himself, now the Speaker of the House, was not immune. With the war nearing its end, Oil Texas launched a serious effort to unseat Rayburn in the 1944 election. Although Rayburn had been prominently mentioned as Roosevelt's running mate that year, he was so alarmed by the oil threat that he stayed in his district until after the Democratic National Convention started in Chicago, thereby killing any chance he'd had for the ticket.

As it turned out, the oil lobby wasn't strong enough to purge Rayburn from his rural north Texas district in 1944, but it had gained considerably more political muscle by 1952, when conservative Tom Connally, the most powerful political remnant of Cotton Texas, was up for reelection to the Senate. Connally, a ranking member of the Senate's Inner Circle and chairman of the Foreign Relations Committee, looked like a Hollywood version of a Southern Senator, with string bowtie and flowing white hair. As Jesse Jones was economic agent for Cotton Texas, Tom Connally was political agent. But he failed to make an accommodation with the state's new political elite. The result of this lack of foresight came, quite literally, in a Texas back room one day early in 1952. Displaying the cash they had col-

---

Secretary of the Navy Frank Knox. Ironically, Johnson was in the position of criticizing Stevenson for being too soft on an oil company. A decade later, Johnson was to attack presidential candidate Stevenson for being antagonistic to the oil industry.

lected to beat him in the Democratic primary, oil's political operatives told Connally the harsh facts of postwar life and simply bludgeoned him out of running.

Lyndon Johnson was determined not to suffer Tom Connally's fate. Although oil men generally regarded Johnson as considerably less dependable than Connally, Johnson soon managed to forge an invaluable link with the new world of gas and oil.

The ambitions of Johnson's up-and-coming friends in the contracting business, George and Herman Brown, went far beyond building dams. The Browns' newly formed Texas Eastern Transmission Corporation emerged as a power in the oil industry after the war when it bought the famed Big Inch Pipeline, built during World War II by the federal government under Harold Ickes' direction to transport Texas oil to the East Coast. On February 14, 1947, the government approved the sale of the Big Inch Pipeline (now converted to transportation of natural gas to the lucrative Eastern market) and the Little Big Inch Pipeline to the Browns' Texas Eastern for $143,127,000. New powers in the oil and gas industry, and already linked to Johnson, they quickly plunged ever deeper into Democratic politics—and became Lyndon Johnson's personal vehicle for a lateral movement into the center of the new oil power. Tom Connally could not do it, but Johnson, with his ties to the Browns, could.

A few years later, Johnson found another vital link to Oil Texas: handsome, debonair John B. Connally (no kin to the Senator). Like Johnson, John Connally came from a family of modest means, growing up in Populistic rural Texas. After a stint in Washington as Congressman Lyndon B. Johnson's administrative assistant, Connally returned to Texas to practice law in a unique Austin firm of political liberals headed by Alvin Wirtz (long since resigned as Under Secretary of the Interior to make room for Abe Fortas). Connally acquired the political coloration of Wirtz—an old-fashioned rural liberalism that was suspicious of, or even hostile to, organized labor, but was wedded to the idea of federal aid for power dams, rural electrification, and irrigation. Moreover, Wirtz was a passionately loyal Democrat, and in those days, so was Connally. As late as June, 1951, when General Douglas MacArthur, fired by Truman as U.S. Commander in Korea, was conducting a triumphal speaking tour of Texas, conservative Democrats were talking about backing him for President on the 1952 Republican ticket. Connally refused to go to San Antonio to hear MacArthur's speech.

But that fall, Wirtz suffered a heart attack and died at the age of sixty-three. His death changed the entire complexion of the law firm and removed its driving force. Without Wirtz and his stimulating energies, Connally lost interest in the firm and started looking for another job. He found it with conservative oil millionaire Syd Richardson. Connally caught Richardson's fancy, and at Richardson's death became executor of his estate—and in the process a millionaire himself. Growing more conservative in principle as well as in political alliances, Connally shed his old Democratic loyalty in 1952 to support Republican Dwight D. Eisenhower for President. He thus became Johnson's second major link to conservative Oil Texas—and just at the time when Alvin Wirtz, Johnson's old friend and deepest influence among the Texas liberals, was gone. Long before this, however, Johnson had made another try for the Senate in 1948, and the Brown brothers by themselves could scarcely make the oil and gas barons his allies. With the whole spectrum of Texas politics moving fast to the right, Johnson needed additional protection and new sources of political financing. It was in his search for this new political support that Johnson's long record in the field of preparedness began to pay dividends.

A new giant, the aircraft industry, was rising on the Texas plains with an even greater stake in Washington's decisions than oil. Johnson's support of Secretary of the Air Force Stuart Symington and General Hoyt Vandenberg, the Air Force Chief of Staff, in battling Truman for more and more bombers, was not inconsistent with Johnson's record as champion of preparedness in Congress. But it had the happy side effect of attracting large sums of campaign money (helped along not a little by Symington) into Johnson's war chest—now building for his second try at the Senate. The overall effect was to compensate for Johnson's lack of oil money.

But as Johnson became more and more a defense specialist in the mid-1940s, he also became less visible in the changing Washington power structure. Roosevelt was dead, and his effervescent Young Guard was dissolved. Under Harry Truman, a more pedestrian crew occupied the White House—serious young men in whom Johnson showed little interest, perhaps because, like most politicians at that time, he regarded the Truman Administration as a brief transitional government. Although he was growing closer again to Rayburn, and the indignities of 1940 were fading, Johnson remained a remote figure in the House. He showed little interest in the impossible task of pushing Truman's program through a hostile Congress. His major business on the floor of the House was an occasional speech demanding a seventy-group Air Force.

It was only in the House Armed Services Committee (successor after 1946 to the Naval Affairs Committee) that Johnson was a formidable figure—a thirty-eight-year-old veteran of ten years in Congress with slightly terrifying self-confidence and undiminished brashness. When a hostile witness testified on a major military bill, Johnson occasionally would set his alarm wristwatch to sound off at a moment calculated to deflate the witness. His aggressiveness sometimes placed "Daddy" Carl Vinson—the chairman—in the position of following Johnson instead of leading him.

For example, in the 1947–48 Republican-controlled 80th Congress, an incisive ex-Army major named Bryce Harlow was appointed chief counsel of the Armed Services Committee. Soon thereafter, during a closed-door committee session, Harlow delivered a detailed Army-style staff memo explaining a pending bill. Without warning, Johnson jumped in with a vicious personal attack on the whole committee staff, including Harlow. Vinson, who was no amateur at tongue-lashing, joined in the attack. Harlow was silent but incensed. After the hearing adjourned, he asked Vinson to instruct the staff exactly what he expected from them—or to hire a new staff. Vinson said it would not happen again. He had only meant to humor Johnson, he told Harlow.

That was Harlow's second run-in with Johnson. In their first encounter, Johnson interrupted Harlow's routine explanation of a minor bill to inquire pointedly whether the bill affected the Reconstruction Finance Corporation—although the bill had not the slightest apparent connection with the RFC. When a befuddled Harlow replied that he hadn't checked the point, Johnson demanded that the committee chairman postpone action on the bill until a "proper investigation" was made.

This harsh personal treatment of Harlow was merely Johnson's way of setting up situations to test Harlow's reflexes, to discover how tough he was. When Johnson satisfied himself about Harlow, they developed a close relationship. But this sort of insensitive treatment of staff members—both in his own office and in his committees—was a personality trait that disfigured every step of Johnson's political rise, all the way to the White House. It is significant that Harlow, though an admirer of Johnson, twice turned down invitations to join his personal staff.

While occasionally hazing staff members, Johnson was also perfecting the art of political back-scratching, often concentrating on Republicans. Thruston B. Morton of Kentucky, for example, long remembered his maiden speech in the House in 1947. Attendance was low, interest lower. The subject was a bill on disposal of the government's surplus rubber plants. Fellow Republicans gossiped with each other.

But Johnson carefully listened and then rose to commend Morton and pledge his support on the point at issue. It was a kindness Morton never forgot, and that, as he climbed the ladder to become an Assistant Secretary of State, a U.S. Senator, and chairman of the Republican National Committee, he had ample opportunity to repay.*

All through these House years Lyndon Johnson's eyes remained on the Senate—and the problem of winning a statewide race in Texas. Now, in his second attempt, he began to do what he would not do in 1941: move rightward with his state, and move fast.

Johnson's overt move to the right may be said to have started in earnest the day of Roosevelt's death. The end of the war was in sight, to be followed eventually by a postwar conservative reaction. Now was the time to shed the New Deal raiment, and as any Democrat had to do if he was ever to be U.S. Senator from Texas, plunge into the mainstream of Texas state politics. In postwar Texas, the mainstream hugged the right-hand bank.

The tip-off came in a *New York Times* interview with Johnson on April 12, 1945—the day of Roosevelt's death. The thirty-six-year-old Johnson was selected by the *Times* as a typical member of Roosevelt's New Guard. He responded with the usual statements of grief and spoke the words that years later would be repeated in a thousand studies of Johnson: "He was just like a daddy to me always." But deeper in the story, Johnson went on in words that had an undeniably defensive quality:

> They called the President a dictator and some of us they called "yes" men. Sure, I yessed him plenty of times—because I thought he was right—and I'm not sorry for a single "yes" I ever gave. I have seen the President in all kinds of moods—at breakfast, at lunch, at dinner—and never once in my five terms did he ever ask me to vote a certain way, or even suggest it. And when I voted against him—as I have plenty of times—he never said a word.

No question about Johnson's grief that day. It was deeply felt. But in his short statement, the automatic, involuntary workings of Lyndon Johnson's political reflexes were discernible. The man who was at

---

* Although Johnson's public kindness toward a young Republican Congressman was unusual, his support for the bill was not. The rubber industry lobbied all Texas Congressmen vociferously, promising to construct rubber plants in Texas towns if rubber manufacturers were allowed to buy the surplus government plants.

FDR's beck-and-call—even to frustrate Sam Rayburn—chose the day of Roosevelt's death to claim his independence of Roosevelt and point out that he never once was asked for a vote by FDR—and in fact often opposed him. Was Johnson looking ahead, quite probably subconsciously, to the new postwar Texas?

Even before the end of World War II, Johnson's own financial status was undergoing profound change. When Johnson returned to Washington in 1942 after his hitch in the Navy, he was neither on the brink of poverty nor financially independent. Most of what little wealth he had was a legacy that Claudia Taylor, whom he married in 1934, inherited from her mother. That inheritance has been variously estimated as between $20,000 and $45,000. By 1943, Lady Bird Johnson's net worth was officially stated to be $64,332, divided between liquid assets and real estate.

In January, 1943, Mrs. Johnson purchased KTBC, an impoverished Austin radio station, for $17,500. The Johnsons quickly won permission from the Federal Communications Commission for unlimited broadcasting hours (KTBC had been limited to the daylight hours) and a thousand watts of transmitting power (four times its previous total). Simultaneously, KTBC won a coveted affiliation with the Columbia Broadcasting System. Almost immediately, KTBC went into the black. Even before the infinitely more profitable television operations of the station began, the Johnsons' Texas Broadcasting Corporation in 1951 had a net worth of $488,116, a profit of $57,983. With these profits, Representative Johnson in the late 1940s began buying land, cattle, and bank stock. As early as 1948, Johnson told a friend that the net worth of his family, based on real market value, was a cool one million dollars. Without anybody really noticing it, and with dazzling speed, Lyndon Johnson had become a millionaire.

Almost all his wealth was in the name of Lady Bird Johnson, who was the applicant of record in all proceedings before the FCC. Later, when Johnson became engrossed in the Senate, Mrs. Johnson was the effective operating head of the family business in fact as well as name. But between 1943 and 1948, when Johnson's political future seemed uncertain, he spent much time himself at their radio station. The station challenged politics as his primary interest. In early 1948, in fact, he told several of his fellow Congressmen from Texas that he did not plan to stay indefinitely in the House. He would make one more run for the Senate, he said, and if that failed, he would quit politics altogether and return to Texas, where he would set about the serious business of making money.

During that period, Johnson sometimes displayed more interest in his radio station than in anything happening in Washington. For example, toward the end of World War II, in 1945, when the Communications Workers of America were threatening to strike KTBC, Johnson was fearful that pickets would damage the valuable transmission equipment at KTBC. Other radio stations in Texas had already suffered. Johnson put out a series of SOSs to his friends, many of whom were just back from the war. Among those summoned were Merrill Connally, John's younger brother and later a state senator himself; J. J. (Jake) Pickle, later to become one of the powers in the Texas Democratic party and, beginning in late 1963, U.S. Representative in Johnson's old district; Joe B. Kilgore, a decorated combat pilot who was to serve in Congress from 1955 to 1965. Still in uniform and wearing sidearms, the Johnson men gathered around the station's transmitter to guard against the violence that never came. Playing the role of strikebreakers in 1945, they became the nub of the Johnson campaign organization for the 1948 Senate race.

During those early years, Johnson's business staff was scarcely distinguishable from his political staff. John Connally and Jake Pickle, lieutenants in the Johnson political organization, had both worked for Texas Broadcasting Corporation. A soft-spoken, competent young Texan named Walter Jenkins served simultaneously on Johnson's public payroll as his administrative assistant and on Johnson's private payroll as treasurer of Texas Broadcasting Corporation.

In the Republican 80th Congress of 1947–48, Johnson didn't lift a finger for Truman but moved resolutely rightward—most notably with votes to pass the Taft-Hartley Labor Act and then to override Truman's veto. It goes without saying that Johnson's second campaign for the Senate was *not* announced from the front steps of the White House. On the contrary, with Truman considered a sure loser in 1948, association with him was to be scrupulously avoided.

Johnson's Senate campaign for the seat being resigned by Pappy O'Daniel did not start until months of agonizing soul-searching had gone by, a procrastination characteristic of many of his important decisions through the years. Pressed by exasperated friends, Johnson refused to say yes or no—and nearly started a boomlet for his handsome young campaign manager, John Connally. But Connally wasn't interested in running. Finally, Johnson announced, and his announcement, despite the long delay, was scarcely a surprise. This was up-or-out for Johnson. Unlike 1941, when he was running in an off-year election, he had to surrender his House seat in 1948, win or lose in the Senate race.

Apart from the defense preparedness theme and the faithful support and backing from Sam Rayburn, the campaign of 1948 bore little resemblance to 1941. This time Johnson was not bound by the handicaps of a pro-administration candidate. Swooping down on voters in his helicopter, Johnson was prepared to say whatever he had to say to win. While never having joined the segregationist bloc in Congress, he now opened fire on Truman's whole civil rights program, and while privately telling friends that he really favored federal control of tidelands oil, he campaigned for a bill to place the tidelands in Texan hands. But nowhere did Johnson display his ability—and willingness —to work both sides of the political fence in order to get into the Senate as he did on the Taft-Hartley issue.

Johnson's vote for Taft-Hartley helped nail down the kind of money support that shunned him seven years earlier—led by the newly oil-rich Brown brothers. Old Wall Street friend Ed Weisl (whose clients included the Hearst Corporation) obtained an endorsement for Johnson from the Hearst newspapers in Texas—an endorsement out of the question if Johnson had voted against Taft-Hartley. That single vote panicked the Texas State AFL into an absurd endorsement of Johnson's right-wing Tory Democratic foe, Governor Coke Stevenson, playing directly into Johnson's hands. Fearful of taking a stand on Taft-Hartley because of the AFL endorsement, Stevenson was a sitting target for Johnson's political arrows aimed at his labor support. Labor-baiting fit snugly into the prevailing anti-labor mood in the Southwest. Challenging Stevenson to repudiate his AFL support, Johnson asked rhetorically: "Does he place his greed for votes above the welfare of his native land?" A major issue of the day, said Johnson, was "whether we should bow our necks to labor dictatorship through the repeal or softening of the anti-Communist Taft-Hartley Bill."

But while the AFL went for Stevenson, a wiser labor official was on the other side. Robert Oliver, a Texas staff member for Walter Reuther's CIO Auto Workers, persuaded state CIO officials not to follow the AFL into the Stevenson camp. In return, Johnson led Oliver to believe that he would take a generally pro-labor stance in the campaign. While Oliver quietly recruited CIO locals behind Johnson (without formally endorsing him), Johnson gradually stepped up his campaign in favor of Taft-Hartley. But Oliver was trapped, because by then it was too late to reverse the CIO, which voted for Johnson. But most important of all, in the August 28, 1948, Democratic primary, Johnson remembered Roosevelt's advice about sitting on the ballot boxes.

Counted out by O'Daniel's ballot-counters in 1941, Johnson was counted in this time by 87 votes out of 988,295 cast, thanks to a late,

late count on September 3, giving him 202 additional votes from the
ballot box in Precinct No. 13 in the hamlet of Alice in Duval County
on the Mexican border. After a long and bitter debate, the State Democratic Executive Committee, meeting in Fort Worth on September
14, certified Johnson as the nominee of the party to be placed on the
general election ballot—as good as election in the Texas of 1948. Stevenson immediately appealed to the federal courts with charges of
fraud, and on September 15, U.S. District Judge T. Whitfield Davidson, a Southern conservative from rural east Texas, issued an injunction denying Johnson a place on the ballot. At a hearing before Davidson in Fort Worth on September 21, Stevenson's lawyers produced
evidence to show that "voters" from the graveyard and from across the
border in Mexico had been recorded for Johnson in Precinct No. 13.
Davidson, clearly intending to rule against Johnson, sent a lawyer into
Duval County to take evidence as a master of chancery for his court.

The full weight of the Truman Administration and the entire liberal
wing of the Democratic party now was thrown behind Johnson. For
all of his conservative transgressions during the 80th Congress, Lyndon Johnson was infinitely preferable to Dixiecrat Coke Stevenson in
the Senate. The President told Johnson precisely that on September
25, when his transcontinental whistle-stop tour passed through Texas
with Representative Johnson as the honored guest. Johnson's old
friends gathered about him as his political career teetered in the balance. John Connally was in overall command. In Texas, Alvin Wirtz
headed his defense. In Washington, Abe Fortas, now in private practice, was his principal attorney. Joining them on a volunteer basis
were prominent liberal lawyers, including Joseph Rauh, a national
leader of the liberal Americans for Democratic Action, who in years
to come was to be one of Johnson's principal antagonists.

Judge Davidson's hearing in Fort Worth reopened on September
28, but it was short-lived. Johnson's lawyers had appealed Davidson's
injunction to the U.S. Court of Appeals in New Orleans. Unable to
get a quick decision there, they went to the Supreme Court in Washington. On September 29, Justice Hugo Black issued an order staying
the Davidson injunction and putting Johnson's name back on the election ballot. Davidson's hearing came to an abrupt end, and further
appeals were moot. Stevenson was beaten—by the disputed 87 votes.
The November election was a formality.

Lyndon Johnson was at last a Senator—a conservative, cautious,
and most discreet Senator, standing, it seemed, a world apart from the
brash New Dealer who had roared into Franklin Roosevelt's Washington eleven years earlier.

Chapter III

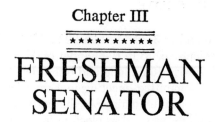

FRESHMAN SENATOR

Lyndon B. Johnson, the junior Senator from Texas, maintains the most rigidly one-track mind in Washington. He is entirely preoccupied with the science of politics. . . . He refuses to be trapped into thinking about or discussing sports, literature, the stage, the movies or anything else in the world of recreation.
>—Paul F. Healy in the *Saturday Evening Post*, May 19, 1951

The hearings have turned into an inquisition. . . . Johnson and his committee colleagues put on a performance reminiscent of the Un-American Activities Committee.
>—Columnist Lowell Mellett in the *Washington Evening Star*, October 1, 1949, commenting on the Leland Olds case

Seldom has so colorful, so varied, and so exceptional a band of new Democratic Senators come at once into the Senate as the Democratic Class of '48—freshman Democrats swept into the Senate in the first postwar presidential election of 1948. That was the election to be remembered in history for the wholly unexpected victory of Harry Truman over Thomas E. Dewey. The Class of '48 Democrats, however, were hardly tied to the Truman coattails. On the contrary, most of them ran far ahead of their party's presidential candidate. Keenly appreciative of that fact, they were not humble followers of Truman but independent personalities whose ambitions, idiosyncrasies and rivalries were to shape the history of the Senate and the nation for the next decade. A partial listing of the Democrats elected in 1948 reveals seven extraordinary men.

Russell Long of Louisiana, 30.   Son of the assassinated Kingfish Huey Long, he was baby of the class. He came to Washington to redeem the reputation of his father and to quiet the inherited Long volatility long enough to carve a niche for himself in the Senate.

Hubert Horatio Humphrey of Minnesota, 37. The crusading reform Mayor of Minneapolis, he had driven the Communists from the state's Democratic party and formed the invincible Democratic-Farmer-Labor party of Minnesota. But he was best known as the leather-lunged young civil rights zealot who had rammed a tough civil rights plank through the 1948 Democratic Convention in Philadelphia, thereby costing Truman the Deep South.

Estes Kefauver of Tennessee, 45. A veteran of ten years in the House, he had impressed himself on the nation as the publicity-wise campaigner with the coonskin cap. Conqueror of the Crump machine of Memphis, he was arch-foe of conservative Tennessee Senator Kenneth McKellar, a high-ranking member of the Senate's inner directory.

Paul Douglas of Illinois, 56. The white-maned professor of economics at the University of Chicago and reform city alderman had enlisted as a Marine private in World War II and emerged as a decorated, wounded lieutenant colonel. To come to the Senate, he had broken the closed circle of one of the most tightly controlled Democratic machines in the nation.

Clinton P. Anderson of New Mexico, 53. This fabulous invalid went West to die of tuberculosis as a young man and instead built a fortune in insurance, served six years in the House, then joined Harry Truman's Cabinet as Secretary of Agriculture before running for the Senate. Washington had become familiar with his no-nonsense manner and intelligence.

Robert S. Kerr of Oklahoma, 52. The swashbuckling oil millionaire who had risen from rural poverty came to the Senate determined to advance both his financial and political interests. Keynoter of the 1944 Democratic National Convention in Chicago and fresh from a stint as Governor of Oklahoma, he brought to the Senate a ruthlessness of mind and character that combined to produce a truly formidable figure.

Lyndon Baines Johnson of Texas, 40. Despite a decade in the House and intimate ties with the great and near-great of the New Deal, he entered the Senate less confidently than his classmates. He was in the most difficult transitional stage of his career, encountering simultaneously a new parliamentary arena and a new constituency requiring basic changes in his political style.

Lyndon Johnson was one of the least publicized members of the Class of '48, which was perhaps the most publicized band of freshmen in Senate history—much to the dismay of Senate elders, who devoutly believed in a long and quiet apprenticeship for their junior colleagues.* Contemporary press evaluation selected Paul Douglas as the member of the class most likely to succeed—clearly presidential timber for 1952. Articulate and fearless, the fighting professor from Chicago seemed to be a throwback to the Roosevelt era and a welcome contrast to the dreary Truman days in Washington. Moving up fast on Douglas in the publicity race was Estes Kefauver, whose placid façade concealed a keen sense of the headlines and deeper longing for the White House than Douglas'.† Within a few years, his titillating investigation of interstate crime over the new, exciting medium of television made him the member of the Class of '48 most easily recognizable in the living rooms of America. And if Douglas and Kefauver were presumptive candidates for President in 1952, Hubert Humphrey was the presidential candidate of the future. His absorbent mind soaked up information on all conceivable subjects, and his facile tongue gave them voice at a moment's notice.

To the outsider, Douglas, Kefauver, and Humphrey were the most promising of the new class. But inside the tight little world of the United States Senate, these three were the farthest outsiders—Kefauver and Douglas to remain so throughout their careers, Humphrey not to be permitted deep into the inner sanctum for six more years. For inside the Senate, Douglas, Kefauver and Humphrey were written off as "liberals" who could dominate the headlines but never the Senate. In the Senate itself, the most promising men of the new Class of '48 were Bob Kerr, Clint Anderson, and Lyndon Johnson.

This threesome moved into the inner directory of the Senate presided over by Senator Richard Russell of Georgia the day they were sworn in. Kerr was a domineering bully, merciless, almost sadistic in his verbal assaults on a cornered foe; Anderson, ever worried about his multiple ailments, was wise and sardonic; Johnson was ebullient and elaborately deferential to his Senate elders. Yet, these three had much in common. All were Southwesterners, cattle owners, self-made men, ambitious to build up their private fortunes. Kerr was one of the richest men in the Southwest, with a fortune that would grow to fifty-five million dollars ten years later. Anderson was many times a millionaire. Johnson was just breaking into the heady category of millionaire.‡

* The only Democratic member of the Class of '48 who met the Senate's tradition of anonymity was Senator Allen Frear of Delaware, who later distinguished himself as one of Lyndon Johnson's most dependable satellites.

† A March 3, 1951, dispatch from Washington in the *New York Times* portrayed the Capital consensus as listing Chief Justice Fred Vinson and Senator Douglas as Truman's most likely successors in 1952. In fact, however, Douglas became Kefauver's campaign manager.

‡ On April 14, 1952, Johnson's Texas Broadcasting Corporation was granted a VHF (very high frequency) television channel in Austin—the only VHF chan-

Although generally liberal in economic policy, these three political and financial buccaneers most decidedly were not committed to any ideological doctrine and knew the value of making common cause with private economic interests. Above all, they knew what power was and were determined to exercise it.

Thus an early arrangement was formed between these strong, hard men—an entente more than an alliance—that was to become increasingly important in running the Senate. The friendship between Johnson and Kerr was rather special. They had a common adversity as the only new Senators whose elections were formally challenged. After both had won their Democratic primary elections, then tantamount to election, charges against them were filed with the Senate Campaign Investigating Subcommittee in the Republican-controlled 80th Congress. The defeated Coke Stevenson charged fraud in Johnson's eighty-seven-vote victory; an investigator for the subcommittee charged Kerr with falsifying his campaign expenditures report and spending more than the law allowed. Had the Republicans retained control of Congress in the general election on November 6, Johnson and Kerr undoubtedly would have been subjected to a penetrating investigation and possibly a delay in being seated. But when Democrats captured the Senate, the lame-duck Republican leadership of the subcommittee on November 8 postponed the Johnson and Kerr investigation until the following January, leaving it to the Democratic 81st Congress. That was the end of the matter but it gave Johnson and Kerr a special kinship.

In the years to come, Johnson, Kerr and Anderson were often to be seen sitting together on the leather couches in the rear of the Senate chamber in full sight of the galleries, discussing cattle breeding in the earthy, obscene language of the Old Frontier or haggling over the trade of a stud bull. Then, without a transitional shifting of gears, they turned to what really mattered—affairs of state and the trade of a vote on pending legislation. All three settled quickly into the inner life of the Senate. Unlike Kerr and Anderson, however, Lyndon Johnson had to confront—and surmount—some formidable political hurdles.

Shortly after Paul Douglas was elected to the Senate, he visited Harold Ickes, his old friend and fellow Chicago progressive, on Ickes'

nel to be granted that city of 100,000 by the FCC. By the early 1960s, this television monopoly was to give the Johnson company (renamed the LBJ Company in 1956) a market value estimated at seven million dollars, with annual profits in excess of five hundred thousand dollars. All the while, Johnson continued to buy more land and bank stock.

farm at Olney, Maryland, outside Washington. The talk turned to the forthcoming session of the Senate, and Ickes pointed out to Douglas that one of his colleagues in the Class of '48 was a Texas New Dealer named Lyndon Johnson. Ickes advised Douglas that Johnson had been close to Roosevelt and should be sought out as a friend.

Paul Douglas and Lyndon Johnson never did become friends. By the time Ickes, his old champion and admirer, spoke the words, Johnson was no longer a New Dealer. His rightward drift following the death of Roosevelt was accentuated in the 1948 Senate campaign and reached its peak in his early Senate years as a necessary accommodation to two political realities—an accommodation that the idealistic Douglas could neither understand nor forgive.

One reality was Johnson's insecure position in conservative postwar Texas. That ludicrous eighty-seven-vote margin over Coke Stevenson in the 1948 election was a constant reminder of how insecure his home base was. When Scott Lucas of Illinois (the newly elected Senate Majority Leader) introduced the freshman Senators of the Class of '48 to the opening session Democratic caucus on January 3, 1949, he good-naturedly referred to Johnson as "Landslide Lyndon." To Johnson's dismay, the term stuck with both politicians and press. To secure his base, and reduce the threat of political annihilation, Johnson had to come to better terms with the power structure of postwar Texas. That meant warming relations with the oil barons, who still distrusted him as Roosevelt's protégé.

Another reality was the fact that the road to power on Capitol Hill no longer passed through the White House.

These were the halcyon days of the Senate's Inner Club. While the two elected Democratic floor leaders were displayed as the *de jure* rulers of the Senate, real power was in the grip of an informal, loosely linked directory of senior Republicans and Southern Democrats. This conservative coalition, born in 1937 in reaction to Franklin D. Roosevelt's Supreme Court-packing plan, by now literally controlled Congress and refused to enact Harry Truman's Fair Deal legislation. The heart of the coalition was a *quid pro quo:* the Republicans agreeing to vote with the South against civil rights legislation, the Southern Democrats agreeing to vote with Republicans against Truman's economic legislation.

But the ruling coalition in the Senate was more than a mere marriage of convenience at the altar of doctrinaire conservatism. While opposed in principle to the underlying doctrine of the New and Fair Deals, the Senate's rulers were not mere ideologues. Rather, they were pragmatic, shrewd, industrious men remarkably well versed in the issues of the day, possessed of accumulated knowledge in their special interests, and adept in the art of legislation—men like Republican Eugene Millikin of Colorado, Republican Robert Alfonso Taft of Ohio and Democrat Walter George of Georgia.

Towering above this informal directory of equals among equals was one figure: Democrat Richard Brevard Russell of Georgia.

Without his approval, no Democratic Senator became his party's floor leader or whip. Thus, Majority Leader Lucas could do Johnson little more good in the Senate than President Truman. He was but the unenthusiastic spokesman for the White House and manager of routine Senate business. The real power in Johnson's new life resided in the informal directors of the conservative coalition—and specifically with the *de facto* director-in-chief, Richard Russell. To get a hand on the reins of power, Johnson had to become intimately involved with Russell and his allies.

Considering Johnson's lack of ideological commitment, the method he could have chosen to deal with these realities might have been straightforward: with the New Deal dead, the Fair Deal stillborn, and liberalism in decline, move all the way to the right. In short, surrender to the realities rather than accommodate to them. But total surrender, while solving Johnson's momentary problems, would cost him his future. For had he gone over completely to the conservatives of Texas and the conservatives in the Senate, he would have destroyed himself as a potential power in the national Democratic party, just as Russell was doing. But at no time did Johnson lose sight of his ultimate goal of national power. Thus, in 1949 a Johnson accommodation emerged that considered the realities. He made new arrangements with the right and shored up his bases in Texas and the Senate, but at no time did he go far enough to box himself in as a hopelessly regional politician.

This tightrope walking was typified by Johnson's ambivalence toward the mighty Southern Democratic Senators. It was important for Johnson to establish himself in the Senate in his old specialty: defense preparedness. That meant persuading the Senate Democratic Steering Committee to give him a seat on the Senate Armed Services Committee, presided over by Russell—no mean task for a freshman Senator in 1949, when rigid standards of seniority still ruled. As the new Majority Leader, Lucas automatically became chairman of the Democratic Steering Committee, which theoretically controlled committee assignments. But the real decisions about committee assignments were made not by Lucas but by Russell and the other directors of the conservative coalition who had seats on the Steering Committee: Walter

George of Georgia, Tom Connally of Texas, Kenneth McKellar of Tennessee, Carl Hayden of Arizona. It was to these Senate grandees, not to Lucas, that Johnson went for help. They responded with assignments unprecedented for a freshman in that day: the Armed Services Committee and the Interstate and Foreign Commerce Committee (which handled legislation affecting the natural gas industry). Lucas was happy to agree with the decision of the Southern Senators.

But while soliciting and securing Southern support for his base in the Senate, Johnson at the same time made an extraordinary departure from established custom to avoid cutting himself off from national Democratic politics and becoming just another Dixie Senator, a junior version of Tom Connally.

Along with the other twenty-one Senators from the eleven states of the Old Confederacy, Texas Senators were expected to attend meetings of Dick Russell's Southern Caucus, which met primarily for the Southerners to get marching orders from Russell on how to defeat civil rights legislation. In his first weeks as a Senator, however, Johnson made clear he would not attend the Southern Caucus.* So did Tennessee's Estes Kefauver. But based on Kefauver's previous political career, Southerners regarded him as something of a scalawag and weren't surprised at his boycott of the Southern Caucus. But Johnson seemed no scalawag, as evidenced by his strong stand against the Truman civil rights program in the 1948 campaign.

Johnson's balancing act was infinitely delicate. While rejecting *formal* membership in the Southern Caucus, he accepted an *informal* membership. Having campaigned in 1948 against federal civil rights legislation, he now reiterated he had no intention of changing that position. During the first days of the 1949 session, he lined up with Russell's Southern legions to beat down the biennial liberal attempt to revise Senate Rule XXII so as to make it easier to apply cloture (the forcible ending of debate) on civil rights bills. The conservatives wanted to hold on to their power to filibuster any civil rights bill to death. Thus did Johnson slip easily into a common law union with the Southern conservatives of the Senate in January, 1949. Having avoided a church wedding, he was free to forsake the South eight years later and pass the first civil rights law since Reconstruction days—an achievement that allowed him to lose his Southern regionalism and pursue his national ambition.

Russell was visibly miffed by the young Texas Senator's secession

---

* Johnson's action set no precedent; of four Senators who have served since then, only one—liberal Democrat Ralph Yarborough—followed his course in seceding from the Confederacy.

from the Southern Caucus, and that was a matter of concern to Johnson. As he always sought the sources of power, he was now promoting with the taciturn Georgia bachelor a new father-son relationship of the kind he had successfully promoted with Franklin Roosevelt, Sam Rayburn, and Carl Vinson.

It was no easy task. Rayburn was an old family friend prejudiced in Johnson's favor from the beginning. Roosevelt and Vinson were gay political rogues who saw in young Johnson a kindred spirit. Not Russell. No two men could have been less alike than the expansive, windy young Texan and the austere, introspective Georgia patrician whose biography in the *Congressional Directory* read in its entirety: "Richard Brevard Russell, Democrat, of Winder, Ga." Russell was almost surely suspicious of Johnson's New Deal background. Indeed, the filial relationship that Johnson sought was never truly achieved. Yet Russell quickly came to admire Johnson—if not to love him—for his energy, his devotion to detail, and his dependability as the hardest working member of Russell's Armed Services Committee. Without Russell's professional patronage, Johnson's career would not have moved so rapidly.

It is doubtful that Johnson could have established any satisfactory relationship with Russell if he had crossed the Capitol from the House to Senate as the same brash, smart-aleck member of Carl Vinson's House Armed Services Committee who had set his wristwatch-alarm to confound the Pentagon brass. Under magnificent self-control, the Lyndon Johnson of the early Senate years was a subdued fellow not seen before and not to be seen again until his painful vice-presidential period. Chastened in part by that eighty-seven-vote win, Johnson also knew enough of the Senate and of Russell to realize that freshmen mind their manners.

He succeeded so well that after his first three years in the Senate, *Newsweek* gave an appraisal of Johnson that would never have fit the pre-Senate Johnson or the Johnson who later became a Senate legend. Said *Newsweek* on December 3, 1951: "His manner is quiet and gentle, and everything he does, he does with great deliberation and care." That was no journalistic error. Years later, Scott Lucas remembered Johnson's first two years in the Senate in these words: "I found him at all times what I would term a gentleman of the old school, and while his activities were negligible, his warm personality and genial conduct made a favorable impression upon all Senators irrespective of their political affiliations."

The most startling word here is "negligible" in describing the man who was to become perhaps the most active figure in the history of the

Senate. But Lucas was right. Johnson was in hibernation, patiently building a new base in the Senate and quietly securing his old base back home. Indeed, the most active member of the Class of '48 was not Johnson, but Robert Samuel Kerr of Oklahoma.

There never had been a freshman Senator quite like Bob Kerr, the burly teetotaler who taught Baptist Sunday school and was born in a log cabin in Indian Territory. It simply was not in Kerr to sit meekly as a neophyte at the knee of Dick Russell. From the beginning, he was deep into every aspect of Senate life: pushing special legislation, opposing presidential nominees, advancing friends as candidates for Senate leadership roles. Perhaps the greatest vote-trader the Senate has ever seen, Kerr was merciless in debate, reckless in promoting the interests of his state, and blessed with an uncanny faculty for digesting and retaining whole huge doses of complex information.

But Robert Kerr was plagued by a fatal flaw—a distorted sense of values. He was a regression to the Senate of the Gilded Age of the nineteenth century when financial freebooters entered public life to protect their private interests. While Johnson as a Senator regarded his growing business investments primarily as insurance against the personal financial crises that had plagued his father, Kerr delighted in the making and accumulating of money. He brazenly wore the lapel button of his Kerr-McGee Company (prompting critics to call him "The Senator from Kerr-McGee"). Although he wanted the presidential nomination in 1952 and made a spectacularly unsuccessful try at it, he did not want it badly enough to tone down his open championship of the oil and gas industry. His authorship of the Kerr Natural Gas bill to end regulation of natural gas prices by the Federal Power Commission (passed by Congress but vetoed by Truman) lost him his chance for Truman's endorsement for President. It was a mistake that Lyndon Johnson never would have made—and never did make.

But while Kerr did the dirty work in winning special treatment for the oil and gas industry, Johnson, staying characteristically in the background, gave Kerr invaluable assistance through a relationship that ripened with the years. In the natural gas fight of 1949, Johnson followed Kerr's lead and raised his standing with both the gas and oil barons and the reigning Senate conservatives. But more important, it was in this same year that Johnson became the chief actor in another cause with results that damaged his standing with the liberals and returned to haunt him years later, long after the cause itself was forgotten. That forgotten cause—the Leland Olds affair—was the point of Lyndon Johnson's maximum activity during his freshman Senate year.

Leland Olds, a native of Rochester, New York, graduated from Amherst College in 1912, served in the Army in 1918, and then spent nine years as an economic consultant and writer for *Labor Letter*, published by Federated Press. (His economic orientation was considerably left of center.) In the following eight years he headed the New York State Power Authority, until President Roosevelt appointed him to the Federal Power Commission in 1939. As a member, then vice-chairman and chairman of the FPC, he was the commission's most militant advocate of tough government regulation of private utility rate-making.

Thomas L. Stokes, the liberal columnist, referred to Olds as a "mild-mannered, tough-minded, zealous old New Dealer." His zeal got him into trouble, and not just with the private utilities. Like all the New Dealers, he loved nothing better than a roaring bureaucratic battle. Unfortunately for Olds, his foes included one of the New Deal's expert infighters: Secretary of the Interior Harold Ickes. Ickes believed that Olds had poisoned President Roosevelt's mind against him, thereby ruining Ickes' chances to become chairman of a new federal Water-Power Commission. The Old Curmudgeon never forgot, nor did his close friends.

By 1949, Olds had served ten years on the FPC and was hoping for still another term. But, in fact, his day was done in Washington. Olds had run afoul of the postwar natural gas boom. Once a relatively unimportant by-product of the oil industry, natural gas had become big business. Interstate pipelines brought gas from the Southwest and revolutionized the home-heating business across the nation. The rise of the oil and gas industry brought a new political power, not just to Texas, but to Washington also. With Bob Kerr leading the way in the Senate, the industry refused to tolerate an FPC dedicated to tough regulation of natural gas prices. The reappointment of Leland Olds for another term on the FPC would have ensured an anti-industry majority on the commission. Olds was a marked man.

Majority Leader Scott Lucas, increasingly harassed in his unhappy role of attempting to chaperone the Fair Deal through a hostile Senate, warned Truman in the fall of 1949 that the Senate would never confirm Olds for another term. He pleaded with the President not to make the nomination, but Truman had become impervious to defeats in Congress. Furthermore, he was increasingly concerned with international affairs. He not only ignored Lucas' advice but, as with so much Fair Deal legislation, just about forgot the Olds nomination once it reached Capitol Hill. Scarcely a telephone call on Olds' behalf was made by the White House. Lucas, who had his own doubts about Olds, went through the motions for the presidential nominee. But it was a hopeless cause. With the indefatigable Kerr beating the drums against Olds and oligarchs Russell and Taft both opposed to him, he had no chance.

What makes the inevitable senatorial lynching of Leland Olds noteworthy was the aggressive part played by the freshman Senator in charge of the special Senate Commerce Subcommittee set up to study the Olds nomination. Lyndon Johnson sought the job—but only when Olds was already clearly marked for extinction.

There seems little doubt that Ickes, nursing his old grudge against Olds, was egging on his protégé, Johnson. Abe Fortas, who had been Ickes' Under Secretary of Interior and was still close to him, although now in private law practice, was the behind-the-scenes counsel for Johnson, supplying him with material and arguments against Olds. But Johnson would scarcely have gone to such lengths just for Harold Ickes. More likely Johnson's motive was tied to his basic political duality: an old New Dealer in a newly conservative Senate representing a newly conservative Texas.

There is no question that as a leader of the Senate pack in full cry against Olds, Johnson erased all lingering doubts in the Senate about his political transformation. For instance, the Olds case drew him close to Senator Edwin C. Johnson of Colorado, a fiercely anti-Communist Democrat who was chairman of the Commerce Committee (parent of Lyndon Johnson's subcommittee) and an intimate of Russell's. At one point in the hearings, Big Ed Johnson passed a note to Lyndon Johnson complaining that the most powerful newspaper in his state, the *Denver Post*, was defending Olds and making life hard for "us Johnson boys." Lyndon Johnson quickly scribbled an answer, assuring Big Ed that he was "taking after *them*"—meaning the *Denver Post*. And to this scribbled answer, Lyndon attached a copy of a confidential letter he had written to the *Denver Post* in which he defended his handling of the Olds investigation—a letter that engaged in some heavy-handed Red-baiting.

In the letter Johnson told the editors of the *Post* that it was not Olds who was in danger of being smeared by the hearings, but Lyndon Johnson, the subcommittee chairman. Olds, wrote Lyndon Johnson, was in league with the "Marcantonio chore boys"—a reference to Representative Vito Marcantonio of New York, the pro-Communist Congressman of the American Labor party. Furthermore, wrote Lyndon Johnson, President Truman had nominated Olds for another FPC term in order to win support from the Communist-leaning American Labor party. The letter was just the sort of missive to warm the heart of an old-line Red-baiter like Ed Johnson (who had gently referred to Olds during the hearings as "a tyrannical, mischievous, egotistical chameleon whose predominant color is pink").

The Olds case, in short, was the ideal instrument for a former Roosevelt New Dealer who wanted to dramatize a new political posture and impress his Senate elders with his new maturity. Even more important, Johnson's well-publicized performance in the Olds investigation was not ignored back home in Texas. The oil and gas barons took due notice when Johnson rose on the floor of the Senate not to sing the Populism of his forefathers but to spout the line of the new conservatism of Texas. Olds, said Johnson, was a rapacious bureaucrat persecuting the entrepreneur:

> Leland Olds' record is an uninterrupted tale of bias, prejudice and hostility, directed against the industry over which he seeks now to assume the powers of life and death. Never once in his long career has Leland Olds experienced, first-hand, the industry's side of the regulatory picture.

That was good political medicine not just for the oil and gas men, but for the whole power structure in Texas. The powerful *Dallas Morning News*, organ of the state's Tory Democrats, recorded Johnson's leading role in the case sympathetically. In return, Johnson leaked to the *News* details of an alleged pressure campaign against him by old New Deal friends who "warned that heavy propaganda weapons would be turned against him if he failed to support Olds"; that the CIO—even Truman himself—were applying the squeeze; and how Johnson was bravely standing firm amid this ordeal. The facts were otherwise; pro-Olds propaganda and pressure were in very short supply.

The Texas newspaper image of Johnson emerged as a courageous independent, standing up against the arm-twisting of his President to obey his own conscience. He told the Senate:

> The lash of a party line may be painful, but as for myself, I know the lash is not as painful as the sting of a conscience which is ignored . . . I do not relish disagreeing with my President and being unable to comply with the requirements of my party, but I can find no comfort in failing to do what I know in my mind is right.

Despite the "lash of a party line," and to absolutely nobody's surprise, on October 13, 1949, the Senate voted 53 to 15 against confirming Leland Olds. Democrats divided 21 to 13 against him.

Johnson's gains from the Olds affair were obvious. His losses were shrouded, immeasurable, indefinable. Any hope of a working relationship with Paul Douglas, one of the few Democratic Senators who genuinely took up Olds' cause, and with other Senate liberals was crippled. Joseph Rauh, the Washington lawyer and ADA leader who had volunteered his legal talents in writing briefs for Johnson when his eighty-seven-vote victory had come before the Supreme Court a year earlier, felt betrayed by the Olds affair and waded into a bitter personal feud with Johnson not concluded until fourteen years later.

Nor did the Ickes-Fortas role in the case indicate that all of Johnson's New Deal comrades were lined up against Leland Olds. On the contrary, Johnson's friends from the Roosevelt White House—Jim Rowe and Tommy Corcoran—were heartsick over his onslaught against Olds. What bothered them was not that Johnson had opposed Olds. That was predictable—and probably politically essential —for a Texas Senator in 1949. What concerned them was Johnson's activist role in the case and his dancing around the edges of what the next year would become known as McCarthyism.

During his subcommittee's hearings on the Olds nomination in September and October, Johnson maintained a public impartiality as subcommittee chairman. He left the Red-baiting to the likes of Senator Homer Capehart, the conservative Republican from Indiana.

But when the Olds nomination reached the Senate floor on October 12, Johnson inexplicably took a harsher tone—a tone that set the liberal community deeply against him for the first time. While insisting that "I do not charge that Mr. Olds is a Communist," Johnson drew heavily from Olds' writings of twenty years earlier.* He concluded his October 12 speech in phrases that linked Olds to un-American political beliefs, adding an innuendo of guilt by association.

> Leland Olds was not taking the only course open then to an American labor liberal. There were Americans of liberal views who expressed their thoughts and maintained their purpose without choosing—as did Leland Olds—to travel with those who proposed the Marxian [sic] answer . . . Leland Olds knew who his friends were and what they stood for . . .

---

* These writings, appearing in the *Labor Letter* of Federated Press in the late 1920s, comprise a naïve portrayal of the class struggle. Olds contended that "the owners exist . . . [as] a privileged class of parasites, whose idleness and dissipation becomes an increasing stench in the nostrils of the people," and warned that "the manipulation of Democratic institutions by this wealthy autocracy forces labor to seek other than Constitutional processes." Testifying before Lyndon Johnson's subcommittee in 1951, Olds asserted that these writings of more than twenty years earlier were designed for shock value. In any event, under direct questioning from Johnson, he unequivocally testified he did *not* now favor public ownership of gas and oil utilities—a most un-Marxist view.

The Olds affair is significant partly as an *atypical* example of Johnsonian techniques—a classic case of political overkill, of detonating an atomic bomb when a whiff of grapeshot would have sufficed. Olds was known to be doomed and Johnson was bound to get a major share of the credit long before he opened fire on the Senate floor. There was no need for Johnson to shoot at all—Homer Capehart and Ed Johnson were already firing at will.

Lyndon Johnson's alienation of the liberals in the Olds affair was unnecessary. It was a mistake that Johnson would not repeat in the Senate. When the Senate condemned Senator Joseph R. McCarthy in 1954, and again when the Senate rejected the nomination of Admiral Lewis L. Strauss as Secretary of Commerce in 1959, Johnson was deeply involved in both actions. But others, not Johnson, served as the shock troops, openly exposed to the political fire.

When the Democratic majority of the United States Senate caucused on the morning of January 2, 1951, to choose new leaders for the 82nd Congress, there was not the slightest indication that a great political career had reached a critical point. Senator Scott Lucas of Illinois and Senator Francis Myers of Pennsylvania, Majority Leader and Majority Whip in the departing 81st Congress, had both been defeated in the 1950 congressional elections. The world outside the caucus had little interest in the Senate Democrats' tribal ritual. For in the postwar years, the official Senate leadership was an unwanted burden, stripped of power and devoid of honor.

The caucus, then, was no free and open forum for the nomination and election of the party's new Senate leaders but simply a formality to ratify those privately selected with Dick Russell's assent.

The Democratic leaders who won that approval in the postwar years were roughly comparable to the "doughface" Democratic Presidents of a century earlier—Northern men with a Southern outlook.* While realizing that the party leaders would have to go through the motions of supporting the liberal Truman program, Russell had no intention of sharing his power with any genuine liberal who might try

---

* The expression "doughface" was coined in 1820 by Representative John Randolph of Virginia during congressional debate over whether to admit Missouri as a slave state. Like many of his fellow Southerners, Randolph had only contempt for the Northern Congressmen who supported the South on slavery, and he could not contain his contempt during debate. "They got scared," Randolph said of the proslavery Northerners. "They saw their dough faces in the glass, and were frightened, and voted against restriction [of slavery] and gave us a majority of three." The term subsequently came into common usage as crafty Southern Democratic leaders used doughface Presidents Franklin Pierce and James Buchanan to protect slaveholding interests prior to the Republican victory in 1860.

to mobilize the Senate's Democrats against the conservative directory.

Certainly, Russell had faced no such threat from aging Alben Barkley of Kentucky, who as Majority Leader during Truman's first term was too preoccupied with his nationwide lecturing to put much effort into the Senate and far too amiable to alter—or even question—the balance of power. When Barkley succeeded to the vice-presidency in the 1948 election, Russell personally approved an even more docile successor. Scott Lucas, a well-liked junior member of the Senate club with the look of a Wall Street lawyer, was a downstate Illinois Democrat whose postures were liberal, but whose visceral instincts often tended to be conservative—particularly on matters concerning civil rights.

Liberals who misjudged Truman's upset victory in 1948 as a mandate for the enactment of the ambitious Fair Deal were stunned when the caucus of January, 1949, accepted Russell's decree without even putting up an opposition candidate and elected Lucas—a man who one year earlier had voted to override Truman's veto of the Taft-Hartley Labor Act and who had fought against the tough civil rights plank at the 1948 Democratic National Convention. Asked by Russell whether he would care to succeed Barkley as Majority Leader, Lucas replied that he would serve but wouldn't lift a finger to get elected. That was enough for Russell. Like Barkley before him, it was simply not in Lucas to ask, much less pressure, another Senator to vote a particular way. The power of the Russells and the Tafts remained undiminished.

By early May, 1949, the liberals' worst fears about Lucas' leadership were realized. Following a conference with a seemingly indifferent Truman, Lucas announced that most of the Fair Deal program was being dropped and that only three "must" items remained on the agenda.*

The job of the Senate Majority Leader in that era was a misery without splendor. While Russell and Taft pulled the strings from the cloakroom, the "leader" was out there on the floor trying to keep the Senate's creaky machinery in operation. While Truman hurled his legislative thunderbolts from the White House—and conveniently all but forgot them—Lucas was required to make a nominal effort to catch and then pass them. Tied down in Washington far from his constituents, he became an easy target for the Republican ex-Congressman, Everett McKinley Dirksen, in the 1950 Illinois Senate election. Years

---

* Of these three "must" bills, one—repeal of the Taft-Hartley Act—was not passed. The other two, ratification of the NATO treaty and renewal of the Reciprocal Trade Agreements Act, did pass.

later, Lucas confided that those two years as leader were the most unhappy of his life. No wonder there was so little interest among other Democrats to take his place.

The climb of the talented Class of '48 to formal positions of power in the Senate hierarchy was considerably short of meteoric. Clinton Anderson and Robert Kerr did not become standing committee chairmen until 1961. In that same year, Hubert Humphrey was elected Senate Majority Whip. Russell Long did not succeed Humphrey as whip until 1965.

It is entirely possible that Lyndon Johnson would have advanced with no greater speed to a position of formal power had it not been for a remarkable chain of events in late 1950 and early 1951. And Johnson, unlike Russell and Kerr, predicated his rise in the Senate on his *formal* position. Whether Johnson would have leaped ahead of the rest of the Class of '48 into national prominence without these fortuitous events is questionable.

The first, of course, was the simultaneous defeats in the 1950 election of both Majority Leader Lucas in Illinois and Majority Whip Myers in Pennsylvania—a startling double slaying of the majority party's Senate leaders. Their defeats were symptomatic of Harry Truman's state of affairs in the Senate, which had dropped from poor to bad. Considering Lucas' utter inability to move the Fair Deal program against the Russell-Taft coalition, his loss in itself did no further damage to Truman in the Senate. As Whip, Myers had been little help to Lucas. But the Lucas-Myers defeats were part of the general Democratic losses in 1950. Those losses were in part due to the drop in Truman's popularity following the upsurge after his 1948 election victory. The United States had intervened in Korea in June, 1950, launching an unpopular war that was to grow increasingly more so as casualty lists mounted. Truman and his leadership in Congress looked forward confidently to two years of hell on Capitol Hill.

Clinton Anderson, Harry Truman's old Secretary of Agriculture, was deeply concerned about the approaching 1951–52 Senate session. Quite apart from the now-discarded Fair Deal program, Lucas' successor as Majority Leader would have no easy time passing such "must" legislation as the foreign aid bill, including the Marshall Plan funds for Western Europe. Anderson worried whether *anybody* could carry Harry Truman's banner in the Senate and hope to survive politically, particularly if he were up for re-election in 1952.

Stewing over this problem, Anderson hit upon an audacious answer: persuade Richard Russell to become the new leader. The idea of the arch-conservative from Georgia, who in league with Robert

Taft had mangled so much Truman legislation, now becoming Truman's Senate chief made a certain sense, quite beyond its boldness. The parts of the Fair Deal legislative program that Russell most objected to—particularly civil rights—were now quite dead. No one was nearly as well equipped as Russell to guide through the Senate the key appropriations bills and a bare-bones legislative program. And if any Democrat could weather close political identification with Truman, it was Russell. In Georgia he was unassailable.

Anderson secretly presented his idea at the White House and got a favorable response from Truman, who was personally fond of most of the Southern Senators and did not resent their opposition. But why should Russell trade the reality of power as director of the ruling coalition for the powerless drudgery of the Majority Leadership? Here again, the facile mind of Anderson conceived a solution for Truman: Russell could be trapped into taking the job.

He proposed that Truman, accompanied by the regular presidential press entourage, visit Russell down in Winder, Georgia. When Truman arrived, he would announce publicly that he wanted Russell for his Majority Leader. As Anderson reasoned, Russell could not say no to the President. Russell was at that time preparing himself for a serious bid for the 1952 Democratic presidential nomination, cautiously edging a bit closer to the national positions of the Democratic party. His refusal of a public request from the President would crush his admittedly slim presidential hopes.

If the Anderson plan had been carried out—and had worked—Lyndon Johnson would have been barred from the Senate leadership indefinitely, because two Senators from the Old Confederacy would never have been allowed to represent the Democratic party as Senate Leader and Whip.

As it turned out, however, Truman was preoccupied with the war in Korea and showed little personal interest in pursuing Anderson's proposal. Instead of making a public expedition personally to Winder as Anderson suggested, Truman dispatched his closest aide—White House counsel Clark Clifford—to put the request to Russell privately. Under those circumstances, Russell could and did decline. Although Russell had no thought of Johnson's future, his refusal was vital to it.

From that point on, White House interest in who would succeed Lucas and Myers was academic. It was Russell who faced the same chore of two years earlier: to pick a sacrificial lamb to replace Lucas, one who would quite probably suffer Lucas' fate at the next election. Russell's choice was Senator Ernest McFarland of Arizona, considerably more of a doughface and a weaker force in the Senate than Lucas. Noting that McFarland faced a struggle for re-election in 1952 anyway, friends advised that to accept Russell's offer of a thankless job identifying him so closely with the Truman Administration would be as fatal to him as it had been to Lucas. Bumbling, genial Ernie McFarland, perhaps yearning for a few moments in the political sun, brushed aside the good advice and accepted. There was no opposition.

Hopeful for one of their own as whip under McFarland, a few liberals began desultory talk in behalf of Senator John J. Sparkman of Alabama, a Southern liberal whose dependable opposition to civil rights might conceivably make his strong support for other aspects of the Fair Deal palatable to Russell. It did not. Sparkman was well outside the Senate's inner circle. Besides, the increasingly powerful Bob Kerr wanted to expand his influence by installing a close friend as whip, and John Sparkman decidedly did not meet these specifications.*

Kerr first felt out Anderson, but the ailing New Mexico millionaire would have sooner taken a job digging Kerr's oil wells. Kerr next turned to Lyndon Johnson. The ambitious Johnson readily agreed, but there remained one possible obstacle: Richard Russell. Russell was skeptical. He had not particularly cottoned to Johnson in 1949–50. Although their relationship was to bloom in 1951–52, Russell said he doubted that an all-Southwest team of McFarland and Johnson had the proper geographical balance. Nevertheless, Kerr doggedly argued for Johnson, and Russell eventually yielded. And so, by an uncertain, unpremeditated course of events, Lyndon Johnson at age forty-two entered the official Senate Democratic leadership—thanks more to Bob Kerr than to Dick Russell, despite the future legend that Russell was the guiding hand who pushed the young Texan along the road to Senate leadership. The team of McFarland and Johnson was elected at the January 2, 1951, caucus of Democratic Senators amid massive inattention from the outside world.

In truth, as the 82nd Congress progressed, McFarland and Johnson didn't make much of a "team." Lacking close ties to the powers in the Senate, McFarland struggled manfully but ineffectively through two dismal years—without much assistance from his young whip. Johnson haunted the cloakrooms sharpening his connections with the leaders

* There is no sign Sparkman wanted the meaningless job. His close friend and senior colleague, liberal Senator Lister Hill of Alabama, was whip for three terms but resigned in January, 1949, fearing close identification with the Truman civil rights program.

of the conservative coalition in both parties. In terms of what the role of whip later became when Johnson himself was leader, Johnson's aloofness might have appeared to be deliberate sabotage of McFarland, but considering the history of the job, it certainly was not. When Russell asked Lucas to become Barkley's whip in 1947, he confided with characteristic honesty that the job was purely honorary. Thus Johnson was doing only what was expected of him, neither more nor less than his immediate predecessors as whip. In the tight little world of Capitol Hill, power is measured partly in the currency of office space, but the only visible trapping of power received by Johnson was a small one-room "hideaway" in the Capitol itself, complete with brown leather couch, small refrigerator and liquor cabinet—a luxury generally reserved only for very senior Senators—that reflected the puniness of the job of whip. Johnson's main work was performed in a five-room suite in the Senate Office Building. With the Senator's staff crowded in on each other and the walls lined with autographed pictures of politicians, the suite was much the same as any other Senator's —with one distinctive difference: a growing collection of baby pictures from parents (many of them Johnson staffers) who had already begun the practice of naming their offspring Lyndon or Lynda.

But even without precise leadership duties or a special office, Lyndon Johnson as whip was a more formidable Senate figure than Francis Myers. He was a person of consequence in the Senate, while McFarland was a mediocrity. That made for an uncomfortable relationship. Sensitive about the prerogatives of his newly achieved office, McFarland would have resented efforts by Johnson to share the duties. Consequently, Johnson made not the slightest effort to vitalize the office of whip, and his life in the Senate proceeded much as it had before. He added to his vital store of information about the Senate and its members, and made mental notes how one day he would improve its operation. With the Korean War reaching a bloody stage, Johnson concentrated more and more on the role which he most enjoyed: the role of national defense expert.

When the troops of the People's Democratic Republic of Korea poured across the 38th parallel into the territory of the Republic of Korea on June 25, 1950, the dramatic decision of Harry Truman to fight back changed the political atmosphere everywhere overnight, and nowhere more than in the United States Congress. For Johnson, the Korean War was a natural opportunity to return to the role of defense expert, incidentally moving him back into the ideologically bland specialty where he felt most comfortable.

Although he had succeeded during 1949 in ingratiating himself with both the conservative barons of the Senate and the oil and gas barons of Texas, this role as protector of the natural gas industry and prosecutor of Leland Olds was not fun for Lyndon Johnson. He had no love for the oil men—although he was constrained to support their legislative projects—or any emotional desire to engage in fierce ideological disputes. These were political responses to his specific situation, not his idea of a good time. Now that he had made his point, and the Korean War was the top issue nationally, it was time to return to familiar ground.

Within days after Truman committed United States troops to Korea, Johnson was urging Russell—as chairman of the Armed Services Committee—to set up a Defense Preparedness Subcommittee to investigate the conduct of the Korean War. Russell thought it a good idea but gave no sign that the first-term Senator from Texas should be given preference as subcommittee chairman. On the contrary, it quickly became clear that Johnson would have competition for the subcommittee chairmanship from a veteran member of Russell's committee: Senator Millard Tydings of Maryland.

A conservative Democrat who split with Franklin D. Roosevelt on the Court-packing issue in 1937, Tydings won renomination and re-election in 1938 against the President's purge of anti-New Deal Democrats. But now, twelve years later, Tydings faced an adversary infinitely more ruthless than Roosevelt: the rampaging Joe McCarthy, who made no bones about his determination to beat Tydings with a Maryland McCarthyite named John Marshall Butler in the 1950 general election. Smeared as soft on Communism, Tydings needed a patriotic issue to rejuvenate himself politically. The obvious answer: an investigation into Truman's conduct of an anti-Communist war.

Not prepared to breach the seniority rule, Russell would have had no choice but to give the subcommittee chairmanship to Tydings—*if* Tydings had pressed the point. But Russell did not ask Johnson to bow out of consideration, and Johnson did not bow out. Tydings, a stiff-backed patrician from Maryland's Eastern Shore, put pride above politics and decided it was beneath his dignity to contest for a subcommittee chairmanship with an upstart freshman Senator. And so Johnson took over the new subcommittee in July, 1950.

Although Johnson constantly consulted Russell on the investigation, it was an LBJ show. He hired his own team to run it. Don Cook, the young Securities and Exchange Commission lawyer who had done such a masterful job with Johnson a decade earlier, was now vice-chairman of the SEC. Johnson wangled a leave of absence for him to run the new investigation as subcommittee counsel. As staff director,

Johnson hired Horace Busby, a twenty-five-year-old reporter for the International News Service in Texas who worked closely with Cook.*

Cook and his staff of investigators were given a free hand with no second-guessing by Johnson. But the Korean investigation bore little resemblance to their World War II effort. The target then was ineffi- ciencies and irregularities. Now it was far bigger game: the basic question of how well the Truman Administration was mobilizing the country for war. Johnson was following the same publicity path that Harry Truman took in the World War II Senate probe that made him Vice-President.

The Korean War wasn't World War II, and the Johnson committee never did match the Truman committee in publicity. But the old issue of defense preparedness that Johnson had studied so hard and plugged so long gave him the widest exposure of his career to date. Reporting the investigation, *Newsweek* of December 3, 1951, put Lyndon Johnson on its cover with the caption, "watchdog-in-chief." His friend and part-time adviser on the defense investigation, Eliot Janeway, wrote a glowing account of "Johnson of the 'Watchdog Committee'" in the *New York Times Magazine* of June 17, 1951. An- other pro-Johnson account appeared in the *Saturday Evening Post* of May 19, 1951.†

These articles stressed the bipartisan nature of the Johnson commit- tee. And indeed, the last thing Johnson could be accused of was overly sympathetic treatment of Harry Truman's handling of the unique problems of the Korean War. The key charge against Truman—that his administration was trying to have both guns *and* butter—was ex- actly what both Republican and Democratic conservatives had been saying and exactly the charge Johnson would face sixteen years later during the Vietnam war. After six months of investigation, Johnson took the Senate floor on December 12, 1950, to denounce "makeshift mobilization" by Truman.

> We are at war and we may well be at war for ten or twenty years more. But we are not getting ready for war. We are in a war but all our effort is seemingly directed toward staying out of the war that we are in already.

---

* Busby, who like many other LBJ intimates always had his troubles working long stretches for Johnson, left the Preparedness Subcommittee after two years to return to Texas. On Busby's recommendation, Johnson hired another newsman— George Reedy, Jr., a pipe-smoking intellectual from the Capitol Hill staff of the United Press—to replace Busby.

† The fact that Johnson was Senate Whip or that there even was such a posi- tion seemed so unimportant to these nationally circulated magazines that they ignored altogether the fact that Johnson held the job.

Johnson's election as whip the following month by no means muted his criticism of the administration's war effort. In November, 1951, Senator Henry Cabot Lodge of Massachusetts was busy promoting General of the Army Dwight D. Eisenhower for President (partly on the grounds of a shoddy Korean War effort by Truman). Johnson joined Republican Lodge's attack on Truman for slow delivery of war matériel to General Eisenhower's European command. On June 18, 1952, the Johnson committee charged that Truman had ignored "the solemn warning" of the Joint Chiefs of Staff that United States air power must be dramatically increased. On September 14, 1952, with the Eisenhower-Stevenson election less than two months away and Eisenhower charging Truman with defense bungling, the Johnson subcommittee blithely attacked the administration's air power program as "abuse, misuse and disuse of power."

What makes that all the more remarkable is that Johnson's private dislike and distrust of the uniformed military deepened even as he took their side in the rambunctious quarreling between civilian and military authority at the Pentagon. It was, in Johnson's opinion, a rerun of the World War II investigation: the high brass appearing before the committee time after time with disorganized, inaccurate, and misleading presentations. Ironically, then, Johnson was becoming the political favorite of the Pentagon generals—and, because of his disregard of partisan Democratic interests, of senior Republican Senators. The top Republican on the Johnson subcommittee, Styles Bridges of New Hampshire (the only veteran of the old Truman committee to serve on the Johnson committee) was delighted with Johnson's criticisms of the Truman Administration. It was undoubtedly here that the Johnson-Bridges alliance started, an alliance that would pay manifold dividends to Lyndon Johnson in years to come.

Harry Truman's escape mechanism during his days in the White House was to gather his friends—male, political, Democratic friends —for long, uninterrupted, gabby sessions of poker. The best of it came in spring and summer when the Truman poker party would spend a lazy weekend on the Potomac River aboard the presidential yacht *Williamsburg;* they would rise late on Saturday for a leisurely brunch and while away the day with political gossip, whiskey, and poker. There were several regulars aboard every weekend: Chief Justice Fred Vinson (whom Truman very much wanted to succeed him); George Allen, the court jester for three Presidents; Senator Clinton Anderson; Secretary of Commerce W. Averell Harriman; White

House Counsel Clark Clifford. Each week Truman would give Clifford a few additional names to round out the weekend party and quite often his instruction would be: "Call Senator Johnson." And Lyndon Johnson, who liked neither to watch nor to play any game except politics, would manfully make the best of the weekend.

But why Lyndon Johnson? Certainly his voting record in Truman's second term didn't qualify him for the presidential inner circle. Truman could scarcely forget Johnson's part in the rejection of Leland Olds, his constant sniping at Truman's conduct of the Korean War, his charge of "dictatorship" when Truman seized the steel industry (Johnson told the Senate on May 21, 1952, that the President was seeking to "override the plain language of the Constitution"), and his down-the-line opposition to Truman's civil rights program. Truman remembered Johnson's vote to pass the restrictive McCarran-Walter Immigration Act and his vote to override the President's veto of it (though he never made a public statement about this highly emotional issue). Why Johnson?

Because Harry Truman had taken a liking to Johnson as an old-style politician with whom he felt comfortable, with or without Johnson's support of his program. Paul Douglas and Estes Kefauver could go down the line for the Fair Deal, but Truman regarded them as holier-than-thou reformers. He could not forgive Douglas' irregularity in blocking Truman's nominations for the federal bench in Illinois, on the ground that they were not qualified. He could not forgive Kefauver's irregularity in permitting his investigation of organized crime to embarrass big-city Democratic machines. That kind of irregularity was not the way to play the political game.

By contrast, Truman understood that Johnson's repeated criticism of his administration was calculated to help Johnson back home in Texas. Political strength back home was one of the first rules of the game. Johnson was only doing what the occasion required, and could be forgiven. That was also the reason why Johnson maintained the warmest personal relations with Majority Leaders McFarland and Lucas while doing little enough to help them out. But Douglas and Kefauver, who usually voted right, were on cool terms with the party leadership.

Therefore, an understanding of the existing political climate is essential in analyzing Johnson's ostensibly anti-administration record during his first four years in the Senate. The President was an ex-Senator who had neither the appetite nor the aptitude to pressure his former colleagues. The Majority Leaders were neither expected nor empowered to pressure rank-and-file Senators. A freshman Senator from

Texas received prodding from neither the White House nor the Majority Leader. In that era, favors for Senators were neither promised nor withheld by the White House or the Majority Leader because of the way a Senator voted. A Senator's vote was his own.

Yet, through those years, Johnson never forgot how the Senate had jumped a decade earlier under the whiplash of Roosevelt and Senator Joe Robinson of Arkansas, the greatest of modern Majority Leaders (who literally worked himself to death trying to pass the Court-packing plan). As events were to show, the rule of leadership and the exercise of power in the White House and in the Senate that Johnson took with him into the future were not the examples of Harry Truman, Scott Lucas, or Ernest McFarland, but of Roosevelt and Robinson.

Chapter IV

★★★★★★★★★★

THE
LEADER

He doesn't have the best mind on the Democratic side of the Senate; he isn't the best orator; he isn't the best parliamentarian. But he's the best combination of all those qualities.
                    —Richard Brevard Russell, describing Minority
                    Leader Lyndon B. Johnson in 1953

On the cold, rainy day of January 3, 1953, a new era, exciting and turbulent, was opening for the United States Senate. To those in the packed galleries, the most vivid figure on the floor was Lyndon B. Johnson, only four years in the Senate and at forty-four the youngest floor leader of either party. Johnson had taken his front-row center-aisle seat on the left (Democratic) side of the aisle as the just-elected Minority Leader, and assumed a physical stance that was to become a Senate trademark in the next eight years: sprawled almost full length, the tip of his spine balanced on the outside edge of his chair, legs crossed, laughing and joking across the center aisle with his Republican opposite number, the reserved Robert A. Taft of Ohio. An inveterate attention-grabber, Johnson kept sliding his chair over to Taft's side, then back to its place. For the first time, he was flexing his muscles as a new Democratic power.

If Johnson was nervous (which he was) or slightly overwhelmed by his sudden new prominence in the Democratic party (which he also was), the view from the gallery gave no hint of it. There was an incongruity, however, about this long, restless bean pole from the Texas hill country conversing as an equal across the narrow aisle with the distinguished, patrician Taft, even then wasting away from cancer.

Like Johnson, Taft had just been elected floor leader of his party. But—unlike Johnson—from the early 1940s Taft had been the *de facto* Republican power in the Senate (just as Richard Russell had been the *de facto* Democratic power). Thus, Taft was now merely getting *de jure* sanction for what had long existed.* Yet it seemed

* Until 1953, Taft held power as chairman of the Senate Republican Policy

strange that newcomer Johnson should be the picture of self-satisfaction as he contemplated battle against the formidable "Mr. Republican."

But the galleries did not realize much about Lyndon Johnson in January, 1953, including how hard he had tried to become Democratic floor leader, the powerless job shunned since the late 1930s.

The polls had scarcely closed on the Eisenhower landslide in the 1952 presidential election two months earlier when Johnson, operating from the LBJ Ranch in Texas, began the maneuvers that led him to the job he coveted—Senate Minority Leader, now that Republicans had won control of the Senate. In that 1952 election, a prominent but not unexpected victim was Senator Ernest McFarland, who lost narrowly to a conservative, young Phoenix department-store owner, Barry M. Goldwater. McFarland's 1952 loss proved to be the first act in a drama to be concluded by Goldwater and Johnson on the presidential stage twelve years later. For 1952, however, the significant point was the indispensability of Goldwater's triumph to Lyndon Johnson's next move up the Democratic party ladder. Just as Scott Lucas' defeat in 1950 and Harry Truman's failure to get Russell to succeed Lucas were necessary, so did McFarland's departure leave Johnson room at the top.

It was only natural that Johnson's first telephone call, after McFarland's defeat, was to Richard Russell. Johnson's proposal: Russell himself should succeed McFarland as Democratic leader and Johnson would be Russell's aide-de-camp.

"I'll do the work and you'll be the boss," Johnson told Russell.

But Russell still preferred to exert his influence in less official but no less significant ways. Besides his unofficial leadership in the conservative coalition, he was chief of the Southern bloc (at that time twenty-two out of forty-seven Democratic Senators) and a senior member of both the Appropriations and the Armed Services Committees. With glacial disdain for the title of leader, Russell said no to Johnson, and then asked Johnson himself to be the new leader. Johnson, who must have had a strong suspicion that this was precisely what Russell would do, quickly agreed. But he extracted a promise that Russell would move his seat in the Senate to the desk directly behind the leader's desk. Johnson wanted Russell's advice available at all times.

Johnson hungered for the leadership for two basic reasons. First, his

---

Committee, preferring that the routine of floor leadership be borne by somebody else (who, of course, would be responsive to Taft's wishes). With the election of a Republican President in 1952, Taft knew that Eisenhower would be dealing primarily with the Majority Leader; he made himself available for that post and was quickly elected to it.

ambition propelled him automatically to the next rung on the ladder. Second, he was afraid that if he—the whip and heir apparent—were not picked to fill the vacancy, his own state of Texas would mark him a failure.

And so, after talking to Russell, Johnson began a series of long-distance telephone calls to Democratic Senators around the country, informing his friends that he had decided to run for leader and letting others know obliquely that, with McFarland gone, Johnson was the natural successor.

One new Senator he called was John F. Kennedy, fresh from an upset first-term victory in Massachusetts, unseating Republican Henry Cabot Lodge. Kennedy and his campaign aides could scarcely believe their ears when the Johnson call came through from Texas even before the polls had closed. Johnson's goal with Kennedy was not to tie down his vote on the leadership question, but to let the new Senator know that Johnson was aware of Kennedy's triumph. Johnson was "romancing" Kennedy, and Kennedy was highly impressed.

He "romanced" a score of other Senators, some of whom he asked outright for support, while handling others as he handled Kennedy. Johnson was careful not to tip his hand to Senators who might end up in someone else's camp. Instead of telephoning direct to Mike Mansfield of Montana, a Congressman elected to the Senate for the first time in 1952, Johnson called one of Mansfield's close friends, Montanan James Rowe—the same Rowe who as a White House aide had helped usher Johnson into Franklin Roosevelt's New Guard in the late 1930s. Johnson and Mansfield had never been close when they served in the House together. So Johnson asked Rowe to find out whether Mansfield would support him for leader. The implication was that Rowe might help out if needed. The Johnson call to Rowe turned out to be superfluous. Mansfield already had wired Johnson on his own with a pledge of support.

The next steps in the Johnson campaign were "spontaneous" public statements by three carefully chosen Senators proposing Johnson for leader while Johnson maintained a shy reticence at the LBJ Ranch. The first of the trio was Russell himself, who declared: "He [Johnson] is highly qualified for the job and, in my opinion, he will be chosen for it." Next was Johnson's faithful follower from the Class of '48, Delaware's Allen Frear. The third endorsement was perhaps the most important. It came from Earle C. Clements, a bald, beefy Kentuckian elected to the Senate two years earlier.*

---

* Johnson's public reaction to the triad of encomiums was suitably modest: "I have been honored and am very grateful to the Senators who have expressed con-

Clements was uniquely valuable to Johnson for his ability to move in two worlds—the inner world of the Senate oligarchy and the outer world of the liberal-oriented, national Democratic party. A former House member well known in Washington, Clements was quickly taken into the Senate's Inner Club through the sponsorship of Virgil Chapman, Kentucky's senior Senator and a minor member of the oligarchy. It was through Chapman that Clements quickly struck up a warm relationship with Johnson. When Virgil Chapman died on March 8, 1951, Johnson pushed Clements—sworn into the Senate little more than two months earlier—to assume Chapman's seat on the Senate Democratic Policy Committee. Two liberals, Herbert Lehman of New York and Paul Douglas of Illinois, applied for the vacancy. Both had seniority over Clements, and Lehman wanted the spot badly. The omnipotent Russell, wanting to keep the Policy Committee in friendly hands, disregarded seniority and selected Clements.

But unlike Johnson and Russell, Clements had liberal credentials hard to assail. His voting record was solidly liberal, his contacts with organized labor were excellent, and his stance on the emotion-charged oil and gas issue was solidly on the side of the consumer. Visceral liberals like Paul Douglas might distrust Clements but they could scarcely brand him a Dixiecrat. Moreover, while Russell stayed home in Georgia during the 1952 presidential campaign and said not a word for Adlai Stevenson, and Johnson only went through the motions of a few speeches for Stevenson in Texas quite late in the campaign, Clements was a bona fide party loyalist. He came out strongly for the Stevenson-Sparkman ticket from beginning to end.

Consequently, Clements' early endorsement of Johnson as leader served a particularly useful purpose. Friendly journalists quickly interpreted it as a sign that all Democrats, liberals as well as conservatives, were closing ranks around Johnson following the 1952 election defeat (even though Clements was certainly not of the Douglas-Lehman school of liberals).

Johnson had an additional use for Clements. He wanted Clements to succeed him as Minority Whip, partly as an ostensible "concession" to liberals, but mainly because he wanted to give the job a new, more powerful dimension. Johnson wanted to take advantage of Clements' proficiency at the back-room political arts. He wanted him to become an assistant to the floor leader, rather than just the assistant floor leader. As a visible sign of this enlarged stature, the whip was given a special office and staff for the first time.

---

fidence in me. It is a matter that the Senate conference [caucus] later will decide."

But Johnson had in mind far more sweeping reforms in Senate leadership than merely giving the whip something to do. Johnson's instinct for the glittering prospects of new political power served him well during those fast-moving days after the 1952 election. With Dwight Eisenhower preparing to move into the White House as head of the first Republican Administration in twenty years, he realized that Democratic leaders in Congress would assume an overnight importance far transcending the congressional role of the Roosevelt-Truman years.

The entire Democratic power structure was in a state of upheaval and Johnson was quick to perceive his opportunity. Sam Rayburn, of course, was secure in the House as number one Democrat. But in the Senate, the liberals were certain to try to elect one of their own as Minority Leader. Johnson sensed that whoever became the party's floor leader in the Senate would be at the center of action in the defeated, demoralized party, able to exert massive influence over party policy and program. Now the Senate Democratic leader had a singular opportunity to rescue that office from its continuing decline since 1938—and Johnson knew it. The Senate liberals, symbolized by Lehman and Douglas but with no real leader, were also aware of the new potential in Senate leadership. Characteristically, however, they were quite unable to organize an effective countermove against Johnson.

The liberal countermove that December, 1952, was marked by an excess of ineptitude that amazed Johnson himself. When Johnson returned to the Capitol from the LBJ Ranch he had far more than one-half the forty-eight Democratic Senators in his pocket committed to vote him in as leader. But now Johnson was aiming higher. He wanted unanimous election, not only to dramatize his new preeminence in the party but also because, with well over a majority already committed to him, he saw no advantage for himself in humiliating a liberal who might be foolish enough to run against him.

Johnson's method was to seek out the Senator with the reputation as the chamber's most militant liberal: Hubert Humphrey of Minnesota. When Humphrey and Johnson entered the Senate together four years earlier, they were worlds apart. To the Senate, Humphrey was not the anti-Communist founder of the Minnesota Democratic-Farmer-Labor party but a radical agitator who in 1948 split his party's national convention in two ("the black knight of civil rights," as Humphrey years later described himself).

By contrast, the skinny young Texan was very much in his element in those early Senate years, very self-assured in Humphrey's somewhat envious eyes. Yet Johnson had spotted in Humphrey a potential ally of value—even when Humphrey's Senate status hit rock bottom his freshman term. Suffering deep frustration as a liberal outsider in the conservative Senate, Humphrey had exploded on the Senate floor with an attack against an unlikely target: mild-mannered Senator Harry Flood Byrd of Virginia, the aging high priest of economic conservatism. Humphrey had shocked the Senate by indicting Byrd's Joint Committee on Nonessential Expenditures (which consisted largely of Byrd press releases decrying federal spending) as the most nonessential expenditure in Washington. Outraged by the freshman Senator's brash attack on a ranking oligarch, the Senate retorted with a withering repudiation of Humphrey's attack from both sides of the aisle.

Johnson, of course, did not defend Humphrey's indiscretion either publicly or privately. But he refused to join the rest of the Senate in treating Humphrey as an untouchable. Asking Humphrey to visit him in the Senate Office Building, Johnson suggested that he might get along better in the Senate if he studied and came to know the Senate's inner directors—instead of attacking them. Smooth some of the rough edges off your liberal politics, he urged Humphrey. Specifically, he suggested that Humphrey make friends with one of the Senate's most imperious grandees—Walter George of Georgia—because some day he might need George's friendship. Humphrey took the suggestion to heart and slowly recovered from the Byrd affair to make friends with Walter George.

That wasn't the only advice Johnson supplied Humphrey. As the year passed, he gave Humphrey a short course on the Senate and how it really functioned. He explained the importance of knowing the strengths and weaknesses of every Senator, of concentrating on committee work and of mastering a specialty. He explained that Muriel Humphrey ought to become friendly with other Senators' wives. Teasing Humphrey about his pals in the ADA and the CIO, Johnson made it clear that Humphrey was *his* kind of liberal.

How far down the road Johnson was looking on that distant day he did not say, but with his instinct for the ebb and flow of politics, and his eye on the long chance, he may well have had in his mind some faint plan that would link himself and Hubert Humphrey. One was a moderate Southerner with a Populistic heritage, the other a militant Northern liberal who, Johnson well knew, would be bound to move toward the middle of the road. Humphrey would become indispensable to Johnson in his rapid rise to power in the Senate, defending him time and again against suspicious liberals. Indeed, as the years went by, Humphrey's own liberal credentials would become slightly blurred, at first just in the eyes of the few political insiders who knew of his generally shrouded relationship with Johnson but later, after the 1964 election, by many more critical liberals.

Now, in December, 1952, seeking liberal acceptance of him as Majority Leader, Johnson turned to Humphrey. In a post-election talk with Humphrey, he carefully avoided specific mention of the leadership question. Instead, Johnson revealed for the first time his daring plan to modify the Senate's historic seniority rule.* He added that the Democrats needed a "good, strong man" on the Foreign Relations Committee, a much sought-after post Humphrey could not demand because of his short Senate tenure, and that Harry Truman, then in his last days as President, had personally recommended Humphrey. For Humphrey, that was heady stuff. He told Johnson he indeed wanted the Foreign Relations Committee slot.

Silent on the leadership question, Johnson's only purpose was to make Humphrey aware of the fact that Johnson regarded him as a rather special fellow. That, thought Johnson, would be enough to cool off Humphrey's participation in the leadership question. But Humphrey already had decided that the liberals must make a bid for the leadership that would display their strength, even though bound to lose. The liberal Democrat whom Humphrey picked (Humphrey himself was far too controversial) was aging, millionaire Montana cattleman James Murray. Never more than a pedestrian politician, Senator Murray by now was in his twilight years, a benign Western liberal who specialized in introducing federal aid to education bills that passed the Senate and died in the House.

Humphrey, Murray, and other liberal Democrats began recruiting and on the eve of the first Senate Democratic caucus of the 83rd Congress, at which the new leader would be elected, they thought they had a respectable seventeen or eighteen votes for Murray and against Johnson, out of the total forty-eight. Then Johnson summoned Humphrey to his office for their second chat.

Johnson came quickly to the point. He wanted Humphrey to back him for leader. He outlined his plans for running the Democratic party in the Senate. He spoke of broadening the Steering and Policy Committees (the leader is automatically chairman of both), so as to give the liberals a larger voice. Humphrey, he said, was a key element in Johnson's grandiose plans for reshaping the Democratic party in the Senate and making it a more vital instrument of party policy and action. When Humphrey explained that he was irrevocably committed to Murray—that he was pledged, locked in, and couldn't change—he got a hard lesson in the Johnson method of doing political business.

* This plan is dealt with fully on pp. 63–64.

Johnson pulled from his pocket the printed list of Democratic Senators of the 83rd Congress. Humphrey, he said bluntly, was foolish to have allowed himself to be sucked in to support Murray. Humphrey hadn't done his homework, Johnson added, because if he had, he wouldn't be talking about seventeen or eighteen votes for Murray. Johnson started down the list, alphabetically.

He got to Rhode Island's octogenarian Theodore Francis Green, who generally was counted in the liberal camp, and asked Humphrey where Green stood. With Murray, Humphrey replied. You see? said Johnson, that's what I mean. You don't know the facts. You don't even know that Green is going to nominate me. And so it went, down the list of forty-eight Democrats, until only a handful was left and Murray's total dwindled. Johnson bore down. Humphrey and the liberals, he said, would look foolish when the vote was taken. Murray would be humiliated. Why make a fight under these conditions? But Humphrey, although thoroughly chastened, could not break his commitment. He changed the subject, and asked Johnson about liberal representation on the Steering and Policy Committees.

Almost curtly, Johnson said: No, I don't want to talk about that now. You put up your man [Murray] and we'll put up our man [Johnson] and we'll see what happens. If you want to talk to me later, I'll discuss these other matters with you. And so, on that rainy January 3, just before the convening of the new Senate, when the Democrats met to elect their new leaders, the result was precisely as Johnson predicted. Murray's total was so small it was not even announced, to spare Murray his humiliation. (No record was kept and the exact number—Humphrey remembers just three votes—is now lost forever.) Humphrey himself moved to make Johnson's selection unanimous.

After the Senate adjourned that day with Johnson now established as Democratic leader, he visited Humphrey's office and offered to talk *now* about the Steering and Policy Committees. Despite his lopsided victory, it rankled Johnson that the liberals hadn't supported him. He told Humphrey: I'll talk to you, but I'm not going to deal with any of those other blankety-blank liberals. I'm not going to talk to those so-and-so's. You tell me what liberals you want on Policy and Steering, and I'll put them on but I won't talk to them.

The Senate organization inherited by Lyndon Johnson was comfortably old-fashioned, dusty with years of tradition and ceremony, and as far behind the times as a Model A Ford. Johnson had quietly scrutinized every cranny of the Senate Establishment. Indeed, on the eve of the Johnson era in the Senate, he knew personally every political power center in the Capital, what made the government work and, most important, which buttons to push to make it work for him. He had spent countless hours grilling old-timers in Congress and in the executive branch on the Washington power struggle. Roosevelt's secretary, Grace Tully, whom Johnson put on the Senate Democratic Policy Committee staff early in 1953, was one of the brains he picked, repeatedly probing her memory to find out how various political leaders, most particularly Roosevelt himself, had handled difficult problems.

Perched near the pinnacle of party leadership, Johnson had a plan fixed in his mind of what he wanted to do. He did not agree with Woodrow Wilson's appraisal of the limitations imposed on the Senate as a legislative body: "The truth is," wrote Wilson, "the Senate is just what the mode of its election and the conditions of public life make it." Johnson had long since decided that the Senate was much more, that it could be mobilized and shaped, depending on the quality of its leaders. Johnson wanted to streamline the Senate's power structure, breaking the power of Russell's conservative coalition and making it part of the regular leadership. That could be accomplished only by stamping the personality of the floor leader on the majority party in the Senate, so that the Senate could speak with a clear voice. Some day, as he looked ahead, that voice would be Lyndon Johnson's. The Senate was made for a man who understood power. The House was unwieldy, but in the Senate a leader could work miracles if he knew how to trade. Johnson was born a trader.

In January, 1953, however, Johnson was not Majority Leader. In the Senate that year were forty-eight Democrats, forty-seven Republicans, and one Independent (Wayne Morse of Oregon, who in disillusionment with Eisenhower bolted the Republicans during the 1952 election). Morse had agreed to vote with the Republicans on which party should run the Senate, and since the Republicans had Vice-President Richard M. Nixon to break the 48–48 tie, Johnson became Minority Leader and Taft Majority Leader.

But even as Minority Leader there were many ways for Johnson to advance his plans. He examined his future within the broader context of his basic political relationships, which were fourfold: 1) with the new Republican President; 2) with the Republican leadership in the Senate (Taft, heir apparent William F. Knowland of California, and Styles Bridges of New Hampshire); 3) with the liberals of his own party (in the Senate and the Democratic National Committee); 4) and, finally, with the badly split Democratic party in his own state of Texas. Any one of these basic relationships, if not handled correctly, could destroy Johnson and gravely damage his party. And on each of them a Johnson policy—drawn from the man's whole history as a politician—emerged rapidly and naturally.

1) Johnson knew that his party, in its relations with the Republican Administration, would be hurt by a basic policy of opposition for the sake of opposition. Eisenhower in 1953 was not Truman in 1952, reviled by the Republicans, falling in the opinion polls, the legatee of "Korea, Communism and corruption." Although it was politically opportune for the Republicans to drag Truman's name into the gutter, it would have been the politics of self-destruction for the Democrats to have handled Eisenhower in the same way. And Johnson would be one of the first victims.

Johnson, of course, didn't explain it quite that way. Soon after his election as leader, he described his basic approach to Eisenhower in statesmanlike words. "There are two courses open to a minority party," he told a Democratic party dinner in New York on February 15. "It can indulge in the politics of partisanship, or it can remain true to the politics of responsibility." "Responsibility" was to be the central thrust of Johnson's "Eisenhower policy" in scores of Senate debates and national crises. And in the guise of "Mr. Responsibility," Johnson never let the majority of his party in the Senate risk the anger of the American people by blind criticism of President Eisenhower, perhaps the most widely popular President in this century. Nor did Johnson, ever mindful of his insecure home base, forget that Texas-born Eisenhower had carried Johnson's Democratic state.

But, contrary to claims by the Democratic liberals, Johnson was far from an Eisenhower stooge. He loudly claimed that right-wing Republicans were Eisenhower's worst enemies, and that he and his band of "responsible" Democrats would "save" the President from his own party—as, in fact, was often the case. But when Johnson felt it was not in his or his party's interest to back Eisenhower, he quickly forgot about "saving" the President. Although Johnson got credit for a nonpartisan stance and avoided a confrontation with the war-hero President, he could be partisan enough on occasion. It was a soundly conceived political posture.

2) Johnson's approach to the Republican leadership in the Senate was no less pragmatic or political. Regardless of what words were spoken in heat of debate or what divisions split Democrats from Republicans, Johnson never allowed a deterioration of relations between himself and the Republican leaders. (Robert Taft, stricken **fatally**

with cancer, was replaced by William Knowland in June, 1953, and Knowland in turn by Everett McKinley Dirksen in January, 1959.) Johnson was in close coordination with the shrewdest horse in the Republican stable, Styles Bridges, although they often voted opposite ways. They knew each other's hand as well as their own. They made their deals over whiskey and soda in remote Capital hideaways, and their intimacy survived the most rancid conflicts on the Senate floor. As Bridges once told Johnson in Johnson's office: "Don't think you can pull the wool over my eyes the way you do with Bill Knowland. I know you as well as you know yourself."

3) But if Johnson found a formula for Eisenhower and for the Senate Republicans, his problem with—and his antipathy for—his own Democratic liberals was infinitely more difficult. The liberals were emotional, idealistic, and firm believers in their own rhetoric, a manifestation of unrealism Johnson could never comprehend. Their roots were not in the Senate, but with the defeated Adlai Stevenson and the Democratic National Committee. They were purist not pragmatic, volatile not self-contained, aggressive not patient. They distrusted Johnson, linked him with oil and gas and segregation, and were thoroughly frightened at the prospect of having to do battle on unequal terms with him in the Senate.

Johnson knew all that in those early days of 1953. He knew his Southern regionalism made him suspect, and it galled him as much as Catholicism galled John F. Kennedy seven years later. But the chasm between Johnson and the Senate's liberal fragment also afforded Johnson an opportunity. Starting at the bottom with them, he had only one way to go, and that was up.

He did not make common cause with the liberals. That would have been ridiculous and would have destroyed his power bases both in the Senate and Texas. The way to play them was to go all out on the liberal issues that Johnson could afford to back. Those were housing, minimum wages, Social Security, farm legislation, rural electrification, reciprocal trade and, occasionally, foreign aid. But on the budget, oil and gas (the tidelands offshore oil bill was the issue of the moment), public power and, above all, civil rights, Johnson had to cash in with his own people in the Senate and in his Texas constituency. Johnson deliberately and, despite the drumfire of liberal criticism, quite successfully used this formula to make himself at least acceptable, if not lovable, to the liberals in his early years as Minority Leader (though his relations with the Democratic National Committee worsened through the years).

"I was against him for leader," Paul Douglas said privately in 1955, "but I think I was wrong. I think now that he's the best man for the job."

4) Finally, Johnson's political policy in his home state, now that he was the leader of the whole Democratic party in the Senate, was more sensitive than before. With a second-term primary election campaign coming up in 1954 and that eighty-seven-vote victory of 1948 so well remembered, Johnson refused to make the slightest move away from the traditional Texas position on oil and gas or the slightest concession to the liberals in the Senate on civil rights. And behind this Texas-first-and-last public posture, Johnson and his chief political agents back home (headed by the increasingly conservative John B. Connally) were plotting to wipe out the memory of 1948 with a massive victory in Johnson's bid for re-election in 1954.

All four of these basic policies were pure Johnsonian politics of expediency. They depended on shifting alliances and a flexible, non-doctrinaire approach. It was within this policy framework that he set about transforming the Senate and himself into sources of more formidable power.

One obvious place to begin was with the broken-down machinery of the Democratic party in the Senate, mainly the party's Policy Committee—virtually inoperative when Johnson took over in January, 1953. "All we got out of the Policy Committee in those days were the little white cards," was the recollection years later of George Reedy, the ex-United Press newsman whom Johnson shortly transferred from staff director of his Defense Preparedness Subcommittee to be staff director of the Democratic Policy Committee.

The "little white cards" told only how each Democratic Senator had voted on previous votes. There was no staff to speak of. Having watched the Policy Committee fail to function during his four years in the Senate, Johnson began to view it as a potentially powerful political instrument, a top strategy board of Senators with staff guidance from outside experts that would compete for ideas and policies with the executive branch of government. With his reflexive ability to relate everything to himself and his own political power, Johnson quickly saw that a revitalized Policy Committee could become the private preserve of the leader, reinforcing his power and adding to his control over the entire Democratic membership.

Actually, the studious Reedy was not the first or even the second Johnson choice for director of the new, sharpened Policy Committee. Johnson's first choice was Don Cook, who had run his defense investigations in both the House and Senate. But Cook had just become chairman of the Securities and Exchange Commission, one of Truman's last major appointments. He declined to leave (and twelve years later would again reject a Johnson offer of employment, that time to be Secretary of the Treasury).

Johnson's second choice was Bryce Harlow, the Oklahoma Republican who had greatly impressed Johnson on the staff of the House Armed Services Committee. But Harlow (who would soon become Eisenhower's top White House lobbyist in Congress) also rejected Johnson's offer, just as four years earlier he had turned down Johnson's invitation to be his administrative assistant in the Senate. Although he had high respect for Johnson's ability, nothing could persuade him to work for the Texan.* The Cook and Harlow refusals pointed up a Johnson deficiency that has always plagued him: the reluctance of highly qualified persons, who knew how ruthlessly Johnson drove his staff, to deliver themselves, their families, and their whole lives into his control. It is significant that Cook, though an LBJ intimate for twenty-five years, never consented to go directly on his payroll. While twice serving as chief counsel on Johnson's investigating committees, Cook had remained on the SEC payroll.

Still, Johnson's vision of a powerful Policy Committee paid off. He brought in as committee counsel Gerald Siegel, a highly competent, imaginative young Yale-trained lawyer and then an assistant to Cook at the SEC. Johnson began to consult with brain-trusters from the Roosevelt years—Benjamin Cohen, James Rowe, Tommy Corcoran. Although the committee never quite achieved the elevation Johnson hoped for it, it did become in time a personal Johnson appendage, and a center of new ideas. Its activities were often vital in leading Johnson to essential legislative compromises.

True to his tip to Humphrey, Johnson added to the Policy Committee two bona fide liberals to join the only holdover liberal, Green of Rhode Island, in those first days of 1953: Thomas Hennings of Missouri, and Johnson's challenger for the leadership, old Jim Murray. He also added Ed Johnson of Colorado, who had been Russell's campaign manager for the presidential nomination the previous year, and Earle Clements. With the four carry-overs, this meant that the liberals now had three out of nine Policy Committee seats, far from a majority but a fair number in proportion to their ratio in the Senate then.†

---

* Harlow was buttressed in his first refusal to serve after Johnson's election to the Senate in 1948 by Representative Carl Vinson, chairman of the House Armed Services Committee and supposedly one of Johnson's political "daddies." Asserting that Johnson liked his employees to be good slaves, Vinson advised Harlow not to take the job.

† Of the four carry-overs, three were to the right of center: Russell of Georgia, Hayden of Arizona, and Kerr of Oklahoma. The fourth, Lister Hill of Alabama,

As for the fifteen-man Steering Committee, Johnson gave Humphrey a seat along with three other liberals, raising the left-of-center ratio to its highest peak, but short of a majority. The Steering Committee had only one function—to assign Senators to standing committees, a seemingly innocuous role. In fact, since the committees were the heart of the Senate, the assignment role could make or break individual Senators.

Nevertheless, despite the new change in the Steering Committee, the inner directorate headed by Russell held the real power over committee assignments, and Russell wasn't even on the Steering Committee.

It was vital, therefore, for Johnson to win Russell's consent before he could carry out his historic reform of the seniority system. With Russell behind him, the Steering Committee presented no problem. Without Russell, the Johnson reform couldn't succeed.

Before Lyndon Johnson's leadership, the criterion for getting assigned to a committee was length of service in the Senate. For example, if two Senators sworn into office the same day were competing for a single committee vacancy, and one of them had served previously in the House, he automatically got preference. Similarly, a former governor had priority over a Senator with equal seniority who had never been a governor. This rigidity made it impossible to place a new Senator where his talents best suited him, if a Senator with one day more seniority happened to want that committee.

A concrete case confronted Johnson in January, 1953. Newly elected Senator Stuart Symington of Missouri, who had grown close to Johnson in fighting alongside him for a seventy-group Air Force as Secretary of the Air Force under Truman, would have been barred by the seniority system from the Senate Armed Services Committee. Johnson had watched the seniority system deprive qualified younger members of committee seats during his fifteen years in the House and Senate. He personally had been immune to it, simply because of patronage by President Roosevelt in the House in 1937 and by Russell and the other Southerners in the Senate in 1949. Now, as the new Senate leader, he decided to risk a major party row by proposing to break the seniority system.

Johnson's first step, naturally enough, was to minimize that risk by talking to Russell. In those days Johnson never made a tactical move without getting—and generally taking—the advice of the dour-faced Georgian whose grasp of Senate politics and innate common sense

---

voted the straight Southern line on all issues touching race but took a strong liberal position on many social welfare issues, particularly in the field of health.

gave him towering prestige among his colleagues. Russell was Johnson's touchstone on every conceivable problem.

When Johnson broached his revolutionary idea, Russell surprised him by replying that he, too, had always favored giving new Senators one good committee instead of making them cool their heels for years on the Post Office and Civil Service Committee. The cautious Russell characteristically added, however, that Johnson would be playing with dynamite in tampering with the hallowed seniority system. As a result of Russell's benign neutrality, the Steering Committee tamely followed Johnson's proposals. Symington was immediately assigned to Armed Services; Humphrey (as Johnson had hinted) to Foreign Relations, along with the just-elected Mike Mansfield; Herbert Lehman of New York to Banking and Currency; and John F. Kennedy to Labor and Public Welfare. With Russell not objecting, this fracturing of the seniority system went by without visible anger from any of the old Senate grandees. Instead, Johnson was praised in the press—and, far more important, collected political IOUs from the freshman Democrats whom he helped. In one blow he had accomplished a multiple increase in the power of his office.

Johnson's tinkering with the committee system didn't stop there. The McCarthy issue was at white heat in early 1953, and with the Republicans now controlling the Senate for the first time in four years, Senator Joseph McCarthy of Wisconsin became the new chairman of the Government Operations Committee and its fearsome arm, the Permanent Investigations Subcommittee. Like most Democrats, Johnson had said nothing publicly about McCarthy's reckless charges against Truman, Secretary of State Dean Acheson, and the State Department. But privately he was deeply worried.

As the Republicans' chief investigator, backed irresponsibly by Taft and by powerful right-wing elements inside the Eisenhower Administration, McCarthy was going to be hard to stop as he delved into the Truman record to back up his charges of subversion and disloyalty in government. To counter McCarthy, Johnson quietly made sure that three new Democrats, none of them wrapped in the orthodox liberal mantle, and none of whom would have to run for re-election for six years, were assigned to the McCarthy Investigations Subcommittee. They were John Kennedy, Stuart Symington, and Washington's Henry M. (Scoop) Jackson. In itself, that was a bold move because, to accomplish it, Johnson had to persuade McCarthy's friend and ally, the forbidding Democratic Senator Pat McCarran of Nevada, past chairman of the witch-hunting Internal Security Subcommittee, to withdraw his own application for a seat on McCarthy's committee.

The fact that Johnson was able to buck McCarran testifies to how rapidly he had consolidated his own power as Democratic leader in those brief, early days of the 83rd Congress.

By the time Johnson went to New York City to give the main address at a Jefferson-Jackson Day dinner on February 15, 1953, his position within the Democratic party in the Senate was secure. The liberals growled, but Johnson already was strengthening his working arrangement with Humphrey, whom he cultivated as his entree into the liberal camp, just as Russell was his agent in the conservative camp. Johnson went to work subtly in his first important New York speech to undermine the liberal dogma that, although Southern, Southwestern, and Western Democrats were welcome in the Democratic party, the party's center of power had to be in the Northern cities and had to be firmly liberal-oriented.

Finding that the Democratic party "has occupied a special position in American life," Johnson added:

> It is only when the voices of a few pressure groups drown out all other voices that the Democratic party loses . . . The American people will never long tolerate a political party dominated exclusively—nor one *that appears to be dominated*—by any special group—be it labor, capital, farm, North, South, East, or West.*

Thus did Johnson, Southerner in a party whose doctrine had been liberal and whose captains had been Northerners since the Civil War, stake his claim for leadership in a different kind of Democratic party. Johnson knew that if he were ever to dominate his party on a national scale as he now dominated it in the Senate, he could not hope to make open common cause with the party's traditional national power centers: labor unions, big-city liberals, the Negro. Down that road lay the quicksand of his native Texas and the quick end of his political career. His target was the great middle-ground of the party, isolating ideological liberals on the left and doctrinaire conservatives on the right. And to this end, also, Johnson began edging away from the party's traditional North-South cleavage. It was in this early period of Johnson's Senate leadership that LBJ aides Reedy and Siegel hammered home the thesis to newspaper reporters and magazine editors that Texas was a *Western* state as well as a Southern state.

Within two months of the opening of Congress, Johnson hungrily

* Emphasis is added.

grabbed the first opportunity to apply two of his basic political principles to a major issue: the question of the Yalta and Potsdam agreements. Ever since the Potsdam Conference in 1945, Republicans had been charging a Roosevelt-Truman "sellout" to the Russians in postwar arrangements for Central Europe. Now that they had come into control of both presidency and Congress, the desire to make political capital out of the Yalta-Potsdam "sellout" simply had to be fulfilled. But Eisenhower, who had been so integral a part of those wartime and postwar settlements, understandably was less eager to delve into Yalta-Potsdam than the Republicans who controlled Congress.

He therefore submitted to Congress an innocuous resolution simply condemning Soviet "enslavement" of Eastern Europe, which Johnson quickly endorsed as having "no trace of the partisanship that could lead to discord and disunity." But the Republicans in the Senate, led by Taft (who in January, 1953, assigned himself to the Foreign Relations Committee for just such a contingency), had no intention of letting a generation of Democratic rule off so easily. Taft demanded that the Foreign Relations Committee stiffen the Eisenhower resolution with language questioning whether the wartime pacts might actually be invalid and illegal from a juridical standpoint.

Here was Johnson's golden opportunity: first, to line up almost all the Senate's Democrats beside Eisenhower and against the dominant Republican conservatives; and second, to make common cause with the liberals in his own party, who were far more emotionally defensive about the Yalta controversy than the moderates and the conservatives. Johnson made the most of it. He accused the Taft Republicans of attempting to "divide us in the face of the enemy," and praised Eisenhower for having issued "a clear call for America to speak with a united voice against the Soviet enslavement of free peoples."

In words that were repeatedly to ring out a fundamental belief in bipartisanship on foreign policy (and that, more than a decade later, he would have occasion to evoke from the Oval Office of the White House), Johnson said:

> It is my intention to support the President's resolution in the nonpartisan spirit in which it was written and sent to Congress. I shall certainly oppose any effort to attach partisan amendments that will jeopardize the President's prestige before the country and the world.

As it happened, the Republicans did (by a two-vote margin in the Foreign Relations Committee) insert harsher language in the resolution, but to no avail. Stalin's sudden death delayed the legislative process for several weeks, and the Taft Republicans lost their initiative. No resolution of any kind was passed.

Johnson returned to his useful theme many times in those early Eisenhower days, portraying himself as a champion of the idolized man in the White House, his protector against the conservative Republicans in Eisenhower's own party. "We shall not permit the Republican Old Guard to use the President's prestige as a shield behind which to tear down the liberty and prosperity our people have built," he promised a Jefferson-Jackson Day dinner in Jackson, Mississippi. Again, on his July 6 weekly radio broadcast taped in Washington for Texas stations, Johnson praised Eisenhower as a "good soldier," who was being safeguarded by "an unusual form of bipartisanship . . . a combination between the President, some elements of his own party, and the Democrats against large groups of Republicans who tried to sabotage his program up and down the line."

On the Senate floor, Johnson was rarely seen sitting quietly in his seat, watching the other actors in the often tiresome legislative debates. Nor did Johnson speak much himself. He had come to this high position of leadership with no reputation as an orator and with precious little experience as a Senate debater. For all his outward self-assurance, he constantly worried that he might be caught in a forensic trap by one of the conservative masters in the Senate—perhaps Eugene Millikin of Colorado who, as chairman of the Senate Finance Committee, divided power on tax bills with Georgia's patriarch, Walter George. Johnson gave those Senate titans a wide berth and never crossed them in debate.

To his own pals—junior Senators such as Florida's George Smathers, Symington, Bob Kerr, and Minority Whip Earle Clements, Johnson often confided his insecurity and asked for guidance. One of them purchased a recording device for Johnson to practice the art of public speaking, and when Johnson's voice was played back his friends listened as critics. So cautious and reserved did these senatorial friends know Johnson to be that once, without his knowledge, they organized a claque of secretaries and sent them to the gallery on a day on which Johnson was planning a speech. When he finished in his indistinct, dry monotone, the claque started a most surprising round of applause that swept through the galleries. Johnson's friends were bucking him up.

It was all part of Johnson's education, a process that drew its inspiration from careful study of the Senate grandees. Johnson seldom left the Senate until long after the last adjournment bell had sounded and he arrived the next morning, driven by his chauffeur, Norman Edwards, in an appropriately shiny Cadillac (a leadership perquisite) long before most other Senators had had their breakfast. Always being available was a tremendous asset. It enabled him to develop quickly the most informed Intelligence System in Senate history. By using this network, Johnson was able to anticipate the result of close votes with astonishing accuracy, to the consternation of both liberal antagonists in his own party and somber, unsophisticated Bill Knowland, who was now his Republican counterpart.

Johnson's Intelligence System quickly found its most apt student in Bobby Gene Baker, a country boy from Pickens, South Carolina, who had come to Washington as a teen-aged Senate page and by 1951 at age twenty-three had become the Senate Democratic cloakroom's chief page. When Johnson became Minority Leader, he immediately promoted Baker, now twenty-five, to become Assistant Secretary to the Minority, a highly strategic position that enabled the precocious Baker to become the leader's eyes and ears. Baker had virtually grown up in the Senate, and his quick mind had by now catalogued every Senator.

Soon after Johnson's election to the Senate in 1948, he called Baker to his Congressman's office on the fifth floor of the Old House Office Building. Johnson and Baker, who soon would become indispensable to each other, discussed such housekeeping matters as what suite Johnson would occupy in the Senate Office Building and what committees he sought. It was the first of many meetings.

By December, 1950, Johnson had found many ways to make use of the sharp-featured, sharp-brained Bobby Baker and simultaneously developed a genuine admiration for him. When Baker's first son was born that month, Johnson gave Baker a fifty-dollar war bond in the son's name. Johnson, who had always wanted a son, told Baker: "You're like a son to me, because I don't have a son of my own." Baker had been urging Johnson to go after the vacant whip job. With laughter, Johnson warned Baker to stop it. "You'll destroy me," he said, "because I can't afford to be identified with the Democratic National party right now." Neither took the warning seriously.

The main mover for Johnson as whip in 1951 had been Bob Kerr, who sold the idea to Russell.* But the rash of newspaper stories that quickly circulated in the Washington rumor mill were important in moving events forward. And these stories—or many of them—came right from Bobby Baker. Throughout 1951 and 1952, with Baker holding the undescriptive title of chief Senate Democratic page, the John-

* See page 43.

son-Baker relationship ripened into an intimate working friendship.

Johnson sometimes included Baker in small dinner parties Mrs. Johnson gave in their house on Thirtieth Place in northwest Washington, parties that played an integral part in Johnson's developing network of allies. The guests invariably included Southern leaders in the Senate, such as Russell or Byrd, and one or two key Republicans, often Bill Knowland. Texan William S. White, then Senate correspondent for the *New York Times,* was another frequent guest. These informal dinners gave Johnson a singular insight into the Senate's inner problems. Senators and their idiosyncrasies were analyzed there as they could never be on the floor and seldom in the cloakroom. At Mrs. Johnson's parties, the men spoke frankly and unguardedly in the intimacy of the dinner table, and Johnson stored up in a few years a penetrating understanding of the world of the Senate. Beyond that, Mrs. Johnson's dinners gave her husband a chance to show off his hostmanship. He was a gregarious politician, unlike Senate leaders Alben Barkley (who almost never had other Senators in for dinner) and Scott Lucas.

Baker had the confidence of all Democrats in the Senate except for a few liberals. It was he who could pass the word to a Senator who wanted to know if it would be safe to take a long weekend, without missing a roll-call vote. It was Baker who knew when the major bills would be taken up, long before any announcement. It was Baker who could tip off a Senator about small-print language in a seemingly innocuous bill. And in transmitting valuable tidbits, Baker would often pick up a tidbit of information in return. Accordingly, Baker knew the Senate's pulse beat as no one else did. Nor was he encumbered by senatorial dignity. Not being a Senator, he could go where he pleased when he pleased. This store of knowledge, fed to Johnson as soon as Baker had it, quickly became Johnson's singular advantage over other Senators.

The six-month 1953 session, Eisenhower's first as President, was devoid of legislative excitement. Johnson continued his traditional support of military spending geared to the demands of the Pentagon brass, and repeatedly warned against the "bigger-bang-for-a-buck" economics (based on an invulnerable force of big bombers) of auto magnate Charles E. Wilson, Eisenhower's Defense Secretary. When the Russians began to show signs of backing a genuine truce in Korea, he told the Senate to guard against a "slow down, cut back, or stretch out" of arms spending. Johnson declared: "We must make certain that we do not let these most recent Communist moves cause us to fold up our military strength. We have made that mistake in the past [and] we are suffering today from the effects of that error."

His support of the President was choppy. He voted to cut Eisenhower's foreign aid spending but backed the President on extension of the Reciprocal (low-tariff) Trade Act and, of course, to give three Gulf-coast states—including Texas—control over off-shore oil resources. But the transcendent issue, as 1953 moved into the heat of a Washington summer and the early adjournment of Congress, scarcely appeared on the Senate floor at all.

This omnipresence was McCarthyism, and it was tearing the country in two. Johnson knew that McCarthyism would be the central problem of his delicate balancing act in 1954.

Chapter V

★★★★★★★★★★

LBJ'S
BALANCING
ACT

Johnson is like a fire chief who doesn't turn on the siren unless he can save the house. When he thinks he can't win, he sits on the side, looking for another weak spot where a successful attack might be launched. This naturally gets him in dutch with many Democrats who think there are fights which should be made even if a loss is certain.

—Frank Tollman in *The New Republic,*
August 9, 1954

There was no question, as the Second Session of the 83rd Congress began in January, 1954, that the Senate must come to grips with Joseph R. McCarthy. The McCarthy issue had assumed proportions that lifted it beyond party politics in the Senate, beyond the Congress itself. It was the most imperative question before the country, not only to Lyndon Johnson and the Senate but to President Eisenhower and the whole nation. But before it became Johnson's lot to devise a weapon to bring down McCarthy, the Democratic leader had other problems no less significant to his own development as a figure of power in his party.

The first of these problems came in January when Senator Estes Kefauver of Tennessee began kicking up trouble for Johnson the moment Congress convened. Kefauver and other liberals were pressing Minority Leader Johnson to call a party caucus at the outset of the new session and adopt a Democratic program far more liberal than President Eisenhower's. Johnson dealt with the Kefauver effort predictably. Publicly silent, he let it be known through newspaper leaks that, no matter how much he was pressed, he would not call a caucus and he would not adopt a program. Even if he had been so inclined, Johnson knew that a majority of the Senate Democrats would never endorse a Kefauver-style liberal program.

Johnson had never liked the ambitious Kefauver, and certainly did not now take kindly to his gratuitous suggestions for bringing democracy to such an inherently undemocratic institution as the Senate. And there was also a personality factor: with less than a year as Democratic floor leader under his belt, Johnson was developing an imperious sensitivity to criticism from his fellow Senators that would cost him dearly in his last two years in the leadership.

But in 1954, Johnson's rejection of Kefauver's idea transcended mere dislike for the Tennessean and hostility to criticism. While Johnson had oiled up the creaky Senate Democratic machinery and established a tentative post-Truman position for his party during the short 1953 session, the long 1954 session posed numerous graver problems: the approaching Armageddon of McCarthyism, Johnson's own re-election in Texas for a second Senate term, the dispensing of favors to both liberals and conservatives among divided Senate Democrats, and the avoidance of an open rupture with the popular Republican President without infuriating partisan Democrats. That was the measure of Lyndon Johnson's balancing act of 1954, and a Kefauver-style program would spoil it.

Commitment to liberal "issues" and "programs" was a booby trap for Johnson. Within the technical minority of forty-eight Democratic Senators, Johnson knew he could build and sustain a consensus only by adopting a "prudent" policy of muted partisanship. The Democrats, he admitted privately, must not engage in head-on attacks against Eisenhower. The way to play the game was to wait for Eisenhower to announce his program and then to oppose, on a highly selective basis, only when politically profitable to the Democrats. As ever, Johnson was fearful of defeat. The Democrats would be in grave difficulty if they proposed a sweeping New Deal-like program, as Kefauver insisted, in direct opposition to Eisenhower's moderate proposals—and then could not pass it. Should that happen, the Democrats, not Eisenhower, would be blamed for stalemating Congress. The chief blametakers would be the Democratic leaders; and the chief Democratic leader was Lyndon Johnson.

For still another reason Johnson was most anxious in those early days of 1954 to keep issues muted. An unknown but rich and eccentric Texas conservative, Dudley T. Dougherty, had filed for the Democratic senatorial nomination against Johnson.* Dougherty was hardly

* In 1965, Dougherty popped up from relative oblivion to call for President Johnson's impeachment.

formidable competition, delivering his speeches from the rear end of a bright red fire truck. Although Johnson did little campaigning, that eighty-seven-vote margin of 1948 still haunted him. Until July, when the primary would be held, Johnson—distrustful of Texas voters after his experiences of 1941 and 1948—felt himself vulnerable. Anything he said might be blown up into a Texas headline to boomerang on him.

But, as party leader in the Senate, Johnson desperately needed some political springboard large enough to accommodate most Northern and Southern Democrats behind him. The Northerners were the chief problem. The 1954 off-year elections lay ahead; the liberals were demanding a fight and Lyndon Johnson had to find an outlet for normal partisan instincts—issues that would alienate neither the South nor the North but appease both.

Johnson's own detachment from issues left him totally flexible. Without a program of his own and committed deep down to no true ideological doctrine (except to his diluted brand of Populism and to the protection of the Texas vested interests essential to his reelection), Johnson could shop around for his issues. (A little something for the South, a little something for the North, a little something for the whole Democratic family.) There were always good and sufficient reasons for issues. There was the ideology of "moderation," in short, no real ideology at all. A student of LBJ and his sometime aide, Michael Janeway, has described this developing Johnson policy: "'Moderation' was a strategy designed to rebuild the Center of the Democratic party at a time when Left and Right were tearing it apart." It was, Janeway added, a strategy "devised by Johnson for his own use."

But what issue could bind Democrats together under the label of "moderation"? The 1954 session had barely started before right-wing Republicans, preparing for the 1954 elections, provided the answer with their theme song of "twenty years of treason" under the Democrats. Joe McCarthy composed the phrase during his Lincoln Day speechmaking around the country, and other Republican campaigners picked it up.

The rebuttal fell partly to the Democratic party's congressional leaders. Sam Rayburn appealed to Eisenhower to halt the Republican attack, which he called "mean, untrue, dastardly." More cautiously, Johnson avoided holding Eisenhower responsible, but pointedly warned that Democratic cooperation with the Eisenhower program might evaporate if the attacks continued. On February 10, under the sting of such Democratic criticism, Eisenhower dissociated himself from the McCarthy attacks, and Johnson, speaking for the entire Democratic party, praised the President as "a gentleman and an American" who was compelled to "rebuke" his own Republican party.

That was Johnson-style politics. He could afford to lead his party against McCarthy's political attacks. Any issue that united most of the Democrats against most of the Republicans was tailor made for Johnson. He was constantly on the search for such issues both in and outside the Senate. The "issue" need not be of transcendent importance, as on the winter evening when a coup by Johnson humiliated Senate Majority Leader William Knowland. Over Knowland's protest, Johnson abruptly adjourned the Senate. That was unprecedented. It dramatized Johnson's position as the new master of the Senate and showed that he could count the votes better than the Republicans; it also took the edge off the biting criticism from his own left wing that he was "soft on Republicans."

The adjournment hassle with Knowland developed over statehood for Hawaii. Although Southern Democrats opposed statehood for multiracial Hawaii and Northern Democrats supported it, Johnson transformed the issue into a simple partisan matter.* Knowland, he told the Senate, had unilaterally scheduled a night session of the Senate; Knowland, Johnson also complained, had simply announced that it would be held, without informing the Democratic leader. That was not only unsportsmanlike, it was humiliating, and Johnson saw a rare opportunity to line up the Democrats and force Knowland to the wall. And so, in a highly unusual challenge, Johnson suddenly moved that the Senate adjourn, preempting the Majority Leader's parliamentary prerogative.

Knowland indignantly blustered that he was "a Majority Leader without a majority," and accused Johnson of trying to filibuster the statehood bill. Nonsense, replied Johnson, he only wanted to make a point: that the Republican "majority" (with only forty-seven seats in the Senate) could not make unilateral decisions dealing with the operation of the Senate. Johnson humorously told Knowland that "the only thing worse" than a Majority Leader *without* a majority was "a Minority Leader *with* a majority."

The banter was routine, but the subsequent roll call on the adjournment question was anything but routine. Johnson won it, 48 to 45, as he knew in advance he would. He had counted his votes secretly and securely, and the issue—for him—was not in doubt. Had it been in doubt, the cautious Johnson would have thought twice about risking his prestige on a matter of such doubtful importance.

* Hawaii's long battle to become a state was not won until 1959, five years after the Johnson-Knowland power play.

The composition of that vote was a harbinger of dozens of other votes taken under Johnson's leadership in the next six years: Not a single Democrat voted against Johnson, and only two Democrats were absent. Johnson accomplished his coup by capturing one Republican, Senator William Langer of North Dakota. (It was the first of many subsequent contests in which Langer, an aging, madcap Populist-Republican—a Son of the Wild Jackass—left his own party and voted with Lyndon Johnson.)

The adjournment vote was a symbolic inroad into Republican solidarity. Even more noteworthy, Senator Styles Bridges, chairman of the Republican Policy Committee but also Johnson's back-room intimate in bipartisan wheeling and dealing, absented himself on the key vote. The "issue" of adjourning or not adjourning was trivial. But immediately after the vote, Johnson accepted the acclaim of his Democratic colleagues. He had brought all elements of his fractured party together by picking an issue without the slightest taint of ideology. He had offered every member of his party in the Senate an easy anti-Republican vote that made headlines the next day.

Senate squabbles over the time of adjournment from one day to the next were rare, however. A more intricate element in Johnson's 1954 balancing act was foreign policy.

By 1954, Johnson had not achieved the stature of a "Senate foreign policy leader" (in the customary phrase of the press). Because he was Democratic floor leader, Johnson's work on the Armed Services and the Appropriations Committees had been curtailed, and these committees only skirted the fringes of foreign policy. Johnson was not a member of the celebrated Foreign Relations Committee—the traditional home of Senate foreign policy experts such as Michigan's Arthur Vandenberg, Walter George, and J. William Fulbright of Arkansas.

If Johnson were to gain a reputation as an expert in foreign affairs, he had to do it by using his role as party leader to make himself heard in the country and by picking the brains of Democrats outside Congress. Dean Acheson, the haughty aristocrat who, as Harry Truman's Secretary of State, was the target of Red-baiting Taft Republicans but in fact was a hard anti-Communist, a few years later would become a key adviser to Johnson. But in 1954, Johnson was relying mainly on such old New Dealers as Benjamin Cohen (a soft-liner) and Tommy Corcoran (a hard-liner).

As Johnson spoke out more and more about foreign policy on the Senate floor, his skillful balancing act evolved: a bit of hard-line anti-Communism, but not enough to make common cause with the Republican neanderthals; help for the Eisenhower foreign policy, but not enough to anger the more partisan Democrats; opportunistic attacks on Eisenhower failures, but not enough to be accused of destroying "bipartisan" foreign policy.

There were occasions, however, when Johnson's use of the hard line against Eisenhower agitated the liberal Democrats—particularly when Johnson went against the President and supported the notorious Bricker Amendment, which limited the President's treaty-making powers (supposedly, to prevent another Yalta Agreement). It is worth noting, however, that Johnson voted *not* for the ultra-Whiggish amendment, sponsored by Old Guard Republican John Bricker of Ohio, but for an innocuous substitute, sponsored by Johnson's friend, Walter George. Some Democrats suspected that Johnson, although voting for the George substitute, had contrived to have it fall one vote short of the two-thirds needed for Constitutional amendments. Johnson had no illusions about the Bricker Amendment. It was a slap at *Democratic* Presidents.

Johnson also took the hard line in coming out against the admission of Communist China to the United Nations—so hard that he riled Fulbright, who was emerging as a liberal foreign policy leader. Johnson predicted flatly that if Red China entered the UN, "the American people will refuse to support the United Nations." Fulbright saw a "political immaturity" in this position, but Johnson's judgment was sound. Having led the counterattack on the McCarthy–right-wing Republican "party of treason" charge, Johnson was shrewd enough to know that anything less than militancy on the question of Communist China and the UN would quickly be snapped up by the Republicans as evidence of Democratic naïveté (since the Democrats, after all, "lost" China to the Communists in the first place).

Johnson again took a hard-line stand in a bold effort to seize Latin American foreign policy initiative from the Republicans. The Communist-dominated government of Guatemala was under siege by pro-U.S. (CIA-financed) rebels. Reflecting the Eisenhower Administration policy, Johnson charged that the Communists were "seeking to establish a beachhead in the Americas now." The "pattern for conquest," he said, was so perfectly evident all over Latin America, and most particularly in embattled Guatemala, that the United States could not stand idly by. Johnson then upstaged the Senate's Republican leaders by introducing a resolution reaffirming the Monroe Doctrine, ruling out Soviet interference with the Guatemalan crisis through the United Nations, and proclaiming that the hemispheric Organization of American States must have sole jurisdiction over "any appropriate action to prevent any further Soviet interference" in the hemisphere. Johnson continued:

This situation imposes upon all of us a new responsibility. I do not refer to the civil war in Guatemala itself. But I do mean the Communist penetration of the Western Hemisphere. That is intolerable from every standpoint and must not be permitted to happen. There is no question here of United States interference in the domestic affairs of any American state. We are concerned only with external aggression.

Johnson's resolution passed, 69 to 1 (the only hold-out being the unpredictable William Langer). By seizing the initiative, Johnson and the Democrats not only beat the Republicans, but Johnson himself, without rippling his party's ideology North or South, placed himself once again at the head of a momentarily united party.

But Lyndon Johnson was certainly no inflexible, doctrinaire hardliner. His position on the most critical foreign policy question in the spring of 1954—the Vietnam (or, as it was then called, the Indochinese) crisis—was a bit on the soft-boiled side. And hard or soft, it surely was not bipartisan.

On May 6, 1954, just one day before the French fortress at Dien Bien Phu fell to a Communist human-wave assault after a fifty-five-day siege, Johnson opened the first of the Democratic party foreign policy attacks on the Eisenhower Administration. In this he centered his fire not on the President but on Secretary of State John Foster Dulles. In the background was a secret bipartisan meeting at the White House, in which Russell, backed by Johnson and most other Democrats, rejected Dulles' proposal for direct United States bombing help to the French from United States carriers then standing by in the Gulf of Tonkin. Russell's condition for Democratic support was implicit in his question to President Eisenhower: "Where do the British stand?" The British stood against intervention, and for that reason the Democrats refused to countenance the already planned United States bombing mission. The air mission was promptly called off.

The occasion of Johnson's sharp criticism of Dulles and his "new, dynamic foreign policy," not long after this pregnant White House meeting, was the annual Jefferson-Jackson Day dinner at Washington's Mayflower Hotel. Johnson's starting point was the Geneva Conference on the settlement of the Indochina war. Dulles, in a transparent effort to dissociate the United States from the Vietnamese partition plan that finally emerged in Geneva, had deserted the U.S. delegation on May 1 and returned to Washington. Because Dulles left Geneva, Johnson said, the United States was "in clear danger of being left naked and alone in a hostile world." It was, said Johnson, "apparent only that American foreign policy has never in all its history suffered such a stunning reversal."

What is American policy on Indochina? All of us have listened to the dismal series of reversals and confusions and alarms and excursions which have emerged from Washington over the past few weeks. . . . We have been caught bluffing by our enemies. Our friends and allies are frightened and wondering, as we do, where we are headed. . . . Only a few days ago we observed our final humiliation in the spectacle of an American Secretary of State backtracking the Atlantic from the conference at Geneva. And yet, a few weeks before, while in Berlin, he had told his own people that Geneva was the world's best hope . . . This picture of our country needlessly weakened in the world today is so painful that we should turn our eyes from abroad and look homeward.*

That was strong language, even for a partisan fund-raising dinner. But to the Democrats assembled there, including Harry Truman, the Johnson attack was sweet music that drowned out the savage Republican attacks of 1951 and 1952 on Acheson. ("Isn't it wonderful," Nixon had said a few months earlier, "that finally we have a Secretary of State who isn't taken in by the Communists, who stands up to them?") At the Mayflower that evening, Johnson's harsh words struck just the right political note, emotionally binding the entire Democratic party together in the half-angry, half-sentimental self-pity that gives a political gathering its sense of unity. Johnson, the catalyst of this unity, had struck another shrewd blow at liberal critics who complained he was "soft on Republicans."

As he scourged John Foster Dulles, Johnson's inner eye was on Texas and the July 24 primary election. If he could clear that hurdle, six years of relative independence stretched ahead. With remarkable skill, he had faultlessly maneuvered around the deepest ideological pitfalls of Senate legislation. Accordingly, poor Dudley Dougherty back in Texas was stymied. But to the very day of the primary, John-

---

* Arthur Krock wrote in the New York Times on May 8 that Johnson "had been under criticism . . . for . . . an excess of caution before joining political battle. On this occasion he did not show that quality. To the contrary, he struck a heavy blow at bipartisanship in the congressional sector of foreign policy. How critical to the non-Communist nations, striving at Geneva to repair their broken front, was the hour in which Senator Johnson did that, was stressed next morning by the fall of Dien Bien Phu."

son let Dougherty's feeble challenge influence his conduct as Senate leader.

The setting on the Senate floor for several days before the Texas primary had been one of unrelieved tension as bipartisan bands of liberals and conservatives fought bitterly over an atomic energy bill. For the first time in decades, the Senate had been held in continuous session—all day and all night—in an effort by Knowland and most of the conservatives to break a filibuster conducted by, of all people, the liberal Democrats.

At issue was an Eisenhower Administration move to give private industry a toehold in atomic power. Further arousing liberals, and particularly the Tennessee Valley Senators, was the Dixon-Yates contract, by which two Southern power companies were authorized to build a private plant that would supply power to the Tennessee Valley Authority complex for the first time.

The liberals were resolved to filibuster the bill until Knowland permitted a vote on amendments that would give Washington regulatory powers over the future sale of atomic power and would soften "giveaway" provisions. For eleven days liberals held the floor in continuous speechmaking. Senate corridors had the look of an overcrowded hospital, with cots and bedding scattered about.

Throughout this filibuster period Johnson kept discreetly silent, although occasionally casting a vote with the liberals. On Saturday, July 24, he talked at length to angry, red-faced Bill Knowland, who was not so quietly raging at the liberals for having tied his Senate in a knot and for damming up major session-end legislation. But Knowland held high cards. The anticipated public outrage against the bill was slow in coming, and the all-night sessions were taking their toll. The liberals found it more and more debilitating to continue.

Late that night, the results of the Johnson-Dougherty primary election were flashed to Johnson in Washington. To nobody's surprise, he beat Dougherty by almost 3 to 1. At that very point, freed from all political repercussions in Texas, Johnson rose on the floor of the Senate and proposed a unanimous consent agreement (a tactic to limit debate by the consent of every Senator present) to end the filibuster. One objection can block a unanimous consent request, and the objection was quickly voiced by Oregon's Wayne Morse. The significance, however, lay not in Morse's objection but in Johnson's proposal. Silent for eleven days during the debate, his sudden decision to seek a vote was a clear signal that his sympathies lay with Knowland and the conservatives. Psychologically, that swiftly cut the ground from under the exhausted liberals and turned the battle into a rout.

That may have surprised some liberals and the press, but not

Knowland. Even before he showed his hand, Johnson had secretly held counsel with Knowland and helped him plan the anti-filibuster strategy of round-the-clock sessions (with Russell in the background giving Johnson advice).*

Johnson's private rationale was spelled out: fifteen of his Democratic Senators, he told intimates, were ready to vote for the Eisenhower bill. The liberals, by holding out, were linked day after day in press headlines with the now partyless Morse, the Senate's unpredictable "Independent" troublemaker. This association, Johnson confided privately, would be political suicide for the Democrats. In short, he claimed that to save the Democratic party the filibuster had to be beaten.

Addressing the Senate moments after he proposed his agreement to end the debate, Johnson sought to calm the anguished spirits of the liberals with an appeal to "reason."

> Through many decades my party has been the truly responsible party. These are times that call for reasonable action by reasonable parties made up of reasonable men. . . . [This is] the hour for each of us to search our hearts and souls and ask the question, "are we exercising the responsibility of which we are capable?"

These words, to be heard in infinite variations from Johnson over the next six years, were the *public* expression of Johnson's *public* view of himself and his party. But they concealed the true nature of his private predicament in the filibuster against the atomic energy bill. As a Texan, he could not alienate his constituency by joining the filibuster. As Democratic leader, he had lost control of his Democrats and was under severe criticism in the press. In self-interest, his only recourse was to join the Republicans and Southern conservatives and smash the filibuster.

Furthermore, Russell and the other Southern Democrats were concerned little about the success or failure of the atomic energy bill. What really concerned them was the possibility that the longer the filibuster ran the greater the chance that frustrated Midwestern Republicans would join in some future effort to liberalize Rule XXII (to make it easier to end filibusters). That, of course, would affect Southern veto power over civil rights bills. Thus, what really drove Johnson to join Knowland were his close ties with Russell and the Southerners and his sensitivity to the press criticism that asserted that he could not lead his Democrats.

* Six years later, confronted by a Southern filibuster against a civil rights bill, Johnson again tried the tactic of all-night sessions to break the filibuster. This time, against Russell's toughly disciplined Southerners, the tactic backfired.

The predictable result of Johnson's move to end the debate was Senate passage of the atomic energy bill on July 27 (after a twelve-and-a-half-hour opposition speech by Morse). But when the bill went to conference with the House, it lost several public-interest amendments the liberals had managed to adopt. Johnson at this point partially retrieved his lost status with the liberals by successfully leading the fight to reclaim the disputed sections. After siding with the conservatives, he was now giving a little something to the liberals.

By the end of 1953, when the depredations of McCarthyism were reaching a climax, a liberal friend of Johnson dropped by his office to lecture him on his responsibilities to his party and his country. Johnson, scolded the friend, must speak out on McCarthy generally and specifically must come down hard against McCarthy's running investigation of "subversion" in the Army.

Johnson listened silently, then broke in on his friend. "We all have to do what we can do," he said. "You are doing what you ought to be doing right now [working against McCarthy]. When the time comes, I'll do what I ought to do."

It was Johnson's conviction that if he, the Minority Leader, were to jump into the vanguard of the public McCarthy-haters, anti-McCarthy Republicans would be forced as an instinctive partisan reaction to come to McCarthy's defense. Beyond that, Johnson had a deeper fear: if the entire Democratic establishment in Congress, led by himself, turned against McCarthy now, when he still had a dangerous and powerful hold on millions of Americans, it might appear that the Democrats were moved by self-interest in trying to cover up some unspeakable wickedness in the Truman Administration. If the whole Democratic party was prematurely arrayed against McCarthy, Johnson believed, McCarthy would win.

That this concern of Johnson's betrayed inordinate caution, and that his true purpose in staying out of the fight was self-preservation, not party preservation, has been charged by some liberals (despite the fact that the liberal politicians attacking McCarthy in 1953 would hardly have filled a telephone booth). But no such indictment can be proved. Johnson, it seems clear enough, wanted to strike at McCarthy —but not until McCarthy could be brought down. He knew how dangerous McCarthy was. As Johnson once said, "Joe will go that extra mile to destroy you."

And so, that day months before the start of the Army-McCarthy hearings on April 22, 1954, Johnson told his critical liberal friend that the vital next step was not for Johnson or any individual Democrat to attack McCarthy, but to make certain that the hearings were tele-vised. Johnson was in close contact with Senator John McClellan of Arkansas, the senior Democrat on McCarthy's Investigating Subcom-mittee. He told McClellan that whatever the concessions the Demo-crats on the subcommittee made to McCarthy, they were to insist on one condition: television coverage. It was Johnson's conviction, and it was proved right, that McCarthy could not survive the brutal ex-posure of television, which would record in millions of American liv-ing rooms his intemperate, paranoiac abuse of American citizens.

The truth is that Johnson was deeply concerned about the excesses of McCarthyism long before the Army-McCarthy hearings. While publicly brushing off the Wisconsin Senator as "a Republican prob-lem" (in much the same manner that Eisenhower told intimates, "I won't get into the gutter with that guy."), Johnson was privately de-bating within himself the most effective means of dealing with both the man and the "ism." He confided his solution, reached sometime early in 1953, in off-the-record remarks to friends in the press.

"If I were the Majority Leader," he said, "I know what I would do about McCarthy. I'd appoint a bipartisan select committee, and I'd put on our side the very best men we have, men who are above re-proach, the wisest men I know in the Senate and the best judges, and I'd ask 'em to make a study of McCarthy and report to the Senate. With the men I'd pick, the Senate would accept their judgment and that would be the end of it."

Johnson knew whom he wanted on this select committee. They would have to be conservatives, such as Walter George of Georgia and John Stennis of Mississippi. (A liberal sitting in judgment on Mc-Carthy would be an easy target for McCarthy and his friends before the first piece of evidence was in.) But, Johnson lamented, he was *not* the Majority Leader. And McCarthy was Bill Knowland's problem, *not* his.

Johnson nursed his solution for months, then brought it up one day to Bill Knowland in a private conversation, in the summer of 1953, in the office of Earle Clements, the Democratic Whip. Knowland, deeply conservative at heart, was skeptical about moving against McCarthy. For although McCarthy was "a Republican problem," he also was regarded by many Republicans as an asset for the 1954 congressional elections in the Midwest and West.

Knowland's reluctance to endorse Johnson's select committee was weakened by the charge of Communist infiltration of the Protestant clergy made in July, 1953, by J. B. Matthews, a McCarthy sub-committee consultant. Johnson happened to be reading the news-ticker in the Senate cloakroom when a bulletin tapped out the inflammatory Matthews attack. He turned to Harry Byrd. "Here, see this," Johnson said. "Joe's gone too far this time."

Almost a year went by before the time was ripe for the Senate to move against McCarthy. Surfeited by McCarthy's excesses during the months of hearings (nationally televised just as Johnson planned) on his dispute with the Army, the Senate finally prepared to act.

On August 3, 1954, in a 75 to 12 vote it agreed to establish a select committee—and Johnson was ready to move. His aides on the Policy Committee had completed elaborate research into Senate record books to see how other Senates had handled situations dealing with other problem Senators. For weeks he had carried in his pocket a smudged compilation of these historical precedents. He had learned all there was to know about select committees, their rules of procedure, the special dignity that attached to their work, and the particular relevance of their findings. (A select committee usually was named for one specific assignment. As the privileged creature of the Senate, its findings invariably carried high authority.) Johnson had done all this in privacy, working out the details with his staff but disclosing precious little of his findings to other Senators. That was the Johnson System: diligent preparation, extraordinary secrecy, nothing left to chance.

As for the qualifications of the members of this select committee, Johnson stuck to his original concept that it should be made up of conservatives in the mold of Walter George. There was an additional Johnson-imposed requirement. Senators who had ever expressed a *public* judgment of McCarthy were vulnerable and should be disqualified.

As it turned out, Walter George, pleading age, fatigue, and too much work, refused a place on the select committee to investigate McCarthy's conduct. Johnson would not take no. He cajoled the old gentleman, stroked his ego, and suggested (with that unique brand of shameless Johnsonian flattery that hardened politicians often found irresistible) that unless George changed his mind, the select committee would fail and McCarthy would continue his tyrannical ways in the Senate. So George finally said yes—with one condition: he would accept if Colorado's Republican Eugene Millikin would also accept a place on the committee. Millikin, however, had already turned down Knowland, on legitimate grounds of bad health, and Knowland could not persuade Millikin to change his mind. So both George and Millikin, who, as Johnson and Knowland knew, could cloak the select committee with the prestige of Jove, were unavailable.

Johnson's second Democratic target was Richard Russell, but Russell also refused. (He lacked time, he said.) That raised a rather alarming prospect. If the Senators with the greatest prestige—the very ones who had stayed farthest away from attacking McCarthy—all said no, the project might indeed fail. This was no job for second-raters.

Johnson's next stop was Colorado's Senator Edwin Johnson, the veteran Westerner so close to the Southern conservatives. Here, at last, was success. He agreed to a place on the committee. So did Mississippi's John Stennis, a highly respected legislator who oozed Southern charm. (Johnson first had to talk him out of a trip abroad with his son, planned months before, that conflicted with the hearings.)

For the third Democratic place, Johnson wanted waggish Sam Ervin, Jr., of North Carolina, a newer member of the Southern clique who was becoming famous for his witty stories and his leaping eyebrows. Ervin had served in every judicial capacity his state had to offer, from the Burke County criminal court to the state supreme court. It was essential that the country accept the select committee as juridically qualified to hear the evidence against McCarthy. Ervin's record was added insurance, and Johnson wanted him for that reason.

Ervin was approached by Johnson and Clements, and Ervin said he would serve. But almost as an afterthought, Clements asked: "Sam, you've never said anything publicly about Joe, have you?" Ervin stared at the ceiling for a long minute. "I wrote a letter once to a constituent and told him what I thought of Joe," he growled.

Through Johnson's mind ran the headline that every newspaper would carry if that letter from Ervin should be discovered and published during the hearings. Ervin might be compromised, and so might the committee—and the entire endeavor.

"Sam," asked Johnson, "you've picked a lot of juries in the past. Would you pick yourself now as a juror to pass judgment on Joe McCarthy?"

Again, a long pause. Finally, Ervin said yes, he would have no scruples about sitting on the McCarthy jury.

The Democratic, all-conservative section of the jury—Stennis, Ed Johnson, and Ervin—was picked in strictest secrecy. Meanwhile, Knowland had named Utah's Senator Arthur Watkins as chairman of the select committee. His other two Republicans were the pleasantly respectable Frank Carlson of Kansas and, from South Dakota, the Senate's most fastidious small-print reader, Francis Case.

Not one of these six men had a feud going with any other Senator. Not one of them was controversial. Not one of them was on record either for or against McCarthy. Not one was up for re-election that year. It was just as Johnson had planned it.

The committee took evidence on the McCarthy case from August 31 to September 13, 1954, and then, six days after the November election, the lame-duck Senate returned to a special session to debate the committee's recommendations. On December 2, the Senate voted to "condemn" McCarthy's conduct as a Senator.*

Throughout all this period, Johnson had held his tongue, revealing nothing of his own feelings toward McCarthy. His parliamentary maneuvers hinted that he had decided to vote "yes" on the resolution of condemnation, but he kept silent. As the case built toward a climax on the Senate floor, however, Johnson was quietly gathering in Democratic votes. Just before the final roll call, he broke his silence.

"In my mind, there is only one issue here—morality and conduct," he said. "Each of us must decide whether we approve or disapprove of certain actions as standard for senatorial integrity. I have made my decision." Referring to McCarthy's description of conservative Republican chairman Arthur Watkins as "stupid" and "cowardly," and his characterization of the select committee as having "done the work of the Communist party," Johnson said: "The words that were used in describing these men do not belong in the pages of the *Congressional Record*. They would be more fittingly inscribed on the wall of a men's room."

Johnson said nothing about the specifics of the charges against McCarthy, the question of Communism in government or the use of "privilege" in a Senate committee to blacken the name of an innocent victim. But when the votes were counted, every single Democrat present voted with Johnson and against McCarthy. It was not accidental.

As Democratic leader, Johnson's handling of the most difficult issue in his new role was beyond reproach. His silence in the Senate set the mood of his party, restrained Democrats from emotional talk, and generously left the floor to debate by Republicans. And on the final roll call he brought off a solid front: from Mississippi's Jim Eastland to New York's Herbert Lehman, a unanimous Democratic vote emerged of 67 to 22.† It was a Johnson tour de force, a taste of what the next four years with Lyndon Johnson as Leader of the *Majority* would be like.

---

* After all this hard work in behalf of the project, Knowland finally could not bring himself to vote censure against McCarthy, and voted "no."

† On the Democratic side of the aisle, there were only three not voting: John Kennedy of Massachusetts, who was hospitalized in Boston recovering from a serious back operation; George Smathers of Florida, and Albert Gore of Tennessee. Smathers and Gore were "paired" with Republican Senators who were unavoidably absent. Thus, of all Democratic Senators, only Kennedy was not announced for the censure of McCarthy.

The political atmosphere was warming in the summer of 1954. Responding to the appeals of Republican partisans who grumbled that their President wasn't political enough, General Eisenhower abruptly warned that if the Democrats won the congressional elections a "cold war of partisan politics" between the Democratic Congress and the Republican administration might undermine the federal government and produce a disastrous stalemate. Congress had adjourned to campaign for the November elections, and Johnson, with his own election assured, toured the country to fight for the election of Democratic Senators. One stop on his tour that fall was a speech for Hubert Humphrey in Madison, Minnesota, where, on October 23, he replied to Eisenhower's warning against the "cold war of partisan politics."

Still anxious to avoid a break with the President himself, Johnson skillfully damned the Republican party without laying a glove on the President. "If there is going to be any 'cold war,' the Republicans will have to declare it themselves. And since they have been practicing on the President for the past two years, they might do exactly that," he said. He then read the telegram that he and Speaker Rayburn had sent the President.

> Your statement of last night is an unwarranted and unjust attack on the many Democrats who have done so much to cooperate with your administration and to defend your program from attacks by members and leaders of your own party. It may be that you have been placed in your position of rigid, unswerving partisanship by the frantic pleas of your political advisers to come to the rescue of a party fearful of repudiation by the voters. Nevertheless, we assure you . . . there will be no cold war conducted against you by the Democrats when we gain control of the Congress.

That speech, typical of Johnson's national campaign effort that fall, was a masterpiece of political judgment. Johnson now commanded headlines as one of his party's chief campaigners, and for the first time he invaded Northern Democratic strongholds that seldom if ever before had heard a Southern accent from the political stump. Fearful that the "cold war" threat might grow into the central campaign theme of the Republicans—and pit the Democrats in that off-year election not against their opponents but against Eisenhower himself— Johnson took pains to kill it before it could grow. Privately, he cautioned Democratic Senators, particularly the militant liberals, not to get into a public dispute with Eisenhower. Publicly, in an effort to prevent the President from making wholesale attacks on all Democrats, he stressed Eisenhower's innate decency.

It worked. There was no more Eisenhower talk about a "cold war" of partisan politics in that campaign and, of utmost importance to Johnson, the Democrats regained control of Congress. The Senate margin was 48 to 47 and the still-Independent Wayne Morse (who announced that this session he would vote with the Democrats, not the Republicans, to decide which party should control the Senate and name the Majority Leader). Thus, after two years as Minority Leader, Johnson was on the threshold of new power in the Senate and new preeminence in his party. He was on the threshold, too, of leading the Senate into four of the most productive and fruitful years of its history.

Chapter VI

★★★★★★★★★★

THE
JOHNSON
SYSTEM

I doubt that if there is a member of the Senate, on either side of
the aisle, who does not look upon Lyndon Johnson as a friend.
— Senator Earle Clements of Kentucky, 1955

Knowledge of the rules isn't too important. What's important is
getting the votes.
— Charles Watkins, Parliamentarian of the
Senate, 1955

On the steamy Washington summer morning of Saturday, July 2,
1955, Senate Majority Leader Lyndon B. Johnson sent word to the
Senate press gallery that he would see the press immediately in his
new "second" office on the top floor of the Capitol. Commandeered
from the Senate-House Economic Committee, headed by Senator Paul
Douglas of Illinois, who was now suffering for his feud with his party's
leader, this two-room suite had become the Majority Leader's office.
In the outer office were secretaries and filing cabinets, but the inner
office was where the real business was conducted in an atmosphere of
leather chairs and couches, tinkling chandeliers and readily accessible
liquor cabinets. It was a corner office, and the view was magnificent,
looking south to well-tended public lawns and fountains and looking
west down the Mall to the Washington Monument and Lincoln Memorial.

The reporters braced themselves for what was coming: a hymn of
praise to the accomplishments of the first session of the 84th Congress,
now drawing to a close after six months.

These sessions of self-congratulation with reporters had become
commonplace. The McCarthy censure vote the previous December
had been only the prelude to the emergence of Lyndon Johnson as
master magician of the Senate when, in January, 1955, he became

Majority Leader of the new and narrowly Democratic Senate. At forty-six, he was the youngest Majority Leader in the chamber's history.

In those six months he had justifiably gained the reputation of the young genius who tamed the turbulent Senate for the first time since the Court-packing fight of 1937. And now, with Congress ready to adjourn for the year, newspapers and magazines were spotted with stories further enriching Johnson's new national reputation.

Newsweek of June 27, in an article aptly entitled "Senator Lyndon Johnson . . . The Texan Who Is Jolting Washington," praised the Senate's record of accomplishment under Johnson's guidance and concluded by suggesting he be considered presidential timber. *The New Republic*, a devoutly liberal publication never before known for praising Johnson, was to carry in its July 4 edition an exuberant panegyric of LBJ by Senator Richard Neuberger of Oregon, a liberal journalist-turned-politician whom Johnson captivated after Neuberger was elected to the Senate in 1954. Martin Andersen, an ex-Texan and old friend of Johnson who now was publisher of the *Sentinel* in Orlando, Florida, was to publish a front-page editorial in his Sunday paper of July 3 endorsing Johnson for President in 1956. But most important by far was the column by Robert C. Albright scheduled to appear in the *Washington Post* the morning of July 3, which would be on every Sunday breakfast table in the Capital. With an advance peek at the Albright column, Johnson had tipped off his friends in the Democratic cloakroom to watch out for it on Sunday morning. He had good reason to be pleased, because Albright's column would be the best trial balloon yet, boosting Johnson for a spot on the national ticket. The Albright column was to begin:

> Senator Lyndon B. Johnson, the first party leader in modern times to tame the independent Senate, last week emerged as something more than a highly skilled legislative technician.
>
> Unless bystanders missed their guess, he was riding a presidential boom.
>
> Whether it would gather force and mature in 1960 or even at some later date was the subject of open speculation in and out of the Senate.
>
> Johnson is only forty-six and can afford to grow and wait. But at least one impatient school of Senate admirers is already talking in terms of 1956. Not for the top spot, they say in the cloakroom, but possibly as a running mate with former Governor Adlai Stevenson.

Albright, a cautious reporter, would go on to compare the Senate's record under Johnson with Franklin Roosevelt's Hundred Days of 1933.

But even with the knowledge of such praise coming the next morning in so influential a newspaper, Johnson was on edge that hot morning of July 2 because of the never-ending liberal criticism that the 84th Congress had accomplished hardly anything. And so he summoned the press to recite once again the litany of accomplishments by his Senate.

The handful of Senate reporters working that Saturday morning filed into his office to confront a man showing the beginnings of an unmistakable middle-aged paunch. But even at two hundred and twenty pounds, the six-foot-three Johnson could still pass as the lean Texan—hard in the chest and shoulders, more angular than fleshy in the face. His full black hair was brushed back slick and close to the scalp, and he dressed like a riverboat gambler: dark silk suit, monogrammed shirt, French cuffs and those long-pointed collars.

As he faced the press on July 2, Lyndon Johnson was bone-weary from six frenetic months of eighteen-hour days. Blowing out great lungfuls of smoke in steamy jets, chain-smoker Johnson made no effort to conceal his irritation with the reporters' singular lack of perception. In slow, weary phrases, filled with pauses, he repeated the list of the Senate's 1955 accomplishments: extension of the Reciprocal Trade Agreements Act, federal aid for highway construction, Upper Colorado River Bill, increase of minimum wage to one dollar an hour, increase of foreign aid appropriations over the President's request. Continuing his slow monologue, Johnson then briefly reviewed the few bills in committee that might yet be considered on the Senate floor in the little time remaining for the session.

John Chadwick, a soft-spoken, veteran reporter for the Associated Press, interrupted the soliloquy with a question. What about Eisenhower's bill to soften the restrictive McCarran-Walter Immigration and Nationality Act and allow more refugees to enter the United States? Chadwick had touched a sore point with Johnson. James Eastland of Mississippi, chairman of the Senate Judiciary Committee and Johnson's good friend, was a foe of liberalized immigration and had no intention of letting the bill out of his committee. Besides, Johnson himself had been a supporter of the McCarran-Walter Act. Coldly, he informed Chadwick that he could scarcely influence a bill until it was out of committee, and the refugee bill was in the province of the Judiciary Committee.

Chadwick persisted. With unassailable logic, he pointed out that Johnson had just finished talking about other bills still in committee and not yet on the Senate floor. Without warning, the six months of hyperactivity and tension boiled over in Johnson, and he exploded in unrestrained invective against Chadwick. For Johnson, that sudden loss of self-control in public was unprecedented. So severe was the tongue-lashing that other reporters rose to defend Chadwick. The press conference came to an abrupt and embarrassing end, with the Majority Leader in an angry mood. It was a signal that he had strained his physical resources to a dangerous degree.

Although his habit was either to skip lunch or to bolt a cold hamburger at his desk in midafternoon, Johnson lunched that day in the Senators' dining room (two floors below his office in the Capitol). There, with Senator Mike Monroney of Oklahoma, Johnson wolfed down frankfurters and beans, after which he set off for a rare, badly needed weekend at the Middleburg country estate of his old Texas friend and supporter, oilman-builder George Brown, in the heart of the exclusive Virginia hunt country.

The Majority Leader's limousine, chauffeured by Norman Edwards, had barely crossed the Potomac River on the hour-long drive when Johnson complained of the heat (though the air conditioner was going full blast) and of feeling sick to his stomach. Stopping at a gasoline station, Johnson gulped an ice-cold Coke but only felt more nauseated. He tried to vomit but couldn't. On arriving at the Brown estate, he turned aside a suggestion that what he needed was a good, cold swim in the Brown pool and went to a downstairs bedroom to rest. Senator Clinton Anderson of New Mexico, another weekend guest, was worried about him.

"My arms are heavy, and I feel like somebody's sitting on my chest," Johnson told Anderson. Anderson, who had weathered almost every disease known to medical science, including a heart attack, professionally ran his fingers down Johnson's chest to locate the source of pain. A second later he announced: "Lyndon, you're having a coronary."

Johnson was furious. A heart attack! Proud of his good health and strong physical constitution, Johnson simply could not believe he was a heart attack victim. Surely, it was only a severe bellyache. And the timing of the heart attack—if indeed Anderson was right in his diagnosis—couldn't have been worse: on the eve of the presidential trial balloon in Sunday's *Washington Post*.

Anderson made Johnson lie down. Host Brown came to help. Johnson started to light a cigarette. "Don't do that," cautioned Anderson. Johnson settled instead for a belt of Scotch. The pain subsided, then returned. Anderson told Brown: "You'd better call a doctor."

"Now, Clint," Brown said, "Lyndon doesn't want us to do that."

"How will you feel tomorrow when you read those big, black headlines saying that Lyndon Johnson died in George Brown's house without a doctor?"

When the doctor arrived, he correctly diagnosed a coronary occlusion. Pointing to Anderson, Johnson wisecracked: "The best diagnostician I know just told me that. Tell me something new." The doctor sent for an ambulance. Johnson again protested; he wanted to be driven back to Washington in his limousine. Nonsense, said Anderson, Brown, and the doctor. In a matter of minutes the still-protesting Johnson climbed into the ambulance.

He was rushed to Bethesda Naval Hospital, in the Maryland suburbs of Washington. Lady Bird Johnson, who had been at their home in Washington, was waiting at the hospital. So was Walter Jenkins, Johnson's faithful administrative assistant, note pad in hand. An expert at shorthand, Jenkins quickly recorded Johnson's instructions.

Johnson was wheeled into the high-speed elevator and taken up to the seventeenth floor. He was still able to banter. Remembering that Scogna, an exclusive Washington tailor, was making two suits for him, one brown, one blue, he told Lady Bird Johnson: "Tell Scogna to go ahead with the blue. I'll need it whichever way it goes." And then Johnson went into deep shock—and into the battle for his life.

Only when the President of the United States suffered a heart attack a few months later in September, 1955, would the shockwaves travel faster or penetrate more deeply than they did on that Saturday evening when the news of Johnson's seizure was announced. The intense concern, bannered in headlines from one side of the country to the other, was no conventional reaction to the sudden illness of a public figure. It went far deeper. It was a practical concern over the fate of the Senate, and of the entire Democratic Congress, without Lyndon Johnson.

In the White House, President Eisenhower made anxious inquiries. Eisenhower, driving to Bethesda on July 15 to spend fifteen minutes with the Senator, was one of Johnson's first visitors. On July 30 Eisenhower dispatched Vice-President Nixon to give Johnson a one-hour briefing on foreign affairs. And the Senate, as though reeling from a blow, found itself unable to proceed as before. Without Johnson driving it from one bill to the next, the Senate quickly reverted to its accustomed languor. The adjournment, confidently expected within a couple of weeks, was pushed back to August 2.

Yet Lyndon Johnson had been serving just six months in a post that for nearly two decades had enjoyed little prestige and even less power. Why, then, was the illness of the new Majority Leader treated as a national calamity?

Johnson made a remarkable recovery from his heart attack, medically designated as "moderately severe." Once out of the oxygen tent, he was soon trying to run the Senate by remote control from Bethesda —and outflanking Republicans. On July 21, during the Summit Conference in Geneva (which Johnson had helped promote), Assistant Secretary of State Thruston Morton, congressional liaison man for the State Department, went to his fellow Kentuckian, Acting Majority Leader Earle Clements, for advice. Would Johnson like a briefing on Eisenhower's forthcoming "Open Skies" proposal (to permit worldwide aerial inspection) so that he could make a statement on it? Or was he still too sick to see Morton? Clements telephoned Lady Bird Johnson and asked her. Knowing how isolated her husband felt at Bethesda, Mrs. Johnson got the doctor's approval and told Clements: yes, by all means send Morton out.

After the briefing by Morton, Johnson immediately dictated a lengthy statement applauding Eisenhower's Open Skies proposal. He instructed Clements to read it to the Senate in Johnson's name the instant Eisenhower formally made his proposal in Geneva. As a result, the hospitalized Johnson's statement was the first by any congressional figure. Senator William Knowland, the Minority Leader, was beaten to the punch, and Johnson again captured the headlines.

On August 7, Johnson's doctors allowed him to leave the hospital and go home to 4921 Thirtieth Place in northwest Washington. There, propped up in a huge leather chair with a reclining back, Johnson began to receive his friends, gradually expanding his circle to include a few reporters.

In each case the ritual was the same. He produced doctors' reports showing to the ounce his weight that morning, the exact calorie intake, meal by meal, the number of trips he was allowed from bed to chair, his precise time for napping in the afternoon and for going to sleep at night, his cardiogram. Johnson was organizing himself for the long pull back to complete health. And by early autumn, having left Washington for his ranch in Texas and the final stage of recuperation, Johnson left no doubt in anyone's mind that he would be back in the Senate when the second session of the 84th Congress convened in January.

But Johnson's recuperation was not an easy one. His father had died of a heart attack in his early sixties, and Johnson, when he was tired and depressed, used to comment that a similar fate probably awaited him. In the post-heart-attack depression that always afflicts a coro-

nary victim, he sometimes mused aloud about retiring from politics at
the end of his term in 1960.* When a British reporter naïvely took the
rumors of a Johnson retirement seriously and wrote about it, the British Foreign Office panicked and sent an urgent cable to its embassy in
Washington asking for verification or denial.

In fact, Johnson's heart attack, far from shortening his political life,
lengthened it. He was forced into a new way of life. He stopped smok-
ing. He was under strict orders to eat a hot lunch—and at *lunch*time—
not a cold hamburger at four o'clock. He counted his calories, reduced
his consumption of Scotch, reduced his weight by thirty-five pounds,
and flew to the LBJ Ranch for regular vacations. And the political
impact of his heart attack was muted by President Eisenhower's own
severe coronary thrombosis in September and re-election a year later.

It remains remarkable, however, that the illness of a Senate Majority Leader could have caused so much concern. The explanation lies in
a parliamentary phenomenon known as the Johnson System.

The new Senate force *implicit* in Johnson's two years as Minority
Leader (culminating in McCarthy's censure) became *explicit* when
Johnson took over as Majority Leader, with narrow Democratic control of the Senate, after the 1954 elections. George A. Smathers, the
debonair young Senator from Florida (who was only dimly aware of
Johnson's presence when they served together in the House), years
later described Johnson's presence in the Senate as "a great, overpowering thunderstorm that consumed you as it closed in around you."
Bryce Harlow, who twice had turned down job offers from Johnson
and by now was President Eisenhower's chief congressional lobbyist,
perceived in Majority Leader Johnson "a new hauteur" that made him
scarcely recognizable to Harlow and other old friends in the House a
decade before. Charles Watkins, the sage parliamentarian of the Senate, watched a new force at work in the Senate. Not long after Johnson became Majority Leader, Watkins remarked: "Lyndon's passed
bills in a few days that I thought would take weeks. He does more
buttonholing and going around than anyone I've ever seen."

Smathers, Harlow, and Watkins each was describing in his own
way the Johnson System by which the young Senator from Texas
stretched the limits of the Majority Leader's inherently meager power
to unimagined boundaries.

The informal directorate of the Senate, headed by Richard B. Rus-

---

* After his gall bladder operation in October, 1965, Johnson made similar remarks about his desire to retire from politics.

sell, insensibly yielded operational control and power to Johnson. It was a remarkable surrender considering that the power ratio of the Senate—evenly divided between Republicans and Democrats, ideologically weighted in favor of the conservatives—was unchanged from the earlier postwar years and was not to be altered until the 1958 elections. When Smathers, Harlow, and Watkins—and many others as well—described the momentous changes of the Senate in terms of Lyndon Johnson's personality, they reported the surprising truth. For the Johnson System was a highly personalized, intensive system of Senate rule adaptable to no successor. Because it involved so little institutional change, the Johnson System vanished overnight once Lyndon B. Johnson himself left the Senate. It was as though it had never existed.

Through most of its history, the Senate had been a cockpit of debaters—Websters and Calhouns, La Follettes and Tafts. Only twice before Johnson's rule had a Majority Leader achieved real power and control. The first occasion was a two-year reign by the imperious Republican aristocrat, Nelson W. Aldrich of Rhode Island, in 1908 and 1909. Under Aldrich, the majority leadership reached its peak of institutional authority. Aldrich had sole power to name all members of standing committees—a power destined for short life in a feudal-like institution whose members possessed baronial equality. Not until the long tenure of Democrat Joseph Robinson of Arkansas—Minority Leader from 1923 to 1928 and Majority Leader from 1928 to 1937— was the Senate again brought under tight control. Robinson utilized his personal authority, born of fourteen years as party floor leader, to compensate for his lack of institutionalized power.

Lacking both Aldrich's institutional power and Robinson's long tenure, Johnson had to concoct his own System. Highly personalized and instinctive as it was, the Johnson System stemmed from no grand master-plan or tightly organized chart. Simply stated, the System can be broken down into two interlocking components: the Johnson Network and the Johnson Procedure. The Network was the source of Johnson's power, the tool essential to put into effect the Procedure that enabled one man to tame the Senate and bring it under control for the first time in eighteen years.

J. Allen Frear, a Delaware farmboy who became a successful small-town, pint-sized banker in Dover, Delaware, was elected to the United States Senate in 1948 and served two terms there before his defeat in 1960. Obscured by his luminous fellow Democrats in the Class of '48,

Frear's trademark was his piercing, high-pitched response to Senate roll calls (much to the amusement of the galleries). Otherwise, he was invisible. Nevertheless, this pleasant little nobody became an important link in the Johnson Network.

At heart a conservative Democrat, Frear generally voted the conservative position—unless Lyndon Johnson wanted him to vote otherwise. Almost without exception, Frear's vote—or non-vote—was Johnson's for the asking, a fact abundantly clear to the astonished gallery in 1959 during the debate on a tax bill. Johnson was supporting an amendment to repeal special tax advantages for dividend income put into law by the Republican-controlled Congress of 1954. In a rare miscalculation, Johnson had miscounted the vote and when the roll call was completed, he found himself beaten by a single vote, 41 to 40. Frear had shrieked "no" on the amendment. Unsolicited by Johnson, he voted as a Delaware conservative. But now Johnson shouted across the Senate floor to Frear: "Change your vote!" Surprised, almost stunned by the command, Frear hesitated. Johnson shouted again, "Change your vote!" Frear did, and the amendment carried.

Indispensable to the Johnson System were generous rewards for consistent good conduct. While distinguished economist Paul Douglas spent years angrily and anxiously waiting for a seat on the tax-writing Finance Committee, Frear went on it quickly (as well as onto the Banking and Currency Committee). Moreover, Johnson did all in his power for Frear's pet bill: a tax-relief measure for Delaware's dominating industry, E. I. Du Pont de Nemours & Company. Du Pont's request was opposed even by the conservative Treasury Department of the Eisenhower Administration.*

Most members of the Johnson Network were not so faithful as Allen Frear. He was the ideal, not a typical, member of the Network—a collection of Republicans and Democrats, Northerners and Southerners, liberals and conservatives, great figures and mediocrities. In varying degree, Johnson could count on them all for help.

At the core of the Johnson Network were his peers—Senate grandees to whom he turned more for advice than for votes. Richard Russell, of course; Clinton Anderson; Styles Bridges, the Senate's senior Republican; and—one to whom he turned far more often than most realized—his old seat-mate from the Class of '48, Robert S. Kerr. Sometimes unsure of himself on the fine points of complex bills, John-

---

* The fact that a combination of liberal Democrats and Eisenhower Administration officials prevented passage of the Du Pont bill contributed to Frear's defeat in 1960. Ironically, the bill passed in 1961, with support from the Kennedy Administration.

son often picked Kerr's retentive brain. Once when White House officials traveled secretly to Capitol Hill to give Johnson a confidential advance peek at a new Eisenhower farm bill, they were taken aback to find Kerr waiting for them with Johnson.

Essential to the Johnson Network was the informal, uncoordinated system of lieutenants that he established soon after becoming Majority Leader. Senator Earle Clements of Kentucky—now the Majority Whip—was general handyman and assistant to Johnson and was still able to move moderately well among all factions of Senate Democrats (though he had become increasingly distrusted by the liberals). Taking up that slack with the liberals was Senator Hubert Humphrey of Minnesota. By 1955, though the general public and even much of the Senate failed to realize it, the one-time stereotype of ADA-style liberalism had become a full-fledged lieutenant of Lyndon Johnson. They still disagreed about many matters, just as Russell and Johnson often disagreed. But as much as Russell, though less openly, Humphrey was a Johnson man.

The most important of Johnson's lieutenants in 1955 was no Senator at all. Bobby G. Baker, now twenty-six, had been promoted to Secretary of the Senate Majority when the Democrats regained control in 1955, approved routinely by the Senate Democratic caucus on the Majority Leader's recommendation. Baker promptly remade that job to fit his own specifications, just as Johnson was remaking the majority leadership to fit his. Thus, a routine housekeeping sinecure became in Baker's hands—and with Johnson's blessing—a position of great authority. Mistakenly shrugged off for years by many Senators as a cloakroom chatterbox, Baker now began to eclipse Senator Clements himself as Johnson's top assistant. When Johnson was running the Senate from the Bethesda hospital bed after his heart attack, he relayed his instructions through Bobby Baker. The bouncy, ingratiating—and immensely able—young man from Pickens, South Carolina, came to be called "the ninety-seventh Senator" and "Lyndon, Jr."

When Clements was defeated by the Republican sweep in Kentucky in 1956, Johnson and Baker together cooked up a scheme intended to give further political substance to the system of lieutenants. Looking ahead to the civil rights fight certainly looming in 1957, Johnson and Baker agreed that the new whip should be a bona fide Southerner who would agree to a moderate civil rights bill.* The only Senator who fit that description was Florida's handsome George Smathers, who was moving closer to Johnson in 1956. Smathers (who had earned the sobriquet "Gorgeous George") had informally filled in

---

* The epochal civil rights fight is dealt with comprehensively in Chapter VII.

for Clements so that Clements could return to Kentucky to mend his fences in a futile effort to save himself in the 1956 election.

True, Johnson and Smathers as leader and whip would place two sons of the Confederacy in the Senate's two top Democratic leadership posts. But Johnson had a countervailing move. The third, and wholly honorific, position in the Senate's Democratic hierarchy, Secretary of the Conference (caucus), would go to Hubert Humphrey. Thus Humphrey would become a working member of the Democratic leadership, not only strengthening his tie to Johnson but giving the liberals their first man on the leadership ladder.

After the 1956 elections and Clements' defeat, Johnson summoned Smathers to a hotel suite in Washington (after first clearing his actions with the traveling Russell by long-distance telephone to Spain), and offered him the whip's job. Worried about the insatiable demands on his life inherent in getting that close to Johnson, Smathers did not flatly agree. But Baker, who had been urging Smathers for whip, was sure he could be persuaded and that the Senate Democratic caucus would approve him in January despite the misgivings the liberals would surely harbor. Moreover, Baker advised Johnson to disregard his old New Deal friends, who pleaded with him not to name Smathers. Though Smathers was a moderate by Southern standards, they simply could not forgive him for what they regarded as McCarthyite tactics against New Deal Senator Claude Pepper, unseated by Smathers in the bitter Florida Democratic primary of 1950.

The anti-Smathers opposition grew too influential for even Baker to overcome when Sam Rayburn joined it. The Speaker heartily disliked Smathers for his campaign against Pepper, and argued vigorously against appointing him whip. The dispute reached a climax on an airplane that both Johnson and Rayburn were taking to Texas. Before the plane left the gate at Washington's National Airport, Rayburn flatly informed Johnson that he could not appoint Smathers. Accordingly, Johnson left the plane and drove back into town to inform Smathers that the offer was withdrawn.

That unhappy episode dulled Johnson's enthusiasm for picking Clements' successor. There was one desultory conversation with Humphrey about becoming whip, but both knew that Russell and his Southerners would never accept Humphrey on the eve of the twentieth-century's greatest civil rights fight. By process of elimination, Johnson finally selected Mike Mansfield of Montana, a devoutly religious former professor of Oriental history who was more interested in the intrigues of Southeast Asia than those of the Senate cloakroom. With no thirst for power, Mansfield accepted only after much urging.

He never became a genuine lieutenant of the Johnson Network in the way that Clements had been. He helped Johnson with all the routine chores, but stayed at arm's length from the center of Johnson operations.

With Mansfield as whip, it would have been hard to sell Humphrey to the South as Conference Secretary. Instead, the job went to ailing Senator Thomas Hennings of Missouri, assuring that the post would remain largely honorific. The failure of a strong Johnson-Smathers-Humphrey leadership team to emerge in 1957 had an unexpected result. It greatly enhanced Bobby Baker's position as Johnson's Number One assistant and drew him still closer to the Majority Leader.

But the Johnson Network was not so much a system of lieutenants as of personal alliances that transcended partisan, ideological, and geographic lines. Johnson slowly built up a cadre of supporters who would vote for LBJ—even, on occasion, against their ideology, their conscience, and their political self-interest, depending on the issue and the Senator. The cadre included: Dennis Chavez, an aging New Mexico Democrat; George (Molly) Malone, an eccentric McCarthyite Republican from Nevada; Democrat Stuart Symington of Missouri, vigorous air power man (whose long relationship with Johnson cooled for personal reasons in the late 1950s); liberal Republican Margaret Chase Smith of Maine; Harry Flood Byrd, conservative Democrat and national high priest of fiscal responsibility; Richard Neuberger, liberal Democrat of Oregon. East, West; rich, poor; left wing, right wing—all in greater or lesser degree were part of the Johnson Network. With other, less conspicuous members of the Network, they made up perhaps one-quarter of the Senate—more than enough to provide the balance of power on most issues.

To build his Network, Johnson stretched the meager power resources of the Majority Leader to the outer limit. The mightiest of these was his influence over committee assignments. Still, it was not comparable to the absolute power enjoyed by Nelson Aldrich a half century before. As chairman of the Democratic Steering Committee, Johnson steadily widened the breach in rigid seniority rules, working delicately with a surgical scalpel, not a stick of dynamite.

In January, 1955, his ally and adviser, Clinton Anderson, pressed his claim for an overdue assignment on either Foreign Relations or Finance. Each committee had one vacancy. But former Vice-President Alben Barkley, who had just returned to the Senate as a "freshman" from Kentucky in the 1954 elections, asked for the Finance Committee

—a request that could scarcely be denied. A further complication was the still unresolved problem of Wayne Morse, the Oregon maverick who had bolted the Republican party in the 1952 campaign and, after two years in the political wilderness as an "Independent," now joined the Democratic caucus in 1955. Morse's decision was vital to Johnson. It provided him with the narrow one-vote margin he needed to cross the bridge, incalculably important in terms of power, from Minority Leader to Majority Leader. Thus, it was incumbent upon Johnson to give Morse a good committee assignment, and Morse wanted Foreign Relations.

Johnson duly explained these facts of life to Anderson, who agreed not to insist (as he well could have) on either Finance or Foreign Relations. But Johnson remembered his old friend's personal loyalty and, on a 1956 speaking engagement in New Mexico, he publicly—and unexpectedly—promised that Clint Anderson would become the next chairman of the Joint Atomic Energy Committee. That post, because of New Mexico's Los Alamos atomic installation, would solidly enhance Anderson's prestige. To make good his promise, Johnson was required to jump Anderson over none other than Richard Russell, who outranked Anderson on the joint committee.

The Foreign Relations maneuvers temporarily drew the sharp-tongued Morse to Johnson, in sharp contrast to a year earlier. In January, 1954, Morse had told an ADA Roosevelt Day Dinner in Texas: "Johnson has the most reactionary record in the Senate. Look at his voting record. If he should ever have a liberal idea, he would have a brain hemorrhage. . . ." * But a little more than a year later, ensconced on the Foreign Relations Committee, Morse gently confided to the Senate: "During the past year, I have been the beneficiary of one kindness after another from Lyndon Johnson. I consider him not only a great statesman but a good man."

And as chairman of the Joint Atomic Energy Committee, Anderson was even more pleased than he would have been on Foreign Relations. The only grumbling over Johnson's ingenious shuffling came from Russell, who had not agreed in advance to step aside for Anderson. But the grumbling was private and soft, not public and bitter. Lyndon Johnson could count on Dick Russell not to make a public fuss about such matters.

Two years later, Anderson was the center of far more devious com-

---

* Johnson retaliated in kind: "Texas doesn't need any outsiders to come in and tell them [sic] how to vote. I don't think Texas will pay any more attention to him than the Senate does." In those early days of his leadership, Johnson was far more ready to engage fellow Senators in a war of words than he would be later.

mittee maneuvers by Johnson. After the presidential election of 1956, Estes Kefauver of Tennessee and John F. Kennedy of Massachusetts, who had competed on the National Convention floor at Chicago for the vice-presidential nomination the previous summer, were competing again—this time for a single vacancy on Foreign Relations. Johnson, who had backed Kennedy against Kefauver at Chicago, was now trying to bring Kennedy closer to his orbit. He was determined to have the vacancy go to Kennedy over Johnson's old foe, Kefauver. But how to get around Kefauver's four-year seniority bulge over Kennedy? In December, 1956, long before Congress convened, Johnson telephoned Anderson with a most curious question: "How are you getting along with your campaign for the Foreign Relations Committee?"

Anderson was puzzled. Could Johnson have forgotten that his "campaign" had ended two years earlier? But Johnson persisted.

"This may be your chance," he said.

Before Anderson could reply that he had his hands full as chairman of Atomic Energy, Johnson rushed on.

"You have seniority now over Jack Kennedy," Johnson explained. "But if you don't claim it, Estes Kefauver may get there first."

Johnson's ploy suddenly came through to Anderson. Both Anderson and Kefauver were members of the Class of '48, and therefore had equal seniority. If they both applied for the one vacancy on the Foreign Relations Committee, Johnson could throw up his hands in the Steering Committee, declare a standoff—and give the vacancy to Kennedy. Anderson went along with this neat strategy, and Kennedy was given the seat, just as Johnson wanted.

Johnson's use of power to influence committee assignments cut both ways. "Good" liberals, such as Humphrey, could be prematurely boosted into the Foreign Relations Committee, and a "bad" liberal, such as Kefauver, could be made to cool his heels for years. A "bad" liberal such as Paul Douglas could be barred from the Finance Committee for eight long years, while five fellow members of the Class of '48 (Kerr, Long, Frear, Anderson and Johnson himself) and one from the Class of '50 (Smathers) were finding places there.* Senators who dared to function too far outside the Johnson Network waited long to get inside the prestige committees.

In these clandestine committee maneuvers, Johnson seldom exposed his hand. But in the routine committee shifts, he enjoyed wringing

---

* This extraordinary treatment of Douglas also reflected Johnson's desire to keep the Finance Committee free of Northern liberals opposing special tax advantages for the oil and gas industry. But if Douglas had been a "good" liberal in the Humphrey mold, Johnson could have shaved a point, since the Finance Committee was already so stacked in favor of the oil and gas industry.

out the last drop of credit. One evening in early January, 1955, shortly after the committee assignments for the 84th Congress had been settled and announced, Johnson invited a couple of friends into his Majority Leader's office in the corner of the Capitol for a political bull session over Scotch and sodas. Nothing relaxed him more than these feet-up, hair-down chats. They invariably lasted well into the night and they invariably ended in long, often hilarious LBJ monologues, full of ribald yarns and racy mimicry.

Suddenly, he interrupted himself. "My God," he said, "I forgot to call Senator Stennis and congratulate him." Stennis had been valuable to Johnson a month earlier in the McCarthy censure fight, and now had just landed a coveted seat on the Appropriations Committee— thanks to Lyndon Johnson. Johnson reached over, cradled the phone between his shoulder and chin, and dialed.

Mrs. Stennis answered the phone, and the conversation commenced. "Ma'm, this is Lyndon Johnson, is your husband there? . . . He isn't? . . . Well, I must tell you, Ma'm, how proud I am of your husband and how proud the Senate is, and you tell him that when he gets home. The Senate paid him a great honor today. The Senate elected your husband to the Appropriations Committee. That's one of the most powerful committees in the whole Senate and a great honor for your husband. I'm so proud of John. He's a great American. And I know you're proud of him, too. He's one of my finest Senators. . . ." Accompanying this monologue were nods and winks in the direction of Johnson's fascinated audience.

Johnson went on to tell Mrs. Stennis how the Steering Committee had selected her husband unanimously for the Appropriations spot and how the full Senate had unanimously concurred, but implicitly he was belaboring the obvious—that it wasn't the Steering Committee or the full Senate that really was responsible. It was LBJ.

Johnson quietly commandeered other bits and pieces of Senate patronage that previous Majority Leaders ignored. To cement his budding alliance with Senator Margaret Chase Smith, for instance, he arranged for a special staff member of the Senate Armed Services Committee to be appointed by her and to be responsible to her alone, even though she was a Republican on the Democratic-controlled committee, and only fourth-ranking Republican at that.

Although in the past, office space for Senators, a source of sometimes intense competition, had been distributed by strict seniority as a routine housekeeping chore of the Senate's Sergeant-at-Arms, Johnson quickly perceived its value as a weapon of influence and fitted it into his growing system of rewards and punishments. When Paul Douglas lost that top-floor Capitol office to Johnson in 1955, the Senate took notice. It was a dramatic sign of the consequences of a lack of rapport with the Majority Leader. Johnson skillfully exploited the gleaming New Senate Office Building in 1958, with its spanking new suites, as an inducement for help on the floor. Senator Mike Monroney of Oklahoma, sometimes troublesome for Johnson, was brought into line on one bill with the award of a handsome corner suite that Johnson knew Monroney coveted.

Johnson also kept his ears open to discover which Senator—or Senator's wife—was really anxious to go on which senatorial junket abroad. At a cocktail party early in 1957, Johnson was chatting with the wife of Frank Church, the young, newly elected liberal Democrat from Idaho. Mrs. Church innocently revealed that she had always wanted to see South America. Knowing that Frank Church might become a valuable addition to the Johnson Network, the Majority Leader saw to it that he was named to the very next delegation of Senators to visit South America.

Even before that, however, Frank Church had reason to be grateful to Lyndon Johnson. Bitterly opposed by the Idaho Power Company and other private-power interests because of his public-power stand, Church was hard-pressed for funds in his 1956 campaign for the Senate. He sent an S.O.S. to the Senate Democratic Campaign Committee in Washington. Senator Smathers, chairman of the Campaign Committee, was dubious about pouring money into what seemed a hopeless cause in a small Mountain State. But Johnson and Bobby Baker argued Church's cause, and their wishes prevailed.*

De facto control of the Campaign Committee's funds was one of Johnson's least obvious but most effective tools in building his Network. He controlled the distribution of committee funds through both its chairman—first Earle Clements and later George Smathers—and through its secretary, Bobby Baker. More often than not, the requests for campaign funds were routinely made to Baker, and the money was physically distributed by him. Johnson further tightened his control when Clements was named the committee's executive director after his Senate defeat in 1956. Johnson got the most out of the committee's limited funds (at that time a mere four hundred thousand dollars) by shrewdly distributing them where they would do the most work. In the small Mountain States like Idaho, a ten-thousand-dollar contribution could change the course of an election. But in New York or Pennsylvania, ten thousand dollars was the merest drop in the bucket.

* For the role Church played in helping Johnson pass a civil rights bill, see Chapter VII.

Johnson and Baker tried to reduce contributions to Democrats in the industrial Northeast to the minimum. Since Senators seldom bite the hand that finances them, these Westerners were naturally drawn into the Johnson Network, while the Eastern liberals tended to remain outside.

But this ingenious stretching of the Majority Leader's limited stock of patronage could not by itself explain the brilliant success of the Johnson Network. The extra, indeed the dominant, ingredient was Johnson's overwhelming personality, reflected in what came to be known as "The Treatment."

The Treatment could last ten minutes or four hours. It came, enveloping its target, at the LBJ Ranch swimming pool, in one of LBJ's offices, in the Senate cloakroom, on the floor of the Senate itself—wherever Johnson might find a fellow Senator within his reach. Its tone could be supplication, accusation, cajolery, exuberance, scorn, tears, complaint, the hint of threat. It was all of these together. It ran the gamut of human emotions. Its velocity was breathtaking, and it was all in one direction. Interjections from the target were rare. Johnson anticipated them before they could be spoken. He moved in close, his face a scant millimeter from his target, his eyes widening and narrowing, his eyebrows rising and falling. From his pockets poured clippings, memos, statistics. Mimicry, humor, and the genius of analogy made The Treatment an almost hypnotic experience and rendered the target stunned and helpless.

In 1957, when Johnson was courting the non-Senate Eastern liberal establishment, he summoned historian and liberal theoretician Arthur Schlesinger, Jr., down from his classroom at Harvard. Wary at the prospect of his first prolonged meeting with Johnson (whom he suspected of disdaining the liberal cause), Schlesinger had in his mind a long list of questions to ask Johnson. Never known for shyness, Schlesinger was nevertheless on his guard when he entered Johnson's Capitol office and sat in front of the great man's desk.

The Treatment began immediately: a brilliant, capsule characterization of every Democratic Senator: his strengths and failings, where he fit into the political spectrum; how far he could be pushed, how far pulled; his hates, his loves. And who (he asked Schlesinger) must oversee all these prima donnas, put them to work, knit them together, know when to tickle this one's vanity, inquire of that one's health, remember this one's five o'clock nip of Scotch, that one's nagging wife? Who must find the hidden legislative path between the South and the North, the public power men and the private power men, the farmers' men and the unions' men, the bomber-boys and the peace-lovers, the eggheads and the fatheads? Nobody but Lyndon Johnson.

Imagine a football team (Johnson hurried on) and I'm the coach, and I'm also the quarterback. I have to call the signals, and I have to center the ball, run the ball, pass the ball. I'm the blocker (he rose out of his chair and threw an imaginary block). I'm the tackler (he crouched and tackled). I'm the passer (he heaved a mighty pass). I have to catch the pass (he reached and caught the pass).

Schlesinger was sitting on the edge of his chair, both fascinated and amused. Here was a view of the Senate he had never seen before.

Johnson next ticked off all the bills he had passed that year, how he'd gotten Dick Russell on this one, Bob Kerr on that one, Hubert Humphrey on another. He reached into his desk drawer and out came the voting record of New Jersey's Clifford Case, a liberal Republican. You liberals, he told Schlesinger, are always talking about my record. You wouldn't question Cliff Case's record, would you? And he ran down the list and compared it to his voting record. Whatever Johnson had on those two lists, he came out with a record more liberal than Case's.

Johnson had anticipated and answered all of Schlesinger's questions. The leader rolled on, reiterating a theme common to The Treatment of that time. He'd had his heart attack, he said, and he knew he'd never be President. He wasn't made for the presidency. If only the Good Lord would just give him enough time to do a few more things in the Senate. Then he'd go back to Texas. That's where he belonged.

Breathless now, ninety minutes later, Schlesinger said good-by and groped his way out of Johnson's office. Eight years later, he was to record his impressions. Johnson had been "a good deal more attractive, more subtle, and more formidable than I expected." And, he might have added, vastly more entertaining.

The Treatment was designed for a single target or, at most, an audience of three or four. In large groups, what was witty sounded crude, what was expansive became arrogant. It was inevitable, then, that when Johnson allowed The Treatment to dominate his "press conferences" a sour note entered his relations with the press. Reporters en masse didn't like being on the receiving end of The Treatment. Johnson's failure to understand that annoyed the press, which in turn made Johnson increasingly wary and suspicious. Unable to tame the press as he tamed so many Senators, he foolishly took offense at routine questions, and was quick to find a double meaning in the most innocent point raised by a reporter. Although Senate reporters and Washington's top columnists were captivated in their *private* sessions with

Johnson in his office or at the LBJ Ranch, his press conferences were fiascoes. They simply could not be harnessed to The Treatment.

One additional bit of Johnson glue held his Network together. Whenever a seventy-five-cent cigar came his way, Johnson would not forget to stick it in his pocket and save it for Senator Carl Hayden of Arizona, a notorious cigar-chomper and chairman of the Senate Appropriations Committee. When William Knowland became a grandfather for the fourth time, Johnson took the floor of the Senate to make the event a historical footnote in the *Congressional Record*. When the wife of Felton (Skeeter) Johnston, a veteran Senate employee who became Secretary of the Senate in 1955, went to the hospital for major surgery, Lyndon Johnson offered to help pay the bill. These small favors and courtesies were elaborately planned by Johnson and graciously carried out. They built Johnson a bottomless reservoir of good will.

Johnson's meticulous attention to such details predated his Senate leadership. In 1952, Westwood, the only daughter of Virginia's Senator Harry Byrd, met a tragic death. Johnson drove from Washington to Winchester, Virginia, for the funeral. As Johnson told the story in 1955, he was amazed to discover that he was the only Senator present. The courtly old Virginian was deeply touched. When Johnson sought Byrd's vote on a labor issue years later, it was Byrd who recalled the funeral and gave Johnson his vote.

While constructing his elaborate Network, the Majority Leader was also building the largest staff ever assembled by a single Senator. Each of the many hats worn by Johnson—Senator from Texas, Senate Majority Leader, chairman of the Democratic Policy Committee, chairman of the Democratic Conference, chairman of the Democratic Steering Committee, chairman of the Defense Preparedness Subcommittee, chairman of the Appropriations Subcommittee on the State, Commerce, and Justice Departments, and (after 1958) chairman of the new Space Committee—each of these hats entitled him to government-paid employees.

Despite the size of this little bureaucracy, the weakest element in the Johnson System was his staff. Throughout his Senate career, he maintained a stable, highly successful relationship with only two staff aides: Walter Jenkins and Bobby Baker.

Jenkins joined Johnson in 1939 fresh from the University of Texas, and except for an unsuccessful race for Congress in a special Texas election in September, 1951, stayed for twenty-five years. He became

Johnson's invaluable first assistant, the steadiest rock on the staff. Jenkins ruled the "Texas office" (Johnson's suite in the Senate Office Building, devoted to Texas affairs, which Johnson seldom visited), but was given highly confidential duties that ranged far afield. He was general office manager, personnel chief, private secretary, shorthand stenographer, and errand boy. Johnson rattled off daily chores, from trivial to top secret, and the uncomplaining, unsmiling Jenkins would jot them down in shorthand and get them accomplished. Privy to every scheme in Johnson's brain, Walter Jenkins never complained about his sixteen-hour days, the abuse the Senator would sometimes fling out to relieve his own tension, or the assignment of the most menial chores. The single clue to the suppressed emotional turbulence inside this devoted poker-faced servant were periodic attacks of a skin rash.

Johnson's other staff intimate was Jenkins' antithesis. Bobby Baker was a natural-born politician who wore his moods on his face; he was gregarious, glad-handing, gossipy, and smart as a fox. If Jenkins would have lost his right arm before revealing a secret Johnson scheme, Baker gloried in passing juicy tidbits to his friends in the Senate and among the press, not to damage but to advance the Majority Leader's objective.

Moreover, the Johnson-Baker relationship was altered subtly by the fact that Baker was technically an employee not of Johnson himself but of all the Democratic Senators. This partially explained why there was about Baker none of the hangdog look of the discreet servant that distinguished Walter Jenkins and most of Johnson's own staff. Baker talked out on his own and on occasion even talked back to Johnson, as one day when Johnson halted a reporter in the reception room just off the Senate floor and upbraided him about a story published that morning. Baker listened for a moment, then interrupted. "Now, Senator, that's silly," he said. "You shouldn't say that. That was a damn good story and you ought to appreciate it." To most members of Johnson's regular staff, talk like that was beyond imagining.

Staff became a deepening problem for Johnson. A select band of informal advisers—James Rowe, Donald Cook, Horace Busby—simply declined to serve him on a permanent basis. They knew all too well that Johnson staffers were literally on call around-the-clock. A private life was out of the question. Johnson spent every waking moment on politics and government and demanded no less from his staff.

But unwillingness to serve Johnson stemmed from more than mere hours of work. Johnson had an unfortunate tendency to waste talent, to assign highly priced and highly educated assistants to menial chores. By 1956, Gerald Siegel was overburdened as counsel of the Democratic Policy Committee and badly needed help. With Johnson's approval, he found and hired an exceptional young lawyer from East Texas named Harry McPherson. McPherson wanted to be a poet, but the McCarthy era so outraged him that he switched to the law to fight McCarthyism. McPherson was an idealist and a humanist with imaginative, sensitive intelligence and a quiet competence.

When he arrived in Washington in the spring of 1956, Johnson was in the midst of an ambitious but incredible project to send a letter of congratulation to every high school graduate in the state of Texas that June. McPherson's first job for his new boss in Washington was to man a bank of robot-typewriters, typing out one address after another manually and then feeding in the tape of a form letter, night after night, sending Johnson's congratulations to all the senior class members in Texas. That set a pattern. McPherson's talent was not really tapped by Johnson for a decade, when he was added to the White House staff.

The experience of Lloyd Hand, another young Texan brought to Washington by Johnson in 1957, was somewhat similar. A University of Texas student leader who worked on the 1948 Johnson Senate campaign, Hand came to Johnson's Washington office in 1957 with strong hints of a high position. When he reported for duty, Johnson handed him a couple of books by Winston Churchill. That's how I want my speeches to come out, he told Hand. And Hand went to work writing, but scarcely for Churchillian occasions. Johnson assigned him to reply to Texas constituents who sent their problems to their Senator. He was placed in the "Texas office" under Walter Jenkins and never did have a chance to do the job he was hired to do: write LBJ speeches.*

Johnson was a ruthless taskmaster. No one who worked for him escaped entirely the slashing rebukes that, in impatience or fatigue, he administered. Later, he would seek to compensate by acts of kindness. But no one was immune, even though others—Senators or reporters— might be present. During one of those unfortunate "press conferences" in his office, Johnson pulled open his desk drawer to read a memorandum carefully prepared for just that occasion. Halfway through, he discovered to his embarrassment that he was reading the wrong memorandum. Embarrassment quickly became rage. He turned on Gerry Siegel, his efficient legal aide, and loudly berated him for his stupidity. The reporters stared, incredulity in their eyes. Siegel, who

---

* After the 1964 presidential election, President Johnson named Lloyd Hand as Chief of Protocol in the State Department. He resigned from that position in early 1966 to run unsuccessfully for Lieutenant-Governor of California.

deeply admired Johnson, candidly told him later that such outbursts did not hurt Gerald Siegel, but did hurt Lyndon Johnson. Other aides were not so philosophical, however, and even Siegel twice resigned from Johnson's staff to return to private employment during a three-year period.

A dreary pattern marked Johnson's recruitment of his staff. First, ardent wooing of the prospective aide—flattery, appeals to conscience and patriotism, promises of rewarding opportunities for public service. Occasionally this variation of The Treatment spilled over beyond the day that the prospective aide went on the payroll, but not for long. More likely, the moment Johnson made his conquest the value of the new aide depreciated. Now that he was bound to Johnson, there was no longer any need to woo him. As inevitable disagreements arose, Johnson invariably became disillusioned with his new acquisition. No one was fired, but middle-level aides recruited with rosy promises of great days ahead were often exiled to drudgery in the "Texas office" under Walter Jenkins' stern eye.

Moreover, internal stresses and rivalries unsettled the Johnson staff in the mid-1950s. A nasty feud developed between Bobby Baker and George Reedy, the affable ex-newspaperman who now held the title of staff director of the Democratic Policy Committee but in fact was an idea man responsible for press relations and speech-writing. Simultaneously, the size of Johnson's overall staff was reaching such proportions that there was a vital need for a chief to pull and hold it together and coordinate the Senator's spreading operations beyond Jenkins' private domain in the "Texas office."

And so in 1956, Johnson laid siege to the man he wanted as chief of staff: James Rowe, Franklin D. Roosevelt's brilliant young aide of the late 1930s who had helped draw Johnson into the New Deal orbit and maintained his friendship for two decades. Johnson asked Rowe to run the staff of the Policy Committee and take charge of policy matters. But Rowe was profitably engaged in a successful Washington law practice with his famous White House colleague of New Deal days, Thomas G. (Tommy the Cork) Corcoran, and he had no desire to return to public life.

Whereupon Johnson set in motion a subtle, implacable campaign of indirection. Tommy Corcoran urgently pressed Rowe to help out Lyndon, for old-time's sake if nothing else. Lyndon needs you, said Corcoran. A third White House insider of the New Deal era, Ben Cohen, telephoned Rowe with the admonition that he was obligated to help Johnson. Then Rowe's wife, Elizabeth, astonished her husband one day with an appeal of her own: give Lyndon Johnson a hand.

Feeling like an ingrate with his law partner, his valued old friend, and his wife all pressing on him with the same advice, Rowe succumbed. He offered to work for Johnson two days a week. Not enough. Four days? No, said Johnson, he wanted Rowe full time. In fact, he went on, Rowe should resign from his law firm. Rowe protested. Johnson, sensing victory, offered personally to call up Rowe's clients to explain. With tears now welling from his eyes, Johnson begged and cajoled. How badly he needed Rowe! Rowe finally surrendered.

The mood changed abruptly. Away went the tears. "Don't forget," Johnson told Rowe, "*I'll* make the decisions."

The Johnson-Rowe friendship was old and strong enough to survive 1956, but Rowe's brief tenure on the Johnson staff was less than entirely happy or successful. He never really did become the boss of the Johnson staff, and in less than a year he was back with his law firm.

Johnson next turned to Colonel Kenneth E. BeLieu, who as chief clerk of the Senate Armed Services Committee had worked closely and amicably with Johnson for the past eight years. A fifteen-year career Army officer with a distinguished battle record who was retired with war wounds (he lost a leg in Korea), BeLieu was now asked by Johnson to put his crumbling staff in order by succeeding Rowe as chief of staff of the Policy Committee. With some misgivings BeLieu accepted—only to find himself without authority and with only minimal contact with Johnson himself. Before the year was over, he returned to the Armed Services Committee.*

From then on, Johnson operated without a chief of staff and turned more and more to outside advisers, particularly drawing for advice on an informal three-man board composed of three of Washington's highest priced lawyers—Jim Rowe, Abe Fortas, and Clark Clifford. They met about once a month in Johnson's house.† Other Washington veterans of the political scene were also frequently consulted, and the more sagacious members of the Johnson Network in the Senate— Kerr, Russell, Anderson—were always on tap for advice.

Although this overlapping directorate of unofficial advisers and con-

* Despite this experience, BeLieu again entered the LBJ orbit in 1959 by becoming staff director of the new Senate Space Committee headed by Johnson. BeLieu was opposed to the idea at first but relented, due partly to a Johnson ploy. BeLieu received a transatlantic telephone call from Senator Styles Bridges in Lisbon. Bridges congratulated BeLieu on his new job. BeLieu protested that he hadn't accepted it. Bridges replied that Johnson felt a man with BeLieu's military background was essential for the Space Committee in order to insure a continued major role for the military in the space program. Surrounded, BeLieu surrendered.

† Clifford, a Missourian who had been President Truman's White House counsel and was now chief political adviser for Senator Stuart Symington, was dropped from the Johnson group after Johnson's split with Symington in the late 1950s. Johnson and Clifford resumed their warm relations after the 1960 election.

sultants was not the same as a well-structured staff with sparkling morale, the fact is that the Johnson System, as contrasted to the Johnson staff, was such a smashing success that the lack of a cohesive staff was scarcely noticed. The implications of its absence were to become clear only years later.

At the opening of the 1951 Senate session, when Richard Russell named Lyndon Johnson as floor manager of the universal military training bill (his first major floor assignment), the Senate could justly claim itself to be "the world's greatest deliberative body." The Korean War was raging, and President Truman badly needed passage of the bill to bring the armed forces to full strength. But the Senate took its time, as it had since its earliest days. Debate on the bill—stretching from February 27 to March 9—had the urgency of a chess game at an exclusive men's club. There was an unhurried discursive tone as the learned Senators—Richard Russell, Wayne Morse, Robert Taft, Henry Cabot Lodge, Herbert Lehman—probed every corner of the bill. The sessions seldom ran beyond six o'clock in the evening, and the chamber was closed over the weekends. Senator Ernest McFarland, the Majority Leader, tried to hurry the Senate along, but he wasn't overly concerned by the languorous pace or the frequency and uncertainty of roll calls on amendments. As floor manager of the bill, Johnson naturally joined in debate, delivering long, rambling speeches. But Johnson did not enter the game with the zest of a Taft or Russell. He seemed impatient with this kind of Senate.

The Senate had always been that way, even in the days of Nelson Aldrich and Joe Robinson. In 1883 the young Woodrow Wilson wrote of the Senate in *Congressional Government*:

> It must be regarded as no inconsiderable addition to the usefulness of the Senate that it enjoys a much greater freedom of discussion than the House can allow itself. It permits itself a good deal of talk in public about what it is doing, and it commonly talks a great deal of sense.

But it would not be hurried, and, without a rule of germaneness, it could not stick to the point, as Senator Lester Hunt of Wyoming perceived in 1952, on the eve of the Johnson System. Hunt complained: "Any state legislature in the United States would make the Senate of the United States look very bad in connection with procedure." Indeed, the "procedure" of the Senate was geared to slow talk, not vital action.

Johnson was quite aware that he could never establish an efficient

procedure by modernizing the encrusted Senate rules. His only recourse, then, as the new Majority Leader, was by trial and error, to
evolve slowly the Johnson Procedure—along with the Network, the
second major component of the Johnson System.

The principal ingredient of the Procedure was flexibility. On any
major piece of legislation, never make a commitment as to what will
pass; determine in advance what is *possible* under the best of circumstances for the Senate to accept; after making this near-mathematical
determination, don't reveal it; keep the leader's intentions carefully
masked; then, exploiting the Johnson Network, start rounding up all
detachable votes; when all is in readiness, strike quickly and pass the
bill with a minimum of debate.

Essential to making the Johnson Procedure work in this fashion was
divided government: a Democratic Majority Leader and a Republican President. Freed of obligation to shepherd a White House program through a Democratic Senate (because the White House was in
Republican hands), Johnson could hold his own cards and play his
own game. Although divided government had come to Washington
before, as recently as the Republican 80th Congress of 1947–48 under
President Truman, no previous leader in a divided government had
had Johnson's political wit. Besides, Johnson genuinely wanted to *pass*
bills, not just block everything sent up by the Republican President.

Johnson had another advantage: the Johnson Intelligence System.
Unlike his predecessors, Johnson was constantly probing beneath the
Senate's bland exterior to discover what the Senate was really thinking. The Intelligence System was a marvel of efficiency. It was also
rather frightening. One evening in the late 1950s, Senator Thruston
Morton of Kentucky (the Republican who defeated Earle Clements in
1956) dined with seven political reporters at the Metropolitan Club.
The meeting was off-the-record. The reporters had been working as a
team for several years. All were sworn to secrecy, and there had never
been a leak. Morton laid bare some fascinating behind-the-scenes divisions in the Republican party. A few days later, one of the reporters
called on Johnson in his Capitol office. Johnson bitterly chided him
and the Washington press corps for writing column after column
about the divisions in the Democratic party while ignoring internal
tensions in the Republican party. To prove his point, Johnson dipped
into one of the deep wire baskets on his desk and fished out a memorandum on the "confidential" Morton session—complete in every detail.

The thoroughness of Johnson's Intelligence System worried his fellow Senators, some of whom began to half doubt the security of their

own telephone conversations. But Johnson needed no help from electronic eavesdropping. His intelligence had a dazzling multiplicity of sources tucked away in surprising places all over Washington. Bobby Baker and his team of cloakroom attendants were in constant touch and conversation with Senators. Johnson's staff was alert to report what they heard on the floor from other Senators and their staffs. The Johnson Network of friendly Senators kept him informed. Johnson himself was constantly probing and questioning other Senators in the cloakrooms, over late-afternoon drinks, during hamburger lunches, in his office. Occasionally aides of other Senators were invited to lunch with the Majority Leader. Immensely flattered, they eagerly volunteered what they—and more important, what their bosses—were thinking.

Speaker Rayburn and the Texas congressional delegation kept Johnson fully informed about what was going on inside the House. Beyond this, moreover, Johnson had loyal friends scattered throughout the government agencies who regularly tipped him on developments.

Johnson took special precautions to maintain a flow of intelligence about the activities of liberal Democrats, his greatest source of trouble in the Senate. Gerry Siegel and later Harry McPherson, his two most liberal staff members, kept lines open to staff members of liberal Senators and sometimes liberal Senators themselves. Robert Oliver, the United Auto Workers staff member from Texas who had maneuvered the CIO behind Johnson in his 1948 campaign and who was now Walter Reuther's chief lobbyist in Washington, was in constant touch with both Johnson and the liberals. But the most important conduit to the liberals was Hubert Humphrey. Johnson had such intimate knowledge of liberal battle plans to reform Rule XXII (the filibuster rule) in January, 1957, that liberals suspected a leak in their own camp. Specifically, they suspected that Humphrey, Bob Oliver, or possibly both, were passing word of their secret meetings to the Majority Leader.

The distillation of intelligence was the head count—the report on how each Senator would vote on a given issue. This delicate judgment of each Senator's intentions was entrusted to Bobby Baker, who compiled the famous head counts in their final form. Baker's head counts were an invaluable asset for Johnson not available to labor, to business, to the Republicans, or even to the White House. Baker's invariably precise count not only gave Johnson the odds on a bill, but what votes he had to switch. This enabled Johnson to energize the Network and get a sufficient number of Senators to change their votes, or at least arrange for Network Senators who opposed the Johnson position to linger in the cloakroom while the roll was called. Johnson controlled the speed of the actual roll call by signaling the reading clerk —slowing it down until the Senator with the deciding vote (on Johnson's side, of course) entered the chamber, then speeding it up (by a quick rotary movement of his forefinger) when the votes he needed were in hand.

Very infrequently the Johnson-Baker count would be off by a single tally. Perhaps an anti-Johnson Senator would return unexpectedly from out of town to vote. If that happened, Johnson would flash an S.O.S. to the cloakroom and a Network Senator would emerge, then signal the reading clerk that he wanted to cast his vote and tip the balance to Johnson.

That was the dramatic culmination of the Johnson Procedure. Never had a Majority Leader maintained so precise a check on the preferences and the possibilities of every colleague. But inherent in the Johnson Procedure were basic changes in the daily operation of the Senate, changes emanating from the personality of the Majority Leader and evolving so slowly that they were ignored by the public and scarcely recognized in the Senate itself. Yet they were insensibly transforming the Senate. No longer was it the deliberative body described by Woodrow Wilson in 1883 and found relatively intact when Lyndon Johnson arrived in 1949.

These were the mechanical devices of the Johnson Procedure that transformed the Senate:

Unanimous Consent. This was merely a matter of getting all Senators to agree in advance to debate a bill for a fixed time and then to vote. It had always been used in the Senate, but used sparingly and mostly for minor bills.

Johnson transmogrified this occasional procedural device into a way of life. He applied it to every major bill. And so, gradually, attention and interest deserted the once stately public debate and centered on the cloakroom where Johnson, in nose-to-nose negotiations, hammered out his unanimous consent agreements to limit debate. Sometimes these were extremely complex, containing an intricate maze of provisos and codicils.

Occasionally Johnson forged a unanimous consent agreement adhered to by all interested parties (or so he thought), only to hear one maverick Senator (perhaps emboldened by too many nips from the bottle) shout "no" when the agreement was formally offered, thereby depriving Johnson of his unanimous consent. Angry at being crossed, Johnson would storm into the cloakroom and when the glass door had swung shut, would let himself go with an angry soliloquy against the nonconformist who was well beyond hearing on the Senate floor. Then, composing himself, the glass door would swing open and Johnson would return to the floor, drape his arm around the offender, find the cause for objection (perhaps nothing more than a desire to make an extra two-hour speech), satisfy him—and then propound another unanimous consent request to the Senate. He seldom was turned down twice on one bill.

Thus did Lyndon Johnson revolutionize the Senate, severely modifying its proud heritage of unlimited debate without changing a single rule. Of course, the filibuster was still available as an ultimate weapon. And of course any Senator could block unanimous consent and keep the debate going. In fact, however, few did. Debates grew shorter—and ever less important.

Aborted Quorum Calls. When Johnson first arrived at the Senate, the Majority Leader still followed the ancient practice of demanding that a quorum of Senators (forty-nine out of ninety-six) be on the floor for an important debate. As Majority Leader, Johnson demanded more and more quorum calls—but with a new purpose: to fill gaps in the Johnson schedule. Instead of recessing the Senate for an hour or two as in the past, Johnson would ask for a quorum call and wait, sometimes for close to an hour, while the reading clerk droned slowly through the names. Then, when Johnson was ready for the Senate to resume, he would suspend the calling of the roll. These aborted quorum calls held the Senate in suspended animation while Johnson worked out his deals in the cloakroom. Soon, nobody answered the quorum calls. The ever-increasing proportion of the Senate's day spent in meaningless recital of names of Senators who did not bother to answer was a symbol of the decay of Senate debate under the Johnson Procedure.

Night Sessions. In the 1920s, the Senate recessed for luncheon and then returned in the afternoon for more debate. That leisurely practice ended long before Johnson's arrival. But before the Johnson Procedure was instituted, the Senate session was a civilized twelve noon to five o'clock, except under extraordinary conditions.

Johnson changed that. When a debate neared completion, he drove the Senate into night session—beyond nine o'clock, to eleven, to midnight. Late hours, he shrewdly calculated, dulled the desire for debate. With senatorial brains addled by fatigue and generous libations poured in anterooms, combativeness diminished. The Senator who was ready to fight Johnson at three o'clock on this line until the snows came was only too ready by midnight to accept a unanimous consent agreement—*any* unanimous consent agreement—if only he could go home to bed. By driving the Senate into night sessions, the Johnson Procedure further reduced and deadened debate.

Stop-and-Go. Born of necessity after his heart attack, this technique became a positive asset to Johnson. Because doctor's orders called for Johnson to make frequent rest trips back to the LBJ Ranch, he compressed packets of complex legislation into a single week or so, then let the Senate limp along with little or no business (under the loose guidance of the Majority Whip). As the years passed, Johnson out of choice began to legislate in bursts of activity followed by spells of torpor—even when he was not home in Texas.

In 1959, Johnson brought this technique to perfection. He drove the Senate into passing important bills on January 5 and 6 during two long sessions. Next followed a lull to March 11 in which the Senate was virtually inoperative. Johnson then harassed the Senate to overtime work and passed four bills between March 11 and 23. Two bills were passed in April, two in late May and then quiet, until a frenetic burst of activity between June 25 and July 9 brought the Senate to the point of exhaustion with the passage of four major bills. Again a long pause, then the frenzied session-end burst of activity with five bills passed between September 5 and 14.

Stop-and-go was the twin sister of the night session. Exhausted by the numbing consideration of one bill after another in a short time span, the Senate was infinitely more pliable and at the mercy of Johnson's debate-limiting, unanimous-consent agreements. It was another nail in the coffin of debate.

The techniques employed by Johnson weakened, very nearly destroyed, the Senate as a debating society. But in place of a debating society, Johnson did not substitute a parliamentary body that functioned with a comprehensive set of rules, such as the House of Representatives or the British House of Commons. For the Senate functioned under Johnson only because of the Johnson System—the Network and the Procedure, both so attuned to one man's genius they had no chance to survive him.

Johnson's Senate procedure was a natural extension of Johnson's personality. Because he was no orator, his genius was not to sway men's minds in forensic debate. Besides, he thought it a waste of time. He knew that Senators seldom revealed their inner nature in public talk, and discovering that inner nature was at the core of the Johnson System. With rare exceptions, the Senate's important work was done in bilateral negotiations, with a premium on secrecy.

But when it came to those rare exceptions when Johnson wanted a single major speech to administer the coup de grace to his opposition, he was a master at setting the stage on the floor of the Senate and at squeezing out the last drop of drama.

Thus, as the annual debate on foreign aid droned to a conclusion and Eisenhower dispatched urgent messages to Johnson and Knowland to hold the line, Johnson carefully staged a debate-closing speech for the bill by the chairman of the Foreign Relations Committee, elder statesman Walter George, whose resonant voice gave off the vibrant timbre of a cathedral organ.

Lesser Senators prepared the way for the chairman's final appeal. As the last of the second-stringers rose to his feet, Johnson sent another Senator into the cloakroom to alert George. Johnson's agent led the old man across the hall to the comfortable quarters of the Secretary of the Senate and poured him a glass of a particular fine old wine that George fancied. Allowing time for George to sip his wine, Johnson finally crossed into the office of the Secretary himself and led George back into the chamber. The Senate quickly filled up—because Johnson had passed the word he wanted a full attendance. Relaxed and lubricated, George spoke for the better part of an hour, excoriating the small minds who opposed the foreign aid bill—his arms pumping the air, his magnificent voice filling the farthest reaches of the chamber. The moment the old man stopped, Johnson signaled to the reading clerk and the roll was called on the foreign aid bill, the conclusion foregone.

The George performance was out of the old pre-Johnson Senate, now becoming extinct, smothered by the Johnson System. Johnson himself seldom attempted a major speech. Instead, he read brief statements from a typewritten sheet of paper, often mumbling inaudibly into his chest.

Just as Thomas Jefferson was a strong President who weakened the presidency as an institution, so did Lyndon Johnson tame the Senate and make it work for him but leave it a weaker institution than he found it.*

---

* Jefferson wielded his power through his leadership of the Republican majority in the House. When Jefferson left the presidency, real power remained in Congress. His successors were unable to continue Jefferson's control of the party in Congress. Presidential power faded for nearly a generation until Andrew Jackson restored the health of the presidency as an institution. This was prophesied two months before Jefferson's inauguration by Chief Justice John Marshall, who wrote in a letter to a friend: "Mr. Jefferson appears to me to be a man who will embody himself with the House of Representatives. By weakening the office of President, he will increase his personal power." Just as Johnson was followed by a weak Majority Leader in Senator Mike Mansfield, so was Jefferson followed by a weak President in James Madison.

Under the Johnson System, the Senate enjoyed a golden era. And the full fruition of the System came in 1957 when it achieved the impossible: the passage of the first civil rights bill since Reconstruction, without a filibuster and without splitting the Democratic party.

Chapter VII

★★★★★★★★★

THE
MIRACLE
OF '57

An effective bill dealing with matters of great delicacy was
passed. The party that seemed about to be torn in two by the
controversy achieved greater unity than it has had in two decades.

> —Richard Rovere in *The New Yorker,*
> August 31, 1957

"I want to run the Senate. I want to pass the bills that need to be
passed. I want my party to do right. But all I ever hear from the
liberals is Nigra, Nigra, Nigra."

In 1957, these were the words of Lyndon Johnson, spoken to friends
in privacy. He was expressing deep frustration at the political and
social disorder, a century in the making, and its corrosive effect on his
own political future. Often, as he contemplated the most difficult
choice of his political career, Johnson would speak these words—bitterly, emotionally, and, indeed, truly. Because the hound of civil
rights nipped ever closer at his heels.

In the early 1950s, when Johnson began to complain increasingly
about the intrusion of the race issue into the Senate's legislative affairs,
his targets were such all-out liberals as Paul Douglas of Illinois and
Herbert Lehman of New York. These liberals, Johnson thought, aggravated the temper of the Senate, forcing Southerners to retaliate in
kind by constantly intruding civil rights into almost every issue that
came to the floor—thereby preventing Johnson from passing the bills
"that need to be passed." * But by 1957, "Nigra, Nigra, Nigra" was the

---

* In one of his most moving speeches in the 1964 presidential campaign, Johnson publicly used these same words—"Nigra, Nigra, Nigra"—to display his impatience not with liberals but with Southern white supremacists. The speech,
in New Orleans, on October 9, 1964, was a deeply emotional appeal to the South
to help, not hinder, the integration of Negroes into the full enjoyment of American life.

fixation not only of the liberal Democrats but of the Republican party, of the Republican President, of the vast, restless, and deprived Negro minority, and of the entire nation. His own South, far from relenting, was stiffening. In 1957, the issue was finally being drawn irrevocably. There could be no escape this time.

Although in Johnson's own Texas hill country the Negro was hardly a political issue, a commitment to the status quo of racial inequality was obligatory for statewide Texas officeholders.* Johnson was conspicuous in fulfilling the obligation, but from his earliest political days there could not be found in him any taint of the personal discrimination against racial minorities that characterized so many of his fellow Southern politicians in the 1940s and 1950s.

Johnson owed much of his electoral success, in fact, to the strong support of another large Texas minority, the hundreds of thousands of Mexican-American voters who lived along the Mexican border in the Rio Grande Valley. They invariably supported Johnson (like any segregated minority, they were a "controlled" and purchasable vote). More intimately, Johnson developed a strong affection for the young Mexican-Americans in his classrooms when he taught the fifth, sixth, and seventh grades at Cotulla, Texas, as a twenty-year-old in 1928.

But from the very first occasion in the House when he confronted a civil rights vote, Johnson voted with the South and backed up his votes with speeches opposing federal intervention in the Southern states and declaring undying loyalty to the racial status quo. After Johnson's loss in the 1941 Senate race pointed out the need to consolidate his position with Texas conservatives, his public position on the race question took on an even deeper Southern accent.

In 1948, for example, Johnson attacked President Truman's civil rights program as "a farce and a sham—an effort to set up a police state in the guise of liberty. . . . I am opposed to the anti-lynching bill because the federal government has no more business enacting a law against one kind of murder than another. I am against the FEPC [Fair Employment Practices Commission] because if a man can tell you whom you must hire, he can tell you whom you cannot employ." That was no more and no less than the straight party line of a Southern Democrat.

---

* Ralph Yarborough, a liberal lawyer from Austin, Texas, elected to the United States Senate in a special election of April, 1957, broke that rule. It should be pointed out, however, that he was a minority candidate who got less than 50 percent of the vote in the special election.

Ever since 1937, when he first entered the House, Johnson had voted *no* on civil rights 100 percent of the time: *no* on an anti-lynching bill in 1940; *no* on a Democratic leadership amendment in 1940 eliminating segregation in the armed services; *no* on anti-poll-tax bills in 1942, 1943, 1945; *no* in 1946 on an anti-discrimination amendment offered by Representative Adam Clayton Powell of Harlem to the federal school-lunch program; *yes* in 1949 on an anti-Negro amendment proposed by Mississippi's Senator James Eastland to the perennial District of Columbia home rule bill. The list was long, the record unbroken.

Actually, all those civil rights bills Lyndon Johnson voted against in the House weren't going anywhere, and everybody knew it. When Rutherford B. Hayes ended military Reconstruction after the election of 1876, Republicans ran up the white flag in the fight for Negro rights. Not since the early 1870s had a civil rights bill been passed by Congress. Woodrow Wilson's New Freedom was not concerned with the Negro, and Franklin Roosevelt's New Deal made only a perfunctory stab at ending segregation. The formation of the Republican-Southern Democratic coalition in the late 1930s made assurance doubly secure that the slowly growing Negro protest movement could not translate its aspirations into legislation. Whatever civil rights bill might pass the House faced the slow death of the Senate filibuster, conducted by Richard Russell's Southerners and buttressed by the benign neutrality of Robert Taft's Republicans.

But with the end of World War II, the Negro cry of protest—chorused by the Douglas-Humphrey new breed of Northern Democratic politicians—could no longer be smothered. The new civil rights movement showed its political muscles at the 1948 Democratic National Convention when Mayor Hubert Humphrey of Minneapolis made an overnight national reputation by taking the convention away from its regular leaders and ramming through the strongest civil rights plank ever adopted by the Democratic party. The result was the predictable bolt of the Deep South from the Truman-Barkley ticket and the Dixiecrat presidential candidacy of South Carolina's Governor J. Strom Thurmond, which carried four Deep South states. Although personally rather suspicious of the Negro protest movement, Truman in 1948 sent to Capitol Hill the strongest package of civil rights legislation since Reconstruction days. Truman's program did not even dent the Russell-Taft line in the Senate, but the civil rights pot on Capitol Hill was warming up.

What brought it to a boil was the Supreme Court decision of May 17, 1954, in the case of *Brown v. Board of Education of Topeka, Kan-*

sas. Reversing a fifty-eight-year-old Supreme Court opinion affirming the constitutionality of "separate but equal" facilities for the two races, a unanimous Court, headed by a new Chief Justice, former Republican Governor Earl Warren of California, declared racial segregation in the public schools to be unconstitutional.

That was the signal flare for the Negro Revolution, though the protest movement would not take to the streets until the early 1960s. By 1957, unrestrainable pressures were growing for a civil rights law. How these pressures would resolve themselves on Capitol Hill depended in large part on the course taken by the new Majority Leader of the United States Senate.

In January, 1957, as the 85th Congress convened with its still slender Democratic majority in the Senate, Lyndon Johnson faced the hardest dilemma of his political career. Either, he could continue in his old ways, and for good and all give up the pretense that he was a Westerner and *national* Democrat, not a Southerner and *regional* Democrat. Or, he could reverse the voting habit of a lifetime and vote for a civil rights bill—and risk a torrent of criticism not only from back home in Texas but from the entire South, as well as the loss of his newly built power as Senate Majority Leader, established with Southern support.

For most of the four years of his first term, Dwight D. Eisenhower had temporized over the festering civil rights issue. Born in the Old Confederacy (in Denison, Texas), President Eisenhower was even more wary of the Negro protest movement than President Truman had been. Prodded by Attorney General Herbert Brownell, Eisenhower finally sent a comprehensive civil rights bill to Congress in the 1956 election year. Whatever the politically inspired motives of such advisers as Brownell were, Eisenhower's own motive was pure enough. Two years after the Supreme Court's historic decision outlawing school segregation, he had come to feel it was high time for Congress to give the executive new tools to carry out the *Brown* decision and also to re-establish the Negro's right to vote, withdrawn from him in the South after 1876. In addition, the President asked for two other provisions: establishment of a new Civil Rights Division in the Justice Department to collect under one roof the growing number of civil rights cases and put them in the care of a specially trained legal staff; and creation of a Commission on Civil Rights, empowered by law to investigate all aspects of the problem and make public reports.

Although the program was scarcely revolutionary, and far less ambitious than Truman's of eight years earlier, to Johnson it posed the politically lethal dilemma. For a man with a weaker power drive and with less imagination and cunning, or one who lacked what Stewart Alsop has called Johnson's "exuberant egotism"—the Eisenhower civil rights program was simply an insoluble problem.

The fact that 1956 was a presidential election year took Johnson off the hook temporarily. When the House duly passed a watered-down Eisenhower bill on July 23, 1956, Johnson cooperated with Mississippi's James Eastland, chairman of the Senate Judiciary Committee, to dispatch the House-passed bill immediately to the Eastland cold storage in the Judiciary Committee. That was consigning the bill to certain death and postponing the great issue until 1957. Although liberals severely criticized Johnson for not holding the bill in the Senate and keeping it out of Jim Eastland's fatal embrace, his decision was the right one.

Congress was due to adjourn in four days for the presidential nominating conventions. If Johnson had bypassed the Judiciary Committee by moving the bill to the floor, it would immediately have tied up the Senate for those last four days and might have blocked final passage of both the foreign aid bill and the bill increasing Social Security benefits, as well as exposing the North-South Democratic party split in an election year. That, however, did not reduce the anger of liberal Democrats, particularly Johnson's old sparring partner, Paul Douglas of Illinois.

On July 23, Senator Douglas walked across the Capitol to the House chamber to be present at the historic passage of the Eisenhower bill. His plan was to walk with the House employee who would be assigned by the Speaker to deliver the bill to the Senate in the accustomed tradition. Instead of traveling at the normal speed, however, the just-passed bill was rushed with unseemly haste out of the House chamber by a side door and over to the Senate, passing Douglas on the way. When Douglas discovered he had been duped by Johnson and the Senate Establishment, he rushed back to the Senate chamber only to find that the bill had already arrived and been sent to Eastland's Judiciary Committee.

With the bill physically in Eastland's hands, Douglas and Herbert Lehman (about to retire after a career of distinguished public service) tried frantically to discharge the bill from the Judiciary Committee. But Russell, backed by Johnson, utilized his encyclopedic knowledge of parliamentary affairs to prevent a vote on Douglas' proposed discharge. The parliamentary situation boiled down to this: for a vote to be taken on discharge, the Senate had to be *adjourned*, not just *recessed*—a decision traditionally reserved for the Majority Leader. And so, on the night of July 24, one day after House passage of the civil rights bill, Douglas moved that the Senate *adjourn*. He was defeated by a humiliating 76 to 6 vote. Thomas Hennings of Missouri was the only other Democrat to join Douglas and Lehman. When Douglas and his young legislative assistant, Howard Shuman, trudged from the Senate chamber that night and reached the Capitol elevator, Douglas bitterly told his aide: "Let's pretend we really *are* Senators and push the bell three times [a signal to the elevator operator that a Senator was ringing]."

What particularly shocked Douglas was the fact that Humphrey had joined Johnson in delaying civil rights action in the Senate until 1957, the first clear evidence to Douglas of the maturing Johnson-Humphrey relationship. Johnson had done his work well in convincing not only Humphrey but the Eisenhower Administration that if the Douglas-Lehman plan worked, the civil rights bill would not be passed and the rest of the legislative program would be doomed.

Based on Johnson's performance in 1956, the politicians and press of Washington believed that hostile neutrality was about the most that could be expected of Johnson in 1957 when Eisenhower sent his civil rights package back to Congress. On January 11, 1957, a *New York Times* dispatch from Washington reported as a matter of fact that Johnson "will oppose" the new Eisenhower bill "as a Senator from Texas." * Both Johnson and George Reedy did nothing to encourage the slightest speculation among the Capitol Hill press that Johnson was preparing a historic shift of position, hoping to keep Johnson in an uncommitted position to give him maximum flexibility in the months ahead.

Even Johnson's intimates doubted how far he would go down the civil rights trail, although early in the year, Johnson confided to Senator Clinton Anderson of New Mexico, the Senate's most ardent supporter of civil rights outside the liberal bloc, that he would make sure a civil rights bill was passed in 1957. As a skeptic and a realist, Anderson didn't think Johnson could or would carry out that pledge.

What neither the press nor most of his fellow legislators (with the exception of Sam Rayburn) realized was how indispensable to Johnson's national political aspirations it was to get credit for passage of the bill, and how fatal it would be for him to oppose it. If he could

---

* The big news contained in the *Times* dispatch was that Johnson "will not attempt to use his position as Democratic floor leader to keep [the civil rights bill] from reaching the floor" and was not expected "to participate in the prospective filibuster or to block efforts to break it."

transform the Eisenhower bill into the Johnson bill, he would once and for all emancipate himself from the Confederate yoke that had destroyed Richard Russell's presidential ambitions. It would move him into the mainstream of the Democratic party for the first time since his early days as a young New Deal Congressman. Unless he plunged into that mainstream, Johnson could not even hope for the presidential nomination in 1960—or ever.

As Eisenhower's new civil rights bill of 1957 slowly made its way through committee hearings, committee sessions, and finally floor debate in the House, Johnson was silent. At no time did he reveal his intentions. Even Ben Cohen, the White House brain-truster of New Deal days whom Johnson turned to for advice on the civil rights bill, never was sure how far Johnson would go on civil rights—indeed, whether he would end up voting for the bill. As in the McCarthy censure fight and just about every major legislative fight since, the absence of a firmly staked-out position for Johnson infinitely enhanced his maneuverability. The strong possibility that, in the case of the civil rights fight, Johnson himself did not quite know where he was going, in no way weakened his legislative position.

Johnson did know that to get a bill passed without destroying himself and his party he must follow a two-part strategy: 1) convince Russell not to use the South's traditional weapon of filibuster; 2) get a majority of the Senate to pull the sharpest fangs from the bill so that Russell could accept it without the need to filibuster.

Johnson's ploy with Russell was to show the dangers to the South if its ultimate weapon, the filibuster, failed to work. Johnson's entirely plausible argument went something like this: the old Dixiecrat-Republican coalition was deteriorating. Without the help of conservative Republicans, Southerners could not be quite so sure of talking the bill to death by a filibuster. For the first time, it was in the realm of the possible that the two-thirds vote required to end a filibuster by imposing cloture was attainable. Would it not be in the South's own self-interest to accept a de-fanged bill without a filibuster, retaining the filibuster as a threat to be used another day against a more onerous civil rights bill? It was perhaps farfetched to talk about cloture being imposed in 1957. But Russell got a graphic demonstration of the old coalition's decomposition in the very first skirmish on the Senate floor.

The House overwhelmingly passed Eisenhower's new bill on June 18, 1957, after a week of perfunctory debate. But this time neither

Douglas nor any other liberal Democrat had to act in order to prevent its burial in Eastland's Judiciary Committee. This time, that safeguarding was to be assured by Senator William F. Knowland, the Senate Republican leader and a conservative, who was now leading one of the most unusual political coalitions in Senate history, a coalition of Republicans and liberal Democrats formed solely to enact the Eisenhower bill. Accordingly, when the bill arrived from the House, the Senate was treated to the extraordinary spectacle of the conservative Republican leader battling against Russell to move the House-passed bill directly to the floor of the Senate (and to bypass Eastland).

On the procedural vote to keep the bill out of committee, Knowland's makeshift coalition beat Russell 45 to 39 (Johnson voting with Russell to send the bill to Eastland's committee), thus launching the Senate into its historic civil rights debate.* Just as Johnson foresaw, the conservative coalition was crumbling under the political pressure exerted by a Republican President (strongly backed this time by the independent-minded Knowland), who was demanding party support for a civil rights bill that conceivably could revolutionize Negro politics and bring the Negro vote back to the party of Lincoln.

The other interlocking component of Johnson's strategy—drafting a sanitized bill that the North would accept and the South need not filibuster against—was more difficult. For weeks, Johnson had been toying with an approach wholly different from Eisenhower's: a Federal Racial Mediation and Conciliation Service, modeled after the Federal Labor Mediation Service. Gerald Siegel, counsel at the Democratic Policy Committee, drafted such a proposal, though it was never introduced. Ben Cohen had told Johnson repeatedly it would never satisfy the liberals. The proposal never left Johnson's pocket.†

By the time the bill passed the House, it was clear to Johnson that two essential modifications in the bill were needed to forestall a filibuster. One was adoption of an amendment requiring a jury trial in contempt-of-court cases arising from violation of the Civil Rights Act. This was an issue of little inherent importance but of symbolic significance, following a heated debate on the House floor that ended with the defeat of a jury trial amendment. The other modification was of far greater significance. It required total elimination of the

---

* On this vote, Johnson voted with Russell to send the bill to Eastland's committee but did nothing to round up votes. Because Russell was beaten so badly, Johnson's vote was meaningless. Johnson's own vote did, however, keep open his lines of communication with Russell and the South and maintain the aura of mystery hovering over his ultimate decision on the bill.

† It was, however, the basis for a section of the Civil Rights Act of 1964.

bill's Part III. Although it was hardly mentioned during a week's debate in the House, Part III was the big gun of the bill. Giving the Attorney General of the United States power to file suit for civil rights injunctions, Part III ensured not only the Negro's right to vote, but was geared to speed desegregation of schools, still proceeding at a most leisurely pace three years after the *Brown* decision.

Thus Johnson was in his own secretive, circuitous way moving toward a trimmed-down bill with three parts: the Commission on Civil Rights, the new Civil Rights Division in the Justice Department, and full use of the federal courts to safeguard the *right to vote*—and no other civil rights. With Part III gone, the bill would sidestep completely the explosive question of school segregation. Playing his cards close to the chest, Johnson privately laid his plans and began to carry them out.

He went first to Russell and then went back to Russell time and again, to probe the South's intention and to seek advice from his old mentor. The advice he got was sound. Russell candidly informed Johnson that if Part III were eliminated and a jury trial amendment added, there probably would be no filibuster. The necessity of stripping out Part III was hammered home. Russell and his Southern cohorts told Johnson: Lyndon, you make that bill a voting rights bill and we'll let it come to a vote. You can vote for it yourself. But if you vote for a bill with Part III in it your name will be mud from the Potomac to the Rio Grande.

In private talks Russell made clear that a bill limited to voting rights could be tolerated in Georgia, where, he insisted, Negroes were not systematically excluded from the polls. Why was Russell so charitable to Johnson? Had he given the word, he could have brought the Senate to chaos by ordering a Southern filibuster.

Russell was, after all, in great degree responsible for Johnson becoming Democratic leader four years earlier. Besides this stake in Johnson's success, he admired the way Johnson had revolutionized and enlarged the floor leader's job (even though it came partly at the expense of Russell's real power). In short, Russell didn't want Johnson to fall on his face.

But Russell would scarcely make so critical a strategic decision out of his sentiment for his old protégé. The real reason lay in the fact that Russell totally agreed with Johnson's warnings about the danger to Southern self-interest of a filibuster now that the coalition was crumbling—on two scores. If the Southerners successfully filibustered the bill to death, the country would rise up in anger and demand that the filibuster rule be changed, causing the South untold misery in the future; but if the civil rights bloc succeeded in breaking a filibuster, the defeat would open the bill to amendments by triumphant liberals far more unacceptable to the South than a mere voting rights bill. On balance, Russell chose to accept (informing only Johnson) a simple voting rights bill rather than risk the far more dangerous course of filibuster.

But that private word from Russell filled only part of Johnson's need (although it was the most important part). Now he needed assurance that when the votes were taken to strip out Part III, and put in the jury trial amendment, there would be sufficient Senators voting his way.

In pursuing his still secret goal, Majority Leader Johnson explored every possibility, hoarded his political IOUs, and spent days quietly persuading Democratic moderates in the civil rights bloc to see it his way. Sometimes the methods were indirect. In early May, for example, Johnson's own subcommittee of the Senate Appropriations Committee was "marking up" the Eisenhower budget request for the State Department—that is, making final recommendations to the full Appropriations Committee and the Senate. It was the height of the 1957 Battle of the Budget, which would culminate in a Johnson vendetta against the United States Information Agency. Johnson was "marking up" the bill with staff aides. Not another Senator was present. Johnson ordered each item reduced throughout the State Department-USIA budget, moving through the bill line by line until he got to a $409,000 request to survey the Passamaquoddy tidal basin on the Maine-Canadian border. The House had entirely eliminated this survey fund from the bill, and staff aides automatically moved along to the next item. They were astonished, then, when Johnson himself *restored* the full $409,000 cut out by the House.

Johnson's purpose was to reinforce his ties with his close friend, Margaret Chase Smith, the Republican Senator from Maine, who always voted an independent line. It was in her vital interest to get close to a half million dollars in federal spending money for that economically depressed part of Maine. Already a member of the Johnson Network, Maggie Smith would, of course, remember Johnson's generosity when he needed votes on the Part III and jury trial amendments. In describing briefly to the Senate on May 15 the exceptional increase for the Passamaquoddy project, while every other Eisenhower request was being slashed, Johnson utilized a curious brand of logic:

> When we inquired of the expert witness on Passamaquoddy they said it would cost more to spread the cost over two years than to include the full item this year. So I voted for economy and I am prepared to defend my action.

THE MIRACLE OF '57

Not a question was asked on the Senate floor. The amount was relatively minor, and it's doubtful whether any Senator was much aware
of what Johnson had done—except Mrs. Smith. The Passamaquoddy
affair had to be multiplied by dozens of favors for other Senators. In
this maneuver, through the winter and spring, Johnson was quietly
storing up IOUs on a bill that would not even come before the Senate
until summer. But the biggest single store of Senate IOUs was piled
up in late June, some two weeks before the civil rights debate, when
the ten-year struggle over Hells Canyon reached a climax on the
Senate floor.

Specifically at issue was who should harness the power from the
waters of the Snake River at Hells Canyon near the Idaho-Oregon
border. Western Democrats pushed a bill authorizing the federal government to build a single high dam at Hells Canyon that would generate low-rate public power for the entire area. Western Republicans,
backed by the Eisenhower Administration, opposed the high dam and
instead proposed that the Idaho Power Company go through with its
plans to build three smaller dams under private financing. But the
fight transcended Hells Canyon. It was the focus for debating the
question of paramount importance through the entire West in the early
1950s: private versus public power. Republican charges of "creeping socialism" were countered by Democratic charges of an Eisenhower "giveaway policy" for natural resources. Carrying the banner of
Hells Canyon, public-power Democrats were breaking the once solid
hegemony of private-power Republicans in the Far West. Fiery, red-
haired Gracie Pfost, campaigning as "Hells' Belle," used the issue to
win election to Congress from Idaho in 1954. It was the high point in
the Oregon Senate campaign of 1956, when Senator Wayne Morse,
the liberal Republican-turned-Democrat, beat back the challenge of
private-power advocate Douglas McKay, who had left the Cabinet as
Eisenhower's Secretary of the Interior to challenge Morse. And also in
1956, an unknown thirty-two-year-old Boise lawyer named Frank
Church crusaded on the Hells Canyon issue to drive McCarthyite Republican Herman Welker from the Senate.

The Hells Canyon high dam bill had cleared the House Interior
Committee in 1956 and seemed a good bet for House passage, but it
was defeated on the Senate floor by a 51 to 41 vote while Lyndon
Johnson made little discernible effort to save it. Frank Church, fore-
runner of a platoon of young Western Democrats who were to revolutionize the Senate's balance of power two years hence, beat Welker in
the 1956 campaign, promising to get the Hells Canyon high dam bill
passed in 1957 if only the voters of Idaho would send him to Washington. Church and his pretty young wife undoubtedly were genuinely

grateful to Johnson for the trip to South America, but that was a personal luxury.* Church's political necessity was Senate passage of the Hells Canyon bill, and only Johnson could do that. To Senators like Church from the Mountain States, where Negroes comprised an infinitesimal share of the population, a high dam at Hells Canyon was infinitely more important than the details of the civil rights bill. And, of course, Lyndon Johnson knew it.

On June 21, the day after Knowland succeeded in keeping the House-passed civil rights bill away from the Judiciary Committee, the Hells Canyon bill was voted on by the Senate with prospects for a very close vote. But in contrast to his nonchalance a year earlier, Johnson this time pulled out every conceivable Democratic vote for Hells Canyon. The bill passed on a 45 to 38 roll call with Democrats showing extraordinary unity in lining up, 40 to 5, for Hells Canyon. The difference came from Dixie.

Johnson convinced Southern conservatives that on the eve of their great civil rights showdown, it would be in their best interests to shave a conservative scruple or two and give their Western colleagues some help. Thus, just as Knowland's Republicans on June 20 bolted from the coalition to block the House civil rights bill from going to committee, so did Russell's Southerners deal the crumbling coalition another blow by abandoning the Republicans on Hells Canyon. Richard Russell himself led the way. Close behind were James Eastland, Sam J. Ervin, Jr., Russell Long, and George Smathers. All five voted *against* the high dam in 1956; all five voted *for* it in 1957. Far from experiencing a miraculous conversion to the cause of public power, these Southerners were merely storing up IOUs for Lyndon Johnson—and themselves—for the days of reckoning on the civil rights bill.†

On July 8, 1957, the opening day for civil rights debate to begin officially in the Senate, Johnson turned control of the Senate over to Knowland, leader of the makeshift, bipartisan, civil rights coalition, and Russell, commanding the South's beleaguered forces. Johnson folded his arms across his chest, sat at his front-row desk, and listened. His grand strategy had by then come far, but there was no proof it would work. Until he had that proof, Johnson was not going to involve himself actively in the civil rights debate.

* See page 103.
† If Russell and his Southerners really cared about the merits of public versus private power, they lost nothing by voting for the Hells Canyon bill. In 1958, the bill was killed by a one-vote margin in the House Interior Committee.

Consequently, Johnson limited himself to brief, statesmanlike speeches on the floor, which were carefully distributed to reporters in the press gallery ahead of time. These short speeches made the same point day after day: the Senate was showing in the high quality of its debate that it would face up to the most difficult issue in years, and Johnson knew that the "reasoned debate" of "reasonable men" would have a fruitful end. He gently rebuked the press and the civil rights bloc for predicting a Southern filibuster. The debate was timely and to the point, he said. At that time, Johnson's work was still off the Senate floor, building a climate that could result in the passage of his two big amendments: Part III elimination and the jury trial amendment.

Part III, incredibly ignored in the drab House debate, was brought to the nation's attention by Russell in his opening speech a week earlier on July 2. Part III, Russell declaimed, was "cunningly designed to vest in the Attorney General unprecedented power to bring to bear the whole might of the federal government, including the armed forces if necessary, to force a co-mingling of white and Negro children in the state-supported schools of the South." But Johnson needed more than Southern oratory to kill Part III. He needed liberal, not Southern support. And it was forthcoming—from some unexpected sources.

The regal Dean Acheson, an original New Dealer under Roosevelt and later Harry Truman's Secretary of State, also happened to be one of Washington's most respected lawyers. He barely knew Johnson when the Majority Leader called him to his office on the Capitol's third floor in the spring of 1957. Acheson spent the entire morning with Johnson and came away enormously impressed.

They went over a draft of the House bill, and Acheson agreed that Part III was dangerous, would deliver too much power to the Justice Department, and should be stricken. Dump Part III, he advised Johnson. Johnson replied he planned to do exactly that. But he cautioned Acheson not to say anything about it. He added: "I can buy a lot with this [from the Southerners], but it has to come out at just the right time."

Acheson's prestige aligned against Part III was valuable. Even more valuable was the support of Senator Clinton Anderson, whose credentials as a fighter for civil rights were impeccable. Anderson had studied the bill himself and volunteered to Johnson the advice that Part III should be eliminated.

"Okay, *you* do it," suggested Johnson.

"How can I?" replied Anderson. "I'm a civil rights man."

Johnson's advice: get a Republican as co-sponsor. Anderson took the advice and came up with Vermont's Senator George Aiken, one of the most senior and most respected of liberal Republicans. Thus the move to eliminate Part III was enhanced because the Senate was not considering the Russell-Eastland Amendment, but the Anderson-Aiken Amendment, sponsored not by segregationists but by moderate liberals.

Yet, perhaps the most important spadework on Part III was accomplished not on Capitol Hill but at the White House. Johnson was working on President Eisenhower himself. It would do no good if the offensive Part III were stripped from the bill by Democratic votes, to be followed by a charge from the President that the Democrats had sold out the Negroes. In fact, if Eisenhower made a strong campaign on behalf of Part III, he might sway enough Republican votes to defeat Johnson.

Aware of Russell's great influence with the President and his rare ability to articulate his point, Johnson encouraged the Southern leader to go to the White House and talk to Eisenhower in early July, well before any votes were taken in the Senate. Russell brought back from Eisenhower reassuring news. Eisenhower told Russell that he could not yield "in my purpose of protecting the citizen's right to vote." This, he said, was "the overriding provision of the Bill" that he "wanted set down to law." Eisenhower stressed to Russell that the Negro could obtain his other basic rights, if once he received the vote.

With no little justification, Russell came back convinced that Eisenhower was agreeable to Johnson's goal of limiting the bill to voting rights by stripping the far-ranging Part III.* Thus, through Russell, Johnson acquired a powerful new weapon for the persuasion of Senators in quiet cloakroom talks: assurance that Eisenhower would not insist on retention of Part III.

The influence of his talks with Johnson and Russell began to show up in Eisenhower's public utterances. On July 3, the day after Russell's Senate attack on Part III, the President was asked at his press conference by James Reston of the *New York Times* whether he wanted the bill "written so that it specifically dealt with the question of right to vote rather than implementing the Supreme Court decision on the integration of the schools." In short, did Eisenhower want to knock out Part III? Eisenhower cut the ground out from under Knowland's battle to retain Part III and stunned the press conference by replying that "before I make any more remarks on that, I would want to talk to the Attorney General and see exactly what [certain

---

* According to the Eisenhower memoirs, *Waging Peace,* he did not intend to give Russell the impression he opposed Part III, though this was the only rational impression to be drawn.

phrases] do mean." But this was nothing compared with the exchange at Eisenhower's July 17 press conference:

Q. Rowland Evans, Jr., *New York Herald Tribune:* . . . are you convinced that it would be a wise extension of federal power at this stage to permit the Attorney General to bring suits on his own motion, to enforce school integration in the South?

The President: Well, no; I have—as a matter of fact, as you state it that way, on his own motion, without any request from local authorities, I suppose is what you are talking about.

Q. Mr. Evans: Yes, sir. I think that that is what the bill would do, Part III.

The President: Well, in that, we will see what they agree on. . . . I personally believe if you try to go too far too fast in laws in this delicate field that has involved the emotions of so many million Americans, you are making a mistake.

That brief exchange ended Knowland's hope of retaining Part III. Just one week later, on July 24, the day of voting on the question, Knowland returned from the White House to report the President did not want Part III eliminated.* It was too little, too late. On July 24, Part III was eliminated by a vote of 52 to 38. Johnson lost only thirteen Democrats and gained eighteen Republicans, a surprisingly large number. It would have taken a switch of seven votes to defeat the amendment and retain Part III. The debate now immediately switched to the jury trial amendment, where Johnson's problems were deeper.

Though of less substantive importance to civil rights than Part III, the jury trial amendment was more easily dramatized for political purposes and thus equally important to Johnson in his fight to stave off a Dixie filibuster. Johnson grasped immediately how important the amendment could be for Southern Senators who faced the ordeal of returning home to tell constituents why they let the first civil rights bill since Reconstruction pass without a filibuster. The jury amendment would give them a nice legal talking point. They would be able to ask their constituents: Can any Southerner fear a Southern jury?

For the most part, the year-long public debate on the jury trial amendment was waged in simplistic terms. Southerners claimed

---

* Throughout the period of debate, Eisenhower seemed confused and ambivalent about Part III. In Cabinet meetings, he expressed doubts about its constitutionality but was apparently swayed from this position by Attorney General Brownell. Despite his hostile statements in the July 3 and July 17 press conferences, the Eisenhower memoirs describe the eventual defeat of Part III as "a blow."

Eisenhower's bill violated the constitutional guarantee of trial by jury. The civil rights coalition retorted that Southern juries never would convict Southerners. With sectional lines drawn on that basis, the jury trial amendment was doomed to defeat (as it had been decisively defeated, 251 to 158, in the House on June 18). Yet Johnson had to add some such amendment in the Senate to avert a filibuster.

To find non-Southern support for the jury trial amendment, Johnson had to convince civil rights advocates it would not wreck the bill. Help came early from an unexpected source: the liberal journal of opinion, the *New Leader*. Gerry Siegel, Johnson's chief legal aide, had noticed an article in the April 29 edition of the *New Leader* written by a law professor at the University of Wisconsin, Carl A. Auerbach. He drew a sharp distinction between civil contempt and criminal contempt arising out of the bill. Auerbach contended that criminal contempt was pure and simple punishment for a violation of law and by all standards of Anglo-Saxon justice, the defendant should have a jury trial. Civil contempt was another matter. The defendant could purge himself of the fine or jail sentence simply by complying with the judge's order, and no jury trial was required. Clearly, civil contempt citations could be used to enforce the bill.

Siegel quickly brought the article to the attention of Johnson, who instantly grasped its importance. Working with Siegel, Johnson's high-priced lawyer friends outside his staff—Dean Acheson, Ben Cohen, and Abe Fortas—put the draft amendment through a half dozen changes before the Senate debate began. At that spring morning meeting in Johnson's office, Acheson had not only advocated elimination of Part III, but agreed with Johnson on the jury trial amendment. The amendment would not undermine the bill, he explained, if it permitted fines and jail terms up to a stated level *without* a jury trial, limiting the jury requirement to cases where a judge imposed higher penalties for criminal (but not civil) contempt.

Again, though, Johnson needed liberal co-sponsors of the jury trial amendment of a caliber to match the Anderson-Aiken sponsorship of the Part III elimination. Bushy-browed, garrulous old Senator Joseph C. O'Mahoney of Wyoming, a neo-Populist crusader against the Eastern money interests, was a natural. He was joined by Senator Estes Kefauver of Tennessee, who despite his Southern background was a member of the Northern liberal bloc in the Senate (and who the previous autumn had been nominated in open convention for his party's vice-presidential nomination). Kefauver was no ally of Johnson's, but needed to water down the bill to satisfy his Border State constituency. The third sponsor of the amendment was none other than Frank

Church. The result was the O'Mahoney-Kefauver-Church Amendment (drafted by Acheson and Cohen).

The amendment had built-in support within the civil rights bloc. Western haters of Wall Street, in the O'Mahoney mold, had always supported the labor union position against court injunctions. For historic reasons, they could not turn their backs on a legislative battle over jury trials. Johnson played every turn he could on this old-fashioned, deep-rooted fear of the injunctive process, invoking memories of famous labor battles before the Norris-LaGuardia Act outlawed anti-strike labor injunctions. As Johnson told it, the jury trial amendment became a sort of beacon of freedom and almost overshadowed the bill itself.

Johnson told the Senate:

> This amendment . . . says only that a man cannot be branded as a criminal, in the sight of his fellow man, without a trial by jury. The tradition of trial by jury is deep within the heart of our liberty-loving people. Repeal that right and our laws will become ineffective, except to incite disobedience. Recognize that right, and we shall have one of the strongest and most effective laws in our history. *

But finding a majority of the Senate was far more difficult here than in the Part III fight. Besides old-style progressives like O'Mahoney, Johnson needed Eastern liberals—and, with the civil rights lobby turning its full fire against the jury trial amendment, they were hard to come by. Nor was there any unwitting help from the White House as there had been in the Part III battle. Eisenhower was unequivocal in his opposition to the jury trial amendment. Thus, Eastern liberal backing for the O'Mahoney-Kefauver-Church Amendment had to be picked up in dribs and drabs.

One vote Johnson particularly wanted was that of Rhode Island's eighty-nine-year-old Senator Theodore Francis Green, a Democratic liberal. With Green's vote in favor of the jury trial amendment, Johnson would surely acquire Senator John Pastore, Green's junior Rhode Island colleague, and perhaps Massachusetts' John F. Kennedy, whose support Johnson desperately wanted. One afternoon in his office, Johnson told Acheson that three votes—Green's, Pastore's and Kennedy's—hung on Green's decision. Green, he felt, was leaning away

---

* In fact, the 1957 Act, although landmark legislation, was totally inadequate as a protection of the Southern Negro's right to vote. It wasn't until eight years later, in 1965, that a truly effective voting-rights law was passed after being sent to Congress by President Johnson.

from the jury trial amendment, but Green did not like to be put under any pressure. Would Acheson have any way of finding out what Green's intention really was?

As Secretary of State, Acheson had spent many hours with the Senate Foreign Relations Committee, of which Green was a senior member. He knew Green well, and they liked each other. On leaving Johnson's office that afternoon, Acheson took the Capitol subway to the Senate Office Building and walked conspicuously and slowly past the open door of Green's outer office. Any meeting with Green must be accidental. He remembered from those earlier days that Green's secretary placed her desk in such a way as to see clearly everyone who walked by the open door. Sure enough, Green's secretary spotted Acheson and called out to him. He made a pretense of pleasant surprise, turned, and entered the office to say hello. The secretary, as Acheson had expected, wouldn't let him go without taking him in to see the Senator. Acheson brightly explained to Green that he had just happened by and had been spotted by Green's secretary, and tell me, Theodore, how the devil are you these days?

After the amenities, the talk quickly turned to the Capitol's only topic of conversation: the civil rights bill. Green confessed to Acheson he was deeply puzzled about certain parts of the bill, particularly the jury trial amendment, and wished that he were a lawyer. Several Senators had asked him how he would vote and he couldn't tell them. Would Dean mind if he asked his advice on that?

Acheson thought a long moment, then replied: "If I were you, Theodore, I'd vote for the jury amendment. Yes, I surely would."

A minute later, Acheson, certain that his mission had succeeded, said farewell to Green, and returned to his walk down the corridor. He stopped at the first pay telephone and called Johnson in the Capitol.

"Lyndon," he said, "don't ask me any questions, but you've got your three votes."

True to Acheson's promise, the New England threesome—Green, Pastore, and Kennedy—ended up voting for the jury trial amendment. It's questionable, however, whether Green's example was really enough to convince Kennedy. Johnson was pulling out all the stops to get support on the jury trial amendment from Kennedy, a rising young figure in the party after his near miss for the vice-presidential nomination against Kefauver the previous year. Johnson dispatched their mutual friend, George Smathers of Florida, to talk Kennedy into backing the jury trial amendment. Smathers reported back that he could get nowhere with Kennedy and Johnson should try himself. Johnson did, but Kennedy's decision remained uncertain until close to roll-call time. The cumulative effect of Johnson, Smathers, and Green, support from Harvard Law School professors, and the fact that Kennedy was then wooing the South for presidential support, eventually delivered his vote.

Still if the vote had been taken immediately after elimination of Part III, the jury trial amendment would have been defeated. Then, unexpectedly, help came from another camp—organized labor. At the Glen Echo Amusement Park just outside Washington a few days after the Part III vote, one of Johnson's assistants ran into Cy Anderson, chief lobbyist for the railroad brotherhoods. "Any labor skate who is against trial by jury ought to have his head examined," Anderson said to Johnson's man when their talk turned to the civil rights bill. Three days later, all twelve brotherhoods wired Johnson their support of the jury trial amendment.

And from old John L. Lewis, President of the United Mine Workers Union, an unsolicited telegram rumbled out of the night: "The injunction has been in the past so often abused and indiscriminately used that enlargement thereof even for worthy purpose must carry with it reasonable protection. . . ." Lewis was backing the jury trial amendment.

Wobbly Democratic liberals who, until then, had refused to join Johnson and the jury trial amendment, out of fear of alienating their liberal constituencies, now had a soft cushion to fall back on: support from an important segment of organized labor.

Labor ended what doubt remained in Johnson's mind. After resisting the vote for ten days, on August 1 Johnson joined Knowland, who had been desperately pressing for the vote, to set the time for decision as late on the night of August 2. Knowland knew his once-solid support was draining away, that the longer he delayed the more he would lose.

Even so, on the threshold of the vote, he thought he had thirty-nine Republicans on his side. Typically and in sharp contrast to Johnson, Knowland had miscounted. He got only thirty-three, and the result was 51 to 42 for Johnson and the jury trial amendment. A switch of only five votes would have beaten the amendment, but Johnson had counted well. He even had a vote or two in reserve. He had also planned well: Passamaquoddy and Hells Canyon paid off.

Senator Margaret Chase Smith was the only moderate-liberal Republican to join him on the jury trial amendment vote. Her Republican companions on that roll call were the arch-conservatives of all the Senate: Goldwater of Arizona, Malone of Nevada, Chapman Revercombe of West Virginia, Schoeppel of Kansas, John Marshall Butler of Maryland, Curtis of Nebraska.

And just as Russell and his Southerners had come to the aid of the
Democratic West on the Hells Canyon bill six weeks earlier, now the
Democratic West came to Russell's aid on the jury trial amendment.
Out of fourteen Western Democratic Senators, all but two (Morse
and Neuberger of Oregon) supported the jury trial amendment.

As he gradually rounded up votes for the two big amendments,
Johnson ended his early passivity in the Senate debate. Without making a public statement, Johnson was signaling that he would indeed
support the bill. More assured, sensing ultimate victory, Johnson was
on his feet now, stalking the Senate floor, correcting extreme statements from both sides, skillfully cooling tempers and disarming angry
antagonists. Again and again he held forth the goal of a "reasonable"
Senate working its way painfully toward a vote and a "reasonable"
solution. In his coat pocket were smudged copies of the Senate roll
call, filled in with checks and x's and dotted with notes and reminders,
that he constantly pulled out to show to this or that Senator. These
were his head counts, and the tallies changed day by day as he gathered in his majorities on the two key amendments.

He began to fill the Senate with his tall, striding presence, his imperious hand waving to an aide. He jollied with this Southerner, com-
miserated with that liberal, confided to his friends, criticized the "extremists" on both sides. By early August, the civil rights bill was no
longer Dwight Eisenhower's or Herbert Brownell's or William Knowland's. It was clearly Lyndon Johnson's—and Republicans resented
it.

On the last evening of debate before the crucial jury trial vote,
Johnson encountered Vice-President Richard M. Nixon in a waiting
room just off the Senate chamber. Cocksure now and in his glory,
Johnson was confronted by an icily controlled Nixon, who knew as
well as Johnson that the jury trial amendment would be adopted, thus
ending any last possibility of a Democratic party civil war on the floor
of the Senate. As the putative Republican presidential nominee for
1960, Nixon, too, had large stakes in the classic struggle.

Smiling tightly, Nixon snapped to Johnson: "You've really got your
bullwhip on your boys tonight, Lyndon," and started to walk primly
on by.

Johnson reared up like an angry steer, "Yes, Dick, and from the way
you've been trying to drive your fellows, you must have a thirty-thirty
strapped to your hip, but it's not doing you any good."

Nixon replied that although Johnson might seem to have won, this
was only the first round, and that before the battle was over he would

lose—an implicit threat that the administration would block final passage when the Senate bill returned to the House.

But that showdown was in the future. The Senate passed the bill on August 7, 72 to 18, after a debate of 121 hours and 31 minutes—no filibuster by any stretch of imagination.* Voting "yes" were five Democrats from the Old Confederacy: Tennessee's Kefauver and Gore, Florida's Smathers, Yarborough of Texas—and Lyndon Johnson. For Johnson, this first vote for civil rights in his twenty years in Congress was the most important vote of his life. Fully aware of its implications and of the implications of the bill, he told the Senate just before the roll was called:

I tell you, out of whatever experience I have, that there is no political capital in this issue. Nothing lasting, nothing enduring has ever been born from hatred and prejudice—except more hatred and prejudice. Political ambition which feeds off hatred of the North or hatred of the South is doomed to frustration. There is a compelling need for a solution that will enable all Americans to live in dignity and in unity. This bill is the greatest step toward that objective that has ever been made.

As for his own vote, he predicted it would be treated "cynically in some quarters" and "misunderstood in others."

"No Texas Senator has cast a vote for Civil Rights since eighteen seventy-six," said Johnson. But the bill about to be passed "is good for every state of the Union, and as far as I am concerned, Texas has been a part of the Union since Appomattox."

Nixon's threat still had to be dealt with. After the bill passed the Senate, the House Republican leadership cried "sellout" and refused to accept the Senate version. But civil rights leaders wanted a bill in 1957—not a campaign issue in 1958—and would not play the Republican game. A modified jury trial plan was finally concocted out of one of Acheson's earlier drafts, permitting a trial by jury for criminal contempt of court only if the judge's sentence exceeded a three-hundred-dollar fine or forty-five days in jail. Johnson pleaded with the Southern Senators to let the bill come back to the Senate without a filibuster.

Finally, on August 23, Johnson called Eisenhower on the telephone. "I can get Ervin [Senator Sam J. Ervin, Jr., of North Carolina] and the others to agree to a compromise of three hundred dollars and forty-five days," he told Eisenhower. Eisenhower checked with Knowland

---

* However, Senator Strom Thurmond of South Carolina at the last moment defied Russell's no-filibuster strategy and staged a futile but headline-grabbing one-man talkathon of twenty-four hours and eighteen minutes against the bill on August 28 and 29—a new Senate record. Thurmond's grandstand play made his Southern colleagues look like slackers to their constituents and insured a filibuster against the next civil rights bill.

and the House Republican Leader, Representative Joseph Martin, Jr., of Massachusetts, and they said "yes." Eisenhower himself agreed. And so the House quickly approved the compromise. On August 29, so did the Senate, sending the bill to the White House.

One or two odds and ends needed cleaning up even then, because the legislative process as practiced by Johnson never stopped. A couple of new United States District judgeships for Kansas and Maryland, long stalled in Eastland's Judiciary Committee, suddenly emerged for quick Senate approval—after Republicans Butler of Maryland and Schoeppel of Kansas had shown their consideration by voting "yes" on the jury trial amendment. And, of course, the Passamaquoddy survey, fully funded, began to lubricate the failing economy of eastern Maine.

It was Lyndon Johnson's Civil Rights Bill, but Lyndon Johnson was no hero to militant liberals of the Paul Douglas variety. Instead of praising Johnson for passing the bill, they condemned him for watering it down. Indeed, this first Civil Rights Bill passed by the Senate in modern times was tame and toothless in comparison with the subsequent Kennedy and Johnson Civil Rights Bills of the 1960s. Nor did it have much real impact on the reality of the civil rights struggle. The new Commission on Civil Rights was without real power. The new Assistant Attorney General for Civil Rights was severely limited by the elimination of Part III. Nor did the bill accomplish its avowed purpose of assuring the Negro the right to vote.

Yet the magnitude of Johnson's performance transcended the details of the legislation. To pass the bill without filibuster was a legislative tour de force. As the years passed, Democratic liberals—even Paul Douglas—questioned their own earlier insistence that much more could have been passed through the Senate in 1957. If Johnson had not extracted Part III and added the jury trial amendment, who could say that the South would not have erupted in a bitter filibuster, defeating the bill altogether? Then subsurface passions would have boiled over and split Southern and Northern Democrats beyond repair.

Johnson's performance in the 1957 civil rights fight was far more than his own emancipation from Southern shackles (though it accomplished that, certainly). It was the full flowering of the Johnson System at a level of proficiency not achieved before. And—though Johnson did not realize it—it was not to be achieved again in his tenure as Majority Leader, even when he was blessed with top-heavy majorities.

Chapter VIII

★★★★★★★★★★

THE
LEGISLATOR

I have always thought of myself as one who has been moderate
in approaching problems.
—Lyndon B. Johnson, December 12, 1955

Under the banner of Senate Majority Leader Johnson, the congressional Democrats have become practically indistinguishable
from the party they allegedly oppose.
—Joseph L. Rauh, national chairman of ADA, March 23, 1956

The unmistakable signal that the second session of the 85th Congress was only hours away from sine die, or final, adjournment came
around ten o'clock on Saturday evening, August 23, 1958, when Lyndon B. Johnson emerged from the Democratic cloakroom, took the
floor, and began reading a statement lauding the accomplishments of
the session—his fourth as Majority Leader. Reading from a double-
spaced typewritten sheet in a barely audible monotone, he began:

This Senate has been a body deeply aware of the obligations
to all the people. It has been creative and constructive. It has
emphasized the substantial rather than the trivial. It has sought
achievement rather than discord.

Johnson documented the ways in which the Senate—*his* Senate—
had achieved a remarkable consensus during 1958 on many issues that
had seemed certain to divide and overwhelm the Democratic majority. He went down the list. Although civilian versus military control of
the new program to explore space should predictably have split Congress down the middle, a compromise bill creating a new Space
Agency passed the Senate by a "unanimous" vote—that is, without a
roll call and without audible dissent. Although President Eisenhower's
proposed reorganization of the Defense Department had brought

warnings from congressional conservatives that a Prussian-style general staff might emerge from it, a compromise plan passed the Senate
by the same kind of "unanimous" vote. And although the question of
tariffs and foreign trade historically was one of the nation's most divisive issues, a bill granting the President four more years of tariff-cutting power passed the 96-member Senate with 72 affirmative votes—
36 Democratic, 36 Republican.

With these statistics out of the way, Johnson went on to propound
his now familiar philosophy of legislation:

> I suppose there are two ways in which a Congress can con-
> duct itself. One is to look at the next election as the objective of
> legislation. The other is to regard the past election as the expres-
> sion of the will of the American people on what should be done.
> The first view would create issues; the second view would re-
> solve issues. By any test, I believe that this is a Senate which has
> tried to resolve issues rather than create them. . . .
> Mr. President, this has been a Congress which conducted it-
> self in the finest traditions of American government. It was calm
> and deliberate. It sought to eliminate rather than to create strife.
> It tried to unify, rather than divide, our people.

Here was more than the self-congratulatory banalities with which a
Majority Leader was expected to applaud himself and his colleagues
upon the conclusion of another session. Johnson was delivering a valedictory not merely for the extraordinarily busy session of 1958, but for
his four years as Majority Leader—his golden years of maximum control over the Senate. But more than a valedictory, it was also a defense
of those four years. For there were Democrats who flatly disagreed
with the Johnson credo that the Democratic-controlled Congress
should "resolve" rather than "create" issues. It was Johnson's obsessive sensitivity to criticism, particularly criticism from within his own
party, that compelled him at the height of his power and authority in
the Senate to justify his strategy of legislation.

Johnson's critics could not deny that almost from his first day as
Majority Leader he had assumed control over the unruly Senate and
ended nearly two decades of feudal disorder. The anti-Johnson argument, on the contrary, was that the Johnson System, splendid and
awesome though it was, produced so little: in short, that although
Johnson had tamed the Senate, he had scarcely come to grips with
and certainly had not broken through the barriers blocking the passage of trail-blazing social legislation. Furthermore, said the critics,
the Johnson System functioned well for precisely the reason that it attempted little. Not even Johnson's tour de force of 1957 in passing a
civil rights act without filibuster (Johnson's compromises gutted the

bill, the critics claimed) stilled the complaint that he had created a mighty legislative machine that produced only trivia.

Without doubt, the legislative output of the Johnson System was less than epochal. The flow of legislative creativity in the New Deal, which ebbed in the late 1930s and dried up with Pearl Harbor, was not resumed in 1955–58. The ambitious liberal goals had been set a full decade earlier with the end of World War II—federal aid to elementary and secondary education, federal health insurance, extension of federal minimum wage coverage, permanent federal programs for economically depressed areas. None of these was achieved in the Democratic 84th and 85th Congresses run by Lyndon Johnson and Sam Rayburn. Each year Johnson was able to assemble long lists of legislative accomplishment, but only a few bills—most notably the Civil Rights Act of 1957—could be called milestones.

Yet, with a Republican in the White House and the political balance in Congress virtually in equilibrium, not even Lyndon Johnson was expected to crash through the legislative deadlock to the long deferred goals. Not his harshest critics argued that he could. They knew that to submit to the Senate a full-blown Democratic program of social welfare would not result in the enactment of bills. They insisted, nonetheless, that Johnson should commit himself and his party to this ideal program of goals, starkly differentiated from President Eisenhower's, and thus build a record. It would surely be a record of failure, but failure could be blamed directly on Republicans in Congress and the Republican in the White House. By building this record, Democrats would then have the perfect strategy for their campaign to regain the White House.

Thus, what contemporary accounts portrayed as a doctrinal struggle between Johnson the "centrist" and the "left wing" of his party was far less doctrinal than tactical. Although Johnson's continuing preoccupation with his shaky Texas base forced him well to the right of the national party, particularly on labor issues, on gas and oil legislation, and, until the 1957 breakthrough, on civil rights, there were few issues that Johnson could not embrace. What he could *not* embrace was the tactic of building a record based on legislative defeat, that is, proposals that could not be enacted. To Johnson this would put the Democratic party in the untenable position of tormenting the benign and well-loved war hero in the White House, would promote discord in an era of national conciliation, and would expose the Democrats to a charge of politics for politics' sake. The road back to power was paved with modest bills actually passed, Johnson believed, and, if he had to meet Eisenhower at least halfway, so be it.

But beyond this lay a more fundamental and highly personal consideration that led Johnson summarily to dismiss the pursuit of a distinctly partisan legislative program. The power of leadership in the Senate was for him an end in itself. To push a maximum program was to undercut the flexibility of a non-program that buttressed the Johnson System. He would have trapped himself in his program and ended up with the impotence of the Democratic Majority Leaders who preceded him. And, perhaps most important to his own ego, he would have no legislative trophies.

Johnson encountered little criticism from his fellow Democratic Senators, and what there was of it bothered him only slightly. Even Paul Douglas of Illinois, his most tenacious liberal critic inside the Senate, was on more than one occasion forced to express admiration for Johnson's accomplishments. Accordingly, the defense of his four years of leadership delivered in the Senate on August 23, 1958, was directed beyond the Capitol to his Democratic critics, and particularly to Paul M. Butler, chairman of the Democratic National Committee. It was Butler, the focus of all Democratic complaints with the Johnson record of legislation, who was making the case for a Democratic alternative to Lyndon Johnson's "creative and constructive" legislative program.

Soon after the 1954 election returned the Democrats to control of Congress, the new Majority Leader marked out his course.

> Naturally, we don't yet know what will be in the program which [President Eisenhower] will present to the next Congress. . . . The only thing that can be said now is that we Democrats will cooperate with the President on any measure which our inner conscience tells us will advance the best interests of the country. . . .

At any other time in the previous two years as Minority Leader, Johnson could have preached his doctrine of moderation without contradiction from the sleepy quarters of the Democratic National Committee, where a low-keyed Chicago lawyer named Stephen Mitchell had been an unobtrusive chairman since his surprise selection at the Democratic National Convention in 1952 by the party's presidential nominee, Adlai Stevenson. Mitchell, an old Stevenson friend, was a political amateur unknown even in his native state and city. After Stevenson's defeat in 1952, he remained as National Chairman and struck up a friendship with Sam Rayburn, which automatically put him on amiable terms with Lyndon Johnson. Partly because of the

Rayburn-Johnson influence, Mitchell's major endeavor as National Chairman was a quiet effort to woo back the Southern Democrats who had bolted their party in 1952. A moderate and a conciliator, Mitchell had no desire to challenge the congressional strategy of Johnson and Rayburn.

But just as Johnson was taking over as Majority Leader, Mitchell was leaving as National Chairman. After the 1954 elections, Mitchell called a meeting of the Democratic National Committee in New Orleans—a Southern site to symbolize his efforts at North-South reunion —to enable the committee to accept his resignation and select his successor. Curiously, the successor, hand-picked by Stevenson and Mitchell, was the antithesis of their soft-pedal style of politics. Paul Mulholland Butler, a South Bend, Indiana, lawyer and party leader, was everything Steve Mitchell wasn't: taut nerved, moody, ambitious, and militantly partisan.

To Butler, the prospect of two "conservative" Texans setting national legislative policy for the Democratic party was absurd. He revealed this attitude a full year before he became National Chairman when he was Democratic National Committeeman from Indiana. At the National Committee meeting at Chicago in September, 1953, Butler proposed that an unprecedented National Convention of the party be convened in 1954 to draw attention to the 1954 congressional elections and to draft a *legislative* program. This was an unmistakable rebuke of Johnson and Rayburn, who were drafting their own legislative program on a day-by-day basis. Rayburn had enough support on the National Committee to kill the proposal.

Remembering the incident of a year earlier, Rayburn and Johnson scarcely savored Butler as Mitchell's successor and tried to postpone selection of a new chairman until early 1955, in hopes of finding an alternative. But whatever his lack of support in the party's congressional wing, Adlai Stevenson then controlled the National Committee and Adlai Stevenson wanted Paul Butler. Butler was elected at New Orleans by an overwhelming margin.

Thus began one of the very few unremitting personal conflicts in Lyndon Johnson's career, a feud not relieved by cease-fires or social amenities. For some six years (Johnson's tenure as Majority Leader coincided almost exactly with Butler's as National Chairman), these two strong, tenacious politicians clashed, mostly at long range, in newspapers and on television and radio. Though their paths collided, Lyndon Johnson and Paul Butler had the same touch of genius for gaining power. Like Johnson, Butler created his power by will and determination, not by institutional change of an inherently powerless job. Never before had a Democratic National Chairman taken upon himself the responsibility to pronounce party policy on the big issues, and never before had a Democratic National Chairman gained so much attention and publicity for his party. Yet, the Johnson-Butler rivalry was in some ways mutually destructive. For Johnson, it heightened the dilemma of a Texas Senator gaining acceptance as a national leader. For Butler, it crushed what slender hope there might have been for his dream to dictate Democratic policy on Capitol Hill (as state party chairmen often do in state legislatures).

The confrontation was quick to come. The predictably bland and moderate recommendations contained in President Eisenhower's State of the Union Message of January 6, 1955, met with a predictably bland and moderate response from Johnson: "The President correctly states a Democratic premise when he says that the general good should be our yardstick on every great issue of our time. We will consider his program in that spirit." Respecting Eisenhower's popularity, Johnson leaned more toward accommodation than conflict in running the legislative half of a divided government.

But Paul Butler, whose acceptance speech as National Chairman a month earlier in New Orleans bristled with contempt for Eisenhower, had other plans. Within a week, the research division at Butler's National Committee issued a withering indictment of the Eisenhower State of the Union Address. Neither Johnson nor Rayburn had been consulted, and they were furious. Nor was Johnson's fury appeased when Senator William F. Knowland, the Senate Minority Leader, emerged from a White House breakfast the morning of January 16 to express mock "concern" lest the Democratic National Committee "attempt to muscle in" on the legislative program. Goaded, Johnson replied publicly via the press that the congressional Democratic leadership was not surrendering and would not surrender its authority to anybody. Simultaneously, Johnson privately encouraged stories to be written that "senior congressional Democrats" were greatly embarrassed by the strange noise emanating from the usually silent Democratic National Committee. The battle was on and would not end for six years.

If Johnson had ever been inclined to follow Butler's advice and pursue a militantly partisan legislative program (and there is no evidence that he had been), it disappeared in his first major legislative floor fight as Majority Leader. Unusual circumstances forced Johnson in that first test to follow the Paul Butler course of partisanship. The result was disaster, and Johnson did not soon forget the lesson.

At issue was a highly political tax cut cooked up by Sam Rayburn as the first major project of the newly elected Democratic Congress. Arguing that the Eisenhower-sponsored 5-billion-dollar cut in income taxes by the Republican 83rd Congress in 1954 mainly benefited corporations and the rich, Rayburn proposed a tax reduction steeped in Texas-style Populism: a twenty-dollar-a-year tax cut for every man, woman, and child in the country, costing the federal Treasury some 2.3 billion dollars a year. Vigorously opposed by Eisenhower as disastrous for his always quixotic balanced budget, the twenty-dollar-a-head cut was viewed by the old Speaker as a *Democratic* plan that would both unite his party and give it a healthy credit for the 1956 presidential campaign. Politically blatant and economically primitive, this raw appeal to the pocketbook was one idea of Sam Rayburn's that meshed with Paul Butler's idea of how to play politics. The Democratic National Committee enthusiastically endorsed the Rayburn plan.

But Lyndon Johnson did not. For Johnson, it was too blatant, too primitive—precisely how the Democrats should not use their new control of Congress. This was no issue for a direct confrontation with Eisenhower, who labeled the Rayburn plan "some kind of a height in fiscal irresponsibility." Johnson's misgivings were reinforced on February 25, when Rayburn barely squeezed the tax cut through the House by 210 to 205, a vote that hugged party lines. The warning was clear. This was a straight party-line issue with little room for compromise, certainly not an issue suitable for the emerging Johnson System, as the Senate Finance Committee clearly demonstrated on March 1. The committee's two Southern patriarchs, Chairman Harry Byrd of Virginia and Walter George of Georgia, joined the committee's seven Republicans to reject the Rayburn plan, 9 to 6.

Justifiably wary of trying to change the tide on the Senate floor, with both Byrd and George against him, Johnson frantically searched for an eleventh-hour compromise around which to create a Senate consensus. But it was too late for that. During the days of late February and early March, when Senate sentiment hardened for or against the Rayburn plan, Johnson was hospitalized for a back operation. By the time he returned, the area for maneuver was severely restricted. Further reducing Johnson's options was the authorship of the tax cut; he could not deviate far from the pet project of his friend and mentor, Sam Rayburn.

When the proposal came to the Senate floor for a vote on March 15, Johnson had devised a small compromise scaling down the amount of the tax reduction.* The Johnson plan was not compromise enough. Three other Southern Democrats joined Byrd and George in opposi-

---

* Johnson's compromise reduced the twenty-dollar cut to ten dollars for dependents and eliminated it for dependent spouses.

tion and only one Republican, old William Langer from North Dakota, broke from Republican ranks. In that closely divided Senate, that was enough to give Johnson a humiliating 50 to 44 defeat. And so, on March 15, 1955, Johnson felt the frustration that so many times afflicted his predecessors in the leader's chair—Alben Barkley, Scott Lucas, Ernest McFarland—"leaders" who bravely but futilely took before the Senate proposals not of their own making and, lacking room for compromise, tasted defeat.

The loss was a watershed for Johnson. Thereafter, his long and intimate relationship with Rayburn underwent subtle change; the younger man now became the dominant partner in the team. Seldom would Johnson again challenge Eisenhower in so raw and elemental a test of power. And not in all his years as Majority Leader would Lyndon Johnson again suffer a defeat so clear and unadorned.

Badly beaten on the tax cut by operating in the open, Johnson now slyly shielded his position on major issues, just as he had concealed his inner purpose on the censure of Joe McCarthy the previous year. He did not reveal—indeed, he did not fully determine in his own mind—what his position would be until the last possible moment, when the conditions of battle were fully known to him. The masterpiece of the 1957 Civil Rights Act was rehearsed a dozen or more times in the passage of minor legislation: the concealed position; the careful head count; the compromise proposal designed to win maximum support; the final triumphant vote, sometimes by a top-heavy or even unanimous margin, often by an exciting single vote. And though Paul Butler and his allies in Congress uttered no word of criticism for Johnson's defeat on the tax cut, they could not forgive his successes—accusing him of selling out Roosevelt-Truman-Stevenson for half a loaf.

A three-year extension of tariff-cutting powers for the President (the Reciprocal Trade Agreements Act), the first major element of the Eisenhower program to reach the Senate floor in 1955, was symbolic of the Johnson strategy. All year long, Johnson had been making Cassandra-like forecasts of impending doom for the program of tariff reduction devised by Cordell Hull and first enacted in 1937. Talking to reporters on March 29, Johnson put on a long face and bemoaned that the bill "is in deep trouble and is getting in more trouble every day." The gloom had some basis in fact. A creeping trend toward protectionism in the postwar years, strong enough to load down the act with a grab bag of protectionist devices, reached a peak in the House on February 17, 1955, when, to Rayburn's surprise and horror, the bill survived by a single vote, 193 to 192. With the Senate historically far more protectionist than the House, Johnson's mournful public comments seemed not far off the mark.

But in fact he was only laying down a smoke screen to deceive the protectionists. Forewarned by Rayburn's close call, Johnson carefully checked sentiment in the Senate, and found ample votes to pass a bill—but a bill loaded down with concessions to protectionism. Johnson did not worry about White House reprisals on that score. The original bill, submitted by President Eisenhower, itself abounded in concessions, and there was no White House outcry when more were tucked in by the House. Accordingly, under Johnson's direction a bill passed the Senate on May 4 so encrusted with protectionist barnacles that Cordell Hull would scarcely have recognized it.* Still, it passed. And it passed by the consensus vote of 75 to 13, an expression of overwhelming support that seemed impossible only a few weeks earlier.

Johnson won no applause from his party's liberals, who had watched Senator Paul Douglas of Illinois fight a lonely battle to liberalize the bill on the floor of the Senate. Had Johnson chosen to help Douglas, the bill might have been improved, but that would have risked defeat on final passage, and Johnson wanted no more defeats.

A clearer case of the techniques of consensus legislation was soon to come in the minimum wage fight. The ostensible issue was whether the $.75-an-hour minimum wage, set by Congress in 1949, would rise to $.90 (as Eisenhower proposed), or to $1.25 (the target of organized labor), or somewhere in between. But the real issue had greater economic significance. This was whether minimum wage coverage should be extended to the vast and unorganized retail and service trades. With the Eisenhower Administration giving lip service to this broad, bitterly contested new coverage, it stood an outside chance of carrying in a Senate roll call.

But Lyndon Johnson wanted no roll call, which would only split the Democratic party down its North-South axis. Working stealthily behind the scenes, Johnson convinced a majority of the subcommittee considering the bill to oppose the subcommittee chairman, Paul Douglas, and approve an LBJ-style compromise: a $1-an-hour minimum (a symbolic dime more than Eisenhower wanted) but no extension of coverage. Having outflanked Douglas, Johnson's strategy was to rush the bill through the Senate so quickly that the liberals could not launch a fight over sweetening the pot.

Thus, on June 8, Senator Herbert Lehman of New York, a Douglas

---

* The bill had become so protectionist that pro-free-trader Senator Albert Gore, who came from Cordell Hull's home town of Carthage, Tennessee, declined to participate in Senate debate.

stalwart inside the Labor Committee, happened to wander into the Senate just as the chair was calling for a voice vote. What's the vote on? he asked. The answer—that the Senate just passed "your" bill— left him speechless. It happened so quickly that Senator Lister Hill of Alabama, chairman of the Labor Committee, was relaxing in the cloakroom, waiting for the bill to come up at the very moment it was being passed. Only two quick voice votes were required: the first, rejecting the Administration's $.90-rate; the second, passing the bill. No roll calls, no amendments, no acrimony.

Yet Douglas and Lehman were in no mood to complain. One day earlier, the Majority Leader had served up his *pièce de résistance* for 1955, a housing bill for which the liberals had no hope of passage at all when the year began. Although Old Guard Republicans were bitterly disillusioned by the failure of the Eisenhower Administration to dismantle the Roosevelt-Truman welfare state, one particular grievance had been satisfied in the drastic reduction of federally subsidized public housing. Restrictions imposed by the Republican Congress of 1954 had virtually killed the program, and there appeared scant chance of reviving it in the Johnson-Rayburn Congress of 1955. Johnson, certainly, did not encourage optimism. He avoided even saying whether he personally favored the program. Herbert Lehman and Paul Douglas were resigned to fighting a lonely, futile battle for public housing.

They failed to recognize Johnson's smoke screen. As early as January, he was thinking hard about housing. He persuaded Senator Mike Monroney of Oklahoma, a strong backer of the housing program as a House member, to take a critical vacancy on the Senate Banking Committee (which handled the bill). In private sessions with the staff of the Banking Committee, Johnson immersed himself in the details of housing legislation (as he seldom did to such extent with any bill). He then began painstaking missionary work among the Southerners.

It came as a surprise then, when, on June 4, Johnson partially showed his hand by endorsing the bill approved three days earlier by the Banking Committee. This bill authorized eight hundred thousand new units of public housing, more than ten times Eisenhower's request. Having endorsed the bill, Johnson poured out his smoke screen of detailed misinformation. Although he had not issued his June 4 endorsement of the bill until a head count by Bobby Baker showed that the bill had an excellent chance, Johnson once again arranged that long face of his, brooded in self-pity, and sadly bemoaned to reporters the hopelessness of his cause. William Knowland, the Republican leader, would win by at least seven votes, he predicted with the air of a man who has tried everything.

The talk lulled Knowland into complacency, as Johnson calculated it would. Indeed, the languid debate on the afternoon of June 7 proceeded as though a Republican victory were a foregone conclusion. What neither Knowland nor the press knew was that Johnson was deliberately stalling the debate until Baker had rounded up every available vote. Then, in early evening, he struck. The tally was 44 to 38 for eight hundred thousand new public housing units. The Republican leadership, lacking the intelligence of a Bobby Baker head count and the shrewdness of a Lyndon Johnson, was astounded by the defection of six moderate Republicans to Johnson. Even more astounding, however, were the pro-Johnson votes of Southern conservatives— Walter George of Georgia, John Stennis of Mississippi, Sam Ervin of North Carolina and Allen Ellender of Louisiana—all of whom turned to support the cause of subsidized low-rent housing.

Exuberant and expansive over the victory, Johnson organized an immediate victory celebration in his office, where he held court far into the evening, a prince surrounded by attendants. On hand were some of the Southerners who had joined him on the vote; Hubert Humphrey, his bridge to the liberals; Bobby Baker, his inside man; two or three reporters—*and* Paul Douglas. This very office, where homage was being paid the leader, had been Douglas' before Johnson appropriated it six months earlier. And now Douglas, himself no regular attendant at Johnson's famous evening sessions of drink and gossip, was there to do obeisance to the benefactor of public housing. Johnson heaped praise on one Senator after another, as a commander does in the flush of victory. Finally, he turned to Douglas. "Well, Paul," he said, "you got what you wanted, didn't you?"

Douglas, grave and dignified, stood directly in front of Johnson and fixed him with a steady gaze. "I didn't think you could do it," he said, "and I will never know *how* you did it, but you did it, and I'm grateful."

Basking in his own glory, Johnson could not stop talking about his great victory. His friends heaped flattery on him. It was a happy party, but Paul Douglas remained aloof, a stranger without pretension in the enemy's camp. The intrigues of Johnson's parliamentary maneuvers, even though in this instance Douglas himself was a beneficiary, were alien to him.

While recuperating from his heart attack on the LBJ Ranch in the autumn of 1955, a restless Lyndon Johnson took steps to bolster his position with the Democratic party outside Congress. On September

27, Adlai Stevenson came to the ranch for the night, and Sam Rayburn made the long drive down from Bonham. The two Texas leaders preached the doctrine of moderation to Stevenson. It was a lesson fully grasped by Stevenson, whose instincts were cautious and restrained, not militant like Paul Butler's.

On November 19, addressing a fund-raising dinner in Chicago, Stevenson uttered words that sounded like Lyndon Johnson's. "I agree that it is a time for catching our breath; I agree that moderation is the spirit of the times. But we best take care lest we confuse moderation with mediocrity, or settle for half answers to hard problems. . . . Moderation, yes! Stagnation, no!" * The fuzzy, impermanent relationship between Johnson and Stevenson was never stronger. Johnson had succeeded in driving a wedge between the party's titular leader and his handpicked National Chairman, who, from the start of his long tenure at the National Committee proved to be far too abrasive to suit the genteel politics preferred by Stevenson.

Just two days later, Johnson took another corrective step, this one calculated to silence the grumbling of Democratic liberals that the party had no set program in Congress. On November 21, Johnson traveled some one hundred and seventy miles from his ranch on the Pedernales to the town of Whitney in Hill County, the heart of the rural cotton country that was the bedrock of his political strength. Addressing a ten-dollar-a-plate turkey-and-dressing dinner, Johnson embellished his theme of positive moderation: "The American people are tired of wrecking crews. They want builders—people who construct. They will entrust their affairs to the party that is constructive. They will turn their backs on the party that is destructive." That was familiar; what followed was something new: a thirteen-point "Program with a Heart"—to be pushed in 1956.

The "Program with a Heart" was a *tour d'horizon* of the year's possible legislative issues: Social Security changes, tax reduction, medical research and hospital construction, school construction, highway construction, farm price supports, housing, water resources projects (first on the list: a high dam at Hells Canyon), aid to depressed areas, elimination of the poll tax by constitutional amendment, immigration law changes, and a bill to return to the oil and gas industry the power to set natural gas prices as high as it liked. Many of the thirteen proposals were ambiguous, and many were unrecognizable from Eisenhower's own proposals—for example, "a school construction program

---

* At the same dinner, Governor Averell Harriman of New York, seeking to take a position left of Stevenson in his futile quest for the presidential nomination, said: "There is no such word as 'moderation' in the Democratic vocabulary."

to meet the needs of our children." Yet it was, for the first time in Johnson's tenure as party floor leader, at least the broad outlines of a legislative program.

The liberal critics who had flushed out the "Program with a Heart" were not mollified by it. Joseph Rauh, national chairman of the ADA, called it a collection of "slogans and promises," adding, ". . . it would make sense to try to figure out just what Eisenhower moderation is versus Johnson moderation, if indeed there is a difference." But Hubert Humphrey, now Lyndon Johnson's favorite liberal, came through with kudos. He described Johnson's thirteen points as a "very fine batting average—twelve hits in thirteen times at bat." The one strikeout, said Humphrey, was the bill to decontrol natural gas prices.

What Humphrey dismissed as a single strikeout was a taint upon Johnson's entire leadership in the eyes of nationally oriented Democratic politicians. Even though the memory of the eighty-seven-vote victory of 1948 should have disappeared in his easy victory in 1954, Johnson was still preoccupied by the political dangers, real and imagined, lurking behind every oil derrick in Texas. But if he could finally pass the natural gas act, after trying for eight years, those dangers would vanish. So it was that he made the natural gas bill, passed by the House in 1955, the Senate's first order of business in 1956. It was a calculated risk, for Johnson was championing a cause supported by only a minority of both the national party and the Senate Democrats, a course alien to his customary strategy.

He could avoid damage only if the bill quickly became law and then, hopefully, the law would be forgotten. Prospects were good as the 1956 session began. Though forced to rely on an unprecedented number of Republican votes, Johnson could already count a comfortable Senate majority for passage of the bill. President Eisenhower's signature was assured. What Johnson had no way of foreseeing was that Senator Francis Case, the caricature of a clerk in an old-fashioned countinghouse, would scramble all his calculations. Taking the Senate floor, the bespectacled, precise little Republican from South Dakota revealed in his flat Midwestern monotone that an oil company lobbyist had offered him twenty-five hundred dollars in cash as a reward for his presumed support of the natural gas bill. This indiscretion, Case said, had convinced him to vote against the bill. Case's revelation created a sensation.

In the face of this melodrama, Johnson retained his outer calm. But in the privacy of his office, he was irreconcilable. He stormed against the fates that seemed to hound this bill, against prissy Francis Case for his old-fashioned purity, against the fourth-rate oil lobbyist who was ruining his plans. The bill passed the Senate by a 53 to 38 vote on February 6 with no evidence that any vote other than Case's had changed. However, Dwight D. Eisenhower was deeply troubled by the Case disclosure. While still endorsing the bill, he nevertheless vetoed it on February 17 because of "arrogant" lobbying practices "in defiance of acceptable standards of propriety." Angry and disappointed, Johnson floated stories among his newspaper friends that the veto had endangered the President's amicable relationship with the Majority Leader, but that was only bluff. It was not Eisenhower, but Johnson who suffered from the veto. The Paul Butler Democrats had the fanciful notion that a "giveaway" of natural resources was the big campaign issue in 1956. They now had the equally fanciful notion that the veto had destroyed the issue; that is, that Eisenhower's veto had purged the Republicans of the "giveaway" sin.

Though overshadowed by the pyrotechnics of the natural gas bill, Johnson's continuing problems with organized labor further strained his relations with the party's liberals. Nowhere was this strain so evident as in a side issue of the new, massive program for a federal interstate highway system. For once, Johnson and the Democratic National Committee had no differences in doctrine or strategy. Both backed Senator Albert Gore's plan to finance the new superhighway system by special user taxes (particularly hitting the trucking industry) rather than the Eisenhower scheme to sell highway bonds. Johnson helped push the Gore bill through the Senate in 1955 (when it was defeated in the House) and again in 1956 (when it became law). But what the liberals remembered about these fights was not Johnson battling Eisenhower but his insistence that the Davis-Bacon Act—requiring that workers on federal projects be paid the "prevailing wage" in their state—*not* apply to the new highway program.

The motivation behind his reluctance was not only the demands of Texas politics but Johnson's quite sincere apprehensions about organized labor. Johnson wanted the *workingman* to improve his lot, but he mistrusted the *leaders* of workingmen. He regarded the question of applying Davis-Bacon wage rates to the highway program not as a matter of dollars and cents for the worker, but as an instrument of expanding labor union power at the expense of hard-pressed small contractors.

He recalled his own experience when, in the late 1920s, before entering college, he took a job on a road gang resurfacing the old Fredericksburg road from Austin to Johnson City. Paradoxically, he remembered not his own low pay but the small profit margin of the contractor, his difficulty in financing new equipment and his trouble in meeting his tax liabilities. From that experience, Johnson developed a sympathy for the small county contractor that colored his attitude toward the Davis-Bacon wage standards.

In 1955, Johnson maneuvered through the Senate an amendment exempting the highway program from Davis-Bacon wage rates. He avoided an embarrassing roll call by convincing Senator Dennis Chavez of New Mexico, chairman of the Senate Public Works Committee, that a floor fight on the amendment might endanger the entire bill. Chavez, torn between his loyalties to the labor unions and his duties as a member of the Johnson Network, succumbed to Johnson. Instead of fighting the amendment, he himself introduced it. Johnson blocked an attempt by Paul Douglas to get a roll call, and the amendment carried on a voice vote.*

By the time the highway program came up again on the Senate floor in 1956, organized labor was better prepared. Its lobbying was so intense that a roll call vote on the Davis-Bacon bill was clearly inevitable. Nor would old Dennis Chavez again be lured by Johnson into an anti-labor stance. This time he would introduce a union-backed proposal to have the Secretary of Labor set the wage rates.

Johnson's closest friend in the labor movement was urging him not to go down the line against organized labor. Texan Robert Oliver, the United Auto Workers lobbyist in Washington who never stopped his quiet campaign to soften Johnson's antipathy toward organized labor, pleaded with Johnson to duck the vote if he couldn't vote labor's way. Johnson resisted. On the afternoon of May 28, 1956, the day before the Davis-Bacon vote, Johnson and Oliver argued for three full hours. That evening Johnson summoned Oliver back to his office for another three-hour session, with Bobby Baker present. With Baker's help, Oliver finally persuaded Johnson to be absent from the Senate the next day. An excellent excuse was there for the taking: Johnson's long-scheduled trip for a checkup at the Mayo Clinic in Rochester, Minnesota. What no one knew at the time was that after his session with Oliver and Baker, Johnson advanced his scheduled 3 P.M. departure for Minnesota to 10 A.M.

With Johnson airborne and unrecorded, the vote was 42 to 37 to give the Secretary of Labor power to set wage rates. Johnson's absence saved him another attack from the unions, but it scarcely won him their praise.

There was also continuing friction between Johnson and the liberals on civil rights. His attempt to substitute a constitutional amendment

* Even Senator Richard Neuberger, Johnson's liberal friend, described this as one of the "lost opportunities" for the Democrats in the 1955 session.

prohibiting the poll tax (contained in his "Program with a Heart") for comprehensive civil rights legislation looked glaringly weak when Eisenhower finally submitted his 1956 civil rights bill.* Johnson's refusal to back the Eisenhower bill in 1956 further soured his relations with the Paul Butler liberals.

Oil and gas, labor, civil rights—this trinity of issues so vital to Johnson in Texas—obscured in the eyes of the Paul Butler Democrats the modest but still impressive body of legislation pushed through the Senate by Johnson in opposition to the President: federal aid to depressed areas (died in the House); high price supports for farm products (vetoed by Eisenhower); and, most important, an election-year sweetening of the Social Security program incorporating one of the most important advances in social legislation since the New Deal.

The first proposal in Lyndon Johnson's "Program with a Heart" read: "A Social Security bill reducing the age limit for women and extending coverage to most self-employed groups." That alone was no more than the normal election-year increase in Social Security benefits that had become a pattern. Johnson studiously did not endorse a proposal for the 1956 Social Security bill that was to bring the hardest Social Security fight since passage of the original program in 1935—the payment of pre-retirement benefits to disabled persons. The reason for this omission from the "Program with a Heart" was simple enough. Keeping flexible in the best manner of the Johnson System, Johnson was not ready to take a position.

When originally enacted in 1935 as the crowning social welfare achievement of the New Deal, Social Security was nothing more than a retirement pension plan for workers at age sixty-five. A 1939 amendment broadened it to provide payments to widows and orphans. For sixteen years thereafter, the Social Security system was basically unchanged, caught in the wartime and postwar legislative deadlock. But pressure was building to use Social Security for wider purposes, pressure that climaxed in 1955 with a liberal-labor proposal to give permanently and totally disabled workers their retirement benefits at age fifty instead of sixty-five—in effect, a federal subsidy for the disabled. The impact of this idea went far beyond the relatively small number of disabled workers. Benefits for the disabled would establish a precedent, ending the Social Security system as a narrow retirement and survivors' benefit plan and converting it into a vehicle for broad social welfare schemes.

* See page 144.

Passage of disability benefits was thus vital to set the stage for the most fundamental liberal-labor program of all: federal health insurance financed by the Social Security system. And that was why the American Medical Association, the doctors' lobby, exerted every ounce of its power against the disability amendment, the thin edge of the wedge.

Despite the misgivings of Speaker Rayburn, the House in 1955 overwhelmingly passed a Social Security program with disability benefits; but that was not surprising in the House. From the beginning, it was the Senate that was expected to be the real battleground. Acting on a personal request from President Eisenhower, Chairman Harry Byrd postponed Senate Finance Committee consideration of the bill until 1956. That gave the doctors' lobby over a year to pressure fence-sitting Senators—particularly those facing re-election in 1956. The AMA pressure was too much for Senator Earle Clements, the Majority Whip, who on most issues was far more inclined to the liberal position than the Majority Leader. But Clements faced a difficult election battle against a popular and handsome Kentucky Republican, Thruston B. Morton. He could not afford to take on the doctors in 1956. Early in the year, Clements gently informed his old friends in organized labor that he could not back them on this one.

If that was true of Clements, it would be even more true of Johnson —or so most of Washington thought. It wasn't known that Johnson and Bobby Baker had been poring over a head count of Senators throughout the spring and early summer of 1956 and had come to a surprising conclusion: there *was* a chance the disability amendment could be carried in the Senate. Shielding his cards, Johnson maintained total silence about the disability amendment. Behind a façade of indifference, he was conducting a laborious, methodical search for Republican votes.

It was no easy job. Although Eisenhower sometimes didn't seem to care whether he won or lost on Capitol Hill in the mid-1950s, he was determined on this issue. Swarms of administration officials soon roamed the Senate corridors to line up votes against the disability amendment. Still, with cajolery and promises, Johnson secretly weaned away conservative Republicans. One was Senator William Purtell of Connecticut. Another, incredibly enough, was Joe McCarthy, no longer the terrifying master of the big smear but a defeated and dying man. Though Johnson had engineered his censure, McCarthy viewed him with considerably less animosity than he did the Eisenhower Administration. And finally, there was Molly Malone.

Senator George W. (Molly) Malone of Nevada was scarcely suited to play the hero's role in the enactment of landmark social welfare legislation. He owed his seat in the Senate primarily to the benevolence of the late Senator Pat McCarran, a right-wing Democrat and Nevada's political liege lord. In the Senate, Malone settled comfortably into the center of a handful of far-right Republican Senators who were an informal cheering squad for Joe McCarthy at the height of his excesses. Florid, bulky Molly Malone was notorious in the Senate for interminable, tendentious harangues on the evils of free trade and the need for a return to the Smoot-Hawley Tariff Act. In short, he was the chamber's most crashing bore.

While Malone would have been near the bottom of any Senate popularity list, one Senator who did not cut him dead was Lyndon Johnson. Ever on the alert to convert friendless Republicans into Johnson votes, Johnson spotted Malone as a natural recruit to be a peripheral member of the Johnson Network, and hence treated him with elaborate courtesy. Malone was not only angry that Eisenhower had deviated from Republican orthodoxy in his support of the Reciprocal Trade Agreements program and foreign aid; he was also suspicious that the White House had been an accessory in the censure of McCarthy. And Johnson recognized Malone's really vulnerable point. Eisenhower's tight budget policy severely limited mineral subsidies, and the tungsten mines in Malone's Nevada desperately needed government purchases to balance the books. A bill requiring at least sixty-nine million dollars in federal tungsten purchases was opposed by Eisenhower and the Republican party. Malone, who had to pass a tungsten bill to have any chance for re-election in 1958, could get his bill only with Democratic help.

Seldom had Johnson made so unsophisticated a back-room deal, but for ex-mining engineer Malone, sophistication was superfluous. He pledged his vote for the disability amendment if Johnson would pass his tungsten bill. Johnson delivered on June 18, when the tungsten subsidy was approved by 32 to 22 votes in the Senate. Only four Republicans joined Malone, but Johnson supplied the votes by making it a party matter. A bewildering array lined up for tungsten subsidies, Senators who were scarcely losing sleep over the plight of Molly Malone or the Nevada mine owners: Green of Rhode Island, Lehman of New York, Frear of Delaware, Humphrey of Minnesota, Kennedy of Massachusetts. Few if any Democrats connected tungsten with the Social Security bill. They were frankly puzzled, but if the Majority Leader needed help, they were willing to give it to him.

Malone's turn to repay the favor came a month later on July 17, when the question of adding disability payments to the Social Security system at long last came to the Senate floor, and it proved harder than Malone had imagined. The faulty intelligence system of William Knowland, the Republican leader, belatedly learned that Johnson had been eroding basic Republican strength for weeks. With the vote only minutes away, Knowland roamed the Senate floor to round up defectors. Malone had no desire to be importuned face to face with earnest arguments by ponderous Bill Knowland. He stayed in the cloakroom, appearing only momentarily to call his "aye" vote for the disability amendment, then fairly ran out of the chamber—disappearing into the corridors of the Capitol before Knowland could get a crack at him.

However, Knowland did get a crack at Joe McCarthy. With McCarthy voting "aye," Bobby Baker's head count showed a 47 to 45 victory for Johnson. But Knowland, who in 1954 collaborated with Johnson on the McCarthy censure and then at the last moment couldn't bring himself to censure a fellow Republican, talked McCarthy into voting "nay." According to Baker's well-worn tally sheet, that made it 46 to 46. The proposal would fail on a tie vote.

Warned by Baker, Johnson reluctantly played his last card. He asked Earle Clements to vote "aye" instead of "nay." Johnson fully recognized that this would subject Clements to the full wrath of the doctors' lobby, which had counted on him to oppose the amendment. Still, he asked Clements to save the amendment at the risk of his own Senate seat. Clements did, and the amendment carried, 47 to 45—a trailblazing victory for Johnson that opened the way for the medical care struggles of the 1960s.

The epilogue to this victory was many-sided. Two days after the disability proposal was passed, President Eisenhower with some misgivings signed into law Malone's mineral subsidy law—never connecting the two wildly unrelated proposals. Two weeks later, Eisenhower signed the Social Security bill with even more misgivings. On the day he signed the bill, he told a news conference that "we are loading on the Social Security System something I don't think should be there, and if it is going to be handled, should be handled another way."

In Kentucky that November, Earle Clements lost to Thruston Morton by less than five thousand votes; no doubt about it, his vote on the disability provision defeated him.* And, ironically, two years later

* After his defeat, Clements was briefly executive director of the Senate Democratic Campaign Committee. He then returned to Kentucky as State Highway Commissioner, and finally—like many other defeated members of Congress—settled in Washington as a lobbyist.

Molly Malone was removed from public life by the Democratic landslide that swept the Rocky Mountain states—tungsten bill or no tungsten bill.

On November 9, 1956, exactly three days after Adlai Stevenson's
second humiliating loss to Dwight D. Eisenhower, Lyndon Johnson returned to Washington. At a press conference at the principal Majority
Leader's office on the third floor of the Capitol, he seemed not at all
perturbed at the prospect of another four years of Eisenhower. He did
not mention the results of the presidential race, concentrating instead
on the continued—but still narrow—Democratic control of Congress,
which he credited to his policy of "responsible cooperation."

He also buried his year-old "Program with a Heart"—which had
failed to accomplish its primary mission of mollifying the liberal critics
—and returned to his more characteristic stance of flexibility, unencumbered by any program at all. ". . . We'll wait for the President,"
Johnson told the reporters. "We'll support him when he is right and
oppose him when he's wrong." And as the press conference neared an
end, reporters tried to draw Johnson into criticism of liberal Democrats—without success. "One reason I don't get into trouble," Johnson
drawled, "is because I don't butt into other people's business." Then
he cupped his hand to his mouth and in his version of a stage whisper
rasped, "Of course, I don't want them butting into mine, either."

To the growing cult of Johnsonologists, the meaning of all that was
clear enough. *He* was the architect of the congressional victory, not
Paul Butler. By the same token, the fiasco of the presidential election
was Paul Butler's responsibility, not his. And Johnson certainly was
not going to stand for Paul Butler telling him how to run Congress.

If Johnson's treatment of Paul Butler seems a bit harsh, the reason
lies in Johnson's reaction to deepening criticism from Butler and his
allies during his two years in the Majority Leader's chair. To Butler,
Johnson's leadership was a disaster, even though the achievements of
1955–56 comprised a better record of social welfare legislation than in
any Congress since Pearl Harbor. The fact was that Johnson's legislative legerdemain, like passing the disability amendment to the Social
Security bill, was quite unappreciated beyond Capitol Hill. Fearful of
antagonizing the doctors' lobby in Texas, the last thing Johnson
wanted was to underscore his own indispensable role in passing the
provision. Even if he had, he could not have narrowed the growing
gap between the congressional Democrats and the National Committee Democrats. Criticism of Johnson had become almost an end in
itself for the committee.

In seeking to explain the contradiction of the second Stevenson catastrophe and the Democratic victory in Congress, the Paul Butler Democrats could not accept obvious facts; that Stevenson was an exceptionally poor national candidate and Eisenhower was a much beloved popular hero. They needed a scapegoat and found one in Johnson's leadership of Congress, thereby exonerating Stevenson from his own defeat. Typical of this sort of election postmortem was the verdict of Herbert Lehman of New York, by now retired from the Senate. "In my judgment, by hindsight, the election of 1956 was lost before the campaign began. . . . The Democrats in Congress failed to *make* the issues during the eighteen months we were in control." *

Accepting this rationale, Butler conceived a novel idea to give the Butler Democrats a strong, new voice in congressional programs. Butler's idea was to establish a new arm of the party, the Democratic Advisory Council, composed of Democratic celebrities both in and out of Congress. He wanted it as a springboard for militant policy positions, including *legislative* policy positions, that would challenge Eisenhower on every front.

Butler complained that the Democrats had failed to fulfill "the true role of an opposition party from 1952 up to the [1956] presidential campaign. . . . It would be different from now on if the advisory group has its way." Butler's creation was sanctioned by the first post-election meeting of the Democratic National Committee, which also rubber-stamped a Butler resolution empowering the chairman to assume "leadership in formulating and enunciating programs."

Johnson and Rayburn predictably responded to this declaration of war by flatly refusing to accept seats on the Democratic Advisory Council. And war it was, for the 1957 session quickly emphasized the split between Johnson and the new Advisory Council. In a year of furious activity on a spurious battle of the budget, and the great civil rights fight, the Advisory Council Democrats were bound to become increasingly disenchanted with Johnson. And with some justification, they scorned his budget-cutting forays.† As for civil rights, they were quite unable to comprehend the fact of Johnson's genius.

Nor did Johnson's reaction to the 1958 recession satisfy the Advisory Council. This most severe of the periodic economic slumps that pock-marked the eight years of Eisenhower, together with the Soviet Union's demonstration of space superiority with the launching of the Sputnik in September, 1957, had ended all talk of budget-cutting.‡ An immense budget deficit, induced by the recession, was assured no

---

* The emphasis is Lehman's.
† Johnson's part in the budget fight is detailed in Chapter IX.
‡ Johnson's space investigation is detailed in Chapter IX.

matter what Congress and the administration did. In the spring, Johnson demanded government action to end the recession. "Personally," he said in a speech to the American Society of Newspaper Editors, "I don't intend to sit it out. I, for one, want to hear America's cash register ring again." That was scarcely unconventional. By 1958, the federal government's responsibility for economic health was well within the consensus and, at least in theory, was proclaimed by even the most conservative elements of the Eisenhower Administration. The question was not "if" but "how."

Paul Douglas, the foremost economist in the Senate, believed the only government action certain to bring a quick business revival would be a tax reduction. Never bashful about expressing an opinion, the Democratic Advisory Council and Paul Butler followed Douglas' lead and called for Johnson and Rayburn to promote a tax cut. Surprisingly, much the same position was taken by the "liberal" faction inside President Eisenhower's own Cabinet. Secretary of Labor James P. Mitchell spelled out the economic justification and Vice-President Richard M. Nixon undertook the political chore of convincing Eisenhower that immediate tax reduction was the only reasonable hope to stem the recession—and avoid a Republican catastrophe in the 1958 congressional elections.

Whatever chance the Nixon-Mitchell faction had with the President was nullified early in the year in a skillful political ploy by Robert B. Anderson, the Secretary of the Treasury. As the Cabinet's most effective conservative, he viewed a tax reduction in the midst of recession as dangerous medicine. This transplanted Texan and ex-Democrat was on intimate terms with Rayburn and had a warm relationship with Johnson. In a series of meetings with Rayburn and Johnson, Anderson convinced them that a tax cut would widen the budget deficit without curing the recession and exacted a pledge that they would not move for tax reduction without contacting him. With Johnson and Rayburn on his side, Anderson was the undisputed winner over Nixon in the Cabinet.

Instead of tax cuts, Johnson proposed massive public works spending of the kind that was tried—with only limited success—in New Deal days. In private sessions, he sold members of the Senate Democratic Policy Committee on the idea. Johnson had all his fingers on the keys to Senate power and, as usual, he counted his votes. As usual, Paul Douglas didn't count his. When Douglas demanded a vote on his tax-cut proposal, he lost by a humiliating vote of 71 to 14 on March 13. After that, Johnson quietly passed the word to Senate Democrats to stop talking about tax cuts, and the issue gradually faded away. But just as Douglas had predicted, public works spending was too cumbersome and slow to have much impact on the 1958 recession.

That was not the Democratic Advisory Council's only grievance with Johnson in 1958. The basic complaint was the same as always: in his zeal to pass bills, Johnson discarded one chance after another to make a partisan record. For instance, he cooperated with Eisenhower to pass a limited post-Sputnik school bill designed to stimulate the study of science and engineering, beating off liberal attempts to convert it into a general education bill at the risk of having no bill at all. The list of such Advisory Council complaints ran to a score or more.

But, as he told the Senate that night of August 23, Johnson had indeed pushed through an exceptional body of legislation in 1958, even if most of it was a bit on the bland side. Never before—and never after, for that matter—was his control over the Senate quite so absolute. Moreover, that control was manifest not only in *passing* bills but also in *defeating* inherently bad legislation.

The failure of Johnson's Majority Leader predecessors to control the Senate was particularly marked by their inability to prevent the Senate from running away with reactionary bills, such as the McCarran-Walter Immigration law. And as the 1958 session drew to a close, Johnson was confronted with a bevy of such bills, any one of which could have damaged the country and all of which were opposed both by the leadership in the Senate and the White House but which, before Johnson applied his wizardry, seemed to have comfortable majorities behind them. That he successfully contrived to kill them all was the Johnson System functioning at its finest.

In the steamy Washington summer of late August, 1958, the Senate was in a restive mood, unhappy at being held in check by Lyndon Johnson during the long, productive but undramatic second session. An early sign of the turbulence popped up August 12 when Senator Charles Potter of Michigan, a Republican facing sure defeat less than three months hence, made an eleventh-hour grab for political glory by trying to attach a special interest tax provision to a routine tax measure. The provision would have given billions of dollars of tax relief to well-heeled, self-employed doctors, lawyers, and other professionals. It had been endorsed by a large majority of the Senate—all of them convinced that the Treasury and the Democratic leadership never would let so outrageous and expensive a raid on the Treasury reach the Senate floor. But Potter, desperate for political help at home, crossed up his colleagues and called up the amendment.

Having blocked tax relief for lower income groups, Johnson couldn't allow a special interest tax bill to pass. But in a cloakroom strategy session with Bobby Baker and Senator Robert Kerr, no way out could be found. Too many Senators had wangled campaign contributions from doctors and lawyers, committing them to vote for the tax grab if it ever came to a vote. Baker's head count showed an overwhelming majority in favor of the Potter amendment. Kerr said he was hooked himself and just couldn't help Johnson.

Then the ingenious Bobby Baker had his brainstorm. Kerr, he proposed, should take the floor sadly and regretfully to make a point of order that the Potter amendment was not germane to the bill under debate. It was audacious, outrageous, ludicrous. There was no rule of germaneness in the Senate and never had been. But it might be the one way out, and Johnson and Kerr seized on Baker's idea. The presiding officer would have to rule against Kerr's point of order. Kerr would challenge the ruling, forcing a roll call on an arcane point of parliamentary practice—not on the amendment itself. Senators supposedly for Potter's amendment could vote for Kerr's point of order. Kerr and his friends would be off the hook—and so would Johnson. By a 52 to 32 vote, the Senate ruled Potter's amendment out of order. There never was a vote on its merits.*

But that was just a warm-up for what Johnson knew was coming: a classic Senate test over the first attempt to cut down the powers of the United States Supreme Court since Franklin Roosevelt's Court-packing scheme in 1937. This time the attack came not from the left but from the right; this time it involved not just the Court but the powers of the federal government itself.

The new threat to the Court began as a Southern reaction to the 1954 *Brown* decision on school desegregation and a series of subsequent racial decisions. But a series of civil liberties decisions by the Court in 1956 and 1957, limiting the impact of federal and state anti-Communist and anti-subversive statutes, brought Northern Republican (and some Northern Democratic) conservatives into the anti-Court faction. Just as the civil rights cases flowed from the *Brown* decision, the Court's key civil liberties decision was *Pennsylvania v. Nelson* in 1956. It held that federal law preempted a state's right to enact anti-subversive laws. These decisions, *Brown* and *Nelson*, momentarily revived the old conservative coalition. By 1958, a substantial majority in both the House and Senate favored anti-Court legislation that would have basically altered the federal system.

* A somewhat modified version of the self-employed tax grab was passed by Congress in 1962 and reluctantly signed by President Kennedy.

As 1958 progressed, the conservative-controlled Senate Judiciary Committee approved a steady stream of anti-Court bills—all of which were put in cold storage in Lyndon Johnson's Democratic Policy Committee. But they could not stay there indefinitely. Although the Policy Committee controlled the flow of legislation to the Senate floor, neither rule nor tradition gave it right to postpone bills forever. Besides, Johnson's Southern friends on the Policy Committee were under intense pressure back home to get the Court-ripping bills to the Senate floor—and get them passed.

It was Johnson's strategy to delay the bills long enough to catch them up in the usual session-end confusion. Thus did the Policy Committee finally approve the bills for floor action in the last week of the session. But late or not, the anti-Court forces had the votes.

Knowing the advantage of momentum in the Senate, Johnson planned to start the debate with a roll call victory. Accordingly, on Monday, August 18, he called up one of the narrowest of the anti-Court bills, a bill that would have reversed a civil liberties decision affecting criminal defendants in the District of Columbia. All through Monday, Johnson delayed a vote until he had commitments from both sides that more important proposals would not be attached to it as riders. The test vote came Tuesday night. Johnson won, 41 to 39.

With the momentum now moving his way, Johnson stalked bigger game: a bill sponsored by two McCarthyite Republicans—William Ezra Jenner of Indiana and John Marshall Butler of Maryland—to curb the appellate powers of the Supreme Court. It was killed early Wednesday evening, 49 to 41.

More confident now, Johnson moved next against the most dangerous of the bills. Previously passed by an overwhelming vote in the House, it would not only have reversed the *Nelson* decision but would have given all state laws preeminence over federal laws whenever they conflicted—thereby perverting the federal system.

Two of Johnson's favorite liberals, Hubert Humphrey of Minnesota and Tom Hennings of Missouri, were acting as his floor managers for the bill. Johnson had instructed Humphrey to pass the word to the rest of the liberals not to interfere with his battle plan by offering amendments of their own. But Paul Douglas apparently didn't get the message. Just as Johnson seemed assured of victory, Douglas offered an amendment to put Congress on record in "full support and approval of the recent, historic decisions of the Supreme Court of the United States holding racial segregation unlawful in public education and transportation. . . ."

That surprise injection of the civil rights issue threw the Senate into a furor. Through a complicated parliamentary device, Johnson managed to sidetrack the Douglas amendment and move the debate back to the states' rights proposal. But by now it was late evening, the Senate was querulous and Johnson's momentum had disappeared. The motion to kill the states' rights proposal failed, 39 to 46. Johnson tried again, and failed, 40 to 47. Had the Senate stayed in session, only a filibuster would have stopped the bill from passing. But Johnson exercised the Majority Leader's prerogative and near midnight adjourned the Senate until noon the next day.

Even after the four bells signaling adjournment sounded that night and reporters swarmed down from the galleries onto the Senate floor, Johnson sat at his front-row desk staring into space—transfixed at the prospect of defeat. Humphrey walked slowly to Johnson's desk.

"Well, Hubert," he drawled, "that's your liberals for you"—a reference to Douglas' amendment. "Now," Johnson continued dreamily, as if in a trance, "if you still want to beat this thing, there's still a way. First of all you—" Then Johnson suddenly awakened to see wide-eyed newsmen gaping at him, all ears.

"I don't know these people," he told Humphrey. "Let's get out of here." He impulsively motioned Anthony Lewis, Supreme Court reporter for the *New York Times* and a known foe of the Court-ripping bills, to come along, although they scarcely knew each other. George Reedy, Johnson's speech writer and press aide, made a foursome for talk and whiskey drinking. Into the small hours of morning, Johnson regaled his three companions with the intricate details of his legislative predicament and how it might be solved. Johnson was thinking out loud, and that thinking was put into effect early the next morning.

First Johnson changed the complexion of the vote. Instead of trying to kill the states' rights bill outright and thereby repeat the same vote that had failed twice the night before, he would ask the Senate to send the bill back to the Judiciary Committee. That would enable Senators to change their position without being recorded as changing. Quickly now, the vote changes started piling up under Johnson's entreaties. Frank Lausche, the conservative Democrat from Ohio, agreed to switch. Kerr, who had voted against Johnson on Wednesday night, agreed to stay in the cloakroom on Thursday afternoon and not vote at all.

When Bobby Baker tallied all the switches, it was still 41 to 40 against sending the bill back to committee. Johnson started frantically searching for the last vital switch. He found it well outside the Johnson Network. Straitlaced, conservative Republican Wallace Bennett of

Utah, a former president of the National Association of Manufacturers, was the last Senator likely to give Johnson a helping hand. But Johnson somehow convinced him that to vote "no" would create a 41 to 41 tie. Such a tie would have to be broken by Vice-President Nixon, the Republican party's prospective presidential candidate for 1960. That would put Nixon in a dilemma. Whichever way he voted he would hurt himself, angering conservatives if he voted "aye" to send the bill back to committee and angering liberals if he voted the other way. Johnson was fully aware that Kerr's agreement to stay in the cloakroom prevented any chance for a tie, but Bennett was not. So to save Nixon embarrassment, Bennett voted "aye" amid gasps from the galleries. The anti-Court legislation went back to the Judiciary Committee and oblivion. With massive Democratic majorities pouring into Congress after the 1958 election, such heroics would never again be necessary—or possible—for Lyndon Johnson.

Chapter IX

★★★★★★★★★★

LBJ
VS.
IKE

Our friendship came of a birth state in common and long personal acquaintance. We had our differences, especially in domestic and economic policy. . . . Yet, when put in perspective, he was far more helpful than obstructive. . . . For this I was grateful and frequently told him so. We remain, on my part at least, good friends.

—Dwight D. Eisenhower in *Waging Peace* (1965)

Lyndon Johnson's masterful burial of the Court bills in August, 1958, warmed the hearts of his New Deal friends who remembered the Leland Olds affair of 1950 but still had kept faith in him through the years. But it really answered none of the complaints of Paul Butler and the Democratic Advisory Council. For, in truth, the root of their quarrel with Johnson was not his occasional doctrinal obeisances to the right, in the direction of his Texas political base, but his refusal to combat Dwight D. Eisenhower. Few of Johnson's legislative masterworks contained partisan attacks against Eisenhower. On the contrary, he often rescued the general from the consequences of his chronic lack of absorption in a President's legislative function. Johnson's performance in the 1958 Court fight saved Eisenhower the task of vetoing a batch of rightist legislation that would have passed with considerable Republican support. Thus, Johnson's great service in the cause of civil liberties scarcely satisfied his critics. They charged him with being entirely too chummy with the Republican President.

Paul Butler would have fairly sizzled had he known of the private intimacy between the members of the famous Texas trio: Dwight Eisenhower, Lyndon Johnson, and Sam Rayburn. At least once a month, and frequently more often, Johnson and Rayburn would drive to the White House at the cocktail hour, enter unseen through the back door, and settle down for a highball or two with the President in the second-floor presidential study. A high White House aide—Sherman Adams, General Wilton B. (Jerry) Persons, or Bryce Harlow—might be present. But attendance was exclusive to prevent these sessions from degenerating into Army-style Eisenhower staff meetings. In the congenial mood of dusk, the Washington Monument a hazy shaft beyond the south lawn, Johnson and Rayburn could talk to Eisenhower in man-to-man fashion about the state of the world and the nation.

Based partly on the convivial mood of these cocktail-hour sessions, Eisenhower and the high-level White House staff came to rely on Johnson and Rayburn to shield them from disaster on Capitol Hill once the Democrats captured control in 1955. Johnson was a vivid contrast to Eisenhower's own Republican leader, William Knowland of California. Sherman Adams, the tough little ex-Governor of New Hampshire who held enormous power as Eisenhower's chief of staff, felt that Knowland "made the weekly meetings of the [Republican] party congressional leaders in the White House an ordeal for Eisenhower" and that "many of the President's aims and hopes actually received more sympathy" from Johnson than from Knowland. Eisenhower himself complained that Knowland "always reacted impulsively to any fancied slight" from the White House staff. "Certainly you do not want the Senate of the United States to become merely a rubber stamp," Knowland would repeatedly tell Eisenhower at the weekly White House breakfasts. In contrast, Eisenhower admired Johnson's "skill in legislative maneuver and negotiation," and so did Eisenhower's intimates.

But the admiring Eisenhower—and, for that matter, the unadmiring Paul Butler—would have been shocked had they heard Johnson among *his* intimates back on the Hill. The chummy bipartisanship of the White House chats turned into ferocious partisanship there. "I've got the committee chairmen and I could make him sweat," Johnson would tell his closest friends in the Senate. He was thinking, among others, of benign Senator Carl Hayden of Arizona, chairman of the Appropriations Committee, who was strictly nonpartisan in dealing with Eisenhower's spending plans. Hayden would have twisted the President's budget out of shape at a word from Johnson, and Johnson would have quickly endeared himself to Paul Butler. The fact that Johnson did not give that word was sometimes self-torture for Johnson himself. Indeed, the fury of Johnson's private discussions about Eisenhower had only one source—Johnson's deep frustration over his unused power.

A major reason why this power remained unused, with a few conspicuous exceptions, was the restraining influence of Senator Richard Russell. An old-fashioned patriot, the Georgia conservative was genuinely worried about the impact on the rest of the world if the Democratic Congress should open hostilities with the Republican President. Whenever Johnson started bragging about how he could smash Eisenhower, Russell warned of grave repercussions if the Democrats broke foreign confidence in the President.

At heart, Johnson agreed with this analysis. But even if he had not and even if Russell had not given such advice, it is doubtful that Johnson would have broken openly with Eisenhower. Johnson's instinct for domestic politics would not permit it. Unlike many Democratic leaders, he had measured the depth and permanence of Eisenhower's popularity beyond the Potomac and foresaw political disaster for any man who broke with the President.

In fact, then, Johnson's true relationship with Eisenhower was not so cordial as the President himself believed nor so collusive as Paul Butler charged. It was a deft and continuing maneuver of probe-and-pierce, ever looking for an opening in the President's armor and then stabbing lightly, to draw no more than a drop or two of blood.

When the 1954 congressional elections elevated Johnson from Minority Leader to Majority Leader, magnifying his power to harass the President, Johnson was asked to what extent he expected to cooperate with President Eisenhower. Buried in his convoluted prose was a hint that subtle guerrilla warfare was in the back of his mind. His reply:

> The only thing that can be said now is that we Democrats will cooperate with the President on any measure which our inner conscience tells us will advance the best interests of the country. But in any event, there will be no personal attacks upon the integrity of the President or upon his intentions.

How this formula could fit a given situation was demonstrated by the way Johnson treated Eisenhower in foreign policy matters during his first months as Majority Leader.

On March 18, 1955, Johnson reacted strongly when the State Department leaked to the *New York Times* hitherto secret papers from the Yalta Conference putting the blame on the Roosevelt Administration and the Democratic party for the loss of Eastern Europe to the Communists—in effect, an official, historical justification for 1952 Republican campaign charges that had been in the air since the end of the war. Johnson's reaction was directed not against the politically untouchable President but against John Foster Dulles, the Secretary of State, whose rigidity was making him a natural target for Democrats. Haughtily suggesting partisan considerations by Dulles, Johnson told the Senate: "We believe that every American would rather win the 'cold war' against Communism than win a 'cold war' against a political party." Eisenhower was not even mentioned.

Five days later, Johnson added a new subtlety by suggesting that any "miscalculations" in the postwar settlement were made not by Roosevelt and Truman, the two Democratic Presidents, but by Eisenhower and MacArthur, the two Republican generals. "I am very proud of the fact," said Johnson, "that no one on my side of the aisle has arisen to question the motives of these military men, whether they be General Eisenhower or General MacArthur, who made miscalculations if any were made."

But a week later, all belated recriminations over the consequences of Yalta faded before the threat of a shooting war in the Formosa Strait separating the Communist-ruled Chinese mainland from Formosa, the stronghold of Chiang Kai-shek's Nationalist Chinese government. Adventurous and confident after surviving the risk of its Korean intervention, Red China was menacing the Nationalist-held offshore islands of Quemoy and Matsu. This threat set off demands by the military and their friends in the Republican party (particularly Knowland, who was often called "the Senator from Formosa") that the United States defend the offshore islands with whatever military power was required.

Johnson leaped to Eisenhower's defense, declaring that the President should have the right to make his own decision without heckling from his Senate leader. Not only that, he implied the Knowland Republicans were a "war party" intent on irresponsible adventure. This cast Johnson's own party in the role of guardian of the peace. "I think we [the Democrats] speak for all the people when they say that they prefer peace to war. And if, when we say that, we find others in disagreement, then if the shoe fits, let them wear it," he told the Senate on March 28.

Less than a month later, Adlai Stevenson suggested that President Eisenhower—though far less bellicose than Knowland wanted—might be leading the nation to war over Quemoy and Matsu and that such miserable real estate wasn't worth it. Johnson came down hard on Stevenson's side. He declared that Stevenson was "correct in asserting that the only real solution lies in the due regard to the realities in Asia rather than in saber rattling and blustering."

Still another month later when the Formosa Strait crisis had subsided without either war or surrender of the offshore islands, Johnson was back on Eisenhower's side on another foreign policy question: a proposed Big Four meeting (the United States, the Soviet Union, Great Britain, and France) at Geneva to ease international tensions. When Eisenhower expressed willingness to attend such a meeting despite objections from conservative Republicans, a leader of the Republican Old Guard—Styles Bridges of New Hampshire—took the Senate floor on May 11 and warned that "appeasement, compromise, and weakness" lurk at all international conferences. Johnson quickly interposed himself between the Republican President and his Republican critics. "I agree with the President," he replied to Bridges on the Senate floor, "that we ought to explore every opportunity for peace."

Johnson showed he meant it soon after the Big Four conference was formally scheduled. Senator Joe McCarthy, more nuisance than menace since his condemnation by the Senate six months earlier, introduced a resolution to put the Senate on record against Eisenhower attending the summit meeting unless he first obtained a commitment from the Soviets promising that the status of the Eastern European Communist satellites would be put on the agenda at Geneva. Never expecting the Senate to consider so outrageous an invasion of the presidential foreign policy realm, McCarthy was just trying to regain a little of the national attention once lavished on him. But Johnson would not let it rest at that. He decided to dig McCarthy's proposal out of its grave in the Foreign Relations Committee and bring it to the floor, thus manufacturing an occasion to protect Eisenhower from members of his own party.

In an unusual appearance as a witness before the Foreign Relations Committee, Johnson orated that McCarthy's proposal "placed a loaded gun at the President's head." But he was not proposing anything so simple as outright defeat of the resolution in the committee. Johnson and Committee Chairman Walter George of Georgia, the Senate's Democratic voice on foreign policy, decided to bring the resolution to the floor of the Senate, where it would be most embarrassing to the Republican party. Eisenhower and Knowland wanted to kill the McCarthy Resolution in the Foreign Relations Committee with a minimum of fuss, but Johnson wouldn't let them. He wanted a more dramatic execution. On June 21, a Republican motion to defeat the McCarthy Resolution was defeated 8 to 7 on a straight party-line vote in the Foreign Relations Committee. Johnson and George had worked hard to invoke party discipline on the issue and bring off this rigged vote.

Republicans were bitter. The next day, when the McCarthy resolution reached the Senate floor, Knowland complained that it should have been disposed of in committee. Senator Homer Capehart of Indiana accused Johnson of "making a field day out of something that should have been thrown into the trash can." Even McCarthy had misgivings and, on Knowland's recommendation, asked permission to withdraw the resolution. But Johnson was adamant. The unanimous consent needed to withdraw it was denied McCarthy, and precisely as Johnson foresaw, the ensuing debate set Republican against Republican. Even two old comrades like Bill Knowland and Joe McCarthy were at each other's throats.* And Johnson? Disavowing political motive, Johnson told the Senate piously: "The issue . . . is whether the President of the United States shall be sent to the Big Four conference in a strait jacket." The resolution was defeated, 74 to 4. Johnson had contrived another situation in which he seemed to save the President.

Thus a loose strategic pattern for handling Eisenhower was slowly evolving. It boiled down to four basic tenets:

1. When it was necessary to attack, as in the release of the Yalta papers, attack the administration generally—or better still, zero in on a single vulnerable component of the administration, such as the State Department or Secretary Dulles—but not at Eisenhower himself.

2. Pose as the protector of Eisenhower from his own party's troglodytes not only when such protection might really be necessary (as when Knowland plotted precipitate action in the Formosa Strait), but also when protection definitely was not necessary, as in the contrived battle over the McCarthy Resolution.

3. While protecting Eisenhower, paint the Republican party in darkest colors—as the "war party," for example, for its stand on the Formosa Strait.

4. But never permit this extraordinarily delicate treatment of the President to prevent opposing him at the right time and on the right issue—even when that right issue happens to be a foreign policy issue. Johnson's support of Adlai Stevenson on Quemoy and Matsu was a signal that he might criticize Eisenhower if a brush-fire war erupted in the Formosa Strait in 1955. And United States involvement in such an action, by no means certain of wide popular support, would be precisely when Eisenhower would most need Johnson's complete support

* McCarthy lashed out at Knowland's opposition to his resolution, declaring bitterly: "It is in accord with the long record of the Democrat [sic] party to whine and whimper whenever the red-hot stove of Communist aggression is touched. . . . But . . . it is not the role of the Republican party to backtrack, to appease, to whine, to whimper." An offended Knowland replied angrily that McCarthy had "no right to say . . . the Minority Leader is whining and whimpering."

—just as Johnson himself would need popular support in Vietnam a decade later. Following this tenet, Johnson denied help to Eisenhower on some key issues where the President needed help the most.

It is clear, then, that the collusion suspected by Paul Butler between Johnson and Eisenhower was more apparent than real. While succeeding in convincing the White House that he and not the Republicans was the President's protector, Johnson often protected Eisenhower from imaginary enemies, such as the McCarthy Resolution of 1955. When the menace was real, Johnson was not so dependable an ally, as he demonstrated in three of the most difficult situations faced by Eisenhower during Johnson's first four years as Majority Leader: the Middle East crisis of 1957, the 1957 Battle of the Budget, and the Sputnik crisis of 1957–58.

On New Year's Day, 1957, Dwight D. Eisenhower summoned congressional leaders of both parties to the White House for a four-hour conference on the turbulent Middle East. Although the summons came on a holiday, there was no immediate crisis. But political unrest there had continued following the Suez Canal crisis the previous autumn. Secretary of State Dulles feared the Middle East could erupt in several ways: renewed warfare between Israel and Egypt triggered by the resumption of Egyptian guerrilla raids; discrimination by Egyptian President Gamal Abdel Nasser against British shipping in the Suez Canal, perhaps followed by renewed British military action against Egypt (despite the disastrous consequences of the Anglo-French-Israeli attack on Egypt in 1956); civil war in Egypt spawned by Moslem fanatics plotting against Nasser.

Any such eruption, Dulles feared, would expand the power vacuum created by the withdrawal of France and Britain and suck in the Soviet Union. Consequently, the fine lawyer's mind of John Foster Dulles conceived the Eisenhower Doctrine to fill the vacuum with United States power and influence. Congress would be asked to authorize the President to send economic aid and, if necessary, military assistance— even troops—to any threatened Middle Eastern country that wanted it. Eisenhower had decided to present the plan formally to Congress on January 5 and wanted to brief the congressional leaders in advance.

In that January 1 meeting, Eisenhower, fresh from his second landslide election victory, stressed the need for speed in enacting his Middle East Resolution. "The existing vacuum in the Middle East," he told the congressional leaders, "must be filled by the United States before it is filled by Russia." There was long and intensive questioning by leaders of both parties, but no sign that the doctrine faced an ordeal in Congress. Ample precedent existed for asking Congress for such open-ended authority, the most recent being the 1955 Formosa Resolution authorizing United States defense of Formosa and the Pescadores. As the New Year's meeting droned on past nightfall, Eisenhower closed on a warm and comradely note to Johnson, Rayburn, and the other Democratic leaders: "You know you are as welcome in this house—in this office—as anyone. . . . When I say Happy New Year to you, I mean it from the bottom of my heart, even though we belong to different clubs."

The President clearly had no idea that he was about to begin his most serious struggle up to that time with Lyndon Johnson. Neither he nor Dulles was able to read the warning signs spelling trouble ahead for the Eisenhower Doctrine. These signs, however, were unmistakable to those in Washington more politically astute than the President and his Secretary of State. Congress never likes to give the executive branch blank-check authorizations for making war, save under circumstances of clear and present danger. Belligerent threats of aggression by Peking pushed the Formosa Resolution through Congress two years earlier, but Moscow's menace to the Middle East was only implicit.

The Eisenhower-Dulles decision the previous autumn to rap the knuckles of their Anglo-French-Israeli allies for the Suez invasion, while doing nothing about the brutal Soviet repression of the Hungarian Revolution, did not sit well with Democratic leaders—or with William Knowland and a good many other Republicans, either. Furthermore, the basic thrust of the Eisenhower Doctrine was a military and economic alliance with the Arab states—a bloc of nations dedicated to the destruction of Israel. That was bound to alarm politicians of both parties sensitive to the Jewish vote.

Finally, Walter George's decision not to seek re-election to the Senate in 1956 radically changed the realities of foreign policy legislation on Capitol Hill. As chairman of the Foreign Relations Committee, George quite probably would have ushered Eisenhower's resolution through the Senate with a minimum of delay and no back talk from Lyndon Johnson. Theodore Francis Green of Rhode Island, George's eighty-nine-year-old successor as chairman, was even more cooperative than George but, unfortunately for Eisenhower, far less influential.

It soon became clear that the central figure the administration would face in the Senate battle over the Middle East Resolution would be Johnson, not Green. Far less devoted to the abstract concept of bipartisanship in foreign policy than either George or Green, Johnson felt no compelling need to rush the resolution through in faithful devotion to the tradition of Republican Senator Arthur Vandenberg's cooperation with Harry Truman. Moreover, as the debate progressed, Johnson ripened his relationship with Dean Acheson, who summarily dismissed the Eisenhower Doctrine in his most Olympian manner as "vague, inadequate, and not very useful."

But Johnson was not even a member of Foreign Relations, the committee that normally would handle all foreign policy business of this nature. Consequently, he cleverly arranged with Senator Russell, chairman of the Armed Services Committee (where Johnson was a senior member), and Senator Green to hold joint hearings. This assured him a highly strategic position.

Johnson stopped well short of those Democratic politicians, including Paul Butler's Democratic Advisory Council, who contemplated outright rejection of the Middle East Resolution. He recognized that congressional failure to pass a resolution would be a severe setback for Eisenhower's prestige in the Middle East and throughout the world. From the standpoint of domestic politics, Johnson believed that rejection of the Eisenhower Doctrine by the Democratic Congress would give his party a neo-isolationist brand that could plague the Democrats for years to come. What both Johnson and Rayburn wanted was a resolution, sharply trimmed, both less specific and less expensive (from the standpoint of foreign aid) than Eisenhower's.

Speaker Rayburn broached the matter to his old friend, Will Clayton, Truman's Under Secretary of State, in a telephone conversation. Clayton did not like the Eisenhower text either. He dictated to Rayburn a radically simplified substitute which, after some editing and refinement, read as follows:

> The United States regards as vital to her interest the preservation of the independence and integrity of the states of the Middle East and, if necessary, will use her armed force to that end.

After getting approval from Johnson and other Democratic leaders in Congress, Rayburn submitted this thirty-four-word declaration to Dulles (without revealing Clayton as its source). Besides eliminating Eisenhower's special economic aid program, it was entirely too simple for a mind so steeped in the complexities of international law as Dulles'. He flatly rejected it.

Since the House was ill-equipped by either tradition or procedure for a subtle foreign policy debate, Rayburn's fight ended forthwith.

The Middle East Resolution passed the House on January 30 without significant change. By then, however, it was obvious that a real battle awaited in the Senate, where Johnson was mounting his most formidable opposition thus far to any Eisenhower foreign policy proposal.

Aware that Johnson would not rubber-stamp the resolution, Dulles in early February finally agreed to several Johnson demands that he had airily rejected a month earlier, including these: instead of a special economic fund for the Middle East, the money would have to come out of regular foreign aid funds; the resolution would not commit Congress to approve extra foreign aid money; the President would have to give Congress fifteen days' notice before granting economic aid under the Eisenhower Doctrine.

Dulles rejected a more important amendment that deleted specific congressional authorization for the President to send troops to the Middle East and that, instead, simply stated that the United States "is prepared" to send troops if *the President* "determines the necessity thereof." But Johnson had the strength inside the Foreign Relations and Armed Services Committees to overrule Dulles and pass this amendment without Dulles' approval; the vote was 15 to 13 along strict party lines. After this was adopted, Johnson let the White House know it would be well advised to accept it without further protest. The advice was followed.

In fact, Johnson was now so thoroughly in command that he saw no reason to delay a mid-winter vacation in Florida. When the two committees voted out the resolution on February 13, Johnson was still vacationing. The resolution probably would have taken a speedy ride through the Senate had not a new diplomatic crisis developed in the Middle East, with reverberations in Washington that deeply strained Johnson's relationship with the Eisenhower Administration.

The new crisis was an outgrowth of the old. Although a United Nations resolution called on Israeli troops to withdraw from Egyptian territory occupied during Israel's lightning invasion of the Gaza Strip the previous September, the government of Prime Minister David Ben Gurion was understandably loathe to lose the security to his nation's frontiers gained by victory on the battlefield. Ben Gurion refused to withdraw his troops until Nasser gave Israel the civil administration and police power in the Gaza Strip, as well as navigation rights in the Gulf of Aqaba. Nasser rejected these conditions. The impasse was leading to a UN debate over Arab demands for economic sanctions against Israel—sanctions strongly favored inside the administration by Dulles. To back down before Israeli demands, Dulles told Eisenhower, would confirm Arab suspicions that the United States government was subservient to Jewish interests and might, therefore, push the Arabs into the arms of Moscow.

But national leaders of the Democratic party were highly sensitive to the heavily Democratic Jewish vote and thus reflected the strong sympathy for Israel inside the American Jewish community. Johnson was no exception. He was unalterably opposed to Dulles on the question of sanctions. On February 11, while still in Florida, he wrote a confidential letter to Dulles that was to inject bizarre new complications into the fight over sanctions. On its face, the letter was an audacious intrusion by the Majority Leader into the presidential realm of foreign policy. It demanded that Dulles "instruct" the United States delegation at the United Nations to oppose "with all its skill" not only sanctions against Israel but even the calling of a vote on sanctions. Johnson was outraged when, upon returning to Washington on February 16, he found that Dulles had not answered his letter.

If Dulles had any excuse for this oversight, it was his preoccupation with the crisis in the Middle East situation, aggravated by the necessity to commute between Washington and Thomasville, Georgia, where Eisenhower was hunting quail at the plantation of George Humphrey, the Secretary of the Treasury. During a conference with Dulles at Thomasville, Eisenhower decided to push firmly for strong economic sanctions against Israel unless Ben Gurion withdrew from the Gaza Strip. It was now necessary to call in the congressional leaders to get their support.

Johnson's mood was growing more truculent. When Eisenhower proposed that the congressional leaders fly to Thomasville to confer with him, Johnson declined. When Eisenhower proposed as an alternative that they confer with Dulles in Washington, Johnson refused. Johnson wanted Eisenhower to come back to Washington, and the President finally agreed to cut his vacation short and come home. The meeting was set for February 20 at the White House.

If ever Eisenhower needed help from Johnson, it was that winter morning. Knowland, supposedly the President's lieutenant, once again had dug himself into an immovable posture of opposition to Eisenhower. He was committed against sanctions. But whatever slim chance Eisenhower might have had to win Johnson's backing vanished on February 19, the day before the meeting. Johnson was furious that morning to read his February 11 confidential letter to Dulles in the *New York Herald Tribune* and the *Chicago Daily News*. He immediately—and incorrectly—jumped to the conclusion that Dulles not only lacked the common courtesy to reply to his letter but had now leaked it to the newspapers. Johnson retaliated by elevating the letter to the status of party doctrine, rushing it through as a formal declaration by the Senate Democratic Policy Committee. Johnson himself was now irrevocably committed on the issue.

After the President made his call for sanctions at the White House the next morning, Johnson turned to Senator Russell with what Sherman Adams viewed as "a determined expression which seemed to say he was not going to yield an inch." When Eisenhower then called on Dulles, Johnson broke in to protest the appearance of his letter in the previous day's *Herald Tribune*. Johnson next pointed out that he and Knowland had reached the same position on this issue without consulting each other, adding, meaningfully:

"After all, there are times when Congress has to express its own views."

"I certainly have no objection to that," Eisenhower replied.

Johnson gazed at the President with a wry smile, then said simply: "Thank you."

Before the meeting ended, all the Democratic leaders politely but firmly refused Eisenhower's request for a public statement backing the administration's efforts to win withdrawal of the Israeli troops.

And now the Middle East Resolution was becalmed in the Senate, held motionless by Johnson pending the outcome of his battle with the administration over sanctions against Israel. If those sanctions were voted by the United Nations with United States support, Johnson made clear privately, the Eisenhower Doctrine was dead. This was power exercised with a vengeance.

Just how far Johnson had become estranged from Dulles on the Middle East question became clear on Friday, February 22, two days after the White House meeting. Seeking to mollify Johnson, Dulles belatedly dictated a courteous acknowledgment of the February 11 letter and assigned a top-level messenger to send it to Capitol Hill— Robert C. Hill, an urbane businessman and Republican politician from New Hampshire who had replaced Thruston Morton as Assistant Secretary of State for congressional relations.

Telephoning Johnson's office from Dulles' house that afternoon, Hill said he was on his way to Capitol Hill to deliver the letter. Juanita Roberts, Johnson's secretary, told him the Senator was in his office. Indeed, Johnson *was* in his office—preparing one of the most chilling and calculated rebuffs ever administered to a Cabinet member by a ranking congressional leader.

When Hill arrived at four o'clock, he was surprised to find the door of the Majority Leader's office bolted—on Johnson's specific orders. Johnson was infuriated to learn from a newspaper reporter, only moments after Johnson himself was informed, that Hill was coming to his office with the Dulles letter. Johnson immediately jumped to the conclusion that Dulles had leaked the fact that his letter was on its way in Hill's pocket to Johnson's office.

But once again, Johnson's oversensitivity led him astray. The reporter's knowledge that the letter was on its way came not from Dulles or the State Department, but from Johnson's own indiscretion. The minute he learned the letter had been dispatched to his office, Johnson confided that fact to a Senate colleague. And the colleague immediately confided it to a reporter, who naturally went to Johnson to ask for a look at the letter when it arrived.

Finding the door locked, Hill stood there momentarily wondering what to do next. He did not have long to wait. Not realizing that Hill had arrived, Johnson came bounding out of his office and smack into Dulles' messenger. Hill reached into his breast pocket, extracted the letter, and offered it to Johnson. "I don't have any time for you now," Johnson snapped. He told Hill to come back the next day, remarking curtly that he was late for an important appointment with other Senators. The appointment turned out to be a date on the masseur's rubdown table in the Senate gymnasium.

Stunned and ashen-faced, Hill took the subway car from the Capitol to see Walter Jenkins in Johnson's "Texas office" in the Senate Office Building. The usually hospitable and amiable Jenkins was icily uncommunicative, treating Hill like a stranger. When Hill explained he was under orders by Dulles to deliver the letter personally to Johnson, Jenkins asked Hill to wait—and wait he did for two hours, without result, before he gave up for the day. When Hill returned to the Majority Leader's office the next morning, Johnson again refused to accept the letter. Only after Hill succeeded in getting Speaker Rayburn to intercede for him did Johnson at long last accept the Secretary of State's letter.

Underlining the almost farcical incident of the Dulles letter was Johnson's deeper anger at the whole question of sanctions against Israel. The Majority Leader and the President seemed to be on a collision course that might have poisoned their relationship for all time. The administration had made a decision to support sanctions unless Israel removed its troops from the Gaza Strip. A United States vote for sanctions would have forced Johnson either to scuttle the Middle East Resolution or else encumber it with a rider attacking Eisenhower's whole Middle East policy.* But open warfare within the

---

* However, Johnson discouraged and suppressed several proposals by Democratic Senators to pass a separate resolution opposing anti-Israel sanctions. That would have been going too far. Johnson was playing a game of maneuver and pressure with Eisenhower. He did not want to tie his hands with a Senate anti-sanctions resolution.

United States government was averted at the last moment on March 1 when Israel capitulated. Mrs. Golda Meir, the Israeli Foreign Minister, announced to the United Nations General Assembly that her country planned a "full and complete withdrawal" of troops.

The sanction question disappeared and the becalmed Middle East Resolution began to move again in the Senate with Johnson back in his old role as Eisenhower's protector. On February 28, Senator Russell was assured of forty-one votes—almost enough to pass an amendment eviscerating the Eisenhower Doctrine. The Russell amendment would have eliminated all mention of military or economic aid to the Middle East. With the sanctions question out of the way, Johnson went to work peeling away Russell's forty-one votes. On March 2, the Russell amendment was beaten by the comfortable margin of 58 to 28. The rest was anticlimax: the Middle East Resolution, whose immediate passage the President had thought important enough to summon congressional leaders to the White House on New Year's Day, was finally signed into law by Eisenhower on March 9.

The Majority Leader's conduct in the Middle East crisis of 1957 was the first clear indication that the President could not always count on Johnson for help even when the political going was toughest. And to underscore the point, the Majority Leader was even more rebellious in a major domestic crisis between the President and Congress that began simultaneously with the fight over the Middle East resolution.

When Eisenhower called congressional leaders to the White House on January 1, 1957, to discuss the Eisenhower Doctrine, he casually mentioned the federal budget he was going to submit to Congress two weeks later. He did not mention his fear, expressed privately to his staff, that the Democrats might find the 71.8 billion dollars in estimated expenditures too low and vote for higher federal spending. Strangely, exactly the opposite occurred, due mainly to Eisenhower's tough, outspoken Secretary of the Treasury, George M. Humphrey.

Humphrey was an aggressively conservative Cleveland steel executive having his first taste of public life and loving it. He had bulled his way past experienced politicians like Attorney General Herbert Brownell, Jr., and Secretary of Commerce Sinclair Weeks to become the strong man of the Eisenhower Cabinet. But for all of his power, Humphrey could not control the federal budget. He became obsessed with the desire to reduce the high level of spending. In that sense, he represented all the shocked Old Guard Republicans who had come to realize that Dwight D. Eisenhower would not—in fact, *could* not—

dismantle the New Deal. After some heavy budget cuts in the early years, Eisenhower's budgets were getting bigger and bigger, just as Truman's did.

Pent-up frustration within the Republican party by caretakers of the Taft tradition was ready to burst on January 15, 1957, when Humphrey held his annual press briefing to explain, and supposedly defend, the new budget. It was a strange defense. Unhappy with a 72-billion-dollar budget and fearful that the Johnson-Rayburn leadership would vote still higher appropriations, Humphrey snapped out that "I would deplore the day that we thought we couldn't ever reduce expenditures of this terrific amount . . . ," then added this memorable, extemporaneous line: "If we don't, over a long period of time, I will predict that you will have a depression that will curl your hair."

If that seemed to be an engraved invitation to Congress to cut the Secretary of the Treasury's budget, it was confirmed by Eisenhower at his January 23 press conference. Not only did he agree with Humphrey that Congress ought to cut the budget, he also declared "it is their duty to do it." To an exasperated Sherman Adams, "that gummed up the sap works." With their thoughtless, impromptu remarks about a budget in preparation for a full year, Humphrey and Eisenhower invited the 1957 Battle of the Budget. Farcical and trivial though it was in substance, it commanded the attention of the nation, the President, and the Congress, and once again aligned Lyndon Johnson against Dwight D. Eisenhower.

Eisenhower quickly realized the self-imposed hazard of a President inviting Congress to whack away at his own budget and began to defend it. But it was too late. The congressional economy demon had been set loose again—particularly among Republicans. Never did Eisenhower so badly need Johnson to save him from his own party. Senior Republicans in the Senate disagreed only as to how much they wanted to slash the Eisenhower budget; William Knowland called for a 2-billion-dollar cut, Styles Bridges 2.5 billion dollars. But just as he did on the question of Israeli sanctions, Johnson took Knowland's side, demanding cuts in the budget and, in one taunting speech on the Senate floor, imploring Eisenhower to show the Democratic Congress exactly where his Republican budget could be cut.

The Battle of the Budget snugly fit Johnson's unwritten rule never to hesitate to attack Eisenhower—at the right time and on the right issue. Certainly, here was a golden opportunity to hint at indecisive leadership, to exacerbate wide differences between George Humphrey and more liberal members of the Cabinet, and generally to confuse a divided administration. But beyond these tactical considerations,

Johnson *believed* in budget cutting for the sake of budget cutting. A product of Capitol Hill, where simplistic veneration of the balanced budget and reduced expenditures provided a daily catechism for members of both parties, Johnson felt that an attack on the Eisenhower budget was good politics—a political orthodoxy that would reappear seven years later in Johnson's first days as President.

In 1957, Johnson wanted to dispel the popular image of a free-spending Democratic party by out-economizing the Republican President. Here then was an opening to the right for the Democratic party —an opening that the Democratic Advisory Council and liberals generally didn't think existed and wouldn't want to enter if it did. Usually critical of Johnson for collusion with Eisenhower, the liberals now wanted Johnson to support the President.

With the Middle East Resolution out of the way, Johnson stepped up his budget-cutting sallies—encouraged by a nationwide splurge of letters to Congress pleading for a slash in the budget. Johnson articulated his budget demands on April 6 before a most conservative and most appreciative forum: the national convention of the American Cotton Manufacturing Institute, meeting in Palm Beach, Florida. Calling the 72 billion dollars a "swollen budget," he hacked away at foreign aid—the budget's most politically vulnerable element, but one that he always had supported—with a pledge to end "foreign giveaways." After the speech, he told interviewers: "The budget must be cut and will be cut."

A month later, Johnson was chipping away at the administration's inconsistent position on the budget. Noting that Eisenhower was so concerned about the budget-cutting hysteria that he felt compelled to make a dramatic radio-television appeal to the country on May 14, Johnson told the Senate on May 2, in a speech spiced with sarcasm:

> In a very real sense that appeal will be welcome. It may help to clarify some of the confusion which has been caused by the conflicting statements by the President's Cabinet officers. I cannot help but wonder, however, whether these appeals are being addressed to the proper source. Instead of appealing to the people, it might be well for the President to appeal to members of his official family, namely the Secretary of the Treasury and the Secretary of State.*

Swept up in the excitement of the Battle of the Budget, Johnson flailed away at programs he had supported throughout his congressional career. On May 25, he refused to give Eisenhower a "blank

* Inside the Cabinet, Dulles had opposed Humphrey's economizing strictures, particularly on foreign aid.

check" on foreign aid. The next day he gave the Pentagon the surprise of the year when, departing from his carefully developed twenty-year position as the apostle of defense preparedness, he asserted the defense budget was not "sacred and untouchable," and indicated he would support heavy cuts in it voted by the House.

The cuts in these national security programs were deep. The 40-billion-dollar defense budget was pared by more than 2 billion dollars. That scarcely compared, however, with the 1.1 billion dollars sliced out of foreign aid, a 30 percent reduction, despite Eisenhower's anguished pleas for help. These major forays in "economizing" were dwarfed by Johnson's ferocity with a relatively minor agency: the United States Information Agency, which encompassed the Voice of America. What happened to the USIA in 1957 is the microcosm of that year's Battle of the Budget.

President Eisenhower had requested 144 million dollars for the USIA. It took a battering in the House, and came to the Senate reduced to 106.1 million dollars. But it was widely assumed that Johnson, who had never before treated the USIA harshly, would restore much of the House cut.

Johnson was chairman of the subcommittee of the Senate Appropriations Committee that regularly handled the appropriation for the State and Justice Departments. Normally, its annual budget hearings were routine, with most of the work in the appropriations process traditionally done in the House. But 1957 was to prove an exception. The Senate appropriations hearing for the USIA, under Johnson's command, turned into a sour, politically inspired investigation, the shabbiest conducted by him since the Leland Olds case eight years earlier.*

Its roots were deeper than the Battle of the Budget, tracing back to an apparently unrelated, distant event: the publication in 1956 of *A Republican Looks at His Party*, a book by a liberal law professor named Arthur Larson. Larson was a Rhodes Scholar originally from South Dakota who first came to Washington in 1941 in a wartime job, leaving in 1945 to teach law. In 1953, Eisenhower plucked him from the University of Pittsburgh Law School, where he was dean, to become Under Secretary of Labor.

While Larson was at the Labor Department, his book was published—with Eisenhower's pre-publication encouragement and post-publication plaudits. Larson tried to make a doctrine out of a vague,

* See Chapter III.

misty political idea called Modern Republicanism. Plagued by the conservative politics of Taft Republicans during his first years in office, Eisenhower and his academician brother, Dr. Milton Eisenhower, along with Sherman Adams, had been desperately trying to define a new kind of Republicanism, broadly characterized as the politics of being liberal in human affairs and conservative in fiscal affairs. Larson's book became the bible of short-lived Modern Republicanism—but also the immediate source of contemptuous irreverence by Democrats of all stripes and Old Guard Republicans as well.

At the tail end of 1956, the furor caused by Larson's book was still echoing in Washington, but Eisenhower nevertheless transferred him from the relative calm of the Labor Department to a notorious hot spot: the USIA. The agency was still suffering the residual agony of Senator Joseph McCarthy's sensational book-burning inquisition in its overseas offices early in the Eisenhower Administration.*

Larson and the Battle of the Budget arrived at USIA together. Despite Democratic irritation at the elevation of "Mr. Modern Republican" to the head of an agency supposedly far removed from politics, Larson might have survived had it not been for a silly political speech he made in Hawaii on April 16, 1957—the day before the House acted on his budget. Inexplicably, the liberal-leaning Republican went beyond usual political restraints in attacking the New and Fair Deals. "Throughout the New and Fair Deals," he said, "this country was in the grasp of a somewhat alien philosophy imported from Europe."

A lawyer and administrator whose understanding of the more subtle aspects of politics was minuscule, Larson lamely defended his Hawaiian blunder by saying he was not talking about the 1957 Democratic party, but the party of Roosevelt and Truman. Whether or not this defense was intended to ingratiate him with Southern Democrats (who sometimes felt the same way), it had just the opposite effect. The Southerners were looking for justification to reduce Eisenhower's budget, and Larson gave them an ideal excuse for attacking the USIA. And he genuinely infuriated Northern liberals, defenders of the Voice of America who simply could not bring themselves to defend its new chief.

Enter Lyndon Johnson. A sweeping Johnson attack on the USIA would please both Northern liberals and Southern conservatives in the Democratic party. Here was both a gift and instrument in Johnson's continuing campaign to nudge the two wings of his party close together. Moreover, it fit into the overall campaign of budget cutting to

---

* McCarthy, a member of Johnson's subcommittee, died on May 2, 1957, the first day that Larson appeared before the subcommittee on the USIA budget.

show the country that the Democratic Congress, not the Republican President, was the true safeguard of fiscal responsibility.

It was the sort of opportunity Johnson had shown on countless occasions he would not pass up. He did not this time. Before the hearings ended on May 10, Larson had become a pathetic object of ridicule and his agency had been so riddled with criticism and so stripped of operating funds that it did not recover for years.

In his opening statement on May 2, subcommittee chairman Johnson welcomed Larson with his customary sarcasm: "We look to you as the distinguished author and spokesman for your party to enlighten us." Everybody, including Larson, knew he was referring to *A Republican Looks at His Party* and the unfortunate Hawaii speech.

Johnson himself led the questioning during the four days of Larson's testimony. Although he preserved a façade of courtesy, the knife of ridicule cut through. Senator Leverett Saltonstall of Massachusetts, an impeccably correct Republican Brahmin, suggested at one point that Larson submit a memorandum containing detailed facts and figures. Johnson intervened. He did not want "the record to show that the chairman [Johnson] invited the head of our propaganda agency to speak orally and then he had to prepare a memorandum." Surely, Johnson was suggesting, Larson was not such a poor witness that he couldn't answer the Saltonstall questions orally. From ridicule, Johnson moved to unction, treating Larson like a kindergarten student.

The question is, how can we do the best job and get the most for our money? I hope your mind is not closed to new avenues. I would gather from the little I know about you that you are an adventurous fellow, imaginative and modern. So I am going to rely on you to help me establish a moderate balance between the modern and the old guard so that we win the propaganda war that we may be in today.

Again, when Larson complained that Johnson was giving an incorrect picture of the USIA in his questioning, Johnson's reply was that of a patient governess.

Larson: Mr. Chairman, that is not correct, and I can demonstrate methodically, point-by-point, figure-by-figure that that is not correct.

Johnson: Let us do it quietly now. Explain these figures in the case of Italy, Pakistan, and in the case of Turkey. These are the three countries. We do not have to be loud about it. You be as quiet as you want to. . . .

Larson: Mr. Clark is here to talk about Italy.

Johnson: Explain Pakistan now quietly.

Larson: I explained Pakistan in great detail. I will do it again.

Johnson: I do not want you to do something that you have already done, but apparently there is considerable confusion here about it. We want to be helpful to you so, if you will, just explain the facts.

Instead of helping Larson with his burden, most of the Republican Senators on the subcommittee figuratively rolled in the aisles with laughter at Larson's discomfiture and at Johnson's sallies.

From the seven Republicans sitting in on the hearings, Larson could not expect help. The mild-mannered Saltonstall was no fighter, particularly when Johnson was on the other side. Margaret Chase Smith of Maine was a member in good standing of the Johnson Network. Four other Republicans on the subcommittee (including Minority Leader Knowland himself) were Old Guard conservatives who—as Johnson well knew—always had been skeptical of USIA and, more important, were contemptuous of all Modern Republicans, particularly Larson. That left Karl Mundt of South Dakota, a hard-shell conservative but a militant anti-Communist who favored well-financed foreign propaganda programs. Paradoxically, Mundt was Larson's only defender. With both Republican and Democratic subcommittee members in his pocket (save for Mundt), Johnson could taunt Larson without fear of rebuttal from other members of the subcommittee.

Larson had been in charge at USIA for less than three months and was an atrociously bad witness. Consequently a huge reduction in Larson's budget was a foregone conclusion. On May 14, two working days after the hearings ended, the subcommittee reported its USIA bill, not only upholding the deep cuts by the House but slicing still another 15 million dollars from Eisenhower's request. This left a meager total of 90.2 million dollars—an overall cut of 38 percent. On the same day, the full committee unanimously approved the subcommittee's cut.

Just one day later, on May 15, the USIA bill came to the Senate floor. Johnson patted himself on the back for having compiled "one of the longest and largest records of any subcommittee in the history of the Senate—1,249 pages of testimony." He was congratulated by Republican Old Guardsman Styles Bridges for having done "a fair, thoughtful job" on the bill. Mike Mansfield, the Majority Whip, agreed, and even went so far as to point out that "some members believed that larger cuts should have been made."

Despite Larson's unpopularity among liberal Democratic Senators following his Hawaii speech, there was some concern in those ranks that Johnson's cut was too close to the bone. Both John F. Kennedy of Massachusetts and Joseph S. Clark, a first-year Senator from Pennsylvania, told Johnson privately that they might try to restore some of the money. The Majority Leader was displeased. "This is a leadership matter," he informed them. In other words, Johnson was cracking the party whip. Kennedy and Clark decided to go along, voting with Johnson for the full 38 percent cut but expressing misgivings on the Senate floor. With a special interest in the new African countries, Kennedy questioned the effect of the reduction there.[*]

Richard Neuberger of Oregon was the only Democrat to oppose the cut, and only fourteen Republicans joined him. By a vote of 61 to 15, the Senate adopted the Johnson-drafted USIA budget without a comma changed—a cut deeper than that any other agency sustained in the 1957 Battle of the Budget. More than all the other skirmishes in the Battle of the Budget, this one strained relations between Eisenhower and Johnson. Irked by the "irresponsible diminution of an agency on the front line of the cold war," the President longed for a Republican Congress as never before.

Johnson's timing made the USIA pill all the more difficult for Eisenhower to swallow. He brought the bill to the floor the very day after Eisenhower's nationwide television defense of his budget and thereby increased the President's humiliation. Less than twenty-four hours after Eisenhower had appealed over the head of Congress against meat-ax budget cuts, the Senate sank its ax deeper than ever before— and by an overwhelming margin.

Johnson, of course, sought to avoid a complete break with the President, even though Eisenhower was furious over the roughing-up of his favorite Republican theoretician. During the May 15 USIA debate when pro-Eisenhower Republican Senators accused Johnson of deserting the President, the Majority Leader replied:

> I never considered it a reflection on me when the President disagrees with me. I do not think it ought to be considered a reflection on the President when I disagree with him. . . . I heard the President's talk last night. I have had to make some TV speeches, at times, to appeal to people to get them to go along with my program. . . . If I know Dwight Eisenhower, the President of the United States, and I think I do, I know he wants me to do my job as a United States Senator as my conscience dictates.

Less exotic federal agencies, with more politically apt directors and better support in Congress, did not suffer so much as USIA. The

---

[*] However, Clark later was to prove considerably less submissive to Johnson's wishes, as shall be seen in Chapter X.

grand total of budget cuts when the 1957 session ended was 4 billion
dollars, unusually large but not enough to warrant all the noise of the
Battle of the Budget. Moreover, the final outcome could not be known
until the fiscal year ended on June 30, 1958. If Congress followed its
usual pattern, some of the 4 billion dollars would likely be restored
by the 1958 session of Congress when no one was looking. But nobody
dreamed how much. For in the early months of 1958, Congress not
only restored *all* of the 4 billion dollars it had cut in the artificial passion of the previous summer, but *added* another 4.5 billion dollars,
elevating spending well above Eisenhower's recommendations.

Thus, the Battle of the Budget, 1957, was sham, farce, and waste. In
the longest sustained assault on Eisenhower during his tenure as Majority Leader, Johnson emerged with no real credit for himself or his
party.

There were, however, two new factors in the 1958 session to reinforce the natural urge of Congress to undo what had been done in the
1957 session. Both these factors were beyond the control of Congress.
The 1958 recession produced a spate of pump-priming programs
pushed by the Democratic leadership.* Simultaneously, the same
Congress that less than a year earlier was all out for slashing defense
spending now furiously voted more for defense—and for the new field
of space. In fact, the 1958 session was popularly known as the Sputnik
Congress. It put Johnson in combat with Eisenhower on a new level.

At seven-thirty on the evening of October 4, 1957, the Soviet Union
opened the Space Age by launching Sputnik I, the first man-made
Earth satellite. Although top administration officials tried to brush off
the significance of the Sputnik (Sherman Adams advised that we were
not about to play the Russians in "an outer space basketball game"),
the Soviet triumph deeply troubled the country. The first impact was a
loss of pride and prestige. Shame soon yielded to fear. Sputnik gave
the Soviet Union a dangerous advantage in missilery that could affect
the balance of power in the Cold War.

For Johnson, the situation held certain obvious political possibilities. During his first year on the Senate Armed Services Committee in
1949, he became interested in space exploration and tried, without
much success, to persuade Defense Department officials to start a research program. He had a long public record as a champion of pure
research, but the Eisenhower Administration was uninterested. While
still a House member in 1948, he had called for "unceasing, never-
ending research, adequate funds for scientists and skilled workmen,

* See page 162.

endless months of trial and error following blind trials." Save for his 1957 budget-cutting spree, he had not only supported defense preparedness but usually favored voting the military services anything they wanted. Now, with Sputnik I circling the globe, Johnson controlled the ideal forum for conducting an inquest into the meaning of Sputnik: his Defense Preparedness Subcommittee, virtually dormant since the Korean War investigations.

Yet in the hours immediately following the Sputnik launching, Johnson hesitated. There was, of course, his habitual caution over challenging the President. Beyond that, however, Johnson was genuinely concerned about international repercussions of an investigation that might reveal Eisenhower and his administration as weak, drifting, and unable to compete with the Soviet Union. Even worse would be an investigation that disclosed dangerous disrepair in United States defenses.

Johnson was on the telephone with old friends and advisers in those hours just after Sputnik was launched—with Donald Cook, Edwin Weisl, and Eliot Janeway in New York City; with Richard Russell in Winder, Georgia. All urged him to go ahead with the investigation. Johnson agreed, and Russell, chairman of the parent Armed Services Committee, announced the probe on October 8. By October 17, when Johnson flew from Washington to Tyler, Texas, to address the annual Rose Festival, he was speaking out strongly on the administration's costly failure in space: "We have got to admit frankly and without evasion that the Soviets have beaten us at our own game—daring scientific advances in the atomic age."

But part of the caution lingered. Wary of grave international consequences, Johnson would not permit the Sputnik hearings to turn into an openly partisan attack on Eisenhower. He was content to make his points against the President's failure in space by implication rather than direct statement. Desiring to emphasize the scientific rather than the military aspects of space, Johnson sought scientists from Rice Institute and the Massachusetts Institute of Technology to run the investigation, but could not persuade them to come to Washington. So he turned to one of his most trusted advisers, Don Cook. But Cook now was in New York as executive vice-president of a major utility, American Electric Power Company, Inc., and could not take a leave. He suggested Weisl. Weisl, too, was reluctant to leave his Wall Street law practice, but succumbed to the magic of the Johnson Treatment and a personal request by Senator Russell. "You're always being critical of me for this or that," Johnson told Weisl. "Now here's your chance to do something for your country." Johnson assured him it would be only a one-week investigation.

The suite in Washington's Mayflower Hotel where Weisl was to live for just one week soon seemed like home. The one week stretched to two weeks, then three weeks and finally two months. With Johnson devoting around three hours a day to the project, he and Weisl put together a textbook example of what a Senate investigation ought to be.

Johnson instructed Weisl and Cyrus Vance, a young lawyer from Weisl's firm whom he brought to Washington as associate subcommittee counsel, to be strictly nonpartisan.* On November 3, Johnson publicly declared the investigation would not attempt "to fix blame" but "to determine what steps can be taken to strengthen our position and restore the leadership we should have in technology." Three days later, when Eisenhower delivered an apologia for the space failure in a nationally televised speech, Johnson was remarkably restrained: "I had hoped that the President would stress what we need to do as well as what we have done. But I am happy that he has noted the necessity for a 'high sense of urgency.'"

But Johnson's avowed nonpartisanship was running afoul of one member of his subcommittee: Senator Stuart Symington of Missouri. Ever since the days when Symington was Secretary of the Air Force under Truman, and Johnson was a high-ranking member of the House Armed Services Committee, they had battled shoulder to shoulder —first against Truman, later against Eisenhower—for a bigger Air Force. But in the mid-1950s, they had grown apart for personal reasons. Moreover, they had sharply different views of the military. Symington trusted and relied on colorful Air Force generals like Hoyt Vandenberg, Thomas Power, and Curtis LeMay; while supporting these generals almost as firmly as Symington did, Johnson was suspicious of them. He didn't really like the brass and wondered about their demands for ever more spending (though he consistently supported them).

It was clear from the beginning that Symington was considerably less interested in a scientific inquiry into space exploration than in an inquisition. His target was Eisenhower's failure to spend money fast enough for the Minuteman and Polaris intercontinental missiles and a half dozen lesser items of military hardware wanted by the Pentagon but denied by the Budget Bureau. Johnson also felt that Symington, seeking to protect his reputation as Secretary of the Air Force, wanted to undercut Republican charges that the Truman Administration was in truth responsible for the lag in missile production. Finally, Symington was gearing up to run for President on a platform of defense preparedness. Thus, Johnson feared that, under the prod of Stu Syming-

* Vance later was President Johnson's Deputy Secretary of Defense.

ton, the hearings might degenerate into a partisan fight over the lack of military hardware and Eisenhower's failure to spend enough money for it.

In hopes of avoiding that, Johnson scheduled two renowned nuclear scientists, Edward Teller and Vannevar Bush, as the subcommittee's first witnesses. The object was to elevate the hearings into the realm of space and away from interservice battles in the Pentagon. In the process, he did not hesitate to sit on Symington even if it violated strict rules of senatorial courtesy.

For instance, when Symington subjected Neil McElroy, the Proctor & Gamble soap manufacturer who was Eisenhower's second Secretary of Defense, to merciless and endless examination about the details of various weapons systems, Johnson fidgeted ostentatiously. Finally, and without ceremony, he flatly interrupted Symington, asking if he weren't about finished. "All I would like to do is get a chance to ask my questions . . . ," Symington shot back. "I believe this analysis is important to national security." The Majority Leader answered with proper Johnsonian irony:

> . . . certainly there is no disposition for anyone to interfere with your questioning or keep you from having a reasonable length of time. We do have plans to conclude the hearings, we want to be fair to all Senators, and certainly lean over backward to be sure that you are accorded equal opportunity to question these witnesses.

Only once did the hearings slip from the model decorum ordained by Johnson and Weisl, and that was Johnson's fault—not Symington's. Lieutenant General James M. Gavin, the Army's research and development chief and a paratrooper hero from World War II who was considered one of the Army's most brilliant—and mercurial—young generals, dramatically resigned from the Army. Gavin departed with a passionate attack upon the Army's failure to modernize for conventional warfare and Eisenhower's reliance on nuclear "New Look" weapons. While seemingly unrelated to the space and missile problems, Gavin's resignation symbolized crosscurrents of unease and suspicion prevailing in the military services under President Eisenhower and was quickly seized upon by Johnson. Acting against the advice of Weisl and Vance, Johnson decided to call Gavin as a witness, and promptly broke all his rules of decorum.

Johnson's suppressed hostility against the professional military caste boiled to the surface as he and Gavin carried on an emotional, sometimes tearful colloquy directed against the beribboned Neanderthals who ran the Army. Johnson finished the exchange with this heated peroration:

> General, I just think this is a horrible situation. I am surprised that it exists. . . .
>
> I am not speaking with regard to any particular military man or any particular civilian. I, as a young man from Texas, who wants to see men like you stay in the service, am making a plea to you. You are a mighty young man to be leaving, getting out.
>
> If men like you, General Gavin—I want you to listen to these words—if you tuck your tail and put up the white flag, say "I can't take it any more," and run from this crowd, we are going to have a second-rate Army, because the first-raters will be getting out.

The Gavin incident was exceptional. Otherwise, Johnson conducted the hearings in a restrained, though properly critical manner, making clear that Eisenhower had done an abysmal job on space and national defense but never directly accusing him. In his "State of the Union Address" delivered on January 7, 1958, the opening day of the second session of the 85th Congress, to the Democratic caucus (beating President Eisenhower's State of the Union by a day), Johnson ignored Symington's emphasis on military hardware and outlined a broad approach, setting space and national defense far above considerations of the budget.* Conveniently neglecting to mention his own role in the Battle of the Budget the previous summer, Johnson challenged the whole concept of the balanced budget. Instead, he spoke of "the appraisal of leaders in the field of science . . . whose valuation of what control of outer space means renders irrelevant the bookkeeping concerns of fiscal matters." The speech gave Johnson and the Democrats the lead in post-Sputnik space policy, a lead they never relinquished.

When the hearings concluded at the end of January, Johnson flatly refused to go along with Symington's demand for a sharply critical report—partly because of his old caution about disgracing Eisenhower in the eyes of the world, partly because he knew Republican members of the subcommittee never would sign such a report. And Johnson wanted unanimity on his subcommittee.

Johnson would actually have preferred that the subcommittee issue nothing at all, but Weisl and Vance convinced him to issue a list of

---

* However, Johnson's speech was not well received by everybody. Professor Clinton Rossiter of Cornell, a staunch champion of presidential authority, ever on guard against congressional incursions, referred to it as "one State of the Union Message too many."

tersely worded, nonpolitical recommendations that the Republicans could support. (One example: "Start work at once on the development of a rocket motor with a million pounds thrust.") The result was a list of seventeen unanimously adopted recommendations urging stepped-up space and missile spending. They didn't satisfy Stuart Symington, but they were soon adopted by Eisenhower as administration policy. Indeed, later in the year Eisenhower acquiesced in the demands of Johnson and Senator Clinton Anderson that space functions be transferred from the Pentagon to a new civilian space agency, the National Aeronautics and Space Administration.* More than in any field, national policy in space was being made by Democrats on Capitol Hill, led by Johnson.

Johnson's handling of the space and missile issue through the 1958 Sputnik Congress, with the single exception of the Gavin incident, was the epitome of what he wanted his relations with Eisenhower to be: damaging to the Republicans and beneficial to the Democrats, without involving himself in a collision with the President. In contrast to his spongy, egotistical conduct in the Middle East crisis, and his demagoguery in the Battle of the Budget, his treatment of the Sputnik Crisis was the peak performance of the Johnson System in dealing with the President. But 1958 was the last year for such a performance. The election of November, 1958, so radically—and surprisingly—revised the power relationships between President and Congress that a minor masterpiece such as Johnson's handling of the Sputnik Crisis was no longer possible. The golden years of his Senate leadership were nearing an end.

---

* Johnson also took the lead in establishing the Senate Committee on Aeronautical and Space Sciences, the Senate's first new standing committee since the Legislative Reorganization Act of 1946. The chairman was Lyndon Johnson, who thereby secured for himself still another power base in the Senate.

Chapter X

★ ★ ★ ★ ★ ★ ★ ★ ★

TOO
MANY
DEMOCRATS

Johnson's jaded generalities are designed to prepare the American public for the inevitable—the inability of this Democratic Congress to resist deficit spending.
> —Meade Alcorn, Chairman of the Republican National Committee, January 8, 1959

Early in the session, Messrs. Rayburn and Johnson snuggled into the strait jacket offered them by the administration. Instead of accepting the challenge to meet the country's needs, the leadership made divided government work by the simple expedient of surrendering to the President.
> —Americans for Democratic Action, October 15, 1959

On a late summer afternoon in 1958, Speaker Sam Rayburn's "board of education" met in his offices, as it did almost every day after work to "strike a blow for freedom"—good political talk accompanied by good whiskey. Lyndon Johnson was present. So were the "board of education" regulars: a half dozen or so Congressmen, most of them from Texas, and one or two trusted newspaper reporters. The topic was the forthcoming congressional elections, and the opinion was unanimous that a major shift was due in the congressional balance of power for the first time since the end of World War II.

A landslide was obviously in prospect. The Republicans were blamed for the recession. President Eisenhower was at a low point of popularity. Sherman Adams' resignation under pressure, after receiving gifts from and intervening with federal agencies in behalf of Boston industrialist Bernard Goldfine, had tarnished the gleam of morality in Eisenhower's Great Crusade. And to make matters worse, business interests had selected just this inopportune time for a national campaign to pass "right-to-work" laws banning all forms of compulsory unionism, thereby rousing the drowsy giant of organized labor into active combat for the 1958 campaign. It was, then, not a matter of *whether* the Democrats would pick up seats, but *how many.*

The very thought of heavy Democratic majorities in Congress for the first time since New Deal days sent the pulse rate soaring for most Democratic politicians. But not Sam Rayburn. Sipping whiskey as the shadows lengthened that afternoon, Rayburn shook his head in unhappy contemplation. "I'd just as soon not have that many Democrats," he murmured. "Believe me, they'll be hard to handle. It won't be easy."

When it came, the landslide surpassed everybody's expectations. The election of November 5, 1958, ended more than a decade of even balance in the national legislature and gave the Democrats margins of nearly 2 to 1 in each chamber: 283 to 153 in the House; 65 to 35 in the Senate. And Sam Rayburn's prophecy that all those Democrats might be a mixed blessing was realized again and again in the next two years, by him—and more particularly, by Lyndon Johnson.

Long before the November 5 election returns were compiled, it was clear that not all the new Democrats pouring into the Senate would be automatic prospects for the Johnson Network. Many were new-breed liberals eager to make common cause with the tiny, beleaguered fraction of liberal Democratic Senators who had fitfully and ineffectively challenged Johnson's leadership from time to time. Indeed, even before the 1958 election, that fraction was growing in numbers and rebelliousness. Each election of the 1950s sent a few more liberals to join Paul Douglas of Illinois, Estes Kefauver of Tennessee, and (until his retirement in 1956) Herbert Lehman of New York.

There was, for instance, Pat McNamara of Michigan, burly ex-plumber and union official from Detroit who was a surprise winner in 1954. Bluff and plainspoken, he had no interest in the ceremonials of Senate courtesy and scoffed at the notion of the Senate as a gentleman's club. Nor did he feel any particular allegiance to the Majority Leader. When Bobby Baker summoned all Democratic Senators for a major Johnson floor speech, as he frequently did, Pat McNamara made it his business to stay away. Handpicked by Johnson in 1957 for a seat on the special eight-member Senate investigating committee on labor misdeeds (the famed Senate Rackets Committee), McNamara fretted that Johnson was using him to give the investigation a pro-labor coloration. McNamara finally quit with a public blast that the committee was persecuting labor. What angered Johnson was not so much that McNamara resigned from the committee as that he quit without first notifying the Majority Leader.

This tendency by McNamara and other Senate liberals to wash the party's dirty linen in public was deeply resented by Johnson. When Johnson called a Democratic caucus on January 7, 1958, to discuss his forthcoming space investigation, McNamara wrote the Majority Leader a blunt letter complaining that caucuses were all too rare— only one a year usually—and that when one was held, it ought to consider more than just the space program. Eschewing elaborate Senate usage, he told Johnson "there are other major issues of concern to the country, and the country depends upon us, as the majority party in Congress, to do something about them." When the letter found its way into Drew Pearson's syndicated newspaper column less than a week after it was written, Johnson telephoned McNamara to inform him curtly that if he had any complaints in the future, it would be best to give him a phone call rather than put his complaints in writing.*

Pat McNamara was too plain and frank to hide his irritation. But other liberal Democrats, though just as rebellious, concealed their true feelings prior to the 1958 election. One was William Proxmire, a mercurial, flamboyant Democrat who replaced Joe McCarthy as junior Senator from Wisconsin. Johnson had taken more than usual interest in Proxmire's uphill campaign for the special Senate election of August 27, 1957—Johnson's forty-ninth birthday—to fill the McCarthy seat. So closely was the Senate divided then that a Republican victory would have given the Republicans control once again, abruptly ending Johnson's tenure as Majority Leader. When Johnson telephoned Proxmire at his Milwaukee hotel suite to congratulate him, the new Senator-elect cracked: "I'm the best birthday present you ever had." A grateful Johnson wangled assignments for Proxmire on three standing committees plus a special Senate group junket to West Germany in the autumn of 1957. In return, Proxmire filled the pages of the *Congressional Record* with lavish praise of the Majority Leader.

A recruit for the Johnson Network? Not quite. Like many of the new liberals entering the Senate, Proxmire simply was not emotionally equipped to sit back and follow the Senate's folkways. A long, quiet freshman apprenticeship was not for him. Craving action and publicity, he chafed under the restraints of the Johnson System. By the

---

* McNamara ignored the advice. But it is worth noting that before his death in 1966, he had acquired enough seniority to become chairman of the Senate Public Works Committee and was no longer considered a rebel in the Senate. McNamara had become a reliable member of the Senate Establishment, not prone to rocking the boat.

summer of 1958, he was speaking more than any freshman should. His relationship with Johnson now frayed, Proxmire was nearing the point of open rebellion at the time of the 1958 elections.

So was Senator Joseph Clark of Pennsylvania, member of a wealthy and aristocratic Main Line family and leader of the liberal Democratic reform movement that had destroyed Philadelphia's corrupt Republican machine in the early postwar years. Elected to the Senate in 1956 after eight distinguished years as Mayor of Philadelphia, Clark had no intention of becoming an ineffectual rebel in the Senate. He sought out the liberal he most admired for advice on how to be an effective Senator. That happened to be Hubert Humphrey, the bridge to the liberals in the Johnson Network.

Humphrey was serving as a part-time United Nations delegate (an honor passed around among Senators) following the 1956 elections, and Clark lunched with him in New York. Humphrey's advice was full and explicit: Take it easy your first months in the Senate. Cooperate with the Majority Leader. Get a copy of William S. White's *The Citadel*, which celebrates Senate folkways and the Senators who adapt to them. Follow White's advice.

Anxious to get off on the right foot, Clark soon after the election dispatched his new administrative assistant, James Sundquist, to Washington to have a chat with Bobby Baker in an effort to learn how the Senate works. Sundquist, an exceptional career public servant who had worked in the Budget Bureau under President Truman, was resigning as a top assistant to Governor Averell Harriman of New York to join Clark's staff. Consequently, he was startled when Bobby Baker asked him to join Johnson's staff as the Majority Leader's main contact man with liberal Northern Democrats.

"But I've already joined Senator Clark's staff," protested Sundquist.

"Don't worry about that," Baker shot back breezily. "We'll take care of it."

Clark was properly indignant when told of the incident by Sundquist, starting his relationship with Johnson off on the wrong foot. Nevertheless, he fully intended to follow Humphrey's instructions and became a cooperative liberal lieutenant for Johnson. Unlike Humphrey, however, the patrician Clark suffered from a culture conflict in dealing with Johnson. He did not like Johnson's salty language; he did not like Johnson's habit of gently pawing at the man he was talking to; he did not like the way Johnson pushed his face up so close to the target when making a hard sell.

More important, in his heart Clark subscribed to the Paul Butler theory that the Democratic majority's function was to enunciate, not necessarily pass, a legislative program in preparation for the day when a Democratic President would be back in the White House. Clark's staff on one occasion in 1957 prepared a proposed policy statement listing Democratic party aims and submitted it to Johnson as a possible Senate Democratic policy document. Johnson shuffled it to Earle Clements, staff director of the Senate Democratic Campaign Committee following his defeat in 1956 but still a key Johnson adviser. Clements promptly edited every meaningful phrase out of the document, and the whole matter was dropped.

By the summer of 1958, Clark had come to the tacit conclusion that Johnson was not his kind of leader, and that it was necessary for Northern liberal Senators, hopefully reinforced by the results of the 1958 elections, to demand he relinquish some of the power he exercised. He made that point clearly on July 24, 1958, in a meeting in Paul Douglas' office attended by Clark, Douglas, Pat McNamara, Senator John Carroll of Colorado and, oddly enough, Humphrey—who always managed to walk in the inner sanctums of the liberal rebels while maintaining intimate relations with Johnson.* They determined it was vital to get a significantly higher ratio of Northern liberals on the Democratic Policy and Steering Committees.

Some two weeks after the election, Clark fired the first shot of the liberal revolt. In a November 18 letter to Johnson, Clark first congratulated him on the great Democratic victory (attributing it to a "constructive record of accomplishment of the Democratic Congress, which was in such a large part your personal product") and then moved on to less pleasant matters. Pointing out that Senators from Western and Southern states controlled the party committees in the Senate, Clark urged that the Northeastern states—which decide presidential elections—get "proportional representation" on these committees. "I can think of nothing that would add more at this time to our party's public relations appeal in the North . . ." said Clark.

Here was the public washing of linen that so annoyed Johnson, for the letter inevitably leaked to the press. Johnson delegated the task of turning down Clark to Majority Whip Mike Mansfield, who did so in a letter of December 9 implying that Clark should rely on "the leadership and parliamentary skill of Lyndon Johnson" rather than restructure the party hierarchy. But the question of Policy Committee and Steering Committee membership specifically and a liberal voice in Senate leadership generally recurred again and again through 1959 and 1960, thanks not so much to Clark as to Bill Proxmire.

* It is revealing of the inadequacy in the intelligence system of the rebels that Humphrey was invited to the secret meeting while Proxmire was not.

A man with a taste for the dramatic and a thirst for headlines, Prox-mire was not content with mere letter-writing. Without advance warn-ing, he took the Senate floor on February 23, 1959, to charge "one-man rule" by Johnson and demand that he start holding regular party cau-cuses.* On March 8, he resumed the attack in another Senate speech accusing Johnson of making party policy "on an ad-lib, off-the-cuff basis." While calling this "a brilliantly instinctive performance by a man who has been called an authentic political genius," Proxmire con-tended the Johnson policy was not responsive to other Democratic Senators or to the party platform.

By themselves, neither Clark nor Proxmire bothered Johnson. What did disturb him was the possibility that the big new class of liberal Democrats brought in by the 1958 landslide would join forces with the rebels. The election returns were scarcely in when Johnson was tele-phoning the new Senators-elect, asking them to spend a weekend at the LBJ Ranch. When some of the new Senators indiscreetly told re-porters of the invitations, Johnson cancelled them in irritation. In-stead, when he returned to Washington, he invited them all to his office for the famed Johnson Treatment.

Some of the new men succumbed to The Treatment at first exposure and were promptly inducted into the Johnson Network. But many of the freshmen were new-breed liberals. They might not be unpredicta-ble mavericks like Proxmire or dauntless reformers like Clark, but they were boldly immune to Johnson's wiles. Edmund Muskie, who had cracked the Republican tradition in Maine as a twice-elected Gover-nor and now had unseated a Republican Senator, fit the mold of the independent new breed who were less than overwhelmed by the Johnson Treatment. After the election, Johnson gave Muskie expert advice on how to be a Senator. For instance, Johnson said, don't make up your mind on a key issue even though you may be pressured. "Wait until they get to the M's in the roll call," the Majority Leader advised.

Muskie left impressed but not seduced, as he soon demonstrated during the first big battle of the new 86th Congress. At stake was the biennial fight by Paul Douglas and his liberals to amend Senate Rule XXII governing filibusters, to make it easier for the Senate to vote cloture, forcibly ending debate; a liberalized Rule XXII would make it markedly easier for civil rights legislation to pass. Douglas always had

* Johnson was resting at the LBJ Ranch at the time of Proxmire's attack. De-fending him against Proxmire was Senator Richard Neuberger of Oregon, a lib-eral member of the Johnson Network. "Unless my memory fails me, the Senator from Wisconsin, during that portion of his career before he was elected to a six-year term [on November 5, 1958] probably 'buttered up' the Majority Leader more than any other Senator," Neuberger told the Senate.

failed, but now, with the Senate top-heavy with Democrats, he had new hope.

Once again, however, Johnson prepared more carefully than the liberals. Senator Richard Russell and his Southerners agreed privately to a slight modification of Rule XXII but nothing so much as Douglas wanted. Thus, Johnson could avoid a session-opening filibuster that would cast a pall over the entire session if only he could table the original proposal of the liberals.* Then he could push through the compromise and get on to more pleasant matters.

Bobby Baker's head count showed Johnson had votes to spare. But he wanted something more: support from the freshman Democratic Senators. If he could win backing from them on the Rule XXII fight, with its emotion-packed civil rights connotations, he could show the Clarks and the Proxmires there really was no base of support inside the Class of '58 for a revolt against him.

Most of the freshman Democrats were invited to Johnson's ornate new suite of offices just off the Senate floor—irreverently called the Taj Mahal because of their Byzantine splendor—for a dose of the Johnson Treatment.† Each was told how a bitter filibuster over Rule XXII could only help the Republican party and particularly Vice-President Nixon, a strong supporter of the liberals against Johnson; how it was important to dispose of this divisive issue as soon as possible and get on to the major business at hand; how no filibuster stopped the 1957 Civil Rights Act and none would stop a civil rights bill in the future.

But included in the Class of '58 were members of a postwar generation of politicians who did not wilt easily. After Johnson completed his argument to Ed Muskie of Maine, for instance, he asked Muskie how he was going to vote. Remembering his previous chat with the Majority Leader, the soft-spoken young Senator replied with a smile: "Well, Senator, I think I'll follow your advice and just wait until they get to the M's." Johnson was not amused.

But behind the soft argument was an unspoken threat. Muskie and all the other freshmen knew that committee assignments would not be

* Specifically, Rule XXII provided for cloture to be voted by two-thirds of the entire Senate. Johnson's compromise eased this slightly by providing cloture to be voted by two-thirds of all Senators *present and voting*. The liberals wanted cloture by a simple majority.

† Johnson moved out of his relatively small, relatively Spartan Majority Leader's office at the beginning of the 1959 session. Commandeering the offices long used by the District of Columbia Committee, Johnson hired an interior decorator in New York. The result was the Taj Mahal, a Hollywood director's conception of what a United States Senator's office ought to look like, resplendent in green and gold.

doled out to them until *after* the Rule XXII questions were settled. There was, then, a large question of how a freshman Senator who voted against Lyndon B. Johnson, Majority Leader, would fare when committee assignments were made by Lyndon B. Johnson, chairman of the Democratic Steering Committee.

The key vote came on January 9, 1959. The liberal motion was killed by a 60 to 36 vote. The fifteen freshmen split 8 to 7 in Johnson's favor. On January 12, the Senate adopted Johnson's compromise, 72 to 22— the votes against coming mainly from the Southern Democrats as a token of opposition—and what had all the earmarks of a divisive issue lasting for months was settled in two weeks. This minor masterpiece indicated that big majority or no big majority, the Johnson System was as effective as ever.*

Paul Douglas was heartsick. Ever since election day, he had dreamed of that big new liberal strength in the Senate passing into law everything he felt had been frustrated by the Johnson System, beginning with reform of Rule XXII. What particularly bothered Douglas was the vote Johnson got from the freshmen. That same concern was expressed loudly to Bobby Baker in a Capitol corridor just after the vote by United Auto Workers official Roy Reuther, Walter's outspoken younger brother. While spectators watched in wonder, Reuther denounced Baker and Johnson for corrupting the new freshman Senators who had been elected with organized labor's campaign contributions.

Yet there were soft spots in Johnson's triumph. Considering his weapon of committee assignments, it was a wonder that even six of the freshmen—Ed Muskie included—dared to vote against the Majority Leader. The threat was not imaginary. Muskie, the former Governor of Maine, was awarded two of the least desirable committees: Government Operations and Public Works. Senator Vance Hartke of Indiana, a freshman who had made the big jump from Mayor of Evansville to the Senate, voted for Johnson on January 9 and found himself on two of the most coveted committees, Finance and Commerce. Moreover, the fight over Rule XXII was fuzzy and procedural, permitting a Senator from Indiana or Wyoming or Connecticut to give the Majority Leader a vote without fear of reprisals back home.

Thus, six freshman defections from Johnson pointed to greater defections ahead on substantive domestic issues unless Johnson was pre-

* That was the general interpretation by reporters covering the Senate. Typical was the *New York Times* account of January 11, which said: "It is . . . clear that Mr. Johnson is now more thoroughly master of the Senate than at any time during the past four years of leadership." Erroneous though this analysis proved to be, it was widely held.

pared to adopt a legislative program far more liberal and ambitious than anything he had pushed during his previous four years as Majority Leader. Such a program, however, would put him in direct conflict with President Eisenhower. On that January 12, 1959, when Johnson once again demonstrated his old mastery over the Senate, no one anticipated how deep that conflict would soon become, and how enthusiastically Eisenhower would join battle with Johnson.

Eugene McCarthy of Minnesota, a prominent liberal in the House who was elected to the Senate in the landslide of 1958, was asked the day after the election whether Lyndon Johnson would move to the left in the wake of the greatest liberal triumph in twenty-two years. A man of biting wit, McCarthy replied: "Lyndon doesn't lean *with* the wind; he leans *ahead* of it." *

Apart from opposing the liberals on Rule XXII, Johnson in the early days of 1959 was fulfilling Gene McCarthy's prophecy of a leftward drift. His "State of the Union" message, delivered for the second straight year to the Senate Democratic caucus one day before the President's constitutionally ordained message, was nothing like the broadly bipartisan discussion of the space program of a year earlier. Instead, it proclaimed that henceforth the size and shape of legislation would be determined exclusively by the Democrats of Capitol Hill with hardly a glance toward the White House. Scoffing at Eisenhower's post-election pleas for Democrats to keep their spending aspirations within the confines of a balanced budget, Johnson told the caucus that there are worse deficits than budget deficits.

> There is between the people and the government a deficit of vigor, a deficit of confidence, and a deficit of will. . . . This is the start of a new era . . . we have—by our majority here—an obligation to lead—we shall honor the mandate.

In chats with reporters, Johnson and Bobby Baker planted the idea that the Majority Leader would use the huge Democratic majorities to pass a package of legislation not seen since Franklin D. Roosevelt's Hundred Days of 1933. Once the Rule XXII fight was out of the way, Johnson announced that the few weeks until Easter—a period usually frittered away in a new Congress—would be used to pass enough major legislation to last a whole session in an ordinary year.

* When the remark got back to him, Johnson failed to see the humor. He urged Speaker Rayburn, who counted McCarthy among his protégés, to caution him about making such public statements. McCarthy later became an admirer of Johnson and an occasional member of the Johnson Network.

Here was a new and bolder Johnson. Never before had he specifically revealed such grandiose plans; that is, just what bills he was supporting and when he wanted them passed. Moreover, on each measure specified by Johnson for pre-Easter passage, the Democratic position was sharply at variance with Eisenhower's. In fact, the Democratic versions of two bills in Johnson's new package—one on airport construction, the other dealing with depressed areas—were almost identical to measures vetoed by the President in 1958.

If Johnson was bolder in challenging Eisenhower, he had ample justification. Never had the old general seemed weaker in the nation, in the Congress, and, most important, in his own party. In a post-election meeting of the Republican National Committee at Des Moines, Iowa, on January 22, 1959, party leaders did not bother concealing their suspicion that Eisenhower's inattention to party matters and domestic affairs generally had produced the debacle the previous November. This rude treatment of the only Republican to be elected President in a generation fulfilled the Constitutional scholars' grim prophecy about the Twenty-second Amendment, limiting the President to two terms. Eisenhower was the first President bound by the change and now he seemed destined to be an impotent lame duck his last two years in office. *

But neither Johnson nor the insolent Republican politicians at Des Moines realized the transformation Eisenhower was undergoing in the Indian summer of his presidency. At the root of the change was the fall of Sherman Adams the previous autumn. More assistant President than chief of staff, Adams relieved Eisenhower of responsibilities he should have carried out himself, particularly in domestic affairs. Now Adams was gone, with nobody to replace him. Eisenhower resumed policy functions he had imperceptibly relinquished to Adams.

Adams' departure also significantly weakened the liberal wing of the Eisenhower Administration. The stony-faced little Yankee had fought hard and well against Eisenhower's two budget-balancing Secretaries of the Treasury, George M. Humphrey and Robert B. Anderson. With Adams gone, the administration's conservative wing—now led more effectively by the clever Anderson than by the overbearing Humphrey—was in ascendancy. Besides, Eisenhower's six years in the White House had made him steadily more conservative. Budget-balancing had now become a sacred cause.

For Eisenhower to crusade for a balanced budget in 1959 seemed to

---

* Eisenhower entered the White House favoring repeal of the Twenty-second Amendment but changed his mind by the time he left. His own experience caused the conversion.

be an incredible display of political naïveté. At precisely the moment when Republican strength was at its lowest in twenty years and his own political power also was waning, he put on the armor of fiscal conservatism. Yet, Eisenhower had certain new resources. The catastrophe of the 1958 election had so reduced Republican ranks that it gave them a new cohesiveness and *esprit de corps*. This new morale was further enhanced by the change in leadership in both Houses of Congress: amiable, fumbling Joseph W. Martin, Jr., of Massachusetts was deposed as House Republican Leader and replaced with partisan, whip-cracking Charles Halleck of Indiana. In the Senate, infinitely flexible Everett McKinley Dirksen of Illinois replaced the stolid Knowland, who ran for Governor of California and crashed in the wreckage of the 1958 elections. Unlike Knowland and Martin, the two new leaders were not above twisting arms to get Republican solidarity.

Within days after the election, Eisenhower remarked to his closest aides that he planned to dedicate himself to halt the imminent spending spree of the Democrats. He kept the promise. On the same day that Johnson declared his legislative independence at the Democratic caucus, Eisenhower met with Republican congressional leaders at the White House. "Every sort of foolish proposal will be advanced in the name of national security and the 'poor fellow,' " he told them. "We've got to convince Americans that thrift is not a bad word."

Yet, skepticism that the lame-duck President could accomplish much against the Democratic Congress ran high in Washington, even among some of the senior Republicans who were at that White House meeting on January 13. No one foresaw the extraordinary resilience of the lame-duck presidency—or what was about to happen to Lyndon Johnson in his last two years as Majority Leader.

In the first weeks of 1959, the Senate followed Johnson's headlong legislative timetable at the pace of the Hundred Days and followed his strategy (enunciated in his January 13 "State of the Union" speech) of enacting bills without concern for Eisenhower's economy strictures. At Johnson's prodding, the Senate Commerce and Banking Committees got off to their earliest start in a generation, working on bills providing federal funds for airport construction and comprehensive housing. By the end of January, both bills had reached the Senate floor and both carried enough money to assure a veto from the new Eisenhower.

But even then, with his intuitive sense of the mood of Capitol Hill,

Johnson was worried that the momentum derived from the November landslide had been lost. For once, Eisenhower was taking a position and sticking to it. In his weekly press conferences, he delivered little sermons on the value of thrift and the evil of profligacy, spiced by threats of vetoes. Privately, he referred to his "veto pistol." A great body of Democrats in Congress, not so committed to social welfare spending as Joe Clark and Paul Douglas, fussed with each other in Capitol Hill cloakrooms about the danger of being labeled the spend-thrift party, and to Johnson these fears were particularly vivid.

In a party fund-raising speech at Albuquerque, New Mexico, on January 24, Johnson subtly modified his previous hard line against budget-balancing. Claiming that the Democrats were the real econo-mizers, Johnson bragged about earlier budget cuts by the Democratic Congress, adding: "To set the present administration up as the guard-ian of the balanced budget is in the same class as hiring a coyote for a watchdog over the sheep." * That was precisely what liberal Demo-crats, inside and outside the Senate, dreaded. In a public relations contest over who had the best record at economizing, they felt the Republicans would always beat the Democrats. Johnson was being lured by Eisenhower to fight on unfavorable terrain.

Anxious to get major legislation passed before an informal congres-sional recess for political speeches the week of February 9, Johnson brought up the housing bill the night of February 5. His handling of that measure showed the success of the President's campaign of exhor-tation. Johnson made short work of efforts by Douglas and Clark to beef up the bill with additional money for urban renewal. Just before final passage, Johnson himself took the floor in a surprise move to ask elimination of some 250 million dollars in spending authority from the bill. Liberals were angry but had no choice except to go along. Clearly, Johnson was trying to pass a veto-proof bill, and the consen-sus-sized 60 to 28 margin indicated he might be succeeding.

Johnson repeated the performance the next night in the Senate when the airport aid bill came up. Just before passage, Johnson again took the floor to cut 100 million dollars from the bill in an unexpected move. Again, Johnson's compromising achieved a consensus vote, 63 to 22, for final passage.

On those two winter evenings in the Senate, Johnson set the course of his last two unhappy years as Majority Leader. The attempts to compromise the housing and airport bills, setting a pattern for the entire 86th Congress, infuriated the liberals but failed to satisfy Eisen-

* Johnson consistently overstated the amount of money cut from Eisenhower's budget by the Democratic Congress.

hower. Despite Johnson's last-minute spending reductions, the President was adamant against both bills. With Dirksen and Halleck enforcing Republican discipline as Knowland and Martin never did, Eisenhower knew the Democrats could not reach the two-thirds vote necessary to override his vetoes.

The housing bill was vetoed. The Democrats promptly sent a substitute to the White House, only slightly scaled down. It too was vetoed. Finally, amid more grumbling from the liberals, Johnson passed a third housing bill tailored to the President's specifications. The airport bill was further trimmed in the House and won the President's approval.

After his capitulation on those first two bills, Johnson slowed the Senate's frenetic pace to a dreary dogtrot. His plan for a huge body of legislation by Easter was abandoned. Long before Easter, it was clear this was to be no Hundred Days. But even more difficult from Johnson's standpoint, the balancing act that was so much a part of the Johnson System in an evenly divided Senate, with a passive Eisenhower, had become impossible. By seeking a middle course, the Majority Leader was whipsawed. Attempting to pass welfare legislation broad enough to satisfy the liberals and still avoid vetoes, Johnson achieved neither goal. Veto after veto came from Eisenhower's pen in a profusion not seen since Grover Cleveland declared war on the pension bills for Civil War veterans. Johnson simply could not make his bills veto-proof without risking rebellion in Democratic ranks. Indeed, his efforts to meet the newly intransigent Eisenhower halfway evoked more Democratic criticism of him in 1959 than in all his previous six years as Democratic floor leader combined.

Proxmire's continued floor attacks on Johnson were publicly supported by Wayne Morse and Paul Douglas. Joe Clark continued to pressure Johnson to liberalize the Steering and Policy Committees. When the Senate passed an unemployment compensation bill tailored to Eisenhower's specifications, Pat McNamara publicly blamed Johnson. These mutterings soon spread beyond the ranks of hard-core liberals. On June 16, Johnson whipped through the Senate an increase in the maximum interest rate on GI home mortgages, avoiding an inevitable floor fight with the liberals by giving no notice that it would be considered. Although Johnson was only trying to bargain with Eisenhower—unsuccessfully, as it turned out—over the fate of the housing bill, he received heated protests on the Senate floor after the bill passed from the two border-state moderates: Albert Gore of Tennessee and Mike Monroney of Oklahoma. A year earlier it would have been inconceivable for either of them to attack Johnson openly.

Democratic National Chairman Paul M. Butler, seeing his old foe in trouble in his own constituency, leaped to the attack. On June 14, his Democratic Advisory Council assailed "time-consuming efforts" in Congress "to water down proposed legislation to the limits the President might accept." Butler himself kept up a steady drumfire. "I hope," he said on July 5, "that we will be laying a bill upon the President's desk even though knowing in advance that he may veto it and letting it be known . . . we will take the issue to the American people."

By late spring, Johnson had become sensitive to sniping from the left. In January he had tolerated Proxmire's assaults with bored amusement. Now they began to draw blood. On May 28, Johnson finally replied to a Proxmire attack. Speaking without a prepared script, Johnson told the Senate that Proxmire needed "a fairy godmother" or a "wet nurse." When a Senator doesn't get his way, said Johnson, "he puts the blame on the leadership." Then looking Proxmire in the face, Johnson told the Senate: "It does not take much courage, I may say, to make the leadership a punching bag."

That Lyndon Johnson would deign to reply to William Proxmire showed how far his situation had deteriorated in five months. Johnson had searched in vain for imaginative new schemes that would avoid trouble with both the newly invigorated President and Johnson's newly unwieldy Democratic majority. Calling his staff together in the Taj Mahal, Johnson would berate them for failing to produce any such Solomonic solutions.

In fact, Johnson's perpetual staffing problem was as acute as ever, in large degree because of himself. James Wilson, a bright young Austin lawyer from Alvin Wirtz's old law firm who had been summoned by Johnson in January, 1959, to fill one of the recurring gaps on his staff, was quickly elevated by the Majority Leader to serve as a key policy adviser. As so frequently happened, however, Wilson's status was only temporary. Johnson soon grew irked with Wilson's independence of mind and unwillingness to follow his leader's every wish. For example, Johnson wanted to help Senator Herman Talmadge of Georgia pass a bill to negate a Supreme Court decision affecting interstate taxation. Johnson strongly hinted he wanted an opinion from Wilson supporting the measure. Instead, Wilson's memorandum flatly opposed the Talmadge Bill, attacking it as a violation of the federal process. "I didn't need to bring you all the way up here from Texas to tell me that," Johnson rasped at his young aide. "I could have got that from any Eastern lawyer." By the end of 1959, Jim Wilson was relegated to largely routine assignments. By summer's end in 1960, he had returned to law practice in Austin.

Gerry Siegel, who had played an invaluable role as a Johnson adviser in passage of the 1957 Civil Rights Act, was lured back to Washington from a position on the Harvard Law faculty by Johnson in 1960 when another civil rights fight was in the offing. But having won Siegel back, Johnson inexplicably ignored him and made little use of him. Along with Wilson, he left Johnson's staff at the end of the summer in 1960.*

Apart from Wilson and Siegel, there were no changes on Johnson's staff in 1959–60. Bobby Baker and George Reedy performed their familiar functions. The "Texas office" was still run by Walter Jenkins with a staff including Lloyd Hand. Harry McPherson continued to work on day-to-day routine legislation. There was no real chief of staff.

Goaded by Johnson, this staff did, in early 1959, produce a proposal for a special commission on unemployment, its members to be chosen by Eisenhower, Johnson, and Rayburn. The commission would be given sixty days to hold hearings around the country and draft recommendations. Based on the theory that the economy was fundamentally sound, now that the recession of 1958 had run its course, Johnson's scheme was really aimed at chronic pockets of poverty.† Here was a Johnson answer to the cross-fire peppering him: a pump-priming welfare program that wouldn't cost much because it was limited to a relatively small number of areas.

Johnson carefully prepared the way in the Senate, collecting sixty-eight co-sponsors—including Minority Leader Dirksen—even before he introduced the resolution to create the commission. On April 10, less than forty-eight hours after its introduction, and with only ten minutes of debate, the resolution was passed by a voice vote of the Senate. It was fast work—too fast. The resolution had scarcely cleared before protest boiled up from organized labor that the commission was a clever gimmick to sweep the problem of unemployment under the rug and appease Eisenhower. The liberal furor over the proposal grew so intense that Speaker Rayburn convinced Johnson to let it die a quiet death in the House. The resolution had cleared the Senate with unanimity and a fanfare of publicity, but it wasn't even referred to committee in the House.

Another Johnson brainstorm to establish liberal Democratic economic policy without running afoul of Eisenhower's vetoes fared little better. Johnson wanted the Joint Economic Committee to conduct a

---

* Wilson returned to the old Wirtz law office. Siegel became a vice-president of the *Washington Post*.

† The commission proposal was an intimation of Lyndon Johnson's War on Poverty less than five years later.

well-publicized inquiry into the problems of unemployment, growth, and inflation, patterned after the famed Temporary National Economic Committee investigation in the late 1930s headed by Senator Joseph O'Mahoney of Wyoming. As Johnson saw it, the Joint Economic Committee would travel the country to take testimony and put the blame for creeping inflation, stunted growth, and chronic unemployment squarely on six years of Republicanism. Calling the shots and getting credit for the inquiry, of course, would be Lyndon Johnson.

But so long as Johnson's old rival, Paul Douglas, was chairman of the Joint Committee, that would be difficult if not impossible. Johnson asked a favor of Senator John Sparkman of Alabama. Would Sparkman invoke seniority over Douglas, take the chairmanship of the Joint Committee, and run the investigation as Johnson's lieutenant? Though no Johnson intimate, Sparkman was infinitely friendlier to Johnson than the uncompromising Douglas. Sparkman mulled the question for days. To take the joint committee chairmanship would mean relinquishing his chairmanship of the Small Business Committee, which might prove more valuable in his campaign for re-election that year. Besides, the courteous Sparkman was a mild man with not an enemy in the Senate. He flinched at the thought of shoving Douglas out of his one place of power in the Senate. Sparkman's answer to Johnson was no.

The investigation was conducted by Douglas, but not the way Johnson wanted. Douglas had no interest in a highly publicized probe, traveling the country coast to coast. The Senate's only professional economist conducted a scholarly, dry inquiry into such esoteric subjects as the Federal Reserve System's open market operations. The hearings and reports of the Douglas investigation were a landmark for economists for years to come, but they weren't the political bombshell that Johnson had been seeking.

Hardly anything seemed to go right for Johnson in 1959 after his virtuoso performance in the Rule XXII fight. Even his fabled political gyroscope seemed occasionally to go out of kilter, as it did when President Eisenhower decided to take the initiative on fiscal responsibility. Cheered by his success with the veto, Eisenhower launched a major legislative effort to remove the 4¼ percent interest ceiling on new government bonds. Interest rates were climbing at such a wild pace that the government was being shut out of the long-term money market. To finance the debt, the Treasury was selling short-term bills (government securities of less than one year's duration) to banks, the highly inflationary equivalent of printing-press money. Robert Ander-

son, the articulate Secretary of the Treasury, told Eisenhower that repeal of the 4¼ percent ceiling (first enacted as a war measure in 1918)
was essential to preservation of the dollar and, indeed, the republic
itself.

On its face, here was a golden opportunity for Johnson to lead the
fight against Eisenhower and tight money. Johnson was ever watchful
for issues that could unite his party's Northern and Southern wing,
and no other issue could bring Hubert Humphrey and Strom Thurmond together so well as a populistic onslaught against the high-
interest bankers of Wall Street. Considering Johnson's double problem
of 1959, the interest limit repealer was ideal. In one stroke, Johnson
could 1) please the swelling ranks of liberals who complained he was
soft on Eisenhower, and 2) score a much-needed victory against
Eisenhower on an issue where the President's veto power would not
come into play.

Finally, there were sound arguments against the interest rate repealer. The conservative tight-money policy practiced by Robert Anderson had helped drive up interest rates in the first place, and, so the
Democrats argued, he could drive them down again by expanding the
supply of money. But repeal of the 4¼ percent ceiling on Governments would only speed up soaring interest rates, to the enrichment of
the bankers. Here was an issue on which a hungry descendant of
Texas Populists could happily gorge.

But Johnson didn't. To the surprise of Capitol Hill, Johnson was
going along with the repealer, even though he made no public announcement. The reason was Bob Anderson, who milked his old relationships with his fellow Texans in Congress. In private conversation,
the persuasive Anderson convinced Rayburn and, not quite so firmly,
Johnson, that the repealer was essential to save the integrity of the
dollar. But in a more profound sense, Johnson's seeming repudiation
of his Populist background was a signal that the initiative in Washington had passed to Dwight D. Eisenhower, that now it was Johnson
going along with Eisenhower, and that incredibly, Johnson had failed
to comprehend that his support of the interest limit repealer would
split the Democratic party down the middle.

Johnson was saved from his error. Donald Cook, his trusted adviser
now an electric utility executive in Wall Street, pleaded with him not
to support the repealer. So did other liberal-oriented friends in the
New York financial community. Johnson began to change his tune. In
late May, he told reporters privately and not for publication that although he didn't have a public position on the repealer, "Paul Douglas is *my* economist, and I always pay close attention to what he has

to say on economics, whatever our differences on other things." The statement was patently absurd. Johnson consulted Douglas on nothing and never asked his opinion on repeal of the interest ceiling. But Douglas was a public foe of repeal, and this was Johnson's circuitous way of flashing his intentions.

By June 9, Johnson was slightly less obtuse. While still not taking an outright position against repeal, he talked about "considerable congressional skepticism" over making "the sky the limit on interest rates." He added in language his Populist grandfather would have admired: "It is difficult to believe that the most powerful government in the free world is powerless to keep the cost of money down to a point where it is within the reach of the average American."

But still, Johnson had not committed himself, and he never did. When liberal Democratic Congressmen threatened an open revolt, Rayburn decided to lay aside Anderson's bill in the interests of party unity. Johnson emerged from the non-fight unscarred, but un-laureled also. He had missed an opportunity to lead his party in a session singularly lacking in opportunities.

As the hot summer approached, Johnson's frustration mounted. And from that frustration came the Majority Leader's only clear victory of 1959, but a victory in a cause of questionable merit.

When President Eisenhower named Admiral Lewis L. Strauss as Secretary of Commerce on October 24, 1958, in the midst of the congressional election campaign, there was no hard comment from Lyndon Johnson or any other Democrat. If, on the other hand, Eisenhower had named him to another term as chairman of the Atomic Energy Commission, a post he had held since 1953, reaction would have been harsh and instantaneous from critical members of the Joint Atomic Energy Commission and particularly from its chairman, Senator Clinton P. Anderson of New Mexico. The AEC and the Joint Committee had a unique relationship, one of unusual intimacy for a congressional committee and an executive agency. For years, the congressional committee had exercised an important influence on the commission.

But Strauss, a stiff-backed financier from Richmond, Virginia, who once was an aide to Herbert Hoover and had served as a rear admiral in World War II, had none of the soft soap needed for congressional relations. He was a man of unquestioned ability with an unfortunate tendency of seeming pompous and vain. Tension between him and the Joint Committee grew over a stormy six years until Clinton

Anderson, a man of pride and passion himself, made it clear he would do all in his power to block Strauss for another six-year term as AEC Chairman in 1958.

Realizing the impossibility of his relationship with Anderson, Strauss declined Eisenhower's proffered reappointment. The President then named him to be Secretary of Commerce. With the Senate in recess, Strauss was sworn in on November 13, 1958. Inside the administration, it was felt that this austere conservative would fill the void left by George Humphrey as strong man of the Cabinet. There was scarcely a hint of deep trouble in the Senate.

Six years later, Eisenhower wrote that "by virtue of his extraordinary experience in government and in business, Lewis Strauss was supremely qualified" and "would have been one of the most outstanding Secretaries of Commerce in the history of the office." Eisenhower added: "It should not have taken the Senate more than three minutes to confirm his appointment. . . ."

Perhaps it wouldn't had it not been for Anderson, one of the most formidable of the Senate elders. So bitter was Anderson's dislike and distrust of Strauss that he dedicated himself to block the confirmation. It became his consuming passion. A figure of great prestige and with many friends in the Senate, Clinton Anderson began stirring up opposition to Strauss. Clearly, the nomination was going to take a good deal more than three minutes.

Hearings did not begin until March 17, and it was immediately clear they would be systematically sabotaged. Delay followed delay. Still, even his tormentors on the Senate Commerce Committee confided that they really did not intend to kill Strauss' nomination, but only scare him a bit and in the process instill in this proud man some respect for Congress as a separate and coordinate branch of government. Indeed, Strauss probably would have been confirmed had it not been for Admiral Lewis Strauss himself. Haughty and unbending, his testimony and general conduct at the hearings turned friends into neutrals and neutrals into foes. Although his nomination was reported to the Senate floor with a 9 to 8 favorable vote (an unusual lack of confidence for a Cabinet nominee), it was now clear that Dwight D. Eisenhower was in danger of becoming the first President in thirty-four years to suffer the indignity of the Senate rejecting a Cabinet nominee.[*]

Lyndon Johnson had no particular interest in Strauss as a public

---

[*] In 1925, the Senate rejected President Coolidge's nomination of Charles B. Warren as Attorney General because of his past association as a lawyer for the "sugar trust."

official, as a conservative ideologist, or as a person. Moreover, all his instincts favored giving a President, any President, unlimited choice in picking his Cabinet, particularly when, as in the case of Strauss, there was no hint of corruption or malfeasance. Had 1959 been anything like Johnson's four previous years as Majority Leader, he quite likely would have supported the Admiral. Unfortunately for Strauss, 1959 was different.

Even before Strauss' nomination was reported by the Commerce Committee, Johnson dispatched Bobby Baker to do a hard head count, making sure that each Senator realized the Majority Leader himself had no position. The result of the head count gave Strauss an edge. But the margin was so close that whichever way Johnson would go might well decide the matter. By now, moreover, the Strauss confirmation hearing had become a liberal witch hunt to rid the Eisenhower Cabinet of its most inflexible conservative. If Johnson should now save Strauss, liberal revolt against his leadership would reach a new crescendo and damage whatever chance he might have for the presidential nomination in 1960. Besides, Johnson had been taking unaccustomed lickings at Eisenhower's hands all year long. He was frustrated, anxious for a victory.

Johnson still said not a word about Strauss, publicly or privately. But when he dispatched Bobby Baker on a head count a second time, Baker informed fence-sitting and pro-Strauss Democratic Senators that "we" are going to be *against* the nomination. When word of this startling development seeped into the cloakrooms, the tide turned against Strauss. Two liberal Democrats who had been for Strauss, John F. Kennedy and Richard Neuberger, now were against him.* Johnson rounded up conservative members of the Johnson Network who might otherwise have supported Strauss: Allen Frear of Delaware, Herman Talmadge of Georgia, Alan Bible of Nevada.

One new member of the Johnson Network, freshman Senator Thomas J. Dodd of Connecticut, was not impressed by a Bobby Baker report that Johnson was against Strauss. A militant anti-Communist conservative in foreign affairs, but a liberal on most domestic issues, Dodd could find nothing in Strauss' record to justify rejection. Strauss' annoying arrogance, coupled with a few contradictions in his testimony, simply could not, in Dodd's view, justify the ultimate weapon of rejection. Even when Johnson himself telephoned, Dodd clung to his independent judgment and reiterated he would vote for Strauss. Dodd then sprained his ankle on a visit home to Connecticut and read the complete Commerce Committee transcript of the Strauss hearings

---

* Kennedy's switch, like Johnson's decision to oppose Strauss, was partly dictated by his presidential ambitions.

while recuperating. The record simply reinforced his conviction that there was nothing to warrant the senatorial lynching of Lewis Strauss.

When he returned to Washington, Dodd informed Johnson he would not only vote for Strauss but would speak in his behalf. When Johnson saw he could not prevail on Dodd, he asked him to delay the speech until he got the word from Johnson. Dodd agreed and found himself waiting out the debate until the final night. Finally, the word came from Johnson. Dodd made his carefully prepared speech during the dinner hour, when the Senate was all but empty. Whether Dodd could have swayed votes anyway was doubtful, but Johnson took no chances.

Lyndon Johnson and Clinton Anderson collaborated closely in rounding up the vote, but it was Johnson who told Anderson when the killing vote was in hand. All the while, the Majority Leader's own position was Washington's deepest conundrum—his decision supposedly not to be made without deepest consideration. Johnson took no part in the debate, revealing his position only when the roll call reached the J's. He did not explain the reason for his vote against Strauss.

At thirty-five minutes past midnight on June 19, 1959, when the vote was taken, the Senate refused to confirm Strauss, 49 to 46. Two Republican votes were needed, and they came from William Langer of North Dakota and Margaret Chase Smith of Maine—neither of whom were strangers to giving Johnson the margin of victory.

In his eight years of friendship and jousting with Johnson, no action of the Majority Leader so angered and so hurt Dwight D. Eisenhower. Yet, it was for Johnson a victory in the old style: dramatic, close, secretive—but somehow also joyless. For the cause was in question.

Senator J. W. Fulbright of Arkansas, subject to the intense lobbying pressures from both sides, never could make up his mind and sat out the vote in the cloakroom. A few days later, he explained: "I just couldn't resolve the question satisfactorily, and under the circumstances I thought it was wiser not to vote, with the outcome as close as it was. It is still a difficult question, and I don't know whether the Senate did right or not."

Some of the Senators who voted against Strauss were to share Fulbright's doubt far into the future.

If rejection of Lewis Strauss was the low point of the 86th Congress for President Eisenhower, the high point of domestic legislation for his entire eight years in the White House was passage of the Landrum-Griffin Labor Reform Act later in 1959. It was steeped in ironies. This conservative piece of legislation, lobbied to a point of frenzy by employer groups and supported by a Republican President, was passed by the most Democratic and liberal Congress in twenty years. Eisenhower, who cared little about fine points of legislation and even less about the legislative process, was primarily responsible for the most important bill to be passed by the 87th Congress. Lyndon B. Johnson, champion of legislative combat and infighting, stood idly by, almost powerless to affect the result—save for one bizarre aspect of the struggle in the Senate quite apart from the mainstream of the labor reform fight.

That fight had its genesis in the revelations of scandal in the Teamsters and other unions, dug up and exposed with lavish publicity by the special Senate Rackets Committee, headed by Senator John L. McClellan of Arkansas with Robert F. Kennedy as chief counsel. Organized labor insisted that public storm over the shocking revelations of the McClellan Committee could be weathered, but the committee's second-ranking Democrat—Senator John F. Kennedy—disagreed. To the tune of heckling from honest and dishonest union leaders alike, Kennedy introduced a relatively mild labor reform bill that attempted to crack down on racketeering and thievery inside the unions without coming to grips with union power. It whizzed through the Senate in 1958 but was killed in the House by a strange coalition of pro-business Congressmen, who thought the bill too easy, and pro-union Congressmen, who found it too tough. Kennedy re-introduced pretty much the same bill in 1959. Once again, it seemed destined for trouble in the House and smooth sailing in the Senate.

But by the time Kennedy's bill reached the Senate floor in mid-April, a new factor had entered the picture: John McClellan, the dour, self-righteous investigative specialist, had backed Kennedy's bill in 1958 but now in 1959 was determined to stiffen it. McClellan's major project was a "Bill of Rights" for union members that would guarantee rank-and-file union members all manner of rights—of membership, of voting, of free speech—enforceable in the federal courts. Anguished labor leaders, who claimed it would turn the labor movement into a madhouse at the whim of dissident union members, were assured the votes would be found to defeat McClellan. As floor manager, Jack Kennedy had no choice but to trust the Majority Leader to get the votes for him.

The result on the night of April 22 was stunning. The McClellan Bill of Rights was adopted by a 47 to 46 vote. Up for reconsideration, there was a 46 to 46 tie, with Vice-President Nixon, as presiding officer of the Senate, breaking the tie to cast the deciding vote in favor of the McClellan Amendment.

A flabbergasted Senator rushed to Bobby Baker. "What the hell happened?" he asked in tones of shock. "I guess I counted wrong," Baker shrugged.

It was a strange miscount. Johnson, of course, voted with Kennedy against McClellan. But usually reliable members of the Johnson Network—Dennis Chavez of New Mexico, Margaret Chase Smith of Maine, Thomas J. Dodd of Connecticut—inexplicably wound up voting for the McClellan Amendment.* Nor did Johnson seem to exhibit the same agitation and involvement he usually did when a close vote was at stake.

Moreover, although the outcome was scarcely detrimental to Johnson, it wounded two potential political opponents. Nixon, the probable Republican candidate for President the next year, was again placed in the uncomfortable position of breaking a tie on a highly controversial issue, a delicate position the Majority Leader had often contrived for him in the past. This time, Nixon cast an anti-union vote. And Kennedy, by now the front-runner for the Democratic presidential nomination, was also hurt politically among labor leaders when the McClellan Amendment was adopted. These labor leaders viewed Kennedy's bill as only barely acceptable without the amendment. They long had worried what would happen to it when it reached the Senate floor. Now their worst fears were realized, and they blamed Kennedy more than Johnson.

Seemingly unperturbed by the stunning defeat, Johnson beckoned staffer James Wilson to his front-row desk. Johnson told him he needed an explanation for his conservative constituents as to why he had voted against the conservative-backed McClellan Amendment. What Johnson expected from Wilson was a routine form letter. He got something quite different.

Sitting down at the typewriter in the Democratic Policy Committee offices on the third floor of the Capitol, Wilson banged out an ingenious apologia for Johnson—or any Southerner. It began:

> The McClellan Amendment passed on April 22 contains a sleeper which is extremely harmful to the South's position on civil rights legislation. In enacting a so-called "labor bill of rights," it follows provisions of the U.S. Constitution. . . .
>
> There are thousands of unions and union locals in the South which have both white and Negro members, but racial segregation is maintained. This amendment effectively prohibits discrimination within the union because of race. The effect will be

* Dodd, however, had represented a dissident group of Teamsters in 1958 before his election to the Senate and had strong convictions about rank-and-file union rights.

widespread. Not only would an integrated union be required, but integrated social activities such as union dances, integrated union youth programs, and integrated union resorts, for example, would also be required.

Wilson, a liberal and an advocate of civil rights, was carried away by his ingenious legal concept. The McClellan Amendment, he continued, could be "the first step of a broad federal FEPC [Fair Employment Practices Commission] program." The amendment provided tools "much broader than any ever proposed under civil rights bills."

He saved the most lurid specter for last. Southern Senators who backed the McClellan Amendment—and almost all did except for pro-labor Olin Johnston of South Carolina—were unwittingly voting to resurrect the detested and rejected Part III of the 1957 civil rights bill, empowering the United States Attorney General to sue in the federal courts for desegregation of Southern schools.* Stripped from the Civil Rights Act by Johnson's patient maneuvers then, it now was sneaking back by the cellar door, according to Wilson's memo:

> . . . damaging precedent has been set for "Part III" type enforcement provisions for school segregation. . . . If the Secretary of Labor can integrate thousands of union locals, the Attorney General would have little trouble integrating the schools of the South.

Wilson tossed the memorandum on the Majority Leader's desk in the Senate chamber the next morning. The full significance of the memorandum hit Johnson immediately. Here was far more than a letter to appease conservative Texans. Here was a weapon that might reverse what had been done the night before, and as a legislative technician Johnson could not pass up such a golden opportunity, even though he had had no prearranged plan to undo the previous night's work.

Wilson's memorandum was typed up verbatim except for substituting "Equal Rights Amendment" for "McClellan Amendment." Johnson saw no need to irritate John McClellan. Passed among Southern Senators, it caused a furor. Solemn John Stennis of Mississippi walked about the Senate floor, deeply concerned over what he had done. "I told you so, I told you so," clucked Olin Johnston. Strom Thurmond, South Carolina's other Senator, who was formidable both as labor-baiter and Negro-baiter, was in a dark mood. Bobby Baker, a South Carolinian himself, had leaked the Wilson memorandum to a correspondent for South Carolina newspapers. Thus, that morning's

---

* See pages 126–127.

front pages back home reported Thurmond voting for civil rights and his arch-rival, Olin Johnston, voting against it.

"Who wrote this?" Thurmond demanded of Johnson.

"Why, that boy from South Carolina over there," said Johnson, pointing to Jim Wilson. Somewhere in the recesses of his memory, Johnson remembered Wilson was born in South Carolina. The remark disarmed Thurmond.

With the Southerners frantic to undo the dastardly deed, a watered-down version of the Bill of Rights was substituted the next day. The Kennedy bill moved to the House with relatively little change.

The massed power of employer interests came, as had been expected, in the House. What started as an anti-racketeering bill now was transformed into a catchall bill to do what had been left undone by the Taft-Hartley Act of 1948—mainly to curb picketing and secondary boycotts. These anti-union Taft-Hartley Amendments, coupled with the anti-racketeering provisions of the Kennedy bill, became the Landrum-Griffin Bill in the House, fully justifying the fears of labor leaders. Public resentment over labor corruption was being skillfully turned by employer interests to their economic gain.

Emboldened by his earlier triumphs, President Eisenhower jumped into the labor fight feet first. Although James P. Mitchell, his liberal-leaning Secretary of Labor was leery about Landrum-Griffin, Eisenhower blessed it. Confusing the economic and anti-racketeering aspects of the bill, he appealed for the nation's support via radio and television on August 6. That settled the issue. Despite Speaker Rayburn's efforts against Landrum-Griffin, it carried in the House by a 229 to 201 vote.

Most galling to Rayburn was the 16 to 4 vote *for* the bill by Democratic Congressmen from Texas—a vote for which many liberals blamed Johnson. In fact, however, Johnson's assistant, Walter Jenkins, was on the phone to the Texas Congressmen urging them to back Rayburn and oppose Landrum-Griffin. Johnson himself tried to talk Representative Joe Kilgore, the whip of the Texas delegation, into supporting the Speaker, but all efforts were hopeless. Anti-labor sentiment in Texas was strong—too strong. It was dangerous for Texas Congressmen to oppose Landrum-Griffin.

Johnson did fully cooperate with Kennedy in keeping the Landrum-Griffin Bill off the Senate floor—where it likely would have passed forthwith—when it returned from the House. Instead, Johnson insisted that a conference committee be given a chance to compromise the House's Landrum-Griffin Bill with the Senate's Kennedy Bill (although Kennedy was forced to yield on almost every key point in conference). The final result was a slightly modified version of the Landrum-Griffin Bill, a bill Kennedy had no desire to put his name to. The session that began with such high liberal hopes ended in September with a glittering conservative triumph.

From the Democratic point of view, nothing had been accomplished in 1959. In 1960, Johnson confronted liberal demands for an indigestible package of legislation: federal aid to education, medical care for the aged, another housing bill, another civil rights bill, and an increase in the minimum wage plus an expansion in its coverage. But the zest had gone out of the 86th Congress. In a sense, all of 1960 was anticlimactic. For, incredibly enough, Eisenhower's late-blooming determination and trigger-quick use of the veto had nullified the huge Democratic majorities.

The early months of the 1960 session were devoted solely to a new civil rights bill, attempting to correct deficiencies of the 1957 bill in safeguarding the Negro's right to vote. But it was no repetition of Johnson's 1957 civil rights masterpiece. While the earlier battle was a dramatically paced legislative tour de force, in 1960 it was laborious drudgery, sapping the strength not only of Johnson but the entire Democratic majority.

Johnson realized from the start of the 86th Congress that the massive Democratic majorities elected in 1958 would demand another civil rights bill to close loopholes in Negro voting protection. Consequently, he hoped to pass a minimal bill as quickly as possible in 1959, again avoiding a Southern filibuster, and well in advance of the 1960 election. On January 20, 1959, Lyndon Johnson introduced his first civil rights bill. A four-part measure, it featured the racial conciliation service he had considered in 1957 but discarded.* The reaction was uniformly unfavorable, from civil rights advocates and segregationists alike. A much broader civil rights bill sponsored by President Eisenhower became the framework for debate.

Finding no time in the Senate's 1959 schedule for the time-consuming business of civil rights, Johnson made it the first order of business in the politically charged year of 1960. From the outset it was clear he could not repeat the miracle of 1957: a civil rights bill without a filibuster. Southern Senators had been hurt at home for their failure to filibuster three years earlier, and they would not make the same political mistake. Moreover, with the big Democratic majority demanding a strong bill, Johnson would be unable to rationalize concessions to the South *unless* there was a filibuster.

* See page 126.

This does not mean there was collusion between Johnson and the Southerners. The Majority Leader tried his best to break the six-week filibuster that began on February 15, 1960. His old mentor and the leader of the Southern forces, Richard B. Russell, had told him in 1954 there was only one way to break the determined liberal filibuster against the 1954 atomic energy bill: around-the-clock sessions.* And in 1954, that back-breaking tactic worked. Remembering that advice, Johnson had cots and bedding moved into the Capitol adjoining the Senate floor, and around-the-clock sessions began on February 29. But disciplined, determined Southerners under Russell's expert generalship in 1960 were not the scattered, leaderless liberals of 1954. Working in teams, the Southerners tied the Senate in a knot. They got away with a minimum of talk themselves by demanding quorum calls whenever the Northerners strayed away from the Senate floor for a bit of shut-eye. It often took hours to rout enough sleepy-eyed Northerners out of their beds to make a quorum and resume the debate. Ironically, it was the filibustering Southerners, dividing the labors in their three-platoon setup, who were sleek and rested and the Northerners who were harassed and fatigued. Johnson was overcome with frustration, his Senate humiliatingly out of his control. He begged his Southern friends for relief, and when they turned him down, he was at the point of nervous exhaustion. For once, Lyndon Johnson simply didn't know what to do next.

Liberals unfairly accused him of staging an elaborate charade with Russell. That false judgment was reinforced when Johnson firmly opposed an effort by Senator Paul Douglas to impose cloture. His open championship of the 1960 act had hurt him far more in the South than his backstage handling of the 1957 act. He was not now prepared to repudiate his Southern support for the presidential nomination by attacking the cherished institution of unlimited debate.

Needing a two-thirds vote, Douglas' cloture motion failed to get even a simple majority on March 10 (42 to 53), and it was clear the filibuster could not be beaten. To appease the triumphant Southerners, Johnson and Eisenhower's Attorney General, William P. Rogers, agreed to delete the bill's two toughest sections (aimed at desegregation of schools and jobs). The principal feature remaining in the bill established a system of court-appointed voting referees, which from the start proved next to useless in protecting Negro votes.† The fight. dragged on until early spring, when President Eisenhower finally

---

* See pages 79–81.
† Effective voting rights legislation was not passed until 1965, when Congress authorized appointment of federal voting registrars—a step proposed by the liberals in 1960 but opposed by Johnson and the Eisenhower Administration.

signed his second civil rights bill into law on May 6. Nobody was particularly elated.

Yet, that was the most solid accomplishment of the second session of the 86th Congress. Instead of a legislative body, the Senate had turned into a cockpit for presidential contenders—Kennedy, Humphrey, Symington, the Majority Leader himself, and as presiding officer, Vice-President Nixon. Their candidacies, plus the pall induced by Eisenhower's vetoes, immobilized Congress.

Nor did Johnson's ventures outside the legislative field pan out in 1960. Ed Weisl and Cy Vance came down from their Wall Street law firm to resume the highly successful 1958 inquiry into space and defense.* This time, the emphasis was on the supposed missile gap between the Soviet Union and the United States. With the presidential elections just around the corner, the inquiry degenerated into a partisan debate over whether Eisenhower had let defenses run down. Even the staff of Johnson's Defense Preparedness Subcommittee conceded it was not remotely comparable to the smooth-functioning 1958 investigation.

When the shooting down of an American U-2 spy plane over Russia threatened to scuttle the summit conference in May, Johnson tried to step into the foreign affairs field. He asked his old friend from New Deal days, Supreme Court Justice William Douglas, to get Adlai Stevenson to come to Washington for a high-level Democratic parley on foreign affairs with Johnson, Rayburn, and Senator J. W. Fulbright of Arkansas, the chairman of the Foreign Relations Committee (who was supporting Johnson for the presidential nomination). John F. Kennedy, front-runner for the nomination and highly critical of Eisenhower in the U-2 incident, was not invited. The Johnson-Rayburn-Stevenson-Fulbright group agreed to send a joint telegram to Soviet Premier Khrushchev urging him not to torpedo the Big Four meeting in Paris—a move viewed privately by Eisenhower as "a somewhat awkward attempt . . . to interfere in the day-to-day conduct of foreign affairs." Awkward it was. Before the cable arrived, Khrushchev had dramatically broken up the conference.

When Johnson saw his 1959–60 cupboard of legislative achievement embarrassingly bare, he hit upon a bold and controversial plan: to recess Congress on July 3 until after the National Conventions that summer, then bring it back in the frenzy of the presidential election

* See pages 189–194.

campaign in August to clean up the unfinished business.* Not only did the move signally fail to increase Johnson's leverage at the Democratic National Convention in Los Angeles, as he hoped it would, but it did inject a sour note into the closing weeks of Johnson's unequaled eight years as floor leader—the short August "rump" session of 1960, as the Senators themselves called it.

In that politically supercharged atmosphere of August, 1960, the Johnson System was inoperative. With presidential nominee Kennedy and running mate Johnson in charge of the legislative program (and Richard Nixon, the Republican nominee, calling his party's signals from the Vice-President's chair), there was scarcely any chance of wooing Republican defectors or engaging in the vital art of compromise. Johnson had a set program of four bills: medical care for the aged, federal aid to education, minimum wage improvement, a new housing bill. The commitments were strong, and they were now backed by the Democratic platform. Thus, there was virtually no room for maneuver, and maneuver was central to the Johnson System.

Then, too, there was the natural though well-concealed embarrassment of Lyndon Johnson, haughty master of the Senate, playing second fiddle to the young Senator from Massachusetts. The Republicans kept rubbing it in. Tart-tongued Senator Hugh Scott of Pennsylvania repeatedly referred to Kennedy as "the Majority Leader's leader." The needling struck home.

One evening during that joyless rump session, Johnson wandered into the back office of Minority Leader Everett Dirksen. Dirksen was gossiping about politics with several Republican Senators and aides. Bone-tired, Johnson slumped into a chair, picked up a Scotch-and-water, and startled his visitors by launching into an emotional critique of Jack Kennedy's shortcomings as a legislator. If *he* wasn't around, Johnson told the embarrassed Republicans, Kennedy would fall on his face.

But such lapses were rare. Johnson and Kennedy worked closely together during the five-week session, without discord. Johnson even showed a touch of his old magic when Kennedy, serving as floor manager for the minimum wage bill, was on the verge of a crushing defeat. An amendment to eviscerate the bill's key provision—extending minimum wage coverage to retail establishments—had more than enough votes for passage, and Kennedy was helpless. Johnson came to the rescue. He talked Clinton Anderson into proposing a substitute

---

* The political significance and background of this remarkable decision are discussed as a part of Johnson's presidential bid in Chapter XII.

that cut the force of the amendment. With that softening step, the original amendment was beaten, 50 to 48, on August 18.

Such victories also were rare. It soon became clear that only massive compromising, if not outright capitulation, would move anything through the Senate. Bobby Baker advised that without heavy concessions on Medicare—even to the point of abandoning the vital Social Security approach—Medicare was dead. Speaker Rayburn urged Kennedy to accept the Republican-designed House bill on minimum wage in preference to no bill at all. Kennedy refused both compromises. It would have undercut the Northern liberal-labor base essential for his presidential campaign.

The dreary record can be swiftly stated. The comprehensive housing bill never got out of committee. Conservatives blocked final action on federal aid to education. Competing Senate and House versions of the minimum wage bill were deadlocked in a Senate-House committee, and nothing passed. Kennedy's medical care bill was beaten in the Senate by a humiliating 54 to 41. Johnson had never worked so hard to round up votes for a bill, but he was stymied by the circumstances that denied him compromise. So tightly were Republican lines drawn behind Nixon's leadership that Johnson could peel off only a single Republican Senator—Clifford Case of New Jersey—for the Kennedy bill.

This defeat finally and sadly informed Kennedy what he and Johnson suspected all along—that the rump session was a fiasco and that there was no time to lose for them to depart the frustrations of the Senate and take to the hustings. On September 1, the rump session adjourned sine die. Not one Kennedy-Johnson goal had been achieved.

It was a most unfitting conclusion to Johnson's leadership. Yet, this drab 86th Congress and its wretched rump session could not erase the fact that Lyndon B. Johnson had tamed the Senate within an eight-year span unmatched in accomplishment or mastery.

Chapter XI

★★★★★★★★★★

"LOVE THAT LYNDON"

Johnson the candidate has grave and probably decisive drawbacks as he, despite the hopes of his supporters, well knows. He has little support in organized labor. He "smells of magnolias," *i.e.*, is a Southerner.

—Life, May 21, 1956

One day in the late 1950s, Lyndon Johnson and the Senate Republican Leader, William F. Knowland, were summoned to the White House from the torpor of a slow Senate debate. A domestic political crisis had blown up on some issue important enough for President Eisenhower to call in the congressional chiefs for urgent consultation.

Side by side they left the Senate; Knowland a stolid bull, head thrust forward and face set in painful concentration; Johnson relaxed, pantslegs flapping at the ankles, eyes on the floor in front of him. Johnson turned to Knowland and invited him to ride the seventeen blocks down Pennsylvania Avenue in Johnson's limousine. In the car with them was a Washington lobbyist, a friend of both men. As the Cadillac nosed under the porte-cochere, swung left away from the Senate wing of the Capitol onto the broad plaza and headed down toward the famous avenue, Johnson asked Knowland if he knew the reason for the sudden summons from the White House. Knowland wasn't certain. Johnson replied *he* knew.

"I know why we're being called down there," he told Knowland. "He's in trouble and he wants us to bail him out. Did you ever think what you'd do as President?"

Knowland said no, he never had.

"Well, *I* have," Johnson said.

There was no precise time when Johnson first began thinking about the presidency. Say, rather, the ambition must have come as naturally to him as his first breath, and with each successive and successful step up the political ladder, it became more insistent, more clamorous, and absorbed more of his attention. Say, too, that Johnson was a practical man whose knowledge of American history, though never profound, always included the hard, unbreakable fact that no Democrat from the Old Confederacy had ever been nominated for President and that only one Texan in all the time since the Civil War had even risen so high as the vice-presidency of the United States. John Nance Garner was that exception, and now Garner, a disillusioned expatriate of the Democratic party, brooded in his home down in Uvalde, out of touch and out of sympathy with the new Democracy.

Knowing all this, Johnson was, from the time he became the Democratic Leader in the Senate, a candidate for President, but a candidate more of the heart than the head. A politician who coveted power, and mastered the techniques for amassing it as Johnson had, could scarcely overcome his desire for the presidency. But the weakness of his credentials for the presidency, as a man of the South and out of the mainstream of national party power, led to presidential schizophrenia in Johnson, an incurable malady that punctuated his uncertain course in presidential politics with sudden stops and starts. At times, his deep-rooted though unarticulated desire for the White House led him to tentative, half-planned starts; then, remembering the burden of his Southern heritage, and further remembering that his shaky political base in conservative Texas might not sustain a bold venture into national politics, he would stop short.

As early as the 1952 Democratic Convention in the Chicago Stadium, Johnson was eyeing the national ticket. That was the year Richard Russell hoped to fill the political vacuum caused by the calamitous fall in popularity and power by President Truman and Truman's decision not to seek another term. In 1952, Russell was making a serious bid for the presidential nomination. Johnson made a secret pact with Russell. He would do all he could to secure Russell's nomination for President. But if Russell failed, Russell then would do all he could to get Johnson on the ticket as Vice-President. Johnson even had a floor lieutenant to help the Russell-Johnson combine. Johnson's old friend Donald Cook, then a member of the Securities and Exchange Commission, was quietly working for Russell and Johnson as a member of the

Michigan delegation under the very nose of that state's militant liberal-labor leadership.

Just as Johnson suspected, Russell's dreams were cruelly smashed; he won few delegates outside the Confederacy. Johnson's hope of winning the vice-presidential nomination as a ticket-balancer proved no more realistic. For all his influence in the Senate, Russell could do Johnson no good among the kingmakers at the Chicago Stadium who helped Stevenson pick his running mate. When Johnson's name was mentioned, he was flatly vetoed by emissaries of both Truman and Stevenson. There had been just too many anti-Truman, anti-Fair Deal votes by Johnson those first four years in the Senate. The party wanted a Southerner, true, to win back the 1948 Deep South defections from Truman, but one with a better record of party regularity. In 1952, some two years before the 1954 court decision on school desegregation, Senator John Sparkman of Alabama admirably met those qualifications.*

Sparkman on the ticket scarcely appeased rebellious Democrats throughout the South—including Texas Governor Allan Shivers, a rigid conservative who was then the most popular politician in Texas. He repudiated the Stevenson-Sparkman ticket and, carrying the state's entire Democratic apparatus with him, supported General Eisenhower. Rayburn and Johnson were among the few prominent Texas Democrats who stayed loyal, but this isolation made Johnson uncomfortable and shaky, as he always was about his position in Texas.

When Adlai Stevenson telephoned Johnson to ask him to introduce the party's presidential candidate at San Antonio during the campaign, Johnson went to Shivers for advice. Would he hurt himself with the dominant conservative wing of the party, he asked Shivers, if he introduced Stevenson? Could he possibly say "no" to Stevenson, pleading another engagement? Shivers suggested that Johnson had absolutely no alternative but to do anything within reason that Stevenson asked him to do in Texas. Well, continued Johnson, would Shivers "protect" him if Texas conservatives criticized him for his proximity to Stevenson? Shivers said: Yes, Lyndon, I'll protect you.

Johnson knew he had no real option. He *had* to introduce the presidential candidate of his party. A refusal by the Senate's Majority Whip to present Stevenson would have been madness and might have cost Johnson his elevation to Democratic Leader in January, 1953.

---

* It will be remembered that a bid in 1951 by Senate liberals to make Sparkman Majority Whip as an alternative to Johnson failed miserably, dramatizing the contrast between power in the Senate and in the national party. See pages 35–36.

Johnson's telephone call to Shivers was simply a shrewd political move to deaden the impact of his forthcoming campaign association with Stevenson and to show Shivers that he, Johnson, appreciated the strength of the right wing in the Texas Democratic party. In fact, Johnson did everything Stevenson asked him to do in 1952.

The overall experience of 1952 discouraged Johnson's unspoken ambitions in 1956. He foresaw political disaster should he make a serious bid for the presidential nomination in 1956. But friends kept pushing him. Early in 1956, Eliot Janeway broached the subject in plain language. Sitting on a bench in an alcove along the Capitol corridor running behind the Senate chamber, Johnson listened with growing impatience as Janeway argued that Johnson should become a serious presidential candidate. While conceding Eisenhower's invincibility, Janeway maintained that Johnson would run a much stronger race against him than would Stevenson and then would be odds-on choice for the nomination in 1960 when the Democrats figured to regain the White House. Johnson flared up in anger. "What are you trying to do? Destroy me?" he snapped.

That judgment was confirmed by James Rowe, Johnson's long-time adviser from New Deal days who had been persuaded by Johnson to serve temporarily on his staff in 1956. Rowe wrote a long, tightly reasoned memorandum advising Johnson not to run for President in 1956. Asserting that he had no chance whatever for the nomination, Rowe warned that the defeat might embitter him against the party and limit his effectiveness in the Senate, just as defeat embittered Russell in 1952. Johnson seemed to agree.[*]

Why, then, in 1956 did Johnson land halfway between Janeway's and Rowe's advice? Why did he neither run the serious campaign proposed by Janeway nor remove himself entirely from the competition as proposed by Rowe? Why, instead, did he wage an ill-planned, ill-conceived, ill-executed campaign as part favorite son, part dark horse under the ludicrous slogan of "Love That Lyndon"? The answer is to be found in Johnson's never-solved problem of Texas politics.

When Allan Shivers backed Eisenhower in 1952, the bolt infuriated the Texas regulars, particularly Speaker Sam Rayburn, by whose good offices the Shivers delegation to the National Convention that year had been seated in preference to a rival delegation of Texas liberals. Rayburn resolved he would never permit another Texas delegation to a National Convention to bolt the party ticket. Johnson agreed.

---

[*] Johnson embarrassed Rowe by giving the memo to Russell to read.

Their first effort was to guard against a repeat performance in 1956 by coming to terms with Shivers, who was still Governor. A Rayburn-Shivers-Johnson agreement on Lieutenant Governor Ben Ramsey to fill the vacant post of Democratic National Committeeman for Texas was cooked up. Ramsey had not bolted to Eisenhower in 1952—but he had not backed Stevenson, either. Nevertheless, over the vain protests of the liberals, Ramsey was selected to fill the vacancy until the following May in an effort to bridge the gap between the Shivercrats and the Johnson-Rayburn loyalists.

It proved to be a delicate spot for Ramsey. When Johnson and Shivers disagreed on a political matter shortly after Ramsey's selection as National Committeeman, Ramsey unexpectedly came down on Johnson's side. He was immediately summoned to the office of Governor Shivers.

"You know my position on that," Shivers told Ramsey. "Why did you take Lyndon's side?"

"Well, Allan, it's this way," said Ramsey. "Lyndon got me by the lapels and put his face on top of mine and talked and talked and talked. I figured it was either getting drowned or joining."

Ramsey was only a stopgap. As the Texas Democratic party moved into the 1956 presidential election year, a more permanent, durable settlement of the battle between the Shivercrats and the loyalists was essential. As their choice to be named National Committeeman by the state party convention in May, Johnson and Shivers tentatively agreed on Representative Joe Kilgore, an intimate of Johnson but also a conservative trusted by Shivers. But Kilgore wanted to get Rayburn's approval, and Rayburn regretfully said no. No Democrat who had voted for Eisenhower in 1952, said Rayburn, could represent Texas in the national Democratic party. The collapse of the Kilgore selection led to more frantic efforts to close the widening split between the Shivercrats and the loyalist-regulars, but all such efforts failed.

The failure presaged an intraparty war. Rayburn, in Washington, cooked up a dramatic plan to elevate Lyndon Johnson to the top of the Democratic heap in Texas, and to eliminate the Shivercrats, all in one bold stroke.

Rayburn's plan was the essence of simplicity: to announce his backing of Johnson not only to head the Texas delegation to the presidential nominating convention that summer (a position that Shivers was counting on for himself), but also to make Johnson the favorite son of Texas for the presidential nomination. If he could bring it off, Rayburn reasoned, the Shivercrats would be excluded from the party's inner circle of decision and power during the infighting that would precede the National Convention, during the convention itself, and during the post-convention presidential campaign. Moreover, with Stevenson running into heavy flak that spring in his campaign for a second presidential nomination, indicating an outside possibility of a free-for-all convention in July, the favorite son of Texas—Lyndon Johnson, the Great Unifier—just conceivably might emerge as the Democratic presidential nominee himself. But it was Texas politics, not national politics, that created the "Love That Lyndon" campaign.

Although Rayburn confided this brave hope to Johnson and a few trusted allies, he did so in strictest secrecy. It was, then, a shock to the Texas Democratic party, and to the entire nation, when in early 1956 Rayburn wrote out a statement in his home in Bonham, Texas, and personally carried it down to the newsroom of the *Bonham Favorite*. The statement committed himself to Johnson both as delegation chairman and as favorite son.

To capture the state convention, scheduled for May 22, the Rayburn-Johnson forces would first have to capture the precinct conventions, which sent delegates to the county conventions, which, in turn, sent delegates to the state convention, which, finally, selected the delegates to the National Convention in Chicago. Of all these ascending steps, the crucial step was the first: election of delegates at the precinct conventions.

On April 10, Johnson opened his formal campaign, after weeks of quiet politicking and organizational work, with a statewide radio and television speech. The speech was a quiet-toned appeal to party unity, complete with his favorite quotations from the Prophet Isaiah ("Come now, let us reason together") and from Psalm 133 ("Behold how good and how pleasant it is to dwell together in unity").

> It should be emphasized once more that this is not a matter of personal ambition. . . . I have made it clear to the leaders of other states that I am seeking none of their delegates. I am a Texan seeking to serve the people of Texas. I will have no part of any move that can create tensions and turmoil in our party. . . . I am appealing to all Democrats without prefixes or suffixes.

Johnson pledged himself to back the nominee of the National Convention and to "work for the election of the nominee." He outlined the complicated process of selecting delegates to the National Convention, then added:

> We must all turn out to the precinct, county, and National Conventions—turn out with our wives and with our sons and our

daughters. Turn out so that for all time to come you can look your fellow man in the eye and tell him that you thought enough of your American heritage to exercise your rights where and when they counted, at the precinct convention.

Quite naturally, considering his influence with Southerners in the United States Senate, Johnson's favorite-son announcement produced an instantaneous flutter of presidential endorsements—almost all with a Southern accent. Harry Flood Byrd and A. Willis Robertson, the patriarchal conservatives from Virginia, issued one of their rare joint statements hailing the Majority Leader as a man of "presidential stature" whose name, once offered to the convention in Chicago, "will draw support not only from the South but from other areas of the nation."

The venerable Walter George called a press conference, a concession to modern communications he rarely made, to announce his support of Johnson. He told reporters that "in the event of a deadlock" at Chicago Johnson could emerge as the nominee. But again, George emphasized Johnson's strength in the South. Richard Russell hailed Johnson now as a possible 1956 nominee and inserted Johnson's Texas speech in the *Congressional Record.* Florida's George Smathers, Louisiana's Russell Long, Arkansas's John McClellan, South Carolina's Strom Thurmond (the Dixiecrat candidate for President in 1948 who later became a Goldwater Republican), and other Southerners endorsed Johnson. From outside the South, only two Senate voices broke the silence: Oklahoma's Robert Kerr and Nevada's Alan Bible.

This deluge of Southern support for Johnson served only to emphasize his serious regional handicap. From the standpoint of his national ambitions, it damaged him. But for the fierce battle about to be fought in Texas, the Southern endorsements were not at all harmful. In challenging the darling of the Texas conservative Democrats, Allan Shivers, Johnson was certain to be tarred, absurdly but vehemently, as a radical who was backed by Big Labor and the Americans for Democratic Action. The public support from such safe conservatives as Harry Byrd and Walter George strengthened his position in Texas.

Here again, the ambivalence of his position as a Texas Democrat who harbored national ambitions plagued every move he made. He could not move sharply into national politics—into his party's mainstream—without alienating the powerful bloc of conservatives back home in Texas. Yet he could not allow this powerful conservative bloc to run out on the national party, as it had in 1952, without raising basic questions in the North about his own convictions.

Two weeks after his statewide appeal for support, Johnson mailed out a "Dear Friends" letter to hundreds of thousands of Texans, enclosing a copy of his television appeal. The letter was mimeographed, and on the reverse side were reproductions of pro-Johnson editorials in twenty-two Texas newspapers. "Telephone your neighbors," Johnson pleaded. "Ask them to join you at the precinct conventions."

As soon as Johnson made his decision to run against Shivers for control of the delegation to the National Convention, his agents began to organize the state, precinct by precinct. John Connally (now a lawyer for oil millionaire Syd Richardson, and with deep ties into the party's conservative wing) was the organizational genius in the Johnson camp. Connally, seeming to grow more conservative each year, had refused to back Stevenson in 1952 and was thought to have voted for Eisenhower, though he made no public commitment. But out of his friendship for Johnson, Connally now opposed Shivers and brought with him such conservatives as Joe Kilgore. Ironically, however, much of the muscle for Johnson's campaign against Shivers was supplied by labor-liberal elements in the larger cities. Though they scarcely loved Johnson, they detested Shivers and, more important, were intent on sending a loyalist delegation to the 1956 convention at Chicago's International Amphitheatre.

Johnson later described the fight as "a campaign of hatred and prejudice . . . without equal in modern times." The Shivers campaign against Johnson—which was not in the best drawing-room style—charged that Johnson and Rayburn were "captives of the radicals" and hand-in-glove with the ADA, the DAC (the liberal Democratic Advisory Council of Texas), the PAC (organized labor's Political Action Committee), the NAACP (National Association for the Advancement of Colored People), and the CIO. But Shivers could not match the Johnson-Rayburn organization. On May 5, Johnson beat Shivers 3 to 1 in the precinct conventions and ran up an even larger margin in the county conventions. When the state convention met at Fairmont Park Auditorium in Dallas on May 22, Johnson held all the cards—or so most Democrats thought.

Having soundly defeated the Shivercrats, Johnson was suddenly hit from the left. With victory in sight, the "liberal liberals," as they were called in Texas (they would have been just plain Democrats in any Northern state), made clear that they were far from satisfied simply to pledge the National Convention delegation to support the party's national ticket. To the liberals, supporting the national party ticket was a clear obligation, the lowest common denominator of any state political party. What the liberals wanted was far more: a Texas Democratic party willing to battle for the social and economic programs of the

national party, not just satisfy the minimum requirements of membership.

The Texas liberals were on the threshold of their most important
battle in years. They had a chance to nominate an unabashed liberal,
Ralph Yarborough, as the Democratic candidate for Governor over
conservative Senator Price Daniel, Johnson's United States Senate colleague and a 1952 party-bolter. With that chance in the background,
they wanted to reform the entire state party and meant to start at the
May 22 convention.

Specifically, the liberals had two objectives: to replace the members
of the state Democratic executive committee, which was loyal to Shivers; and to elect their gallant, colorful leader in Houston, Mrs. Frankie
Randolph, as National Committeewoman. They had agreed with
Johnson on liberal-leaning Byron Skelton, chairman of the state Democratic Advisory Council, as National Committeeman to replace Ben
Ramsey.

To Johnson, these two objectives were folly. Having defeated Shivers in the primary and the precinct conventions, Johnson was now
prepared to make major concessions to his old friend Shivers. Here his
national ambitions conflicted with Texas politics, specifically the important objective of making peace with the right-wing faction he had
just vanquished. Besides, it was widely believed in Texas that when
the *"liberal* liberals" joined the Johnson-Rayburn-Connally loyalists in
the precinct-convention battle against Shivers, the two factions had
made an agreement: Johnson to pick the National Committeewoman,
the liberals to pick the National Committeeman. Johnson had quickly
accepted Byron Skelton. Now, when the liberals, led by Mrs. Randolph herself, refused to go along with his choice of a National Committeewoman—Mrs. Lloyd Bentsen, wife of a former conservative
Congressman—Johnson made no effort to conceal his anger.

The ouster of the Shivers-controlled executive committee, he said,
would exacerbate the break between loyalists and Shivercrats and
lead to a court fight which would embarrass the whole party. When
Johnson made this point to a pre-convention rally in Dallas' Adolphus
Hotel, he was booed for forty seconds, so high was the tension. Cries
of "Traitor" and "Throw him out" came from the liberals. Displaying
anger, Johnson held his ground and pleaded for party unity. When the
convention formally met the next day, he won his point to keep the
old executive committee, but he could not raise the votes to defeat
Mrs. Randolph with Mrs. Bentsen, partly because the Randolph liberals had found a 1952 newspaper clipping that quoted Representative
Bentsen as saying he would not vote for Stevenson.

Nevertheless, when the May convention ended in Dallas, the outstanding fact was not Mrs. Randolph's election as committeewoman over Johnson's opposition but Johnson's flowering as favorite-son presidential candidate and unchallenged leader of the fifty-six-vote Texas delegation to the National Convention less than three months away. He now seemed a more potent factor in national politics, perhaps a kingmaker or even a dark-horse possibility for the nomination himself.

On returning triumphantly to Washington, Johnson was greeted by Senate colleagues, by the press, and by his friends as a full-fledged presidential candidate. Encountering Senator Walter George in the Senate, he joshed: "I'm going to have first call on you to be my Secretary of State." Jim Rowe was set to work as an inside political adviser in the ten weeks remaining before the August convention in Chicago.

But despite these surface manifestations, Johnson's intimates could not know what was going on in his mind. Did he really want to make an all-out fight against the overwhelmingly favored Adlai Stevenson? Would Johnson risk nationally what he had refused to risk in the Senate: publicly stake his prestige in a fight when the odds were all but locked against him, when the power was in other hands?

These questions had no clear answers. The ambivalence that was to plague Johnson in all his excursions into national politics was now dramatized by the doubts surrounding his true intentions at Chicago in August—doubts, some of his closest friends believed, fully shared by Johnson himself. Publicly, he told the press he was not a candidate, but he carefully did not endorse Stevenson. After a disastrous loss in the Minnesota primary to Estes Kefauver, Stevenson had come back strong to beat Kefauver in Florida, Oregon, and most important, in California. The candidacy of Governor Averell Harriman of New York, though backed by Harry Truman, had not lifted off the ground. That left scarcely any doubt that Stevenson would win a second nomination. There was no room to maneuver, no deals to be made, no trades to be offered.

And yet, Johnson nursed an absolutely serious hope in those few weeks before the convention opened on August 13 that, somehow, lightning would strike and that, somehow, the convention would deadlock and he would be tapped.

With Congress adjourning sine die on July 27, the leaders of the Democratic party had ample time to make their way to Chicago well before the nominating convention opened on August 13. The Suez crisis, which broke out on July 26 with nationalization of the canal by

Egyptian President Gamal Abdel Nasser, worsened during the first ten days of August, and President Eisenhower dispatched his plane to Chicago on August 12 to bring congressional leaders back to Washington for a top-secret briefing.

On the trip east to Washington, Johnson sat across from Speaker Rayburn and gave his old friend a heavy dose of the Johnson Treatment. What Johnson seemed to want now was nothing less than a serious Johnson presidential candidacy led by Sam Rayburn, the most prestigious, active Democrat in the country after Stevenson himself.

Truman had issued his ringing endorsement of Harriman in Chicago the day before, throwing the convention delegates (the convention had not yet formally met) into disorder. The political impact of the Truman endorsement, and of Truman's biting commentary about Stevenson, was still uncertain. Could Truman deadlock the convention? No one knew. But Johnson, whose instinct for power was acutely attuned to any new opportunity, quickly sensed a remote possibility that Truman's attack on Stevenson might so confuse the convention as to make it a genuine battleground. He wanted to be prepared.

And so, with Rayburn his captive audience on the presidential plane and other congressional leaders occasionally lending an ear, Johnson brought out every argument he could think of to persuade Mr. Sam to convert the Johnson favorite-son candidacy to a serious candidacy. Rayburn listened, occasionally issued a grunt, puffed on his cigarette—and said nothing. Rayburn knew, perhaps, what Johnson did not: that the time was late, too late to risk throwing the convention into turmoil. Because, as the convention's elected permanent chairman, Rayburn knew that any serious move by him in Johnson's direction would set off a mighty revolution in the party. And so Rayburn just listened.

After the White House briefing, Johnson made his next move, adding another piece of evidence to show his true intention. He asked the Southern leader, Richard Russell, to fly back to Chicago and help him round up Southern delegates to back him as a serious candidate.

Russell had not gone to Chicago after Congress adjourned but had returned home to Winder. Nor had Russell any intention of going to Chicago at all. Disillusioned by his own experience as a presidential candidate in 1952, Dick Russell long since had decided to go fishing during the 1956 convention. Now, his vacation temporarily interrupted by Eisenhower's summons to the White House, he was preparing to return home.

Johnson turned on The Treatment. Russell, he said, must come out to Chicago with him. He needed his help, his advice, his resourcefulness.

Nonsense, said Russell. Even if there were a hopeful prospect for a Johnson nomination, Russell could not help bring it about. Why, even the Georgia delegation itself was beyond Russell's influence. The delegation was under the thumb of Governor Marvin Griffin, a hard-shell segregationist who would never give Johnson so much as half a vote. For Russell to go to Chicago, he said, would be a waste of Russell's time and an encumbrance to Johnson.

Johnson persisted. All right, he said, Griffin is hopeless. But please, *please*, come out with me anyway. Come with me and sit with me in my headquarters and talk to me and eat with me and be with me. The tone was beseeching, pleading. And Russell finally succumbed. All right, he'd go to Chicago with Lyndon but he'd only stay one and a half days. For the patriarchal Georgian, it was an astonishing concession. Robert E. Lee could not have dragged Dick Russell to the Democratic National Convention in that year 1956. But Lyndon Johnson did.

Meanwhile, out in Chicago, James Rowe had come to exactly the same conclusion as Rayburn. James Finnegan, Stevenson's crafty, talented floor manager from Philadelphia, was skillfully proselytizing the Johnson people and the conservative Southern wing of the party, convincing them Stevenson had the nomination locked up with the assured support of the big-city liberals. Kefauver had withdrawn and was backing Stevenson. If the conservatives, said Finnegan, did not hop aboard the Stevenson bandwagon they might find themselves left out altogether, and would risk losing a voice in the direction and tone of the whole campaign. Finnegan spoke with just the right amount of assurance. If the South and the conservatives wanted to keep a handle on Adlai, he said, they had better join up while the joining was good.

And to the liberals in the North, Finnegan was craftily peddling the same line. The Southerners, he said, were ready to back Adlai. If the liberals let the Southerners supply the small increment of votes needed to put him over on the first ballot, Stevenson's first obligation would be not to the industrial states of the North but to the Old Confederacy.

The Finnegan gambit worked. Even with Truman's backing, Harriman's candidacy continued to sag. Rowe knew, just as Rayburn and Russell knew, that in these circumstances, Johnson was out of the running. But Johnson—always so wary about running for the presidency —refused to give up, not because of illusions that he might win, but because he feared a premature surrender in Chicago would diminish his stature with his supporters in Texas.

Back in Chicago now, holed up in his Conrad Hilton Hotel headquarters, Johnson and his lieutenants (led by John Connally) pumped the telephone. Johnson fastidiously concealed his own hopes. He would not risk public statements that he was seriously seeking the nomination. If he personally saw a single delegate outside of his Texas delegation to ask for support, it was the best-kept secret at the convention. But when Senator Albert Gore of Tennessee and Senator Mike Monroney of Oklahoma asked him to back Stevenson, he was furious, and told them so. He operated out of sight in his suite at the Hilton. For one thing, he did not want to risk humiliation by coming into the open and then losing. For another, the political schizophrenia that always dogged his ventures into national politics was at work here. He had promised the Democratic party in Texas that he was seeking "none" of the delegates of other states. Exposure of his true purpose might damage him back home in the anti-Johnson wing of the party, just as pulling out might damage him with his Texas friends.

As Rayburn, Russell, and Rowe all foresaw, when the first roll was called on August 16 Stevenson went over the top when Pennsylvania recorded its votes. Johnson got only eighty votes—all but two of them from Texas and Mississippi.

The contest for the Democratic vice-presidential nomination that year was the most thrilling in history. Stevenson confounded some friends and angered others by throwing the nomination open, and when he confided his plan to the party leaders (including Johnson) there was consternation. Johnson was under heavy pressure from the South—from both Rayburn and, by long-distance telephone, from Russell and other Southern friends—to demand the vice-presidential spot for himself. No Southern Democrat wanted Estes Kefauver, who, as Stevenson's main competitor in the spring primaries, was the obvious choice. Kefauver was a scalawag; Johnson was a true Southerner. They wanted Johnson.

Momentarily attracted to the idea, Johnson ordered Rowe to inform Stevenson that Johnson *would* be receptive to a vice-presidential offer, but then suddenly changed his mind and called Rowe off. At the emotional party meeting when Stevenson unveiled his idea not to pick a running mate, but to give the convention its head, Johnson and Rayburn argued heatedly against the plan. Finally, realizing Stevenson was adamant, Johnson turned to Mr. Sam and said: "It's the Governor's decision. After all, he has to live with it, not us."

In the open contest, Johnson probably wanted to throw the Texas delegation's votes to Senator Hubert Humphrey, his liberal lieutenant in the Johnson Network. But when he checked his delegation, he couldn't sell Humphrey because of the memory of Humphrey's political coup in 1948, when he forced a strong civil rights plank on the National Convention and part of the South walked out. Humphrey, at least, was convinced afterward that Johnson had tried to swing the Texas delegation to him on the first vice-presidential ballot.

Some Democrats, however, suspected that Johnson was playing the field, as Senator John F. Kennedy suggested later.

> I talked to Lyndon, too, but he gave me a noncommittal answer. Maybe Hubert thought Lyndon was for him and maybe Symington thought the same thing and maybe Gore thought that too and maybe Lyndon wanted them all to think that. We never knew how that one [Johnson] would turn out.

"That one," working closely with Rayburn, decided to give the Texas votes to Governor Frank Clement of Tennessee on the first ballot. Clement, however, was committed to his fellow Tennessean Gore, and wasn't running himself. Consequently, Texas went for Gore on the first ballot, even though Johnson and Gore were notorious antagonists on the Senate floor.

Johnson and Rayburn, however, still wanted Humphrey and hoped to swing the Texas delegation to him on the second ballot. Rayburn composed a brief talk to give the Texas delegation after the first roll call, cleverly eliminating each of the possible candidates—except Hubert Humphrey. This little speech, never delivered, praised Kennedy, then neatly ruled him out because of his religion. But as the first ballot progressed, Kennedy showed unexpected strength in the South. Georgia, Louisiana, South Carolina, Virginia, for example, gave him all or some of their votes—and Rayburn changed his mind.

Even before the roll call ended, everyone knew it would be a Kefauver-Kennedy battle. Rayburn was incommunicado as convention chairman and sent Texas labor lobbyist Robert Oliver rushing down from the platform to find out whether the Texas delegation would accept Kennedy. In the Texas caucus, Johnson made the appeal for Kennedy. The answer from the caucus: not only would Texas accept Kennedy, Texas *wanted* Kennedy. On the second ballot, when the call of the roll reached Texas, Johnson grabbed the floor microphone and shouted: "Texas proudly casts its fifty-six votes for the fighting sailor who wears the scars of battle. . . ."

Kennedy seemed to have the nomination locked up at the end of the second ballot. Then, just as all was lost for Kefauver, Minnesota switched from Humphrey to Kefauver, and Tennessee, which had stuck with Gore, finally was released by Gore (its junior Senator) and switched to Kefauver (its senior Senator). That started the switches. Kefauver went over the top. Johnson was only a spectator, his availability for the vice-presidency scarcely mentioned.

To Johnson, the Chicago convention was a faintly hostile place filled with strange and faintly hostile people. The Blackstone and Conrad Hilton Hotels, even the International Amphitheatre down in the stockyards, were alien to him. He kept to himself in the Hilton, sitting for hours with the telephone cradled on his shoulder, working on the movers and shakers of the United States Senate—Democrats who had no more influence on the political power at a National Convention than a Senate page boy had on a roll call vote in the Senate. This convention world, the world of big-city pols, labor skates, minority groups, and eggheads had no relevance to the bitter intramural politics of Texas. Instead of moving aggressively among the big-state delegations, Johnson waited uneasily, impatiently in his suite at the Hilton, waited vainly for the power to come to him, as the powers came to him in the Senate and, on occasion, back home in Texas. But in Chicago, the power was scarcely aware of Lyndon Johnson.

If the National Convention was an anticlimax for Lyndon Johnson, after his take-over of the Texas delegation in May, his return to Texas from the Stevenson-Kefauver campaign was even worse. In the party's fall convention—the "Governors' Convention" in Fort Worth, at which the incoming Governor has his first chance to put together a party structure to suit himself and his faction—Johnson deserted his liberal allies of the spring convention and lined up with Price Daniel, the Democratic nominee for Governor, and the outgoing Shivers conservatives to humiliate Mrs. Randolph and the liberals. The liberals, who had come within a whisker of beating Daniel with Ralph Yarborough in the Democratic primary for Governor, were at the peak of their power. Johnson felt it necessary to take them down a couple of notches. The fact that he succeeded poisoned his relations with them forever, further weakening his Texas political base.

During the summer, Johnson had advised Daniel's managers not to issue an invitation to Mrs. Randolph, the National Committeewoman, to attend the September Governors' Convention. This singular treatment of the woman who held the highest distaff post in the state party organization was partly the result of her defiance of Johnson and Rayburn in May. But it went deeper. The sudden flowering of the liberal faction terrified the Daniel conservatives. Johnson's basic support was deep in that wing of the party, not really with the liberals, despite their springtime dalliance. A headline the day after the convention opened, in the September 11 *Fort Worth Star-Telegram*, betrayed the deep unease among the conservatives: DANIEL'S CONTROL OF CONVENTION APPEARS SHAKY.

Considering the fact that Daniel had just been nominated for Governor (tantamount to election in those days), it was an extraordinary turn of events. Propelled into action to assure their dominance, the Johnson-Daniel forces, helped now by outgoing Governor Allan Shivers, maneuvered to bar Mrs. Randolph's Harris County (Houston) delegation from being seated at the convention and to replace it with a conservative delegation.

While in the midst of successfully putting together enough votes to unseat Mrs. Randolph's Houston delegation, Johnson was surprised by a visit from an opportunistic liberal from El Paso named Woodrow Bean. County Judge Bean's liberal delegation from El Paso was under challenge from a conservative delegation, and he wanted to deal with Johnson. Would Johnson help seat Bean's liberals, asked Bean, if they then agreed to back Johnson on any other issue coming before the convention? Johnson, always ready to deal, asked Bean whether he would back him in voting against Mrs. Randolph in the Harris County fight. Bean agreed. Johnson immediately saw to it that the Convention Credentials Committee certified Bean's El Paso delegation to be seated.

The only trouble was that Bean couldn't deliver on his end of the bargain. His liberals flatly refused to back Lyndon Johnson and oppose Frankie Randolph. Johnson got wind of the revolt, and called in Bean.

"Judge," said Johnson, "I hear you've decided not to go along with me on the Houston matter."

"I'd *like* to, Lyndon," said Bean, "but I'm having a little trouble with some of the boys."

"Well, can you deliver or not?"

"I can try, Senator."

"Trying don't count," Johnson shot back. "You with me or against me?"

Johnson, poking a finger in Bean's chest, said: "Woodrow Bean, I'm gonna give you a little three-minute lesson in integrity. And then I'm gonna *ruin* you!"

True to his word, Johnson lectured Bean briefly on the virtues and, indeed, the political necessity, of keeping a bargain with Lyndon B. Johnson. He then summoned the Credentials Committee, which had no further meetings scheduled, into emergency session. Bean's El Paso liberals were unseated and replaced by the conservative delegation.

Mrs. Randolph's Houston liberals were then denied their seats. Retaliatory action was also taken against Mrs. Kathleen Voigt of San Antonio for having dared to distribute pamphlets charging that Shivers and Daniel had a "deal" to steal the convention at the expense of the liberals. The conservatives had a close but safe margin of 1,006 to 869 to relieve Mrs. Voigt of her job as director of the Democratic Campaign Committee for the November election—the position to which Johnson himself had appointed her in May after she had supported him in the spring convention.

The rage of the liberals ran high after this twin humiliation, and much of their wrath was directed at Johnson and Rayburn. But for Johnson, what the convention once again demonstrated was not that he had to make his alliance with the conservatives but that he was still quite unable to stake out a durable, tenable middle position of his own in the Texas Democratic party without alienating either the left or the right. Johnson had no solid *Johnson position* in Texas (as, for example, John Kennedy had in Massachusetts or Hubert Humphrey in Minnesota). This lack of independence emphasized the split in his political personality and heightened his ambivalence beyond the borders of Texas. He could not afford to take a single step in national politics without looking over his shoulder to catch the reaction back home.

An immediate consequence of the autumn convention was that Johnson's support of the Stevenson-Kefauver ticket in Texas lacked enthusiasm.* His campaign speeches were for the *Democratic party*, rather than for *Adlai Stevenson*. At one point, Johnson's political agents published and distributed a syndicated column, nasty about Stevenson but friendly toward Johnson, written by Holmes Alexander, a conservative, and at that time a close friend and admirer of Johnson.

Johnson's uninspired course through the 1956 presidential campaign was dotted with concealed gimmicks like this, designed to put his campaign efforts for Stevenson in the most favorable cast in Texas. He was, as it were, acting and reacting all in one motion and never per-

---

* But Johnson did not in 1956 face his 1952 problem of having to introduce Stevenson at a campaign rally. With Texas certain to go for Eisenhower again, Stevenson did not bother to campaign there in 1956.

mitting the blasphemy to take root that Lyndon Johnson had been "had" by the ADA crowd.

Throughout the meanderings of the 1956 national political season, Johnson was unable to transcend the fiercely competitive struggle of Texas politics. That was why, during the pre-convention period of 1956 and, to a much greater degree, four years later before the 1960 National Convention, Johnson seemed so often unable to make up his mind whether he did or did not want to become a serious presidential candidate. The boiling stew of Texas politics constantly threatened to spill over on him. Even a decade later, backed by the power of the presidency, Johnson was still unable to take hold of the Texas Democratic party, shake it, and make it his own.

Thus, Johnson's 1956 entry into national Democratic politics was scarcely a success. Now, stretching ahead, were four more years of divided government in Washington, to be followed by two predictable events: the presidential nomination in 1960 of a fresh face in the Democratic party and (because of the two-term limit) the certainty that a new President would be elected. Johnson returned to Washington at the turn of the year a wiser man, armed by the failures of 1956 and eyeing the more glittering opportunity of 1960. But paradoxically, instead of profiting from 1956, Johnson soon demonstrated that he still had not mastered the realities of national Democratic politics. If 1956 was a disappointment, 1960 was to approach disaster.

Chapter XII

★★★★★★★★★★

COMEDY
OF
ERRORS

Lyndon Johnson in Brooklyn is almost as pathetic a spectacle as a Brooklyn Congressman in Washington. Neither has the slightest thing to do with the reality of the environment.
—Murray Kempton in the *New York Post,* January 22, 1960

With the eight Republican years of Dwight D. Eisenhower nearing an end, 1959 was a year of feverish anticipation for ambitious Democrats who aspired to the 1960 presidential nomination. The Democrats were still the nation's majority party. They had managed to win Congress in 1954, in 1956 and—by landslide proportions—in 1958, despite Eisenhower's great popularity. Eisenhower could not run for a third term and his probable successor as Republican party leader, Vice-President Richard M. Nixon, lacked popular appeal. Whereas Eisenhower had transcended party, Nixon was a party man. But he could not win the presidency with Republican votes alone. Accordingly, the Democratic party, hungry to enter the White House after eight years on the outside, seethed with internal turmoil for the right to contest Nixon.

The list of aspirants was long, and at the top of it was Senator John F. Kennedy of Massachusetts, an active though unannounced candidate following his re-election to the Senate by a record plurality in 1958. Senator Hubert H. Humphrey of Minnesota was the candidate of the liberals. Senator Stuart Symington of Missouri, the advocate of air power, was certain to run. Adlai Stevenson would not make another overt try for nomination, but he was obviously receptive. Then there were dark horses galore: Governor Edmund G. (Pat) Brown of California, Governor G. Mennen (Soapy) Williams of Michigan, Senator Albert Gore of Tennessee, Governor Robert Meyner of New Jersey.

And finally, in the opinion of sophisticated politicians of both parties in 1959, the list could not be complete without the name of Lyndon B. Johnson. Indeed, he was assumed to be every bit as active a candidate as Kennedy or Humphrey or Symington.

To his colleagues in the Senate, one proof of this activity was the funny things going on over in the Senate Democratic Campaign Committee. Johnson had levers of power there in Bobby Baker, who was committee secretary, and in a Johnson Network member, Senator George Smathers, the committee chairman. Through them, Johnson was quietly arranging for sizable sums to be sent to states with 1960 senatorial elections in which Johnson's presidential interests might be engaged. That little push from Johnson might just win the support in these states of the local Democratic hierarchy by providing them with extra campaign funds. Their gratitude, a natural enough result of Johnson's helping hand, would give him an advantage over other Democratic presidential contenders in the battle for the nomination.

One interstate transfer of campaign funds was particularly interesting. The previous autumn, in his national campaign on behalf of 1958 Democratic candidates for the Senate, Johnson spoke at a fundraising dinner in Nashville, Tennessee. Soon thereafter, ten thousand dollars from the proceeds of that Tennessee dinner were sent to West Virginia. In West Virginia, Senator Robert Byrd, newly elected in 1958 and rapidly becoming the most powerful Democrat in the state, was a Johnson man. Moreover, West Virginia was a good bet to become one of the early presidential primary battlegrounds for the 1960 presidential nomination. Any politician could sense the potential importance of little West Virginia, a state with very many Protestants and very few Catholics. The hollows of West Virginia were ideal to bait the trap for John Kennedy.

That only confirmed high-level political opinion. For example, Senator Kennedy felt privately that Johnson was "running very hard" but didn't have a chance. Adlai Stevenson, still the party's titular leader, confided that he regarded Johnson as a candidate and as the best qualified Democrat for the presidency from the standpoint of performance and ability, but plagued with a grave weakness: he was a Southerner. The Republican Senator closest to Johnson, Styles Bridges of New Hampshire, privately described him as a "very active" candidate. He based that judgment on the fact that Johnson was asking him many questions about New Hampshire, where the first presidential primary election of 1960 would be held.

To this consensus, there was one important dissenter: Lyndon Johnson. Seated in his newly decorated Taj Mahal in the Capitol on January 7, 1959, the Majority Leader told a visitor: "I don't want to get a bug in my mouth that I can't swallow. I don't have the disposition, the training or the temperament for the presidency."

No such disavowals came from Kennedy, Humphrey, or Symington. Nor was this just public posturing. Johnson was frustratingly negative when confronted straight-out with the question of whether he was running, even in intimate conversations with trusted friends. Johnson would not say, "Yes, I'm running," or even, "Yes, I *may* run."

So uncooperative was Johnson with friends who wanted him to run that he began to lose supporters indispensable in any campaign for President. One was James H. Rowe, Jr., the New Dealer who had recommended against a Johnson-for-President race in 1956.* But 1960 was another matter as far as Rowe was concerned.

In early 1959, Rowe talked long and earnestly to his old friend. Johnson, he argued, must make a private commitment to run for the nomination. He need not announce, but he must decide within himself that he was a candidate and be prepared to do what was necessary. Johnson listened as he was then listening to other friends bearing the same message, but he seemed to be adamant— No, he said. And again, No. He would not be a candidate. Never forget, he told Rowe, the power of Texas and the power of the South were here in Congress, not down there in the White House.

Rowe persisted. Johnson, he continued, was the best hope of the Democratic party to run for President, not just because he was ideally suited to hold the Democratic party together, as he had proved he could do as Majority Leader, but because he could hold the *country* together. The presidency, he pressed on, should not be decided on the basis of narrow sectionalism or geography, any more than it should be decided on the basis of religion. Rowe thought that 1960 was the right year to test the political truism that a Southerner could not be nominated and elected President, and Johnson was the right man to do the testing. Furthermore, said Rowe, sooner or later Johnson would find himself dragged into the presidential race whether he wanted to be dragged in or not. Far better to come in under his own power.

Still, Johnson said No.

Rowe was a Johnson man, but he did not want to stand on the sidelines in the most exciting race for the Democratic nomination since 1932. With Johnson adamant, Rowe turned to Hubert Humphrey. He explained his feelings in a candid letter to Humphrey, giving the background of his efforts to persuade Johnson to run and Johnson's refusal. He ended by offering his services to Humphrey. Rowe's letter to Hum-

* See page 228.

phrey anticipated what he knew would be a reflexive reaction by politicians to his signing on with Humphrey: that he was in fact a Johnson agent, working with Humphrey only to destroy the Kennedy candidacy, after which he would rejoin Johnson. To deal with that reaction, Rowe pledged in his letter to Humphrey that he was signing up for the duration and that he would not leave the Humphrey camp, no matter what Johnson might do, so long as Humphrey was an avowed candidate.

Rowe's experience was duplicated by other Johnson men, including Dean Acheson. Acheson informed Truman, Sam Rayburn, and Adlai Stevenson in 1959 that they had enough combined power within the party to dictate the party's 1960 nominee. In Acheson's mind was Lyndon Johnson, whose skill in threading through the political maze of the Senate had won his confidence. But any plan Acheson might have had to form a pro-Johnson phalanx around these three party giants was soon abandoned. Johnson would not give the word. Two Johnson intimates—former Senator Earle Clements and John Connally—drove out to Acheson's country place at Sandy Springs, Maryland, some months later, to ask him to back Johnson. Acheson told them it was too late. Feeling Johnson would not move, Acheson had thrown his lot in with his old chief, Harry Truman, whose candidate was Symington.

Johnson's potential competitors were getting the same message. It was, of course, in Kennedy's interest to know just what Johnson's intentions were. So, in late 1959, he dispatched his brother Bobby to find out the Majority Leader's plans for 1960. Robert F. Kennedy, thirty-four, now his older brother's campaign manager after resigning as chief counsel for the Senate Rackets Committee, went on a flying mission to the LBJ Ranch on the Pedernales River. Whatever his difficulties with Johnson were to be in the future, that overnight visit was most cordial.

After a long talk with Johnson, Bobby Kennedy left Texas with three distinct impressions: Johnson was not going to run himself; he would do nothing to help or hinder Jack Kennedy's candidacy; and, finally, what concerned Johnson most was that Adlai Stevenson not be given a third nomination.

How did Johnson's coolness to Jim Rowe's overtures square with his pouring campaign funds into West Virginia? How could he tell Bobby Kennedy he was no candidate but pump Styles Bridges for information about New Hampshire politics? Which was the real Lyndon Johnson?

He was, in fact, torn by indecision whether to run or not to run, torn between hope and despair. Haunting him was that same old question of Texas. Could he run without jeopardizing, perhaps wrecking his position in Texas? Indecision was complicated by the fact that 1960 would be a political doubleheader for Johnson in Texas. He not only would have to defend party control won at precinct conventions in 1956, but also would be up for a third term in the Senate. That the precinct conventions promised nothing like the 1956 furor, and that no strong challenger to Johnson's Senate seat was in sight, mattered not at all to Johnson. In a sense, he was still haunted by the nightmare of that eighty-seven-vote victory in 1948.

Through 1959 and into the spring of 1960, Johnson agonized over the question of whether to run or not to run week after week, month after month. When he finally gave his answer, it was too late. Thus, his strategy for 1960 was reduced to the non-strategy of postponement, delay, procrastination—and hope. That doomed Johnson against fiercely competitive Jack Kennedy, who had taken the hard, determined first step—the mental commitment to run for President no matter the odds or obstacles—almost as soon as the shouting died away in Chicago's International Amphitheatre in August, 1956.

Here was the fatal defect of the Johnson candidacy in 1960. For Johnson could have mapped a campaign starting in that spring of 1959 that would have made the 1960 convention a contest and that just conceivably might have succeeded. Instead, he condemned himself to a year of misery, humiliation and, in the end, the worst political defeat of his career.

While Lyndon Johnson was locked in the vice of indecision, and 1959 turned into 1960, Speaker Sam Rayburn was growing more certain each day that his protégé must run for President for the sake of the nation and the party, even if he did not want to. The reason was that John F. Kennedy was now the clear front-runner. Like other veterans of the Al Smith debacle of 1928, Rayburn was convinced his beloved Democratic party would confront disaster if it nominated another Roman Catholic from the eastern seaboard for President. To Rayburn, the prospect of Richard M. Nixon in the White House was too awful to comprehend.

Private conversations revealed the intensity of Rayburn's feelings. In December, 1959, when the congressional recess was drawing to a close, Senator Vance Hartke of Indiana strolled across the Capitol to pay a visit to the Speaker in his office. Hartke, just completing his first year in the Senate but a confirmed member of the Johnson Network, told the Speaker he had pleaded with Johnson to cooperate with him in getting a presidential campaign going in Indiana. Johnson's reply was a flat "no." Rayburn grunted that he received the same negative reaction from Johnson. But then, the old Speaker made fists of his small hands, pounded them on the desk, and said fervently: "He *has* to run. He just *has* to run. He just owes it to his country."

Rayburn was making this same point to Harry Truman, who disliked Kennedy and regarded him as a young upstart. Clark Clifford, Truman's old White House aide, was managing the soft-sell campaign of Stuart Symington and naturally took pains to solicit the former President's support. He and Symington traveled to Independence, Missouri, in late 1959 to nail down the old man's allegiance to his fellow Missourian. But a suspicion lingered in the Symington camp that Truman had doubts about Symington's ability to get nominated— doubts fanned by Rayburn's intensive operations. If Truman were uncertain about Symington's staying power, Rayburn reasoned, his natural second choice might be Johnson. Rayburn beat a steady track to Truman's door to convince him: first, that Kennedy had to be stopped at all costs; and second, that Symington was a sure loser.

Rayburn was not the only Johnson man who wouldn't take "no" as the Majority Leader's answer. Unlike Jim Rowe and Dean Acheson, a small group of Johnson intimates never gave up. As the campaign year of 1960 began, they were badgering Johnson to commit himself, trying to drum up support behind his back, planting stories in the press.

In Texas, John Connally was the leader of the Johnson-for-President band. In New York, Edwin Weisl and Eliot Janeway, who nurtured an intense dislike for the Kennedys, invited Johnson for cozy lunches on Wall Street with the nation's financial powers. In the Senate, there were senior members of the Johnson Network such as Robert Kerr and Clinton Anderson (when Johnson appeared at a party dinner in Albuquerque, New Mexico, on January 24, 1959, Anderson introduced him as "the next President of the United States"). And closest of all to Johnson was Bobby Baker, who never lost his vision of the Majority Leader in the White House.

The broad lines of the battle plan drafted by these Johnson men made sense: wait for Humphrey and Kennedy to destroy each other in the primaries; keep on good terms with all the candidates; quietly build up a base of delegate support in the South and West.

A variation of this plan was offered in Indiana by Senator Hartke. He and other Indiana Democrats felt that Kennedy had taken an unwise risk in entering the Indiana presidential primary to be held in May. A basically conservative state with strong ties to the South, Indiana had the Ku Klux Klan in its past and a lingering mood of anti-Catholicism. If Johnson would enter just this one primary, Hartke told him, he could beat Kennedy. And so precarious was Kennedy's hold on the party leaders that one primary defeat might destroy him.

Johnson would have no part of the Indiana primary. In fact, Hartke's plan never attracted much favor inside the Johnson camp. They wanted Johnson to announce his candidacy—as Kennedy, Humphrey, and Symington announced theirs early in 1960—but stay out of the primaries, as Symington did. He could plead that his duties as Majority Leader required him to stay on the Senate floor.

Johnson played the game, but only halfheartedly, and he refused to announce. He began to portray himself as the statesman, rooted to his post in the Senate, while lesser Democrats paraded around the country soliciting convention votes. Somebody, he kept saying, had to "tend the store."

Johnson felt that whatever chance he had for the nomination would come in quiet arrangements with state party leaders, or perhaps in a deadlocked convention with a back-room compromise choice, not in an open primary. His Texas accent, for example, would win few votes in New Hampshire and Wisconsin, the first two presidential primary battlegrounds. Johnson backers argued in vain that he could announce his candidacy without entering the primaries. Ever apprehensive about the impact in Texas of such a move, Johnson refused.

Operating a presidential campaign without an announced candidate is difficult in any case. But compounding the difficulty for Johnson's backers were tactical blunders of enormous magnitude. Applied for the first time across the wide range of national politics, the tightly controlled system that gave Johnson his unique mastery over the Senate broke down completely.

The breakdown stemmed from two basic causes: the political ambivalence that prevented Johnson from doing the right thing in Detroit or Chicago because the right thing there was the wrong thing in Texas; and Johnson's erroneous belief, shared by intimates in the Senate, that the base of national power in the various states was there in the Senate—not in the city precincts, in the minority groups, and in the delegates who would actually pick the presidential nominee. The blunders arising from these two factors made a comedy of errors out of his unannounced candidacy.

In August, 1959, when the House (and a vast majority of Texas Democratic Congressmen) passed the Landrum-Griffin Labor Reform

Act, Johnson joined with Kennedy in opposing its anti-union features
—and promptly found himself in hot water back home in Texas.*
Conservatives to whom no labor bill could be anti-labor enough,
swamped the Johnson office with protesting letters and telegrams.

On August 22, Johnson and his assistants composed a reply praising
the milder Kennedy Bill passed by the Senate as "the fairest and most
effective bill we could pass"—a statement that labor leaders could not
fault. But Johnson's letter proceeded from there to say what should
have been the unsayable for a national politician. It boasted of the
fact that Johnson had voted for all the labor-hated bills of the preceding twenty years—the Vinson Bill, the Smith-Connally Act, the Taft-
Hartley Act "and, in the last two instances . . . to override a Democratic President to make these measures law." Inevitably, the letter got
out and was duly published in the newspapers.

For his constituency in Texas, Johnson's letter was ideal. But for his
presidential constituency, it was suicidal. The leaders of organized
labor—Walter Reuther, George Meany, and many others whom Johnson had come to know well in the Senate—understood the political
realities of Johnson and Texas. They liked Johnson, took account of
the fact that he had to pay homage to his Texas constituency, and felt
in their bones that if Johnson could ever be freed from the Texas
albatross, they could live quite happily with him. But that was their
private view, and it was a view of Johnson held only at the topmost
ranks of the union hierarchy.

Now, however, with Johnson crowing about his old votes for labor
bills universally hated by all the labor unions—and citing, as the letter
did, an analysis of the Labor Reform Bill by the arch-conservative
Republican, Senator Barry Goldwater—the union chiefs were put on
the defensive. Although they knew Johnson had not really betrayed
their interests, the "Dear Friend" letter to his Texas constituents
nailed his old anti-labor record across his chest and made it impossible for his labor friends to explain Lyndon Johnson to *their* constituencies.

Precisely that sort of political embarrassment was caused again and
again by well-meaning Johnson assistants in the "Texas office" in the
Old Senate Office Building, whose first reaction to political crisis was
always to look to Texas, never to Johnson's national aspirations.

The most bizarre of the many events in which Johnson and/or his
office were caught on the horns of his political ambivalence concerned the main liberal-labor goal for 1960: medical care for the aged
financed by the Social Security system. On March 8, 1960, Johnson

* See page 219.

received a brief air-mail letter from Murphy Hebert, president of Texas Local 4-23 of the AFL-CIO Oil Workers Union. It read:

> Sir: In action adopted by this Local Union at its regular business meeting on Monday, March 7, 1960, I have been requested to write you to ask assistance in the use of your offices to work and vote for the passage of Forand Bill HR-4700.* Your consideration in the above matter will be greatly appreciated. Respectfully yours . . .

Johnson's "Dear Friend" answer, dated March 11, began: "I am glad to have your views in *opposition* to the Forand Bill. . . ." † It continued:

> You may know the House Ways and Means Committee held hearings on this bill last year. Thus far, the committee has taken no action on the bill and it is doubtful that it will be acted upon at this session. I happen to know that the Texas member of that committee, Congressman Frank Ikard, is opposing the measure. In the unlikely event the bill should reach the Senate this session, you may be sure I will review it carefully in the light of your views and also in the light of my consistent opposition to the socialization of the medical profession. . . .

On March 16, a telegram arrived in Johnson's office from the surprised union, signed not by Hebert but by the Local's secretary-treasurer, Frank J. Arnaud.

"Apparently some mistake has been made," wired Arnaud. "We requested your assistance to work for and vote for the Forand Bill."

When the gaffe in Johnson's office came to the Senator's attention with the arrival of Arnaud's telegram, Johnson sent back another routine form letter, again with the "Dear Friend" salutation. It read:

> Thank you for giving me your views. I believe some plan must be evolved which would permit the average American to be able to provide a measure of security for his medical needs in his advancing years. I'll do all I can to be fair and helpful. Best wishes . . .

Magically, the "consistent opposition to the socialization of the medical profession" that Johnson boasted about to his regular Texas constituents turned into support for "some plan" to help every American "provide a measure of security for his medical needs." That was the Johnson Medicare position reserved for the *national* Democratic

---

* This is a reference to Representative Aime Forand of Rhode Island, sponsor of the original Medicare plan.
† The emphasis is ours.

party. There is no more graphic example of the ambivalence that cut across every line of Lyndon Johnson's political philosophy, and plagued his chances for the presidency.

Apart from the blunders, the contradictions inherent in a Texas moderate seeking the presidential nomination of an increasingly liberal party were revealed again and again—and never more so than in late March at Detroit, the site of a full-scale convention of the Midwestern Democratic Conference, the most liberal of the party's regional groups. Bobby Baker, whose fertile brain was constantly dreaming up schemes to advance his boss's presidential ambition, begged Johnson to attend the meeting. All the other candidates would be there. A rip-snorting partisan speech in labor's hometown might help erase the memory of Johnson's letter to his Texas constituents on the Labor Reform Bill. But Johnson would not be budged.

Substituting for him were Clifton Carter, one of Johnson's old political hands in Texas, and Warren Woodward, who worked for the Johnson-owned KTBC television station in Austin. At Detroit's Sheraton-Cadillac Hotel, they opened a Johnson hospitality suite conspicuously manned by Texas politicians wearing white ten-gallon hats, sporting ALL THE WAY WITH LBJ buttons, and addicted to loud and genial "Ha y'all" yells to any stray politician who happened by. At the most liberal-oriented political meeting of the spring, it was an anomaly—and the subject of amusement.

Baker himself arrived at Detroit on Sunday, March 27, when the meeting was nearly finished. The sensitive Baker antenna that picked up the inner secrets of the Senate was useless in Detroit. Baker paced the corridors, looking for friendly faces and finding precious few. It was another world, and neither Baker nor any other Johnson ally was familiar in it or with it.

Johnson's speech writer and press man, George Reedy, could have been the one exception. Brought up in Chicago, Reedy spoke the language of the Northern liberals who were minutely studying Kennedy, Humphrey, and Symington, all of whom were in Detroit that weekend. But Reedy was hampered by Johnson's ambivalence. Thus, while the three candidates on the scene were pledging their political lives to Medicare, Reedy was cautiously leaking stories to the press that Johnson was not really unfriendly to Medicare. Although the contrast was detrimental to Johnson, Reedy's hands were tied. Johnson could be for Medicare in Detroit, but not in Texas, and there was no way to separate the two places.

The big news out of Detroit was a published story, leaked by President Walter Reuther of the United Auto Workers, but not attributed to him, that the liberals must stick together. The target of the story were UAW leaders in Wisconsin who were supporting Humphrey against Kennedy in a primary battle that was growing nastier. What worried Reuther was that anti-Kennedy attacks might open wounds too deep to close and cause a rift in liberal ranks that conceivably could lead to the nomination of Johnson. The leaked story said just that.

When this story was published in the *Washington Evening Star*, Eliot Janeway prevailed on Reuther to send Johnson a telegram that described the dispatch as "completely erroneous," and to send a separate detailed denial to the *Star*. But the story *was* accurate, and everyone in Detroit knew it. It summed up Johnson's disorientation from the party's liberal-labor wing. It was soon to make itself felt in the unsuccessful search for Johnson delegates.

If the Democratic members of the United States Senate had balloted on their party's nominee for President in 1960, the winner would have been Lyndon Johnson by a wide margin. Only two Democratic Senators—Edmund S. Muskie of Maine and Henry M. (Scoop) Jackson of Washington—publicly supported Kennedy. In the simplistic political reasoning of Johnson and his friends, these Senators spoke for their state parties, and therefore could woo their state delegations to back Johnson. This gross exaggeration of the political importance back home of a United States Senator undermined the whole ephemeral Johnson campaign plan.

That plan was to hold the South, Southwest, and Border States, take a sharp offensive in the small Mountain States of the West, and to keep some big industrial states neutral, that is, non-Kennedy. It quickly became apparent that this was a dream, quite removed from reality. Its bedrock—strength in the Western states to coalesce with the South—was a total misreading of the political realities.

Consider, for example, the state of Arizona. Here the venerable Carl Hayden, President Pro Tempore of the United States Senate and a member of Congress ever since Arizona was admitted to the Union, was solidly for Johnson. So was Ernest McFarland, Johnson's predecessor as Majority Leader and now Governor of Arizona. With Hayden and McFarland supporting him, Johnson felt assured of Arizona's delegates.

Johnson was unaware of a small event that occurred the last night of the 1959 session. On a sudden impulse, Representative Stewart L. Udall of Arizona (later Secretary of the Interior to both Kennedy and

Johnson) walked over to the Senate to call on John F. Kennedy. Udall had been brooding about the approaching struggle for the presidential nomination. He scarcely knew Kennedy but had been impressed by his part in the labor reform fight. Before that night ended, Udall had enlisted in the Kennedy campaign for the duration. Naturally, there were no announcements. Working quietly, Udall organized Arizona so efficiently that Kennedy had its delegates all but locked up before the Johnson managers were aware what was happening.

One afternoon in the House several months later, Udall was summoned by Speaker Rayburn, presiding over the House from his seat on the rostrum. Gently but quite firmly, Rayburn warned Udall not to do anything in Arizona that would damage Senator Hayden's effort to bring the delegation into the Johnson camp. Udall immediately explained that he had been plotting on Kennedy's behalf for several months and was doing rather well at it. Rayburn was stunned. So must Johnson have been when he learned that Udall was making off with the booty out the backdoor while the aging Hayden and McFarland stood guard at the front.

The Johnson camp's unhappy experience in Arizona was duplicated in neighboring Colorado. Udall and ex-football star Byron (Whizzer) White, working with a transplanted New Yorker named Joe Dolan, toured Colorado in an old car lining up Kennedy delegates to the state convention, which would select the delegation to the National Convention. Johnson was relying on his old Senate colleague, Edwin Johnson, to carry the state for him.* In fact, Big Ed Johnson was completely surprised by the successful Udall-White-Dolan maneuver, and the state went to Kennedy.

The pattern was repeated in Montana. There Kennedy men organized the Irish Catholics in the Butte iron mines, and Representative Lee Metcalf, a liberal leader in the House who was working aggressively for Kennedy, outflanked the state's two Senators, Mike Mansfield and James Murray, both of them passively for Johnson.

Sometimes the Johnson camp counted on Senators it didn't have. In the early spring of 1960, a Johnson agent was dispatched to Wyoming with a list of party leaders supposedly friendly to Johnson. The agent found that, to a man, they were committed for Kennedy. Informing Walter Jenkins of this startling news, the agent was told to check with "Johnson's man" in Wyoming: freshman Senator Gale McGee. When the agent did so, he was informed politely by McGee that he was not committed to the Majority Leader, and, in fact, intended to remain

---

* Johnson was one of the three Democrats Lyndon Johnson placed on the McCarthy censure committee. See page 84.

scrupulously neutral. The Johnson camp did not even know that Democratic State Chairman Teno Roncalio had been on the ground floor of the Kennedy operation from the start and had wrapped up the state for him.*

Reliance on the wrong political figures was endemic. Johnson men looked at Iowa as one Midwestern state where the Democratic party was neither very liberal nor inclined to Kennedy. Consequently, Johnson's political handyman, Cliff Carter, flew out to Des Moines to line up Governor Herschel Loveless. He returned with what he thought were pretty hard commitments. What Carter didn't know was that Democratic State Chairman Duke Norberg was already in the Kennedy camp. Moreover, Norberg worked on Loveless to separate him from Johnson. Loveless, who could see which way the wind was blowing, began to lobby the Kennedy camp for the vice-presidency.

Johnson's failure to break through in the West was surpassed by the bungling of his agents in the East, where his men were quite ignorant of the power realities. Connecticut was the New England state that the Johnson camp hoped to woo from Kennedy, and the reason was Senator Thomas J. Dodd, a new but enthusiastic member of the Johnson Network. In fact, however, the power in Connecticut was not Dodd, but Governor Abraham Ribicoff, one of the first major figures in the party to declare for Kennedy outside his home state of Massachusetts. With State Chairman John Bailey (a Kennedy insider) at his side, Ribicoff sewed up Connecticut for Kennedy months before the convention.

In New York, Johnson pinned his banner to the sinking mast of Carmine DeSapio, boss of Tammany Hall, but losing power rapidly. Johnson's men never realized that DeSapio controlled the party only in Manhattan, a single borough of New York City, and that that control was undermined by the rising reform movement. In the meantime, Kennedy had cornered party support in Brooklyn, the Bronx, and Queens, plus Albany, Rochester, and other upstate power centers. In the face of such solid Kennedy support, DeSapio never delivered on his early pledge to help Johnson.

New Jersey was in the Connecticut–New York mold, but for a different reason. No friend of Kennedy, Governor Robert B. Meyner had taken a high fancy to Johnson—and perhaps a Johnson-Meyner ticket. But Meyner was a political loner, not a professional. Attempting to keep his delegation away from Kennedy, Meyner faced rebellion from his party leaders. It was clear the delegation was Kennedy's if he really needed it.

* Wyoming's vote put Kennedy over the top on the first ballot at Los Angeles.

The plan wasn't working. While Johnson held fast to the Senate helm, his crew scurried around the country, to and fro, desperately trying to round up delegates in what may have been the least coordinated, worst managed pre-convention campaign in history.

The self-doubt about whether to run or not to run seemed to increase in the spring of 1960. The mishaps of his friends in trying to win delegate support only confirmed Johnson's feelings that a Texan could be neither nominated nor elected as President and that he would be destroying himself and his power in the Senate if he ran. Thus, on one day he chastised Bobby Baker or Sam Rayburn or John Connally, and everyone else trying to draw him into the presidential tangle. But on the next, he seemed every inch the candidate, talking of how he could once again unite the Democratic party on a North-South basis. And as 1960 wore on, he seemed more and more resentful when his friends picked an *announced* horse in the presidential derby.

For example, a liberal Democrat who worked for a Texas Congressman close to Johnson signed up to work in the unpublicized Kennedy headquarters in the Esso Building, two blocks west of the Capitol. He was convinced Johnson was not a candidate and never would be. When Johnson heard that the assistant of his Congressman friend from Texas was in the enemy camp, he ordered him out. There was a certain bitterness, too, over the fact that Senator Mike Monroney of Oklahoma was now taking the leading role in the drive to nominate Adlai Stevenson for a third try.

Without great relish, and with considerably less optimism than his supporters, Johnson was edging inexorably toward a bid for the nomination. Two impending events propelled him in that direction: the presidential primary election in West Virginia May 10 and the Senate primary election in Texas on May 7.

To the anguish of the Kennedy camp, Humphrey had stayed in the race for the presidential nomination, despite his loss to Kennedy in the Wisconsin primary on April 5, and now, according to the polls, was a heavy favorite to ride a seeming wave of anti-Catholic prejudice to victory over Kennedy in Protestant West Virginia. Such an outcome would all but eliminate Kennedy but scarcely restore Humphrey as a viable candidate. It would, instead, create a wide-open convention at Los Angeles that just might wind up nominating Lyndon Johnson.

The Texas primary three days earlier was even more important to Johnson. He faced no opponent for a third-term Senate nomination. Moreover, his forces seemed certain to win the precinct conventions without the battle of four years earlier. Never had Johnson's Texas base seemed less shaky.

These events gave Johnson both the motive and the security to start traveling. And such travels were essential. Even in Indiana, where Vance Hartke had been assuring him he could topple Kennedy, his image was foggy. A secret poll of Indiana by pollster Louis Harris taken for Kennedy showed that only 38 percent of Indiana's voters were familiar enough with Johnson to have any opinion of him at all. Furthermore, of those who had an opinion fully 53 percent were "not sure" how they regarded him. But perhaps most harmful, Johnson came through in Indiana as a "politician's politician," not as a "people's politician," a distinction that Harris described in his confidential report to Kennedy as "critical." Said Harris:

> As a politician's politician, a man is known and even admired for his cool, calculating skill but never for his warmth toward the rank and file of people. He is a cunning and clever individual, but not one who evokes the kind of warmth or confidence of which presidential majorities are born.

Johnson finally woke up to a fact visible to others for many months: that if he was to have any chance at all, he must get around the country himself. And so, in his first concession to reality, he set out on a two-day, three-state tour of the Appalachian region on May 6 and 7. Surrounded by a panoply of Senate reporters and the other accouterments of a major candidate for the presidency, he flew first to Liverpool, Ohio; then to Pittsburgh and finally into the Kennedy-Humphrey West Virginia battleground itself at Clarksburg.

Wearing his new contact lenses for the first time at a political appearance, Johnson talked like a candidate. In East Liverpool, the home of his chief Ohio backer, the mercurial Representative Wayne Hays (who had started out as a Kennedy man and then switched to Johnson), he took a slightly protectionist line—far removed from his free trade record—to please his host. In Pittsburgh, he spoke out strongly in favor of the reappointment to the Federal Power Commission of William Connole, a liberal whom President Eisenhower announced he would not reappoint. Johnson's defense of Connole, numbered high among the public enemies of the oil and gas industry, was an uncharacteristically bold affront to Texas. It marked him as a putative presidential candidate, as did his hard-hitting attack—also out of character—on Eisenhower in East Liverpool. He told a story in Ohio about how two cannons had been sent from there to Sam Houston's Texans in the revolution against Mexico. "When Texans are looking for heavy artillery," he said, "the place they look for it is Ohio." It sounded very much like a bid for delegates.

Spending the night in Pittsburgh's new Hilton Hotel at the tip of the Golden Triangle, Johnson invited the traveling press to his suite, ordered up a bar and buffet and launched into a monologue that was alternately funny, teasing, and sorrowful. Johnson was obviously enjoying himself out on the stump. Suddenly, without explanation, he reached for the telephone after midnight and asked for long distance.

"I'm going to call John Connally," he announced. "If I was ever in trouble I'd want John Connally by my side.

"Don't you know John?" he asked his surprised audience. "I'll say that nominating speech he made for me in 1956 was the best at the convention." The monologue continued, with Connally cut in down in Texas.

The next day, in his formal speech in Pittsburgh, he captured the crowd with his unabashed enthusiasm. In another unscheduled talk to veterans of Bataan and Corregidor (who happened to be meeting at the Hilton), he brought tears to some eyes with a moving, sentimental flashback to the Pacific War. Later in West Virginia (where he carefully skirted the Kennedy-Humphrey race) he handled himself well. His theme there was his work in the Senate to give the Democratic party a record to run on that fall. "Somebody's got to tend the store," he said, in a dig at his two colleagues who had exhausted themselves for a month in West Virginia.

From West Virginia, the Senator flew on to the LBJ Ranch, arriving Saturday night, May 7, the day of the Texas primary. He stayed up half the night listening to the radio and telephoning for results that, as expected, showed that Johnson men had done exceptionally well in the precinct conventions. He was tired from long hours in the Senate, but he had enjoyed his three-state swing. He liked campaigning, once he got out of Washington, and now in that soft Texas night on the banks of the Pedernales, he began to think deeply about announcing for the presidency. But the time was later than he knew. In truth, he had little to be pleased about even in the three states he had just visited.

Before Johnson left East Liverpool, Representative Hays had told him he could count on at least twenty delegates from Ohio after it completed its first-ballot commitment to Kennedy. In fact, he had no more than three.

In Pittsburgh, Mayor Joseph Barr had indicated his liking and respect for Johnson, hinting that the Majority Leader was his secret choice for the nomination. But Barr had to face the reality of the recent primary election results in Pittsburgh. Kennedy received 75,951 write-ins; Richard M. Nixon, 7,243 (*Democratic* write-ins, that is), and Johnson, 745. With that showing, no Pennsylvania Democrat could risk supporting Johnson. Predictions of thirty Johnson delegates by his volunteer workers in Pennsylvania were as unrealistic as Hays' predictions in Ohio.

Only West Virginia, of the three states visited, seemed likely to give Johnson delegate support—and, far more important, a real break-through because of Humphrey's expected victory three days later. With Humphrey virtually eliminated from the nomination because of his defeat in Wisconsin, the stakes in a Humphrey triumph in West Virginia actually were higher for Johnson than for Humphrey himself. A Humphrey victory would open up the party to a whole series of new arrangements and deals, a fluid situation tailored to Johnson's special skills.

It was no wonder, then, that some curious and secretive work was being done in West Virginia by Johnson men. Humphrey and, con-ceivably, Johnson himself may have been unaware of it, but Johnson agents were coming and going during those last few days of the cam-paign. Their contacts were Charleston business and banking interests, a scattering of local politicians who had tied up with Humphrey—and Senator Robert Byrd. In New York, Janeway and other New York businessmen raised money for the concealed Johnson operation and sent it down to Charleston to help Humphrey win the primary. Earle Clements appeared mysteriously in West Virginia just before the elec-tion, his apparent purpose to line up delegates to the National Con-vention. (The primary did not bind the twenty-five delegates.)

All these clandestine efforts for shadow-candidate Johnson came to naught. Instead of winning, Humphrey lost to a lavishly financed Kennedy campaign in West Virginia even more decisively than in Wisconsin, and Humphrey retired from the presidential race to begin a long, indecisive, emotional struggle as to what he would do with his handful of delegates from Wisconsin, South Dakota, Utah, Nebraska, and Minnesota. But if West Virginia was the end of Humphrey's 1960 presidential hope, it was a sharp, painful beginning for Johnson. Now he could not back into the nomination. If he did not act, he was through.

The first overt sign of a shift in Johnson's thinking came later in May when, on a political trip to California, he stopped in Idaho Falls for a confidential talk with Idaho Democratic leaders. Johnson carefully instructed the Idaho Democrats to pay no attention to what the newspapers were saying, *i.e.*, that he was not a candidate for President. The fact was, he said, that although he couldn't announce it yet, he most definitely *was* a candidate. Yet, so plagued by misfortune was the Johnson campaign that this revelation backfired on the Majority Leader.

He engaged in a little private public relations game after his meeting with the Idaho Democrats that resulted in an embarrassing front-page story in the *New York Times*. Johnson instructed Irving Hoff, chief assistant to Senator Warren Magnuson of Washington and on loan to Johnson, to tip off Robert Baskin of the *Dallas Morning News* that he had privately told the Idaho Democrats he would soon bring his candidacy into the open. Johnson was bothered by growing doubts in Texas that in the end he would not announce his candidacy and would not run, leaving the Texas delegation in limbo. Johnson, in other words, wanted to leak the accurate story that he had tipped his hand in Idaho, but he wanted the story printed only in Texas. News is almost impossible to contain, and Hoff's leak to Baskin quickly leaked to John Morris of the *New York Times*, who also published the story.

When Johnson was told of the Morris story, he angrily summoned Morris and accused him of betraying a trust by writing the story. As a "guest" on Johnson's campaign plane, Johnson continued, Morris had written a story that was out of line. Morris, embarrassed at Johnson's anger but sure of his own ground, told Philip Potter of the *Baltimore Sun*, a friend and admirer of Johnson, about his run-in with Johnson, and Potter was enraged. He confronted Johnson and announced he was leaving the trip. "If I'm a guest, I don't want to be here. I thought I was a working reporter," said Potter. Johnson took refuge in the oldest of all political dodges: he denied that he was angry at Morris and backed down. Potter stayed.

In truth, it was so late in the game that it scarcely made much difference whether Johnson did or did not announce his candidacy. His visit to California, following the Idaho incident, showed how vain was his hope for winning any significant part of that state's big delegation. State Representative Jesse (Big Daddy) Unruh, just emerging as a new Democratic power in California, admired Johnson and had been in touch with Johnson agents. But even before Johnson was playing games in Idaho over whether he was or wasn't a candidate, Unruh had signed up in the Kennedy camp. Unruh had no intention of trading political alliance with Kennedy for Johnson's procrastination.

Furthermore, the overall Johnson plan was no longer a matter of getting delegates for himself but of stopping Kennedy from getting any more. Following the West Virginia primary on May 10, Johnson's only hope was to stop Kennedy. And this entailed a change in the ambiguous relationship between Lyndon Johnson and John Kennedy.

That relationship was warm enough on the surface, particularly after Johnson helped deliver the Texas delegation to Kennedy for the vice-presidency at the 1956 convention in Chicago and the next year maneuvered a seat for him on the Senate Foreign Relations Committee. But even so, Johnson could be cutting about Kennedy—as he could about anybody. During those informal gab sessions when President Eisenhower invited Johnson and Rayburn over to the White House for cocktails, the two Texans often mocked Kennedy as a dilettante and an upstart, not really a Senate type at all and certainly not presidential timber.

As the 1960 contest approached, the relationship warmed. In the spring of 1959, Kennedy remarked to friends that Johnson had been treating him extremely well. In early 1960, when Johnson in private conversation made a habit of ridiculing other potential nominees— Symington, Stevenson, and even his old friend Humphrey—he seldom included Kennedy. There was a reason. In his unguarded moments, the Majority Leader sometimes mused about his political "dream ticket": Johnson for President and Kennedy for Vice-President. Bobby Baker was rhapsodic about binding up the old North-South rupture in the Democratic party with this ideally balanced ticket. And why not? Hadn't Kennedy himself described Johnson as the best qualified Democrat to be President? Wouldn't Jack Kennedy be more apt to throw his support to Johnson, rather than to Symington or Stevenson, once he slipped in the primaries? But that was just the point. The dream of a Johnson-Kennedy ticket was predicated on Kennedy losing in the primaries.

When Kennedy won all seven primaries, Johnson was forced to seek alliances with the other candidates. It became essential for him to persuade *all* candidates to hold their delegates and prevent them from hopping on the Kennedy bandwagon. Thus, Humphrey must not throw his support to Kennedy.* Equally important, Adlai Stevenson must not be allowed to rule out the possibility of a Stevenson draft. When Stevenson visited Washington on May 16 to testify on the bill authorizing televised debates between presidential nominees, he was invited to the Taj Mahal for a confidential chat with Johnson. Stevenson, who had been described by Johnson as an unacceptable nominee

---

* This interesting aspect of the Johnson-Humphrey relationship is described in more detail in Chapter XIII.

when Bobby Kennedy visited the LBJ Ranch several months earlier, was led to believe that Johnson would throw him his delegate strength if he could not make it himself. Forgetting his earlier irritation with Senator Mike Monroney for leading the Draft Stevenson movement, Johnson now began to collaborate with Monroney. Monroney's politically astute aide, Tom Finney, exchanged information with Walter Jenkins on a regular basis. If and when Kennedy was stopped, it would be time enough to determine whether Stevenson or Johnson would be nominated.

With a Johnson-for-President campaign headquarters now operating full speed at the Ambassador Hotel in midtown Washington under John Connally's supervision, the still-unannounced Johnson candidacy was taking on the earmarks of a Stop Kennedy movement. Yet, dogged by the ineptitude that marked all of Johnson's presidential efforts, the Stop Kennedy drive accomplished nothing except to poison relationships with the entire Kennedy camp—a development that was to have repercussions in American public life for years to come.*

The Ambassador Hotel headquarters reproduced a bitingly satirical "open letter" to Kennedy written by Senator Hugh Scott of Pennsylvania, a former National Chairman of the Republican party, which chided him as an "absentee Senator." Form letters asserting that Kennedy couldn't beat Nixon were mailed to every convention delegate.

But attacking Kennedy was not enough. The Ambassador Hotel headquarters also had to convince the delegates that he did not have a first-ballot victory wrapped up, as more and more politicians were coming to believe. To counter this bandwagon psychology, the Ambassador Hotel headquarters issued more and more optimistic reports of Johnson's delegate strength. They backfired. They were quite simply beyond the credibility of informed politicians and were taken as evidence of deep Johnson weakness. For example, as early as March, stories leaked to sympathetic newspapers, and reported as bona fide political information, claimed for Johnson five hundred and thirty convention votes on the first ballot or "more firm support than . . . Kennedy . . . will have."

These absurd estimates of Johnson's strength were accompanied by fanciful predictions that once he announced there would be a great national rising-up, a spontaneous demand from coast to coast for the man who had made the Senate work and now would make the country work. But that, too, was a pipe dream that fooled only the gullible and certainly not Johnson himself. Winners of nominating conven-

* These attacks did not hit their peak until the Los Angeles convention itself, as will be seen in Chapter XIII.

tions are those who have the delegates, and Kennedy had spent four years accumulating delegates.

Worst of all, the Ambassador Hotel headquarters made the fatal mistake of believing its own propaganda. One inflated tally of delegate votes, prepared by Bobby Baker and Walter Jenkins, showed Johnson with five hundred and two votes. That propaganda actually became the factual basis of a work sheet used by Johnson's advisers in drafting strategy. Bobby Baker, the gifted Senate head-counter and intelligence chief of the Johnson System, was committing the same error that used to amuse and amaze him when committed by the liberal Senators: overestimating his strength. Beyond the Senate, the Johnson System was simply inoperative.

Another basic mistake was the effort to apply the System's reward-and-punishment technique, so basic to control of the Senate, to the politics of a presidential convention. When the annual Governors' Conference met June 26 at Glacier Park, Montana, grumbling over Johnson strong-arm tactics was getting louder. As a result, the earlier resentment of political pressure from the Kennedy camp was now transferred to Johnson.

Particularly upset were several Democratic candidates for the Senate who were either supporting Kennedy or verging toward support—Representative Lee Metcalf of Montana, Governor Herschel Loveless of Iowa, and Thorn Lord of New Jersey. Hints from Johnson aides had led them to believe that if they backed Kennedy they might have trouble obtaining campaign funds from the Johnson-controlled Senate Democratic Campaign Committee and, further, that if they got elected, they might find the better committee assignments closed to them. That sort of threat only angered its targets, each of whom joined the Kennedy bandwagon.

There is evidence that Johnson himself was responsible for one complaint that broke into the open at Glacier Park. Eliot Janeway was publicly accused of conveying a thinly covered threat, tinged with political blackmail, to Governor G. Mennen Williams of Michigan on June 2 to prevent him from endorsing Kennedy. Asked about it three weeks later at Glacier Park for the first time, Williams answered candidly. The threat, he said, came from "a New York ally" of Johnson (Janeway) and went directly to Walter Reuther, Williams' most important political adjunct in Michigan, as follows: if Williams came out for Kennedy on June 2 (as everyone knew he planned to do and as he actually did), Johnson might find it impossible to persuade the Senate to pass a Medicare bill—the very bill that Johnson had forthrightly opposed in his first answer to the Texas unionist. The effect of all this was to create a pervasive anti-Johnson aura at Glacier Park.

Back in Washington, the Ambassador Hotel operation was also hurting Johnson. Now that Humphrey was out of the race for President, Jim Rowe, released from his commitment, was back masterminding Johnson. But for others, the time was too late to collect on well-intentioned offers of assistance made a year earlier. Johnson telephoned his old lieutenant, Earle Clements, in Kentucky to ask him to come back and work full time on the campaign. Clements would have jumped at the offer six months earlier, but he had just become Kentucky State Highway Commissioner and could help Johnson only on a part-time basis.

Thus, except for the talented Jim Rowe, the headquarters at the Ambassador Hotel took on a purely Texas flavor that did Johnson's cause no good. Handsome, suave John B. Connally was in charge. Also from Texas were Cliff Carter and an executive of the union-baiting Lone Star Steel Company, W. Marvin Watson, Jr., who was a rising figure in the conservative wing of the Texas Democratic party. Wives of Texas Congressmen manned the telephones and served as receptionists. Aides of Texas Congressmen were impressed into service as field men. But even if some of his supporters basked in optimism, Johnson knew his campaign—still *unannounced*—was still not off the ground. He searched for something new, something different, for some dramatic breakthrough. Instinctively, he reached deep into what he knew best: the legislative process.

Johnson and Bobby Baker had cooked up the audacious plan together sometime after Kennedy's win in West Virginia. By late June, Johnson was broaching it secretly in the nightly "board of education" sessions in Speaker Rayburn's office. His daring ploy was not to *adjourn* the Senate sine die before the Democratic convention opened, but to *recess* it for five weeks only, beginning around the Fourth of July, and then bring it back into session after the nominations for President and Vice-President had been made.

Here was blatant political blackmail, and an extreme exercise of power. If the party had to return to a post-convention session of the Senate, it would be submitting its final pre-election record—such issues as Medicare and the minimum wage—largely to the dictates of Lyndon B. Johnson, the only Democrat who could make the Senate work. It would give Johnson a unique influence over the convention itself, because of his power over the legislative process. Johnson hoped that convention delegates might be alarmed just enough by the prospect of a Johnson-dominated post-convention session of Congress only weeks before the November election to give him the nomination for President.

When Johnson first broached the scheme at a "board of education" session, he encountered fierce objections from Representative Richard Bolling of Missouri, who often served as the Speaker's bridge to the liberals in the House and was one of the few non-Texan regulars at the nightly drink-and-talk sessions. Bolling had suspected Johnson's motives and never tried to hide his antagonism. Bolling strongly advised Rayburn that the scheme would result neither in Johnson's nomination nor in passage of the pending bills.

Habitually cautious, Rayburn at first was inclined to follow Bolling's advice rather than Johnson's. But in the end he could not deny his old friend this last maneuver that Johnson felt he needed in a drive for the presidency which the Speaker had been urging for a year. So Rayburn went along. The Johnson-Rayburn move for a pre-convention recess on July 2 came as a shock to the Kennedy Democrats when it was unveiled late in June. Johnson's control of the Senate, which so greatly exceeded his control of the party at large, was sufficient to force the plan through with the loss of only six Democratic votes. But far from aiding Johnson, the maneuver was just one more burden on his shoulders. The party took it exactly for what it was—a power play—and, naturally enough, resented it.*

Despite the unsavory taste left by the recess ploy, the excitement was high not only among his supporters but throughout the party when, on July 5, Lyndon Johnson finally met the press and several hundred Democratic friends in the elaborate theater of the New Senate Office Building to announce his candidacy. At last, he was a real, live, announced, running presidential candidate.

The Majority Leader was dressed in a custom-made blue suit with a three-pointed white handkerchief in the breast pocket, a white shirt with a long, pointed collar, and a blue tie. He had that slight diffidence as he stepped up to the podium, as befitted a man about to offer himself for the presidency. There, in the New Senate Office Building that was so much his monument (it was completed during his leadership), confronting the cynical Washington press corps, behind whom sat his senatorial friends, old colleagues from the House, and a generous proportion of all the Texans living in Washington, he read his announcement, his voice high-pitched, dry.

* The details of what became known as the "rump session" are found in Chapter X. See pages 222–224.

In the accustomed tradition, he hit hard at the front-runner, Kennedy, but only by indirection. Delegates to the convention, he said, would not permit the convention to be bound "in advance" to one candidate, because that was not the tradition of the Democratic party. Woodrow Wilson, Al Smith, Franklin D. Roosevelt—all were nominated after, not on, the first ballot. Some of the candidates this year had been in the field for months, but as for himself: "I am not going to go elbowing through 179 million Americans, pushing aside other Senators and Governors and Congressmen to shout 'Look at me —and nobody else.' " He continued: "Those who have engaged in active campaigns since January have missed hundreds of . . . votes. This I could not do—for my country or my party. Someone has to tend the store."

Here was the voice of responsibility towering above those others who, in their arrogance and youth, had sought to rig the convention before it even convened.

But one question asked him that July 5, 1960, drew a strangely equivocal answer. Would he, if he failed in his quest for the presidential nomination, agree to run for Vice-President? Would he trade his vote as leader in the Senate for the gavel of the President of the Senate, the Vice-President of the United States?

The first time it was asked, Johnson took refuge in the time-honored response of no response at all. He was a candidate for President, period. But the reporters pressed him. Would he reject the vice-presidency, if it were offered him, as Kennedy had already announced *he* would? Johnson's reply, though generally overlooked in the confusion, was prophetic:

> . . . I would never reject something that hasn't been offered to me. I have been prepared throughout my adult life to serve my country in any capacity where my country thought my services were essential.

Was that a hint that Johnson knew he could not win the presidential nomination and would settle for the second spot? Or was it a subtle undermining of Kennedy, painting the vivid contrast between himself —modest, unassuming, and ready to answer any call—and the man who missed "hundreds of votes," elbowed his way through millions of Americans, and publicly rejected in advance the vice-presidential nomination?

Almost certainly, everyone thought it was the latter. To overtake Kennedy at this all-too-late date, Johnson's only weapon was psychological warfare. He was leaving the seat of his power and going to a place where he had no power. In Los Angeles, there would be no big delegations to break through now, or to steal from under Kennedy's nose. They could be won only by shaking them loose, by shocking the party back into its senses. Or so it seemed to everyone on July 5.

Two days later, Johnson was driven to Friendship Airport near Baltimore in his Senate limousine. In the car with him were Lady Bird Johnson, his two daughters, and Colonel Ken BeLieu, staff director of Johnson's Senate Space Committee.

Johnson was in a meditative mood on that thirty-five-mile drive through the Maryland countryside. Never again, he knew, would life be quite the same as the life he was leaving. He talked about the convention. Frankly, he doubted if he had much chance to win in Los Angeles. But he had to go, he had to make the effort, they were counting on him, Sam Rayburn particularly was depending on him. He could not back out now. But he knew, and faced up to it, that he was not close to the five hundred and two delegates his managers were claiming for him. Johnson was a realist, and now, as he sped through the hot summer's day to Friendship, his realism was revealed.

Suddenly he interrupted himself. "I left my contact lenses on the top of the bureau," he said. He described exactly where they were. BeLieu, who had persuaded Johnson to wear contact lenses only a few months earlier, was sent back to the house on Thirtieth Place to find them, wrap them, and mail them to Los Angeles. The incident, of course, was utterly without importance. Yet, it was curiously symbolic. Like so much else in Lyndon B. Johnson's unhappy bid for the presidency, it was one more thing undone, one more thing forgotten.

Chapter XIII

DEFEAT— AND EMANCIPATION

By changing Lyndon Johnson from a Texan to a national politician, Kennedy frees him to take more liberal positions if, as Johnson's old friends in Washington have always vowed, those are the
true beliefs of the inner man.

—*The New Republic*, July 25, 1960

Los Angeles, on that sultry, smoggy July 8 when the Johnson family
arrived there, was a Kennedy town, but nothing in the conduct of
candidate Johnson and his managers betrayed an inner sense of defeat.

Here, at a National Convention of his party, Lyndon B. Johnson's
potential for exercising power was infinitesimal, as he had learned to
his sorrow four years earlier in Chicago. Here there were few levers
that Johnson knew how to get his hands on. Most of the deals had
been made long ago. As for those not quite closed, Johnson was at a
distinct disadvantage. The Kennedy forces, manning every state delegation in depth, were a field army compared to Johnson's platoon.

It was an overhurried, underorganized effort for Johnson at Los Angeles. Marvin Watson, the conservative Texas steel executive, was
handling public relations—an alien field to him. Ed Weisl, the Wall
Street lawyer, was put in charge of wooing perfect strangers in Far
Western delegations. One Texas politician who at the last moment
decided not to make the trip to Los Angeles was assigned to mother
several delegations. A replacement never was named.

But the fever in the Johnson camp welled hot as he made his entry
into the convention city and to his seventh-floor suite in the Biltmore
Hotel, two floors below Kennedy's suite. Despite the overwhelming
odds against them, the Johnson camp nourished their hope on illusion
and sought action, any action, that might upset the smooth pace of the
Kennedy juggernaut.

Johnson's key strategists believed that Kennedy had to win on the first ballot if he was to win at all. He would, in fact, suffer second-ballot defections from states—primarily Ohio and Indiana—whose delegates were pledged to Kennedy only for one ballot. Thus, the Johnson plan, of necessity, was to stop Kennedy on the first ballot and worry about the second ballot later. This was the plan:

1. Convince Hubert Humphrey, still agonizing over what to do, to hang on his forty-odd delegates. If he did not release them, they could not go to Kennedy.

2. Encourage Adlai Stevenson to act more like a candidate and less like a shy violet. Using Stevenson as a shadow candidate, Johnson's hope was to split away loose Kennedy delegates and move them into the Stevenson camp. There would be ample time after that first ballot to arrange for a switch of Stevenson delegates to Johnson. For now, however, the Johnson and Draft Stevenson staffs were meeting jointly.

3. Prevent the favorite sons from releasing their delegations. Governor Robert Meyner of New Jersey was a covert Johnson man and could be counted on to prevent the New Jersey delegation from breaking away. But Governor Herschel Loveless of Iowa and Governor George Docking of Kansas both were leaning toward Kennedy and posed problems.

4. Smear Kennedy. The campaign smear is scarcely unique as a political weapon. Few candidates will eschew the smear *if* they think they can get away with it (as the Kennedy camp smeared Humphrey in the West Virginia primary by making an issue out of his World War II draft deferment). Kennedy, it was thought by the Johnson managers, was vulnerable on two counts: the condition of his health, arising out of an adrenaline deficiency that required regular but limited treatment with cortisone; and the candidate's strong-minded father, Joseph P. Kennedy, who as United States Ambassador to Great Britain at the outbreak of World War II in Europe was accused of favoring the Germans and of harboring anti-Semitic sentiments. Johnson himself had no part in planning the smear campaign, but that did not stop his high command, led by John Connally.

Hubert Humphrey arrived in Los Angeles on the same day as Johnson and checked in at the Statler-Hilton. As a non-candidate, Humphrey didn't rate a suite in the Biltmore, the convention headquarters hotel.

Already in Los Angeles were two liberals who had been longtime, fervent supporters of Humphrey: Joseph L. Rauh, Jr., a national leader in the Americans for Democratic Action, and Marvin Rosenberg, a New York manufacturer. Both had backed Humphrey against

Kennedy in Wisconsin and West Virginia with passion and determination and, after the West Virginia debacle, had switched to Kennedy. Eyeing a possible Kennedy-Humphrey ticket, they had urged Humphrey to endorse Kennedy after West Virginia. On one occasion, Rauh thought Humphrey was persuaded.

But Humphrey stayed neutral. Now, on July 8, three days before the convention formally convened, Rauh and Rosenberg had an urgent mission: to persuade Humphrey to endorse Kennedy and bid for the second spot himself. They drove to Los Angeles International Airport to meet Humphrey's plane. But they missed Humphrey in the confusion of the airport and quickly hired a taxicab to take them to the Statler-Hilton. They did not telephone to say they were coming.

Taking the elevator to Humphrey's floor, Rauh hurried to his suite and knocked on the door. No answer. He knocked again. Still no answer. He turned to walk back down the corridor to the elevator. Rauh then heard the unmistakable sound of Hubert Humphrey's exuberant laughter coming from behind a closed door as he moved down the corridor. Rauh stopped and knocked. The laughter stopped. Then the next door down the hallway, leading into another room of the same suite, opened a crack. Pat O'Connor, a Minneapolis businessman and Humphrey intimate, poked his head out and scanned the corridor.

Seeing O'Connor, Rauh walked quickly toward him and, with a smile of recognition, said, "Oh, here he is. I stopped at the wrong suite." But when Rauh started through the half-open door, O'Connor blocked his way. Inside, Rauh caught a glimpse of James Rowe, another veteran of Humphrey's campaigns in Wisconsin and West Virginia. That surprised Rauh. After the West Virginia primary, Rowe had joined the Johnson-for-President effort and was a ranking member of the Johnson high command.

Next, Rauh found himself physically ejected from the doorway by O'Connor. Rauh was momentarily astounded at this unfriendly treatment. Astonishment quickly turned to anger. He took a swing at O'Connor, but O'Connor fended him off, stepped back in through the door and slammed it behind him. Rauh stood there for a moment, speechless.

Then, in a sudden flash of intuition, he knew what was happening. Lyndon B. Johnson was in Humphrey's suite! He also realized, at that same instant, that Humphrey now could not possibly go on the Kennedy ticket as vice-presidential nominee. Rauh had stumbled on a top-secret meeting between Johnson, Humphrey, and Rowe. While Humphrey was wanted by Joe Rauh to give the ADA liberals a trusted friend on the presidential ticket, Humphrey was needed by

Johnson as essential to stop Kennedy on the first ballot. As soon as
he saw Humphrey with Johnson, Rauh and Rosenberg (who had
waited downstairs in the lobby) tossed their vice-presidential plan
into the wastebasket.*

Johnson's pressure on Humphrey was symptomatic of the furious
but futile energy expended those last few days before the roll would
be called on Wednesday night, July 13. Another major target was the
big California delegation, where Johnson had little open backing but
important undercover support. It was impolitic in California's liberal-
oriented party to be for Johnson. How then could the covert Johnson
men fight Kennedy?

The answer was Adlai Stevenson. A Stevenson freshet was running
strong in California when the delegates gathered in Los Angeles, not
only among the delegates themselves but among thousands of Stevenson rooters, most of them from California, who were in Los Angeles
for the convention. Among the liberal, volunteer Democratic club
movement of California, Stevenson was far stronger than Kennedy.

For weeks, then, Johnson agents in California had solicited Kennedy delegates and sought to attach them, not to Johnson but to Stevenson. One important conquest was made: William Munnell, California Democratic State Chairman and Majority Leader of the State
Assembly. Although he pledged himself to Kennedy in a secret meeting at Carmel, California, that spring, Munnell now became an
avowed Stevenson man and a crypto-Johnson man. When Kennedy
walked down the line of the California delegation in a routine handshaking ceremony before the convention opened, he refused to shake
Munnell's outstretched hand. Kennedy smiled evenly and told Munnell: "You're the only delegate in the country that we locked up who
didn't stay locked up."

With Johnson operating beneath the Stevenson cover, the California operation was his one mark of success at the convention. Counting
on a big majority in California, Kennedy was stunned when a delegation caucus on July 11 showed him running second to Stevenson, with
considerably less than a majority. It was the high point of the convention for the Johnson forces. California's defection, they hoped, would
stop the Kennedy bandwagon.†

---

* Although Rauh didn't know it, the Kennedy camp had by then discarded the
possibility of inviting Humphrey on the ticket. The Kennedys felt Humphrey had
waited too long.

† California was indeed Kennedy's one major pre-convention miscalculation.
He had counted on Governor Edmund G. (Pat) Brown to deliver the delegation
to him and therefore stayed out of the California primary campaign. Had he
known of Brown's weakness in his own delegation, Kennedy would have entered
the California primary.

Apart from California, detaching delegates from the hard blocs of pro-Kennedy Democrats at Los Angeles was fruitless. With the exception of Munnell and a few others who yielded to the blandishments of the Johnson people, they were frozen in.

The drive to keep the favorite-son delegations committed to their favorite sons was hardly more successful. Loveless in Iowa and Docking in Kansas both went over to Kennedy. Kennedy men in the New Jersey delegation were prepared to desert Governor Meyner as soon as the first ballot was completed.

The fourth weapon of the Johnson camp, the smear campaign, was actually self-defeating. Its main architect was John Connally, and he struck principally at two targets: John F. Kennedy's health and his father.

On July 4, in a press conference, India Edwards, the National Democratic women's chairman of the Truman era and now an ardent Johnson supporter, charged that Kennedy had Addison's disease and "would not be alive today if it were not for cortisone." The Kennedy camp issued an immediate denial, and on July 5, Johnson himself, when asked about Mrs. Edwards' accusation, said all the Democratic candidates were in good health.

But Johnson could not restrain himself from joining the attack on Joseph P. Kennedy. Ever since delegates started arriving in Los Angeles, Connally had been spreading a campaign of innuendo against the Senator's father, charging that he had harbored pro-Nazi sympathies as ambassador in London just before World War II. On the very day of the balloting, July 14, Johnson took up the cry: "I wasn't any Chamberlain-umbrella policy man. I never thought Hitler was right."

The accelerating shrillness of the smear effort was a sign that the Johnson camp was desperate. The power available in the Senate to the Majority Leader could not be drawn on in Los Angeles. There, power resided with the big-city machines, the labor unions, the Negroes. Those late, flailing attempts to split open the solid Kennedy strength probably weakened Johnson's overall position.

On Monday, July 12, the first day of the convention, this desperation led the Johnson camp to a clear mistake in judgment seeking to capitalize on a rare error by the Kennedy camp. A telegram from candidate Kennedy to uncommitted delegations requesting permission for Kennedy to address their caucuses was mistakenly sent to the Texas delegation. The inadvertent Kennedy "request" was quickly granted by the Texas delegation. On the curious theory that young Jack Kennedy wasn't up to the rough-and-tumble of a face-to-face debate, Johnson tacticians sought a confrontation before a joint session of the Texas and Massachusetts delegations. Kennedy first refused, but Johnson persisted. In a telegram to Kennedy, he declared: "May I earnestly, Jack, urge you to reconsider your refusal and permit your delegation to join with ours for this important discussion of issues." Much to the surprise and the delight of the Johnson strategists, Kennedy turned up at the last moment Monday afternoon to debate Johnson in the Biltmore ballroom before hundreds of delegates and a television audience of millions.

The debate was scarcely what John Connally anticipated. Johnson tried to break down Kennedy with cumbersome innuendo, attacking his support of the Eisenhower Administration's low price-support policy for farmers during all but the last two of his eight years in the Senate. ". . . I hope that you will never forget that I have never at any time during my public career embraced any of the policies of Ezra Taft Benson [Eisenhower's Secretary of Agriculture] and his farm program," said Johnson. A smiling Kennedy brushed aside Johnson's thrusts, airily remarking that "I don't think I will argue because I don't think Senator Johnson and I disagree on the great issues that face us."

Johnson's main tactic in the debate was to portray himself as the responsible legislative leader and, by implication, to paint Kennedy as a dilettante. Pointing out that he had answered *all* fifty quorum calls and voted on *all* forty-five roll calls during a six-day stretch of round-the-clock Senate sessions called by Johnson to combat a Southern filibuster against the 1960 Civil Rights Bill, Johnson added that "some Senators" (Kennedy) answered no quorum calls and missed thirty-four of the roll calls.* Kennedy again used the light touch, mixed with a little sarcasm. Assuming that Johnson was "talking of someone else," he praised the Majority Leader's "wonderful record" of answering quorum calls. Johnson's central debating point was that his experience as Democratic Leader in the Senate and his unanimous election to that post, not just once but four times, qualified him for the presidency.† Kennedy's riposte: "I strongly support him for Majority Leader." In other words: he can keep the Senate, I'll take the White House.

Even if the forty-minute debate *had* provoked Kennedy into a major error as Connally had hoped, it would not have changed the out-

---

* During the 1960 civil rights filibuster, Johnson had been genuinely angry not only at Kennedy but at his friend Hubert Humphrey. Both were campaigning in Wisconsin, and neither helped Johnson much in the round-the-clock sessions.

† Johnson always referred to his four-time *unanimous* election as floor leader, apparently forgetting that Senator James Murray of Montana received a smattering of votes against him in 1953. See page 57.

come at Los Angeles. The debate did dramatize, however, the difference in political comprehension and sophistication between Kennedy and Johnson at that time. Again, Johnson was confusing the realities of a Democratic convention with the obscure, mysterious, esoteric workings of the Senate, of which he was master. He was unaware that a candidate's standing in the Senate cloakrooms counted for nothing at a National Convention. Kennedy was well aware of the realities.

The failure of the much-publicized Johnson-Kennedy confrontation to do anything but bemuse a bored convention snuffed out the last flickering hope inside the Johnson camp. That evening, key staff men of the Johnson camp and the Draft Stevenson movement held a joint meeting in the Biltmore, compared tally sheets and came to the conclusion that John Kennedy had the nomination salted down. Lyndon Johnson knew it, too, without the benefit of tally sheets. That Monday night marked the convention's first formal session, and Johnson watched it over television from his suite in the Biltmore. As Senator Frank Church of Idaho delivered the keynote address, Johnson turned to Jim Rowe seated beside him and commented casually: I don't see how we can stop him now.

Yet, the noisy, sleepless hysteria of National Conventions breeds a unique illogic that drives beaten candidates into self-defeating efforts in the face of hopeless odds. And so, two days after privately conceding defeat, Johnson unleashed his attack on Joseph P. Kennedy. And so, just moments before the balloting began on Wednesday night in the Los Angeles Sports Arena, John Connally and Bobby Baker held a final strategy session a few feet off the convention floor. The drive to "Stop Kennedy" had become entirely detached from Johnson. It was disembodied. Now, when it really was all over, Baker and Connally talked of uniting all non-Kennedy delegates behind one man—perhaps Stevenson or Symington. Johnson himself was out of it. A campaign steeped in illusion concluded with a conversation divested of the slightest touch of reality.

John F. Kennedy went over the top on the first ballot at "Wyoming." He collected 806 votes, with 761 required for the nomination. Johnson's score was 409, far below the unrealistic claims that had been made for him. The anger of frustration could be seen on the faces of Johnson's rank-and-file supporters. "Okay, okay, okay," muttered one Texas delegate, close to tears, pounding his fist into his palm. "They can have Kennedy and get beat. But we'll be back here in four years to nominate Lyndon." It was assuredly the worst political defeat in Johnson's long career.

Or *was* it? Was it just barely possible that that master-planner, Lyndon Johnson, whose sense of timing was legendary, whose ego did not court defeat and who always knew the odds, knew from the beginning that he could not beat Kennedy? Could he have been angling not for the presidency but for something less? Can a case be made that not the presidential nomination but the nomination for *Vice-President* was his secret goal?

In no sense was Lyndon B. Johnson's interest in the vice-presidency overt or explicit. There is no record that on any occasion he told a friend or ally: "I want to be Vice-President." Yet, multiple clues can be assembled bearing on the mystery of Johnson and the vice-presidency.

Clue Number 1: On March 12, 1960, Johnson and several friends shared his limousine and drove to Far Hills, New Jersey, to attend the wedding of the daughter of Charles Englehart, New Jersey industrialist, owner of South African diamond mines and dabbler in high level Democratic party politics. Johnson's mood was pensive, introspective, and serious as he discussed the approaching battle of Los Angeles. He talked about all the Democratic possibilities for President, but most of all about John F. Kennedy. Kennedy had class and Kennedy had education, Johnson mused aloud. Kennedy's instincts, as he had observed him for almost eight years in the Senate, were sound. But did Kennedy have guts? he asked. His companions had their own special views of Kennedy. The consensus in the automobile was that, yes, Kennedy also had guts. It was then that Johnson said:

"A fellow from my part of the country probably couldn't be anything more than another John Nance Garner."

To those driving to New Jersey, Johnson seemed to be thinking of the vice-presidency for himself. It was not stated, but it was felt.

Clue Number 2: Three weeks before the convention opened, Representative Hale Boggs of Louisiana, an influential back-room strategist for the Democratic party on excellent terms with both John Kennedy and Lyndon Johnson, made a bet with a friend that the ticket emerging from the convention would be Kennedy-Johnson—in that order.

Clue Number 3: At a Washington social gathering in June less than a month before the convention, Bobby Baker met by chance with Theodore Sorensen, Senator Kennedy's chief policy aide. For a year now, Baker had been singing the praises of a Johnson-Kennedy "dream ticket." But now, he reversed the order of that "dream ticket," telling Sorensen as their conversation ended:

"Maybe the ticket will turn out to be Kennedy and Johnson."

"I think that would be wonderful," Sorensen replied, "But I doubt very much that the second man on that ticket [Johnson] would agree to it."

"Don't be too sure," Baker replied, cryptically.

That was the only clue that John F. Kennedy had of Johnson's possible availability for the second position. He never confided Ted Sorensen's intelligence about Bobby Baker's remark to his brother Robert or to his chief political aides, Lawrence F. O'Brien and Kenneth P. O'Donnell, who were to become famous as the leading figures in the Kennedy Irish Mafia. Nor did Kennedy ever so much as mention the possibility of Johnson for Vice-President to them.

Clue Number 4: In 1960, as the contest for the nomination was heating up, Johnson passed some surprising confidential information to Tim McInerney, a friend of Johnson and a lobbyist who operated in the higher reaches of official Washington. Johnson confided that he regarded Kennedy as the Democrat in all the party who was best suited temperamentally for the presidency. As McInerney interpreted this, Johnson had the second spot on the ticket in the back of his own mind.

Clue Number Five: Representative Joe Kilgore, one of Johnson's strongest allies in the conservative wing of the Texas Democratic party, left Los Angeles immediately after Kennedy won the nomination. Back in Texas the next day, Kilgore was flabbergasted when he heard that Kennedy had offered Johnson the vice-presidency and Johnson had accepted. He phoned Walter Jenkins in Los Angeles. Usually close-mouthed, Jenkins for once was revealing. He told Kilgore: "This is what we've been waiting for all this time."

Kennedy had been using the lure of the vice-presidency throughout the pre-convention period to gain maximum political advantage for his own presidential campaign. In the finest tradition of candidate blarney, he had carefully planted the hope of the vice-presidency in many Democratic breasts—including Senator Stuart Symington, an announced candidate for President. Kennedy dangled the vice-presidency for Symington in two separate conversations that spring with Clark Clifford, Symington's campaign manager. Clifford came away from those conversations convinced that Symington could be Kennedy's running mate if he withdrew from the race for President and threw his support to Kennedy. Although vitally interested in the vice-presidency, Symington felt he still had a chance for the top spot. He did not take the bait. Less explicitly, perhaps, the same bait was presented to—and taken by—other would-be Vice-Presidents: Governor Herschel Loveless of Iowa, Governor George Docking of Kansas, Senator Henry M. Jackson of Washington, Senator Albert Gore of Tennessee.

A more serious prospect than any of these, however, was Governor Orville Freeman of Minnesota, who had fought shoulder to shoulder with Hubert Humphrey against the Republicans on the one hand and the Communists on the other in the Minnesota postwar political battles. When Humphrey did not overcome his bitterness at the smear against him in the West Virginia primary and refused to back Kennedy, the Kennedy camp turned to Freeman. Breaking with Humphrey, Freeman endorsed Kennedy before Los Angeles and agreed to make the major nominating speech for him.

Yet, there was another factor. John Kennedy had made a secret decision in consultation with his most intimate confidant and adviser, brother Robert F. Kennedy. Before Los Angeles, the Kennedy brothers had decided that if Johnson ever indicated he wanted to be *asked* to take the second spot—if, in other words, he wanted the right of first refusal—then he must be asked. But not in their wildest dreams did the Kennedys think he genuinely wanted the vice-presidential nomination.

In the momentary passion of Los Angeles in July, 1960, it seemed inconceivable that Lyndon Johnson would want to be asked to be John F. Kennedy's running mate. Pierre Salinger, Kennedy's press secretary, had been one of the few Kennedy aides who favored a Kennedy-Johnson ticket—*before* Los Angeles, that is. Now, embittered by the Johnson camp's attacks on Kennedy's health and father, he thought it out of the question. Nor did the prospect seem any closer to reality inside the Johnson camp.

After Kennedy's nomination on Wednesday night, Johnson's followers gathered in their headquarters at the Sports Arena, despondent, exhausted, angry. The gloom thickened until Johnson's elder daughter, Lynda, arrived and made a little speech thanking them all for what they had tried to do. Lynda's speech was tonic, a badly needed pep talk with the ancient theme of the defeated warrior: "We'll live to fight another day." Spirits in the Johnson camp visibly lifted, but there was no talk of reconciliation with the Kennedys.

In the Biltmore, Johnson himself changed into pajamas and lounged in an easy chair, talking over the events of the disappointing day with neither anger nor resentment, sipping a Scotch-and-water, quietly giving orders to a battery of secretaries. There was no talk about the vice-presidency. But the previous day, when a close friend arrived and asked a question about the vice-presidency, Johnson replied with a four-letter word: "Oh,____."

Yet, by Wednesday night, Kennedy had definitely decided that indeed he would ask Johnson to go on the ticket. He had many reasons. Johnson was first on a list of vice-presidential possibilities submitted to Kennedy by Ted Sorensen and Myer Feldman, Kennedy's legislative aide. On Wednesday, two journalist friends and admirers of *both* Kennedy and Johnson—Philip Graham, publisher of the *Washington Post,* and syndicated columnist Joseph Alsop— were advising Kennedy not only to ask Johnson but to urge him to accept. On Wednesday night, Joseph P. Kennedy, target of an attack that day from Johnson, plugged for a Kennedy-Johnson ticket. All this buttressed a decision made sometime before that by the Kennedy brothers: Johnson wanted to be asked and ought to be asked.

Thus, it was frosting on the cake Thursday morning, when Kennedy received several Southern party leaders in his ninth-floor suite in the Biltmore. Among them were William Battle, a Kennedy stalwart from Virginia and son of a former Governor of Virginia; Governor Lindsay Almond of Virginia, nominally a Johnson man but sympathetic to Kennedy; and Governor Ernest F. (Fritz) Hollings of South Carolina, another Johnson man with a soft spot for Kennedy. It was essential for Southern support in the election, they told Kennedy, to get Johnson on the ticket.*

About the same time, Robert F. Kennedy urgently summoned aides Kenny O'Donnell and Pierre Salinger to his hotel room. Bobby was in the bathtub, calling instructions and discussing for the first time with O'Donnell and Salinger the possibility of Johnson to round out the ticket. Salinger was told to tote up the electoral vote of the North and add Texas to it, along with other Southern states that Johnson's name on the ticket would presumably add to the Democratic column.

O'Donnell and Salinger, both indignant over the Johnson anti-Kennedy smears at Los Angeles, were astonished. O'Donnell asked if Johnson was seriously being considered. Calmly and without emotion, Bobby replied that he was. O'Donnell left the room and ran up one flight of steps to Senator Kennedy's suite for confirmation. He got it.

Meanwhile, Johnson was well aware of the activity in his behalf by Alsop and Graham but seemed uninterested and unimpressed, at least on the surface. That was before a telephone call started a frantically

* Late Thursday night, when he arrived at a party for Kennedy, Bill Battle encountered Joe Kennedy, who told him in high excitement that his son's choice of Johnson was "the smartest political move he ever made." The elder Kennedy credited the visit of Battle, Almond and Hollings that morning as having helped John Kennedy make his decision.

confused day that was to influence so greatly the course of American history.

At 8:35 A.M., Kennedy telephoned Johnson's suite, two flights beneath his own. Mrs. Johnson answered the phone, then put the Senator on. Kennedy asked if he could come down and see him. Johnson said he would come up and see Kennedy. No, said Kennedy, he'd come down at 9:30 A.M. They hung up.

Johnson, still in his pajamas, told Mrs. Johnson that it looked to him as though Kennedy was going to offer him the vice-presidential nomination. Mrs. Johnson did not say no. Since the 1955 heart attack, his health had never been far from the mind of Lady Bird Johnson, a woman of great charm and intelligence, spiced with a keen sense of the practical. Then, after these few words with his wife, Johnson characteristically leaped into action. He summoned trusted lieutenants and began a peripatetic series of telephone calls to the usual Senators, Texas politicians, and confidants whose judgment he always tapped before making large decisions. One he called was Representative Homer Thornberry, the Texas Congressman closest to him. Thornberry was shaving when Johnson's call came in. The dialogue went like this:

Johnson: "Jack Kennedy's coming down to see me at nine-thirty."

Thornberry: "Yes, Lyndon."

Johnson: "He may offer me the vice-presidential nomination."

Thornberry: "Yes, Lyndon."

Johnson: "What do you think I should say?"

Thornberry: "Why, Lyndon, I wouldn't touch it with a ten-foot pole."

Johnson: "But what will I tell Jack?"

Thornberry: "You know what to tell him better than I do, Lyndon. Tell him anything you want, but don't take it."

Thornberry, the lather drying on his cheeks, hung up and resumed his shaving. But now, in a flash of insight, Thornberry decided he'd given Johnson the wrong advice. He rushed back to the telephone, still unshaven, and frantically tried to get through the jammed Johnson telephone switchboard. Finally, Johnson was back on the phone with him.

"Lyndon, I've been thinking this over. I was wrong. You ought to take the vice-presidency."

On the other end of the line, there was a long pause, then Johnson's puzzled question: "But, Homer, what'll I tell Sam?"

Sam Rayburn had telephoned Johnson late Wednesday night, to extract a promise that he would not accept the vice-presidency under any circumstances. Johnson had told Rayburn then that it was a moot question, because he hadn't been offered it. But he promised the

Speaker that if it were offered he wouldn't say yes without consulting him.

Kennedy arrived in Johnson's suite at 10:05 A.M., thirty-five minutes late. He thanked Johnson for his congratulatory telegram of the night before, composed by Johnson when the roll call reached "Iowa."

Kennedy quickly got down to business. He told Johnson that many of the party's most eminent leaders thought Johnson ought to be on the ticket. They were concerned, said Kennedy, about the implications of Kennedy's nomination with only nine and one-half delegate votes from the Southern states. Kennedy named names: Mayor Richard J. Daley of Chicago; State Chairman John Bailey of Connecticut; Governor Michael DiSalle of Ohio; State Chairman Michael Prendergast and Tammany Hall leader Carmine DeSapio, both of New York; Governor David Lawrence of Pennsylvania.

That was all fine, said Johnson, but a lot of Johnson's friends were *against* his taking the vice-presidential nomination. Besides, he said, there were Stu Symington, Scoop Jackson, and all the others who thought Kennedy was planning to pick them. Johnson didn't want to get in their way. Then Johnson asked Kennedy point-blank: if you don't pick me, who will you pick? Kennedy replied that his second choice was Governor Orville Freeman of Minnesota.*

Kennedy next asked Johnson whether he would accept the vice-presidency. To Kennedy's surprise, Johnson asked for a little time to think it over. With so many of his political allies in Texas and the Senate dead set against it, he must consult them. Now suddenly obvious to Kennedy was a fact he had not dreamed could be true. Johnson not only was willing, he was eager to give up the enormous power he had built in eight years of Senate leadership to take a job that John Adams had called "the most insignificant office that ever the invention of man contrived or his imagination conceived" and that Texan John Nance Garner dismissed as not being "worth a pitcher of warm spit."

Having made his offer, Kennedy returned to his own suite to report the surprising news of Johnson's interest. Johnson went into action. Cradling the telephone between his shoulder and chin, he alternately talked on the phone and to the friends who came crowding into the large bedroom of his suite.

To one, who warned him not to exchange the vast power of the Majority Leader of the Senate for the emptiness of the vice-presidency, Johnson said: "Power is where power goes." Clearly, he was already thinking that, as Vice-President, the power he had gathered to

---

* To the press, Freeman's selection would have been nearly as much a surprise as Johnson's. The press corps had considered all but certain that Kennedy's running mate would be either Symington or Jackson.

himself in the Senate would not disappear but would follow him. "He was thinking," said the friend, "that he could run Congress from the vice-presidency."

Few agreed with him. In one corner of the bedroom, Governor Price Daniel of Texas and Senators Robert Kerr and Clinton Anderson were in a barely controlled dispute over Kennedy's offer.

"We can't carry this boy [Kennedy]," drawled Daniel.

"You're young," argued Clinton Anderson. "You'll be elected some day yourself. Don't take a chance on getting messed up now."

Kerr, a powerful lay leader in the Baptist church, said to no one in particular that he was "afraid" Johnson was going to say yes. Kerr argued strongly and bitterly. With a Catholic heading the ticket, Oklahoma would go Republican. But more important to Kerr was what was left unsaid. If Johnson left the Senate, the politically profitable Kerr-Johnson partnership of twelve years' standing would end forthwith. With Johnson's backing as Majority Leader, Kerr had pushed through the Congress one of the most ambitious water-development programs in the country's history. Kerr wanted Johnson to stay in the Senate because he feared Johnson's departure might drastically reduce his own influence there.

Another negative response came from Senator George Smathers, a close personal friend of Kennedy. Earlier that morning, Smathers had told Kennedy that Johnson would strengthen the ticket in Florida more than any other running mate but would be foolish to accept. Now, in Johnson's suite, Smathers told Johnson what he had told Kennedy; that is, although he would strengthen the ticket, he would be foolish to accept.

Ed Weisl wandered in and quietly added a powerful dissent of his own. Weisl had engaged in a bitter corporate battle with Joseph P. Kennedy years before for control of Paramount Pictures, during which Kennedy was accused of making anti-Semitic remarks about Weisl. He did not want his friend Johnson going on any Kennedy ticket.

With Weisl was Cyrus Vance, his young law partner in New York and assistant on the Defense Preparedness Subcommittee. Vance argued that Johnson should say yes. Not many others agreed. Bobby Baker and Representative Hale Boggs were among the exceptions.

As more and more of Johnson's old political allies, personal friends, Senate staffers, and Texas cronies crowded into the Johnson suite, the mood became charged with emotion. But one by one, each of them learned the astonishing fact that Kennedy himself had learned at ten o'clock that morning: Johnson very much wanted to run on the ticket. Indeed, Johnson *would* run on the ticket.

Although nothing could really change his mind, there were, nevertheless, two opinions of special importance to Johnson. He wanted the approval of his two most intimate advisers: Sam Rayburn and Lady Bird Johnson.

It was Hale Boggs who quietly persuaded the Speaker, so adamant against a Kennedy-Johnson ticket the night before. Rayburn himself, Boggs reminded the old man, had hankered for the vice-presidential nomination in 1956 but Stevenson had told him: Mr. Speaker, I wish I could, but you're too old. But what really changed Rayburn's mind was Boggs' argument that with anybody other than Johnson on the ticket, Kennedy would lose. That meant Rayburn's hated enemy, Richard M. Nixon, would become President.

When Boggs brought Rayburn around, he telephoned Kennedy to tell him. Boggs knew speed in nailing down the Kennedy-Johnson ticket was essential to prevent an anti-Johnson outbreak among liberal delegations. Boggs told Kennedy that the Speaker wanted to come and see him, overruling Kennedy's demurrer that he instead would call on Rayburn. When Rayburn, Boggs, and Rayburn's assistant, John Holton, arrived at Kennedy's suite, Rayburn and Kennedy disappeared into an inner room, leaving the other two outside with Kenny O'Donnell. The conversation was successful.

Rayburn returned to Johnson's suite and advised him to accept. When Johnson twitted him about changing his mind overnight, the Speaker cracked: "I'm a damn sight smarter this morning than I was last night." In truth, Rayburn's instinctive fear of a Catholic candidate was outweighed by his cerebral horror of a Nixon presidency.

Lady Bird Johnson had quite different reasons for saying yes. She loved her husband and wanted him to live out a full life. For five years since his heart attack, she had worried about the all but intolerable strain on the Majority Leader, the crazy, irregular hours, the endless telephone calls far after midnight to make certain that the last arrangement had been completed for tomorrow's battle on the floor, the meals turned cold, the constant pressure, pressure and yet more pressure. Mrs. Johnson wanted her husband to say yes. A new life as Vice-President would deprive her husband of the power he sought, but it would slow the reckless pace.

That should have been the end of the story. The fact that it wasn't had momentous repercussions. A poorly conceived, poorly executed rebellion by the liberals against Johnson, and the way the Kennedy camp reacted to it, sowed seeds of discord at the very moment the union was being formed. The alliance between John F. Kennedy and Lyndon B. Johnson that opened to Johnson the door of national power set in motion the mutual suspicion between Lyndon B. Johnson and Robert F. Kennedy that would grow in importance and depth as the years went by.

John Kennedy dispersed his top political lieutenants—Bobby Kennedy, Larry O'Brien, Kenny O'Donnell—to pave the way for smooth acceptance of Johnson. But delegates and delegation leaders were scattered everywhere.

There was no way to bring everyone together at once—the big-city leaders, the labor leaders, the liberal leaders—to pass the word and calm the fears.

The press quickly picked up angry complaints, centered in Michigan and the District of Columbia, and made the most of them. Although unable to measure the depth of the anti-Johnson reaction, Senator Kennedy was deeply worried. Finally, long after noon, he dispatched Robert F. Kennedy to inform Johnson of the gathering storm. Johnson, isolated in his suite and surrounded by Southern and Western political allies, had no idea of the depth of the anti-Johnson revolt.

The heart of the revolt was the Michigan delegation, headed by Governor G. Mennen (Soapy) Williams, an incessant critic of Lyndon Johnson the past eight years. No other delegation was so committed to liberalism. Behind Williams were such firebrands as Walter Reuther, President of the United Auto Workers; Gus Scholle, President of the Michigan AFL-CIO; Democratic State Chairman Neil Staebler, and many others, including more Negroes than any other delegation.

At two o'clock on that Thursday afternoon, July 15, the Michigan delegation caucused at its headquarters in the Statler-Hilton. Williams ordered the room cleared of all but bona fide delegates, then for the first time reported on his just finished visit with Kennedy, revealing to his delegation the possibility that Johnson was going to be tapped. Standing on a box, Williams told his delegates:

A large group of Southern governors and others urged Lyndon Johnson as nominee for Vice-President. That is preposterous. After our remarkable achievement in obtaining the civil rights plank in the platform, it is like stepping down from the clouds. For some of us the suggestion was catastrophic, and we have made it known in no uncertain terms.

But when pressed by the delegates to be more precise, Williams said he just could not believe that Johnson was a serious "contemplative possibility," despite the "people" urging Johnson on Kennedy.

Williams recessed his caucus and returned to his own suite in the Statler-Hilton to await more definitive word. At 3:30 P.M. Robert F. Kennedy arrived. He gave Williams the amazing message: "Jack wants Lyndon." Williams was stunned (although he later denied saying that he was "double-crossed"). Williams' reaction was reflected throughout the Michigan delegation. Labor leader Gus Scholle termed the selection "totally unnecessary." Alex Fuller, a Detroit Negro leader, said that Johnson was "wrong on more things than civil rights. He will be tough to sell among my people."

The Michigan rebels received some support from the tiny District of Columbia delegation, where Joseph Rauh—feeling he had been betrayed first by Humphrey and now by Kennedy—was the dominant force. "Say it isn't so, Jack," Rauh shouted over national television when he heard the news. A few Wisconsin delegates also kicked up their heels in revolt. But that was the extent of it.

Michigan was a special case. The state party was a coalition of liberal intellectuals and organized labor, wholly distinctive from the conventional party power structures in other industrial states, where professional politicians wanted a winner above all and were not fastidious about doctrine. In those other states—Pennsylvania, New York, Ohio, Illinois, Indiana—there may have been individual unhappiness, but the delegation leaders were sold on Johnson.

When members of the Michigan delegation, growing more and more embittered, contacted these other delegations to find a competing candidate against Johnson, they found nobody. Orville Freeman, though badly disappointed, accepted Kennedy's decision without blinking. He was not about to challenge Johnson. Governor James T. Blair, chairman of the Missouri delegation, told Michigan it was "the prerogative of the nominee to name his running mate" and that Symington backers would all go along.

But John F. Kennedy may have been misled by the sound and fury from Michigan. He could not be certain about the dimensions of the anti-Johnson revolt. If the revolt got out of hand, he pondered, would he be stuck with Johnson? Or was there some way out? He temporized momentarily. It was then that he made the decision with fateful implications. He sent his brother to see Johnson.

Bobby Kennedy set out on this errand after his 3:30 report to Soapy Williams. It was only one of very many errands Jack Kennedy had given his brother, and it took some time to get to Johnson's suite. Unknown to him, when he arrived at Johnson's suite, Senator Kennedy in that interval had decided the anti-Johnson revolt was *not* going to get out of hand. In short, he decided he would definitely put

Johnson on the ticket with him. Johnson had been informed of this hard fact by Jack Kennedy *before* his brother arrived with the shocking suggestion that perhaps Johnson ought to take himself out of the vice-presidential picture.

That, then, is the reason the Lyndon Johnson–Robert Kennedy confrontation in Johnson's suite was so pregnant with emotion. In the first place, Johnson was deeply upset that so important a state as Michigan would reject him. But beyond that, Johnson now believed that Bobby Kennedy was unilaterally trying to ease him off the ticket after John Kennedy had put him on. They talked briefly together, and Bobby, unaware that his brother's decision was now final, told Johnson that if he chose not to go through with the vice-presidency, he could be National Chairman "or anything else" he wanted.

Johnson was stunned. Sam Rayburn came in and was outraged, expressing his sentiment in four-letter words. Johnson told Bobby not only that he did not wish to withdraw, but indicated that he wanted very, very, very strongly to go on the ticket.

Now, in the new confusion caused by Bobby's visit, Johnson became alarmed all over again. He wanted final, definitive word from Kennedy himself, as the hour grew later and later. Johnson was throwing a party in his suite that afternoon. When Phil Graham of the *Washington Post* arrived, Johnson told Graham about his concern. Graham immediately phoned Jack Kennedy, who shrugged off Johnson's trepidations about Bobby's visit. "Oh!" he told Graham, "that's all right, Bobby's been out of touch and doesn't know what's been happening." Kennedy thereupon read Johnson the statement he was about to make over television.

The precise timing of the events of that frenetic day became confused almost immediately in the memories of the major actors, but soon after hearing Senator Kennedy's statement over the phone, Johnson slipped out of his bedroom and walked up to Kennedy's suite to seal their arrangement with a handshake. In the room were the two party leaders and Larry O'Brien. Kennedy was standing at a window, staring out into the haze of Los Angeles. He turned when Johnson entered, and they spoke a few words. Then Johnson came over to O'Brien, grabbed his right hand in both of his, swore fealty to the Kennedy cause, and told O'Brien that he, Johnson, would work his heart out in the campaign. The Kennedy camp, said Johnson, could be certain that he would be a full member of the team.

Johnson then returned to his own suite, where his party was in full swing, and switched on the television set to watch Kennedy make his electrifying public announcement that it would be Johnson. A few minutes later, Johnson walked out of his suite into the sweaty herd of reporters and television cameras and read his own statement, signifying his desire to go on the ticket.

But Bobby Kennedy's last-hour visit to him was not forgotten. Johnson and some of his intimates bitterly resented it. In fact, Bobby was carrying out his brother's outdated orders, quite unaware that the issue was moot when he sat down with Johnson. Johnson never realized it. Nearly four years later, Robert F. Kennedy was to remember well those few moments with Johnson in 1960, as he sat alone with Johnson in the Oval Office of the White House to be told by President Johnson he was not wanted on the 1964 ticket.

House Majority Leader John W. McCormack of Massachusetts, though nominally the convention "floor manager" for the young Senator from his state, was really closer to Johnson than to Kennedy. Consequently, he gladly accepted a special assignment given him when the convention convened at the Sports Arena Thursday night.

On the seething floor, the anger and disappointment of the Michigan and District of Columbia delegates plus scattered others were smothered by McCormack's sudden, unexpected call on behalf of the Massachusetts delegation for a "voice vote" on Johnson's nomination, instead of the usual state-by-state roll call. A two-thirds vote was needed to suspend the rules of the convention to permit the voice vote. Governor LeRoy Collins of Florida, the convention chairman, paused uncertainly when he put the question and heard the roar of response. The convention parliamentarian, octogenarian Representative Clarence Cannon of Missouri, nodded his head, and Collins announced that, with two-thirds concurring, "the motion is adopted . . ." (yells and boos filled the hall) ". . . and Senator Lyndon B. Johnson of Texas has been nominated for the vice-presidency of the United States by acclamation." *

Some of Lyndon Johnson's most loyal supporters reeled from the developments of July 15, 1960. Governor Price Daniel and the Texas

---

* One bizarre aspect of the furious pace of events early Thursday evening at the Sports Arena was the activity of Senator William Proxmire of Wisconsin, Johnson's arch-critic in the Senate. Unpredictable as ever, Proxmire helped quell an incipient rebellion against the Kennedy-Johnson ticket among Wisconsin delegates. In a speech to a delegation caucus, Proxmire argued that Johnson would do the liberal cause less damage in the vice-presidency than in the Majority Leader's chair.

Democratic delegation were devastated, more disillusioned by Johnson going on the ticket than Johnson losing the presidential nomination. Senator Robert Kerr was so angered when Bobby Baker told
him that Johnson had accepted the vice-presidential nomination he
slapped Baker across the face. Ed Weisl, heartbroken to see his old
friend allied with the hated Kennedys, left Los Angeles without seeing Johnson again. Eliot Janeway, who surpassed Weisl in his dislike
for the Kennedys, decided to support Nixon for President.*

Yet, one of Lyndon Johnson's shrewdest friends and advisers who
was not in Los Angeles saw clearly the meaning of his decision. In
New York, Donald Cook immediately supported Johnson for he knew
what Johnson knew: he had emancipated himself from Texas. It was,
almost certainly, the only way he could do so.

Johnson knew, and had often remarked, that the odds were long
against a Texan ever being nominated for President. Accordingly, the
only possible way to get to be President was to become Vice-President
first. As Vice-President, Johnson could accomplish two things beyond
his grasp as Senate Majority Leader: first, it was at least conceivable
that he would become heir apparent, and run for President in 1968 at
the end of Kennedy's two terms. Second, as Vice-President he could
cast off the Southern regionalism that had plagued him all those years
in the Senate and become a *national* politician. As Vice-President, he
would speak for the *nation*, not just for Texas.

Although the record of Vice-Presidents becoming President by the
normal route of nomination and election was poor (not once in this
century), three Presidents had died in office and been succeeded by
their Vice-Presidents since 1901. "Today I am nothing," John Adams
said during his vice-presidency, "but tomorrow I may be everything."

Furthermore, Johnson's preeminence in the nation as Majority
Leader of the Senate stemmed in part from the fact that the White
House was in Republican hands, and, moreover, in the hands of a
benign Republican President. But what would become of the Majority
Leader's power if the White House went Democratic? Then John F.
Kennedy would be the focal point of power and influence in the Dem-
ocratic party, not the Senate Majority Leader. With Kennedy in the
White House, Johnson remaining as Majority Leader could choose be-
tween two roles: he could be one of about a dozen or more Kennedy
lieutenants, all with roughly equal influence; or he could build his own

* That reaction extended to some of Johnson's conservative Republican friends
in the Senate, who had been assured by him he would not take the vice-presidency. Senator Barry Goldwater of Arizona scribbled Johnson a two-word note:
"I'm nauseated."

Democratic fortress in the Senate and try to dictate to the Democratic President from Capitol Hill, a most hazardous course.

If Johnson had turned down the vice-presidential nomination after Kennedy's offer and Kennedy lost the election, his shaky standing in the Northern wing of the party would be still shakier and he might well be blamed for the Kennedy loss. If he accepted, and then the ticket lost, he would still be Majority Leader. The Texas legislature had made it possible for Johnson to run simultaneously for President (or Vice-President) *and* for a third term in the United States Senate. Yet, it would not be the same with Richard Nixon in the White House. Johnson once remarked to a friend that with Nixon as President, he did not know whether the Majority Leader's job would be worth having.

Given, then, the political realities once Kennedy was nominated for President, to run for Vice-President was the best of all possible worlds for Lyndon Johnson. It unchained him from Texas. It opened the door a crack toward power so awful as to make Johnson's carefully nursed power as Majority Leader seem puny.

Chapter XIV

CAMPAIGNING
FOR
KENNEDY

I didn't run for Vice-President, but I'll tell you why I'm proud
to be on this ticket. A strong, dedicated man walked into my
room one morning and said, "I want you to help me." It took a
pretty big man to walk down two flights of stairs to ask that of
the man who had opposed him all the way down to the Canal
Zone.
>   —Lyndon Johnson, campaign speech in
>   Hartford, Connecticut, September 9, 1960

On Friday morning, July 16, 1960, John F. Kennedy exercised his sudden new power as national party leader and summoned the Democratic National Committee into session at the Biltmore Hotel in Los Angeles for the purpose of replacing Paul M. Butler as chairman. Obediently, the committee followed Kennedy's instructions to the letter and elected Senator Henry M. Jackson of Washington, one of the many disappointed suitors for the vice-presidency, as Democratic National Chairman—the first Protestant to hold that office since Cordell Hull in 1925.

Although Jackson was not picked until Los Angeles, Kennedy had long since decided he needed a Protestant for the job and that the new chairman would be used primarily as a front-man and speech-maker. The National Committee's headquarters in Washington would actually be run by Lawrence F. O'Brien, Kennedy's political aide, with the title of Director of Organization. His selection, along with Jackson's, was announced to the National Committee at the Friday morning meeting.

Understandably, Kennedy quite forgot about Lyndon Johnson, his running mate for all of twelve hours, when he called that meeting of the National Committee for Friday morning. Also understandably,

Johnson was piqued. Johnson would have appreciated hearing the news about Jackson and O'Brien first from Kennedy. Instead, he heard it with the rest of the world.

"I think I'll go back to Texas, make a couple of speeches, and the hell with it," Johnson complained to a friend. He didn't mean a word of it. Nevertheless, the dull ache of the morning after was real enough. The adjustment from Number One to Number Two could not be accomplished overnight. Yet, many of his friends were surprised that Johnson held his public composure so masterfully.

Although Johnson's power emanated from the Senate, he had made the Senate felt across the land. For the past half dozen years, Johnson felt he, more than any other single Democrat, spoke for his party. He yielded to no man. Now he would have to yield, not just today and tomorrow but as far as time stretched ahead, to John F. Kennedy. That prospect, crowding in after his long preeminence, would have galled a man less proud than Johnson. And so, understandably, Johnson was easily irritated those first days after the Kennedy-Johnson ticket was nominated.

But he did not show it, except among close friends. In that immediate post-convention period, he gave no outward sign he had not reconciled himself to second place with the best grace of the good loser. In the twenty-four hours before the untidy exodus of Democrats from Los Angeles on Saturday, Johnson was lost in the throngs of Kennedy admirers but did not betray by any public gesture the pain he must have felt. He walked behind the new leader, and he walked in step.

Robert C. Hill, the United States Ambassador to Mexico, had telephoned Johnson in Los Angeles on Thursday—after Kennedy won the nomination but before he completed the ticket—and asked Johnson and his family to come down to Acapulco for a short vacation.* Johnson said no, it was out of the question. A few days later, however, Mexico beckoned, a place far away from the turbulent climax of Los Angeles and the complaints of his friends. He called Hill by long distance and accepted.

After leaving Los Angeles on the weekend of July 17, the Johnsons, with Representative Homer Thornberry and his wife, George Reedy, and several secretaries, flew down to Acapulco for a few days' rest in a guest house that belonged to the President of Mexico. There he was immune from the sharp, cutting criticism of Texas Democrats that he had "sold out" by going on the ticket with a Catholic boy from Boston still wet behind the ears. There he could commune and take stock and

* Hill was the Assistant Secretary of State who served as John Foster Dulles' messenger during the 1957 Middle East crisis. See pages 179–180.

prepare himself for the self-discipline which he would rigidly have to apply for the foreseeable future. From that day to the end of the campaign, and, if the ticket was successful, to the end of Kennedy's presidency, Lyndon Johnson would not be his own man. He would be Jack Kennedy's man. To steel himself for that, and to learn to live with it, would take all the self-control that Johnson possessed.

On Friday evening, July 30, vice-presidential candidate Johnson and his retinue of campaign aides swept into Hyannis, Massachusetts, on Cape Cod, with a plane-load of Texas newspapermen and editors, some of them still rankling over Johnson's decision to go on the ticket. On his return to the LBJ Ranch from the brief respite in Acapulco, Johnson characteristically moved his Texas organization into quiet action to beat down the rising protests. He argued persuasively with old friends in the right wing of the Democratic party, trying to make them understand the *Realpolitik* of his decision. But the bitterness was hard to dispel. It would break out later in the campaign in a virulent form in the new-rich Texas city of Dallas, with important repercussions on the presidential election itself.

In the tiny residential village of Hyannisport adjoining the town of Hyannis that soft summer's evening of July 30, Johnson drove to Kennedy's modest, clapboard summer cottage on the edge of the Kennedy family's compound overlooking Nantucket Sound to dine with Kennedy. Also attending were James H. Rowe, who had arrived in Hyannis earlier to serve as liaison man between the Kennedy and Johnson campaigns, and Myer Feldman, Kennedy's legislative aide. Johnson had not seen Kennedy since Los Angeles, although they had talked by telephone.

Now they faced two problems: the special "rump" session of Congress beginning nine days hence on August 8, Johnson's creation which had now come back to haunt him; and the planning of the campaign itself, which would start officially on Labor Day.

Johnson, consulting memoranda on a variety of subjects specially prepared for the meeting with Kennedy, did most of the talking that evening, which started with a long, relaxed cocktail hour, followed by dinner and then more talk. But it was Kennedy who summed up, in quick, precise phrases, the basic political problem that confronted the Kennedy-Johnson campaign. Kennedy had already demonstrated to the total satisfaction of the Johnson men that he knew more about the American political scene than any politician since Franklin D. Roosevelt. Having crisscrossed the country innumerable times in his quest for the nomination, he knew where the ethnic bodies were buried, how the expanding suburban vote should be played, where and how the civil rights issue could be exploited. While Johnson was running the Senate, Kennedy was learning national politics.

But Johnson knew the Senate and sensed disaster ahead. He warned that the rump session held potential dangers for the Democratic ticket. Not much would be achieved, he predicted. He advised against both a new farm bill and an additional three billion dollars to the 1961 defense appropriation as Kennedy had promised at Los Angeles. Johnson also flatly opposed any new civil rights bill, as the Negro organizations were demanding. Instead, the program must be limited, he said, to the four major bills pending when he recessed the Senate for the Los Angeles convention: Medicare, minimum wage, housing, and education.*

Apart from the rump session, Johnson cautioned Kennedy to go slow on civil rights in the campaign itself. Johnson's task was to restore the Democratic party's ancient hegemony in the Old Confederacy, and this task would be far more difficult in the South if civil rights were a major issue in the campaign.

Johnson worried, too, about his own civil rights record as a Texas Democrat, notwithstanding the remarkable Johnson breakthrough in passing the 1957 Civil Rights Act. Johnson advised Kennedy to play up the fact that he had always opposed the Texas poll tax and not to forget his long friendship with and support from the Mexican-American community in Texas.

Kennedy agreed with all of that—but only up to a point. Kennedy also knew that civil rights contained the possible seed of Democratic victory in November. That part of the Negro vote which had slipped toward Dwight D. Eisenhower in 1952 and 1956 must be recovered. Too much soft-pedaling of Negro rights, Kennedy said, would be counterproductive.

Kennedy's general plan for the campaign conflicted with Johnson's in one other important respect. He wanted Johnson to confine himself largely to the South. Kennedy would beat for votes in the great urban strongholds of the North, in the suburbs, among the ethnic minorities.

But on behalf of Johnson, Jim Rowe disagreed. With experience in national politics dating back to the Roosevelt years and a base in Montana that gave him a vantage point quite distinct from Kennedy's, Rowe argued forcefully against this basic campaign plan. Kennedy was still not known in the West and Southwest, he said, despite his

* The failure of even these bills to move through the election-bound Congress is described in Chapter X. See pages 223–224.

four-year perambulations around the country. A Catholic himself, Rowe explained: "You've got to let these people see you. You've got to show them that Catholics don't have horns." By the same token, Rowe insisted that Johnson could not be confined to the South. He, too, must display himself where he was not known.

What finally resulted was a compromise. Kennedy campaigned all over the country, but heavily in the East and not nearly enough in the West, in the opinion of politicians there. Johnson was by no means restricted to the South, but he did his most effective campaigning there.

So did the evening of July 30, with John F. Kennedy and Lyndon B. Johnson in a new and potentially embarrassing relationship, pass pleasantly enough. For all of his worry about the rump session, Johnson was wound up and exuberant. His voice, rising and falling, could be distinctly heard through the open windows by reporters waiting outside in the country lane.

Leaving Kennedy's house late that evening, Johnson was gay, relaxed, and ready to embark on one of his periodic talking jags. He drove back to the Yankee Inn in Hyannis, where he and his staff were spending the night, and with him went Pierre Salinger, Kennedy's genial, rotund press secretary. Johnson credited Salinger with having helped create Kennedy's image.

Into the early hours of the morning Johnson talked and talked, with Salinger and others listening. He seemed fully recovered now from the defeat of the convention and looking forward to the first campaign in his life in which he would be freed from at least some of the parochial restraints of Texas and could move around the country as a *national* candidate on a *national* ticket. But he brooded over his image—his Texas image.

Johnson went on: Palmer Hoyt, publisher of the *Denver Post*, once told him he ought to present himself as a Matt Dillon type, a law-and-order man from the old frontier, not a gas-and-oil man from the new Texas. "You know," Johnson kidded Salinger, "like Matt Dillon, big, six-feet-three, good looking." What he really needed, Johnson continued, was a press secretary like Pierre Salinger. George Reedy, a large and learned man with a huge head, thick and unruly hair, and tortoise-shell glasses, listened solemnly. Reedy, who was many things to Johnson, including his *de facto* press secretary, was silent as Johnson confided his need for a new image-maker—like Salinger, Johnson said. Salinger tossed a name into Johnson's lap, Joseph Lastelic, who was a political reporter for the *Kansas City Star*. Johnson was impressed and actually hired Lastelic.

Before Johnson and company departed Hyannisport the next day, the two candidates held a joint press conference Saturday morning in the living room of Ambassador Kennedy's house. Again, Johnson did most of the talking. He wanted at all cost to avoid any impression that he was sulking, or unhappy in his role of Number Two. He was positively ebullient at that press conference, and Kennedy was well satisfied to have him just that way. It was vital to the coming campaign that the Kennedy-Johnson team show a mutual delight at being linked after the passion of the convention, to dispel the rumors that they made an incongruous team and could never pull together in the same harness. Before the meeting with the press ended, Johnson cracked: "I was sure that we had arrived on the New Frontier when I walked out of Senator Kennedy's house last night and saw [reporters for] the *Wall Street Journal* and *Time* waiting for me."

But deeper thoughts filled Johnson's restless imagination. Not long after his visit to Hyannisport and after the rump session had started, Johnson sat one evening with a friend and talked again of Jack Kennedy. Clearly, this new relationship was not an easy one for Johnson. Suddenly, he turned to his friend and said without a trace of sarcasm: "Tell me, just what is it that people like so much in Jack Kennedy?"

It was a natural enough question, but it betrayed a sense of unfulfillment in Johnson. This ambitious, exciting, vain, temperamental, insecure, powerful politician had tamed the Senate, but underneath the tough exterior, and more keenly than anyone could know, he felt the pain and anguish of not being loved. What Johnson was asking in that innocent question—"what is it that people like so much in Jack Kennedy"—was really this: why do they love Jack, but not me?

Briefly, the headquarters of the Kennedy-Johnson campaign was housed in a cramped little office in the Senate wing of the Capitol that Joseph Duke, the Senate Sergeant-at-Arms, had loaned to Kennedy for the duration of the rump session. On the other side of the Senate chamber was the grand vista of Johnson's own Taj Mahal, but it simply would not do for the Number One man to use the office space of the Number Two man, no matter how much grander it was. Thus, in the all-important scheduling sessions to plan where each of the two candidates would be at each hour of every day from September 1 to the election, the initial work was done in Joe Duke's postage-stamp office. The confusion, habitual to a presidential campaign, was aggravated by Johnson's congenital inability to be satisfied for long with a set, inflexible schedule.

The first significant scheduling meeting, held just after the rump session got underway, was symptomatic. At issue was a campaign trip that Kennedy had planned to make to Hawaii but which, because of the congressional session, he felt he would have to cancel. Not enough time. As the only possible substitute, Kennedy suggested that Johnson go to Hawaii. Before the convention, Johnson often talked about wanting to go to Hawaii. Johnson had sponsored a bill for an East-West University there.

And so, when it was brought up that day in Kennedy's borrowed cubbyhole office, the Honolulu trip was laid out for Johnson without a word of protest from Johnson himself. But not long after the meeting adjourned, Johnson called a meeting of his own in the Taj Mahal. There with Johnson and Rowe were Walter Jenkins, from Johnson's own staff; Richard Maguire, a politician and Kennedy staffer from Massachusetts; Rein Vander Zee, a young ex-FBI agent from Texas who had just signed on as Johnson's scheduling man.

To this gathering, Johnson announced that he was *not* going to Honolulu. Surprised in view of the apparent agreement concluded across the Senate chamber in Kennedy's office, Rowe told Johnson he had understood Johnson to say definitely that he would make the trip. Further, Rowe said he had ordered Vander Zee to hire an airplane from American Airlines. Johnson turned to Vander Zee. Is that right? he asked. Vander Zee said, Yes, sir, that was the way he understood it. Johnson then turned to his trusted personal aide, Walter Jenkins, and asked Jenkins *his* recollection of the meeting in Kennedy's office. Jenkins, obviously briefed by Johnson, said that Johnson had only discussed the *possibility* of going to Hawaii but had never finally agreed. Taken off the hook by Jenkins, Johnson announced finally and firmly he would not go to Hawaii, and he did not, even though Salinger had announced publicly that Johnson would substitute for Kennedy on the trip.

Time and again, Johnson pulled the rug from under firm plans or plans that everyone else thought were firm, canceling appearances at the last minute. Often, alarmed by an impromptu talk with a fellow Senator about how bad the political conditions were back in his state —or prodded by another Senator to come out to his state and take advantage of the state fair or what-have-you—Johnson would suddenly order his schedule rearranged. That never helps any campaign, and for Johnson, a Southerner campaigning often in alien Northern lands, it was particularly damaging. In canceling out a speech at the last moment, he infuriated all the local Democrats who had worked for a large turnout, and frustrated his advance men. On the other hand, by appearing in unscheduled cities without proper forewarning, Johnson assured low turnouts and thin publicity.

Throughout Johnson's campaign, nagging incidents plagued the relations between the candidate and his closest campaign aides. There was continuing tension between Johnson and his speech writers. The basic speech-writing team stayed in Washington, headed by Charles Murphy, a Truman speech writer ten years earlier. But, Johnson often scrapped their carefully constructed speeches and put his own traveling staff to work composing speeches under the most difficult circumstances.

Constantly, he was torn between the expert advice of national politicians and the conflicting advice from parochial politicians in the Senate who could glimpse only a small corner of the broad canvas. Thus, it was decided by the national professionals, including Kennedy himself and Jim Rowe, that an ideal format for Johnson would be the fourteen-state Midwestern Democratic Conference in Oklahoma City on September 16. Johnson's instinct was to say no. Those Democratic liberals from Michigan and Wisconsin who had protested furiously against him at Los Angeles would be at Oklahoma. It looked risky to Johnson. He equivocated.

But to Rowe and the others, it was precisely because the Midwest meeting would be filled with liberals that Johnson should go there. It was, thought Rowe, an essential forum if Johnson were to shake off the thick layers of Texas politics and put on the new raiment of national Democrat. Rowe convinced Johnson, told the Midwestern conference Johnson would be there, and made reservations. To Senator Robert Kerr, however, the Oklahoma trip was folly. Kerr knew that his arch-rival in the Oklahoma Democratic party, James Arrington, the state's National Committeeman and a liberal, was sponsoring the fourteen-state conference. Arrington was a strong supporter of the Kennedy-Johnson ticket. Never reconciled to the decisions made at Los Angeles, Kerr sat on his hands during the campaign. Kerr advised Johnson not to come, but too late to change the plan.

When Johnson and his entourage arrived in Oklahoma City three hours before the dinner speech, he and Kerr huddled with Rowe in Johnson's hotel room. Big and bellicose, Bob Kerr was angry. He asked Johnson, What idiot told you to come out here? Rowe answered that he was that idiot.

Kerr complained that if he had had a little more time, he could have packed the hall for Johnson's appearance, with employees of the Kerr-McGee Company if need be, but that now it was too late. Johnson, he said, would have a very poor house. Kerr then suggested that the occasion be presented to the press not as a major speech, but as a televised pep talk by Johnson to the select group of Democratic leaders from the fourteen states, thus obviating the inevitable reaction that Johnson couldn't fill up the hall. Kerr ordered tons of television equipment into the hall, to take up space and make it more difficult to judge the audience. All this made Johnson distinctly uncomfortable. Arriving at the hall on schedule, he saw many empty seats. He strode to the podium, delivered a hard-hitting political speech that was reminiscent of Harry Truman's 1948 campaign, and then, without a backward glance, strode out again, furious at what he considered a loss of face.

Rowe worked around the clock to keep relations smooth between Johnson and all the elements of his campaign, but the strain took its toll. A series of irritations, some of them seemingly insignificant, began to wear down the old harmonious relationship between Johnson and Rowe. Indeed, they contributed to one of Johnson's recurring problems: alienation of a friend. The friend in this instance was the faithful Jim Rowe, but there had been other estranged friends at earlier periods of Johnson's life—even Sam Rayburn himself, to whom Johnson refused to speak for a time during 1956, communicating only by a go-between. Johnson's coolness toward Rowe, as with all the others, passed away in time, but while it lasted—throughout Johnson's vice-presidency—it was strong enough to keep these two old friends apart.

For all of the scheduling and speech-writing problems, Johnson threw himself into the battle with an exuberance and enthusiasm that more than justified Kennedy's decision to take him on the ticket. Robert F. Kennedy felt no need to fault Johnson's campaign effort. Johnson held up his end of the Los Angeles bargain in a manner beyond criticism.

His role in the campaign was, as it had been in the Senate, to bind together North and South. On the opening day of his campaign, on September 8 in Boston, an exuberant Johnson coined a campaign phrase that he repeated time and again: this was a campaign linking Austin, Texas, with Boston, Massachusetts, and the Boston-Austin Axis combined the best of the North with the best of the West and would be invincible in November.

Behind the Boston-Austin Axis was the reality of twenty-four electoral votes in Texas. In 1952, Texas went Republican for the first time in history by well over one hundred thousand votes. That margin was repeated in 1956. If Johnson could not return his state to the

Democratic column in 1960, the whole point of naming him to the ticket would be lost. Indeed, the election might well be lost. But much had changed since 1956 when Dwight Eisenhower was on the ticket. In 1956 the Dallas County Democratic executive committee did not even meet to plan a campaign for Adlai Stevenson. Chairman Edward J. Drake was openly for Eisenhower, as were hundreds of other Democratic party officials in Texas. A powerful Businessmen-for-Eisenhower committee raised thousands of dollars against Stevenson in 1956. Now, in early September, 1960, Johnson, Rayburn, and the Democratic party loyalists had already moved successfully to cut down on this sort of defection by non-loyalist "Democrats." They neutralized the Dallas Businessmen's Committee so that it would not support the Nixon-Lodge ticket. The county executive committee in Dallas, heartland of conservatism, might not work very hard for the Kennedy-Johnson ticket, but neither would it engage in sabotage, as it had in 1952 and 1956.

Moreover, Sam Rayburn, moved to unusual exertions now that his protégé was on the Democratic ticket, openly threatened legislative retaliation against the oil-and-gas industry if it worked against the Democratic ticket. The Texas oil moguls, warned Rayburn, could not be Democrats for 3 years and 364 days, and then vote Republican in the presidential election. If they did, they might find their precious depletion allowance exposed to sudden change in Congress. Coming from Speaker Rayburn, the oil barons' most powerful protector in Congress, that was advice not to be ignored.

But in 1960, there was a new burden that Adlai Stevenson had not borne in 1952 and 1956 and that now threatened the Boston-Austin Axis and Lyndon Johnson's campaign to return Texas and the rest of the Old Confederacy to its home in the Democratic party. It was the religious issue.*

Even as Johnson opened his campaign in Boston on September 8, it was clear that this was *the* cutting issue of the campaign. The day before Johnson's arrival in Boston, one hundred and fifty Protestant clergymen headed by the Reverend Dr. Norman Vincent Peale met in Washington and warned that a Roman Catholic President would be "under extreme pressure by the hierarchy of his church" to follow the Vatican's foreign policy. They claimed that the religious issue had become the "most significant" of the campaign and that no matter what Kennedy said, his church "insists that he is duty-bound to admit to its direction."

---

* It was thought for much of the campaign that anti-Catholic prejudice would hurt Kennedy most in the South, just as it had Al Smith in 1928. Actually, Kennedy probably suffered more from it in the Midwest.

Johnson hit the religious issue head-on in Boston and continued to hit it in Hartford, Connecticut, in New York City and, after he met Kennedy four days later on September 12, across the state of Texas. Johnson handled the issue as a Texas cowman, not with the sophisticated subtleties of a Protestant theologian. He said in Hartford on September 9:

If it develops that people do apply a religious test as a qualification for office, then we tear up the Bill of Rights and throw our Constitution into the wastebasket. In the next election, the Baptists will be out, and next a Jew or a Methodist or a Christian cannot be President, and soon we will disqualify everyone who believes in God and only the atheists will be left as eligible, and that's not the American way.

Unsubtle, even crude, but a child could understand it. Moreover, Johnson spoke the lines not from a ghostwritten text but from his own cuff, his high-pitched voice spelling the doom of the Republic if religion were permitted to interfere with the free choice of the people.

From New York, on September 10, Johnson flew in his twin-engine Convair down to the LBJ Ranch, landing on the runway that ended a few yards from his backdoor. In Texas, a crucial confrontation was about to take place. For days, he and Kennedy had pondered the religious dilemma. Should Kennedy appear before the Greater Houston Ministerial Association on September 12 and submit to questions from fundamentalist Baptist ministers, over statewide television, or should the issue be handled quietly, and the creeping hate campaign be allowed to run its course without a confrontation?

The issue was discussed by Ted Sorensen and Myer Feldman for Kennedy, and a bright new staff man for Johnson. He was Bill D. Moyers, an ordained Baptist himself, at age twenty-five. Moyers had answered mail for Senator Johnson one summer during his college days and later worked for his station KTBC in Austin before getting his Bachelor of Divinity degree at Southwestern Baptist Theological Seminary in Fort Worth in December, 1959. He returned to the Johnson staff in early 1960 and, seated in the outer office of the Taj Mahal, was assigned to answer important mail (much to the merriment of Johnson's pretty secretaries, who giggled and wisecracked over having a preacher on the staff). Moyers leaped up the steps of the Johnson staff ladder, serving Johnson as a combination valet-messenger-administrative assistant during the wild days at the Biltmore in Los Angeles and living in the bathroom of the suite. Now, in September, he had become a key political adviser to Johnson on the thorny religious issue.

Moyers gathered in the religious statistics of Texas. Thirty-nine percent of all Texans, or almost 3.5 million, were Protestants. Of these,
nearly half were Southern Baptists and 788,000 were Methodists.
Texas Catholics totaled about 1.3 million. Moyers told Johnson that an
estimated 95 percent of the 3,700 Baptist preachers in Texas would
actively oppose the Kennedy-Johnson ticket, but that less than one-
half their parishioners would follow them. The age breakdown ex-
trapolated by Moyers' research was that those under forty, who had
matured during World War II and who included many war veterans,
would stay with the Democratic ticket, while the older Protestants
would follow the clergy. But all that was predicated on the assumption that Kennedy would not stumble in the confrontation with the
Baptist preachers.

For days, Kennedy discussed with Sorensen and Feldman the question of whether to appear before the ministers in Houston. Johnson
discussed it with Moyers. Finally, Kennedy relayed a tentative "yes"
to Johnson via telephone. Johnson concurred but warned Kennedy
about "mine fields."

"We must be careful about where we walk," Johnson told Kennedy.
In the back of his mind was a conviction that Kennedy's performance
before the Houston ministers would make or break the campaign in
Texas, and perhaps in the nation.

The climactic meeting with the ministers was only two days away as
Johnson flew from New York to the LBJ Ranch. Here was the first
climax of the campaign, in Johnson's own backyard, and as he flew
South he repeatedly praised Kennedy's courage in risking a public
meeting with the suspicious ministers. Johnson was pleased with the
results of his New England trip. He pulled one newspaper clipping
after another from his pocket and gleefully read aloud glowing accounts of his performance.

That night at the ranch, long after Mrs. Johnson and the Senator's
staff had gone to bed exhausted from the long day that started in
New York early that morning, Johnson took two reporters out to the
edge of his heated swimming pool, where a row of hammocks
stretched alongside the pool. He dropped into one of the hammocks
and his two companions occupied hammocks on either side of him.
The candidate wanted to talk, and the reporters wanted to listen. But
now, long after midnight, with the soft strumming of crickets and the
gentle droning of insect life under the pale moon, the reporters found
it impossible to keep their eyes open and drifted off to sleep. The
Democratic vice-presidential candidate talked on and on into the
small hours of Sunday morning, September 11, buoyed by his restless

energy, untired despite the hard day of campaign-and-travel just completed and exhilarated by the prospect of guiding Kennedy through
the dangerous reefs of Texas little more than twenty-four hours hence,
on Monday, September 12.

The day began in West Texas, at El Paso and Lubbock. From
there, the two candidates flew to San Antonio. At noon, September 12,
the square in front of the Alamo was filled with pickets. "We want the
Bible and the Constitution," one proclaimed. "We don't want the
Kremlin or the Vatican," said another. When Johnson introduced
Kennedy, the sign-holders waved their messages in his face. With
Kennedy at his side, Johnson shouted above the hecklers. He told of
young naval Lieutenant Jack Kennedy, his PT boat cut in two by a
Japanese destroyer, rescuing a wounded crew mate and swimming
him to shore by clenching the sailor's belt in his teeth. Then came
Johnson's dramatic punch line: "When Jack Kennedy was saving
those Americans, they didn't ask him what church he belonged to."

The Kennedy-Johnson tour was brought to a successful climax that
night when Kennedy confronted the ministers in Houston's Rice Hotel. From that point on, the religious issue lost its respectability. Fresh
from that triumph, Kennedy, escorted by Johnson and Rayburn, barn-
stormed Texas the following day and when Johnson said farewell to
his chief on September 13 he felt far more secure than he had just two
days earlier that Texas might indeed return to the Democratic column
in November. In fact, however, Texas almost certainly would have
stayed Republican had it not been for an unpredictable, explosive incident in Dallas almost two months later on November 4, just four
days before the election, in which Johnson was cast in the role of
hero.

In the first week of November, Lyndon Johnson returned to Texas
to close out his end of the campaign and fulfill his end of the bargain:
win Texas for Kennedy. The polls showed Texas a toss-up. Things had
not gone as well as anticipated. Instead of quieting the post-convention clamor of conservative Texans that Johnson had betrayed his state
by going on the ticket with Kennedy, the campaign had intensified it.

The state's mood was nasty when Lyndon and Lady Bird Johnson
came to Dallas on November 4 to attend a Democratic rally in the
Adolphus Hotel. They arrived at the Adolphus around noon, an hour
after a Republican rally for Richard M. Nixon had ended. Republicans
and an assortment of Johnson-hating Democrats crowded into the
lobby of the Adolphus several hundred strong. As they waited for

Johnson, their mood went from unruly to ugly to threatening. Many were women, dressed in special Nixon costumes and wearing colorful straw hats. Some were members of the Dallas Junior League: rich, smug, prejudiced. When the Johnsons entered the lobby and started to cross to the elevator, the placard-bearing crowd pressed in on them, swearing, shouting insults, spitting on the floor. In the crowd was Representative Bruce Alger of Dallas, the only Republican Congressman from Texas, carrying a sign that read: LBJ SOLD OUT TO YANKEE SO-CIALISTS. As the Johnsons moved deeper into the crowd, it became bolder. It bristled, now, with hostility. Showing admirable coolness in a dangerous situation, Johnson kept moving slowly through his fellow Texans, bringing Lady Bird after him, and finally, nearly thirty minutes after they had entered the lobby, they reached the staircase and walked to the second floor.

The incident was unique in American political history. In one sudden revelation, it portrayed Johnson to the critical North in a wholly new light. The stereotyped Johnson was a Texas rancher with cowboy boots and Stetson, owned by oil and gas, possessed of a Deep South racial prejudice, arrogant toward the labor unions, moved only by the pretensions of great wealth. Now, that stereotype, for years the target of ridicule and suspicion by Northern intellectuals and liberals, was *himself* under attack, and in his own state and by the very crowd that was supposed to own him! Suddenly, a "new Johnson" appeared to those who always thought they had his number.

But beyond that, the ugly incident in the Adolphus outraged thousands of Texans and many more thousands of Southerners in other states. Senator Richard Russell, who had not campaigned for his party's national ticket since 1944, telephoned Johnson that evening to offer his services in the few days remaining in the campaign. Johnson readily accepted, and Russell campaigned through Texas with Johnson.

Indeed, the shockwaves of the outrage at the Adolphus spread across the South. Four days later on Election Day, Republicans were stunned by their poor showing in Dixie. They carried only three states of the Old Confederacy: Tennessee, Florida, and Virginia. A segregationist ticket of independent electors carried Mississippi (and voted for Senator Harry F. Byrd of Virginia in the electoral college). But the Kennedy-Johnson ticket had carried Georgia, North Carolina, South Carolina, Alabama, Louisiana, and—above all—Texas.

John F. Kennedy could not have been elected President without the South. Could he have carried enough Southern states to win with Orville Freeman or Stuart Symington or Scoop Jackson as his running mate? Probably not. At any rate, key members of the Irish Mafia felt Kennedy could not have been elected without Johnson. Although at Los Angeles in July they had not seen Lyndon Johnson as the key to victory, they viewed him in retrospect as essential.

Johnson's mere presence on the ticket had helped Kennedy in the South. His colorful whistle-stop train ride through Dixie in October, blaring "The Yellow Rose of Texas" over the loudspeaker at every stop and dubbed the "Cornpone Special," not only made good newspaper copy but corralled the courthouse politicians who ran Democratic politics in the South.

For example, as his eleven-car train jerked to a stop at Culpepper, Virginia, local Democratic politicians climbed aboard near the observation car and made their way back to the vice-presidential candidate for a handshake and a word or two on how to stir up the folks of Culpepper. After a couple of minutes, during which the crowd of several hundred waited in suspense, a dark blue curtain parted and Johnson stepped out on the observation platform. "We're mighty glad you came out to howdy and shake with us," Johnson said, his face wreathed in a wide grin. "You make us feel so wonderful to come out here and look us in the eye and press the flesh . . . now, what has Dick Nixon ever done for Culpepper?" Here, Johnson felt at home, among his own people, with a common idiom and a common history. And Culpepper was special, because in the crowd that day were thirty or forty city slickers imported for the occasion from nearby Washington, D.C., by Johnson to whoop it up for him. Dressed in proper country-boy style, they were recruited from the staffs of Johnson's Texan Congressman friends. They made a lot of noise for Johnson (but in the election, Nixon carried Culpepper).

At stop after stop Johnson ridiculed the Republican nominee. Again and again, he told the story how Nixon's face had been made up for the first Kennedy-Nixon debate. "Of course," he would say, "all of us Democrats who have been around him for eight years have known all along he's made up." But it was serious business, this tour of the Southland. Kennedy here was suspect, alien, and feared. Johnson's mission was to expose the other half of the Kennedy ticket and to make voters tell themselves, If Lyndon's runnin' with him, maybe Jack ain't so bad after all.

Yet, it may well be that the Adolphus outrage, not the whistle stop, saved the South for Kennedy and defeated Nixon. In South Carolina, what happened in Dallas almost certainly cracked the excellent prospects that Nixon would take that state. In Louisiana, any doubt there might have been about the election disappeared overnight.

But most important was Texas itself, where the lynch-mob spirit of the Johnson-haters in the Adolphus lobby changed votes overnight. Considering the fact that Texas went Kennedy-Johnson by only forty-five thousand votes, it is a credible hypothesis that the Adolphus incident swung Texas into the Democratic column.

And so, this first national campaign by Lyndon Johnson, who had sought for a decade to throw off the political shackles of his home state, ended on a symbolic note: even now, as his party's vice-presidential candidate, he could be reviled and ridiculed by the element in Texas he had always feared and often appeased. The incident pointed up the source of the old ambivalence that dogged all his earlier political ventures beyond the borders of Texas, inhibiting him in national politics.

Four days later, elected to the second highest office in the country, Johnson would never again have cause to trim his politics to satisfy the demands of the Texas conservatives. Four days later, Johnson would be truly emancipated, no longer a Texas Democrat but, from then on, a national Democrat, the second in his party—but now, for the foreseeable future, stripped of all power.

Chapter XV

★★★★★★★★★★

THE VICE-PRESIDENT

Th' prisidincy is th' highest office in th' gift iv th' people. Th' vice-prisidincy is th' next highest an' th' lowest. It isn't a crime exactly. Ye can't be sint to jail for it, but it's a kind iv disgrace. . . .
    —Finley Peter Dunne (Mr. Dooley)

. . . The chief embarrassment in discussing his [the Vice-President's] office is that in explaining how little there is to be said about it, one has evidently said all there is to say.
    —Woodrow Wilson in *Congressional Government*

With an audacity that astonished both friends and some confidential advisers, the Vice-President-elect moved swiftly to stake out a power base even before the inauguration of John Kennedy. Having possessed for eight years one of the mightiest voices in the Democratic party, it was only natural that Lyndon Johnson would refuse to accept the historic fact that Vice-Presidents were made to be neither seen nor heard, only to wait. He did not agree with Thomas R. Marshall, Woodrow Wilson's undistinguished Vice-President, that the Vice-President "is like a man in a cataleptic state. He cannot speak. He cannot move. He suffers no pain. And yet he is conscious of all that goes on around him."

Yet for Johnson to seek new avenues to vice-presidential power was a contradiction in terms. His effort's total failure was a foregone conclusion.

Johnson's first target was the United States Senate, for so long his base of power. When the sixty-four Democratic Senators met on January 3, 1961, for the regular party conference that always preceded the beginning of a new Congress, Senator Mike Mansfield of Montana was moved up the ladder from Majority Whip and, without opposition, was elected Majority Leader replacing Johnson. Immediately thereafter, Mansfield, who owed his prominence in the Senate entirely to Johnson's selection of him as whip in 1957, made a motion to the caucus. Mansfield's motion, which he had discussed with no one except Johnson, was a shocking interruption to the usually formalistic proceedings of the caucus. He proposed formally that Johnson be empowered to preside over Senate Democratic caucuses—in effect become *de facto* chairman—even though in seventeen days he would be Vice-President.*

The Constitution gives the Vice-President only three functions: to preside over the Senate as its President; to vote in the Senate to break a tie; and to succeed to the presidency in the case of the President's death "or inability to fulfill the powers and duties of his office." Now, Mansfield was proposing that the Senate of the 87th Congress do what no other Senate had done: breach the constitutional separation of powers by making the Vice-President the presiding officer of all the Senate Democrats whenever they met in a formal conference.

Mansfield's unexpected move in the caucus confirmed the fears of Johnson's old liberal critics in the Senate. Ever since the election, they had been brooding that Johnson would try to run the Senate from the Vice-President's chair, with Mansfield, the self-effacing and introspective former professor who was uncomfortable with power, deferring to him. Although they had neither the strength nor the organization to oppose Mansfield for Majority Leader, their apprehensions over his independence were heightened by two small events in December, 1960.

First, word seeped out that Johnson and Mansfield had agreed that Johnson would retain the spacious splendor of his Taj Mahal. Johnson originally justified his take-over of that splendid office on grounds that the Majority Leader needed it. Now, he decided that Lyndon Johnson needed it more. Mansfield was quite content to take an office across the Senate chamber that would have fit twice over into the Taj Mahal.

Second, Mansfield made it known that he would retain Bobby Baker as Secretary to the Senate Majority. The liberals could not forget that Baker was far more a personal aide to Johnson than he was an agent of all the Senate Democrats. They would have preferred that Mansfield get his own man.

When Mansfield made his motion at the January 3 caucus there was

---

* Johnson resigned from the Senate just after the Democratic conference on January 3. He had been re-elected to the Senate under the new Texas law that enabled him to run simultaneously for Vice-President and Senator in 1960.

a moment of stunned silence, but only a moment, followed by a wave of opposition. Five Senators rose from their chairs to challenge the proposition that a non-Senator should preside over them. Included among the protesters were two liberals who had been feuding with Johnson for years: Joseph Clark, the Pennsylvania reformer, and Albert Gore, the Tennessee Populist. That was expected. The depth of the revolt against Mansfield's motion, however, was discernible only in the identity of the other three: Clinton Anderson of New Mexico, Olin Johnston of South Carolina, and A. Willis Robertson of Virginia. All these were senior members of the Senate Establishment and standing committee chairmen. All three had supported Johnson for the presidential nomination six months earlier. Most important, Clinton Anderson was a true power in the Senate and had been an inner member of the Johnson Network.

Anderson specifically noted his support of Johnson at Los Angeles and the debt all Democratic Senators owed Johnson for his leadership in the Senate the past eight years. But the office of the Vice-President, said Anderson, was more a creature of the executive branch than the legislative branch. Therefore, quite apart from the fact that the Senate Democrats would look ridiculous electing a non-Senator to preside over them, to do so would violate the spirit of the separation of powers.

The debate continued in a mood of embarrassment. Johnson was present. Not only that, but in just seventeen days, Johnson would be one step away from the presidency itself. The Senators who rose to speak against him were fully aware of the risks they took. When the vote was called, seventeen Senators voted against the Mansfield motion. It was supported by forty-six, but even among these there was an undercurrent of discontent.

That undercurrent, together with the outright opposition of seventeen Senators, was a humiliating rebuff for Johnson. But why were there seventeen negative votes? In the first place, the liberals had hoped Johnson's election as Vice-President would free them of his pervasive influence. They wanted no vestigial operation of the Johnson System. Others agreed with Clinton Anderson's constitutional argument about separation of powers. But beyond that, an unspoken sentiment among many Senators was the fear that if Johnson became de facto chairman of the conference he would use that position as a lever to become de facto Majority Leader, with tentacles of power into both the Steering and Policy Committees (newly headed but not controlled by Mansfield).*

---

* Stung by rumors that he would be a front-man for Johnson, Mansfield quickly put out the word to the press that he would run his own kind of Senate,

That suspicion was unprovable and undoubtedly exaggerated, but it demonstrated the acute sense of uneasiness about Johnson in the place he once ruled. Having watched him operate for eight years, Democratic Senators were fearful of what he might do now if he got a toe in the door.

Actually, Johnson never confided to anybody a grand design for seizing Senate power from Mansfield. It is unlikely that he had any detailed scheme in his mind. Yet, his desire to preside over the conference was a sign he intended to maintain a large influence in Senate affairs. And the seventeen votes cast against him—particularly the votes of Anderson, Johnston, and Robertson—were a sign to Johnson that his leadership in the Senate was no longer welcome.

Johnson grieved deeply and emotionally over those seventeen votes. No other single event in those formative days of the New Frontier cut deeper, and none more influenced his conduct as Vice-President after January 20. Indeed, he retired from the Senate—physically as well as legally.

Although he seldom mentioned the humiliation of that January 3 conference, he never forgot it. And when, much later, he was accused by the liberal *New York Post* of not working hard enough to help pass the Kennedy program, Johnson took a certain grim delight in recalling that the same newspaper had criticized him for a power grab at the first Democratic conference of the session.

Johnson's second target of power was in the executive branch. Shortly after the inauguration on January 20, one of Johnson's aides drew up an executive order for President Kennedy's signature. It stipulated that the Vice-President was to have "general supervision" over certain large areas of the government, including the National Aeronautics and Space Administration, the new space agency. It was drafted for the President's signature, after which it was to be distributed as a presidential directive to various departments and agencies, directing that Johnson receive all reports, information, plans, and policy that these agencies customarily sent to the President himself.

Johnson himself was a bit skittish about so unprecedented an order, but he approved it and sent it to the White House. Within hours after its transmittal to the White House, Johnson showed a copy to a friend in the Taj Mahal. The friend was flabbergasted. It was, he said

---

eliminating such mechanisms of the Johnson System as night sessions and stop-and-go scheduling. He did, and the Senate's efficiency suffered.

frankly, the most presumptuous document any Vice-President had ever sent to his President.

At the White House, the document quickly found its way to President Kennedy's staff, where the reaction was precisely that of Johnson's friend. The President never signed it. The memorandum disappeared into some dusty bin, never to be seen or heard of again.

Perhaps Johnson did not realize the import of the memorandum. Certainly he knew that Kennedy was no Mansfield, and could not be dominated by Johnson. He also knew Kennedy was surrounded by a high-powered staff who had no affinity for Johnson. These men were led by Robert F. Kennedy, who was well aware of Johnson's ability as an infighter and was determined to keep a sharp eye on him. Considering Johnson's appreciation of these facts and relationships, the proposed executive order may well have appeared to the White House as more of a power grab than Johnson had intended it to be. The Vice-President may have been the victim of an overeager staff rather than a calculating bidder for executive power.

But the incident did strain relations somewhat between the White House and the Taj Mahal. And it led to some backstairs remarks in the White House that compared Johnson to William H. Seward, who, as Abraham Lincoln's Secretary of State, constantly sought to expand his power at the expense of the President. When Johnson heard about these remarks from White House aides, he complained to the President. John Kennedy himself was more amused than bothered by Johnson's grab for power. Still, he may have been just a shade apprehensive when he asked his aides why Johnson spent so much time in the working wing of the White House.

Most important, the White House rejection of Johnson's proposed executive order, coming on top of the fiasco in the January 3 caucus, bred a caution into the Vice-President that was to dominate his actions for nearly three years.

In the early days of the New Frontier, the new President and the new Vice-President each called his staff together to deliver little speeches. Kennedy's remarks involved Johnson: You are to treat him, he told his staff, exactly as you would want me to be treated by him if our positions were reversed. If you ever stray from this rule, Kennedy said, you'll lose your job.

Johnson's remarks to his staff were in the same vein. He had signed on as Vice-President, he told them, and he was going to be the best Vice-President he knew how to be. He meant it. In private, serious talks about John F. Kennedy, there was never a hint of criticism from the Vice-President. Reporters who had spent a lifetime learning how to detect slight differences of opinion among politicians came up against a stone wall when they cross-examined Johnson about the President. Even old Johnson friends in the Senate did not receive from him any signal by word or inflection of significant disagreement with Kennedy. Whenever the press claimed that a disagreement existed, both Kennedy and Johnson went far beyond routine denials to repudiate it. For Johnson, whose pleasure in mocking competitors and politicians behind their backs was legendary in Washington, that self-control must have stretched his endurance.

Johnson had no intention of being a breakaway Vice-President like John Nance Garner, who became a thorn in Franklin Roosevelt's side.* In Johnson's view (which did not change when Hubert Humphrey became *his* Vice-President), the Vice-President ought to be a perfect servant to the President. Johnson knew that all strong Presidents sooner or later found some reason to split away from their Vice-Presidents, and that most Vice-Presidents sooner or later found the relationship untenable. Woodrow Wilson wanted to change Vice-Presidents in 1916. Franklin Roosevelt did change Vice-Presidents in 1940, and again in 1944. Harry Truman and Alben Barkley, as comfortable as old shoes together in the Senate, drew apart within months after their inauguration in 1949. Dwight D. Eisenhower and Richard Nixon maintained a relationship unruffled on the outside, but they were scarcely close, and it was no secret that Eisenhower resented the subtle pressures exerted by Nixon in his efforts to influence policy. Johnson wanted to avoid all such pitfalls.

Johnson knew that his best chance for the presidency lay in keeping Kennedy's good will through 1968 and hoping for Kennedy's blessing at that year's National Convention. No minutes were kept of the conversation between the two men in Los Angeles on July 15, 1960, but there are strong indications that Kennedy hinted to Johnson that he would have an eight-year contract as Number Two man. However, that wasn't the same as being Kennedy's heir apparent. Thus, Johnson knew that if he were to succeed to the nomination in 1968 (as Nixon succeeded Eisenhower as Republican nominee in 1960) it would be by his own efforts, and by far the most important effort he now could make was to keep Kennedy's goodwill.

To a great degree, Johnson retained presidential goodwill. But his relations with the President, and to a greater extent with the Presi-

---

* As a young Congressman, Johnson had been Roosevelt's hatchet man against Garner. See pages 11–12.

dent's brother and staff, could not be described as joyful. Indeed, his unsuccessful power maneuvers of January, 1961, caused Johnson to take a cautious stance and badly distorted his relationship with the New Frontier.

John F. Kennedy pondered much, in the days just after the election, how he should use his Vice-President. Kennedy was well aware that Johnson was not, as Kennedy once said, "interested in issues." Johnson's passion was to get things done, to confront a problem, regardless of its ideological content, and solve it. Kennedy decided that he would exploit Johnson's genius where it worked best—on Capitol Hill. Johnson, he thought, would be an invaluable presidential asset when the Kennedy program got into hot water in the House and Senate.

But Johnson was so hurt and angry at the large number of votes against him on the Mansfield motion on January 3 that his usefulness as a legislative helper to Kennedy turned out to be minimal. As Senate Majority Leader, Johnson's dominant mood always had been the mood of the master, the levers of power held firmly and employed unsparingly. Now, as Vice-President, the dominant mood was caution. On matters dealing with foreign policy, where Johnson's expertise was limited, such restraint was understandable. But on legislative affairs, where his mastery was unequaled, his withdrawal puzzled Kennedy and frustrated his plans for the Vice-President.

With a few exceptions, Johnson did absolutely nothing to advance the Kennedy legislative program.* He did not try to exert his influence on his old friends in the Senate, seldom if ever employing the Johnson Treatment as of old on Richard Russell or members of the vestigial Johnson Network. He did not wheel and deal. White House staff members responsible for passage of the program privately complained on occasion of this lack of zeal and energy. Even when Johnson noticed and lamented to friends that telephone calls from Capitol Hill for favors from the administration were starting to come to Lawrence O'Brien, the chief presidential lobbyist on Capitol Hill, instead of him, he did not bestir himself. He simply brooded over his fallen state.

Johnson had a stake of his own in the success of the Kennedy Administration, and that stake would have gone up in value had he been able to exert a recognizable influence in Congress. Consequently, his nonparticipation was surely not sabotage. Rather, it was the memory of how the Senate Democrats had treated him on January 3, 1961.

---

* One of the exceptions was a series of constructive suggestions Johnson made as Vice-President in what was to become the Civil Rights Act of 1964. See Chapter XVII.

Having absorbed that experience, Johnson felt that a Vice-President, even Vice-President Lyndon Johnson, simply could not play a large role in Congress.

The painfulness of Johnson's brooding was not eased by the instant disintegration of the Johnson System under Mike Mansfield's permissive leadership. The intelligence apparatus, the system of reward-and-punishment, the special mechanisms for speeding up the Senate—all disappeared, and the office of Majority Leader once again diminished in stature. Johnson never publicly second-guessed Mansfield. Nor did he counsel him. Only in private among intimates did he occasionally complain about the way the Senate was being run.

However, early in 1963, Johnson did obliquely criticize the reticent Mansfield manner to a wider audience, though still privately and strictly off-the-record. In the biennial liberal effort to change Senate Rule XXII, the cloture rule, Johnson—acting in his constitutional role as presiding officer of the Senate—had made a ruling that civil rights leaders believed would doom chances for liberalization of Rule XXII.*

Stung by his critics, Johnson called a top-drawer assortment of civil rights leaders into the Taj Mahal and explained that he had been compelled to make the ruling he did because it was the right ruling. But, he went on, that did not end the fight. Johnson argued that a Southern filibuster against amending Rule XXII could be broken if the Senate went into round-the-clock sessions—an extreme and physically taxing procedure that Mansfield would not employ. Johnson told the civil rights leaders that Richard Russell and his Southern brigade had aged since their disciplined team effort maintained a filibuster against the 1960 Civil Rights Bill in the face of round-the-clock sessions.† In the colorful style of the Johnson Treatment, the Vice-President outlined to the civil rights leaders the physical deficiencies of each of the Southern patriarchs.

A group of young Democratic Senators who visited Johnson in the Taj Mahal shortly thereafter were given a similar exposition. The inference drawn by both groups was that *Johnson* could change Rule XXII if he were still Majority Leader. There is no evidence that he ever advised round-the-clock sessions in 1963, directly or indirectly, to

---

* Johnson refused to rule that the Senate was not a "continuing body." If sustained by the Senate, such a ruling would have made it possible to break a filibuster against changing Rule XXII by a simple majority vote. Liberal Republicans shrilly attacked Johnson, pointing out that, as Vice-President, Richard Nixon had made such a ruling. It should be pointed out, however, that Nixon's ruling contributed nothing to liberalization of Rule XXII in 1959, while Johnson's careful efforts that year did. See pages 200–202.

† See pages 220–221.

either Mansfield or the White House. Indeed, Johnson's reluctance to give advice on any conceivable subject had become ingrained by the time of the Rule XXII fight of 1963.

In his office one day in early 1962, Johnson described his concept of the vice-presidency. The President, he said, has *his* job. The Speaker runs the House. And the Vice-President presides over the Senate and does whatever the President tells him to do. Then, he added: "I always hope that the President won't turn to me and ask, Lyndon, what would you do?" As Majority Leader, Johnson continued, he was so cocksure on so many things. But now, sitting in the inner councils of the executive branch, he was not sure at all. There were, he said, difficult, terrible decisions to make and there was only one person to make them: the President. That attitude of utmost caution was to cause tensions between Johnson and Kennedy that neither wanted.

At the President's weekly breakfasts for Democratic legislative leaders, Johnson was a sphinx. He seldom offered a suggestion. When asked directly by Kennedy for his opinion on a bill, he answered in monosyllables so low he could scarcely be heard. At meetings of the National Security Council, he often replied to Kennedy's invariable effort to draw him out by saying he didn't have enough information on the subject to contribute anything.

Nevertheless, President Kennedy insisted that Johnson be invited to all top-level meetings. If on occasion the invitation was not delivered or Johnson failed to receive it, Bobby Kennedy—now Attorney General but also the President's chief assistant—followed up with a telephone call of his own. Thus, President Kennedy constantly sought to draw Johnson close to the decision-making process, not so much in quest of his help on the actual decisions, but to have him there while the decision was being made—to take partial responsibility and to be prepared in case he should suddenly become President. For his part, Johnson constantly sought to avoid direct participation in the decision-making process, not because he did not want to be at the table when the decisions were made but because he did not want to go on the record with *Johnson* proposals and *Johnson* recommendations.

To old friends in the Senate who had known and studied Lyndon Johnson for a decade, Johnson had gone into the job reluctant to be part of the team. He wanted to stay off, keep his own counsel, play his own role in his own way. But Kennedy would not let him. He made Johnson take part, pulling him into the center of the New Frontier.

That unarticulated conflict between President and Vice-President was irritating to both Kennedy and Johnson, but neither put his feelings into words. Instead, the derogatory impact of Johnson's policy of supercaution registered most keenly on Bobby Kennedy and the Kennedy staff, and reflected badly and unfairly on the Johnson vice-presidency.

Johnson's gloomy silence at Cabinet and Security Council meetings was misinterpreted by Robert Kennedy as a sign of inability to cope with the great problems of the day. The Attorney General was a central figure in setting the tone of the New Frontier, and his ideas, sometimes exaggerated, were transmitted widely through the administration. With Johnson's golden days as Majority Leader forgotten or not known by the young lions of the New Frontier, the Vice-President began to be marked down in a grossly unfair and wildly incorrect appraisal as a lightweight—a back-room politician ill-equipped to meet the challenge of the 1960s.

From there, it was one easy step for Lyndon Johnson to become the butt of jokes throughout Washington. "Whatever happened to Lyndon?" became the fatuous cliché of the early 1960s. Deeply sensitive to any hint of criticism, such abuse deeply hurt Johnson, some of whose friends promptly blamed "the Kennedys" for starting it. That further raised Johnson's guard and increased his caution, which in turn further lowered regard for him inside the administration.

On top of it all was the recurring strain of federal patronage. Kennedy gave Johnson the power to veto any Texas appointment he didn't like. Within that broad patronage power, Johnson had to take account of the prerogatives of his old liberal Texas enemy, Senator Ralph Yarborough; of his old friend in the House, Speaker Rayburn; and of Johnson men back in Texas. Johnson was deadly serious about patronage. He kept an elaborate chart showing exactly which Texans were appointed to what jobs and under whose patronage—his own, Yarborough's, Rayburn's, or someone else's.

In the spring of 1961, Johnson proposed Sarah T. Hughes, a liberal Dallas lawyer and a strong Johnson ally who was co-chairman of the Kennedy-Johnson Campaign Committee in Texas in 1960, for a vacancy on the United States District Court.* Besides being a Johnson supporter, she had valuable political credentials of her own outside the Johnson orbit and her appointment to the federal bench under Johnson's patronage would be a political asset for him back home. But when the name of Sarah Hughes arrived in the Justice Department for a routine check, Attorney General Kennedy vetoed her on grounds of

---

* A little more than two years later, Judge Hughes swore in Lyndon Johnson as President at Love Field in Dallas.

age. She was sixty-four, far beyond the age which the Kennedy Administration thought proper for new federal judges. Johnson could not change Bobby Kennedy's verdict. Shortly thereafter, while Johnson was abroad on a trip, the Attorney General bumped into Speaker Rayburn in the Capitol and asked why it was that one of his pet anticrime bills was stymied in the House. Rayburn replied: "That bill of yours will pass as soon as Sarah Hughes becomes a federal judge."

Taken aback, Bobby Kennedy said that he had nothing against Sarah Hughes except her age. Rayburn turned a withering eye on the thirty-five-year-old Attorney General. "Sonny, everybody seems old to you," he said. Kennedy laughed and suggested that maybe, in view of the Speaker's personal interest, an exception could be made for Sarah Hughes. The nomination was quickly cleared by the President and readied for the Senate.

When Johnson returned from his trip and found that Sarah Hughes had made the grade in his absence, he confronted an unpleasant political situation. As Vice-President he lacked the power to make the Attorney General waive his arbitrary age requirement. But in Johnson's absence, the Speaker demonstated that *he* possessed that much power and could exercise it in a one-minute conversation with Bobby Kennedy. Johnson put a funny face on it in the President's office, complaining about this sorry state of affairs. The Vice-President, he stormed to John Kennedy in mock anger, asks the President for one little teeny favor and is turned down! And along comes that old man up there in the House, the Speaker, and gets it right away! Johnson played out the roles of himself and Rayburn. But underneath the mock anger and the amusing mimicry, Johnson felt that the whole affair had hurt his reputation, both in Washington and back home in Texas, where the story of how Sarah Hughes got to be a judge quickly made the rounds.

Shortly before his death in 1961, Rayburn again demonstrated just how much more power he possessed than the Vice-President. At issue this time was a Rayburn protégé whom the Speaker proposed to fill a vacancy as an Agriculture Department conservation service agent in Texas. Johnson opposed the man. Rayburn insisted. Hard-boiled Kenneth O'Donnell, Kennedy's increasingly powerful appointments secretary and confidential assistant, asked the President what should be done. Kennedy, with O'Donnell in his office, summoned Johnson. O'Donnell described the situation in detail, reminding the President of the arrangement with Johnson that no Texas patronage appointment would be made without his consent. The President asked Johnson what his preference was. Johnson said: This man is not reliable.

He may get us all in trouble. Don't appoint him. O'Donnell reached for the telephone on the President's desk, saying to Johnson: "If you don't want him, he's dead, Mr. Vice-President." He dialed a number.

"Who are you calling?" Johnson asked.

"The Speaker," said O'Donnell.

"What for?" said Johnson.

"To tell him that the Vice-President has vetoed his man."

"You're not going to blame it on *me*, are you?" said an aroused Johnson. Kennedy, relaxing in his chair, was enjoying the scene hugely. O'Donnell said:

"You don't think that *we're* going to take the blame, do you? Our agreement with you is that you can veto anyone in Texas. You're vetoing this guy. We've got to give the Speaker the facts."

Johnson was, by now, thoroughly agitated. Wait a minute . . . he said. Let's not go so fast.

Within twenty-four hours, Walter Jenkins telephoned O'Donnell to say the Vice-President had cleared the Speaker's man for conservation agent. But Lyndon Johnson's attitude toward Kenny O'Donnell and the New Frontier may have soured just a bit more.

As Woodrow Wilson's little-noticed Vice-President, Thomas Marshall of Indiana spent much of his time on the lecture circuit making quite a comfortable living. For Marshall, his predecessors, and most of his successors, there was simply nothing to do. Not until Henry Wallace twenty years later was any Vice-President assigned specific, statutory tasks that might otherwise be handled by a Cabinet member, a White House aide, or someone specially appointed for the job. Not until Richard Nixon, another twelve years later, did these statutory tasks take on major dimension.

What Eisenhower did with Nixon, Kennedy expanded with Johnson. Early in 1961, the new Vice-President was given two statutory positions. Based on Johnson's background as a congressional pioneer in space and founding father of the 1958 Space Act, Johnson was named chairman of the Space Council—which was supposed to shape overall space policy and mediate disputes between military and civilian leaders but which had been relatively unimportant under the chairmanship of President Eisenhower. The other post designated for Johnson was similar to the major assignment Eisenhower had delegated to Nixon. He was named chairman of the new President's Committee on Equal Employment, designed to prevent racial discrimination in employment by businesses having contracts with the federal government.

In contrast to Johnson's subtle tug-of-war with Kennedy over speaking out forcefully at White House meetings, and the embarrassing squabbles over patronage, these permanent assignments filled the empty hours of Lyndon Johnson's vice-presidency with productive work. But they were not entirely free from trouble.

As chairman of the Committee on Equal Employment, he was faced from the beginning with conflict inside its staff. Jerry R. Holleman, state president of the AFL-CIO in Texas, was brought to Washington—with Johnson's consent but not at his recommendation—as Assistant Secretary of Labor. He also became executive vice-chairman of the Equal Employment Committee. Holleman, who came out of the labor-liberal faction of the Texas Democratic party, was no Johnson man, and friction developed between him and the Johnson-oriented staff. This friction increased when Holleman brought in John Feild from Michigan's Fair Employment Practices Commission as the committee's executive director. Feild's sponsors were Michigan's liberal Democratic Senators, Pat McNamara and Philip Hart—no friends of Johnson. Moreover, Feild's policy was more militant than that of Johnson, who felt the best federal weapon to end discrimination in employment was conciliation.

Johnson moved to consolidate control of the staff in May, 1962, when Holleman resigned under fire from the government after acknowledging that he had accepted one thousand dollars for "personal expenses" from fellow Texan Billie Sol Estes, the financier-swindler. To replace Holleman, Johnson brought in one of his own staff aides, Hobart Taylor, Jr., a Negro lawyer from Detroit whose family roots were in Texas and who strongly supported Johnson for President in 1960. Like Johnson, Taylor was a gradualist.

Feild's days were numbered. The committee now would have two executives with differing philosophies: Executive Vice-Chairman Taylor and Executive Director Feild. Johnson wanted Taylor to move into the middle of the road outflanking Feild, agent of the liberals from the state that revolted against Johnson's vice-presidential selection at Los Angeles. When Feild made an issue of the two executives and asked the committee to choose one or the other, Johnson naturally chose Taylor.

The turmoil on the committee went beyond personalities and into the realm of grand strategy. The Vice-President's primary effort was conciliation and mediation, not coercion. Although he could and occasionally did threaten cancellation of a recalcitrant employer's government contract, that was not his style. He would tell the committee staff: "Let's make it *fashionable* to end discrimination."

Furthermore, Johnson was under pressure from old friends in the

Senate not to be too aggressive. Richard Russell had sponsored an amendment in the Truman Administration sharply curtailing the amount of federal funds to be spent on contract compliance, and the Russell Amendment was still law in 1961. Senator Willis Robertson, a senior member of the Senate Appropriations Subcommittee handling military funds, also kept a critical eye on activities of the President's Committee.

Johnson's cautious approach had more formidable critics than Jerry Holleman and John Feild. Robert Kennedy, who as Attorney General maintained general supervision over all civil rights matters, felt Johnson's tendency was to reduce the problem of equal employment to statistics. Although major improvements were made in the hiring of Negroes, Bobby Kennedy felt there was too much emphasis on pretty statistical pictures and too little on progress. The President's brother was no diplomat. He issued peremptory orders to Johnson to get moving in the employment field and Johnson resented this direction, further straining their relations.

Joining Bobby Kennedy in his criticism of Johnson's methods was Willard Wirtz, a former intimate of Adlai Stevenson who was named Under Secretary of Labor in 1961 and became Secretary in the fall of 1962. Wirtz began to strip the committee of its operational powers, transferring them into the government agencies that had the most contracts with private business, and using funds from these agencies to supplement the meager resources of the committee itself. Johnson and Wirtz often had it out at meetings of the Equal Employment Committee.[*]

Johnson's experience as chairman of the Space Council was far less entangled in bureaucratic feuding. Indeed, space was the one area of executive policy where John F. Kennedy clearly intended to give his Vice-President a major role. To begin with, he asked Johnson in the early months of 1961 for a recommendation on the proper role of the United States in space.

Johnson invited three resourceful and imaginative executives from the fields of communications and industry to study the space program, still in its infancy because of budget hold-downs in the Eisenhower Administration. They were General David Sarnoff of the Radio Corporation of America; Dr. Frank Stanton of the Columbia Broadcasting System, an old friend of Johnson's; and Donald C. Cook, now president of American Electric Power. Without publicity, Sarnoff, Stanton, and Cook made a complete study of the entire United

---

[*] Friends of Wirtz expected Johnson to drop him from the Cabinet after Kennedy's assassination, but instead the two became close.

States space program and recommended to Johnson greatly accelerated spending. Johnson passed their recommendations on to the President and they helped Kennedy make a vital decision in early 1961 to
shoot for the moon in "this decade."

Moreover, the directorship of the National Aeronautics and Space
Administration was one high-level job Kennedy gave to Johnson to fill.
After Don Cook turned down a feeler, Johnson proposed another old
friend, James E. Webb, who became the New Frontier's space boss in
early 1961. Webb had served as Director of the Budget and later
Under Secretary of State in the Truman Administration. During the
Eisenhower years, he became a director and part of the top management of Kerr-McGee, the fabulous oil empire of Senator Robert Kerr,
who had succeeded Johnson as chairman of the Senate Space Committee.

Working closely with Webb, the Vice-President was in on all the
decisions as NASA became one of the government's major operating
agencies during the early 1960s. Self-assured in this field, Johnson ran
the proceedings of the Space Council with an iron hand, occasionally
treating Secretary of Defense Robert S. McNamara as a top sergeant
handles a raw recruit.

But even space was not without its difficulties for Johnson as Vice-
President. Such an intense interest did Johnson take in space exploration that on February 20, 1962, when Colonel John Glenn became the
first American to orbit the earth, the Vice-President astonished and
then angered President Kennedy by asking to fly to Grand Turk Island in the Bahamas, near the spot in the Caribbean where Glenn
would come down at the end of his three-orbit space flight. Johnson
wanted to be there when Glenn came ashore. The President flatly refused.

But on March 1, when New York City prepared a hero's welcome
for Glenn with a ticker-tape parade up Broadway, Johnson again informed the President he wished to go along for the ride. Again Kennedy said no. This was Colonel Glenn's day, the President told Johnson, and he ought to be able to bask in the glory alone! But Johnson
persisted, and Kennedy finally yielded. As it turned out, Glenn and
Johnson were a great hit on Broadway.

As an outgrowth of the Space Council, Johnson also presided over a
special committee to study the supersonic transport or SST that someday would fly at 1,750 to 2,000 miles an hour on intercontinental hops.
The question of how to finance the SST led to deep disagreement
between Johnson and three of the administration's biggest guns:
McNamara, Walter Heller, chairman of the President's Council of

Economic Advisers, and Kermit Gordon, director of the Budget Bureau.*

All were members of the special SST committee. McNamara, Heller, and Gordon insisted that private industry should put up at least 25 percent to 30 percent of the development costs in the form of risk capital for the vastly expensive SST. Johnson favored a far larger federal subsidy, even, if necessary, a complete federal underwriting. But McNamara, who was regarded by Johnson as the smartest man in the Kennedy Cabinet despite their lack of rapport, was adamant. The Pentagon, he insisted, should not put up a nickel for the SST because the Pentagon would not get a nickel's worth out of it when built. It was Johnson's contention that, considering the high risk of the project, private capital would never agree to so large an investment, but the SST committee refused to endorse the project as Johnson wanted. For no matter how many jobs Kennedy might assign him, the power was not his.

In the earliest days of the Republic, Vice-President Thomas Jefferson refused to go abroad at the request of President John Adams. No Vice-President in history, according to the research of Vice-President Lyndon Johnson's staff, had gone abroad during his incumbency until John Nance Garner visited China in the early 1930s. The new style in traveling Vice-Presidents came into vogue during Eisenhower's presidency, when Richard Nixon traveled to Latin America, the Soviet Union, and many other parts of the world. But if Nixon-Eisenhower changed the style, it was Johnson-Kennedy who made it fashionable. Vice-President Johnson made eleven separate tours outside the United States during his two years and ten months in that office, a record that may never be broken.

What happened on these trips, and why they were undertaken, tells much about the torment of the vice-presidency. Johnson's travels from December, 1960, even before he was inaugurated, to November, 1963, when he made his last voyage abroad as Vice-President, were a reflection of the man himself in the most uncomfortable period of his life. For during the void of the vice-presidency, Lyndon Johnson could be close to his own impulsive, bigger-than-life self only when beyond the borders of the United States.

By all odds his most important foreign trip as Vice-President came

---

* But during the 1964 presidential campaign, Johnson described McNamara and Heller as his "best secret weapons." Later, he was to ask Gordon to be his Secretary of the Treasury. Gordon turned the offer down.

in the spring of 1961 against an ominous backdrop of Communist insurrection in the kingdom of Laos—one of the successor states of French Indochina—that threatened to immerse all of Southeast Asia. Johnson left for Saigon, the capital of South Vietnam, on May 9, four days after cease-fire talks started between the pro-Western Royal Laotian government and the Communist Pathet Lao. Despite the start of these talks, fighting was to go on for months and years. Johnson's mission was to show the American flag in South Vietnam and elsewhere in Asia; to demonstrate, in short, that the United States had a vital interest and would not abandon its friends. To give the mission still more prestige, Kennedy sent his sister and brother-in-law, Jean and Stephen Smith, with Johnson.

Johnson's somber and confidential report to President Kennedy, dated May 23, one day before he returned to Washington, captured the mood of crisis that hung over South Vietnam:

> The public, or more precisely, the political reaction to Laos has drastically weakened the ability to maintain any strongly pro-U.S. orientation. Neutralism in Thailand, collapse in Vietnam, anti-American oratory in the Philippines were all developing prior to our visit. The show of strength and sincerity—partly because you had sent the Vice-President and partly, to a greater extent than you may believe, because you had sent your sister—gave the friendly leaders something to "hang their hats on" for awhile. Our mission arrested the decline of confidence in the United States. It did not—in my judgment—restore any confidence already lost. The leaders were as explicit, as courteous and courtly as men could be in making it clear that deeds must follow words—soon. We didn't buy time. We were given it.

Johnson's report was simple and realistic. If Southeast Asia were permitted to fall to Communism, he went on, "the United States, inevitably, must surrender the Pacific and take up our defense on our own shores." The Philippines, Japan, and Formosa would be without security if the free nations of the Indian subcontinent—India and Pakistan—were not able to provide an "inhibitory influence" on Asian Communism.

In words similar to those that three years later, as President, Johnson would utter in the White House, the Vice-President made his case for continued and rising United States involvement in the battleground of Southeast Asia.

> There is no alternative to United States leadership in Southeast Asia. . . . We should consider an alliance of all the free nations of the Pacific and Asia.

As for United States ground forces, Johnson anticipated the difficult situation he would confront in July, 1965.

> Asian leaders, at this time, do not want American troops involved in Southeast Asia other than on training missions. American combat troop involvement is not only not required, it is not desirable. Possibly Americans fail to appreciate fully the subtlety that recently colonial peoples would not look with favor upon governments which invited or accepted the return this soon of Western troops. To the extent that fear of ground-troop involvement dominates our political responses to Asia in Congress or elsewhere, it seems most desirable to me to allay those paralyzing fears in confidence, on the strength of the individual statements made by leaders consulted on this trip. *This does not minimize or disregard the probability that open attack would bring calls for U.S. combat troops.* *

There followed, in this report from Johnson to Kennedy, a deep conviction, perhaps finding part of its roots in Johnson's own childhood in the hill country of Texas and his Populist heritage, that the "greatest danger" to the United States in Asia was not "the momentary threat of Communism itself" but the danger of "hunger, ignorance, poverty, and disease." Whatever strategy the United States adopted, said Johnson, "we must . . . keep these enemies the point of our attack."

In Vietnam and Thailand, the basic decision must be made: whether to help these countries "to the best of our ability" or "to throw in the towel in the area and pull back our defenses to San Francisco and a 'Fortress America' concept." He added:

> More important, we would say to the world in this case that we don't live up to treaties and don't stand by our friends. This is not my concept.

Johnson was not so unreservedly enthusiastic about Ngo Dinh Diem, South Vietnam's authoritarian President, as he was later portrayed to be. All he had to say to Kennedy about Diem was that he had "admirable qualities" but was "remote from the people [and] surrounded by persons less admirable and capable than he." The closing paragraph of the Vice-President's confidential report to President Kennedy was prescient in its glimpse of the hard decision he himself would have to make four years later:

> The fundamental decision required of the United States is whether we are to attempt to meet the challenge of Communist

* The emphasis is added.

expansion now in Southeast Asia by a major effort in support of the forces of freedom in the area or throw in the towel. This decision must be made in a full realization of the very heavy and continuing costs involved in terms of money, of effort, and of United States prestige. It must be made with the knowledge that at some point we may be faced with the further decision of whether we commit major United States forces to the area or cut our losses and withdraw should our efforts fail. We must remain master in this decision. . . . I recommend we proceed with a clear-cut and strong program of action.

Johnson himself would finally have to make this "fundamental decision."

Later, in India, the second most important stop on his itinerary, Johnson made a good impression on Prime Minister Jawaharlal Nehru, who on occasion could be one of the world's most exasperating persons. John Kenneth Galbraith, the Harvard economist-author who was now United States Ambassador in New Delhi, reported in his diary that the first session between Nehru and Johnson was an "outstanding success." * He continued:

Both Nehru and Johnson spoke rather formally on education, which they favored; poverty, which they opposed; freedom, which they endorsed; peace, which they wanted; and the third Five-Year Plan, which they praised.

Through Johnson, the Indians saw something fresh and new in America. He and Nehru got into a long conversation about the importance of electricity and Johnson explained at length how he had been responsible for the first electric cooperative in the Pedernales Valley. In short trips outside New Delhi, Johnson campaigned as though he were running for the House back in 1937. As Galbraith recorded it:

Then we took off for Agra, the press having already been dispatched in advance. At the airport . . . LBJ did some electioneering which he followed up a few minutes later with a ride on a bullock cart and lifting water from a well. Then we went to see a couple of villages where he campaigned in earnest. At one, a brass band boomed us down the village street to a wedding march with many garlands and marigold petals and an infinity of handshaking. I left the Vice-President to his own devices and time schedule and was comforted by the thought that the campaigning was coming out of his afternoon rest period. There is

* Ambassador Galbraith's diary was made available to the authors at their request.

no doubt that the villagers liked it. And their smiles will show up in the photographs.

In his confidential report to President Kennedy, Johnson spoke of "an intellectual affinity or an affinity of spirit" between India and the United States. He added, in a vein not lacking political sophistication:

This, in my opinion, should be exploited not with the hope of drawing India into our sphere—which might be as unnecessary as it would be improbable—but, chiefly, with the hope of cementing under Nehru an India–U.S. friendship which would endure beyond any transition of power in India.

Johnson's impressive performance on his Asian journey was in many ways the high point of his foreign travels. With one exception, his subsequent travels were anticlimactic. The exception was the one trip overseas that Lyndon Johnson did not want to take.

On August 13, 1961, Communist East Germany closed all routes between East and West Berlin. On August 15, the Berlin Wall, made of cinder block and concrete, began to replace barbed-wire fences. Another world crisis was on, and Berlin again was threatened.

In the midst of frantic top-level meetings in the White House, Kennedy summoned Johnson and asked him to make an emergency trip to West Berlin to hold up the American flag. Johnson was not only unenthusiastic; he was positively against the trip. Kennedy dismissed him, saying he would think it over.

Johnson's strong reluctance increased after leaving the President's office. The sudden, dangerous pressure brought by the Communists on Berlin could lead to war at any moment. Kennedy, he suspected, was throwing him into the breach without any clear view of what the United States would do next. He feared the trip might have unfortunate political results that would severely damage his own career. He telephoned several of his friends in the Senate to ask their advice, making it clear to them he did not want to go to Berlin.

It was shortsighted for Johnson to exhibit such fears when asked to perform one of the most important duties of his vice-presidency. But Johnson above all was a cautious man, and underlying the caution was insecurity. On the day when Kennedy asked him to go to Berlin, his insecurity momentarily crowded out the normal response to the challenge of high adventure.

Kennedy quickly decided that the United States must send somebody to Berlin and that Johnson, as the second-highest official in the nation, must be that someone. He dispatched brother Bobby—the instrument for so many unpleasant chores—to see Johnson and tell him it was the President's *command* that he make the trip. The Attorney General carried out this odious mission, overriding Johnson's continuing objections. It was a most unpleasant confrontation. That Bobby Kennedy, once again, was the agent of his brother's bad news further exacerbated his relationship with Lyndon Johnson.

Berlin was the most spectacular mission of his vice-presidency. Landing at the Bonn-Cologne Airport on August 19, he told a welcoming crowd of West Germans that he was on his way to Berlin to "express a conviction, to convey a pledge, to sound a warning and to reiterate a policy." That same day, standing before a special session of the West Berlin Parliament, Johnson borrowed from the Declaration of Independence and pledged "our lives, our fortunes, and our sacred honor" to maintain the freedom of West Berlin. On August 20, in a moment of high drama, he greeted the first arrivals of a contingent of fifteen hundred United States troops ordered from West Germany to West Berlin, traveling across East Germany at the moment of maximum peril in the Berlin crisis. Early on August 21, he left Berlin and flew back to Washington to report to the President. His visit accomplished precisely what was intended, and his earlier fears that somehow he was being used as a sacrificial goat were quickly forgotten. But the expression of those fears, at such a climactic and dangerous moment of history, revealed once more his reluctance as Vice-President to become fully engaged, the tendency to draw away and the fear that, somehow, he was being taken advantage of.

Johnson's cogent reports to Kennedy from Southeast Asia, his masterful handling of Nehru in India, and his triumphant reassurance to the worried citizens of West Berlin comprised the brighter side of his foreign travels. There was a grayer side, and it was clearly evident both to the reporters who accompanied him and to the United States officials in the countries he visited. Inasmuch as these reporters scarcely saw the Vice-President except on his foreign travels, their impression of him was understandably discolored and their reports did not help the public image of Johnson as Vice-President.

In sum, the problem of Johnson's overseas traveling was this: constrained and frustrated in the isolation booth of the vice-presidency, Johnson could stretch his legs and revert to a semblance of the vigorous freewheeler only when he traveled. Pent-up energies and excesses of personality burst forth on these trips.

Johnson's journeys around the world took him twice to Rome, to Great Britain, to Independence Day fetes in Senegal and Jamaica, to the Middle East, to the Dominican Republic for the inauguration of later-deposed Juan Bosch, to Scandinavia, to the Benelux nations, to Turkey, Cyprus, and Greece, to Sweden for Dag Hammarskjold's funeral. While performing his mission on each of these trips, Johnson left behind him a trail of disgruntled Americans sucked for the brief space of a day or two into the Johnson vortex.

The self-effacing Vice-President of Washington, D.C., shed his mantle of restraint preparing for foreign travel. On each trip, Johnson sent a check-off list of requirements ahead of him to the embassy involved. An oversized bed was a must to accommodate his six-foot-four-inch frame. Also on his regular list were shower attachments that emitted a hard, needlepoint spray. On occasion, he sent his official vice-presidential automobile ahead, as is the practice of the President. Always on the checklist was plenty of Scotch whiskey, Cutty Sark preferred. That caused a problem in Formosa on the 1961 Far Eastern trip just after President Kennedy instituted his Buy-American policy to ease the deficit in the balance of payments. On Johnson's orders, a Navy plane was dispatched from Taipeh to Hong Kong to purchase a case of Scotch and return it to Taipeh for the Vice-President's party.

Such incidents became legend in the Foreign Service. Indeed, the legends began when Johnson was still Vice-President-elect. On November 20, 1960, Johnson flew to Paris for a meeting of the North Atlantic Treaty Organization. On Thanksgiving night, the United States Embassy in London received word that the Vice-President-elect was unexpectedly dropping in on the British Isles on his way back home. Johnson arrived the next afternoon in a large Air Force plane, which drew up at the VIP gate at London Airport in pouring rain. A United States sergeant emerged, ran over to where Minister Walworth Barbour waited, and motioned him on the plane. Johnson shook hands with Barbour and asked his invariable first question, carried over from campaign days and continued in his foreign travels: How large is the crowd? There was no crowd, replied Barbour, but there were many newspapermen. All right, said Johnson, I'll have a statement but no questions.

The British, who had been informed early that morning, were thrown into a maelstrom of activity. Prime Minister Harold Macmillan canceled a weekend trip to be in London to see the Vice-President-elect. Following his example, so did other members of the Conservative government. Lord Home, the Foreign Secretary, invited the cream of British politics to a dinner in Johnson's honor at Home's official residence that evening. The dinner went smoothly, but before ten o'clock Johnson rose from his easy chair, stretched, and announced he was tired—he had a heavy schedule the next day and had to go off to bed. The early departure was a blow to the British officials who had canceled their weekend plans and hoped to get a preview of the Kennedy Administration, but perhaps, under the circumstances, it was understandable. What was not understandable were pictures in the newspapers the next day showing Johnson at a snappy Park Lane nightclub late the previous night. Secret Service agents, in their routine report to the embassy the next day, clocked Johnson at four hours in the nightclub. The British government was not amused.

At 8:30 the next morning, the entire embassy staff was assembled at Winfield House, the ambassador's residence, to say good-by to Johnson before his eleven o'clock departure for Washington. The press was clamoring for an early-morning question session. Johnson at first refused, but then at the last moment canceled departure plans and announced he would hold a press conference at 4:30 that afternoon. Despite the inconvenient time, forty-three or forty-four reporters invited to Winfield House showed up.* But Johnson put the whole session off-the-record.

Embodied in Johnson's twenty-four-hour stop in London were the principal elements of all his subsequent foreign travels: sudden change of plans, total confusion within the host embassy, and a casting off of the humility and quiet dignity that generally marked his vice-presidency.

His first trip as Vice-President, two and a half months after the inauguration, contained all these elements. Kennedy sent Johnson to Senegal to represent the United States at Independence Day ceremonies for the new African country. Johnson asked Kennedy if there was not some special mission he might accomplish in Europe after the celebration at Dakar. Kennedy said yes, drop in at Geneva and take a sounding on the nuclear test-ban talks then in progress.

But Johnson also wanted to visit Spain, particularly since Mrs. Johnson had never been there. He called Secretary McNamara at the Pentagon and asked if there was not some mission he might accomplish in Spain. McNamara said he could think of only one: an inspection of United States bases there, but he asked that it be done informally. Just to keep the record straight, Johnson wrote a "Dear Mr. Vice-President" letter for McNamara's signature, and had it taken by his chauffeur to McNamara's office for the Secretary to sign. The letter simply asked the Vice-President, in view of his forthcoming flight

---

* The one absentee was C.B.S. commentator Eric Sevareid. Johnson, who had a list of the forty-four invited, took out a fat dark pencil, circled Sevareid's name, and stuck it back in his pocket.

from Dakar to Geneva, to be kind enough to stop off for a day or two in Spain.

Innocent enough, but that arrangement almost led to an international incident, because on March 28, 1961, the President had issued a startling announcement: he was ordering the closing of seventy-three military bases, including several abroad. Their identity was secret. Thus when, two days later, it was announced that at McNamara's request Johnson's schedule was being changed to include an informal inspection of United States bases in Spain, the Spanish embassy in Washington received an urgent cable from Madrid: Does this mean that Kennedy is closing down a base in Spain? Convinced that it did, and convinced also that the Kennedy Administration would not admit it, the Spanish Embassy in Washington mounted a fierce counteroffensive. The Spaniards could learn nothing. Unaware of Johnson's intention to visit Spain, the President had ordered a tight security lid on all the projected base-closings. It took considerable time to discover that nothing more was involved than a comedy of errors, much to the relief of General Franco.

As the trips continued, tensions grew between the Vice-President on the one hand and the Foreign Service, the State Department, and the White House on the other. For instance, in Bangkok on his generally successful Far Eastern trip of 1961, Johnson was the despair of State Department officers who accompanied him. In their view, he refused to stick to schedule, confused diplomacy with a campaign tour, and was oblivious to the normal courtesies and protocol of any visitor from abroad. But Johnson's own assistants took a different view. The State Department, they thought, had loaded him down with an impossible schedule, was more concerned with protocol than performance, and simply did not appreciate the value of a forthright approach to the people.

On that same trip during his stop in Formosa, State Department officials were unnerved when the ageless Generalissimo Chiang Kai-shek momentarily convinced Johnson of his ageless refrain—totally refuted by United States intelligence—that unrest on the Communist mainland was about to explode into revolt.

Johnson's sudden irascibilities kept popping up in embarrassing places and at embarrassing moments. As he was leaving Prime Minister Nehru's office, after a long, cordial talk, Johnson turned to one of his aides and asked whether the press conference had been arranged. Apparently, there had been a misunderstanding or a change of plans that had not been conveyed to the aide, for he replied that he knew nothing about a press conference. Johnson bore down hard on the unfortunate aide, in Nehru's presence, for being unable to handle the most trivial task, such as setting up a press conference, and said: The only way to deal with you is to handcuff you to my belt so you'll be there when I need you.

For Johnson's swing through the Middle East, the White House assigned one of its top National Security staffers, Robert Komer, as a high-level escort officer. Johnson was quite aware that Komer's assigned mission was to keep an eye on him and he wasn't pleased by it.* Soon after the Vice-President's party reached Rome after the Middle East tour, word arrived of a severe earthquake in Iran, where tumultuous throngs had greeted Johnson a few days earlier. Johnson proposed that he and his Air Force jet take off immediately for Teheran on a relief mission. The entire embassy quietly counseled against it. Komer was promptly on the telephone back to Washington to buttress his own feeling that nothing good could come from such a trip. It was finally ruled out by a cable from the White House, but only after hours of confusion. Smiling wryly, Johnson told a high official in the United States Embassy: "I knew all the time they wouldn't let me go. I just wanted to give them something to do." Whether he was or was not serious, the incident was a reflection of the administration lack of confidence in Johnson by this point.

Perhaps more damaging were some of Johnson's private performances that embassy officials promptly relayed back to Washington by word-of-mouth. The list of incidents was endless—some hilarious, some damaging, all of them Johnsonian. In Rome, a CIA agent was required to locate the owner of a famous shop, closed for the night, to ask him to be at the Excelsior Hotel at 8:30 the next morning to present a large display of ties for the Vice-President. In Istanbul, Johnson's staff ordered a plywood partition to be hastily constructed in the hotel a day before Johnson arrived to separate the Vice-President from others traveling in his party. In Copenhagen, he haggled with an artist in his hotel suite over the price of oil paintings.

Based on such incidents, the press began to confuse Johnson's deficiencies as a Private Person with his accomplishments as a Public Person. It was a problem that bothered him with the press somewhat in his days as Majority Leader, but the press corps on Capitol Hill—part of the family, really—seldom printed unflattering portraits of the Private Person. In contrast, the press accompanying him on his round-the-world travels contained strangers, and, inevitably, they wrote harsh, if

---

* During Johnson's presidency, he established a most congenial relationship with Komer and in 1966 named him a Special Assistant on Vietnam problems.

truthful, accounts of the Private Person. It was a problem that would reach crisis proportions during his presidency.

One night after a party at The Elms (the mansion in northwest Washington purchased by Johnson from party-giver Perle Mesta after he became Vice-President), Johnson walked to the front door with the last remaining guest to say good-by. It was raining. As the guest started out the door, Johnson held him back. "Wait a minute," he said. "I'll send my chauffeur to get your car and you won't get wet." Chauffeur Norman Edwards was dispatched for the automobile. Johnson and his guest chatted.

"That's a smart man, my chauffeur," he said. "He's been driving Senate Majority Leaders since Joe Robinson, and when I got elected Vice-President, I asked him to come with me.* At first he said no. I said, 'Why?' He said he liked to drive the Majority Leader because there was a man with real power. He said the Vice-President doesn't have any power at all." Johnson paused. "He's a pretty smart fellow, my driver. I wish I'd had him with me in Los Angeles."

As an experienced student and wielder of power, Lyndon Johnson fully shared Norman Edwards' appreciation of the vice-presidency. Except for the space program, he exerted little influence inside the Kennedy Administration. One sign was the fact that among the top echelon, only James Webb, the NASA director, owed his job to Johnson. True enough, former Johnson staffers were spotted in second-level jobs throughout the Kennedy Administration—John B. Connally as Secretary of the Navy; Cyrus Vance as General Counsel of the Defense Department and later Secretary of the Army; Bill D. Moyers as Deputy Director of the Peace Corps; Harry McPherson as Deputy Under Secretary of the Army. But contrary to the opinion then widespread in Washington, Johnson himself placed *none* of these former aides. Robert McNamara, for example, picked Connally for the Navy job, then cleared it with Johnson. Moreover, Johnson mourned that some of his aides, particularly Moyers, had left his staff for the heady excitement of the New Frontier.

Indeed, in his blue moments, Johnson felt all his friends and protégés were abandoning him in this, the lowest point of his public career. Perhaps his biggest disappointment came in 1962 when John Connally resigned as Secretary of the Navy to run for Governor of Texas. Connally was elected, but he virtually repudiated Johnson

* Senator Joseph T. Robinson of Arkansas was Majority Leader of the Senate at the time of his death in 1937.

during the campaign. Johnson had been making strong civil rights speeches, and was, of course, closely identified in Texas with the New Frontier. Sensing a Texas reaction against the Kennedys *and* Johnson, Connally wanted to divorce himself from the New Frontier. His campaign treatment of Johnson was acutely painful to the Vice-President, who confided one day that he would never turn the picture of an old friend face-to-the-wall just to win a couple of votes.

Similarly, Johnson's old relationship with Senator Robert Kerr became frayed at the edges. Although Kerr had vigorously opposed Johnson taking second place on the ticket at Los Angeles, partly because he himself might lose power if Johnson left the Senate, the New Frontier raised the brilliant, belligerent Oklahoma oil baron to new heights of power. Kennedy badly needed a lieutenant to guide his program through the Senate. Neither Johnson nor Mansfield, the new Majority Leader, could do the job. Kennedy turned for help to Kerr, his 1960 convention foe, and Kerr gave it in exchange for political concessions that enhanced his power. As the "uncrowned king of the Senate," in Senator Paul Douglas' rueful phrase, Kerr pulled away from Johnson and even downgraded him in conversations with his friends in big business. Kerr's thoughtless remarks inevitably got back to Johnson.

Nor did Johnson take full advantage of his emancipation from Texas to become for the first time a national Democratic politician. President Kennedy's political experts became frustrated by his reluctance to fulfill speaking engagements in the North, where, they thought, he would want to be seen and heard. Kenny O'Donnell repeatedly set up dates for Johnson in such cities as Cleveland and Chicago, only to find the Vice-President did not wish to go "where they don't like me." Johnson's reluctance about domestic political excursions had become endemic by 1963. He was still essentially a *Washington* politician, still without the services of an experienced *national* politician—of the caliber of Larry O'Brien—on his staff.

Furthermore, Kennedy intimates felt that Johnson was drawing ever further away from the semblance of partnership with the New Frontier. It was their theory that Johnson was losing confidence that he would ever get Kennedy's blessing for President in 1968—an entirely reasonable assumption. Friends of Johnson played on this corrosive concern, seeding the idea that the Kennedys were planning a dynastic succession, with Robert Kennedy to succeed John Kennedy in 1968. These thoughts rankled the Vice-President.

Toward the end of 1963 he was more restless and less reconciled than he had been in 1961. He was hurt by what he took to be social slights by the Kennedys. After a Democratic party fund-raising gala in Washington early in 1963, he and Mrs. Johnson gave a late-evening party for the Hollywood stars and entertainers at The Elms. Neither Bobby Kennedy nor Senator Edward M. (Teddy) Kennedy of Massachusetts came, and Johnson remarked on their absence. Shortly thereafter, Johnson talked about it late one evening in the Senate with Bobby Baker, who suggested to Johnson that perhaps he should run for the Senate in 1964 against Ralph Yarborough and spare himself another four years of frustration.

Johnson himself thought about signing off as a one-term Vice-President. He talked vaguely about leaving politics altogether in 1964 and returning to Texas. He mentioned the possibility of becoming President of his alma mater, Southwest Texas State Teachers College in San Marcos.

Returning from one of his last trips abroad in the autumn of 1963, before President Kennedy's assassination, Johnson was gloomy and morose about his future. In truth, his friends felt he was concerned more about being dumped from the ticket in 1964 than in dropping off it voluntarily. He walked into the office of a Texas Congressman in early October, plunked himself down in a chair and complained that he had lost the President's confidence. "Why does the White House have it in for me?" he asked. He became preoccupied with fears that Kennedy would pick someone else for his running mate in 1964.

These fears were heightened by the eruption of the most bizarre Washington scandal of the 1960s. In 1961, Bobby Baker had remained as Secretary of the Senate Majority under Majority Leader Mansfield. But he neither built a new close working relationship with Mansfield nor maintained his old intimacy with Johnson. Instead, his new patron was Senator Robert Kerr. Kerr never troubled to segregate his swashbuckling business enterprises from his freewheeling activities in government. Neither did Baker, who now began to spend more time on private than on public affairs.

The storm broke in the fall of 1963 when the *Washington Post* reported that a lawsuit had been filed against Baker charging him with using his Senate job for financial gain. From that beginning flowed an ever more sensational series of stories about the financial dealings of the boy-wonder from Pickens, South Carolina, with implications, not entirely relevant, of fast-and-loose living in the higher reaches of official Washington. A *Post* court reporter had happened by chance across the lawsuit that triggered the Baker affair. But Baker believed the *Post* had been put onto the story by Attorney General Robert F. Kennedy who (in Baker's view) had planned the whole affair. That view, to a great extent, was shared by Johnson. He suspected that the

Justice Department and Bobby Kennedy were hounding Baker to embarrass Johnson and ease him off the ticket in 1964. Particularly significant to Johnson was the fact that Robert Kennedy was using some of his same crack Justice Department lawyers to run down the Baker case who were prosecuting Teamster leader James R. Hoffa, the Attorney General's arch-foe.

But, in fact, the President, the Attorney General, and the entire Irish Mafia were certain that if the Baker case blew up into a scandal of Teapot Dome proportions, John F. Kennedy as President would be far more damaged politically than Lyndon B. Johnson as Vice-President.*

President Kennedy was well aware of Johnson's fears. To curious friends, however, he repeatedly emphasized that changing Vice-Presidents would cost him more than it would gain. Besides, Kennedy added, he had no complaints about Johnson. At a press conference in early November, the President was asked two questions: Did he want Johnson on the ticket in 1964 and "do you expect that he would be on" if Kennedy himself ran for re-election? Kennedy's reply was quick: "Yes to both questions."

Still, Johnson was apprehensive and he saw new trouble coming, as ever, from Texas. His difficulties with liberal Senator Ralph Yarborough had continued throughout his vice-presidency. Convinced that somehow Yarborough was part of a Texas-based plot to remove him from the ticket in 1964, Johnson secretly worked on Representative James Wright, a moderate Johnson man from Fort Worth, to run against Yarborough in the 1964 Democratic senatorial primary, promising him financial backing. Liberal Don Yarborough (no relation to the Senator) had narrowly lost to Connally in the 1962 Democratic primary for Governor and also was suspected by Johnson of encouraging anti-Johnson hostility back in Texas in preparing to take on Connally again in 1964. Although the old Johnson-Connally relationship now was at a low point, Connally was infinitely preferable to Don Yarborough in Johnson's view.

Actually, the Irish Mafia was sympathetic to the Vice-President's political problems in Texas. On one occasion Kenny O'Donnell said he would block Don Yarborough from seeing the President unless he stopped criticizing Johnson back in Texas. But that was small comfort to the troubled Johnson.

That, then, was the mood of the Vice-President, in late November,

* However, if Johnson had been Vice-President instead of President in January, 1964, when, as an offshoot of the Baker case, the gift to Johnson by his insurance agent of an expensive stereo player was revealed, he might well have been dumped from the 1964 ticket. That was the opinion of high-ranking politicians not unfriendly to Johnson.

1963—a mingling of apprehension and loneliness—when President Kennedy arranged a political trip to Texas. Kennedy's purpose was to make peace between the Texas Democrats—Governor Connally and his conservatives on one side, Senator Yarborough and the Texas liberals on the other, and Vice-President Johnson in the middle.

Johnson went to Texas ahead of the President and spent his last weekend as Vice-President on the LBJ Ranch. He joined the President at Fort Worth on November 21. The next day was Dallas.

Never was there a more difficult union of man and job than the joining of Lyndon Johnson, the supreme connoisseur of power, with the vice-presidency, the place without power. Accordingly, his record of those years must be judged not in terms of his failure to play a major part in the Kennedy Administration or in his frictions with Bobby Kennedy or in his conduct on overseas assignments. It must be judged by the fact that, for the greater part, he kept his temper, his dignity, and his reputation during three trying years.

A White House official who worked for John F. Kennedy for nearly three years and then continued on with Lyndon Johnson, exposed for the first time to Johnson's "enormous, restless energy," captured the essential meaning of what the vice-presidency meant to Johnson. "The greatest tribute to him," the official said, "is that he had the self-discipline and patience to accept political impotency and stay out of trouble."

Chapter XVI

★ ★ ★ ★ ★ ★ ★ ★ ★

"LET US CONTINUE"

. . . This is the time when our whole public system could go awry, not just the Republican party and the Democratic party but the American system of government.
—Lyndon Johnson, November 25, 1963

Lyndon Johnson, trained to the use of power, his whole life geared to his driving ambition, had come now to the presidency itself, but under circumstances that could not conceivably have been more ominous. Driving through the sunny streets of Dallas in a motorcade on November 22, 1963, President John F. Kennedy was murdered by a mail-order rifle fired by Lee Harvey Oswald. Tragedy struck in Johnson's own Texas, in the very city where, almost exactly three years earlier, he himself had been mobbed by screaming Republicans.

Now, when the nation mourned its dead President, the burden of binding the wound, of creating a sympathetic response between the new President and the millions of American citizens who loved the old, of reassuring Kennedy's Administration that he was worthy of its support, of showing a resolute face to the world, of moving a nation wrapped in sorrow out of its tears—the whole burden fell on this one man.

Here was Lyndon Johnson, the first Southern President since the Civil War, not elected but come to the office by an assassin's bullet; Lyndon Johnson, born in Texas and now the sudden repository of all the hopes of twenty million Negroes battling for equality; Lyndon Johnson, hotly opposed for the *second* office at the last convention by the liberal core of his own party; Lyndon Johnson, the legislative genius now challenged with the highest responsibility of *executive* power. Paradox crowded on paradox. The forbidding quality of these paradoxes was forgotten after the event, but they bore heavily on Johnson that November day.

Of all the imperatives for Johnson in that worst of times, there was one that towered highest; that was the imperative of confidence. Here was his preeminent concern, first as he waited in a cubicle with the blinds drawn near the emergency room at Parkland Hospital, minutes later as he sat stone-faced in the car of Dallas Police Chief Jesse Curry who drove him, incognito, to the President's Air Force One—now *his* Air Force One—at Love Field; still later, now sworn in as President, as the great plane took off and returned to the Capital. Johnson knew that above all else, he needed the confidence of the American people. He knew how that other Johnson, Andrew Johnson, who succeeded Abraham Lincoln in another time of racial crisis, was vilely accused of having himself plotted against Lincoln. He knew, too, that that other Johnson had lost the confidence of the people before he had fairly had a chance to gain it. And so this Johnson, Lyndon Baines Johnson, the Thirty-sixth President, began at once, as by instinct, to restore the confidence of the people in their country and to gain their confidence for himself.

Yet, in those days and early weeks of transition between the Kennedy and Johnson Administrations, the new President's quest for confidence was always accompanied by the reality of his power. Although he knew he had yet to gain the confidence of the nation and the world, he did not hesitate to use his new power. He was the lawful President, and he made the decisions and gave the orders from the very outset of those fearful early moments.

Air Force One waited at the end of the runway at Love Field in Dallas. Brigadier General Chester V. Clifton, President Kennedy's Army aide, ordered the pilot to take off immediately. Malcolm Kilduff, Kennedy's assistant press secretary, canceled the order and told the pilot to delay. Johnson had ordered Kilduff to keep the plane on the field until Federal Judge Sarah Hughes arrived to swear him in as President.

Back in the main compartment of the plane where Kennedy's body lay in its casket and where Jacqueline Kennedy and her husband's former aides—Dave Powers, Kenny O'Donnell, and Larry O'Brien— huddled together in their grief, there was first surprise, then consternation at the long delay. Brigadier General Godfrey T. McHugh, President Kennedy's Air Force aide, rushed up to the pilot's cabin to repeat Clifton's order. "Mrs. Kennedy and Kenny O'Donnell want it," he said, his voice edged with impatience and emotion.

But again, Mac Kilduff countermanded the order. "But, Mac," McHugh said, "Mrs. Kennedy and Kenny want it." Kilduff, acting under higher authority, said what had to be said: "General, they're not in charge anymore."

Johnson *was* in charge. For he had become President, not when sworn in aboard Air Force One by Sarah Hughes, but the moment Kennedy died.

There was first the question of the assassination itself. Inevitably, irresponsible demagogues of the left and right spread the notion that not one assassin but a conspiracy had killed John Kennedy. That it occurred in Johnson's own state on a political mission urgently requested and promoted by Johnson only embellished rancid conspiratorial theories. If he were to gain the confidence of the people, the ghost of Dallas must be shrugged off.

In his earliest hours as President, then, Johnson, assisted by Abe Fortas and other counselors, conceived his plan for a blue-ribbon commission composed of the nation's most eminent citizens to make a painstaking investigation of the tragic events of November 22 and exorcise the demons of conspiracy. Moreover, it had to be a commission of consensus, skillfully drawn from contrasting segments of the population. He made the choices and telephoned them himself: from the Eastern Establishment, John McCloy, an esteemed banker and diplomat; from the liberal Republicans, Senator John Sherman Cooper of Kentucky, Kennedy's close friend; from the orthodox Republicans, Representative Gerald Ford, Jr., of Michigan; from the Democratic party House leadership, Representative Hale Boggs of Louisiana;* from the top echelon in the world of international intelligence, Allen W. Dulles, the former director of the Central Intelligence Agency.

The two most important members of the commission were the hardest to get. To symbolize his hope for national reconciliation, binding together the distraught nation, Johnson wanted opposites: Chief Justice Earl Warren (who would head the commission and give it its name) and Senator Richard Russell. It was the Supreme Court under Warren's vigorous leadership that, through its civil rights decisions, brought about the Negro Revolution that whittled down the political power of Russell's South. In hour upon hour of Senate oratory, Russell had denounced the judicial usurpation of the "Warren Court." Now, Johnson wanted these two antagonists side by side in a moment of national peril.

Warren protested. He knew that past members of the Supreme Court had been subject to heavy criticism when they accepted nonjudicial assignments. He told Johnson that neither he nor any member of the federal judiciary should serve on the commission. Seated across

---

* When he finally reached Boggs at his suburban home in Bethesda, Maryland, the new President grumbled that Boggs' phone had been busy for too long.

the desk from Warren in the White House, Johnson declared: You wore the uniform of a first lieutenant in World War I and served your country with honor. Are you now going to refuse to serve your country in another critical situation? Tears in his eyes, Warren reluctantly agreed.

Russell was far more reluctant. When the President reached him by telephone at his home in Winder, Georgia, Johnson's old mentor stiffened. He had no desire to serve next to Earl Warren. In addition, he was suffering from a chronic lung disorder and wanted to conserve his energies for the Senate filibuster over civil rights that surely lay ahead in 1964.* He remembered that he had managed to decline Johnson's pleadings a decade before to serve on the special Senate committee to serve as judge and jury for Joe McCarthy.†

But the occasion now was far more compelling. In a conversation lasting most of an hour, Johnson unleashed The Treatment, dormant now for three years. Emotionally, he recalled their long, intimate association. He appealed to Russell as his friend, and he appealed as the President of the United States. "If you say 'no,'" Johnson said, "I'll have you drafted." Russell accepted, and the commission was complete.

The very selection of the commission stilled doubts about Dallas. Its report buried them for long past the period of transition. The Warren Commission was a rudiment in the battle for confidence, a simple maneuver compared to the subtle weavings of Lyndon Johnson in the early days after the assassination.

There were the Kennedy men in and out of the government proper: the Irish Mafia, Harvard professors, labor leaders, the Kennedy Cabinet, the White House technicians, big-city politicians. All these, with no time to lose, had to be brought within the compass of the new President. Those in the government had to be persuaded to stay on the job. For if, as Johnson moved into his new job, some or most of these moved out of their old jobs, the country would draw an obvious conclusion: these Kennedy men did not choose to work for Johnson. That could destroy confidence. Thus, Johnson's first important move as President was to prevent even the appearance of an exodus, and to reinforce his still-tentative ties with the Northern power blocs that made up the power of the Democratic party: Negro organizations, labor unions, big-city machines—plus the liberal intellectuals.

* The long hours devoted by Russell to the Warren Commission's work were, in fact, partly responsible for his serious illness in early 1965.
† See page 84.

From the beginning as President, Johnson never entertained the remote possibility of following Harry Truman's example when he succeeded to the presidency in 1945 at the death of Franklin Roosevelt.
Truman cleaned out his predecessor's Cabinet and White House staff
and moved in his own. For two reasons, Johnson simply did not enjoy
the option that had been open to Truman. First, it was too late in
Kennedy's term and the mood of the hour was too black. And second,
he would have been hard put to find replacements. He *had* to keep
the Kennedy team intact.

The extraordinary intensity and persistence of the new President in
carrying out this job was symbolic of the extraordinary success of the
transition period. There was no hesitation, no ceremony, no delay. As
President, Johnson could now persuade with an authority never before possessed, and persuasion had always been a sharp instrument in
his exercise of power.

But persuasion, in the first few days at least, could not be too exuberant. Johnson subdued his energy, lowered his voice, and assumed a
posture of humility. The merest semblance of exuberance in a period
of a national grief and mourning could trigger the mass exodus of
New Frontiersmen that he must avoid at all costs. It could mean an
abrupt resignation as Attorney General by Robert F. Kennedy that
would split the Democratic party in two. For immediately upon the
death of his brother, Bobby Kennedy assumed leadership not only of
the family but of a substantial portion of the Democratic party.

Thus, in those early days of Johnson's presidency, the old acrimony
between him and Bobby Kennedy was absent. Talking to Kennedy on
the telephone from Dallas and then in Washington on Saturday, November 23, at his first Cabinet meeting, the new President was
thoughtful and understanding of the young Attorney General's personal loss. As Johnson told another New Frontiersman that evening,
he had kept the Saturday Cabinet meeting short mainly out of respect
for Bobby Kennedy. Eventually deep discord between these two figures who had been on the ragged edge of civility for some three years
was inevitable, rather sooner than later. But the fact that Johnson was
able to maintain that civility on November 23, 1963, saved the transition from disaster at the outset. Bobby stayed.

Bobby Kennedy was not the only potentially troubling member of
the administration inherited by Johnson. He distrusted the brisk Ivy
League manner of two Eastern Establishment Republicans who
played vital policy-making roles for President Kennedy: Douglas Dillon, Secretary of the Treasury, and McGeorge Bundy, White House
aide for National Security. He resented the fact that he was greeted in
his first hours in the White House by memoranda pleading with him

not to reduce expenditures from two Cabinet members: Secretary of Agriculture Orville Freeman and Secretary of Labor Willard Wirtz. The speculation throughout Washington was that Dillon, Bundy, Freeman, Wirtz, Secretary of the Interior Stewart Udall and quite likely many, many more would all be gone by year's end. The fact that they stayed is testimony to the magnificent restraint of Johnson in those transition days. Old friends and aides remarked they had never seen him so self-possessed, so humble. Talking to a quick-witted New Frontiersman on Saturday night, Johnson asked for patience. He could not, he said, absorb things as swiftly as Jack Kennedy.

With each key Kennedy man, Johnson used a different technique to try to make him a Johnson man. Walter Heller, the chairman of the President's Council of Economic Advisers, had sat next to Vice-President Johnson regularly at President Kennedy's weekly "briefing sessions" preceding his press conferences. For three years, Heller invariably made a point of giving Johnson a copy of his economic briefing paper for Kennedy when the President called in his experts to bone up for the press conference. As a result, Johnson developed a special relationship with the lean professor from the University of Minnesota whose New Economics set the tone of domestic policy in the Kennedy Administration.

Late in the evening on Saturday, November 23, Heller was called to the temporary office of the new President in the Executive Office Building just across West Executive Avenue from the White House. What ensued there was an essence of the new President's first few weeks in office as, one by one, he exerted the highly individualistic Johnsonian charm and persuasion to prevent the exceptional men brought to Washington by Kennedy from leaving.

As his chat with Heller progressed, Johnson was particularly anxious about the stock market decline following the assassination. Was there anything he could do or say to instill confidence? Heller told him the number of points the market had dropped in the few moments between the assassination and the close of the market and was mentally computing the percentage of decline when Johnson himself figured it out. The drop had been about 3 percent, Johnson said, and now the important thing was to create a general sense of confidence and assurance that the Johnson Administration was going to "move forward," not slide backward.

After touching on economic subjects, President Johnson came to the important point. Heller had left his chair and was walking to the door to leave, when Johnson came over, pulled him away from the door and shut it. He wanted to tell Heller what he had told a dozen others already: that he was not a conservative, a budget-slasher, who would take the government back to the laissez-faire of the Eisenhower Administration. No, far from it. The new President was, he said, a Roosevelt New Dealer, and anyone who studied his record would find that out. It was, he continued, vital that the economic and political liberals understand that fact. He asked Heller to make that clear to his liberal friends, to such Kennedy intellectuals from Harvard as historian Arthur Schlesinger, Jr., a White House assistant, and economist J. Kenneth Galbraith, Ambassador to India, who was in Washington for Kennedy's funeral.

As for Heller, said the President, there must be no question about his leaving the administration. Johnson needed him—needed him more than Kennedy had because Johnson had far more to learn than Kennedy. Heller's response echoed the words that the new President was hearing that day, and for many days thereafter, from every Kennedy man he appealed to: Heller would stay, he was eager to do everything he could to smooth the transition period for the new President, and he would stay not just out of a sense of duty but with a sense of warmth and friendship. That, Johnson knew, was establishing confidence.

Heller was essential to the new President not only because he had friends throughout the academic community and was a symbol of the New Economics, but because an indispensable part of government was in his charge and Johnson could not do without him all at once. In establishing confidence he must, then, establish a confidential relationship with Heller, with the Cabinet, and with the other main blocks in the arch of which Johnson himself had now become the keystone.

With Schlesinger, the emphasis was different. Schlesinger was important not because of what he was doing in the White House but because of his symbolic quality as a liberal's liberal. If Johnson could not let a Heller leave because the departure would make a gaping hole in the government itself, he could not let a Schlesinger leave because the departure would make a gaping hole in the new administration's ideological image.

On Tuesday, November 26, he asked Schlesinger, who had sent in his resignation the day after the assassination, to join him in the East Room of the White House, where the President made a speech to the Latin American ambassadors, pledging his support of the Alliance for Progress in graceful, sensitive words that evoked the memory both of John F. Kennedy and Franklin D. Roosevelt. Now, as he walked out of the East Room, he took Schlesinger back with him to the Oval Office in the White House, where by now Johnson was installed.

Sitting on opposite sofas by the fireplace, the President made what must have been a difficult appeal to Schlesinger. He and Schlesinger had never been close, and the man from the Texas frontier on occasion resented the blunt rhetoric and intellectualism of the Harvard professor on the New Frontier. He needed Schlesinger, said Johnson, because Schlesinger had a profound knowledge of the programs, the purposes, and the history of this country and of the progressive policies that distinguished Democratic administrations. Schlesinger knew the writers and the liberals, and Johnson needed that. He had Schlesinger's letter of resignation, he said, but he regarded it as nothing but a gesture, a formal offer. He rejected it. "If you act on it," Johnson told Schlesinger, "I will have you arrested."

Schlesinger, who really *wanted* to resign when he submitted his letter to Johnson, pointed out that every President had a right to have his own people, particularly in the White House. Johnson replied that he now regarded Schlesinger as one of his own men, that he had complete confidence in him, and that although it undoubtedly would be a sacrifice for Schlesinger, he must stay for the President's sake and for the country's. Johnson said all this with simplicity, dignity, and conviction.

Schlesinger stayed on for four months. He was given no jobs to do and saw the President only infrequently before he left. He was, then, a symbol, but an important one for Johnson.

Johnson's wooing of administration officials went to extremes at times, as it did with Adlai Stevenson, Ambassador to the United Nations and still an idol to the Democratic party's liberal wing. Johnson's private opinion of Stevenson had never been high, but their relations had generally been cordial and now he needed him. So ardent was his wooing that Stevenson, who had far less policy-making influence under Kennedy than he had hoped for, felt a new and major role was destined for him in this new administration.

Stevenson went to President Johnson's office in the Executive Office Building on Monday, November 25, the day of Kennedy's funeral. "I know and you know that you should be sitting behind this desk rather than me," Johnson told Stevenson. "You could have had the vice-presidential nomination in Los Angeles, but you kept your word to me that you wouldn't back any of the candidates and as a result I am here instead of you." What Johnson was saying—correctly or not—was that if Stevenson had endorsed Kennedy, the second place on the ticket would have been his for the asking.

Then Johnson went on: the late President had not been consulting Stevenson, but "all that is going to be changed from now on." Stevenson must not hesitate to telephone Johnson any time he had a recommendation. "I want you to play a large role in the formation of policy," Johnson said. Recalling that conversation to a friend a few weeks later, Stevenson said he genuinely believed that if he had given the word, Johnson would have replaced both Secretary of State Dean Rusk and McGeorge Bundy. But Stevenson told the President he should retain both Rusk and Bundy. Notwithstanding the President's glowing invitation for Stevenson to play that "large role" in policy-making, he found his influence progressively reduced, even below its level with Kennedy.*

The effort to encompass the entire New Frontier was so successful that no Kennedy man left until Ted Sorensen, Kennedy's Special Counsel at the White House, resigned effective February 29 to write a history of the Kennedy Administration. Nor was Sorensen's departure followed by a mass exodus. The key faces of the New Frontier remained in Washington into 1965 and even beyond.

Yet, Johnson's valiant achievement in retaining the entire Kennedy team had its unpleasant side. Edward R. Murrow, the brilliant radio-television commentator, had come to government from broadcasting in 1961 to take over the United States Information Agency. Some time in early 1963, he became ill. The illness was diagnosed as cancer, and from that moment, it was simply a question of picking an appropriate time to resign. Shortly before President Johnson went to Texas for the Christmas holiday, Murrow was advised by his doctors he must soon leave Washington for good and enter a clinic. Murrow had not wanted to resign during the transition, but now he had no choice. He informed Johnson that he would remain for one more month and that, three or four days before leaving, he would alert the President so that the usual statement could be issued at the White House.

But Murrow's health deteriorated faster than expected. Soon after New Year's Day his doctors ordered him into a clinic. On each of seven successive days, Murrow attempted to arrange an appointment with the President. He could not contact the President on the telephone. He booked a seat on a plane to California for January 17. Still the White House was silent. Finally, less than six hours before he left for the airport, Johnson telephoned him to say good-by and read the statement that the White House would issue.

Why did Johnson handle Murrow's departure in that way? Not because he wasn't sensitive to Murrow's health (although obviously he

---

* By 1965, Stevenson was reduced to asking Vice-President Hubert Humphrey for advice on how to get in touch with the President. Humphrey suggested that Stevenson try to work through Bill Moyers, the leading presidential aide.

had not been fully briefed on its seriousness). Not because he didn't appreciate Murrow's work in the government. What concerned Johnson was the prestige of the presidency after the shock of Dallas. Johnson wanted to delay Murrow's departure until he could find an appropriate replacement. He felt the presidency could not risk top-level vacancies. *Any* vacancy could impair confidence, and confidence after Dallas was the first imperative.

On the night of November 23, after his long series of meetings in the old vice-presidential suite in the Executive Office Building, Lyndon Johnson went home to The Elms, exhilarated but exhausted and burdened by the weight of many things to be done. Shortly before midnight, he and Lady Bird Johnson went upstairs to their bedroom in The Elms.

Johnson asked Horace Busby, his close friend and former aide, to sit with him upstairs while he had his regular nightly massage—and then to stay until Johnson went to sleep. There might be something he would want to say, and Busby would be there to receive it. The three talked for a few minutes after the lights had been put out. Then Busby, sitting in an overstuffed armchair, waited for the President to doze off. Thinking after half an hour that the President had fallen asleep, he quietly lifted himself out of the chair and tiptoed around the end of the bed toward the door.

"Buz," the voice came from the darkness. "Buz, is that you?" Busby said yes, it was him.

"Buz, I'm not asleep yet." And Busby returned to his chair. More minutes passed in the early morning. Now certain that he was listening to the rhythmic breathing of deep sleep, again Busby gently moved out of his chair and toward the door.

"Buz, are you still there?"

This time, embarrassed at his second miscalculation, Busby said yes, he was still there and he was just moving over to the window to adjust the curtain. It was fully an hour later that Busby finally left the sleeping President to return to his own temporary quarters in The Elms.

That was not the self-confident, self-possessed Johnson who had spent the past thirty-six hours reassuring a nation and winning its confidence. For his deeper mood was more tentative than revealed on the surface. Even though this man had pointed so long toward the White House and had recorded in his memory the history of so many of its occupants, the sudden weight of total responsibility was unaccustomed and unsettling. Having come to the White House not by the voice of the people, Johnson's insecurity showed itself in those first days, but never publicly. Harry Truman, far less skilled in the arts of government and politics, slept the sleep of peace during his own presidential transition. But Johnson, though he gloried in power, was not made like Truman, and the uncertainties he confronted came down hard on him. It was then that he reached out his hand to old and trusted aides like Horace Busby.

But these were difficult days for the old Johnson aides. Johnson was telling the Kennedy men he planned to graft only three or four of his own men onto the existing White House staff to justify his argument that true loyalty to the memory of President Kennedy required them to stay on. Johnson's own staff, he told Schlesinger, was composed of able men but not in the same class as the White House staff Kennedy had gathered around him. This repeated theme of Johnson's—that his own staff wasn't quite up to Kennedy's—naturally got back to the old Johnson hands who moved into the White House with him. Well as they understood him, it hurt and galled them, even though most of them appreciated the transcendent importance of Johnson's appeal to the New Frontier.

From the start, the few Johnson men who did move into the White House were far from unimportant. While Kennedy's New Frontiersmen stayed on as symbols of continuity, the duties of some of them soon fell to Johnson's men. The faithful, ever-present Walter Jenkins assumed administrative command at the White House. Bill Moyers, who happened to have been in Texas on November 22 and immediately flew by private plane to Dallas, returned with Johnson to the White House to stay (though for over a year he maintained the fiction that he was still deputy director of the Peace Corps and soon would return there). Soon, Moyers began to fill Kenny O'Donnell's function as appointments secretary (though O'Donnell was to stay at that desk for another year). Jack Valenti, the bouncy little Houston advertising man who had married Johnson's private secretary and traveled abroad when Johnson was Vice-President, also returned from the Texas trip. Starting out primarily as a speech writer, he became a White House fixture until his departure in May, 1966. Although Busby didn't sell his businessman's newsletter and join the Johnson staff for four more months, he was speech-writing for Johnson from the beginning (as he was during the vice-presidency). It was Busby who wrote Johnson's televised Thanksgiving Day message to the country on November 28.

While ingratiating himself with the New Frontiersmen, Johnson took pains to strengthen his links, some gone rusty these past three years, with unofficial advisers. Dean Acheson was consulted about foreign policy. Johnson's old friendship with Edwin Weisl in New York, cool ever since Weisl had objected to Johnson taking second place on the ticket in 1960, was renewed in the first week of Johnson's presidency when he flew to New York for the funeral of former Senator Herbert Lehman.° Johnson sought out all three members of that triumvirate of shrewd Washington lawyers—Abe Fortas, Clark Clifford, and James Rowe—who had advised him in the mid-1950s.

Fortas had remained on intimate terms with Johnson all during the vice-presidency. When White House lawyers prepared the fair housing order to be enforced by Vice-President Johnson's Committee on Equal Employment Opportunity, Johnson asked them to let Abe Fortas have a look at it, even though he had no official government position. Now with Johnson as President, Fortas—still without official status—was constantly on the scene after November 22: writing speeches, giving advice, keeping Johnson company.†

But Johnson needed more than Abe Fortases. He summoned help from the past. Clark Clifford had seen little of Johnson since that time a decade earlier when his closest political associate, Senator Stuart Symington, broke with Johnson. But Clifford, Harry Truman's White House counsel, was an expert in the inner mechanics of the executive branch. Moreover, he had worked for President-elect John F. Kennedy after the 1960 election in effecting the smooth transition between Eisenhower and Kennedy. Now, late on the afternoon of Wednesday, November 27, Clifford was asked to the White House to see the new President. Into the night, they talked for some five hours. Johnson pumped Clifford for information about the Truman White House, about Truman's attitude, about the Eisenhower-to-Kennedy transition. "Clark," the President said, "you've become the transition expert." In the next month, Clifford saw far more of Johnson than he had in the preceding eight years.

And the foolish break with Jim Rowe that began in the 1960 campaign at last was healed. Rowe was invited to the White House on Sunday, December 1. Johnson, who never found it easy to apologize to anybody, apologized to Rowe for what had gone before. Rowe protested that apologies were not necessary. "Jim," persisted Johnson, "you're not going to deprive your President of the chance to say he's

---

° At the President's urging, Weisl became Democratic National Committeeman from New York in August, 1964.

† Fortas had been retained by Bobby Baker as his counsel in the multiple legal complications that began late in the summer of 1963, but Fortas dropped Baker as a client when Johnson became President.

sorry to an old friend, are you?" It was a time for renewing old friendships.

Johnson's capacity for work in those first few days after he became President was superhuman. All but overlooked in the funereal atmosphere of Sunday and Monday, when millions of Americans could think only of Kennedy and grieve in front of their television sets, Johnson worked at building confidence. On Monday evening after the last sound of muffled drums, he went to the State Department auditorium for a lugubrious reception for foreign heads of state, foreign ministers, prime ministers. Included were Anastas Mikoyan, Deputy Premier of the Soviet Union; Ludwig Erhard, Chancellor of West Germany; Charles de Gaulle, President of France; Sir Alec Douglas-Home, Prime Minister of England, and others comprising one of the most celebrated aggregations of foreign statesmen since the funeral of Britain's Edward VII in 1910. Johnson knew it was important to be seen by these foreign politicians, who would soon be testing the strength and responses of the new American President. And he surprised Secretary of State Rusk with his knowledge of names, his memory for faces, and his ability to recall pertinent experiences during his many travels as Vice-President.

The next morning he invited Mikoyan, Erhard, and Sir Alec to separate conversations in the White House. To secure confidence, he needed to display to his own countrymen his capacity to deal with these foreign powers. At the same time, he wanted to show the statesmen from abroad that President Kennedy had chosen wisely when he chose Lyndon Johnson as his running mate.

He called in the Governors of the fifty states after the funeral on Monday evening, and warned them that without confidence in the new administration "our whole system could go awry. . . ." He described the "American System" in phrases of one syllable as far from the high style of Kennedy as the Pedernales is from the Charles. It was a country man's idiom, explicit, to the point, unadorned. It would be heard again and again in the Johnson presidency:

> . . . We think we have the best system. We think that where a capitalist can put up a dollar, he can get a return on it. A manager can get up early to work and with money and men he can build a better mousetrap. A laborer who is worthy of his hire stands a chance of getting attention and maybe a little profit-sharing system, and the highest minimum wages of any nation in the world.

The Governors may have been surprised to hear these earthy Americanisms from the new President, but they were strangely comforted, too. There was no uncertain stammering here, no outward sign of hesitation, but obvious and deep sincerity to get on with a difficult job, and there was an atmosphere of confidence, a *presidential* atmosphere of latent power and decision.

But the high point of Johnson's bid for confidence came two days later, when he rode to the Capitol to address a joint session of Congress. That, the first full-dress presidential message to the nation, was of supreme importance to Johnson. How it was to be made—as a "fireside chat" from the White House or from the rostrum of the House to a joint session of Congress—was the subject of a most serious discussion. Ted Sorensen preferred the congressional approach, and Johnson, his roots deep on Capitol Hill, agreed.

On Saturday, November 23, Johnson asked Sorensen to write this first major speech—the same task he had performed so well for Kennedy. Later that day, Johnson by accident ran into Galbraith in an elevator in the Executive Office Building. Worried about the speech to Congress four days later, Johnson asked Galbraith whether he worked well with Sorensen. When the answer was yes, Johnson asked him to collaborate on the address. That night, Sorensen and Galbraith got together in the handsome Georgetown house of Katherine Graham, widow of Philip Graham and now publisher of the *Washington Post*. Galbraith hatched ideas and Sorensen put them in writing.

When Sorensen prepared his speeches for Kennedy, the draft was circulated, amendments were made, and it was then returned to Sorensen for final polishing. With Johnson, it was different. After the Sorensen-Galbraith draft was submitted to Johnson, they never saw it again. Johnson gave it to Abe Fortas, who did a top-to-bottom rewrite. "I corned it up a little," Fortas said later. The result was an amalgam that was neither pure Kennedy nor pure Johnson. It was a transition address.

But in those days when appearances meant so much, the speech itself was only part of a larger ceremony. There was the ritualistic question of who would accompany the new President during the slow ride up Pennsylvania Avenue to Capitol Hill. The fact that Johnson's old friend, Representative Joe Kilgore, was *not* in the presidential limousine on November 27 was a sign of the mood in Washington during the transition.

On November 22, Kilgore put away his tan Stetson hat. For Joe Kilgore sensed what Johnson was seeking after the assassination. The image of Texas had always irritated and sometimes infuriated the

Eastern Seaboard, and the Eastern Seaboard dominated Washington and the New Frontier. Thus, Kilgore knew how important it was to dilute the old image of Texas now that a Texan was President. The worst service his friends could perform for Johnson would be to strut around the streets of Washington and in and out of the White House wearing Stetson hats.

When the President announced he would address Congress November 27, Kilgore telephoned Elizabeth Carpenter, Mrs. Johnson's press secretary and one of the most prominent Texans in Washington. He told Mrs. Carpenter that the speech Johnson would make to Congress was the most important speech he would ever give. This speech, said Kilgore, would fix the President forever in the minds of millions of Americans who, until November 22, had been all but unaware of his existence. Not only that, said Kilgore, but it also would set the tone of his administration and establish its credentials. Every American who could find a television set would be watching and every American would form his first impression of the new President on the basis of this first speech. Kilgore asked Mrs. Carpenter to tell the President all that, and to tell him further that he must not wave his arms from the rostrum of the House, he must not shout or speak too fast, and he must say the right things.

Informed of Kilgore's call, the President invited him to the White House to hear the draft of the all-important speech. Then, he invited the conservative Texas Congressman to ride to Capitol Hill with him when he went to give his speech. No, said Kilgore, that wouldn't do. The best help he could give his old friend, he told the President, was to stay away from him in public. Everything was changed now, and the President must do nothing to convey the impression that his closest friends were conservative Texas politicians. The next day, when Johnson went to the Capitol to deliver his speech, Ted Sorensen was in the presidential limousine. Joe Kilgore took a taxicab.

Speaking from the rostrum of the House, President Johnson achieved a tour de force in the most important address of his life. The words that counted were these: "Today, in this moment of new resolve, I would say to all my fellow Americans, *let us continue*." Who could not recapture, on hearing those words, the phrase that gave them birth, uttered by John Kennedy on the steps of the Capitol January 20, 1961: "*Let us begin*." The new President, with that link between the dead and the quick, rang with conviction and captured precisely the mood of the country. The speech had been written by Sorensen, Galbraith, and Fortas, but the heart of it—"let us continue"—was President Johnson's own. And then the President examined the unfinished business: "Our most immediate tasks," he said, "are here on this Hill." He moved quickly to show that Kennedy's projects were his projects. He told Congress:

> First, no memorial oration or eulogy could more eloquently honor President Kennedy's memory than the earliest possible passage of the civil rights bill for which he fought so long. We have talked long enough about equal rights in this country. We have talked for one hundred years or more. It is time now to write the next chapter and to write it in the books of law. I urge you again, as I did in 1957 and again in 1960, to enact a civil rights law so that we can move forward to eliminate from this nation every trace of discrimination and oppression that is based upon race or color.

And then to the next unfinished task that Kennedy had placed high on his congressional program:

> And second, no act of ours could more fittingly continue the work of President Kennedy than the early passage of the tax bill for which he fought all this long year. . . . This is no time for delay. It is a time for action.

Finally, a strong appeal to the nation's hope and faith:

> Let us put an end to the teaching and the preaching of hate and evil and violence. Let us turn away from the fanatics of the far left and the far right, from the apostles of bitterness and bigotry, from those defiant of law and those who pour venom into our nation's bloodstream. . . . So let us here highly resolve that John Fitzgerald Kennedy did not live—or die—in vain.

Sitting with Mrs. Johnson, in the place of honor in the overflowing galleries of the House chamber, were three men: Governor Carl Sanders of Georgia, a voice of the New South; Mayor Robert Wagner of New York, a Catholic and a voice of the big-city Democrats; and Arthur Schlesinger, Jr., a voice of the third great component of the Democratic party: the liberal-intellectuals.

Who had the time and forethought to make those selections? Probably Johnson himself. It was a last-minute decision. Schlesinger was telephoned from the White House with his invitation late Tuesday evening, the night before the speech. He was out but returned the call at 1:00 A.M. Clifton Carter, Johnson's long-time political agent in Texas, gave him the invitation. Schlesinger had not intended to go to the speech. As it was, he returned from Capitol Hill convinced the President had "achieved a genuine success." Johnson, thought Schlesinger, had never spoken so well before.

By the time Lyndon Johnson finished his address to Congress on November 27, he had indisputably gained the confidence not only of the nation but of the liberals who had always distrusted him. Johnson went out of his way to be pleasant to Joseph Rauh of the Americans for Democratic Action, inviting his arch-critic aboard Air Force One to attend Senator Lehman's funeral in New York.

Yet, there remained one place where confidence was incomplete. Those Texas liberals who had never forgiven Johnson for turning against them in 1956 were still unforgiving. He might be a liberal in Washington, they said, but Lyndon Johnson was still in league with his conservative pals and the money interests back home. Senator Ralph Yarborough, leader of the liberal faction in Texas, faced a possibly difficult fight for renomination in 1964. Should Governor John Connally and the new President's other old friends bring down the South's only Senator with an unbroken record of all-out support for the New Frontier, the old, nagging liberal-labor suspicion of Johnson would return in every Northern Democratic stronghold.

Prior to the assassination, Johnson became more and more distracted with worry that Yarborough was working against him. Yarborough, thought Johnson, was plotting to have him dumped from the 1964 ticket. Accordingly, Johnson had been spending more and more time searching for a pro-Johnson Texas Democrat to beat Yarborough in the 1964 Senate primary.* Much to Johnson's irritation, Representative Jim Wright, the ideal candidate, was shying away from the race. Two other possibilities were considerably more conservative than Wright: Representative Joe Kilgore and Lloyd Bentsen, a former Congressman.†

Although the primary purpose of President Kennedy's political journey to Texas was to make peace among the warring Democrats of the Vice-President's state, Johnson and Yarborough were never more antagonistic than during the first day of the trip on November 21. Knowing full well that Johnson was scouring Texas for a foe to run against him, Yarborough flatly refused to ride in the Vice-President's car in the Houston and San Antonio caravans. Only when an exasperated Kennedy personally insisted did Yarborough consent to enter Johnson's limousine in the fatal Dallas motorcade.

* See page 333.
† The liberals had beaten Johnson's efforts to elect Bentsen's wife as Democratic National Committeewoman from Texas in 1956. See page 233.

On Air Force One before the landing in Dallas, Johnson discussed Yarborough with Jim Wright and Joe Kilgore. Noting Yarborough's refusal to ride with the Vice-President in Houston, Kilgore needled Johnson and asked what he was going to do about the state's senior Senator.

"Well," drawled Johnson, looking evenly at Wright and Kilgore, "up until now, nobody has had the guts to run against him, and maybe now it's too late."

After Dallas, everything changed. Yarborough telegraphed the new President his pledge of support. Before that first weekend ended, the two old enemies chatted amiably over the telephone. Overnight it became Johnson's highest interest to end the miserable feuding of the Texas Democrats. His solution was simple and equitable: a nonaggression pact between liberals and conservatives. Liberals would not oppose the re-election of Governor Connally, who had been seriously wounded by Lee Harvey Oswald as he sat in front of President Kennedy and was now politically invincible. Conservatives would not oppose Ralph Yarborough for re-election as Senator.

That nonaggression pact was broken, not by the conservatives, but by the other liberal Yarborough, Don Yarborough, who announced his candidacy against Connally. Don Yarborough, a glib young man, had run a surprisingly close race against Connally for Governor in 1962 but now he was doomed to overwhelming defeat against the survivor of Dallas. Nevertheless, the Connally conservatives regarded Don Yarborough's challenge as a declaration of war, opening the way for one of their own to run against Ralph Yarborough.*

But who would it be? Bentsen removed himself from consideration. Wright put himself back into the picture, then took himself out. That left Kilgore, who wanted to retire from Congress anyway, had less to lose, and felt keenly that Ralph Yarborough should be retired from the Senate.

Here was an unhappy problem for the new President. To block his good friend Joe Kilgore from running against a blood enemy like Ralph Yarborough was not easy. Lady Bird Johnson was deeply upset to see her husband aligned against his old friend and made her views known inside the White House. But Bill Moyers and other presidential assistants argued that Johnson simply could not afford to take part in a right-wing purge of Yarborough. The repercussions would be national and nasty.

---

* Actually, Connally never was a party to the nonaggression pact but simply felt the defeat of Ralph Yarborough was no longer attainable after the assassination.

The Texas problem persisted into January, long after other problems of the transition had been disposed of. At one point, Kilgore received a telephone call from Walter Jenkins that the White House did not mind if there were an opponent against Ralph Yarborough now that Don Yarborough had announced against Connally.

As the February 4 filing deadline neared, Kilgore announced his retirement from Congress and his availability for the Senate but soon picked up soundings of opposition from the President. Kilgore immediately telephoned Jenkins. After checking with Johnson, Jenkins apologetically reported back to Kilgore, his friend of so many years, to say the President did not want him to run. Jenkins explained that the President was concerned first about party unity; and second, about Joe Kilgore's well-being. Kilgore replied softly that he could take care of himself and he wondered out loud whether what the President was really concerned about was Lyndon Johnson's well-being. In any event, said Kilgore, he wanted to talk to Johnson personally.

They did talk over the telephone, and it was a talk Kilgore would never forget. The President was positive. He absolutely would not have any of his old friends opposing Ralph Yarborough, and that's all there was to it. If Kilgore persisted, said Johnson, he would throw against him all the power in Texas: newspapers, businessmen, campaign financing. Then, in a softer tone, Johnson appealed to Kilgore. If Yarborough were purged, the President said mournfully, the liberal wing of the party might conspire to nominate somebody else at Atlantic City in August. For the country's sake, wasn't it more important to have Lyndon Johnson in the White House than Joe Kilgore in the Senate?

Shaken and undecided, Kilgore flew from Washington to Austin on Saturday, February 2, less than forty-eight hours before the filing deadline. The issue was settled at the Governor's Mansion in a tense conference between Kilgore, Connally, and the Governor's aides. Kilgore was one of Connally's closest friends. The Governor was bitter at Johnson's intervention. But he knew the realities. Connally told Kilgore that he would support him all the way if he decided to run but that he must know that most of the Texas power structure would not. Wouldn't his old friends in industry and the Texas power structure back him? Kilgore asked. Hardly, Connally replied, considering the fact that the power of the federal government was at Johnson's fingertips. Kilgore did not file.

At the cost of weakening his friendship with John Connally and destroying for the time being, at least, his relationship with Joe Kilgore, President Johnson had saved Yarborough from a dangerous primary fight.* It did not make the *Texas* liberals love him or even trust him. But it achieved the fundamental purpose. It convinced the *national* liberals that Johnson had moved far beyond the orbit of the Texas Tories.

Texas politics, then, was the last spasm of Johnson's Operation Confidence begun on November 22.

Even as he sought confidence, Johnson exercised his new power from his very first days as President. Not permitted in those early days to show itself publicly, it cropped up privately in odd moments. When an intimate of President Kennedy went to the White House to talk to Johnson alone for the first time, he brought up two items of unfinished business. Kennedy, he said, had planned to name two distinguished Harvard professors to high office. Economist Seymour Harris was to be a member of the Federal Reserve Board. Samuel Beer, a professor of government, was to be Ambassador to Uruguay. The appointments had been cleared by the White House shortly before Kennedy left for Texas. Arthur Schlesinger, Kennedy's friend told Johnson, was confident that Beer was an excellent choice for Uruguay. Johnson replied: "Arthur Schlesinger isn't running Latin American policy anymore." In 1960, as national chairman of the ADA, Beer had prepared an attack on Johnson as a presidential candidate. Neither Beer nor Harris was appointed.

Another Latin American ambassadorial appointment planned by Kennedy was at an even more advanced stage on November 22. On the President's desk in the White House the day he flew to Texas was a commission, ready for the presidential signature, nominating Frank Coffin as Ambassador to Panama. A former Democratic Congressman from Maine, Coffin had been a foreign aid official in Washington for three years and now was slated for advancement. But back in 1961, he had privately disagreed with Vice-President Johnson over a technical provision in Kennedy's new foreign aid bill. Several Congressmen were present during an argument between the two men. Coffin told Johnson: "You're wrong." Johnson did not forget that he had been so addressed by a middle-echelon official. For a month after Johnson became President, Coffin waited for Johnson to sign his commission. It never was signed.†

---

* Gordon McClendon, a right-wing owner of radio stations, did file against Yarborough. A political neophyte without lines into the Texas conservative establishment, McClendon was not a serious contender.

† Coffin later was named by Johnson to a relatively minor post in the Export-Import Bank in Paris and still later was appointed as a federal judge.

It was inevitable, of course, that Johnson run his presidency his own way, and appoint his own men. It was inevitable that many of his *private* actions in the days following the assassination would not go down well with Kennedy men. That was particularly true of those at the second level of government whose allegiance was not essential to Johnson's major purpose of establishing continuity and of demonstrating his ability to keep the main actors of the New Frontier on the Johnson stage. Johnson would go to any length to prevent Bobby Kennedy or Bob McNamara or Walter Heller from leaving. But he need not humble himself before middle-echelon officials such as Frank Coffin—or the public relations officers of the administration.

Two days before Christmas, Johnson directed Press Secretary Pierre Salinger to summon the government's top public affairs specialists to the White House. These men, most of whom held the rank of Assistant Secretary, were image-makers for their departments and for the administration. Among those called to the White House by Salinger, for example, were Assistant Secretary of State Robert Manning; Assistant Secretary of Defense Arthur Sylvester; the Deputy Director of the United States Information Agency, Donald Wilson, and seven or eight others. They waited for half an hour, and when the President arrived it was quickly apparent that he was out of sorts. He didn't know the exact job description of all this high-priced talent, he said, but he knew that none of them was earning his pay. "You're not getting my picture on the front page the way you did Kennedy's," the President scolded. That day, he went on, the only front-page display featuring the President of the United States was a story about the annual ceremony in which the President lights the Christmas tree on the ellipse south of the White House. He was going down to Texas for a Christmas holiday, Johnson said, and he didn't want any major news announcements in Washington while he was gone. They were to be sent to him in Texas and they would be made there from the Texas White House.

Considering the terrific strain on President Johnson during those first four weeks of his presidency, an outburst like that was understandable (although, in fact, the "play" that he had been receiving in the press was pervasive). But in lecturing the government's top public relations men, Johnson was subtly enhancing his power by driving the point home that these men were under his personal scrutiny and had better watch their step if they wanted to keep their jobs. He made them become *his* men.

Although the high-echelon Kennedy staff was treated with infinitely more respect, they found it difficult to adjust to the new President's working habits. Kennedy delegated a great deal of routine, daily work. Johnson did not like to delegate anything. He wanted reports from his advisers in writing, and they had been accustomed to brief, succinct verbal communication with Kennedy. Johnson had a habit of walking round and round a problem, analyzing it this way and that and seeking advice on how to deal with it from many different advisers, none of whom knew the identity of the others.

In those early days, Johnson also frequently invited Senators to come to the Oval Office to get their advice. Thus a reply from the President to a letter from Premier Khrushchev was held up for several hours while the President discussed it at lunch with Senator Russell Long. On another occasion, the White House staff wanted to instruct the Pentagon to have several helicopters ready for possible emergency use in a new crisis in the Congo. Bill Moyers, who was rapidly becoming the President's foremost adviser, said that was a matter about which the President himself should be consulted. The President, in turn, asked for a formal, joint State Department–Defense Department recommendation on the plan. The plan was lost in the bureaucracy and nothing ever came of it.

Similarly, appointments piled up in bewildering confusion on the President's desk. Once Kennedy had got his office in order and running smoothly, he left much of the routine appointive power to Ralph Dungan, a Kennedy aide dating back to Senate days. Not surprisingly, Johnson was skeptical about this sort of delegation during his first weeks in office. Consequently, Secretary of State Rusk instructed his own staff not to push the President on appointments. Let the appointments pile up on his desk for a while, Rusk said, and leave the President alone. Rusk knew it would take months before the White House could operate with the old efficiency.

The Cabinet, too, found it necessary to change the habits of three years to accommodate to the new President. Kennedy liked his Cabinet to float trial balloons, often without checking with him. But under Johnson, Cabinet members who floated trial balloons quickly found out, sometimes to their sorrow, that Johnson preferred to float the trial balloons himself. It took time, too, for Johnson to master the complexities of issues that, as Vice-President, he was aware of but which, because he had never been deeply involved in them, he did not fully understand. One day he turned to Bromley Smith, an assistant on McGeorge Bundy's National Security staff in the White House, and asked plaintively: "Can you tell me in one clear sentence what the Kennedy Round is?" *

* The "Kennedy Round" was the negotiation scheduled to start in 1964 on tariff reductions, made possible by the passage of the Kennedy Trade Act of 1962.

Moreover, as the poignant mood of transition faded and the Johnson presidency began to take on its own color, the President reverted to the old, imperious Johnsonian style in his handling of even high-echelon Kennedy holdovers. When he returned to the LBJ Ranch for Christmas, 1963, day and night conferences were held in the living room to prepare for the first Johnson State of the Union Message to Congress on January 8. For the better part of a week, the ranch resembled a Grand Central Station of Washington officials. In these meetings at the ranch, the veneer of self-restraint and humility that marked the transition President was wearing thin. The zesty, irrepressible Johnson of Majority Leader days was beginning to emerge.

Bill Moyers, Walter Heller, Budget Director Kermit Gordon, and other top officials were seated at the dinner table one night along with the entire Johnson family. Johnson suddenly switched the conversation from the poverty program to sagging beef prices. Three local cattle barons magically appeared at Johnson's invitation and were introduced to Heller, Gordon, and the other city slickers from Washington. Johnson sat them down, then extracted a memorandum written for him by Heller and Gordon and read it aloud. The subject was the decline of prices for domestic beef, and the memorandum argued that imports from abroad were only one factor in the decline and not even a major factor. The true reason for falling beef prices, the President read, was increased domestic production, which accounted for four-fifths of the total decline.

As he read, the three Texas cattlemen became more and more agitated. When he finished reading, the President got up and paced the floor in a parody of a man about to go through the roof with frustration. This memorandum, he told the cattlemen, lifting his arms high in mock fury, is typical of what you get from a bunch of eggheads. What is an egghead? An egghead is a man with strong opinions on things he knows nothing about. All this was hyperbole, delivered in excellent humor. Then the President produced figures on the rise in imports, and turning triumphantly to Heller, Gordon, and the others from Washington, told them to listen to what the cattlemen had to say.

One by one, Johnson's Texas neighbors said the same thing: the problem was imports, not domestic production. One of the President's friends said the price drop would cost him fifty thousand dollars in a single year. With that, the President turned to his twenty-thousand-dollar-a-year economists. "You see?" he exclaimed. "I just want you to be aware of the problem. Now, if there was a twenty percent decline in the wages of Walter Reuther's auto workers, you gentlemen would be asking me for action."

Christmas week at the ranch was the beginning of the end of Johnson's transition as President. There remained only the President's address to the opening of the second session of the 88th Congress on
January 8, 1964. Returning to Washington, the President called in his
chief advisers on foreign policy for a final session in the Cabinet Room
on the State of the Union Message, already in draft form.

There, gathered in the Cabinet Room, were three layers of advisers,
each separate from the other, each with its uncommon tradition but
all now joined together. The first layer was the Kennedy-holdover
layer: Rusk and McNamara, the CIA's John McCone, McGeorge
Bundy, Arthur Schlesinger, Walt Rostow of the State Department
Policy Planning staff, Don Wilson of the USIA; the second layer was
the core of Johnson's new, inside advisers: Moyers, Valenti, and, of
course, Walter Jenkins; finally, the third layer—the triumvirate of
Fortas, Clifford, and Rowe.

One common purpose united this diverse group: to help Lyndon
Johnson. Johnson took the floor. Remember, he said, I still talk two
and a half times as slow as Kennedy. Keep it short. The President
wanted his advisers to understand what he was thinking. Kennedy, he
said, had left the nation in excellent military condition (a complete
military inventory had been made for Johnson by McNamara). Then
Johnson launched into a highly subjective discourse about peace. He
did not want to be in the position, he said, where at breakfast "I get a
new message from Khrushchev saying how much *he* is for peace when
all I read from the United States is how we are strong enough to blow
up the world." That was the tone the President wanted to establish
before the final draft of the speech was written.

He touched on foreign aid, because foreign aid was always a problem in Congress and always a difficult program to explain and justify
in the State of the Union Message. Foreign aid, said Johnson, could
not be fought out "on the basis that it helps our national security" but
rather because it is an "obligation" of the richer nations to help the
poorer nations. "It is better to give than to receive," said the President.
"We've got to talk about rich nations and poor nations."

After this long, revealing monologue, Johnson talked briefly about
his domestic program: housing, urban affairs, and his brand new poverty program. He still worried about the word "poverty." Wasn't there
some better way to describe it? Apparently not—so Johnson agreed it
would have to be the *poverty* program. "But it's not poverty," he said,
"it's wastage of resources and human lives."

Far into the evening, the meeting went on. There was no question
here about who was in charge. In six weeks, Lyndon Johnson had

pulled into his own hands all the threads of the United States government. The presidency was his, the transition was over. The bitter memory of Dallas was still overpowering, but the new President had achieved his first imperative. There was confidence again in the land.

Chapter XVII

★★★★★★★★★

TAMING
THE
CONGRESS

We have in 1964 a unique opportunity and obligation to prove
the success of our system, to disprove those cynics and critics at
home and abroad who question our purpose and our competence.
—President Lyndon B. Johnson, State of the
Union Message to Congress, January 8, 1964

It was a simple statement of fact when President Lyndon B. Johnson
told Congress on November 27, 1963: "For thirty-two years, Capitol
Hill has been my home."

During the critical days that followed, the new President treated
Capitol Hill, so often inhospitable to Chief Executives, almost as if it
were still his home. His decision to speak to the nation from the rostrum of the House, rather than from his desk in the White House,
partly reflected his love of the place. The mood persisted. Although
Presidents seldom care to travel those seventeen-odd blocks more than
absolutely necessary, Johnson was back and forth between the White
House and Capitol Hill in those early days as though his life depended
on it. Without advance warning during his first week in office, he
dropped in on the weekly luncheon meeting of the Texas congressional delegation that he used to attend unfailingly as Congressman,
Senator, and Vice-President. The next day he paid a surprise call on
Speaker John McCormack of Massachusetts and stayed to have a
drink with House leaders in the room where so often he had sat as a
member of the late Sam Rayburn's "board of education."

The traffic on Pennsylvania Avenue also moved in the other direction. Senators and Congressmen who seldom if ever had been in the
White House except for formal ceremonies suddenly found themselves
sitting down with the President and Mrs. Johnson at intimate, quickly
arranged dinner parties. When Senator Hubert Humphrey telephoned

Johnson on November 26 to report the first Johnson victory in the Senate as President, Johnson was elated and impulsively asked Humphrey over for dinner that evening.*

Johnson went out of his way to ingratiate himself with the opposition. Kennedy had never had much use for Representative Charles A. Halleck of Indiana, the House Minority Leader, a gut fighter who asked and gave no quarter in his often bitterly partisan style of legislative combat. But in that first week as President, Johnson dispatched his limousine to pick up Halleck at his home one morning and bring him to The Elms for a leisurely, pleasant breakfast with the new President. A beaming Halleck emerged from The Elms full of praise for the President who had served him "thick bacon, just the kind a fellow like me from Indiana would like."

In the early weeks of the Johnson presidency and, in fact, right up to the election of 1964, relations between the President and individual members of Congress were closer than at any time in memory. Senior Democrats who had seen President Kennedy only on official business or at social events had easy and casual access to President Johnson. The informal tone of the White House under Lyndon and Lady Bird Johnson was more congenial to middle-aged legislators from the South and West than the high, dashing style of the Kennedys.

This marked change in relations between Capitol Hill and the White House was inevitable with Lyndon Johnson as President, no matter what the prevailing problems. After all, Capitol Hill was Johnson's political home. In the first weeks of his presidency, his attentions naturally would turn there. Besides, Johnson had never had a *social* life distinct from his political life. The two were inextricably blended.

This congressional emphasis was deeply underscored by the fact that in the late autumn of 1963, Congress was widely regarded as Problem Number One for the White House. For Johnson inherited from Kennedy what seemed on the surface to be the worst congressional revolt since the days of Harry Truman, resulting in an atrophy of the New Frontier's legislative dreams. Some of Johnson's advisers who were less than admiring of the Kennedy presidency actually believed the congressional stalemate was undermining foreign confidence in the administration's ability to run its own country. Even a few New Frontiersmen now felt that the Kennedy legislative record was the weak spot of his presidency. They were coming to believe that his place in history would be assured by his brilliant victory in the 1962 Cuban missile crisis and the skillful negotiations that brought off

---

* This was the defeat of the bill restricting sale of American farm products behind the Iron Curtain. It is described in detail later in this chapter.

the 1963 test-ban treaty but that history would not record him as one of those few Presidents who tamed Congress.

In fact, Kennedy's record in Congress had its own triumphs. No President had devoted so much attention to the details of legislation and the interests of legislators. The office of legislative liaison instituted in the White House by Eisenhower was expanded and refined by Kennedy under the astute direction of Lawrence O'Brien. Nor was Kennedy a doctrinaire, reflexive liberal who plunged into the congressional thickets with the unfulfilled dreams of generations. In a successful ploy aimed at detaching Southern Democratic Congressmen from the conservative coalition they formed with Republicans in the late 1930s, Kennedy delayed a comprehensive civil rights bill until well into 1963 at the cost of a specific campaign pledge that he would press for new civil rights legislation early in 1961.

In short, while sharing Truman's and Eisenhower's preoccupation with international affairs, Kennedy was infinitely more attentive than his two predecessors in promoting a legislative program. Moreover, his majority in Congress, though not awesome, was more comfortable than either Truman's or Eisenhower's. Republicans had not recovered from the 1958 debacle. In 1960, they scored net gains of only twenty-two seats in the House and one seat in the Senate. That left the Democrats with majorities of 262 to 174 in the House and 65 to 35 in the Senate.

Subtracting a variable number of Democratic defectors on each bill, these majorities—plus the immeasurable help of the activist Democratic President in the White House—were enough to break, at least partially, the deadlock on liberal legislation that had been building ever since Roosevelt's defeat on the Court-packing issue in 1937. Projects pending for a decade or more became law in 1961: a program of economic aid for depressed areas to be administered by the new Area Redevelopment Administration; a comprehensive new housing program with easy mortgage terms for the poor; extension of the federal minimum wage–maximum hour law into the retail and service trades.

In 1962, Kennedy won approval of two proposals that had not been blocked in that earlier period of deadlock, but carried his own special brand: a Trade Expansion Act that gave the President unprecedented new power to cut tariffs; and a limited tax revision bill carrying special tax credits for businessmen who were willing to invest in their own expansion.* In the fall of 1962, Ted Sorensen and Larry O'Brien were telling the press that the congressional output under two years of Kennedy was greater than in Roosevelt's time.

* This bill was wholly separate from the major tax reduction bill introduced the next year.

Statistically, they were right, but what they failed to spell out was the other side of the coin. The most imaginative New Frontier proposals were treated harshly in Congress. Bills to streamline and modernize the regulatory commissions, create a Cabinet-level Department of Urban Affairs, establish a new concept of "supply management" to stabilize the farm economy, enact standby powers for the President to reduce taxes in times of recession—all these died in Congress. Even more significant was the death of two far more important proposals that had been pending for at least a decade and were on the agenda of the "rump" session back in August, 1960: federal aid for elementary and secondary schools and Medicare for the aged under Social Security. These two bills were really the core of Kennedy's first-term legislative program and their defeat was a bitter pill for the President.

Republican hopes of massive off-year gains in the 1962 elections were cruelly disappointed; the Republicans won only two seats in the House and *lost* four seats in the Senate. Kennedy's plan, then, was to pass his landmark tax reduction bill in 1963 and the Medicare bill in 1964 (with consideration of the education bill postponed until after the 1964 election, in anticipation of Democratic gains that year). But this timetable was overtaken by the breadth and intensity of conservative opposition to tax reduction at a time of budget deficits. Kennedy, surprised, now realized that passage of the tax bill might have to be delayed until 1964.

That possibility became a certainty when the simmering Negro Revolution exploded in the Birmingham riots of May, 1963. Now, any further delay of civil rights legislation was out of the question, and the civil rights bill would have to be the most far-reaching ever sent to Congress. It was quickly submitted. Thus, what Kennedy had feared during his first two years in office came to pass. Frightened by the political uncertainties at home caused by the Negro Revolution and the Southern White Backlash, Southern Democratic Congressmen who had been supporting Kennedy on many bills now shied away and deserted him—not only on the civil rights bill but on *all* legislation.

On top of that, John F. Kennedy in the spring and summer of 1963 was suffering from a strange, inexplicable malady that strikes all Presidents, usually more than once. The New Frontier was stalled. It would rise in spirit again in the early autumn of 1963, with hopes for a full recovery. But in the spring and summer—despite Kennedy's triumph in the test-ban treaty—there was an ill-defined sensation of going downhill.

How keenly this sensation was felt on Capitol Hill became clear on June 12, when the House voted 209 to 204 against authorizing further funds for the Area Redevelopment Administration, the depressed areas program passed with such high hopes just two years earlier. That taste of blood fed the spirit of revolt, which always lurks near the surface at the first sign of presidential weakness. Frightened congressional leaders led by Speaker McCormack advised the White House it would be foolhardy to risk even the most innocuous presidential proposal—for instance, a limited program of federal assistance for urban mass transit—on the floor of the House. By that standard, there could be no thought of risking the mighty tax bill. And until the tax bill was disposed of, it would be impossible to consider the civil rights bill, which had not yet picked up the necessary Republican support anyway. In brief, John F. Kennedy midway through his third year in the presidency confronted legislative stalemate of the magnitude that habitually plagued Harry Truman.

But whereas Truman threw up his hands in dismay and cursed the haughty barons of Capitol Hill, Kennedy tried to put the legislative pieces back together again. He maintained a public profile of optimism and a mood of cordiality quite different from the open feuding of the Truman era, while Congress idled in sullen rebellion and Larry O'Brien went about the tedious business of collecting enough votes to pass the tax and civil rights bills. By September, the New Frontier was beginning to get its second wind and the climate on Capitol Hill was improving. On September 25, the House at long last passed the tax bill after narrowly rejecting—226 to 199—a Republican alternative that would have gutted it. The White House and congressional leaders of both parties knew that the great legislative logjam of 1963 was beginning to crack.

But the general public didn't understand that, and neither did much of official Washington. Thus, when John F. Kennedy was assassinated, the inaccurate image of a Congress rebelliously running out of control was still the prevailing image, and it was shared to some degree even by the new President himself and the aides he brought to the White House. To a President so much a product of Congress, it was essential to demonstrate that the executive branch could control the legislative branch, and to demonstrate it speedily, not just in order to pass the Kennedy legislative program but also to convince the watching world, both Western and Communist, that a leader capable of running the entire federal government had succeeded to the presidency of the United States.

For that reason, Johnson insisted on keeping the Congress in session, even though a recess was long overdue and the tragedy of Dallas afforded a justifiable reason for adjournment until the first of the new year. During the first weekend, Hubert Humphrey advised Johnson privately to send Congress home, arguing that a cooling-off period was precisely what the overworked, querulous legislators needed. But Johnson rejected the advice. He insisted that Congress be kept in session so that he could show the world a spirit of national unity and purpose before year's end.

Substantial progress on the tax and civil rights bills was impossible until 1964. The new President's first goal then was to whip through all the appropriation bills during December as a sign of renewed presidential-congressional cooperation. In reaching for this goal, Johnson ran head-on into a limited yet hotly disputed question that offered him a quick opportunity to show the country that the man who had tamed the Senate had not lost the key to power on Capitol Hill, despite three years of isolation as Vice-President.

By the summer of 1963, the Soviet Union's chronic agricultural problem had reached a crisis. The Soviets put out a tentative feeler for the purchase of American wheat, and it was immediately snapped up by President Kennedy. His public justification for the proposed deal was economic. Australia and Canada had just completed wheat deals with the Soviets, so why shouldn't the United States get some of Moscow's business and, in the process, deplete the immense United States wheat surplus? Kennedy's deeper purpose was not economic but his hope of establishing a *détente* between Washington and Moscow, a transcendent goal of his foreign policy. Commercial transactions such as the wheat deal might help. At 4:00 P.M. on October 9, he informed a bipartisan meeting of congressional leaders at the White House of his decision, just two hours before he announced it to the world at a press conference. Adding to their deep suspicion of any dealings with the Communist bloc, congressional conservatives in both parties were irritated that Kennedy had not consulted the legislative branch before setting forth on this major effort to thaw East-West relations.

While United States and Soviet officials bickered over the details of the wheat transaction, the conservative critics evolved a strategy in early November, led by Senator Karl Mundt of South Dakota. Mundt, an Old Guard Republican and hard-line anti-Communist, attacked the plan to finance the wheat purchase through the United States government's Export-Import Bank—a necessary arrangement in view of Moscow's lack of foreign exchange and poor credit rating with American banking. Contending that Soviet purchase of American wheat was "bad" and that United States government financing of it was "indefensible," Mundt drafted an amendment to block Export-Import Bank participation. He proposed to attach it to the foreign aid authorization bill.

The strength behind the Mundt Amendment was evident on November 14, when the Kennedy Administration failed to kill it in the Senate by a vote of 40 to 46. On November 15, Mundt was persuaded to withdraw his amendment in return for a promise that the Senate would consider it as a separate bill prior to the adjournment of Congress. On November 21, at his last breakfast meeting with Democratic legislative leaders before leaving for Texas, John F. Kennedy emphasized that the Mundt Bill must be killed because of broader foreign policy considerations. But at that time, Mundt seemed to have enough votes to carry his bill.

All changed after the assassination. President Johnson insisted that the Mundt Bill be reported, as scheduled, by the Foreign Relations Committee on Monday, November 25, the day of President Kennedy's funeral, and put before the Senate the next day. What two weeks earlier had been a basic question of foreign policy toward Moscow now was transformed into a vote of confidence in the new President. Nine Democrats and one Republican who had backed Mundt November 14 now opposed him. The 57 to 35 defeat of the Mundt Bill was a quick legislative triumph for Johnson accomplished with a minimum of effort.

But the wheat battle was far from finished. By December 16, with the period of mourning nearing an end and politics-as-usual returning, the troublesome House added the equivalent of the Mundt Bill as an amendment to the foreign aid appropriations bill by a vote of 218 to 169. When a Senate-House conference deleted the amendment, the House rejected the conference report, 141 to 136, returning the bill to the conference committee. Congress seemed to be ready to resume its rebellion against presidential authority. Charles Halleck, cracking the party whip, was his old, partisan self. Responding to Republican criticism that he had "sold out" to Johnson over breakfast at The Elms, Halleck retorted: "I guess this shows it takes more than a piece of thick bacon to buy me."

Time was running out in the long, unhappy session of 1963. Speaker McCormack advised Johnson to take a brief recess for Christmas and worry about foreign aid and wheat to Russia in 1964. Again, the President refused. For this was a different Lyndon Johnson. This was not the Majority Leader who always proceeded with extreme caution. He was different, too, from John F. Kennedy, who as President felt he possessed a finite store of credit with Congress and that that store must not be spent all at once. Now as President, Johnson acted as if there were no tomorrow, demanding of Congress what Congress had made clear it would not give. But in his lifetime on Capitol Hill, Johnson had understood well the natural enmity of Congress for the presidency.

To his staff, the President explained that he must gain the upper hand. He insisted that the Senate-House conference committee keep working on the foreign aid appropriations bill. When the conferees devised a new bill December 21 without the ban against wheat to Russia, Johnson instructed his horrified House Democratic leaders to order the House, now scattered around the nation and the world for a brief Christmas holiday, to return forthwith for an unprecedented Christmas Eve vote. Though furious at that presidential summons, most Congressmen came at once to Washington.

But Johnson characteristically softened the whiplash. On December 23, he telephoned Representative Hale Boggs, the House Majority Whip, to ask whether it would be a good idea to invite all House members then in Washington—*all*, not just Democrats—to the White House for a party that night (the end of the official mourning period for John Kennedy). No, replied Boggs, everybody was too tired. And further, he said, the House was not in the best of moods with the vote on the wheat amendment scheduled for the next day. Maybe so, Johnson said, but they'll want to come to the White House for a party and I'm going to ask them.

Despite the fatigue and a snowstorm, the first of some two hundred Congressmen started arriving at the White House within two hours after Johnson had placed the call to Boggs. The festive warmth of a Christmas party in the White House deflated the anger on Capitol Hill. And the President drew Halleck aside to apologize for uncomplimentary newspaper stories that gave the White House as the source. These dispatches had indeed originated in the White House, and the President promised Halleck his staff would not make that mistake again. As the party was breaking up, Johnson stood on a gold chair upholstered in velvet in the State Dining Room to thank his guests for coming. "You have labored through the vineyard and plowed through the snow," he shouted. The President's party was a smash hit.

Some twenty-four hours later, the House reversed itself, accepting the report of the conference committee by a 189 to 158 vote. But nobody had changed his mind from the vote of three days earlier. It was strictly a matter of more Democrats than Republicans making the long trip back for the Christmas Eve session, and that was the direct result of the President's insistence that members of *his* party be located and returned to Washington.

That insistence told much about how Johnson would function as a legislative leader from the White House. Unlike Kennedy, Johnson was not particularly interested in the wheat transaction as an instrument of foreign policy. He had no burning concern over the substantive questions behind the Mundt Amendment. His interest was simply to reassert presidential dominion over Congress, as a signal to the nation and the world. If Congress were permitted to adjourn without acting on the wheat-to-Russia question, Johnson believed, then Congress might run wild in 1964.

Indeed, for all of Johnson's efforts to ingratiate himself with Halleck, he viewed the Republican leader's attempt to kill the wheat transaction as a serious challenge to his power and was bitter about it in private conversation. "Halleck tried to cut me a little bit," said Johnson, adding that Halleck was "unfair" to him and "wouldn't give me the same break he gave Kennedy." *

Johnson's victory in the wheat fight also showed that the mood of reconciliation following the tragedy of Dallas could not suspend for long hostilities between President and Congress. True enough, throughout 1964, Johnson would appeal privately and publicly to pass the program of the martyred President. But such pleas by themselves were not what passed the tax and civil rights bill. The fact that the House twice had voted against the new President during the period of official mourning showed Congress was not going to play dead for Johnson.

In that first weekend after the assassination, Lyndon Johnson had to rush through much the same thought process on tax policy that, because of its revolutionary nature, John F. Kennedy had deliberated over for two full years. For it was not until December, 1962, that Kennedy finally decided to defy fiscal and political orthodoxy and all historical precedent and ask for a 10-billion-dollar tax reduction at a time when the economy was on the upswing and the budget remained unbalanced. Fearing the inevitable reaction from the bulk of the business community and conservatives in both parties, Kennedy twice during 1961 had rejected recommendations by his economic advisers for a massive tax cut to stimulate the economy.

---

* However, Johnson continued his efforts to woo Halleck well into 1964. On June 5, 1964, Johnson appointed Hamer Budge, a former right-wing Republican Congressman from Idaho who had been defeated in 1960, to a vacancy on the Securities and Exchange Commission. Budge's only apparent qualification for the job was his intimate friendship with Charley Halleck. The appointment led to much Washington conversation that Johnson was about to gear his major appointments to the exigencies of Congressional politics, but the Budge appointment proved to be one of a kind.

It was well into 1962 before Kennedy fully accepted the theory of Walter Heller, his chief economic adviser, that high tax rates were a drag on investment, preventing faster growth and lower unemployment rates. Even accepting Heller's theory of fiscal drag, Kennedy agreed with Douglas Dillon, his Republican Secretary of the Treasury, that the tax cut must be accompanied by great restraint in spending. The result was a hold-down on federal expenditures far more severe than Heller and other liberal economists thought wise. In effect, Kennedy was compromising between the Heller and Dillon views.

Despite that fiscal restraint, however, Kennedy's tax cut was greeted with predictable opposition by business conservatives and their allies in Congress. Business had preached the gospel of the balanced budget for so many years that it now had pushed itself into the anomalous position of opposing a tax reduction that, as the bill took shape in the House Ways and Means Committee, favored business far more than the consumer.

This orthodox attachment to the balanced budget was shared to a surprising degree by Johnson, particularly because he had not been a listener or a participant in the administration's internal debates over the proposed tax cut in 1961 and 1962. As Vice-President, he privately told friends he was highly skeptical about Kennedy's entire tax package, both the reduction and the accompanying revenue-raising reforms (included largely to pacify the tax-reform bloc on Capitol Hill). After a generation of defending the oil and gas industry's inequitable depletion allowance, Johnson could not easily accept the evisceration of this fifty-year-old tax advantage.

The fact that Washington politicians and lobbyists were incorrectly interpreting this provision in the bill as a sign that Kennedy might dump Johnson from the 1964 ticket, just at Johnson's peak period of insecurity, did not enhance the Vice-President's regard for the tax bill. One day in the summer of 1963 when Johnson expressed his fear about being dropped from the 1964 ticket, a friend suggested that he come out loud and clear for the tax bill, thereby identifying himself more clearly with the top legislative proposal of the Kennedy Administration. Johnson ignored the advice and restrained his comments about the bill.

Thus, in those crowded early hours after the assassination, nobody knew how Johnson really felt about the tax bill. Certainly, two conversations in that period reinforced his reservations over tax cutting at a time of deficit financing. On Saturday, November 23, Dwight D. Eisenhower, who at Johnson's request came to Washington from his Gettysburg, Pennsylvania, farm to see the new President, lectured

Johnson on the need to cut spending and reduce the deficit. The next day, Johnson got a more explicit lecture in conservative economics from a more forceful disciple of orthodoxy. Robert B. Anderson, the Texas financier who as Eisenhower's Secretary of the Treasury had talked Majority Leader Johnson into opposing an emergency tax cut during the 1958 recession,* spent four hours with Johnson on Sunday in the vice-presidential office in the Executive Office Building. Anderson did not disguise his lack of enthusiasm for the tax cut. The best thing Johnson could do to restore national unity and confidence, Anderson told him, was to cut the budget and pare down the deficit. When Bob Anderson left, Johnson was by no means certain about the wisdom of Kennedy's tax cut.

The antidote to Eisenhower and Anderson came Sunday night at The Elms in a long, meandering discussion with an older and closer adviser, Donald Cook, who as a utility executive had developed a progressive, imaginative economic policy. Cook argued that fears over tax reduction were hobgoblins scared up by conservative businessmen who had made a fetish of the balanced budget. To free the economy of high tax rates, he said, tax reduction was essential. But he joined Eisenhower and Anderson in recommending a simultaneous reduction in appropriations.

Based on these conversations, and memoranda supplied him by the administration's top economic policy-makers, Johnson knew what he wanted when he met for the first time with Kennedy's economic "troika": the Council of Economic Advisers, the Treasury, and the Budget Bureau. Present at the meeting Monday night, November 25, were Secretary of the Treasury Douglas Dillon; Under Secretary of the Treasury Henry H. Fowler; Walter Heller, chairman of the Council of Economic Advisers; Gardner Ackley, a member of the Council; Budget Director Kermit Gordon, and Deputy Budget Director Elmer Staats.

The memoranda they had prepared for Johnson showed Dillon and Heller still in conflict over the old question: how much federal spending should be sacrificed in order to get a tax cut? Kennedy had set an arbitrary ceiling of 101.5 billion dollars in the budget to be submitted in January, which, if that figure held, would make it the first peacetime budget in history to break the 100-billion-dollar mark. Heller believed that was an irreducible minimum, and he was backed by Budget Director Gordon, a liberal economist who had served on the Council before being moved to the Budget Bureau. Dillon's memorandum to the President, on the other hand, argued that for political rea-

* See page 162.

sons the spending figure must be reduced in order to assure Senate passage of the tax bill. Since its passage by the House on September 25, the bill had been imprisoned in the Senate Finance Committee headed by Senator Harry Byrd, apostle of economic orthodoxy and arch-foe of the tax cut.

Quickly, Johnson showed which way he was thinking. "What about your tax bill?" he asked Dillon. And before Dillon had a chance to answer, Johnson gave his own answer: "We won't even get it to the Senate floor unless we tell Congress that the new budget will be about one hundred billion dollars." Johnson had taken the advice of Cook and Dillon. He would push the tax cut—but only with a dramatic show of budget cutting.

Although he had been President for only three days, Johnson informed the "troika" he had been checking around on Capitol Hill and had come to the conclusion that to get the 11-billion-dollar tax cut contained in the bill he would have to give up 1.5 billion dollars in expenditures. He talked about further Defense Department cuts plus some budget gimmicks that made the cuts seem deeper than they really were. Johnson's question: which would you rather have? The 1.5 billion dollars in expenditures or a tax cut? He threw the question out for anyone to answer.

Heller grabbed it. If that was really the question, Heller said, the answer was easy. He would naturally sacrifice 1.5 billion dollars in spending. But he questioned, first, whether the liberals would accept such a trade-off; and second, whether the conservatives, and particularly Senator Byrd, would stay hitched after the bargain was made. Byrd was a close friend of Johnson's, but friendship could not compete with fiscal solvency.

The discussion turned to how low the budget *could* go. Fowler argued that the spending figure must be kept below 100 billion dollars. Dillon felt that would be most difficult. A figure just over 100 billion dollars, but not high enough to round off at 101 billion dollars would do the trick.

Now Gordon talked. To reduce the budget even as low as 101.5 billion dollars, he had had to cut out all new irrigation projects and cut back on rural electrification. Defense, he thought, could be lowered another 750 million dollars—but Secretary of Defense Robert McNamara didn't agree.

Johnson interrupted. He knew all about the troubles of cutting the budget even to 101.5 billion dollars, he said. He'd been hearing from "Heller's liberal friends"—Secretary of Agriculture Orville Freeman and Secretary of Labor Willard Wirtz. He turned on Heller: "Tell them to lay off, Walter. Tell them to quit lobbying. I'm for them. I know they have good programs and the economy needs to have money pumped in. I want an expanding economy, too, and I'd like a budget at 108 billion dollars. They don't need to waste my time and theirs with their memos and phone calls." The President was not an angry governess but an impatient father.

A moment of embarrassed silence, and then Dillon began again. Even if McNamara would accept still a further reduction in Defense, the military services would make a terrible fuss and lobby Congress and the President for more money. But, added Dillon, McNamara thought that if the President backed him he could handle the services.

At that, Johnson said his Cabinet was made up of nine salesmen and a credit manager.

Heller handed the President an eight-point memorandum, and told him a budget pegged at 101.5 billion dollars *could* be defended. The President replied with a laugh:

"I can defend 101.5 billion dollars—you take on Senator Byrd." Besides, he continued, he had been talking to Eisenhower and to Bob Anderson, and they both were worried about federal expenditures. If you don't get this budget down around 100 billion dollars, Johnson went on, "you won't pee one drop" (nervous laughter).

Then, reading from Heller's memorandum, the President said: "This represents my philosophy. You're writing about what's desirable. Doug Dillon [whose separate memorandum Johnson had already devoured] is writing about what's possible." And then Johnson dipped into a little history. He could take a 100-billion-dollar-plus budget and go to the country with it, he said, but Roosevelt tried that, going to the country in the 1937 Court-packing fight, and Roosevelt got licked. It wouldn't work now either, he added. You simply had to give something to buy off Harry Byrd. Of course, if all his advisers *told* him he should go to Congress and ask for 101.5 billion dollars, Johnson continued, he would do it. But his advisers ought to know what the price for this was and be willing to take responsibility for it. In other words, Johnson was saying to Heller, if you want to keep spending at a 101.5-billion-dollar level you better be prepared to take the blame for losing the tax bill.

Dillon bolstered the President's argument. Reducing spending was a price to be paid for getting the tax cut, but it was well worth it. Once you have the tax cut, Johnson added, you can do what you want just like Eisenhower did. Eisenhower talked economy and then spent, Johnson said wryly.

Heller was coming around to Johnson's position, pushed by the President's arguments. Heller agreed that if it were a real choice between an immediate tax cut and a 1.5-billion-dollar cut in spending achieved by Kermit Gordon's Budget gimmicks and Bob McNamara's Defense cutbacks and no real reductions in non-defense spending, *then* he would have to agree that from an economist's standpoint the tax cut was worth a reduction in spending.

Johnson then further soothed Heller's doubts by promising that even though the budget would be pared down to around 100 billion dollars, he would actually spend at a rate of 101 billion dollars and then come in for the extra 1 billion dollars after the 1964 election.* The President said he would tell Congress the budget really should be around 108 billion dollars but that he had sacrificed deeply to slice it down that much.

Gordon was skeptical that a 100-billion-dollar budget full of gimmicks would satisfy Harry Byrd. Rather, Gordon said, Byrd would want to see the details. Johnson brushed this aside by instructing Dillon and Fowler to sound out Byrd and other Finance Committee members. He would do the same thing.

The meeting ended, and Johnson shook everyone's hand as they filed out. Later, one of the "troika" summed up Johnson's performance this way: "He pulled all of us to his way of thinking and left not the slightest doubt which way he was going." In fact, Johnson had summoned the "troika" not to get its advice but to influence it. He succeeded. The skills used so often as Majority Leader were intact, as though his long, dreary period as Vice-President had never been.

With that meeting out of the way, Johnson took over the budget as his personal property—cutting, patching, splicing, and ending up with proposed spending for fiscal year 1965 of only 97.9 billion dollars. That was Johnson's weapon in selling the tax cut to the conservatives, both in Congress and in the business community.

Seeking to speed up Finance Committee consideration of the bill, Johnson used the revised budget to woo Byrd, giving him an advance peek at the surprise figures before the budget was made public on January 21. The old Virginian was delighted that at last a President was trying to do some real economizing. But the tax cut was not approved by the Finance Committee before the end of 1963, as Johnson had hoped. The committee, moving with the speed of a tortoise, finally approved the bill by a 12 to 5 vote (Byrd among the dissenters) on January 23, 1964—about six months behind President Kennedy's original schedule.

But with all this fastidious planning and careful choice of strategy,

---

* As matters turned out, McNamara cut so heavily into Defense Department spending that actual spending was kept well below 100 billion dollars, much to almost everybody's surprise.

Johnson's budget cutting and the ardent courtship of Byrd were not the magic combination that brought the tax cut out of the Finance Committee. Weeks before the assassination, the administration's friends on the Finance Committee had estimated the bill would reach the floor toward the end of January. They felt they had Byrd's agreement to that timetable. Besides, Everett McKinley Dirksen, Senate Minority Leader and a committee member, had promised the administration not to stall the bill. By early November, Dirksen believed the tax bill's time had come and nothing would stop it.

But the new President was taking no chances, and he did contribute some typically Johnsonian flourishes. When the Finance Committee staff finally completed drafting its report on the bill on the Friday following committee approval, Johnson himself telephoned startled officials at the Government Printing Office and warned them to expect weekend work. He wanted to be sure the GPO would be open to rush the long-delayed report into print so the bill could get to the floor as soon as possible. Then he flabbergasted Elizabeth Springer, the chief clerk of the Finance Committee, by telephoning her that the Government Printing office was on alert waiting for the manuscript of the report! No other President of the United States had been quite so familiar with the minutiae of the legislative process. But on the bill itself, Johnson's succession to the presidency made not one whit of difference in either its timing or its size, notwithstanding the legend that he had saved it from certain death. He did, however, personally effect two changes in what otherwise would have transpired—one minor, one major.

The minor change involved a remarkable personal effort in congressional lobbying by Johnson, an exercise of power in the grand manner. On the morning of January 23, 1964, Senator Dirksen submitted a surprise amendment in the Finance Committee to repeal excise taxes on a variety of "luxury" items: jewelry, furs, cosmetics, handbags, luggage, mechanical pens and pencils. With administration forces off guard, Dirksen's amendment carried by a 10 to 7 vote, increasing the tax reduction another 445 million dollars. The administration, which had already promised an excise-tax reduction in 1965, feared that the Dirksen Amendment might open the floodgates on the Senate floor for repeal of the automobile and telephone excises.* A multibillion-dollar tax-cutting binge of that sort could endanger the entire bill. Accordingly, Larry O'Brien wanted to amputate the amendment before the bill got out of the Finance Committee. There was just one little problem: a lack of votes.

* When President Johnson did propose excise-tax revision in 1965, the final version of the bill passed by Congress did call for cuts deeper than he had intended.

For the first and only time in the tax battle, O'Brien called on the President for help when the Finance Committee recessed at noon on January 23. Reached while eating lunch at the White House, Johnson snapped into action. He telephoned every one of the Finance Committee's seventeen members and argued that the Dirksen Amendment must be reconsidered and defeated when the committee reconvened in the afternoon—appealing to Democrats to be loyal to their party and President and to Republicans to be loyal to their presumed fiscal responsibility. Kennedy was the first President to start the practice of telephoning individual members of Congress for their votes on specific issues, but never had he carried it to this extreme. Johnson's telephone barrage worked in an overpowering display of presidential power. When the committee reassembled in the afternoon, the Dirksen Amendment was reconsidered and defeated by a 9 to 8 vote.

The President's second individual contribution to the tax bill was significant far beyond its effect on that one bill. Powerful elements of the business community, of Congress, and of the public still had not accepted—as, in fact, Johnson himself did not accept until he became President—the profound change in economic policy that dictated cutting taxes in the full knowledge that it would increase the budget deficit. Such an unreconciled minority conflicted with Johnson's grand design of reconciliation and consensus.

Accordingly, Johnson's expenditure-cutting exercises, reducing the budget below 100 billion dollars, though not necessary to pass the bill, made it far more palatable to its foes in and out of Congress. That, together with untiring personal contacts by Johnson with big businessmen, gave the tax cut a degree of acceptability in the business community that Kennedy never had achieved. Even Senator Byrd was artfully stripped by Johnson of his sense of outrage over the New Economics. Of course, the old man could not actually vote for the tax cut without giving the lie to the doctrine of fiscal orthodoxy he had preached in Washington for some thirty-five years. But Johnson made of Byrd virtually a secret ally. Sharing a late-evening drink at the White House with Johnson the night his committee approved the bill, Byrd told the President: "I'm going to have to vote against the bill, but I'll be working for you behind the scenes."

The rest was anticlimax. The Senate passed the bill by a consensus-sized vote of 77 to 21 after a week's debate. Another three weeks were needed to reconcile the Senate and House versions. When the President signed the bill on February 26, he further wooed the conservatives by appealing for consensus. In the closing moments of the long struggle on this bill of such historic significance, Johnson's intent was to mollify the defeated prophets of orthodox economic policies. Pledg-

ing "earnest attempts" to reduce federal spending, he had special
words of praise for none other than Harry Byrd, who had never publicly endorsed the bill at all. This was the epitome of Lyndon Johnson's early presidency.

Within hours after President Kennedy's death, there were quiet
conversations in Washington about whether President Johnson would
scuttle or at least dilute the civil rights bill. Remembering Johnson's
compromising style in pushing through the Civil Rights Act of 1957,
civil rights advocates feared and Southerners hoped that he somehow
would perform the same miracle of consensus with the bill that had
been submitted by Kennedy in June and just reported on November
20 by the House Judiciary Committee.

But this was not 1957, and Johnson was not Majority Leader. The
passion unleashed by the Birmingham riots in May, 1963, ruled out
legislative surgery on the Kennedy civil rights bill. Moreover, Lyndon Johnson was now President. If as Vice-President he still worried
about parochial political feuds in Texas between John Connally and
Ralph Yarborough and if he still was overly protective toward oil-and-
gas depletion allowance, his emancipation from Texas was complete
in the crucial field of civil rights. Anybody who thought on November
22 that he might be tempted to scuttle the civil rights bill simply had
not been listening to Lyndon Johnson the past three years.

In speeches throughout the winter and early spring of 1963, he
spelled out his new, firm—almost militant—civil rights stance. On
January 6 at Wayne State University in Detroit: "To strike the chains
of a slave is noble. To leave him the captive of the color of his skin is
hypocrisy." On January 26 before the Cleveland Urban League:
"These next hundred years of our national experience demand of us
that we resolve the problems left unresolved when the Emancipation
Proclamation freed the slaves." On May 18 before the Capital Press
Club in Washington: "It seems to me that in the field of human rights,
we are well past the stage where half a loaf will do." The capstone of
this series of speeches came on May 30, Memorial Day, in Gettysburg,
Pennsylvania, with this peroration:

> Until justice is blind to color, until education is unaware of
> race, until opportunity is unconcerned with the color of men's
> skins, emancipation will be a proclamation but not a fact. To the
> extent that the proclamation of emancipation is not fulfilled in
> fact, to that extent we shall have fallen short of assuring freedom
> to the free.

Inside the Kennedy Administration's councils, Johnson had become something of a champion for Negro rights. In contrast to moody silence on most questions, the Vice-President volunteered his contributions frequently and forcefully in the long discussions during the winter and early spring of 1963 over just what kind of civil rights bill should be submitted. He drew from his experience as chairman of the President's Committee on Equal Employment Opportunity to propose ideas dealing with Negro employment. He promoted his old recommendation of 1957 and 1960 to establish a federal racial mediation service, now to be called the Community Relations Service.* Most important, he took a hard line—surprising to many on the White House staff—for a tough, no-compromise bill at a time when President Kennedy was apprehensive about the harmful effect on his overall legislative program of a tough civil rights bill. The full flowering of the Negro Revolution, brought about by the brutal repression of the Birmingham demonstrations in May, ruled out any further compromise, in Johnson's view.

At the same time, however, the Vice-President clashed again with Robert F. Kennedy. Johnson felt that the Attorney General had been unduly influenced by a private meeting with author James Baldwin and Negro militants in New York on May 24 and was pushing too fast to get the bill to Congress. He proposed careful preparation, both with Congress and the South, delaying introduction of the bill until President Kennedy and his Vice-President could explain it on a proposed barnstorming tour of the South. Johnson was overruled, and the bill was dispatched to Capitol Hill.

The bill finally sent to Congress by Kennedy on June 19, 1963, was a compromise at its birth. It was by far the most comprehensive civil rights bill ever submitted to Congress by a President and included a public accommodations section guaranteeing Negroes the right of access to hotels, restaurants, and other such facilities. But it fell short, in the opinion of civil rights leaders, in two respects. It contained no mandatory Fair Employment Practices proposal and it did not resurrect "Part III"—the section of the 1957 bill that would have given the federal government power to intervene in civil rights cases but which was skillfully excised by Majority Leader Lyndon Johnson.†

Two days later in June when civil rights leaders met at the White House to discuss the bill with the President and his top advisers, they were surprised by the Vice-President's friendly tone toward their efforts to improve the bill. Kennedy had left the room after a brief

* See pages 127, 200
† See page 127ff.

discussion, and Johnson was presiding over the meeting. Joseph Rauh of the Americans for Democratic Action—one of the Capital's most experienced and accomplished Johnson-baiters—rose to ask a question. What would the administration's attitude be if civil rights leaders tried to add FEPC and "Part III" to the bill? Would this produce friction? Johnson replied quickly that he saw no reason why it should. There was a need for "flexibility," he said.

Thus, though Johnson in his first hours as President was ambiguous about the tax cut proposal, there was no doubt where he stood on the civil rights bill. He made this clear to all the civil rights leaders—Dr. Martin Luther King, Roy Wilkins of the NAACP, Whitney Young of the Urban League, Joe Rauh—in the first days after November 22. Summoning them to his office individually, he left no doubt he would at the very minimum stand with the bill approved on November 20 by the House Judiciary Committee.

But the myth that Johnson saved the civil rights bill from slow death has little relation to reality. The great breakthrough in the civil rights legislative fight came a few days before President Kennedy's assassination when the White House, after weeks of wooing, finally obtained Charley Halleck's promise of support for the bill. That celebrated "thick bacon" breakfast between the new President and the House Minority Leader at The Elms a few days later came after the fact of Halleck's decision on civil rights. Beyond that, there was little doubt that the civil rights bill ultimately would have been passed late in 1964—after much debate, much acrimony, and much horse-trading.

Johnson's contribution—and it was a highly significant one—was to pass the civil rights bill *without* much horse-trading. "Part III" had been added to the bill in the House Judiciary Committee and FEPC was adopted on the House floor, bringing the bill up to the highest hopes of the civil rights leaders. Under Kennedy, it is quite probable that one or both of these sections would have been sacrificed in the Senate in exchange for the public accommodations section and to eliminate or at least shorten a Senate filibuster. But Johnson refused any compromise whatsoever.

Even before the bill passed the House on February 10 by a vote of 290 to 130, Johnson had laid down the no-compromise edict. In a private session in his office with Clarence Mitchell of the NAACP and Joe Rauh of ADA, Johnson pledged there would be no changes in the bill even if that required suspending all other activity in the Senate for months. When the House adopted the FEPC provision on February 6 in the last doubtful vote on the bill there, Johnson immediately telephoned Rauh on the Hill. His opening question pleased Rauh. "What are you fellows doing about the Senate?" Johnson reiterated he wanted the Senate to pass the bill intact—*including* FEPC. That meant rounding up support to break the inevitable filibuster that lay ahead, either by sapping the will of the Southerners, or, more likely, by voting cloture.* Simultaneously, Johnson told his Senate leaders, Majority Leader Mansfield and Majority Whip Humphrey, that he was prepared to sacrifice all other legislation in the Senate if necessary to break the civil rights filibuster.

Now fully emancipated from his Southern base, there was no need to trim his civil rights position to please Dixie. On the contrary, if he trimmed away as Kennedy probably would have done to wedge the bill through the Senate, Johnson would be excoriated by the civil rights movement, by organized labor, and by liberals. On this issue, Johnson's political imperatives as a *Southern* President foreclosed compromise, whereas Kennedy's would not have. But beyond that, Johnson was now functioning from his new presidential power base, and he was determined to exercise control over Congress with no thought of compromise.

Almost incredibly, Johnson won the whole package. The death of Kennedy had robbed the civil rights opposition of much of its sting. The emotional reaction to Dallas changed the climate of opinion, both in Congress and the country, and intangibly brought it into far more sympathetic response to the Negro Revolution. Nor did Johnson feel any embarrassment in appealing to the country and to the Congress to pass this bill out of respect for John Kennedy.

Another important asset to the President in the spectacular civil rights breakthrough was his no-compromise rule. Richard Russell, older now and ailing, organized his Southern Senators in platoons, just as he had done in the 1960 civil rights fight, in a 1962 fight over state literacy tests which effectively disfranchised Negroes, and in the 1961 and 1963 struggles over Rule XXII. But his tiring legions had no zest for battle in 1964. Once the President ruled out the possibility of compromise and declared his intention to suspend all other Senate business to outwait the filibusters, the Southerners knew they were beaten. It is doubtful whether Russell could have maintained a filibuster had Mansfield ordered around-the-clock sessions as Johnson desired, but Mansfield refused.

The question, then, boiled down to this: where could Humphrey,

---

* Skeptical that the Senate ever would invoke cloture on a civil rights bill, Johnson at first believed around-the-clock sessions would be needed to break the filibuster, but by the time of his talk with Rauh he had accepted the cloture strategy.

the floor manager for the bill, find the two-thirds vote necessary for cloture under Rule XXII? That required support from Dirksen, who became another hero of the civil rights battle when he finally declared himself for cloture. And so, after fifty-seven days of Senate debate beginning March 26 and ending June 10, the longest filibuster in Senate history was ended by a 71 to 29 vote for cloture, marking the first time the Senate had ever forcibly closed debate on a civil rights question.

On July 2, Lyndon Johnson signed the final version of the bill—not greatly different from the bill approved by the House on February 10 and certainly no weaker. For the first time, Congress had passed a civil rights bill without significantly compromising it. Lyndon Johnson, exchanging the methods of maneuver for inflexible determination, was in great part responsible. Russell himself, the wise old commander of the battered Southern legions, had predicted just this result when Johnson moved into the White House. With Johnson now President, he was asked, would the civil rights bill be watered down? "No," said Russell, "the way that fellow operates, he'll get the whole bill, every last bit of it." And he did.

President Johnson was not satisfied with the tax cut and Civil Rights Act, landmark legislation though they were, as final accomplishments of the 88th Congress. Here again the presidential Johnson contrasted sharply with the senatorial Johnson. Although congressional leaders yearned for an early adjournment in election-year 1964 after the all-year session of 1963, Johnson kept their feet to the fire until October 3. Bill after bill was passed, including bills written off as dead in 1963. The bill to provide federal aid for mass transit facilities was revived and passed. Many of Kennedy's proposals for additional federal help to college students were passed. Although Kennedy had not planned an all-out drive in Congress for his Anti-Poverty Program until after the 1964 election, Johnson rushed a program to Congress and got it passed.*

To some of Johnson's closest advisers, however, his most remarkable legislative achievement in the 88th Congress was enactment of a wheat price-support bill. In May, 1963, in a self-damaging assertion of independence, the nation's wheat farmers voted in a referendum to reject the wheat program passed by Congress in 1962 that required tight planting controls. The result, unless a substitute proposal was enacted, would be no program at all, a precipitous drop in wheat

* The Anti-Poverty Program is dealt with in greater detail in Chapter XIX.

prices, and perhaps an incipient farm depression. In the early winter of 1964, prominent Democrats advised Johnson not to risk his prestige in attempting to enact farm legislation, but rather to let the wheat growers stew in their own juice. A large number of Democratic Congressmen from the South and the Northern big cities agreed. Farmer-oriented Hubert Humphrey gave Johnson different advice. Humphrey pleaded with the President at least to make an effort for a new bill. At the last moment, Johnson followed Humphrey's course and backed a measure not greatly different from the scheme rejected in the 1963 wheat referendum.

On this issue, House Republican opposition was monolithic. Consequently, the defection of not very many House Democrats could defeat the bill. With Johnson personally helping to prepare the measure, it was calculated to attract the Democrats. A cotton bill was added to win Southern votes. A food-stamp plan for distribution of food to the needy was tossed in to win over big-city Democrats from the North. Other ingredients of the legislative recipe were a dozen or more presidential telephone calls to the recalcitrant Democrats just before the wheat-cotton-food stamp bill came to a vote in the House on April 8. The result—a 211 to 203 squeaker—tasted delicious and Johnson was elated. He regarded the vote on this issue which had always lacked consensus as a much clearer sign of his mastery over Congress than either the tax or civil rights bills.

There were, of course, notable exceptions to that mastery, one of which was medical care for the aged financed by the Social Security system. The key to victory here was the enigmatic, brilliant Representative Wilbur Mills of Arkansas, who as chairman of the House Ways and Means Committee held life-or-death power over the bill. At the outset of the Kennedy Administration, the White House staff had come to the conclusion that Medicare could not be passed without active cooperation from the Harvard-educated Mills, who possessed that rare combination of encyclopedic knowledge of issues, high accomplishment in the art of legislative chicanery, and ideological flexibility that enabled him to change position whenever he pleased.

Kennedy had been wooing Mills since January, 1961, and a strange partnership had been growing stronger and warmer. To the surprise of Washington, Mills had become the enthusiastic and effective congressional patron of Kennedy's most important legislation: the Trade Expansion Act in 1962, the Tax Revision Act in 1962, and the tax cut in 1963. By November of 1963, the White House was certain that Mills was about to abandon his long and lethal opposition to Medicare and guide a compromise bill through the House in 1964.

Kennedy's death changed that. For all they had in common in legislative craftmanship and ideological flexibility, Lyndon Johnson and
Wilbur Mills never had been close. Mills' self-possessed urbanity
seemed to intimidate Johnson. Although House Democratic leaders
urged the President to start working on Mills quickly and often, their
meetings were few and unproductive. Mills did not abandon his opposition to Medicare.

Even with Mills' help, passing the bill in the House would not have
been assured. Without Mills, it was hopeless. Nevertheless, Johnson
insisted on making a stab at Medicare in the closing weeks of the 88th
Congress. His failure revealed that there were, after all, finite limits to
Lyndon Johnson's control of Congress.

The failure of Medicare caused little stir. The presidential campaign
of 1964 was in full swing, the interminable 88th Congress was about
to adjourn and, by that time, the image of President Johnson's mastery
over Congress was too well planted in the public mind to be uprooted
by a single defeat.

For the real difference between what Johnson did and what Kennedy probably would have done in the 88th Congress was a matter of
image—no trifling matter for the President of the United States. Quite
beyond passing the tax bill in a spirit of consensus, beyond his dramatic success with the civil rights bill, and beyond his passage of an
unpopular farm bill, Johnson's most significant legislative breakthrough was to establish an image in Congress, as with the public, of
presidential mastery over Congress. Just as no mere listing of bills
passed could do justice to Johnson's record as Senate Majority Leader,
so his record as President in the 88th Congress transcended any tabu-
lation. He had cautiously hoarded the meager powers of Majority
Leader to tame the Senate, and now he lustily expended the enormous
powers of the presidency to tame the Congress. And in so doing, he
strengthened his presidency.

Chapter XVIII

CHIEF
DIPLOMAT

My plane has landed in many continents, touched down in more than thirty countries in the last three years. The wheels have never stopped and the door has never opened and I have never looked upon any faces that I didn't think would like to trade citizenship with me.

—President Lyndon B. Johnson, February 11, 1964

When President Charles de Gaulle of France surprised the world by announcing that he would fly to Washington for the funeral of John F. Kennedy on November 25, 1963, the new President of the United States glimpsed a rare opportunity to mend his nation's tattered relations with its oldest ally. Four months before the assassination, Franco-American relations had dropped to their lowest point in a century and a half. Personal relations between Kennedy and de Gaulle had become cool since their inconclusive though cordial meeting in Paris in June, 1961.

More and more, the French leader emphasized the depth of his opposition to the North Atlantic Treaty Organization as an instrument to insure American domination of the European continent. He had challenged not only London but also Washington in blocking the British from joining the European Economic Community (Common Market). And then, on August 4, 1963, diplomatic civility itself was strained almost to the breaking point between Kennedy and de Gaulle when the French President rejected the test-ban treaty signed by the other three nuclear powers—the United States, the Soviet Union, and Great Britain—together with most of the non-nuclear powers.

De Gaulle viewed the treaty as a violation of French sovereignty. His intransigence doomed Kennedy's plans to make the treaty the basic international tool for halting worldwide proliferation of nuclear weapons.* Laying aside his customary caution in public statements

* Communist China, soon to become the fifth member of the nuclear club, rejected the treaty too.

about world leaders, Kennedy told a television interviewer: "Charles de Gaulle will be remembered for one thing only, his refusal to take that treaty."

However, Franco-American relations were warming in the early autumn of 1964, and secret plans were afoot for a de Gaulle visit to Washington.

And now de Gaulle seemed to be engaged in an act of reconciliation by flying to Washington for Kennedy's funeral. Johnson felt he could make de Gaulle see reason where Kennedy had failed, just as he felt he could make Charley Halleck and Harry Byrd see reason on Capitol Hill. Like Halleck and Byrd, de Gaulle was closer to Johnson's generation than Kennedy's. In his first State Department briefings after the assassination, Johnson was warned that nothing could be done with *le grand Charles*. But Johnson was optimistic. His rare combination of persuasion, intimidation, and charm, he believed, could be as effective in the international sphere as it had been in the Senate, reinforced as it now was by presidential power.

There was ample opportunity for Johnson to test himself in the international sphere within seventy-two hours after becoming President. Washington swarmed with presidents, prime ministers, foreign ministers, and what was left of the monarchy of the world. They had come not only to show their grief for the fallen young leader, but to size up his successor. Johnson granted private audiences to the most important, including Anastas Mikoyan, the Armenian Bolshevik who had survived Soviet Russia's Byzantine power struggles and was now a deputy premier. To Mikoyan, Johnson offered no deviation from the Kennedy line, carefully mixing firmness with a desire for *détente*.

Something quite different from Kennedy's style was exhibited, however, when the new President conferred with A. Z. Bhutto, Pakistan's brash young foreign minister. When Bhutto had the bad taste to make critical remarks about United States foreign policy during their interview, Johnson dressed him down as he had reporters who had written stories displeasing him in his Majority Leader days. Attacking Pakistan's courtship of Communist China to become an ally against India, Johnson warned that he would use what power he had to frustrate Pakistan. He was quite prepared, said Johnson, to curtail United States foreign aid payments essential to Pakistan's economy. Unaccustomed to such plain talk from a Western head of government, the usually voluble Bhutto was speechless. Although Bhutto's brashness invited Johnson's response, the new President had a deeper purpose. He wanted to dispel any notion that might have been carried over from his Senate years that he favored Pakistan over India, and would so transform Kennedy's foreign policy.

But the foreign luminaries at the funeral were dominated by Charles de Gaulle, a little stooped now but still a towering, imperious figure in his uniform of a French Army brigadier. His air of self-esteem seemed all the greater now that the other three powers of the Western Big Four had suddenly acquired new leaders, none of whom had yet been elected in his own right—Douglas-Home in Britain, Erhard in Germany, and now Johnson in the United States. Thus, de Gaulle posed the first true test for Johnson in the art of personal diplomacy that Woodrow Wilson and Franklin D. Roosevelt had made obligatory for all Presidents.

The two tall leaders met in the White House, alone except for their translators, and Johnson felt they got along extraordinarily well as they discussed world issues in generalities. As Johnson was to tell the story later to his associates, de Gaulle said during their talk: "I will be meeting with you here." But when they shook hands and said good-by at the door of the White House, according to Johnson, de Gaulle said simply: "I will be meeting with you"—omitting the word "here." Whether de Gaulle really changed his mind after his talk with Johnson, or there had merely been some error in translation, never will be known.

But on November 25, 1963, Johnson was certain he would soon be meeting with de Gaulle in a prolonged face-to-face session in Washington that would go far to restore health to Franco-American relations. Going directly from his post-funeral meeting with de Gaulle at the White House to greet state governors next door in the Executive Office Building, the President told them:

> I am sorry I am late. General de Gaulle had to return to Paris. He has had a long day of it and he is flying back tonight. We talked a little longer than I anticipated. Even then we did not finish, so *we have another meeting set up for early in the year when he comes back to this country.**

Johnson was convinced he had insured the long-delayed return visit to President Kennedy's Paris trip in 1961, and beyond that, a beginning toward rehabilitating the Western alliance. Shortly thereafter he told friends: "I think he likes *me*. I'm going to try to work *with* him—not force something down his throat. If you force three Bourbons into Luci [the President's younger daughter], it will all come up. I've told everyone who has anything to do with it: stop telling Europeans they have to do *this* or *that*—or *else*."

Even as he addressed the governors, Johnson's hope was being dashed. De Gaulle had left the White House suspecting there was a

* Emphasis is added.

certain confusion as to just what he had or had not agreed to. In truth, he had no intention of coming back to Washington for a full-scale meeting with Johnson and did not want Johnson to think so. At Andrews Air Force Base outside Washington, before boarding a jet for Paris, de Gaulle instructed his Ambassador in Washington, Hervé Alphand, to convey that fact to Johnson. But by the time Alphand returned to town, the President had made his remarks to the Governors. With Alphand now requiring further instructions from Paris, it was four days before he could inform the State Department, and Secretary of State Rusk then could inform Johnson, that de Gaulle had no intention of coming back to Washington. As senior chief-of-government in the West and a recent visitor to Washington, he felt Johnson should come to Paris if there was any visiting to do, and he was not especially eager for that, either.

Indeed, it was soon evident that de Gaulle had no desire to patch up Franco-American relations. In January, 1964, France defied United States wishes by granting diplomatic recognition to Communist China. De Gaulle had not mentioned this possibility during his November 25 talk with Johnson. Nor did he ever communicate directly with Johnson about this drastic change in French policy. Instead, he sent Ambassador Alphand to the White House to inform Johnson of it in routine fashion shortly before the formal announcement.

President Johnson's first attempt to transplant the techniques he had employed in the Senate to the international scene was a failure. Although White House aides who had served both Kennedy and Johnson generally agreed with Johnson that de Gaulle did get along better with him than with Kennedy, that point was irrelevant. For de Gaulle's quarrel with the United States had nothing to do with his personal feeling for the man who happened to occupy the White House. The root of his anti-Americanism was his strong, emotional spirit of French nationalism and his conception of Europe for the Europeans, aggravated by the shabby manner in which he was handled during World War II by President Roosevelt. Those days when he was an underprivileged client of the Anglo-American partnership nourished his determination to drive the United States and Britain—the Anglo-Saxons, as he called them—from the Continent. De Gaulle's ambition was French hegemony over Western Europe, preferably in partnership with West Germany.

Thus, the simple application of the Johnson Treatment could not in the slightest deflect de Gaulle from a project twenty years in the making. Johnson was to discover that de Gaulle's reaction to the Johnson Treatment was the rule, not the exception, for foreign leaders. World problems, whether he dealt with one man, as with de Gaulle, or with the complicated interworkings of many leaders and many nations, were seldom susceptible to solution at the head-of-government level. With all the power of the presidency at his disposal, Johnson was unable to tame the world as he had tamed Congress.

President Johnson's unhappy encounter with de Gaulle on November 25 was only his first effort at personal diplomacy. When on December 24 he flew from Washington to the LBJ Ranch, he was going home not only for the holiday but to a heavy work schedule, not the least of which was an informal meeting with the new Chancellor of the German Federal Republic, Ludwig Erhard. Particularly in view of his failure to soften de Gaulle, Johnson desperately wanted to display to the world, the nation, and himself that he was in full command as the nation's chief diplomat. The Erhard visit to Texas was important far beyond the issues to be discussed by the two leaders.

Dr. Erhard, jowly and *gemütlich,* was a far less formidable diplomatic figure than General de Gaulle. Having succeeded to the chancellorship less than a month before Johnson became President, upon the reluctant and belated resignation of Konrad Adenauer, Erhard had points in common with the new President. He was trained not in foreign affairs but as a professional economist; Erhard was the chief architect of the postwar "economic miracle" in Germany as Adenauer's Minister of Economics. Like Johnson, he had not yet stood for election as head of his party. He did not yet have a mandate from the voters. He too needed the prestige that would come from successful bilateral negotiations with the head of the Western alliance.

There were other fortuitous circumstances in the Johnson-Erhard talks. Erhard held a different view of Europe from de Gaulle's and Adenauer's. He opposed Franco-German dominance in Western Europe. He looked to the Atlantic, and to closer relations with the British and Americans. Then, too, the selection of the LBJ Ranch, with its surrounding clusters of German-American communities, as the site for the Johnson-Erhard meeting was a clever move. The idea, curiously enough, was not Johnson's but Secretary of State Rusk's.

For two days, December 28 and 29, the President and the Chancellor, accompanied by their entourages, swooped around the brown hills of central Texas, driven in presidential limousines, dashing from one ranch house to another, looking for deer, politicking in the German-American communities, swapping stories with Johnson's cousins and aunts.

The joint communiqué on the Johnson-Erhard talks, issued December 29, was filled with the conventionally turgid prose of diplomacy and offered little glimpse into the freewheeling Johnson diplomacy of the previous two days. It was their unreported secret talks that revealed so much of Johnson's style and substance as chief diplomat.

Johnson's principal message to Erhard was clear: the United States is "going down the road to peace" and "we are going to do it with or without others." Remembering how Adenauer had lectured Presidents Eisenhower and Kennedy on the need for a firm stand against Moscow, Johnson told Adenauer's successor that the United States and its President knew all about Communism. Furthermore, Johnson continued, as President, he had no intention of spending all his time "talking about it," or about the past. Peace is essential, he said, because he didn't want the United States killing one hundred million Russians and the Russians killing one hundred million Americans. For his part, Erhard did not sound like Adenauer. He indicated that Bonn would soon be taking a more flexible attitude toward Eastern Europe. Johnson did not hide the fact that he *expected* Erhard to be more flexible than Adenauer.

Erhard informed Johnson that Premier Khrushchev had asked him to visit Moscow but that he had declined, feeling it would be better if Johnson, as the head of the alliance, visited the Soviet leader first. But Johnson replied he had no intention of encouraging a meeting with Khrushchev until such time as he thought "some good would come of it." As for de Gaulle, Johnson's warmth of a month earlier was gone. "I am not going to fuss at him or over him," the President told Erhard. "If necessary, I will ignore him for a while."

From these lofty considerations, Johnson progressed to matters of dollars-and-marks importance between Washington and Bonn. He emphasized how much the United States was sacrificing to keep the free world strong. Nor, he went on, does Kennedy's death in any way diminish the United States commitment to West Germany and Western Europe. Remember, he told the Chancellor, Kennedy not only picked the right man for Vice-President in 1960 but also had the foresight to send that man to Berlin at the right time during the 1961 crisis. That trip, Johnson continued, gave him the chance to see for himself how vital the commitment to Berlin really was.

Germany, he said, must understand the importance of "paying" the United States to maintain six Army divisions there. Erhard earnestly agreed. The "payment" would consist of a larger German purchase of military equipment from the United States. Of course, this would have adverse political repercussions for Erhard. But if it were not done,

Johnson made clear, there would be adverse political repercussions in the United States. "This is very important to the continued good will of the American Congress and public," he said pointedly.

There were no hard agreements as the two leaders sat in the living room of the ranch, surrounded by their staffs. But later Johnson again brought up the question of German military purchases as he and Erhard sat in the President's limousine, speeding across the Texas hill country. Johnson was embroidering his point that it was a genuine sacrifice for the United States to keep American divisions in Europe.

"Give me one reason we should keep those divisions in Europe," Johnson challenged Erhard.

"They like it there," the Chancellor replied.

"Don't tell me that," the President shot back. "Every one of them would like to come home to his mother, wife, and sweetheart."

Finally, still riding across the Texas plains, Erhard agreed to the Buy American plan while cautioning the President not to make the agreement public lest he raise a storm in the German Parliament. At the same time, Erhard agreed to Johnson's pleas for an increase in the West German defense budget.

Johnson was also successful on the question of Cuba. Washington's economic embargo against Fidel Castro was regularly violated by America's NATO partners—including West Germany. Would Erhard agree to stop shipping goods to Cuba? Erhard agreed.

There was no such easy agreement, nor was any expected, on the touchy question of Germany's semi-embargo of American chickens, accomplished through various health and tariff restrictions. Johnson wanted it stopped. Otherwise, he indicated to Erhard, Congress might retaliate. For the ban was hurting Arkansas, a major poultry-producing state, and Arkansas was the home of J. William Fulbright, chairman of the Senate Foreign Relations Committee. Johnson also argued for lower tariff walls against American grains. Reminding Erhard that American farmers represent thirty-five million Americans, Johnson told the Chancellor: "I am not going to sell them short."

Instead of resenting Johnson's undiplomatic candor, Erhard was exhilarated and impressed. So was Johnson, confident that he was exploiting the international power of the presidency. Those Texas talks with Ludwig Erhard went exactly the way Johnson wanted. He would have liked to conduct all his foreign affairs in that tone and style, a style as different from that of his predecessors as the LBJ Ranch was different from the polished floors of diplomacy in Washington.

But it was not to be. The Erhard talks were a high point in personal Johnsonian diplomacy. For seldom if ever again would a foreign visitor be so pliable as the German Chancellor, the environment so comfortable as the LBJ Ranch, and the time so leisurely.

Johnson did not get along at all well in February with Sir Alec Douglas-Home of Britain (the name assumed by Lord Home after he renounced the peerage to become prime minister), a charming but stiff, politically untutored aristocrat. Johnson not only failed to persuade the British leader to stop British trade with Cuba. He also felt Sir Alec was indiscreet in making light of a much-criticized sale of English buses to Castro. In an attempt to be lighthearted over a matter of sensitivity to his host's country, Sir Alec included these words in a toast at the White House state dinner in his honor February 13, 1964: "Occasionally we may, perhaps, send buses to Cuba, but never will anything interfere fundamentally with the friendship and delight which we feel in the company of a great ally and a great partner." It made Johnson angry.

Despite the early rebuff from de Gaulle, Johnson continued his efforts of personal diplomacy to renew the old friendship with France. Johnson's friend and Eisenhower's Secretary of the Treasury, Robert Anderson, was to be used by Johnson more as diplomatic troubleshooter than as economic adviser. The President sent Anderson and Under Secretary of State George Ball separately to Paris to sound out discreetly the possibilities for a Johnson–de Gaulle meeting. Nothing came of it.

Most disappointing to Johnson was the failure of his personal diplomacy to bring about an understanding with Moscow. In view of Khrushchev's blow-up in 1960 at the summit meeting with President Eisenhower at Paris, which killed the meeting altogether, and his bellicosity at the 1961 meeting with President Kennedy at Vienna, Johnson was—as he told Chancellor Erhard in Texas—in no mood to meet the Soviet Premier. But from the very beginning of his presidency, Johnson continued Kennedy's secret correspondence with Khrushchev. It produced pitifully little—certainly not enough to justify the convening of a Johnson-Khrushchev conference.

A great part of Johnson's correspondence with Khrushchev concerned the insoluble question of Russia's refusal to pay her share of the United Nations peace-keeping operations in the Congo and the Gaza Strip. As an old Senate man, Johnson wanted a compromise that would avoid a showdown in the UN, but compromise failed. Despite Johnson's efforts, Moscow gradually grew more intransigent on the UN dues question, and the 1964 session of the General Assembly was shortened to avoid a United States–Soviet showdown. The only tangible result of the Johnson-Khrushchev correspondence was a mutual reduction by both the United States and the Soviet Union in the production of enriched uranium, used in nuclear weapons, during the early months of 1964. The importance of this exercise in bilateral disarmament was somewhat diminished by the fact that both countries had a surplus of enriched uranium and needed to cut down. It was a Liliputian achievement.

By mid-1964, Johnson had become wary of personal diplomacy, his zest for face-to-face encounters with other captains of the world clearly diminished.* World affairs, of course, would continue to plague him and eventually dominate him. But the notion that he could operate as spectacularly on the world scene as he had in the Senate soon died.

There is no preparatory school to teach a President how to run the foreign policy of the United States. John F. Kennedy in 1961 brought to the office a consuming interest in world affairs. This interest combined with three difficult years in the presidency that began with the fiasco of the Bay of Pigs invasion of Cuba, had, by November 22, 1963, given Kennedy a significant familiarity with the problems and possibilities of foreign policy. When an international crisis broke out, no matter where, Kennedy quickly grasped the options. After the Bay of Pigs debacle, his reactions were manifestations of a coherent and consistent foreign policy.

Lyndon Johnson had no such background. Although he had spoken out on almost every international event during his eight years as Majority Leader, he viewed these events narrowly, within the special political and senatorial exigencies of the day. He had no Johnson policy or Johnson philosophy to guide him years later when he became Chief Diplomat. At first, he seemed to take rather a softer than a harder line toward Communism and *détente*. He was no fancier of "brinkmanship." But these were not deeply held principles. In his early presidency, the pressure of immediate crisis would on occasion undercut them altogether. One close friend of Johnson described him as a "nationalist," not in the usual sense of that word (as de Gaulle was a nationalist), but in the sense that his first interest was national, not international, affairs.

---

* This disinclination for face-to-face dealing with heads of government became even more pronounced after Johnson's election on November 2, 1964. In 1965, he had an unfortunate session with the Prime Minister of Canada and peremptorily postponed visits to the United States from the President of Pakistan and the Prime Minister of India. See Chapter XXIV.

Such a President of necessity would have to rely heavily on advisers to sketch the background of international questions for him, and Johnson in his first weeks as President cast about for advice on foreign policy questions in many different places.

The search for advice reached a peak of sorts when Johnson, heeding Adlai Stevenson's recommendation in their first conversation after Dallas, agreed to address the General Assembly of the United Nations on December 17, 1963, and requested Dean Acheson to draft a speech for him. Although Acheson had been advising Johnson informally and sporadically on foreign policy matters for nearly a decade, it was an odd choice that reflected Johnson's lack of insight into the politics of foreign policy. No two Democrats were further apart in regard to the UN, and most other foreign policy questions, than Adlai Stevenson and Dean Acheson. Furthermore, it would have been difficult to find a prominent Democrat with a more critical view of the United Nations than Acheson. Predictably, the speech written by Acheson was put aside, and a staff-written effort was substituted.

Unhappy with the staff draft, which the new President felt was too bland and needed flavoring, Johnson tried to spice it up at an informal White House dinner party a few nights before his appearance at the UN. The guests included Senators J. W. Fulbright and Eugene Mc-Carthy, friends of Johnson during the Majority Leader days; Representative Homer Thornberry, Johnson's closest friend in the House, who had just resigned from Congress to become a federal judge in Texas; Representative Jack Brooks, who was filling Thornberry's place as the Johnson man on the Texas congressional delegation; Clark Clifford, the transition expert; and Thomas C. Mann, an Assistant Secretary of State just appointed as Johnson's policy czar for Latin American affairs.

After dinner, over coffee, Johnson startled his guests by tossing the draft of his speech on the great table in the Treaty Room on the second floor of the White House, and asking each of them to take a shot at improving it. Whereupon the six men scribbled away on the margins of the speech in high good humor—some only changing a word, others writing in substantive revisions. Of the half dozen, only Mann was in the executive branch of the government, and only Mann and Fulbright had any particular expertise in foreign affairs. As later events were to show, a consensus between Fulbright and Mann was every bit as difficult to achieve as a consensus between Stevenson and Acheson. The final, heavily edited version of the speech emphasized disarmament and East-West cooperation generally—just the kind of speech Stevenson wanted for the UN but in a prose style that was both turgid and jumpy.

Such madcap procedure in writing a major foreign policy speech could not long survive. In the mid-twentieth century, a President could obtain solid and continuing advice on international affairs only from persons with access to secret embassy cables and intelligence reports. That restricted the President's use of advisers from private life and from the Senate after the transition period ended, although well into 1964 Johnson still liked on occasion to dispatch a private person on a diplomatic mission. Months after his unsuccessful secret mission to Paris, Robert Anderson headed the United States team to negotiate a new Panama Canal treaty. Acheson was sent as a presidential envoy in the late summer of 1964 in an unsuccessful search for a political solution to the battling between Greek and Turkish ethnic groups on Cyprus, a crisis that threatened war between Greece and Turkey. By and large, however, Johnson relied on the official foreign policy advisers he had inherited from Kennedy.

That meant relying primarily on Dean Rusk at the State Department and McGeorge Bundy at the White House. In fact, lacking Kennedy's all-consuming interest in foreign policy, Johnson leaned more heavily on both Rusk and Bundy for policy decisions in noncrisis situations. Rusk, who had been extraordinarily attentive in assuring that Johnson was briefed on foreign policy during the vice-presidential days, found himself in a much closer and more intimate relationship with Johnson than he had ever enjoyed with Kennedy. The State Department bureaucracy, which had just about written off Rusk as a power in the New Frontier, began to look at the Secretary with new respect.

Even without a clear design as to exactly where he wanted to go in international policy, the pervasive power of the presidency was insensibly altering that policy. Within days after the assassination, high State Department officials perceived a change in the most important idea men under Kennedy: McGeorge Bundy and Under Secretary of State George Ball. Without receiving explicit instructions from the new President, their private advice to him became more cautious and tentative than with Kennedy. They scrupulously avoided anticipating the wishes of the new President, waiting for him to reveal his inner thoughts.

On December 14, the first clear signal came that the President was indeed planning a change, both of style and substance, in the way the foreign policy of the United States would be conducted in his administration. On that day, three weeks after he became President, Johnson nominated Thomas C. Mann as Assistant Secretary of State for Inter-American Affairs, an appointment with immediate and sensational reverberations.

The Latin American policy of John F. Kennedy typified the New Frontier at both its best and its worst. With its ideal of rebuilding and reforming impoverished, ravaged Latin America, Kennedy's Alliance for Progress raised the *Yanqui* in the esteem of Latin America as had nothing since Franklin Roosevelt's Good Neighbor Policy. Through the Eisenhower years, a single-minded United States emphasis on developing Latin America by private investment, and only private investment, had actively sustained the hemisphere's most reactionary elements in order to make it safe for Americans to risk capital. One result was a positive United States support of unsavory dictatorships throughout Latin America. Thanks to the influence of Dr. Milton Eisenhower, and a growing alarm beginning in 1959 that Washington's support of the Latin right wing was only encouraging Castro-style revolutions, the policy began to unfreeze during the last two years of the Eisenhower Administration. But not until Kennedy became President did the United States government officially align itself with the new revolutionary impulse sweeping the hemisphere. With the adventure of the Bay of Pigs fading into the background the United States' standing in Latin America was higher on November 22, 1963, than at any point since World War II.

But that did not mean the Alliance for Progress was succeeding. By the end of 1963, complaints of inefficient administration and confusion were growing throughout the hemisphere. At the heart of the complaints was a chaotic chain of command in Latin American policy that divided authority between policy-makers at three points: the White House, the State Department, and the Agency for International Development.

The organizational confusion derived initially from President Kennedy's failure to persuade New Dealer Adolph Berle to become his Assistant Secretary of State for Inter-American Affairs. Berle, who in that post under Roosevelt was an architect of the Good Neighbor Policy, insisted the job be upgraded to the level of Under Secretary. When Kennedy would not make that change, Berle declined the job. Kennedy then named Berle to head an official Latin American task force that also included two White House aides: Arthur Schlesinger, Jr., and Richard Goodwin, a bright, clever but abrasive twenty-nine-year-old Kennedy speech writer. With such a high-powered triumvirate setting policy, Kennedy was hard put to find anybody of much stature to take the job of Assistant Secretary. In mid-1961, Goodwin was sent to the State Department as Deputy Assistant Secretary, further undercutting the authority of the Assistant Secretary. Proliferation of authority grew. Ralph Dungan, a quietly competent White House aide, was given a share of authority with Schlesinger in the Latin American field. Teodoro Moscoso, a strong-minded Puerto Rican who had run his island's highly successful development program, was put in charge of the Washington end of the Alliance for Progress with the position of a deputy administrator in AID.

At the time of the assassination, the White House was moving toward an overdue consolidation of these tangled lines. Senator Hubert Humphrey, who had made Latin America one of his many special interests, had privately trotted out Berle's old suggestion that the top Latin American job be upgraded to Under Secretary of State with increased powers that would make him a czar. Simultaneously, Schlesinger and Goodwin renewed the idea. At their urging, Kennedy sent Rusk a memo saying he wanted to create the job and asking for a report on its *positive* possibilities. When Rusk bucked the President's memo into the State Department bureaucracy and no answer was forthcoming, Kennedy repeated his request—shortly before his death. Both Averell Harriman, at that time Under Secretary of State for Political Affairs, and Sargent Shriver, President Kennedy's brother-in-law who had enjoyed a conspicuous success as director of the Peace Corps, were considered for the new post.

The question of tidying up the Latin American staff was one of the first matters of business on Lyndon Johnson's presidential desk. Humphrey reiterated to Johnson his proposal to create a new under secretaryship. Fulbright and Rusk objected that such a change would create an organizational imbalance, giving one geographic area an Under Secretary while Assistant Secretaries held sway for each of the other regions of the world. The idea was discarded. But Johnson was nevertheless determined to name a director for Latin American affairs with whatever title. Shriver's name came up again, but Johnson wanted his own man for the job. He wanted a wiry, tough, bilingual career foreign-service officer from Laredo, Texas, Thomas C. Mann, then serving as Ambassador to Mexico.

No development during the transition so disturbed New Frontiersmen and liberals generally as the appointment of Tom Mann. It seemed to sustain the worst fears about Lyndon Johnson harbored by the Kennedy liberals. Even that old *Johnson* liberal, Hubert Humphrey, was dismayed. Humphrey, a militant champion of the non-Communist left and of reform in Latin America, had been battling what he regarded as perceptible backsliding by President Kennedy toward toleration of military dictatorships, and now he privately advised Johnson against appointing Mann because he feared it would be a further trend in that direction.* But when Mann was named, Humphrey did not protest, publicly or privately. Other liberals, however, laid down a heavy barrage against Mann. Newspaper stories described him as a Texas crony of the President who had helped draft Eisenhower's disastrous Latin American policy and championed the Latin American status quo. Many liberals regarded him as a reactionary champion of American business interests who would betray and destroy the Alliance for Progress.

The truth was quite different. As Assistant Secretary for Economic Affairs and, from August, 1960, as Assistant Secretary for Inter-American Affairs, Mann had in fact been a liberalizing influence on Eisenhower's Latin American policy. He was a foe of dictators and an advocate of reform, on close terms with liberal reformers throughout the hemisphere. In January, 1961, when Berle turned down the job, President Kennedy asked him to remain as Assistant Secretary. When Mann declined for personal reasons, Kennedy enlisted the aid of Vice-President Johnson to change Mann's mind—not because they were old friends but because they both were Texans. Johnson could not persuade Mann to stay in Washington but did talk him into staying in the foreign service as Ambassador to Mexico. From that time on, Johnson and Mann started on the road toward a warm friendship.

There was a basic difference between Mann, on the one hand, and Schlesinger, Goodwin, and Moscoso on the other hand, though not so vivid a contrast as much of Washington believed. The difference came down to one of emphasis. Desiring no return to the Eisenhower policy, Mann was concerned that Kennedy's Alliance for Progress, in its zeal to put the United States on the side of reform, had moved too far away from encouraging private investment in the hemisphere. Mann put more emphasis on stabilizing Latin American currencies and fighting inflation than did the New Frontier. Influenced by his admiration for the one-party Mexican system, Mann was less dedicated to pure democracy in Latin America than were Kennedy's policy-makers. By the same token, he was less disturbed by the prospect of temporary military regimes.

At the root of the liberals' concern over Mann was style more than substance. They winced at his habit, common to foreign service officers with Latin American experience, of using the diminutive phrase "Commies." Tom Mann and Arthur Schlesinger might not be all that

---

* As Vice-President, however, Humphrey became one of Washington's strongest supporters of Mann.

far apart on a particular point, but Mann would sound like a tough Esso oil-company executive talking about the need for stability and Schlesinger would sound like a liberal poet talking about the revolutionary impulse. Thus did the gulf between them seem wider than it was.

One matter of substance dividing Mann from the New Frontier was his greater emphasis on the anti-Communist aspects of the Alliance for Progress. When Dick Goodwin traveled to Mexico City in 1961, he and Ambassador Mann clashed over Goodwin's desire to confer with Mexican left-wingers. Mann had a more serious dispute in 1962 with Edward M. Kennedy, the President's youngest brother who was then running for the Senate from Massachusetts. Arriving in Mexico City, Teddy Kennedy proposed a dinner party at the Ambassador's residency for Mexican Communists and other leftists. His intention was to discuss and debate the issues with them, perhaps softening their anti-Americanism in the process. Mann flatly refused to permit such a guest list in his home, advising Kennedy it would neither sit well with the Mexican government nor have the slightest influence on the left. Kennedy went ahead with the dinner anyway, in a private home.*

There was, then, a difference between Tom Mann and the New Frontier. When President Johnson gave to Mann all the reins of Latin American policy that had been held by so many under Kennedy, he was not only effecting an overdue consolidation but declaring his own independence from the Kennedy foreign policy.

On December 18, 1963, four days after Mann was named Assistant Secretary of State, Johnson appointed him a Special Assistant to the President. No White House aide would challenge his decisions, as they did in Kennedy's day. Johnson bestowed upon Mann an extraordinary grant of power. "We expect to speak with one voice on all matters affecting the hemisphere," the President told a press conference. "Mr. Mann . . . will be that voice." To give Mann absolute control over Latin American policy, it remained necessary for him to take over Teodoro Moscoso's job at AID, running the Alliance for Progress. Moscoso and his friends started a backfire, encouraging newspaper stories that the purge of Moscoso would damage the new President not only in Latin America but with Spanish-speaking voters at home. Once again, Humphrey intervened with the President, urging him to retain Moscoso. Once again, Humphrey's advice was

* The same disagreement over tactics was repeated in late 1965 when Mann, then Under Secretary of State for Economic Affairs, objected to Senator Robert F. Kennedy's unofficial visit to Latin America partly on the grounds that Kennedy would engage in futile debates with leftist leaders.

ignored. On December 27, Johnson gave Mann his third job, replacing Moscoso.

Johnson was well aware that his reorganization went far beyond Latin America. It was a declaration of independence from the New Frontier. A private letter* from a Kennedy intimate to a Kennedy Cabinet member revealed the emotions stirred in the Kennedy camp by the Mann appointment. The letter began by suggesting that the Mann appointment was subject to two interpretations, one minimum and one maximum. The minimum interpretation was that "Johnson wanted a trusted Johnson man in a critical spot." The maximum interpretation was the more interesting:

> That Johnson seized the occasion to make a declaration of independence to show that this is *his* administration and that he is master of his own house and strong enough to take charge in a field that had been of special concern to President Kennedy and appoint a man who was unacceptable to the Kennedy group and do so without consultation. Consider the reverse situation—JFK would look for an opportunity to do just what Johnson has done —to demonstrate his own control of the government, to disperse and isolate the Johnson forces, to render the Johnson loyalists impotent. It is thus quite inevitable in the situation that LBJ should move in this direction.
>
> . . . Thus, Johnson has won the first round. He has shown his power to move in a field of special concern to the Kennedys without consulting the Kennedys. This will lead people all over the government to conclude that their future lies with Johnson. . . . If he wishes, he will be able to pick off the Kennedy people one by one and either sidetrack them or drive them out of government and so long as he maintains an ostensibly liberal position on issues, it will be very difficult to do anything about it.
>
> I had supposed that Johnson so badly needed the Kennedy people for the election that we would retain a measure of power for eleven months. I am now inclined to believe that this supposition is optimistic. I think we have underestimated the power of the presidency. The President has nearly all the cards in his hand. . . . [But] I do not think LBJ intends to go . . . far at this point. My guess is that, having succeeded in this power play, he will try to be propitiatory on small issues because it is to his advantage to keep the Kennedy forces in the government in his camp. But he has shown, I believe, that we are weaker—a good deal weaker—than we had supposed. He has understood that the sanctions we have are resignation and/or revolt—and that both sanctions are meaningless and would seem sour grapes. . . .

* The letter was made available to the authors with a stipulation for anonymity.

The symbolic importance of the Mann appointment was not soon forgotten. For, by chance, Mann was at the very center of Johnson's first foreign policy crisis. The way that crisis was handled provided positive proof for the New Frontier that a different way of conducting foreign policy had arrived in Washington.

President Johnson's first full-blown foreign crisis came in the steamy, unhappy Republic of Panama, as luck would have it, in Mann's area of responsibility. Beginning in early January with street rioting, the crisis did not reach its diplomatic climax until March. By then, those who considered themselves preservers of the Kennedy tradition in Latin American policy—in the State Department, Congress, and the press—felt their worst fears about Mann had been justified. However, the New Frontier's concern with Mann's policy in office preceded the Panama crisis.

On December 14, 1963, the United States recognized the military regime which on September 25 had overthrown the reformist government of President Juan Bosch, the intellectual and writer chosen by the Dominican Republic ten months earlier in its first free election since the dictatorship of Rafael Trujillo began in 1928. Liberal New Frontiersmen such as Ted Moscoso had counseled against recognizing the military regime, insisting that economic pressure from Washington could restore Bosch to the presidency. The liberals regarded the recognition of the military government as a betrayal of the Alliance for Progress and a Johnson-Mann retrogression toward Eisenhower days. In fact, however, recognition was inevitable. Washington could not let the Dominican Republic drift unaided toward chaos and, conceivably, Communism. On November 22, 1963, the White House staff had drafted a memorandum recommending diplomatic recognition of the military regime for these very reasons, awaiting inspection by President Kennedy upon his return from Texas.

The Johnson-Mann policy was again criticized by the New Frontier inside the government in an early February spite contest with Fidel Castro. In reprisal for the United States seizure of four Cuban vessels sailing in Florida waters, Castro cut off the water supply to the U.S. Navy's Guantanamo base on Cuba. Johnson immediately ordered the base to stop getting its water from Castro. Fresh water was brought in by tankers, and plans were made for a permanent water supply by converting sea water. Simultaneously, Johnson reduced American dollars going into Cuba by firing some twenty-five hundred Cubans who worked for the Navy at Guantanamo, but lived and spent their salaries in Cuba. It was an effective solution to a sticky problem that Barry Goldwater proposed should be solved by a Marine expedition to turn *on* the water. But Kennedy men in the State Department grumbled privately that Mann had overreacted and made the United States look petty by firing the Cuban employees.

Thus, by the time the United States–Panamanian crisis reached its climax of tortuous negotiations in March, critics of Mann were poised to blame him for all policies that they thought veered from Kennedy doctrine. Yet, the basic decisions regarding Panama were made not by Mann but by the President. In this first major foreign policy crisis, as in the others to follow, Johnson assumed complete power and, often in opposition to his advisers, personally dictated the government's step-by-step response. If Mann received much of the New Frontier's criticism about Panama, it was because in March, 1964, there was still some hesitancy inside the administration to criticize the new President. Accordingly, in those early months of the Johnson presidency, Mann was not only the symbol of the Johnson control of governmental power but a lightning rod for liberal criticism.

The roots of the 1964 Panama crisis could be traced back sixty years to America's fling at turn-of-the-century imperialism under Theodore Roosevelt. When Roosevelt could not come to terms with the Republic of Colombia for cutting a ship canal across the Isthmus of Panama, he fomented an artificial Panamanian revolution, and in 1903 signed a contract with the new Republic of Panama for United States jurisdiction "in perpetuity" over a Panama Canal Zone. For an initial payment of ten million dollars, and an annual fee of two hundred and fifty thousand dollars, the United States had full control over a ten-mile-wide zone. Manned by a hereditary caste of colonial civil servants called the "Zonians," who resembled nothing so much as a bit of Kansas transplanted in the tropics, the Canal Zone was a well-manicured colonial anachronism sitting primly next to the wretched squalor of Panama City. It became a natural and convenient whipping boy for the Panamanian oligarchy, which preferred to orate about the Canal Zone rather than institute genuine social reform.

The real issue was renegotiation of the 1903 treaty on terms of greater equity for Panama. But congressional sentiment, whipped up by skillful Zonian lobbying, had enshrined Teddy Roosevelt's treaty as an inviolate artifact, immune from change. The merest suggestion of amendment would endanger United States security and tarnish United States honor. Consequently, the Canal Zone question in the late 1950s and into the 1960s centered on the symbolic issue of whether the flag of Panama should be permitted to fly in the Canal Zone as a manifestation of sovereignty.

On October 10, 1962, President Kennedy and President Roberto Chiari of Panama finally agreed on equal, impartial display of the American and Panamanian flags side by side at fifty sites throughout the Canal Zone—a plan denounced by angry Zonians and their patrons on Capitol Hill as a sellout. The order would apply to American high schools in the Zone on January 6, 1964. But as an attempted compromise, United States authorities decreed that after students returned to classes on January 6, 1964, after the holidays, *no* flags would fly at the schools.

In defiance of this order, a group of Zonian teen-agers hoisted the Stars and Stripes at Balboa High School on Tuesday, January 7. A protest march into the Canal Zone by Panamanian students was skillfully escalated by Communist agitators into a full-scale riot on January 9. More than twenty Panamanians were killed, some by gunfire from Canal Zone police, and over three hundred were wounded. President Chiari, a member of Panama's ruling oligarchy, was fearful that the disorders could be fanned by Communist activists into a revolution. He postured as a supernationalist to endear himself to his country's miserable citizens. It soon became apparent that he was demanding nothing less than renegotiation of the 1903 treaty.

Lyndon Johnson faced his first foreign crisis at Washington under anomalous conditions. With the majesty and strength of the world's greatest power at his fingertips, he was powerless to deal with an impoverished banana republic. He was utterly unfamiliar with the politics, the problems, and the realities of the situation. In desperation at 11:35 A.M. on Friday, January 10, Johnson instinctively reached for the telephone to call President Chiari in Panama City. Here was an extraordinary example of personal diplomacy, President-to-President, between two nations which at that moment had no diplomatic relations. On the phone, Johnson asked for an end to violence and an attempt at restraint. Chiari agreed, but insisted that treaty revision was essential to United States–Panamanian amity, a proposition to which Johnson did not agree. Once again, the President's attempt to apply the Johnson Treatment to international affairs was not a success. On that very day, violence resumed in Panama City and a mob attacked the American Embassy.

Now, a ludicrous sight unfolded for the hemisphere and the world: the mighty U.S.A. locked in mortal diplomatic conflict with tiny Panama. Apprehensive about the oligarchy's power in the Panamanian elections coming in May, Chiari needed a commitment that Johnson would renegotiate the treaty. But that was precisely what Johnson felt he could not give. More keenly attuned to the opinion of Congress than world opinion, he felt he could not succumb to a Communist-tinged mob in his first foreign crisis though, substantively, he had no objection to treaty revision. This hard line, incorrectly attributed by the New Frontiersmen to Mann, was Johnson's own.

The crisis soon boiled down to an agonizing semantical debate. Chiari wanted the United States to agree to "negotiate" a new treaty. Johnson would agree only to "discuss" causes of conflict between the two countries. Anything else, he felt, would cause a revolt in Congress at precisely the moment he was trying to pass his tax and civil rights bills. As the Organization of American States continued its futile attempts to break the impasse, Johnson's own attitude seemed to harden and grow more vexed. At a February 29 press conference, while conceding that the 1903 treaty might "require adjustment," the President added:

> . . . We are not going to make any precommitments before we sit down on what we are going to do in the way of rewriting new treaties with a nation we do not have diplomatic relations with. Once these relations are restored, we will be glad . . . to _discuss_ anything, any time, anywhere, and do what's just and what's fair and what's right.*
>
> And just because Panama happens to be a small nation no larger than the city of St. Louis—is no reason why we shouldn't try in every way to be equable and fair and just and we're going to insist on that. But we are going to be equally insistent on no preconditions.

These remarks were not considered particularly helpful in bringing a settlement—particularly the comparison of a sovereign republic with an American city. Nevertheless, the OAS pressed on, with Johnson now agonizing over every word, every comma in the plan of settlement. On March 10, agreement to restore diplomatic relations at last seemed imminent, but Johnson objected that the imposition of one word—"international," in describing the agreement to end the crisis—implied the very "precommitment" toward negotiation of a new treaty that he had ruled out. On March 12, Chiari agreed to drop the word "international" but urged the United States to use any word besides "discuss" (he suggested "review"), in order to avoid the impression of capitulation by Panama. Mann and Johnson's other advisers urged him to accept this easy way out, but the President prevailed as a minority of one. There was no agreement.

* Emphasis is added.

On Sunday, March 15, the persistent OAS negotiators felt they had Mann's concurrence in an agreement between the United States and Panama to designate ambassadors for "discussions and negotiations." At 6:45 P.M., the OAS announced United States and Panamanian approval of this wording. Summoning Rusk and Mann to the White House that night, Johnson seemed ready to accept the OAS solution.

But Johnson, still unsure of himself, continued to gaze toward Capitol Hill for guidance. That very night, he invited legislative leaders to a secret meeting at the White House. Senators Hubert Humphrey, Mike Mansfield, and J. W. Fulbright all advised him to accept the OAS doctrine. But more conservative congressional leaders, Republican and Democratic, pressed on him opposing advice in strong language.

If Johnson gave an inch in this, his first major crisis abroad, they told him, it would indelibly stamp him at the outset of his administration as "weak" and give him a reputation that would haunt him for the rest of his days in the White House. This warning was conveyed to the President most vehemently by Senator Everett McKinley Dirksen, the Senate Republican Leader, who warned Johnson not to give in to "every little country." Dirksen was firmly seconded by Johnson's old Senate intimate, Richard Russell. Johnson was confronting the same parochial senatorial line in foreign policy that he himself used to take in the Senate, an outlook affected by domestic politics and senatorial exigencies. Alarmed by the stern warning of Dirksen and Russell, Johnson hardened his position.

Whatever Mann had told the OAS, the President was rejecting the statement. At 11 P.M., the White House announced that there was no agreement, a flat contradiction of the OAS statement of four hours earlier.

At noon the next day, Monday, March 16, Johnson by coincidence was scheduled to address Latin American diplomats at the Pan American Union to mark the third anniversary of the Alliance for Progress. The speech pledging commitment to the Alliance attempted to put a new emphasis on private investment to accompany government investment in the hemisphere, in line with Mann's views. Couched in the pedestrian prose that prevailed briefly at the White House after speech writer Ted Sorensen's departure, the prepared speech did not set too well with the Latins. But what really startled them was not the speech but a stunning impromptu digression by Johnson on the Panama crisis. Once again, he repudiated the OAS statement of the previous night by saying there had not been "a genuine meeting of the minds between the two Presidents of the two countries involved."

Then, in terms that could only infuriate the Latins, the President added:

> Press reports indicate that the government of Panama feels that the language which has been under consideration for many days commits the United States to a rewriting and a revision of the 1903 treaty. We have made no such commitment and we would not think of doing so before diplomatic relations are resumed and unless a fair and satisfactory adjustment is agreed upon.

The "press reports" Johnson referred to were Panamanian radio broadcasts of the previous night. Bone-tired OAS mediators were appalled that the President had pulled them into a critical diplomatic situation. But Johnson felt above all that he could not be placed in the United States election-year position of submitting to Panamanian election-year pressure.

But Lyndon Johnson the politician was not one to freeze in a posture of intransigence. The reaction, both domestically and internationally, to his wrecking of the OAS efforts was adverse. At noon on Saturday, March 21, Dean Rusk met with Juan Baptista de Lavalle of Peru, chairman of the OAS Council, to reveal a softening in the United States position. One hour later, Johnson surprised newsmen by walking into a routine press briefing by Press Secretary George Reedy and reading a letter to de Lavalle most conciliatory in tone:

> We are well aware that the claims of the government of Panama and the majority of the Panamanian people do not spring from malice or hatred of America.
> They are based on a deeply felt sense of the honest and fair needs of Panama. It is therefore our obligation as allies and partners to review these claims and to meet them, when meeting them is both just and possible.
> We are prepared to *review* every issue which now divides us, and every problem which the Panamanian government wishes to raise. . . .[*]

Here was the solution—substituting the word "review" for either "discuss" or "negotiate"—suggested more than a week earlier by Chiari before Johnson's repudiation of the OAS agreement and his Pan American Union speech. Those two events had built up a store of ill will in the hemisphere, all of which would have been avoidable had Johnson softened his position a few days earlier. "I don't say discuss," Johnson told the White House reporters, "because that is a sticky

---

[*] Emphasis is added.

word. Some of them [apparently, Panamanian officials] do not quite understand what it means. But I say review. We are glad to do that." On April 3, an accord was signed between Panama and the United States, diplomatic relations were restored, and Robert Anderson was dispatched by Johnson as a special ambassador to "review" the sixty-three-year-old treaty.

The epilogue to the Panama crisis is a happier story. After months of painstaking negotiations by Anderson, and after both the American and Panamanian presidential elections, President Johnson announced over television on December 18, 1964, that the two nations would *negotiate* a new treaty. The only ripple of protest in Congress came from self-appointed spokesmen for the Zonians. The Canal issue had steamed for so long in Johnson's pressure cooker that it had almost completely boiled itself away.

Comparisons with the way President Kennedy might have handled the Panama crisis were inevitable. Kennedy probably would have been more sparing at the outset in applying the nation's might against little Panama. He likely would have agreed more quickly to what Johnson finally accepted after agonizing months and rising tension. To safeguard warm relations with the Latin American nations, Kennedy likely would have risked the outbreak in Congress that Johnson, at the cost of hemispheric relations, avoided. But by taking a hard line against Panama from January through March, Johnson did open the door to full public acceptance of treaty revision the following December. As in the case of the tax bill, Johnson finally wound up in about the same place Kennedy would have but with less domestic criticism and with a deeper consensus in Congress and throughout the country.

However, the early months of the 1964 Panama crisis did reveal characteristics of the new President, and these would govern his conduct in far more difficult crises ahead: an insistence on deciding every detail himself; a tendency to encourage the most frantic mood of emergency in the government; and a willingness to employ massive American power to the fullest.

After April, 1964, when the Panamanian question was on the road to settlement, no foreign crisis of any magnitude personally engaged Lyndon Johnson in his first full year of the presidency to anything like the extent of Panama. Cyprus, Laos, and the Congo were major problems, but their handling in Washington was entrusted in great part to subordinates.

As for the continued guerrilla war in South Vietnam, where a few thousand United States military "advisers" were fighting beside the South Vietnamese Army, Johnson neither fully understood it nor was much interested in it. In his first State of the Union Message on January 8, he mentioned Vietnam only tangentially.* In a televised hour-long conversation with network correspondents on March 15, he mentioned it not at all. Thus, 1964 gave Lyndon Johnson only the skimpiest preparation of what he would face internationally in the years ahead.

The truth was that the President did not have his eye abroad in that first year of his presidency. His eye was on the 1964 election, and his inner timing mechanism was set only for that one monumental event. That was the year to run for President. In 1965, the weight of crises in the Caribbean and Southeast Asia would end a year of grace.

* The fact that Vietnam was mentioned at all seemed dictated more by considerations of rhetoric than policy. His first reference: "Today, Americans of all races stand side by side in Berlin and in Vietnam." His second was that the United States would defend freedom against "infiltration practiced by those in Hanoi and Havana."

Chapter XIX

★★★★★★★★★★

THE GREAT SOCIETY

LBJ has been hurling himself about Washington like an elemental force. To be plain about it, he has won our admiration in the last fortnight.
—T. R. B. in *The New Republic*, May 2, 1964
It is quite obvious that every day in every way Mr. Johnson is liking the presidency better and better. Not only liking it—he is beginning to shape the office for his unique brand of leadership.
—*The Reporter*, May 7, 1964

On the Easter weekend of March 28–29, 1964, Lyndon B. Johnson drove his Lincoln Continental at high speed near the LBJ Ranch in an uninhibited joyride that had a most unfortunate impact on his infant presidency. Fast rides over the smooth, empty black-tops in the Texas hill country had always been part of the entertainment for Johnson's guests on the ranch. With one hand on the wheel and the other holding the speaker of his radio-telephone, shouting orders to secretaries and ranch hands, Johnson displayed himself in all his elemental exuberance.

It was, quite simply, great fun. But now Johnson was President of the United States, and his passengers that Easter weekend were four members of the Washington press corps—three of them female. Later, one of the girls related the hilarious events of the day to her colleagues in the press and the story of the President's daredevil driving began to find its way into the newspapers. At a press conference on Saturday, April 4, the President was asked about published reports "that you had hit speeds of perhaps up to ninety miles an hour in a zone with a speed limit of seventy miles an hour." These reports, the questioner continued, were creating "concern that you are putting yourself in danger."

Bristling, the President replied with neither patience nor accuracy: "I am unaware that I have ever driven past seventy."

All this made the White House staff distinctly uneasy, but the Texas joyride over Easter did not reach crisis proportions until Monday, April 6, when the new edition of *Time* reached the newsstands. Entitled " 'Mr. President, You're Fun,' " the article began:

A cream-colored Lincoln Continental driven by the President of the U.S. flashed up a long Texas hill, swung into the left lane to pass two cars poking along under 85 m.p.h., and thundered on over the crest of the hill—squarely into the path of an oncoming car. The President charged on, his paper cup of Pearl beer within easy sipping distance. The other motorist veered off the paved surface to safety on the road's shoulder. Groaned a passenger in the President's car when the ride was over: "That's the closest John McCormack has come to the White House yet."

Describing Johnson as "a cross between a teen-age Grand Prix driver and a back-to-nature Thoreau in cowboy boots" when he inhales springtime on the ranch, *Time* told the story of the ride:

. . . [The President] hopped into his Continental to play tour guide, invited in four reporters, including Hearst's pretty blonde Marianne Means and two other newswomen. More reporters and photographers scrambled into five other Johnson-owned vehicles and the whole caravan jounced at high speeds across a pasture, zigzagging around dung mounds and clusters of fat white-faced cattle.

At one point, Johnson pulled up near a small gathering of cattle, pushed a button under the dashboard—and a cow horn bawled from beneath the gleaming hood. Heifers galloped toward the car while photographers clicked away and the President looked pleased. As he drove, Johnson talked about his cattle, once plunged into what one startled newswoman called a "very graphic description of the sex life of a bull."

. . . During the tour, Reporter Means, her baby-blue eyes fastened on Johnson, cooed: "Mr. President, you're fun."

Through all the fun, the President sipped beer from his paper cup. Eventually, he ran dry, refilled once from Marianne's supply, emptied his cup again, and took off at speeds up to 90 m.p.h. to get more. . . . Someone gasped at how fast Johnson was driving. Quickly, Lyndon took one hand from the wheel, removed his five-gallon hat and flopped it on the dashboard to cover the speedometer . . .*

* We have quoted the *Time* account at such length because at the White House, this account, not the actual events that inspired it, was the source of all the trouble.

The President was outraged by this account, and telephoned angry protests to the editors of *Time* in Washington and New York. In the past, Johnson's staff used to chuckle about their chief's incurable sensitivity to press criticism, but not this time. They, too, were upset by such a story in a mass-circulation news magazine. Indeed, they feared that the *Time* article might conceivably be one of those rare pieces of journalism that could fundamentally change the course of history by creating an indelible image of a reckless President, cutting away his popular support. Inevitably, the *Time* account inspired moralizing editorials across the country that deplored the beer-drinking, fast-driving President. Republican orators sanctimoniously exploited the incident as proof of moral decay in the Johnson Administration.

The anxiety of the White House staff stemmed from the fact that Lyndon Johnson was still emerging from the transition and had not yet put his own distinctive imprimatur on the administration. As a human being, he was still something of an enigma to most Americans. He had successfully, perhaps brilliantly, passed the test of transition; he had gone far toward taming Congress; he had displayed a great determination, if not great finesse, in handling the Panama problem and thus surmounting his first foreign crisis. But he had not yet made this administration his own, had not yet put his unique stamp on it. The transition was finished, but the Great Society had not yet been born.

It was in this tentative, inconclusive period that, suddenly, the destructive image of the Texas joyrider, so different from what he and his aides wanted, was growing spontaneously in the public consciousness. It seemed all of a part with Johnson's reputation as a Texas wheeler-dealer, and the Easter weekend was fully compatible with this lingering image that the President was trying so hard to wipe from the record.

Johnson's deep interest in his image and his concern to improve it were evident within hours after the assassination, and his proposed instrument of image-making in the beginning was Pierre Salinger, the stubby, gregarious ex-reporter inherited from Kennedy as the White House press secretary.

On November 22, 1963, Salinger had accompanied much of the Cabinet on a trip to Tokyo that was interrupted in mid-Pacific flight by Kennedy's assassination. The plane immediately returned to Washington, arriving in the early hours of November 23. At seven-thirty A.M. after only a few hours' sleep, Salinger answered his bedside phone and was momentarily stunned to hear an operator tell him the President was calling, followed by an unfamiliar Southwestern voice.

Salinger was to hear that voice often in the coming weeks. Johnson assigned two of his Texas aides, Horace Busby (then not yet on the White House staff) and Jack Valenti, to draft background papers putting his position on various matters in the most favorable light and then directed Salinger to peddle this material to reporters. In short, the President wanted Salinger openly and blatantly to proselytize reporters. Johnson also used Salinger to complain—not in the President's name but in his own—to reporters about stories the White House did not like, an old habit of Presidents that Johnson carried to a new extreme. In December, Salinger was ordered by Johnson to phone a reporter who had been close to Kennedy, upbraid him because of a dispatch that had angered Johnson, and tell him: "You used to have a pipeline over here, but you don't anymore." Reporters treated this way were not impressed by any great finesse.

Attempts to manage the news and cultivate the press were as old as politics, but Johnson was pressing too hard. Although he permitted no word of criticism to seep out publicly, Salinger privately protested to the President. He told Johnson good publicity could seldom be manufactured. Good publicity, continued the press secretary, followed good works. The President should let his accomplishments speak for themselves. Besides, Salinger said, Johnson was receiving excellent treatment from the press during the transition days.* But the President was convinced that only through manipulation of the press could he and his administration be assured of fair treatment. The relationship between Johnson and Salinger, so warm in December when the President dined at Salinger's home on Lake Barcroft in the Virginia suburbs (something Kennedy had never done), began to cool. On March 18, 1964, Salinger resigned as press secretary to run for the United States Senate from California, and that was the end of Johnson's plan to have Pierre Salinger do for him what he mistakenly believed Salinger had done for John F. Kennedy.

Salinger's departure increased Johnson's freedom to attempt to manipulate the press corps as though it were a commodity for sale, with personal favors in return for favorable stories. In his years on Capitol Hill, Johnson had developed a fine contempt for reporters, regarding them as underpaid victims of a system requiring them to reflect faithfully the views of their employers, or, in some cases, of politicians. It

---

* It was at this time that Johnson called in the top-echelon public information officers to complain that he was not getting enough favorable publicity. See page 355.

was difficult for him to conceive of a reporter developing and presenting a view of his own.

Accordingly, a critical report in a newspaper or magazine was seldom viewed by Johnson as an objective analysis, but as a plant by some political foe or the result of an order from a hostile publisher. The important corollary of that proposition was that Johnson could generate favorable stories by the simple expedient of courting influential reporters and then feeding them appropriately pro-Johnson tidbits and background information. Both the proposition and the corollary contained a nugget of truth. Johnson's success as Majority Leader in cultivating a number of submissive correspondents led him to the erroneous conclusion that his press relations could be solved by the art of seduction.

Hence, in the early months of the Johnson presidency, both before and after Salinger's departure, journalists had unprecedented access to the Oval Office, to the living quarters, and to the manicured lawns and macadam driveways on the White House grounds. James Reston and Walter Lippmann, Brahmins of the Washington press, were sought out for advice at the White House as they never had been in the Kennedy and Eisenhower days. The President sent his own plane to pick up Reston and his wife in Phoenix, Arizona, and fly them to the LBJ Ranch during the 1963 Christmas holidays.

But Johnson's early courting of newsmen was by no means limited to the princes of Washington journalism. An equal object was to make Johnson men of its front-line soldiers as well. During the Eisenhower and Kennedy Administrations, the news correspondents assigned to the White House on a regular basis had seen increasingly less of the President, outside of the formal press conference, and consequently had found themselves diminished in function and prestige. Within weeks after becoming President, Johnson consciously resolved to upgrade the White House correspondents and thereby gain important allies in the news media. White House correspondents were called in for private interviews with the President, occasionally over luncheon in the White House. Only the White House regulars were in a position to attend Johnson's unannounced Saturday press conferences.

The contrast between Johnson and his immediate predecessors was particularly vivid during his first few visits to the LBJ Ranch as President. When Eisenhower went to Gettysburg and Palm Springs and Kennedy to Hyannisport and Palm Beach, the traveling White House press seldom saw the President, relying for news on briefings from the press secretary. Not so at Johnson City. On that first Christmas trip to the ranch, three correspondents—Tom Wicker of the *New York*

Times, Douglas Kiker of the *New York Herald Tribune,* and Philip Potter of the *Baltimore Sun*—were suddenly summoned from Austin, fifty miles away, to attend a fish fry at the ranch. It was an extraordinary visit. The President administered a long, relaxed version of The Treatment, discoursing for hours over every conceivable subject of public policy. Other reporters on other occasions, reporters who had scarcely known Johnson, were privileged listeners to confidential chats on the front porch of the ranch house, high-speed tours of the hill country, and hilarious parties aboard the President's motor launch.*

But the effort to seduce the press failed. It was bound to fail, for Johnson's basic premise was wrong. Only in rare instances could a reporter be softened, no matter how lavish the President's attentions. Moreover, Johnson's unprecedented courtship of the press during his early months backfired. Any White House correspondent who had been wined and dined at the presidential table and was regarded by Johnson as his man was castigated by Johnson as an ingrate and a traitor when he failed to echo the Johnson line in his reports. Intimacy between two such natural antagonists as the President, any President, and the press could only damage the President's relations with the press. But a far more significant hazard in Johnson's early wooing of reporters was not just the deterioration of his press relations, but of his overall image in the country.

It resulted from confusion between the President's Private Person and his Public Person. As Majority Leader in the Senate, Johnson was uninhibited in the presence of the regular Senate correspondents. He invited them into his office for a few highballs in the evening and let his hair down, talking in his colorful and racy idiom and turning his gift of mimicry against every leading political figure in the country. But these Senate correspondents were, in a sense, themselves a part of the Senate Establishment. Johnson could trust them not to reveal too much of his Private Person in their reports about his Public Person— that is, as Senate Majority Leader.

This strict demarcation line between the Private and Public Person began to crumble during Johnson's freewheeling overseas trips as Vice-President. But the problem was magnified beyond control in his early presidency when he tried to deal with fifty or more White House correspondents in the same style that he had dealt with a dozen Senate regulars. Stories inevitably were published that concentrated on the Private Person and displayed the new President as a whiskey-drinking

---

* But when the telescopic lens of a wire-service photographer produced a picture showing Johnson in white yachting cap surrounded by visitors holding glasses on the deck of his cruiser, a presidential order resulted. From that time on, glasses were to be left below deck, even if all they had in them was root beer.

Texas primitive, who told dirty jokes and mistreated his Secret Service bodyguard.

Johnson's aides knew all too well that such exposés in the press fitted neatly with the image of the President as a Texas wheeler-dealer that began to emerge in early 1964 quite apart from his treatment in the press. Two long, meticulously researched articles in the *Wall Street Journal* on March 23 and 24 by Louis M. Kohlmeier described how Lyndon and Lady Bird Johnson had made their fortune in the government-regulated communications industry. The Kohlmeier articles, which won him a Pulitzer Prize, set off a year-long discussion of Johnson's personal fortune—a subject related to the Private Person, not the Public Person.

Furthermore, the Bobby Baker case was warming up. On January 17, 1964, the Senate Rules Committee published incendiary testimony in its Baker investigation from Don B. Reynolds, a garrulous insurance salesman from the Washington suburb of Silver Spring, Maryland, who said he had taken Baker into his insurance firm as a vice-president in the late 1950s to exploit his invaluable political contacts. Baker suggested in 1957, Reynolds testified, that Reynolds sell a life insurance policy to Senator Johnson, two years after his severe heart attack. Johnson was obviously a high risk, but Reynolds placed $100,000 in life insurance with an underwriter. Shortly thereafter, Reynolds testified, Walter Jenkins suggested that he purchase advertising time from KTBC, the Johnsons' television station in Austin. The clear implication was that Reynolds owed Johnson a favor for the commissions he would receive as broker for the $100,000 of life insurance. Reynolds bought the television advertising at a cost of $1,208. Two years later, in 1959, according to Reynolds' testimony, Baker suggested that he give Johnson a high-fidelity stereophonic phonograph of a particular type desired by Mrs. Johnson. Reynolds said he sent such a set, costing him $584.75 for purchase and installation, to Johnson's home in Washington accompanied by invoices that indicated Reynolds was the buyer. In 1961, after he became Vice-President, Johnson bought another $100,000 life insurance policy from Reynolds.

As he often did when trouble loomed, Johnson turned to those two canny Washington lawyers, Abe Fortas and Clark Clifford. Their advice boiled down to this: Jenkins should not testify before the Rules Committee and risk a cross-examination that might escalate Reynolds' testimony into a full-fledged crisis.* But, Fortas and Clifford went on,

* While declining to testify, Jenkins did send the Rules Committee a memorandum asserting that he never had suggested to either Baker or Reynolds that Reynolds buy advertising time on KTBC, that he did not know Baker was associated in Reynolds' insurance firm, and that he had believed the stereo set was a gift to Johnson from Baker, not Reynolds.

the President must reply to Reynolds' charges and innuendo. That's precisely what Johnson did. At an impromptu press conference on January 23, the President gave a brief history of the life insurance policies purchased from Reynolds but said nothing at all about the advertising bought by Reynolds from KTBC. As for the stereo set, Johnson described it first as "a gift . . . that an employee of mine [Baker] made to me and Mrs. Johnson" and then as a gift of "the Baker family."

Democratic politicians generally disagreed with the Fortas-Clifford advice. Anything the President said, they believed, would elevate the whole matter and build it up as a political issue. Nor were these politicians happy when, at another presidential press conference on January 25, Johnson clumsily tried to equate the Reynolds-Baker stereo set with a miniature television set received from his office staff by Senator Barry Goldwater, then campaigning in the New Hampshire primary for the presidential nomination. "I am a little amused when you talk about the stereo and the miniature television," said Johnson with deep irony. "I don't know what the difference is, but I guess there is some difference."

Most certainly there *was* a difference, but Johnson could not control his instinct to strike at someone else when in trouble himself. Finally, the President exposed himself to serious criticism when confidential files containing derogatory information about Reynolds' record as an Air Force officer were leaked to the press.

The life insurance policies, the advertising purchased from KTBC, and the stereo set were soon forgotten, but Johnson's clumsy manner of dealing with the minor crises in late January inevitably strengthened public suspicions about his association with Bobby Baker, with the election only nine months away. Lyndon Johnson was no Harry Truman, who foolishly but gallantly endangered his own prestige by refusing to disown wayward aides in their time of trouble. Since becoming President, Johnson had neither seen nor spoken a single word to Bobby Baker, and he did not plan to. Feeling no remorse in abandoning Baker to his just deserts, the President told friends that Baker had betrayed him by getting involved in so many shady business operations—including Don Reynolds' insurance business—after Johnson left the Senate in January, 1961. This irritation with his former protégé was heightened by the President's deep concern over whether Attorney General Robert F. Kennedy would use the Baker case against him in some way. Thus, it became the President's highest aim to divorce himself both in spirit and deed from the aide who had been so much his intimate adviser, confidant, and lieutenant for eight years.

Over national television on March 15, an interviewer asked Johnson to comment on "the investigation of Bobby Baker in the Senate, [which is] aimed at you because he was your protégé and your friend." With breathtaking audacity, the President replied that "one of the finest committees in the Senate . . . have [sic] been conducting this investigation of an employee of theirs—no protégé of anyone; he was there before I came to the Senate for ten years, doing a job substantially the same as he is doing now; he was elected by all the Senators, . . . including the Republican Senators. . . ." * On January 23, however, Johnson had described Baker as the donor of the stereo set and, at the time of the gift, "an employee of mine."

But Johnson could not so easily shrug off Bobby Baker and his aura of fast living. The *Time* account of the President's freewheeling life down on the ranch disturbed the White House because it fit so neatly with what the public had been reading about the fast and loose living of Bobby Baker and his friends. Thus, the overriding concern at the White House was that the image of Lyndon Johnson, some five months after the assassination, was becoming not only unpleasant but a potentially dangerous political liability.

The immediate steps taken to resolve the crisis after Easter were simple enough. Johnson exercised a new and uncharacteristic caution with the press. Newsmen were no longer invited to uninhibited parties at the ranch or aboard the motor launch. The President no longer drank with the correspondents or was seen drinking by them. Access to Johnson, the Private Person, narrowed.

But in addition to protecting the Private Person, there was also the question of what to do about the Public Person, now that the transition was over. Two rival groups of presidential aides had conflicting policies, which, for the sake of simplification, can be called the policy of Containment and the policy of Exposure. Both agreed that Johnson's original plan of seducing the press had failed. But they offered widely varying alternatives.

The advisers counseling Containment hypothesized that Lyndon Johnson, so much bigger than life, simply could not be digested whole by the American public. He must be dispensed to the American voters in small pieces at generally formal occasions—carefully written

---

* In his zeal to put as much distance as possible between himself and Baker, the President drew upon his encyclopedic knowledge of Senate minutiae. Actually, Baker was selected by the Democratic caucus at Majority Leader Johnson's recommendation. The ratification of this selection by the full Senate, Republicans and Democrats, was mere formality without meaning.

speeches, carefully rehearsed television appearances, a rare press conference or two. The voters and the press would see little of the Public Person and never the Private Person under the policy of Containment.

Advocates of the Exposure policy agreed that the Private Person and the press were a disastrous mixture that must be stopped. But they felt it was essential to expose Johnson's charm and exuberance to the American public—"to show the American people what kind of President they have," in the words of one White House staffer who felt that only the politicians knew the real Johnson. There must be greater, not less, exposure of Johnson to the *public* but in carefully planned and more attractive ways than the beer-sipping, fast-driving image of the Easter weekend.

But Johnson never made a conscious choice between Exposure and Containment, for an event seemingly far removed from the image problem made the decision for him, ended all the morbid "image" planning, and changed the nature of his presidency.

On April 8, 1964, railroad unions struck the Illinois Central, thereby forcing resolution of a most difficult question that had been hanging over the heads of railway labor and management for seven years. Plagued by outmoded work rules that cost an extra six hundred million dollars a year, the railroads had demanded modernized contracts with labor in 1959, eliminating firemen on diesel locomotives and reducing the number of trainmen on crews. Presidential commissions appointed by both Eisenhower and Kennedy made formal recommendations which, in both instances, were accepted by management and rejected by labor.

Acting on a suit filed by the unions, the United States Supreme Court ruled on March 4, 1963, that the railroads had a right to change the work rules but that the unions had a right to protest by striking. On August 28, 1963, faced with a midnight strike deadline, Congress passed a law barring a railroad strike until February 25, 1964, and referring the principal issues to an arbitration board. When three months later the arbitration board ruled that the railroads could legally eliminate the worst of the featherbedding and the railroads began dropping workers, the unions were geared for a strike—against individual carriers, not all carriers at once.

But the April 8 strike call against the Illinois Central brought instant retaliation from the railroads, which announced they would put all the new work rules into effect. The union replied by threatening a nationwide strike. A nationwide strike would have idled two hundred thousand railway workers, reduced employment for another five hundred thousand and, in the opinion of the Johnson Administration, affected no fewer than six million citizens.

With the railroads scheduled to post their new work rules at one minute after midnight on April 10, Secretary of Labor Willard Wirtz visited the White House on Wednesday, April 8. Johnson instructed him to do all in his power to mediate a settlement. At Wirtz' instance, an emergency negotiation session was convened in Washington that night. It adjourned at 3:00 A.M. with nothing accomplished.

Now a strike was all but certain unless the President himself intervened. Talking with the President and Bill Moyers on Thursday, April 9, Wirtz advised the President against asking labor and management for an extension of the deadline set for that night. There were valid reasons for Wirtz' caution. Johnson had had no experience whatever in collective bargaining at this level and no particular standing either in the labor movement or the railway industry. Accordingly, it was entirely possible that the President might suffer a humiliating refusal if he asked for an extension. Besides, the government's own labor experts, including members of the National Mediation Board, were convinced that a brief strike might actually contribute to a settlement. Some of them believed that labor and management negotiators might come up with a settlement in forty-eight hours if the President stayed out.

But the passive approach to problem-solving was not Johnson's way. Furthermore, he was mightily impressed with the arguments of Walter Heller, chairman of the Council of Economic Advisers, who painted a woeful picture of disaster if the President did not intervene. Among other things, Heller told the President that food shipments to New York City could be cut off. Impressed, the President decided to intervene.

At 6:00 P.M. with the deadline six hours away, Johnson assumed his role as the nation's chief labor negotiator for the first time. The hard-bitten bargainers of rail labor and rail management, seated in the Cabinet Room at the White House, got their first whiff of the Johnson Treatment. Recalling that labor and management had pledged their support to him "on that tragic day in November," he asked for that support now, reminding them he was the only President they had. The industry and its labor unions had been battling for four years, he continued, and had lost faith in each other. "Have you lost faith in me?" he asked. The question was put separately to Roy E. Davidson of the Brotherhood of Locomotive Engineers, and to J. E. Wolfe, the top industry negotiator. The answer, of course, was "No." Pleading for the same chance they had given President Kennedy in 1963, Johnson asked for an extension of the deadline.

Both sides withdrew to consider the matter separately, then, two hours later, returned to the Cabinet Room. Wolfe announced that management was agreeable to a delay in the effective date of the long-awaited showdown. But labor balked and the President applied a more concentrated dose of The Treatment. "I am your President," he told the heads of the railway brotherhoods. "All I want is for you to give me a chance. Just give me a chance." Johnson read verbatim from a memorandum he had directed Heller to prepare that morning, detailing the economic impact of a strike—including the prediction that six million people would be adversely affected.

The President then separated the labor leaders from the management spokesmen, herding them into his own office. He pressed harder, telling the labor leaders that they *owed* him a chance. He turned to Charles Luna, head of the Brotherhood of Railway Trainmen, and a fellow Texan. "Charley," Johnson implored, "it's not one of those damn Yankees asking you." He appealed to the brotherhood leaders for both the future of collective bargaining and in the overriding national interest. As patriotic Americans, he said, they must agree to his wishes.

Meanwhile, the railroad presidents grumbled among themselves that the President of the United States ought not to beg labor leaders for favors. But this was Johnson's way, and once again he got what he wanted. The labor leaders agreed to a fifteen-day delay. Properly elated, Johnson took to television from the White House at 10:30 that night to tell the country that instead of a strike there would be negotiations.

That was only the beginning. Now began what must rank among the strangest labor negotiations in United States history. The negotiators for both sides, and two presidentially appointed mediators, met in the Executive Office Building next door to the White House, frequently and without warning interrupted by visits—and words of encouragement—from the President. On Friday, April 9, the first day of renewed bargaining, Johnson swept into the bargaining room at one point to acknowledge that both sides had hard decisions to make:

The hardest decision I ever had to make was in California four years ago when I lost the presidential nomination and had to decide whether to take the vice-presidential nomination. I decided to, because I felt it was necessary to a Democratic victory. I know what it's like to make a hard decision.

That was the pattern for most of the next two weeks. Johnson would pop into the talks and stand behind the negotiators, inspecting what each side was writing on their little pads of paper, doodles and all. On Sunday, April 19, with the new deadline of April 25 nearing and the talks still deadlocked, Johnson gave another pep talk. He told the union leaders they must find the courage to tell their members they couldn't have everything they wanted. He told the industry negotiators: "Don't let the almighty dollar stand in the way of a settlement."

But Johnson was doing more than delivering pep talks. Without a briefing paper or summary from his own mediators, he was carrying on private talks with individual members of the labor and management teams, looking for small disagreements within each side that could be exploited for a settlement. The technique was the very one that Johnson had brought to such high polish in the Senate as Majority Leader. The swift, sure way in which Johnson began to push the opposing sides closer together startled and delighted administration officials who had never seen Johnson in action. At the same time, Johnson worked overtime to stamp out rumors that he would, as Kennedy did in 1963, ask Congress to authorize compulsory arbitration if the talks failed. Once both sides were certain that the alternative to settlement was not a strike but compulsory arbitration, they would simply quit bargaining.

At around three in the morning on Wednesday, April 22, after a hard night of negotiations, the labor representatives asked Johnson's mediators to draft a proposal. It was finally and most unenthusiastically approved by the union negotiators, subject to ratifications by at least five brotherhoods. But railroad management was far from satisfied, particularly because it did not resolve their demand for longer runs for some train crews.

Early that morning after a few hours of sleep, Wolfe went to the White House to see the President. Excusing himself from his weekly breakfast meeting with the legislative leaders in the private dining room, Johnson stepped into a room nearby to confer with the industry negotiator and Wirtz. Wolfe protested that the settlement proposal did not mention the vital question of longer runs for train crews. Wirtz assured him that the omission did not mean the issue was being ignored, but Wolfe wanted more than assurances.

He brought up two matters dear to the hearts of the railroad industry but unrelated to the work-rules controversy with labor. Wolfe expressed concern that a bill granting the railroad industry greater freedom to set rates was stalled in the House Rules Committee, and then complained that the Internal Revenue Service had refused to allow depreciation for tunnel and bridge construction at an annual savings to the industry of from twenty-five million to thirty million dollars. Johnson knew a horse trade when he saw it. He quickly promised all-out administration support for the rate bill and prompt Treasury consideration of the tax question. *

But despite Johnson's offer to help on these bread-and-butter matters, the rail presidents still felt Wolfe had given away too much in the draft statement. Over coffee in the White House Oval Office that afternoon, rail executives told Johnson they meant no disrespect or disloyalty to the President of the United States, but they were genuinely concerned by the failure of the draft proposal to mention longer runs.

Once again Johnson applied The Treatment, but this time in a fashion markedly more restrained than his April 9 pleadings with the union chiefs to postpone the strike. Johnson had been upset by an account in the April 17 issue of *Time* quoting an anonymous railroad president as saying that Johnson "was practically on his knees" in his supplications to the union leaders and adding that "the President really demeaned himself with his begging and pleading." The word "demeaned" upset the President. On the afternoon of Wednesday, April 22, he coolly informed the rail heads that their refusal to accept the compromise would constitute no disloyalty or disrespect. Nor, the President added pointedly, would there be any "demeaning" of the office so long as he was President. Still, he *did* want a settlement and promised the railroad men that the negotiations for the issue missing from the draft statement—longer runs for the same crew—would definitely be pressed.

Then, jubilation! Half an hour after his meeting with the rail presidents, Johnson was informed by Wolfe that the industry agreed to the compromise. In a triumphant mood, Johnson wanted to announce the good news immediately to the nation. Informed that it would take an hour for television cameras to be set up in the White House, he packed Wolfe and Davidson into the presidential limousine and drove through rush-hour traffic to station WTOP two miles up Wisconsin Avenue to make the announcement to the country. In words that no speech writer could have prepared for him, Johnson heaped praise on both rail management and rail labor in just the way he used to praise the Senate after a particularly bitter debate concluded with passage of a bill. The President told the country:

* President Johnson's sympathy did not, however, result in any help for the railroads. The rate bill was killed by an 8 to 7 House Rules Committee vote on April 28, six days after the threat of a rail strike was averted. As for depreciation of bridges and tunnels, the Internal Revenue Service had not approved it as this book went to press.

This agreement is American business and American labor operating at its [sic] very best at the highest levels of public responsibility. This is the face of American industrial democracy that we can proudly show to the entire world, that free enterprise, free collective bargaining, really works in this country, and that the needs and demands of the people's interest are understood and those needs and those demands come first. For, says the Old Testament, "he that keepeth understanding shall find good."

Lyndon Johnson had won a signal victory that went far beyond settlement of the railroad dispute and, more significant, solved a far more basic problem.

Throughout the two long weeks of rail negotiations in the Executive Office Building, President Johnson repeatedly emphasized the need to protect the integrity of collective bargaining. Yet, this was presidential high-style intervention as surely as Kennedy's forcing arbitration of the rail labor dispute in 1963, its saving grace being the final settlement of the dispute rather than compulsory arbitration ordered by Congress. Thus, a good case could have been made, and, indeed, was made by labor experts, that the cause of collective bargaining would have been better served had Johnson left the railroads and the brotherhoods to their own ends, even if a strike resulted. If that were so, and if Johnson's own labor experts were correct in their estimate that a strike would have been brief, then the President's intervention, brilliant and impressive though it was, was a questionable step.

But the deeper meaning of the rail intervention had less to do with the future of collective bargaining than with the Johnson presidency itself. It was Johnson's presidential takeoff. Magically, the depressing self-analysis and image-preoccupation of transition days were for the time being no longer relevant. By one positive act, Johnson had established a distinctive image for his administration. The intervention in the rail dispute was singularly fitted to Johnson's personal style: the absence of ideological considerations; the uniting of seemingly irreconcilable elements; the horse-trading and bargaining; the appeal to diverse elements of society to lay aside their differences for the sake of the country; the underlying scent of consensus; the appeal to patriotism. The fact that he had triumphed immeasurably bolstered his confidence, further changing the tone of his presidency, which now became both resilient and resonant.

Most important, perhaps, was the timing of the rail intervention. Thrust upon the President at precisely the moment the White House was steeped in gloom, it solved the disagreement between the policy of Exposure and the policy of Containment. Buoyed and exhilarated by his success in the rail dispute, Johnson followed the blueprint of the Exposure advocates. He showed the people what kind of a President they had, and it was Johnson at his most charming.

On April 10, the day after his intervention gained the fifteen-day delay in the rail dispute, the President was exuberant. Reporters waiting to see him in the Rose Garden were startled to hear a shout from the Truman Balcony overlooking the garden and South Lawn. "Hey, down there!" shouted Johnson. "Here's Carl Sandburg. Don't you want to ask some questions?" The octogenarian poet-historian was standing on the President's left in the bright spring sunshine with bearded Edward Steichen, the distinguished photographer, on his right.

Excited and beaming, Johnson joked about the Easter joyride that had been causing him so much anguish only a day earlier. "How about coming for another drive with us?" he yelled to Dorothy McCardle of the *Washington Post,* one of the four reporters on the notorious ride. After a few minutes of banter, Johnson raised his arms and said: "Well, back to the salt mines." He then burst into the rail negotiations with Sandburg and Steichen, introducing the labor and management representatives as "some of the toughest people in the world," with enough power to toss six million people out of work.

That was only a foretaste. The next day the President and Bill Moyers took a stroll before lunch down to the Southeast Gate of the White House where tourists were peering through the wrought-iron bars. "Would you like to take a walk with me?" Johnson asked. The answer was a shriek of delight, and Johnson ordered the gates opened. A hundred tourists swarmed about him. "All of you ugly men get up front and all of you pretty girls come back here with me," he shouted. Then they all took a memorable stroll around the South Lawn. Half an hour later, the President turned up in the receiving line for a party given by Luci Johnson for her classmates at the National Cathedral School. Still later, the President drove up Massachusetts Avenue to visit Felix Frankfurter, the retired and ailing Supreme Court Justice.

And on the next day, much to the distress of the Secret Service agents charged with his protection, Johnson walked across Pennsylvania Avenue from Blair House (where visiting King Hussein of Jordan was staying) to the White House and was quickly engulfed by handshaking tourists and passers-by. With all this meticulously reported by the press and television, Lyndon Johnson was putting himself on exhibit. What the people saw was not the stereotyped Texas wheeler-dealer, but an outgoing, compulsively gregarious, peripatetic President.

Another sign of renewed confidence came on April 16. Impressed by the advice of the Containment school of advisers in the White House, and heeding his own self-doubts, Johnson had avoided holding press conferences in the large and elegant auditorium of the new State Department Building over live television—the format used by John F. Kennedy to transform himself from a minority President into a popular national hero. Not only to avoid invidious comparisons with Kennedy, but also because of well-grounded doubts of his ability as a television performer, Johnson preferred limiting his press conferences to untelevised, informal sessions in his office with the relatively small circle of White House correspondents.* But on April 16, as part of the shift to Exposure, he held his first televised press conference in the State Department auditorium.

In his present state of self-confidence, Johnson was magnificent. He even made a little fun of himself. "I did not drive myself over here," he said solemnly. "But I did have to cancel an informal meeting with some tourists at the [White House] gate." † What followed was only one of five news conferences that Johnson held in a span of thirteen days in keeping with his new policy of exposing the Public Person.

The President's high sense of control and confidence was clearly visible on April 27 when he addressed the United States Chamber of Commerce, a business organization not known for cordial relations with Democratic Presidents, at Constitution Hall. An appreciative audience heard Johnson, fresh from his railroad victory, preach the doctrine of consensus, of all conflicting elements in the society working together. And again, he made a joke at his own expense. He told the businessmen: "Everybody is going to *walk* at the LBJ [Ranch] from now on, and I am going to do what Lady Bird tells me, and we are going to make everybody drink nothing but pure rain water or Pepsi-Cola."

---

* Truman had removed the press conference from the intimacy of the President's private office to the Old Indian Treaty Room of the Executive Office Building to accommodate more reporters. Eisenhower first permitted the President's remarks to be quoted directly and allowed cameramen to film his press conferences which, after editing, were shown over television. Kennedy completed the transformation by moving the press conference to the more spacious State Department auditorium and permitting live television. Johnson tried to turn the clock back to Truman but, apart from the White House regulars, the Washington press corps bitterly protested.

† However, once Johnson had shown the press corps and the nation he could conduct a Kennedy-style press conference and do a splendid job of it, he returned to the more intimate format and, as this book goes to press, has not held another press conference in the State Department auditorium.

Not only was the crisis over, but Johnson for the first time had presented an appealing Public Person to the American people. Thus, there seemed to be, in the spring of 1964, a possibility of genuine affection between the country and its President. The rail settlement had opened the door for Johnson to make the administration something more than a continuation of the New Frontier, an administration truly his own—the Great Society administration.

On March 15, 1964, in a televised interview marking the end of Lyndon Johnson's first hundred days as President, the President was asked if he had thought up a slogan to follow the New Deal, the Fair Deal, and the New Frontier. "I have had a lot of things to deal with the first hundred days," Johnson replied, "and I haven't thought of any slogan, but I suppose all of us want a Better Deal, don't we?"

The "Better Deal" slogan popped up in a few of the President's speeches after that, but it did not catch hold as a slogan. The absence of a slogan was symptomatic of Johnson's failure at that time to give a distinctive post-New Frontier profile to the administration. And until he did this, his full power as President would be incomplete.

Johnson's most important collaborator in finding both a slogan and an image was, ironically, not an old Johnson hand at all but a young man who epitomized the New Frontier. Precocious, impudent, brilliant, and iconoclastic, Richard Goodwin had taken his law degree at Harvard in 1958, clerked for Justice Felix Frankfurter, was an investigator in the House 1958–59 hearings on television quiz scandals, and wrote speeches in the 1960 campaign for Senator John F. Kennedy before emerging in 1961 as Latin American policy-maker, first at the White House and then at the State Department.*

But Goodwin was losing influence as Kennedy's Latin American policy started to grow more conservative in 1963. Exiled from the State Department and assigned to the Peace Corps, Goodwin was a bureaucratic meteor who seemed to have reached his apogee at the tender age of thirty-one. In late 1963, a rehabilitation plan for Goodwin vanished in the tragedy of Dallas. On November 23, 1963, President Kennedy was to have announced that Goodwin would be reassigned to the White House, not in his old role of foreign policy adviser but in the less exalted position of Special Assistant on the Arts. After the assassination, Goodwin wrote the new President a note relieving him of all obligation for the appointment.†

* See page 394.
† Roger Stevens, a Broadway angel and ex-real estate tycoon, was given the job.

But Bill Moyers had worked closely and well with Goodwin at the Peace Corps and, remembering his background in Latin American affairs, called on him to write the President's speech to Latin American diplomats on November 25, reaffirming the United States commitment to the Alliance for Progress. After that single chore, Goodwin disappeared from the transition scene and was swallowed up in the obscurity of the Peace Corps.

But one day late in January, he was at the White House while Shriver reported to the President on an overseas inspection trip he and Goodwin had just completed. By chance, Johnson caught sight of Goodwin in a White House corridor. The President, whose public prose at that stage was in desperate need of eloquence, whisked Goodwin into his office. Would he prepare a presidential statement on the Panama crisis? He did. The statement was delivered to the press on January 23, and the former *enfant terrible* of the New Frontier left the Peace Corps forever to take a coveted position as *sub rosa* speech writer for Lyndon Johnson. No announcement was made, and for weeks both Johnson and Goodwin denied he was writing presidential speeches.

Johnson was soon calling on him for more than speeches. In a monologue delivered in the White House swimming pool in March, with Moyers and Goodwin his audience, Johnson expressed his need for new ideas, for a new thrust, for some dramatic departure in government that would go beyond the Kennedy Administration. As a direct outgrowth of that and other conversations, Goodwin prepared a speech to be delivered by Johnson in presenting the first Eleanor Roosevelt Memorial Award to Judge Anna M. Kross of New York at the White House on March 4.

In his draft, Goodwin wrote of the challenge for America to resolve such problems as poverty that were hidden beneath middle-class prosperity and to move forward not just toward a rich and powerful society but to the "great society"—a phrase and a concept frequently discussed by social theoreticians of the past half century.* Jack Valenti, then serving as the President's principal speech writer, liked Goodwin's draft but not for that occasion. He preferred a speech about the role of women in modern life as more appropriate for the occasion of presenting the Eleanor Roosevelt Award.

The Goodwin draft was not delivered, but Johnson never forgot its key phrase. When the "better deal" failed to get a stirring response,

* To their great glee, conservative Republicans discovered that an English Fabian socialist named Graham Wallas wrote a book called *The Great Society* in 1914. This socialist doctrine, they contended, was the model for Johnson's slogan. It wasn't. Goodwin had not even read the book.

Johnson gradually began to weave the "great society" theme into his speeches, both prepared and extemporaneous. On March 17, to a delegation at the White House in connection with the Montana Territorial Centennial, he said: "We want to have the glorious kind of society." On April 21, in the White House Rose Garden, he asked a group of broadcasters and editors to "accept with me the responsibility of developing a greater society." On April 23, the night after settlement of the railway crisis, he told a Democratic fund-raising dinner in Chicago: "We have been called upon—are you listening?—to build a great society of the highest order, a society not just for today or tomorrow, but for three or four generations to come." During the next month, Johnson mentioned the "great society" in sixteen separate speeches and statements.

Lyndon Johnson had found his slogan, but it was not recognized as such until Goodwin wrote his May 22 speech at the University of Michigan graduation exercises. It began by saying:

> Your imagination, your initiative, and your indignation will determine whether we build a society where progress is the servant of our needs, or a society where old values and new visions are buried under unbridled growth. For in your time we have the opportunity to move not only toward the rich society and the powerful society, but upward to the Great Society.*
>
> The Great Society rests on abundance and liberty for all. It demands an end to poverty and racial injustice, to which we are totally committed in our time. But that is just the beginning.
>
> The Great Society is a place where every child can find knowledge to enrich his mind and to enlarge his talents. It is a place where leisure is a welcome chance to build and reflect, not a feared cause of boredom and restlessness. It is a place where the city of man serves not only the needs of the body and the demands of commerce but the desire for beauty and the hunger for community. . . .
>
> But most of all, the Great Society is not a safe harbor, a resting place, a final objective, a finished work. It is a challenge constantly renewed, beckoning us toward a destiny where the meaning of our lives matches the marvelous products of our labor.

The Great Society was more than Dick Goodwin's words said it was. Like the New Deal and the New Frontier, it was the badge of *this* particular President and *this* particular administration, of the uninhibited Johnsonian style, of the restless quest for new ways in which to

---

* The capitalization of "Great Society" in the advance texts of the Michigan speech distributed to the press left little room for doubt that Johnson was proclaiming a slogan.

use the presidential power, of the search for consensus, of government programs made by Johnson, as distinguished from those inherited from Kennedy. And of those programs, none was so much a symbol of the Great Society as the War on Poverty.

When Walter Heller saw the new President on Saturday night, November 23, 1963, he spoke favorably and earnestly of the poverty program in embryonic form at the moment of John F. Kennedy's death. Heller told Johnson of his last talk with President Kennedy, in which Kennedy had expressed hope that anti-poverty proposals could be incorporated in the 1964 legislative program. In view of that conversation, Heller continued, the Council of Economic Advisers had been working on poverty as an important part of the 1964 program and hopefully would continue to do so within budgetary restraints.

Actually, Kennedy felt he had as much or more than he could handle in the civil rights and tax bills before the 1964 election. He was bearish about confronting a rebellious Congress with a spanking new program that had undergone no gestation period. For that reason (as well as the need for budgetary restraint to create the proper atmosphere to cut taxes) it was generally thought inside the administration, prior to November 22, that the anti-poverty proposals would be included in the Kennedy program for 1964 but would not be pressed very hard. Rather, they were to become a major talking point in the 1964 campaign.

If Kennedy was that bearish about the new program, New Frontiersmen feared the worst from a President whose entire career, they believed, had been characterized by caution and restraint. With that background, Heller might have been a shade guilty of overstating to Johnson how hard Kennedy had planned to push the anti-poverty program in 1964. But Johnson's first response to Heller was surprisingly strong. He expressed both his interest in a poverty program and his sympathy for it. Taking advantage of the moment, Heller asked if he should push the project full speed ahead for the 1964 session of Congress. The answer from Johnson was yes.

But events a month later during Johnson's visit to the LBJ Ranch over the Christmas holidays bothered supporters of the poverty program. In conversations with Johnson, the Texas cattlemen who had come that day to the ranch to teach the Eastern professors the truth about beef prices and imports were critical of the whole poverty idea. Certainly they did not want a new government program to eliminate poverty, and they reminded Johnson that his country was a middle-class country. Johnson had also been hearing skeptical comments from some of the more conservative members of the administration. John McCone, the Republican businessman who now headed the Central Intelligence Agency, commented wryly that he had relations who were poor but that the best antidote for them probably was hard work, not a new government program.

And for his own part, Johnson seemed to be having second thoughts that Christmas week at the ranch about the commitment he made to Heller on November 23. He hounded Heller at mealtime, sitting on the porch, chasing after deer on the ranch in his Lincoln Continental: "How are you going to spend all this money?" Talking with friends, Johnson speculated about limiting the entire poverty program to nine months, after which state and local governments would pick up the burden as best they could. As a result of all this deflating talk, Budget Director Kermit Gordon left the LBJ Ranch to return to Washington deeply worried about the fate of the poverty program.

But Gordon and other administration officials were misinterpreting Johnson's characteristic probing, mulling, and incessant talking whenever he was about to embark on a major political voyage. In fact, Johnson even then was looking at the poverty program as potentially *his* program, quite distinct from the programs inherited from John F. Kennedy under the transition pledge of "Let Us Continue."

On paper, the poverty program had all the ingredients. It coincided with Johnson's visceral sympathy for the problems of the poor. Yet, as he envisioned it, the poverty program was scarcely revolutionary. It could be sold to the business community as a sensible step toward building the Great Society with abundance—including profits—for all. And the coincidental timing of a simultaneous tax cut would help.

Thus, the aura of skepticism at the LBJ Ranch that worried Heller and Gordon soon yielded to boundless enthusiasm for what Johnson was already proclaiming as his own creation. The President shrugged off the advice of his conservative rancher friends in Texas and told Congress in his State of the Union Address on January 8:

> This administration today, here and now, declares unconditional war on poverty in America. I urge this Congress and Americans to join with me in that effort.
> It will not be a short or easy struggle, no single weapon or strategy will suffice, but we shall not rest until that war is won.

Such well-meant but high-flown rhetoric continued through much of the year, exciting vast expectations of help among the poor—particularly the impoverished Negro in the slums of the big cities. But Johnson's War on Poverty was more a slogan, a concept, a laudable desire than a carefully structured plan of action.

Its formlessness assured a classic struggle within the Washington bureaucracy, the intensity of which was unwittingly heightened with the selection of Sargent Shriver as director of the Office of Economic Opportunity, the new agency of the poverty program. Moyers, Shriver's former deputy at the Peace Corps, had been urging a high post in the administration for Shriver, possibly Secretary of Health, Education and Welfare or the contemplated but never created post of Under Secretary of State for Inter-American Affairs. But Shriver, whose Peace Corps was by all odds the most successful new agency of the Kennedy Administration, seemed singularly fitted to head Johnson's first great undertaking of his own. Independently, both Heller and Gordon privately urged Johnson to give Shriver the job at least of organizing the poverty program. And so Shriver was named by Johnson February 1, with a rather vague commission of undetermined length. He was also to remain as director of the Peace Corps.

Shriver's shining asset as a public official was his inspirational talent, his ability to infuse subordinates with a high level of enthusiasm and to draw from them prodigious amounts of work. He was, however, considerably less skilled in the arts of administration and bureaucratic infighting, and these were precisely the talents most in demand in the War on Poverty.

The early planning of the poverty program was a babel of discord from the program-builders and advisers brought in to draft it. Michael Harrington, the eloquent socialist writer whose account of poverty amid plenty in *The Other America* had opened President Kennedy's eyes to the full extent of poverty in the United States, advocated radical changes in the economic system. Daniel P. (Pat) Moynihan, an articulate sociologist who was Assistant Secretary of Labor, advocated mass educational and vocational training for the one-third of the nation's youth who flunked the draft test because of educational deficiencies. James P. Sundquist, a veteran and a distinguished career civil servant who was Deputy Under Secretary of Agriculture, argued for special programs to save rural America from extinction. These and many others all came to the poverty program, and they left when their ideas were rejected or drastically reshaped.

One who apparently came to stay was Adam Yarmolinsky, an exceedingly able but abrasive and tough liberal intellectual who left his job as special assistant to Secretary of Defense McNamara to help Shriver draft the program. Working closely with McNamara, Yarmolinsky proposed that the poverty program take over abandoned

Army camps to educate semiliterate school dropouts. Enveloped by this plan was a three-year-old Department of Labor proposal for a Youth Conservation Corps patterned after the old Civilian Conservation Corps of New Deal days.

By early March, Shriver was the target of bureaucratic sniping from every quarter. Senator Hubert Humphrey, who was the chief congressional patron of the proposed Youth Conservation Corps, personally protested to the President over the theft of his dream by Shriver's poverty program. The day after Humphrey's protest, at the most tumultuous Cabinet meeting of Johnson's Administration, the Shriver-Yarmolinsky approach came under vicious fire from Wirtz of Labor, Freeman of Agriculture, and Anthony Celebrezze of Health, Education, and Welfare, all of whom charged that the program was acquiring an unhealthy military pallor. Wirtz and Celebrezze strongly objected to the creation of a separate federal poverty agency under Shriver's control, arguing that the program would be handled within existing departments—*their* departments.

The President played the peacemaker. Heeding the argument against too much emphasis on Army training camps, he told Shriver at the Cabinet meeting: "Sarge, we shouldn't give this too much of a military flavor." With that statement, Bob McNamara disappeared from the poverty program and the emphasis on Army camps was diminished. But Johnson was determined to have an independent agency run the program. "The best way to kill a new idea is to put it in an old-line agency," he commented one day. As for the Youth Conservation Corps, Humphrey's protests could not save it and it more or less became the Job Corps of the poverty program. On the other hand, the Neighborhood Youth Corps, which had been in the planning stage in the Labor Department, remained there under Wirtz' control, not Shriver's. The result, then, was the archetypal mishmash of a Washington compromise.

Through all these bureaucratic struggles the President seemed largely disinterested and dispassionate. Nor was he to take much of a personal hand in differences between Shriver and the established bureaucracy. He was, in other words, considerably less interested in the content of the program than in his determination to achieve a great national consensus to eradicate poverty. To Johnson, the means were less important than the end.

Government officials soon discovered how little interested Johnson really was in the differences between Shriver and Wirtz and how consumed he was by an evangelical mission to persuade prosperous America that the poor must be helped. By late April, the anti-poverty concept was the pivot of Johnson's Great Society. Having just completed a tour of the poverty-struck Appalachian area, Johnson preached a strong anti-poverty sermon to the hard-bitten businessmen of the United States Chamber of Commerce in Washington on April 27:

> I don't know how many of you live on the side of the track where you even see this [poverty]. I wish you could have gone with me and looked into their eyes and seen the faith and hope that they have in their country, when I traveled into Pittsburgh and saw the unemployed steelworkers, and into South Bend and saw the eighty-three hundred men all of whom lost their jobs Christmas Eve—auto workers—and into eastern Kentucky and West Virginia and saw the unemployed miners. One man with eleven children told me that he had four days' work last month at four dollars a day, not because he does not want work but because it is not there. . . .
>
> So I have gone into these schools and these slums and I have seen these insidious enemies of a stable economy and the ones that really promote recessions and inflation. I want to tell you that no segment of our society has a greater stake in these people than folks who are well enough, can afford to come to Washington, and belong to the United States Chamber of Commerce.

That speech was the start of an intensive campaign to lobby all economic segments of the nation on the *mission,* not the details, of the poverty program. It was no easy task. The very idea of a war on poverty was new. The program had no suitable growing period, no testing in the intellectual marketplace, as had the civil rights bill or the tax reduction bill. Furthermore, it was coming before a Congress that had never even debated the hard fact of poverty and it was to arrive there on the eve of the 1964 election when Republicans would not rejoice at the prospect of supporting the pet program of the Democratic candidate for President.

Yet, Johnson insisted that the poverty package be passed by Congress before the 1964 election, and for reasons that went well beyond the presidential election. Just as Johnson prematurely rushed the poverty program into being far faster than Kennedy would have, he now employed every technique of pressure to rush its passage, for this was *his* bill, not Jack Kennedy's. He needed it now, in the summer of 1964, to put the Great Society imprint on the administration and dramatize his consolidation of power.

Passage in the Senate was no problem, but a close vote loomed in the less pliable House in the first week of August. Republican Congressmen from Pennsylvania were incredulous when Stuart Saunders, the president of the Pennsylvania Railroad, personally telephoned them to solicit support for the poverty bill. President Johnson, of course, was the voice behind Saunders' voice. He had recruited a powerful, irresistible phalanx of industrialists, businessmen, and newspaper editors to telephone reluctant Congressmen and urge their votes for the poverty program. None of these amateur lobbyists had the vaguest idea of the highly debatable contents of the program, but Johnson had convinced them that something, *anything*, must be passed in this field.

The subordination of all else to passage of the bill was tragically underscored in a kangaroo court held that week in Speaker McCormack's office. Adam Yarmolinsky, a liberal with impeccably anti-Communist credentials, had been the victim for years of an absurd but vicious right-wing smear painting him as a subversive and a security risk. This outrageous smear had seeped into the consciousness of conservative Congressmen. Now, on Thursday, August 6, in the privacy of McCormack's office with Shriver present, conservative Democrats from North and South Carolina delivered an ultimatum: They would vote "no" on the crucial vote the next day unless they had absolute assurance that Yarmolinsky would be excluded from any part in administering the new program.

Yarmolinsky, who was the administrative dynamo behind Shriver, was slated to be Deputy Director of the new Office of Economic Opportunity. But Shriver tried to put off the head-hunting Southern Congressmen by saying that even his own role in the new agency was uncertain and that only the President himself could decide whether and to what position Yarmolinsky might be named. The Congressmen would not accept that. They insisted that a call be placed to Johnson. Shriver called the White House. He returned from the telephone to report: "The President has no objection to my saying that if I were appointed I would not recommend Yarmolinsky." Thus, an additional eight votes were secured—but at unpardonable cost to Yarmolinsky's reputation.[*]

All the while, Johnson himself was furiously lobbying his friends in the House. He did not hesitate to call Representative Joe Kilgore of Texas, who still ached from having been crowded out of a run for the Senate earlier that year by Johnson. Johnson promised Kilgore: If you vote for the poverty program, I will repay you three times over. Kilgore, about to retire from public life, decided to support a friend for old-time's sake and vote for the bill.

[*] Yarmolinsky returned for some months as an aide to McNamara in the Pentagon, where, as before, he had complete access to all the nation's military secrets.

The calls Johnson had promoted via the industrialists helped pick up twenty Republican votes. The critical roll call on Friday, August 7, was 228 to 190 for the bill. The eight votes from the Carolinas were superfluous. The sacrifice of Adam Yarmolinsky was unnecessary.

On the next day, Saturday, August 8, the Yarmolinsky affair was raised at a presidential press conference by Edward T. Folliard, White House correspondent for the *Washington Post*, as follows:

Q. Mr. President, I want to ask a question about Adam Yarmolinsky, if I pronounce it correctly. He had been with the Department of Defense.

The President: He still is.

Q. I thought he had been working . . . on the poverty bill.

The President: No, your thoughts are wrong, Eddie. He is still with the Department of Defense.

Q. I was also asked to ask you, sir, if he was going back to the Pentagon, but you say he is still there.

The President: He never left.

An annoyed Johnson was once again bothered by the Yarmolinsky affair on August 15 during a press conference in the White House Rose Garden after two newspaper columns appeared recounting the whole sordid business.* Johnson asserted:

> Mr. Yarmolinsky is employed by the Defense Department. . . . No one, to repeat, to emphasize, no one at any time, any place, anywhere suggested to me anyone for any of these places [in the anti-poverty program]. The first information that I had that Mr. Yarmolinsky was, in effect, appointed to one of these places that did not exist was the columnist rumor that you talked about. . . . We [do not] plan to make any assignment because some columnists think we ought to.

Yarmolinsky was only one of many sacrifices that Lyndon Johnson was willing to make to secure the first big bill of the Great Society. The package had been put together too quickly to have much coherence. The excruciating problems of how the poor could best and most systematically be lifted from the rut of poverty were glossed over in the mad rush to put a program on paper and hurry it through Congress. The high priority on quick congressional approval subverted intelligent debate in Congress, which might have improved the program. But even more significantly, the President seemed willing to mortgage the future by planting hopes and expectations among the poor of such magnitude that they could not be met.

Yet, these sacrifices did produce results of considerable value. The

* By the authors. Published August 11 and 12, 1964.

scope of the poverty program passed by Congress exceeded any level that could have been adopted in 1964 under Kennedy. Public awareness of poverty in the United States, virtually nonexistent a year earlier, was now pervasive. But most important, Johnson had made the War on Poverty part of the national consensus. It was not only bad politics but quite immoral to question the propriety of the government's attack on poverty.

And finally, the poverty program indelibly stamped the imprint of Johnson's Great Society on the government. The incredibly complex details of the program could wait until after the election.

Chapter XX

★★★★★★★★★★

PICKING A
VICE-PRESIDENT

There is only one bitter, inescapable appreciation of American politics which the two men—Kennedy and Johnson—share: the knowledge that Lyndon Johnson was never able before 1964 to become President on his own . . . the Kennedys opened power to him.

—Theodore White in *The Making of the President 1964*

What came soon to be known in the Johnson White House as The Bobby Problem commanded more attention and consumed more energy and raw emotion than any other single concern of state that the new President confronted after Dallas. It *was* a matter of state, transcending the old and deepening conflict of personality between Lyndon B. Johnson and Robert F. Kennedy. In his heart Johnson regarded Bobby Kennedy as the one possible obstacle to his complete take-over of the Democratic party, and unless he could assume control of the party in his own right and on his own terms, he could not feel secure in exercising the full powers of the presidency.

Johnson made no secret of his determination to cut down Bobby Kennedy. The forlornness that had always accompanied his efforts to compete with John F. Kennedy for the affection of the American people now transferred itself to Robert Kennedy.* Bobby stirred more controversy and engendered less affection than did his older brother, and ran well behind the new President in simplistic Gallup Poll competition. But Bobby was the symbol now of the emotion and sentimentality that swept the country after Dallas. He was custodian of the Kennedy dream, a dream now embedded in the Democratic party. Understandably, Johnson did not relish the prospect of becoming preserver of that dream between the presidencies of John and Robert Kennedy. He was dreaming Johnson dreams, and those dreams

* See page 294.

required a distinctively Johnson Administration start in 1965, not a Johnson-Kennedy Administration.

The President spent hour after hour discussing The Bobby Problem in the early months of 1964. He told intimates he had devoted three years' service to John Kennedy and the time now had come for total independence from the Kennedys. He spoke of the "great palace of light" that President Kennedy had made of the White House, casting its reflection over the world—a phenomenon of which Lyndon Johnson had been so small a part. If he took Bobby Kennedy on the presidential ticket with him, he continued, his presidency would become a transitory episode between two Kennedys. He rejected that out of hand. He wanted a Great Society Administration, a Johnson Administration, that irrevocably excluded Bobby Kennedy.

Even to Kennedy's own political allies, President Johnson poignantly revealed this yearning for independence. "I don't want to get elected because of the Kennedys," he told a member of the Irish Mafia in the spring of 1964. "I want to get elected on my own. That's a perfectly normal feeling, isn't it?"

But to Johnson himself, there seemed grave danger that his "perfectly normal feeling" might be frustrated. If Bobby Kennedy was the custodian of the Kennedy dream, the President worried, his exclusion from the ticket might cost Johnson support where he needed it most: with organized labor, with the Negroes, and other minority voting blocs; with the Eastern intellectuals; with the Catholics. The Democratic National Convention would be dominated by these forces, the very forces who opposed Johnson at Los Angeles in 1960. Could Johnson arbitrarily exclude Bobby Kennedy without provoking a revolt fueled by the emotions that welled up from Dallas?

The answer was: of course he could. But Johnson was uncertain. Johnson conjured up one picture after another of what might happen to him if, as he thought, he overplayed his hand in excluding Kennedy from the ticket. The Bobby Problem became an obsession, and all the Texas-based politicians who now surrounded him in Washington and who, like Johnson himself, had not learned how complete the power of the presidency really was, played on that obsession and magnified it. Nor was Johnson comforted by increasing talk early in 1964 on the Washington cocktail circuit and in the press that in the end he would have to put Kennedy on the ticket or risk defeat at Republican hands in November.

This concern was typified by an incident at the Gridiron Club's annual dinner on April 25, 1964, in Washington. Walter Jenkins spotted Larry O'Brien. Taking O'Brien off to a corner, Jenkins gravely argued that President Johnson should have total freedom to select his own running mate. O'Brien gravely listened, but he was astonished at Jenkins' nervousness. O'Brien knew that the President could pick his second man by the merest flick of his finger. But Johnson and his Texas politicians hadn't learned that rule of American politics.

Lacking this confidence in the political power of the President, Johnson's agonizing search for an answer to The Bobby Problem led to a series of astonishing political maneuvers, all of them derived from Johnson's insecurity and apprehension about a Kennedy second front forming within the Democratic party.

There was one small kernel of reality in the shadows of the President's fears. If Kennedy had quit as Attorney General when Johnson moved into the White House and taken the cream of the New Frontier with him, Johnson could have been in deep trouble. But this was a highly unlikely eventuality. Any such walkout not only would have split the Democratic party but also would have ended Kennedy's political career, because Johnson would have held all the cards, from the ace of presidential power to the trump of moral position.

The first of Johnson's series of maneuvers to keep Bobby Kennedy off the ticket with a minimum of damage to himself and his party came within two weeks of the assassination. Presidential intimates—and the President himself—began quietly to plug Sargent Shriver for second place on the ticket.

Shriver had become friendly with Johnson during his vice-presidency through Bill Moyers, Shriver's deputy at the Peace Corps until the assassination. As a Kennedy in-law, he would strengthen the ticket, without confronting Johnson with the emotional trauma of Bobby Kennedy. His selection would foreclose a Kennedy countermove, Johnson reasoned, because he was of the Kennedys himself. He was a Catholic from the Midwest. He was young, vigorous, good-looking, and worked well with Johnson.

Yet the liabilities outweighed these assets, and the first of these was the very fact that Shriver *was* of the Kennedy family. If a Kennedy was going to be picked for vice-presidential candidate, the Kennedys would insist it be Bobby. Much as President Johnson would like to have split this powerful, closely knit family and thereby weakened it as a political force within the Democratic party, picking Shriver was just too obvious—and, instinctively, Johnson sensed it from the start. A lesser defect was the fact that Shriver had never run for political office and had no standing with the powerful Democratic machine of

Mayor Richard Daley of Chicago, Shriver's home. Daley took pains to let the White House know that Shriver was definitely not his first choice, his second, or even this third.

Assume, however, that the Kennedy family and Daley had approved and supported Shriver. Would Johnson then have selected him? Probably not. For essentially Shriver was an escape hatch—a "Kennedy" but not Bobby. Even a Kennedy in-law on the ticket was a concession to the Kennedys that Johnson wanted to avoid. The politicians would have seen in Shriver's selection an indication that Johnson was uneasy in his new power, worried about his election, and convinced that he needed Kennedy help. When, after his first few months in the White House, Johnson determined that no Kennedy—not even a Kennedy in-law—was vital for the ticket, Shriver's chances ended.

With Shriver excluded from Johnson's secret plans, the President turned with far more seriousness to Secretary of Defense Robert Strange McNamara. At face value, Bob McNamara for Vice-President on the Democratic ticket strained credulity. McNamara had consistently voted Republican until 1960 and still had not joined the Democratic party; he had been president of the Ford Motor Company, an industrial enterprise of great economic power whose management always had been associated with the Republican party; he had never run for office or taken the slightest interest in elective politics; his blunt, terse manner was the antithesis of political amiability. Here then was a vice-presidential prospect to quicken the pulse of one who, like Lyndon Johnson, gloried in springing sudden surprises and confounding the prophets.

But Johnson's interest in McNamara as his running mate went beyond shock value. Although they disagreed on occasion during Johnson's vice-presidency, Johnson deeply respected the management expert who had for the first time brought the Pentagon under full civilian control. Returning from the first meeting of the Kennedy Cabinet, Vice-President Johnson told friends "that fellow with the Staycomb" (a reference to McNamara's slicked-down black hair) was Kennedy's smartest Cabinet member. Now, in the early weeks of Johnson's presidency, the respect had deepened. Johnson admired the manner in which McNamara controlled his vast defense budget himself, keeping in his own fingers all the different threads of management and policy. He admired his candor and his courage in making decisions repellent to Capitol Hill.

Johnson thought seriously not only of putting McNamara on the ticket but of giving him unprecedented operational power within the federal government, roughly akin to the authority exercised by an executive vice-president in a large corporation. The President pondered the large vision of Vice-President McNamara reorganizing the entire executive branch and applying his managerial genius to the staggering problems of population, the rising federal budget, and the accelerating pace of federal involvement with state, city, and local governments.

Offsetting his political inexperience were solid advantages. McNamara had never been caught up in the civil rights battles, and would cost Johnson nothing in the South. Furthermore, with a former Republican industrialist as his running mate, Johnson's chance of capturing Republican-oriented big businessmen would be enhanced. Finally, though this was not at all a paramount reason for Johnson's interest in McNamara, he also might help solve The Bobby Problem. McNamara was Kennedy's closest friend in the Cabinet. Thus, a Kennedy counterattack against a Johnson-McNamara ticket was unlikely.

Johnson discussed McNamara privately with Democratic politicians. With McNamara himself, he went further than discussion. In feeling him out, Johnson all but offered him second place on the ticket.

The reaction among the party leaders was indignantly, though predictably, negative. They made it clear to Johnson that although they couldn't stop him from selecting McNamara, they wouldn't lift a finger to help sell him to the party. That would be Johnson's job. But the prospect of a lifetime Republican with unknown political ideology suddenly elevated to the second highest position in the Democratic party and becoming heir apparent to the presidency itself filled these politicians with alarm. The President was informed that if he chose McNamara, he was telling the country that the Democratic party did not have a single member eligible for the vice-presidency. Furthermore, they added, McNamara, as a lifelong Republican, would only supplement rather than complement Johnson. His strength with business duplicated the President's. His weakness with labor, minority groups and big-city party leaders was precisely Johnson's weakness— or so it seemed in early 1964.

McNamara's own reaction to the President's private overtures was far less predictable but just as negative. He gently informed the President that he was not available. The overriding reason was his intimacy with Bobby Kennedy. McNamara was not going to help the President solve The Bobby Problem.

When the period of official mourning for John F. Kennedy had ended, Robert F. Kennedy met with some of his brother's trusted political lieutenants to appraise the political future. They emphasized the difficulties inherent in "running" for Vice-President. Difficult as it was, they told him, an effort could be made to encourage vice-presidential support from the hard-core Kennedy organization across the country. But if any such thing as a serious campaign was to be mounted, it would have to start quickly. Bobby Kennedy was non-committal. He had never shared Jack Kennedy's zest for party politics and party politicians. Now, shaken by grief, he had no taste for political combat. Subsequently, neither Bobby nor his brother's old aides ever took personal command of any Kennedy-for-Vice-President movement anywhere in the country. Efforts on his behalf, accordingly, took on an amateurish, haphazard quality not remotely comparable to the Kennedy-for-President pre-convention operations of 1960. The New Hampshire presidential primary election on March 10 was the beginning.

Shortly before the New Hampshire election, Robert B. Shaine, a Democratic ward leader and public relations man in Manchester, New Hampshire, announced that he was organizing a write-in campaign for Kennedy for the vice-presidential nomination. The campaign was presumptuous for two reasons: first, any party underling who tries to second-guess the party leader—the President in this case —or force his hand is playing with political dynamite; second, the campaign was undertaken without Kennedy's consent and without the help of the formidable political power in the state that Kennedy had at his disposal. In fact, Shaine was not part of the state's Kennedy organization set up in 1960. Nevertheless, news of the Kennedy write-in effort had electric repercussions in the White House.

The President and his political advisers were absolutely certain that Kennedy was stage-managing the New Hampshire write-in and were understandably concerned. Nobody was formally entered in the Democratic primary, either for President or Vice-President. In the absence of a presidential write-in campaign for Johnson, the Kennedy write-in for Vice-President would dominate the March 11 headlines across the country and might trigger a grass roots movement to put Kennedy on the ticket.

Cliff Carter, the President's political handyman, placed a telephone call to Hugh Bownes, the Democratic National Committeeman from New Hampshire. There quickly followed a statement by Bownes asserting that Johnson—"and he alone"—had the right to pick a running mate. Accordingly, said Bownes, New Hampshire Democrats should not write in Kennedy's name. But it was too late to stop what Shaine had started.

Within days, the Democratic Governor of New Hampshire, John

King, joined the write-in campaign but simultaneously called on all New Hampshire Democrats to show their feelings about the President by writing "Lyndon Johnson" on the presidential line. As it turned out, Johnson got 29,635 write-ins for President, almost 4,000 more than Kennedy received for Vice-President, but the episode both angered and bothered the President.

Publicly, Kennedy deplored the New Hampshire write-in. The Justice Department issued a statement saying the Attorney General felt the choice of a running mate "should be made by the Democratic convention in August, guided by the wishes of President Johnson." Privately, he told friends that if he really wanted to organize a campaign for Vice-President, it certainly would be a great deal more effective and professional than the slapdash New Hampshire effort. But by then, Kennedy genuinely believed that the choice at Atlantic City would be Johnson's alone.

There is no question that Bobby Kennedy wanted to be asked by Johnson to go on the ticket. Although he said privately that he would accept only if the President agreed to specific conditions, outlining precisely what his duties would be, it is virtually certain that if he had been asked by Johnson, he would have accepted. But Kennedy knew that no write-in campaign or other clumsy power play would put him on the ticket. It was essential, then, that he keep at least a veneer of cordial relations with Johnson.

That was not difficult in early 1964, for policy disagreements that were to break out between them came much later. Kennedy truly regarded Johnson's first months in office as a period of thorough accomplishment. Johnson was working closely with him on the civil rights front, never once turning down a suggestion from the Attorney General on that subject. Kennedy said publicly on March 12 that he had the "highest regard" for the President. "Our relations are friendly," he said. "He has always been kind to me, to my family, and to Mrs. [John F.] Kennedy, both as Vice-President and since then."

But those words scarcely eased the concern in the Johnson camp, especially when an abortive Draft Kennedy movement sprang up in Wisconsin immediately after New Hampshire.* Johnson felt the Kennedys closing in on him. When an old political friend from Texas visited the White House, Johnson told him: "If they try to push Bobby

---

* The amateurish quality of the efforts in Kennedy's behalf is shown by the effort of the Wisconsin Draft Kennedy group to conduct a write-in campaign for him in the Wisconsin presidential primary on April 7 even though Wisconsin law permitted no such write-in. The leaders of John F. Kennedy's successful Wisconsin primary campaign in 1960 got no green light from Robert Kennedy in 1964 and did not join the Draft Kennedy group.

Kennedy down my throat for Vice-President, I'll tell them to nominate him for the *presidency* and leave me out of it." The hyperbole showed how unrealistic—even naïve—was Kennedy's hope that he would be asked to go on the ticket.

The President decided drastic action was needed. It took the form of an unprecedented pressure play that not even Franklin Roosevelt at the height of his power had contemplated.* In mid-April, one month after the New Hampshire primary, former Senator Scott Lucas of Illinois, who found himself clothed in new political power by virtue of Johnson's accession to the presidency, persuaded all nine county Democratic chairmen in his downstate Illinois congressional district to sign a pledge. The pledge was the essence of simplicity:

> Be it . . . resolved that President Lyndon B. Johnson, when nominated for President on the Democratic ticket, shall have the free choice of selecting his running mate as Vice-President.

Lucas did not discuss this resolution with the President himself, but the President knew about it through Cliff Carter, who had discussed the idea with Lucas. Carter saw to it that the resolution was quickly sent around the country, *sub rosa,* to key Johnson politicians who, it was hoped, would have it adopted by *all* delegations to the National Convention at Atlantic City. Thus, during the first week in May it was taken up and passed, despite an undercurrent of complaint against presidential dictation, at the Midwest Democratic Conference in Des Moines, Iowa.

On May 1, on a trip to Atlantic City to discuss National Convention arrangements with New Jersey's Democratic leaders, Carter carried a copy of the Lucas Resolution in his pocket. At lunch he pulled it out, showed it to Governor Richard Hughes, and pointedly suggested that perhaps the New Jersey delegation would like to subscribe to it, too. The reaction was unpleasant. State Democratic Chairman Thorn Lord protested. Other leaders in the New Jersey delegation said they wouldn't touch it. To give the President a blank check in advance of the convention would demean the whole selection process, even if, as everyone acknowledged, the delegates would vote for the President's choice in the end anyway. In Rhode Island, where one final effort was made to have the delegation pass the resolution, the New Jersey experience was repeated. The Rhode Island delegation would have nothing to do with it.

So that was the inglorious end of another of Johnson's maneuvers to

---

* In fact, Roosevelt encountered severe opposition to his choice for Vice-President from two separate Democratic conventions, when he selected Henry A. Wallace in 1940 and when he picked Harry Truman in 1944.

solve The Bobby Problem. Clearly, some other way—a cleaner, less ponderous way—must be found to eliminate Robert F. Kennedy.

Once Shriver and McNamara had been ruled out, Johnson began to pay increasing attention to his old friend and liberal lieutenant, Senator Hubert Horatio Humphrey. At his regular Tuesday morning meetings with the Democratic congressional leaders, Johnson frequently praised Humphrey for a speech reported in the newspaper that morning, or the disclosure of a poll that showed Humphrey with support for Vice-President. There was not all that much joy for Humphrey to be found in the polls. Although he was supported heavily for Vice-President in polls of the county leaders (who might well have been anticipating the President's own decision), the more important public-opinion surveys showed Kennedy ahead of Humphrey in every instance. Yet, at the Tuesday morning meetings, Johnson would find one element in a new poll which showed strength for Humphrey and praise Humphrey for that. It became clear to the congressional leaders that Johnson was encouraging Humphrey to show his stuff. They made a mental note of it. All of Washington made a mental note when on March 8, seconds after Humphrey finished a "Meet the Press" interview, the President telephoned him at the studio and congratulated both him and his wife, Muriel. The telephone call was immediately made known and news of it was published.

Starting in late January, Johnson privately encouraged Humphrey to take confidential soundings around the nation and discover how much support he might have for Vice-President—and shore up his weak spots. The message was delivered by the President's old friend and Humphrey's 1960 campaign manager, James Rowe.

Humphrey was quick to react. In one typical period during February, he campaigned, without any announcement, for three days in New York City, one day in New Jersey, four days in California, and one day each in Oregon and Florida—all in a space of some three weeks. In these and other travels, Humphrey was put in contact with elements who distrusted him most: mainly the South and big business. For what Johnson wanted was evidence that if he chose Humphrey, he would not damage the ticket in the South, where the Senator's identification with civil rights was strong and pungent, or with the business community, which regarded Humphrey as a radical. Humphrey's successful missionary work convinced the President that if he *did* end up taking Humphrey, support from the South and business would not be much reduced.

By spring, Hubert Humphrey was clearly the front-runner in the competition for Vice-President. But this competition would be settled by the vote of one man only. It would never be fully settled until that one man firmly made up his mind. Before Lyndon Johnson would get down to that decision, there remained the unfinished task of disposing of Bobby Kennedy.

John Kenneth Galbraith had resigned as Ambassador to India and, since his part in drafting Johnson's first speech to Congress on November 27, 1963, had become a frequent visitor to the White House and adviser to the President. On July 21, 1964, the eve of his departure for a lengthy trip to Europe, Galbraith is known to have written President Johnson along the following lines: recalling a conversation he had with Johnson several days earlier on the subject of the vice-presidency, he praised Bobby Kennedy as a calm, competent person of great ability. The Kennedys, wrote Galbraith, had made one special contribution to the country: they had involved the new generation in politics on the grand scale, just as Franklin Roosevelt had done in those days when Galbraith had first met Johnson in Washington.[*] The enthusiasm of youth, wrote Galbraith, is a vital campaign asset. Moreover, youth and the involvement of youth would be even more important to the Johnson Administration in the forthcoming four-year period. In fact, concluded Galbraith, whether youth were enthusiastic for the Johnson ticket or disappointed in it could determine the result of the election.

In his letter to the President, Galbraith was lobbying for Bobby Kennedy, and Galbraith had one of those eloquent liberal voices that, if sounded out loud, could attract much attention and make much trouble for Lyndon Johnson. Here it was, some five weeks before the Atlantic City convention. The Bobby Problem remained unsolved, and one of the most skilled publicists in the Democratic party was writing a letter as if there really were a possibility that Johnson would give second place on the ticket to Kennedy.

Such continued persistence by Kennedy men made it clear to Johnson that the last feeble beating of Bobby-for-Vice-President hopes could not be permitted to continue into the National Convention itself, when the confusion and grief for John Kennedy among the delegates might somehow produce a climate of revolt at Atlantic City.

Thus, during the week of July 27, one week after receiving Galbraith's letter and four weeks before the convention opened, Johnson quietly moved to prevent an emotionally supercharged atmosphere from developing at the big Convention Hall on the boardwalk.

[*] See page 9.

The Arrangements Committee for the convention had scheduled an opening day documentary film in memory of John F. Kennedy. It would, no doubt, be a deeply moving, tearful review for the three thousand delegates and alternates and would be carried across the country over television. Fearful it might start a vice-presidential bandwagon for Bobby Kennedy, Johnson ordered the memorial film postponed from the first to the last day of the convention—the night *after* the candidate for Vice-President had been nominated. Then, all the emotion in the world would avail for nothing.

But changing the date of a movie by no means removed The Bobby Problem. For weeks, the President had quietly discussed various alternatives for removing Kennedy from all consideration for the vice-presidential nomination. Now he was ready to act. The best of all possible worlds from Johnson's point of view would have been for Kennedy to voluntarily disqualify himself from vice-presidential consideration, but that plainly was not going to happen. Johnson, still insecure in wielding the full political power of the presidency, did not want to risk alienating the Kennedy wing of the party by ruling out Bobby Kennedy in a simple statement. Thus it was that Johnson in secret consultation with his triumvirate of senior political advisers—Abe Fortas, Clark Clifford, and James Rowe—hit upon the final solution to The Bobby Problem.

On Monday, July 27, the President telephoned the Attorney General and arranged for a meeting at the White House on Wednesday, July 29.

When Bobby Kennedy walked into the President's Oval Office at 1 P.M. on Wednesday, Johnson came at once to the point. Kennedy, said the President, would probably run the country on his own someday but Johnson wanted him to know that he did not plan to put him on the ticket in 1964. The reason, Johnson said, was that he had decided Kennedy was not the Democrat who as Vice-President could contribute the most to the party, to the country, or to the President. Johnson offered Kennedy any foreign diplomatic post he wanted, and any Cabinet post, if and when incumbent Cabinet members resigned.

Kennedy accepted this verdict quietly and told Johnson he would do everything he could to help in the election. Johnson then asked him to become the campaign manager, as he had done for his brother.

Kennedy replied he would have to resign as Attorney General to do that, and he wouldn't resign unless Johnson named Nicholas Katzenbach, then Deputy Attorney General, to succeed him.*

---

* Kennedy did resign as Attorney General on September 3, 1964, to run for the Senate in New York. After five months of soul-searching, Johnson finally named Katzenbach to take his place.

Kennedy now had been informed, but the larger problem—chewed over in such great detail with the Fortas-Clifford-Rowe triumvirate—of informing the world remained for Johnson. At that Wednesday afternoon confrontation with Kennedy in the White House, there was some discussion of how the President's decision would be announced, but nothing was decided. Johnson still hoped to solve The Bobby Problem in the most expeditious way: a voluntary withdrawal by Kennedy himself.

After the Wednesday meeting, he sought the help of Kenny O'Donnell to urge Kennedy to make such a statement. But O'Donnell, in an anomalous position through all of 1964 as presidential assistant with far closer ties to the Attorney General than to the President, declined. He told Johnson that Kennedy felt it was the President's responsibility to make whatever announcement he wanted, not Kennedy's. The President next enlisted his chief National Security aide, McGeorge Bundy, a nominal Republican who had never been ordered to engage in party politics before. On behalf of the President, Bundy asked Kennedy to announce he was not a candidate. Kennedy was both hurt and angry by Bundy's intervention and refused.

With Kennedy refusing to jump overboard, Johnson now moved to the alternative strategy he had devised with Fortas-Clifford-Rowe to push Bobby over with a minimum political risk. On Thursday evening, July 30, the President unexpectedly went before television cameras at the White House and read an announcement without precedent in American history: "I have reached the conclusion that it would be inadvisable for me to recommend to the convention any member of my Cabinet or any of those who meet regularly with the Cabinet." *

Politicians who had tuned in on the President could scarcely believe their own ears. In shooting down Bobby Kennedy, the President had performed a mass execution of his entire Cabinet as well as two vice-presidential dark horses "who meet regularly with the Cabinet," Adlai Stevenson and Sargent Shriver.

All of Washington guffawed at the clumsiness and transparency of the ploy. Yet, it was not without political logic. A case could be made that the Cabinet caper did muffle the blow against the Kennedys and thereby minimized the reaction of Kennedy forces in the party. Al-

---

* Humphrey had not been informed of the Cabinet's wholesale elimination in advance, did not tune in his television set to watch the President on July 30, and was first informed of Johnson's startling announcement by a telephone call from a reporter. After hanging up the phone, Humphrey remarked to an aide that the reporter who had called him was invariably reliable but must be having hallucinations now. Humphrey could not believe the story.

though every politician and newsman in the country knew Johnson was aiming only at Bobby Kennedy, the President had a plausible argument to the contrary. He claimed that his decision grew out of the larger consideration of good government. He couldn't spare any of his valued Cabinet aides, and that was as true of the other nine as it was of Bobby Kennedy.*

Noting that Kennedy's elimination from the vice-presidential contest had produced remarkably little adverse reaction in the party, Johnson felt The Bobby Problem was solved. And if Johnson felt it was solved, then it *was* solved. For from the beginning, it had existed primarily in the President's own mind, bred from his lack of confidence in national Democratic politics, from his haunting fear that Bobby Kennedy at Atlantic City somehow would amass the same forces commanded by Jack Kennedy at Los Angeles. Yet, ironically, the feeling that The Bobby Problem had been disposed of unshackled Johnson in a way that was to have implications for years to come.

For all of its tension, the July 29 meeting between the President and the Attorney General had been cordial enough. Kennedy told close friends, while pledging them to secrecy, that Johnson had gone out of his way that afternoon to avoid a rupture with him. But the President could not leave it at that. On Friday, July 31, convinced that at last he had found the final solution to The Bobby Problem, he could contain himself no longer. Eight months of caution and restraint in dealing with the dead President's brother ended in explosive Johnsonian exuberance. Johnson invited newsmen to his office throughout that day to relate his showdown with Kennedy in terms that were highly favorable to himself and considerably less favorable to Kennedy. Mimicry, exaggeration, overvivid description—all Johnson's conversational techniques—were brought to bear on Bobby Kennedy for the first time since the assassination in the presence of newsmen. Newspaper accounts giving details, as supplied by the President, of the Wednesday meeting began to appear in print as Kennedy went off to Hyannisport for the weekend.

Kennedy was furious and let Johnson know about it. Whatever slim hope existed for a Johnson-Kennedy *rapprochement* vanished that weekend. Now, Kennedy was convinced that Johnson saw poetic justice in their face-to-face encounter in the Oval Office. Johnson wanted to humiliate him, Kennedy believed, because Johnson had not forgot-

* Johnson was so eager to prove that the exclusion was aimed at Cabinet members other than Bobby Kennedy that he told White House reporters in a background session on July 31 that covert vice-presidential campaigns were under way for Dean Rusk and Orville Freeman in their respective home states of Georgia and Minnesota. This marked the first—and last—report of any such efforts.

ten that hot day in July, 1960, when Robert Kennedy, unaware that his brother's plan had changed, went to Johnson's suite in the Biltmore at Los Angeles to tell him he did not have to run for Vice-President if he did not want to risk a floor fight.*

In fact, a top presidential aide in the Johnson White House, who was not overly fond of Bobby Kennedy, found similar evidence that Johnson had positively relished the opportunity to put Bobby down. This Johnson aide was called into the Oval Office on Thursday, July 30, after the Johnson-Kennedy talk, but before the President's mass elimination of the Cabinet. The President asked Walter Jenkins to fetch the memorandum he had dictated the previous afternoon on his conversation with Kennedy. Jenkins got it, and Johnson read from it. The precise language in the memorandum sounded like an exact reproduction of the entire conversation, word for word. Having heard the memorandum, the aide was certain that the whole interview had been taped, and that Jenkins had transcribed the tape onto paper— backing up Kennedy's recollection of a recording device on the President's desk.

Bobby Kennedy was eliminated, but that did not reveal whom the President *did* want. And it was still to be twenty-six days, with the convention to convene in twenty-four days, before that question was finally, irrevocably decided. Master of timing and lover of surprise, Johnson did not want to tip his hand until the last possible moment. The convention promised to be the dullest since 1936, when the Roosevelt-Garner ticket was nominated by acclamation. To have allowed his choice for Vice-President to become known ahead of time would have obliterated what seemed the one possible element of excitement.

In Johnson's mind, as in everybody else's mind, Humphrey was the leading candidate. During the last week of July, the President deputized James Rowe to interrogate Humphrey about any defects in his personal life that might make him a liability on the ticket. There were none. Yet, even then Johnson did not truly close his mind, and not wholly for the reason of maintaining suspense.

Although Southern opposition to Humphrey had diminished significantly, Humphrey presented special problems in the President's own state of Texas. Governor John Connally and the Texas conservatives had felt as early as March that Humphrey was emerging as the most likely choice for Vice-President, and the prospect was forbidding not only because of the drag they thought he would exert on the ticket in Texas but also for a deeper reason. If Humphrey were elected Vice-

* See pages 283ff.

President, he would become heir apparent to Lyndon Johnson, and if at some future time, perhaps at the end of two Johnson terms in 1972, Humphrey did succeed to the national party leadership, he would move it to the left. Looking far ahead, the Connally conservatives knew that a Democratic party headed by Humphrey would drastically reduce their influence.

Ironically, Connally's candidate was Humphrey's junior colleague from Minnesota, Senator Eugene McCarthy, Catholic, handsome, suave, witty, a brilliant orator when moved by the occasion (as in his nomination speech for Adlai Stevenson at Los Angeles in 1960). A former college professor whose voting record in Congress was fully as liberal as Humphrey's, McCarthy was still infinitely less ominous to the Texas Establishment. The Texans felt that McCarthy, lacking the power base in the Democratic party's liberal-labor wing that Humphrey had built, would be more malleable and more congenial to their own future interests.

President Johnson and Governor Connally had patched up their quarrel over the Texas senatorial nomination, and Connally now was ducking in and out of the White House. On those trips, he argued on behalf of McCarthy. He had a powerful ally in Lady Bird Johnson, who, along with Lynda and Luci, was charmed by the courtly manner and quiet intelligence of Gene McCarthy. As between Humphrey and McCarthy, there was no doubt how a majority of the Johnson family would decide. Furthermore, McCarthy had been led to believe by the President himself that if Johnson had a truly free hand at Atlantic City, he would prefer McCarthy to anybody else.

Many times, Johnson and the Fortas-Clifford-Rowe triumvirate sat sipping a drink and discussing the merits of Humphrey versus McCarthy. McCarthy was less aggressive than Humphrey and did not seek the public limelight as Humphrey did. That pleased Johnson, who did not care for limelight-sharing. McCarthy was a Catholic, and, with Bobby Kennedy now out of it, his selection would smooth any ruffled Catholic feathers. However, an advantage for Humphrey was a large and vocal constituency growing out of long, intimate association with the labor unions, the Negroes, and the Jewish community. In contrast, McCarthy had no national constituency. Finally, Humphrey now had become the unanimous candidate of the Kennedys after the mass Cabinet elimination of July 30. They felt Humphrey had earned it, going all the way back to his defeat in the hollows of West Virginia in 1960, and they knew he had been a faithful lieutenant of President Kennedy for three years as Senate Majority Whip. McCarthy, on the other hand, was the candidate of Johnson's Texas allies.

President Johnson couldn't understand the Kennedy commitment to

Humphrey. In a long, amiable chat in the Oval Office one night in early August with the Irish Mafia still on the White House staff, Johnson expressed amazement at the Kennedy-Humphrey alliance. Don't the Kennedys know, the President asked, that Humphrey is an ambitious and aggressive politician who will try to take over the party after me? Don't they understand that if Bobby wants to become President, Humphrey will block him? Why, Johnson persisted, don't the Kennedys want Mike Mansfield—or better still, Gene McCarthy? But the Irish Mafia could not be budged toward McCarthy. They well remembered that McCarthy had never liked Jack Kennedy in the Senate days, and the Kennedys had never liked him.

Nevertheless, as convention time neared, Johnson sought to whip up party interest in McCarthy to give the appearance of a Humphrey-McCarthy contest at Atlantic City. Not long after his exclusion of the Cabinet, he called a meeting of John Bailey and Richard Maguire, chairman and treasurer, respectively, of the Democratic National Committee, along with Cliff Carter, Kenny O'Donnell, Walter Jenkins, and Jim Rowe. The President opened by saying that he was worried about the Catholic issue. Without a Catholic on the ticket, he said, politicians had been telling him he would be in trouble. This was particularly true, he said, because the Republicans had nominated a Catholic, Representative William Miller of New York, for Vice-President. Johnson said he had been getting reports that he ought to have a Catholic, too. Isn't that right, Walter? the President asked Jenkins. Jenkins, often used to backing up Johnson's unprovable assertions, said, Yes, Mr. President, that's right.

With that introduction, Johnson went around the room, one by one, asking whether a Catholic was needed on the ticket. With the single exception of Walter Jenkins, every man there said no, and every man there recommended Humphrey. Johnson's effort to have someone other than himself or Connally promote McCarthy failed.

Still, as the convention grew still nearer, it was clear Johnson retained his option to switch to McCarthy—or anyone else, for that matter—if he wanted to. He had more raw political power than any Democratic leader since Franklin Roosevelt in 1936. The Republicans had nominated a ticket that even Barry Goldwater knew was doomed. The Kennedy power had been neutralized for the time being. The economy was in its fourth straight year of steady upward spiral; the prognosis was good. The murder in Dallas had produced a yearning for atonement, a mass reaction across the nation that puzzled the psychologists and that would seek an outlet—a Democratic outlet—in the November election. All these factors added to one conclusion:

Johnson had close to total power on the eve of the Democratic convention when, for the first time, he would be mandated to run the country in his own right.

This, then, was Lyndon Johnson's convention. Rebuffed at Chicago in 1956 and at Los Angeles in 1960, he now controlled every party lever, with power to stage-manage Atlantic City to the color of the popcorn wrapping. He could arrange the program, write the platform, pick the Vice-President. Moreover, this was to be a Great Society convention, and, in the summer of 1964, that meant a consensus convention. Controversy, dispute, and rancor were forbidden. The only trouble was that an aspect of the Negro Revolution intruded at Atlantic City without invitation, not only threatening consensus but even casting a shadow over the vice-presidential selection.

What threatened to spoil Lyndon Johnson's convention was the famed Mississippi Summer Project of 1964, participated in by a coalition of civil rights groups ranging from the moderate National Association for the Advancement of Colored People to the radical Student Non-Violent Coordinating Committee. Unable to register Negro voters in the country's fortress of white supremacy, the Summer Project formed its own political party: the Mississippi Freedom Democratic party, composed of Mississippi Negroes plus a few white civil rights workers. The MFDP elected its own slate of delegates and alternates to the Democratic National Convention, consisting of sixty-four Negroes and four whites, and sent them to Atlantic City to challenge the regular lily-white delegation from Mississippi for recognition by the convention.

Lacking a compromise, one of two dire events was certain to occur. Either the South would walk out in protest over too *many* concessions to the MFDP; or liberals would take the issue to the floor in a party-splitting floor fight if too *few* concessions were made. Either event might kick up the White Backlash against the Negro Revolution, then much feared by Democratic politicians as Barry Goldwater's not-so-secret weapon. Either event would make a mockery of Johnson's consensus convention. Thus, the President laid down the basic strategy from the White House well before the convention began. The Johnson strategy seemed simple enough: compromise between the white regulars and the MFDP was absolutely essential.

Yet, this was not the simple fight between the downtrodden Mississippi Negroes and the Jim Crow Democratic party as it seemed to be. Deep strains inside the MFDP, between the moderate NAACP elements and the radical SNCC elements, made agreement on a compromise impossible. Aaron Henry, a courageous and dedicated Negro druggist from Clarksdale, Mississippi, who was both state president of the NAACP and state chairman of the MFDP, was a reasonable man. But the MFDP's real power was Bob Moses, a youthful Harvard-educated civil rights worker from New York and a nationally known figure in the emerging New Left, where compromise was a dirty word.* The dichotomy carried over to the important area of legal advice for the MFDP. Its nominal counsel was Joseph Rauh, the ADA civil rights expert who bitterly opposed the far left influences hovering around the MFDP at Atlantic City. But far more influential with Moses were veteran attorneys from the National Lawyers Guild, often cited as Communist-infiltrated. The MFDP never really survived these strains at Atlantic City. Within six months, the NAACP and Aaron Henry had pulled out, leaving the MFDP to SNCC and the radicals.

If that were not enough trouble for Johnson, further complication derived from the tie-in of the Mississippi seating fight with Hubert Humphrey and the vice-presidential nomination. Humphrey, with his deep involvement in the politics of civil rights, would be inevitably drawn into the center of the struggle. Johnson did not *order* Humphrey to take charge of this delicate operation, but the President knew he would be forced into it. If a compromise could not be found, Humphrey would be damaged. Indeed, the vice-presidential dreams cherished by Humphrey could be deeply affected by his ability or inability to prevent a Mississippi explosion at Convention Hall before the eyes of the nation.

In Washington on August 20, four days before the convention officially opened, the President had one of his last face-to-face talks with Humphrey about the increasingly dangerous politics of the MFDP challenge. On that very day, the President received ominous warnings from national Negro leaders, including officials of both the NAACP and SNCC. They told Johnson the MFDP challenge was no propaganda stunt but deadly serious political business. If concessions weren't made, the President was told, the tenuous racial peace that he needed so badly throughout the campaign to avert a White Backlash would be shattered. After August 20, Humphrey was to hear no more about the matter from Johnson. The President was determined not to show his hand in the difficult fight.

---

* Before the year was over, Moses had left Mississippi and, under the name of Bob Parris, was concentrating not on civil rights but on opposition to United States involvement in Vietnam.

This backstage management was a typical exercise of Johnsonian power, perfected through long years of Senate leadership. In breaking a deadlock in the Senate between opposing groups of Senators, his strategy was to stay out of sight and use leading figures on either side, whose loyalty was unquestioned, to work out the compromise. He prodded, pleaded, scolded—in private—but until the compromise began to take form, he stayed in the shadows. That was the Johnsonian strategy for the battle of Mississippi. The legal and moral issues were secondary. The object was to gain a compromise, any compromise, that would prevent either a walkout of the South or a liberal floor fight. Specifically, the easy compromise first glimpsed by Johnson was to seat the Jim Crow delegation, provided it pledged to support the presidential ticket; to give the MFDP the privilege of the floor of the convention, but no votes; and to adopt a new rule making it mandatory for Democratic parties in the Southern states to open the party rolls and procedures to Negroes, ending generations of lily-white party politics and insuring racially mixed Southern delegations at future conventions. This last part of the hoped-for compromise came directly from the President.

To arrange the compromise at Atlantic City, the President employed two highly trusted agents to carry out his secret orders. One was Walter Jenkins. The other was a young lawyer named Tom Finney, who as Senator Mike Monroney's administrative assistant had managed the Draft Stevenson operation at Los Angeles in 1960 and had become well acquainted with the Johnson inner circle during the futile Stop Kennedy drive. Now a member of Clark Clifford's law firm, Finney was chosen by Johnson to work with Humphrey on the Mississippi problem. For the better part of a week before the convention began, Finney devoted twenty hours a day to the MFDP issue. Finney had no direct contact with the President. *His* instructions were relayed through Jenkins and Clifford.

But this was a predominantly liberal convention, and to the Northern liberal delegates, the explosive Mississippi issue was not a matter easily compromised—not like splitting up the Texas delegation between rival power factions, as Johnson had done so many times in bygone days. The *legal* standing of the MFDP was nonexistent. But liberal delegates felt the *moral* standing of the regular Mississippi delegation was equally nonexistent.

How Mississippi Negroes had been systematically denied participation in the regular Democratic party was propounded forcefully at Atlantic City by the MFDP counsel, Joseph Rauh, a member of the Credentials Committee himself. Rauh pleaded the MFDP case before that committee and aroused the entire nation by taking televised testimony from MFDP delegates on Saturday, August 22, that turned a ruthless searchlight on the methods used in Mississippi to deny Negroes their fundamental right to vote.

So effective was the testimony of these MFDP delegates that the Johnson compromise became wholly inadequate not only for the MFDP but for hundreds of liberal delegates, outraged by the vivid descriptions of life in Mississippi given by the MFDP delegates put on the stand by Rauh. Enough members of the Credentials Committee refused to accept the initial Johnson compromise to assure a minority report and force a full-scale debate on the floor of the convention.

That meant the convention would open on a sour note—a murderous civil rights battle—precisely what Johnson wanted to avoid at all costs. Here then, on Monday night, August 24, the first day of the convention, was a major crisis. At Johnson's request, Clark Clifford put in an emergency telephone call to Walter Reuther, president of the United Auto Workers, then in the midst of tense contract negotiations of his own with General Motors Corporation in Detroit. Just before midnight Monday, Reuther broke off his Detroit talks, chartered an airplane, and rushed to Atlantic City. Reuther's credentials as a fighter for Negro rights were unquestioned and, Johnson believed, would be invaluable in helping cool off liberal delegates.

Humphrey's credentials were of a part with Reuther's. Thus, after midnight on Monday, Humphrey was inevitably pulled into the vortex of the back-room negotiations. He knew the risk he took and he made no effort to conceal his unhappiness at becoming a principal in the dispute, but it was impossible for him to sit this one out. At one point that night, fearful that his vice-presidential bid would be torn to shreds in a civil rights floor fight, he pleaded with Jenkins for authority to call the President directly. Jenkins said no, the President had specifically ordered that he did not want to talk to any of the principals except Jenkins and, through Clifford, Finney.

When Reuther arrived, he joined Humphrey, Finney, and Jenkins in a meeting in Jenkins' suite lasting the rest of that long night. Stunned by the rejection of their first compromise effort, they decided that a true compromise was now impossible. They now realized, in short, that the MFDP was split between responsible and irresponsible Negro leaders and that the irresponsibles would settle for nothing less than total surrender by the convention. Thus, instead of *compromise*, the requirement now was for a final *solution* that would satisfy the non-radicals inside the MFDP and, more important, the liberal delegates.

This solution, in other words, had to be such that fewer than eleven members of the one-hundred-member Credentials Committee would demand a minority report. Proof that compromise had now been discarded as impossible was evident in the fact that when the solution was finally agreed on, as the sun began to rise over the Atlantic Ocean Tuesday morning, the quartet of compromisers—Humphrey, Jenkins, Finney, and Reuther—barred all discussion of it with MFDP officials, including Joe Rauh. Instead, the most powerful political leaders in the party were privately briefed on the solution and informed that this was it, whatever the MFDP did.

The solution, going beyond Johnson's original compromise, gave the MFDP far more than even its most optimistic supporters had thought possible. In addition to two elements of the rejected compromise—the loyalty pledge by the white delegation and the new convention rule banning segregated Democratic parties—the sweetener gave the delegation two at-large votes in the 1964 convention. All Tuesday morning this solution was explained to political powers of the Democratic party. They accepted it, and early in the afternoon it was adopted in the Credentials Committee. Out of the one hundred members, fewer than eleven opposed it and a floor fight was thus avoided.

The country's most prestigious civil rights leaders—Roy Wilkins, Dr. Martin Luther King, Bayard Rustin—all accepted the solution. So did Joe Rauh and Aaron Henry, but Henry controlled only one-third of the MFDP delegation. Under terrific pressure from Bob Moses and the dominant radicals, he reversed his position.

But for Johnson's purpose, rejection of the solution by two-thirds of the MFDP was unimportant. What counted was that the solution was accepted by all the liberal delegates and every Southern delegation, except Mississippi and Alabama. There was no Dixie walkout. There was no floor fight. President Johnson had won an impressive victory. Yet, the interaction of civil rights radicals on Texas conservatives very nearly deprived him of his consensus convention just when it seemed assured.

Although Johnson's agents were quite aware that the MFDP wouldn't like the solution, they were not quite prepared for what happened Tuesday afternoon and evening. When delegate credentials for the two MFDP members were taken to their own caucus, they were rejected. The radicals—Bob Moses and the National Lawyers Guild—were fully in control of the MFDP, and Rauh resigned. Bent on inflaming the issue, the radicals staged an illegal "walk-in" on the convention floor Tuesday and, in full view of the television cameras, appropriated the vacant seats of the regular Mississippi delegation (which had left Atlantic City in protest to the Johnson solution to the

Mississippi problem). On Wednesday night, convention aides were seated in the empty Mississippi chairs, but the MFDP delegates staged a sit-in on the floor.

A great many delegates, Southerners certainly but a few Northerners as well, were outraged. They took it as ill grace or worse on the part of the MFDP hotheads to try deliberately to sabotage the convention after their spectacular triumph. In particular, an angry murmur of protest was audible in Governor John Connally's conservative-oriented Texas delegation, seated in the place of honor in front of Convention Hall. Connally, who had come to Atlantic City fresh from an unpublicized stay at the White House as the President's guest, was worried about the White Backlash—particularly if Humphrey were Johnson's running mate, as now seemed increasingly probable. The television spectacle of a Negro sit-in on the convention floor, Connally grumbled, could only contribute to the backlash. If he were running this convention, said the Governor, he would have the police eject the MFDP interlopers from Convention Hall, with whatever force was required. Exactly those views were held by another Texas conservative named W. Marvin Watson, Jr., who happened to be in a position to act.* Watson, a steel executive and a leader in the Texas Democratic party's right wing, had been named by Johnson to handle physical arrangements for the Atlantic City convention—his baptism of fire in national politics.

Watching the Wednesday night invasion of the MFDP delegates over television from their vantage point in the White House communications center in Convention Hall, Walter Jenkins and Tom Finney were flabbergasted to hear an unmistakably Texan voice come over the private radio intercom. The voice of Marvin Watson shouted an order to the convention police force to "clear out" the Negro interlopers. Jenkins and Finney leaped into action, simultaneously reaching for their own telephone connection with the intercom to countermand the order. They weren't going to jeopardize a solution so tortuously patched together. If the Negroes were forcibly evicted, the convention might slip out of control and shatter consensus. The MFDP sit-in was all but ignored. Lyndon Johnson's convention had survived its first and last real crisis.

Before President Johnson could pick his running mate, there still remained the often sticky formality of adopting a party platform.

---

* Watson was subsequently to become President Johnson's appointments secretary and a figure of much controversy at the White House.

Adoption of the platform split the party wide open in 1948 and triggered floor fights in 1952, 1956, and 1960. But here, the Consensus Convention functioned as Johnson wanted it to.

Johnson was insisting on a bland though liberal diet that would digest easily and without controversy on the floor. He took great pains to get it. In mid-spring, Bill Moyers had asked Frederick Dutton, Assistant Secretary of State for Congressional Relations and a former political aide to Governor Edmund G. Brown of California, to resign from the State Department in order to draft the party platform at the Democratic National Committee months in advance of the convention.

Again, the President kept his hand hidden. The directives and memoranda received from the White House by Dutton at the National Committee were signed by Moyers, not Johnson. But Johnson himself was dictating not only broad outlines of the platform but some of the specifics as well. For instance, at the same time that the convention Platform Committee chairman, Representative Carl Albert of Oklahoma, was saying privately that he opposed mentioning specific extremist groups in the platform and adding that they probably would not be named, Johnson had decreed that they be named. Indeed, they already were in Dutton's draft. By identifying the Ku Klux Klan, the John Birch Society, and the Communist party, the President meant to show up the Republicans, who in their platform had refused to attack extremism in any form.

With the platform written and approved by the President long before the Platform Committee met in Atlantic City, little presidential pressure was required to keep it inoffensively bland. Senator Joseph S. Clark, the liberal from Pennsylvania, was unable to persuade the Platform Committee to accept a clause endorsing "general and complete" disarmament, and he threatened to take the issue to the floor. Word quickly came back from the President himself that to stir up a floor fight would only jeopardize a disarmament bill that the Senate would be debating when it reconvened in Washington shortly after the convention. And so again, operating behind the scenes from his command post in the White House, Johnson achieved his second objective: a party platform without a floor fight.

The reports of the Credentials and Platform Committees were approved Tuesday night. Now the stage was set for what the President had been planning for so long. All that was left was the vice-presidency.

By Tuesday night, August 25, everyone assumed Humphrey would be the choice—if only because now there was no reason why he should *not* be. The Mississippi credentials fight, which had made

Humphrey so apprehensive, had ended satisfactorily; Eugene McCarthy had failed to pick up support;* and far from attempting any late coup for Robert F. Kennedy, the Kennedys were actively for Humphrey. Yet, the delegates who were so confident of a Johnson-Humphrey ticket on August 25 might have harbored doubts had they been aware of all the hidden events that occurred the previous week.

On Saturday, August 22, the President asked Kenneth O'Donnell to "set the wheels in motion" for a possible last-minute switch to an entirely new and highly unlikely vice-presidential prospect, Senate Majority Leader Mike Mansfield. The President was flatly advised by O'Donnell that Mansfield would not accept the vice-presidency for all the copper in Montana, but Johnson just smiled. "Yeah," he said, "that's what they said about me."

After this conversation with O'Donnell, the President dispatched Walter Jenkins on a strange mission to James Rowe, a fellow Montanan and close political associate of Mansfield. Johnson, said Jenkins, wanted Rowe's opinion on two points. First, did he think Mansfield would be preferable to Humphrey on the ticket? Second, did he think Mansfield would go on the ticket if asked? Rowe was incredulous, but Jenkins insisted the President was serious. Rowe replied he was certain Mansfield would never take the vice-presidential nomination, skirting the question of whether he would or would not be better than Humphrey on the ticket. Jenkins reported back to Johnson with the negative answer.

What was happening here? Was Johnson just teasing O'Donnell and Rowe, to build up a new element of suspense? The evidence is that the President was more serious than that. He was not particularly pleased with the way Mansfield had been running the Senate the past four years. Moving him into the vice-presidency would open the way for the more aggressive, more skillful Humphrey to become Majority Leader.

But what if Mansfield had replied, "Yes, I'll be happy to serve"? It seems unthinkable that Johnson would have dumped Humphrey at that late date. Within these unanswerable questions can be found the essence of Lyndon Johnson's style in the use of power. For the mystery, the confusion, and even the fear engendered by these eleventh-hour overtures to Mansfield—and news of them did spread quickly among the politicians in Atlantic City who counted—somehow heightened the power of the man in the White House and made of him an even more formidable leader.

---

* Frank Smith, boss of the still formidable Philadelphia Democratic machine, tried to start a McCarthy-for-Vice-President boom on the convention floor but could not find sufficient allies.

The news that Johnson was feeling out Mansfield and still had Mc-Carthy under consideration quickly found its way to Humphrey and made him ever more uneasy about Johnson's plans for him. Thus, if it accomplished nothing else, Johnson's sly build-up for one potential candidate after another was a macabre cat-and-mouse game that irritated and worried Humphrey's supporters and kept Humphrey himself in a state of high nervousness.

While Humphrey fretted in Atlantic City, an ebullient, irrepressible Johnson was presiding over an open-house carnival at the White House, leading the press on extended walks in the hot sun around the oval driveway on the South Lawn, inviting reporters to his private quarters for drinks and, all the while, talking, talking, talking. Over and over again, he talked about the vice-presidential nominee. Telephone calls went out around the country to seek advice from old friends. The lines between the White House and Atlantic City hummed with the presidential voice asking Governors, National Committeemen, Senators, whether they had any last bit of advice for the President of the United States.

To reporters who hurried to keep up with him on those interminable parades around the oval driveway, he reviewed again and again the requirements he had set for the man he would pick. He must be this, and he must have a flair for that, and he must be ready to take over the presidency, and on and on. But who was he? The President hadn't decided, because, he insisted, this was a fateful decision not to be taken lightly. And always present in the back of his mind was delicious anticipation of the political circus that awaited his arrival in Atlantic City, where thousands of Democrats at the convention and millions of Americans would watch his nomination by thunderous acclamation. It was all his. He was savoring it to the last sweet morsel.

By early Wednesday afternoon, he was finally ready to let the first tangible evidence of his choice for the vice-presidential nominee be squeezed out of him, drop by drop. Humphrey? he said rhetorically to a reporter probing the presidential mind on yet another lap around the White House lawn. Well, he'd asked Humphrey to come down from Atlantic City that very Wednesday afternoon to talk to him. He said it casually, as though it were a commonplace, but in fact it was the first hard news of Humphrey's imminent selection. Reporters rushed to their typewriters to tell the world Humphrey would be coming to the White House within hours.

Up in Atlantic City, the invitation to Humphrey had been delivered in supersecrecy to Walter Jenkins more than twenty-four hours earlier, shortly before noon on Tuesday, with final settlement of the Mississippi case by then in clear view. Jenkins made elaborate shorthand notes of every syllable uttered by the President over the telephone, typed them out, and handed them to Jim Rowe, who was to inform Humphrey. Rushing out of Jenkins' office to find Humphrey, Rowe finally located the Senator, told him the good news, and took Humphrey to Rowe's suite in the Colonial Motel, along with Muriel Humphrey, William Connell, the Senator's administrative assistant, and Max Kampelman, his closest political adviser.

Rowe took Humphrey into his bedroom and closed the door, leaving the others in the sitting room. He recited from the long instructions given to Jenkins by Johnson, including a suggestion that Rowe show Humphrey a copy of that day's *Washington Evening Star* which carried a meticulously worded interview of Johnson laying down the elaborate guidelines he had in mind for his Vice-President. The guidelines covered every responsibility and duty that Johnson planned for his Number Two man and included the statement that Johnson's Vice-President would have a higher standing in the administration than any other in history. Humphrey had read the interview in another newspaper with a less complete version than the *Star*, and Rowe discovered there were no issues of the *Star* left in Atlantic City. But Rowe needed no newspaper. He was in possession of and ready to relay the most exhaustive "do's" and "don't's" that any prospective nominee for Vice-President ever had received from the head of the ticket.

With the long, anguished wait now at an end, Humphrey was bubbling with euphoria himself. His excitement mounting, he started to open the door of Rowe's bedroom to tell his wife the news. Rowe stopped him. The President had ordered total secrecy. No one was to know. But my *wife?* moaned Humphrey. This is terribly embarrassing, Humphrey said. You've got to tell my wife! Now Rowe was embarrassed. He, too, regarded the secrecy as irrelevant. All right, he said, you can tell Muriel, but no one else.

Still, however, the world was not to know Johnson's secret because, as that final act staged by Johnson played out, one scene remained. Johnson's original plan had been to invite Humphrey *and* McCarthy to the White House together, sustaining the suspense for still a few more hours.

But McCarthy had tired of the cat-and-mouse game. By Tuesday morning he knew he would not be Vice-President. Deeply hurt, now, and convinced that Johnson had been leading him down a blind alley all those months, he sent the President an extraordinary telegram that he was withdrawing from contention. Shrewd and well-versed in the President's ways, McCarthy suspected that as soon as Johnson received his wire, he would order him not to release it to the press. For once McCarthy's wire was released, only Humphrey would be left in contention and all residual suspense would be gone.

Sure enough, McCarthy did get a call from the White House. The President, he was told, was unhappy to have received the telegram and he would be most displeased if it were made public. Such a request from the President of the United States could not be refused. But McCarthy, anticipating Johnson, made the wire public before he sent it. Humiliated and angry, Gene McCarthy in the years immediately ahead did not really resume his friendship with Johnson. And yet, had the Mississippi dispute not been settled, McCarthy might well have been chosen to run for Vice-President instead of Hubert Humphrey.

With McCarthy out, Johnson needed a substitute to maintain the semblance of suspense. He invited Senator Thomas J. Dodd of Connecticut, a close friend and, in the Senate, a faithful member of the Johnson Network, to fly to Washington on the same plane with Humphrey—in the seat he had intended for McCarthy.

The convention floor buzzed. Humphrey *and* Dodd to the White House? Dodd for Vice-President?* Would Johnson do *that?* Incredible, thought the politicians. Impossible, thought the press. But with Johnson's insatiable appetite for the surprise, anything seemed possible.

The plane to Washington arrived in mid-afternoon Wednesday, at just the time Mrs. Johnson was arriving by plane in Atlantic City. The President wanted his wife to have the television screens to herself. So Humphrey and Dodd, who were met at the Washington airport by Jack Valenti, drove haplessly around for an hour, waiting for their summons from the White House. When it came, they drove to the South Portico and waited another twenty minutes in the car. Then Johnson himself walked to the car and tapped on the window at Hubert Humphrey, who was dozing in the back seat.

The rest was anticlimax. After a brief and insignificant talk with Dodd, Johnson took Humphrey into the Oval Office for a long exchange about the vice-presidency. Presidents and Vice-Presidents seldom got along well, Johnson said, but he and Humphrey must. Humphrey must be exactly the Vice-President that Johnson wanted him to

---

* Such speculation was encouraged when some delegates discovered, shortly after the announcement that Dodd would accompany Humphrey to Washington, that the official convention painters in the basement of Convention Hall were preparing "Dodd for Vice-President" placards suitable for demonstrations. Actually, the painters had no inside information. They merely wanted to be prepared for any contingency.

be. He must be Johnson's man down to the tips of his toes, and he must do whatever Johnson asked him to; he must be able to share secrets that no one else would know; he must be prepared for special duties in space, civil rights, education and welfare, agriculture. Humphrey responded in kind. *If* he were chosen as the vice-presidential nominee on the following day, Humphrey said, he would be the most loyal partner any President could have.

Then ceremony followed ceremony. First into the Cabinet Room, where Johnson presented his running mate to McNamara, Rusk, and McGeorge Bundy. Then a presidential telephone call to Muriel Humphrey in Atlantic City. Then a press conference with the White House reporters. Then the ceremony of several fast laps around the South Lawn, the press following. Then everyone upstairs in the White House, with plenty of drinks and food for all—White House aides, reporters, and both members of the Democratic party's national ticket. Johnson was gay, exuberant, teasing, and understandably self-satisfied.

Lyndon Johnson and Hubert Humphrey flew to Atlantic City that Wednesday night. The President had not been scheduled to appear at Convention Hall until Thursday night, the last night of the convention, to make his acceptance speech. But Johnson correctly felt the convention was getting sluggish and dull—particularly for the television viewers. It needed a lift.

Two enormous pictures of Johnson, floor to ceiling, flanked the Speaker's rostrum on the wall to its rear. Filling the space above them were three much smaller photographs of Roosevelt, Truman, and Kennedy. At 11:03 P.M. on Wednesday, August 26, Johnson was nominated for President by acclamation. Johnson immediately entered the cheering Convention Hall and, flanked by his huge likenesses, mounted the rostrum to reveal what smiling delegates already knew: Hubert Humphrey would be his running mate.

It was Lyndon Johnson's convention—*his* Mississippi compromise, *his* platform, *his* vice-presidential nominee. With all that, a faintly disturbing note was still to come on Thursday night, the anticlimactic final evening of the convention.

The first order of business that night was the John F. Kennedy memorial film that Johnson had postponed from Monday night. Robert F. Kennedy, about to run for the Senate from New York, mounted the rostrum. The emotion so carefully contained through four days of a controlled convention burst forth. In a rare, spontaneous demonstration, the convention cheered and clapped for ten full minutes. Then, minutes later, the memorial film itself evoked an unrestrained weeping seldom seen on the floor of any National Convention.

The demonstration for Bobby Kennedy and the emotional reaction to the film was no rebellion against Johnson. It was an uncontrollable surge of regret and grief for the young President killed nine months before. And yet it brought second thoughts to the politicians who had accused Johnson of overkill in deploying the powers of the presidency on The Bobby Problem. They pondered, now, whether at least some of Johnson's maneuvers—the Shriver ploy; the Lucas resolution; postponement of the memorial movie; and, finally, mass execution of the Cabinet—might have been necessary to head off revolt on the boardwalk at Atlantic City.

Perhaps not. But Lyndon Johnson took no chances. He did not leave a margin for even the *possibility* of that latent Kennedy emotion at Convention Hall transforming itself into revolt. At last, Lyndon Johnson had gained full control of the Democratic party. He had accomplished it himself, in his own way.

Chapter XXI

★★★★★★★★★★

IN SEARCH
OF A RECORD

It has been suggested that if he [Johnson] learned on the morning of November 4 that he had lost ten states, he might decline to serve, saying that he just didn't want to be President unless he could be President of *all* the people.

—Richard H. Rovere in
The Goldwater Caper

Campaigning in Indiana early in October, 1964, Lydon Johnson flew the short hop from East Chicago to Indianapolis with Matthew Welsh, the Democratic Governor of Indiana, as his guest aboard Air Force One. Not since Franklin D. Roosevelt beat Alf Landon in 1936 had a Democratic candidate for President carried Indiana. Not since Harry Truman came within striking distance of Thomas E. Dewey in 1948 had the presidential contest there been close. Now, a beaming Welsh carried glad tidings for his party's leader. Based on his own political survey of the state, the Governor predicted the President would carry Indiana with a comfortable 55 percent of the vote. Johnson's face darkened at the news. "God, that's close," he said without a trace of humor.

Thus, the presidential campaign of 1964 was a contest not just for victory, for Johnson's victory was assured on July 16 at the Republican National Convention in San Francisco. The very moment the party's right wing seized control for the first time since 1924, ignored the consensus, and nominated Senator Barry Goldwater of Arizona, the November result was assured. The campaign for President, 1964, was never a contest at all, as ill-matched as Harding and Cox in 1920, or Roosevelt and Landon in 1936.

The Republican nominee was running not only against Johnson but also the ghost of John F. Kennedy and the tragedy of Dallas. It is doubtful that any Republican nominee would have had much chance, but certainly not Goldwater, who was beaten almost 2 to 1 in public-opinion polls among his own party's rank-and-file by Governor William Scranton of Pennsylvania, his last opponent for the nomination. But Goldwater had the delegates, representing conservative control of the party's machinery after a generation of dominance by the Republican kingmakers from the Eastern Seaboard. And Goldwater, the voice of the renascent Republican right, was the antithesis of Lyndon Johnson: uninterested in power, inflexible, doctrinaire, essentially nonpolitical. He was, in short, everything a candidate for President of the United States should not be. All these weaknesses had been aggravated by his unsuccessful Republican foes, who had planted in the public mind the caricature of Barry Goldwater as a political Neanderthal who would risk nuclear war and abolish the Social Security system.

Johnson knew full well that no miracle could save Goldwater. But once the Republicans had done the unthinkable and nominated him, Johnson became a man possessed with ambition not just to win, not just to win handsomely, but to win the *largest* presidential victory in the history of the country. As early as January, Lawrence O'Brien, the shrewd student and manager of Democratic politics whom Johnson had inherited from Kennedy, predicted privately that Johnson might indeed exceed Franklin Roosevelt's 63 percent of the popular vote in 1936, or even Warren Harding's 64 percent in 1920. That became Johnson's goal. Not until they understood it did his aides and advisers also understand how a candidate so far ahead could worry and fret as much as did Lyndon Johnson in the 1964 campaign.

A landslide would be the last and mightiest step in his consolidation of power. He had survived the crisis of confidence during the transition, put the stamp of the Great Society on his administration, disposed of The Bobby Problem, and dictated the one-man convention at Atlantic City. Here now was the final goal: to win by so large a margin that the consensus he sought as the means to power would be ratified by an unprecedented electoral landslide.

That was the goal, but the means were unknown. Campaign organization, strategy, and tactics were unsettled, as murky and as disorganized for President Johnson in 1964 as they had been for Senator Johnson in his disastrous attempt at the nomination in 1960. What had changed, and changed drastically, were Johnson's power position and Johnson's foes.

Hoping to profit by the invaluable experience of the cliff-hanger against Nixon in 1960, John F. Kennedy was building the best-oiled, most efficient campaign organization of all time a whole year before the 1964 election. During the week before he went to Dallas, the first pre-campaign meeting was held at the White House. With Robert F. Kennedy kept busy as Attorney General, brother-in-law Stephen Smith was to have taken over as campaign manager. Larry O'Brien would have had the same job he held in 1960: director of organization, dealing with state party leaders. Kenny O'Donnell would have been in charge of scheduling. Even at that early date, campaign coordinators were named for troublesome states. By January, 1964, the organization was to have been a going concern.

As President, Lyndon Johnson had other concerns and other ways of going about politics. Kennedy's ambitious plan was forgotten. Johnson had not even named a campaign manager by the time the convention rolled around. Even after Atlantic City, he named no overall director of the campaign. His campaign organization—disorganization was the better word—defied schematic description. Johnson simply could not decide who should be the campaign manager,* first inclining toward Governor John Connally, then switching to Clark Clifford, then, unsatisfied with their advice, looking elsewhere—and everywhere. He ended up with no campaign manager at all, except Lyndon Johnson.

O'Donnell, who was still a White House aide, was sent over to the Democratic National Committee as its executive director and given the assignment of arranging the President's schedule. Scheduling was also assigned to Jack Valenti at the White House. But the President played havoc with his schedules, and O'Donnell wound up spending much of the autumn working for Bobby Kennedy's Senate campaign in New York.

Speech writers appeared and disappeared, both inside and outside the White House. Most prominent inside the government were four White House aides—Bill Moyers, Richard Goodwin, Horace Busby, and Douglass Cater—plus Secretary of Labor Willard Wirtz. Wirtz's role was kept under a strict secrecy injunction by Johnson, who feared a bad reaction if the press were to learn he was employing a Cabinet member to write speeches. Outside government, the President assigned speeches to magazine writer John Bartlow Martin, who had served Kennedy as a speech writer in 1960 and later as Ambassador to the Dominican Republic; to Frank Gibney, a former editor of *Time;* and occasionally to Abe Fortas.

A dozen or more lesser lights, from both inside and outside the gov-

---

* Johnson's offer of July 29 to make Bobby Kennedy his campaign manager was, of course, quickly forgotten. See page 445.

ernment, also wrote speeches. They worked in teams, one headed by Cater and the other by Wirtz. But at the President's insistence, one group did not know of the other's existence until they all met at a speech writers' cocktail party after the election. All these stagehands worked in an atmosphere of nearly total confusion, with little central direction or clear idea of what the star performer was going to do next. The duplication of effort was appalling. Members of the Wirtz and Cater teams might be assigned to write a speech on the same subject, only to have the final product written by Bill Moyers or Abe Fortas. Finally, the President might discard the speech altogether.

On top of this madcap disorder, Larry O'Brien had a position of his own. Nominally, he was director of organization—the same job he held under Kennedy in 1960. But in 1964, there were no organizational lines to direct. When O'Brien finally managed to free himself of his duties as chief congressional lobbyist in September, he served as a high-level political agent for Johnson.

In early September, Johnson instructed O'Brien to arrange a series of some twenty-one confidential regional meetings, in which he could take the measure of the political situation in every state. Until then, Johnson had done nothing about the campaign. Now he felt "out of touch," as he put it, and assigned O'Brien to be the presidential eyes and ears. As such, O'Brien took off on an intermittent tour that covered six weeks.

The object was to talk politics to a dozen or so top leaders in every state. In sessions behind locked doors, lasting three or four hours, every detail of the campaign was ruthlessly laid out. O'Brien then locked himself in his hotel room and wrote a voluminous confidential report for the President, which was sent by Western Union to the White House the instant it was finished.

To the President, who had never had the benefit of such professional political help, the O'Brien reports became The Word. Their recommendations were carved up and passed among the staff of the White House. The Democratic National Committee and Walter Jenkins were ordered to follow through. In the White House, the O'Brien reports came quickly to have the same urgent classification as a National Intelligence Estimate from the CIA. Johnson soon ordered Jenkins to have O'Brien's traveling staff, usually one secretary and one assistant, telephone his report to White House stenographers page-by-page, as it was finished, no matter how late at night, so that the recommendations could be carried out at once. In all, O'Brien's reports gave Johnson what he had never had before: a political map of the United States, each area filled in with facts and figures. Even if his organiza-

tion remained chaotic as in 1960, his intelligence—based on reports
from O'Brien and pollster Oliver Quayle—was excellent.

Behind this slapdash, jerry-built campaign structure, one element of
strategy was devised in comparatively orderly—and extremely secretive—fashion. It was what was known as the Anti-Campaign. Conceived and watched over by Lyndon Johnson, it was his unique contribution to presidential campaigning.

No political operation in history was ever conducted with such secrecy. The Anti-Campaign was clandestine "black propaganda" organized by a dozen brainy Washington-based Democrats, some in and
some out of the government. It had no chairman, kept no minutes,
issued no statements, revealed no strategy. No word of the Anti-
Campaign leaked out. It operated out of a small conference room on
the second floor of the West Wing of the White House, almost directly
above the President's own Oval Office.

Its members were security-conscious and well-versed in the propaganda of politics. They were: Myer Feldman, the President's special
counsel; Adam Yarmolinsky, back at the Defense Department after
his purge from the War on Poverty; Daniel P. Moynihan, an Assistant
Secretary of Labor; Leonard Marks, an old friend of Johnson and an
attorney who specialized in communications law;* Tyler Abel, Assistant Postmaster General and husband of Mrs. Johnson's social secretary: James Sundquist, an Assistant Secretary of Agriculture and
former Truman speech writer; Hyman Bookbinder, a former labor
lobbyist and lieutenant of Hubert Humphrey; D. B. Hardeman, confidential assistant to the late Speaker Sam Rayburn; Myer Rashish, an
expert on international trade. And then there were three Washington
lawyers: Tom Finney, fresh from his work at the Atlantic City convention, John Sharon, a former Adlai Stevenson campaign aide and,
like Finney, a member of Clark Clifford's law firm, and Robert Martin,
who had worked for Johnson's campaign in 1960.

Not often did all these members of the Anti-Campaign meet at the
same time. They came and went, and Feldman and Sharon were first
among equals. The job was easily defined: embarrass the Republicans,
get under Barry Goldwater's skin, thereby achieving Johnson's overall
goal of winning by the biggest possible margin.

For example, it was learned early in the campaign that half a dozen
small liberal church journals, one of them published by the Protestant
theologian, Reinhold Niebuhr, had scathingly editorialized against
Barry Goldwater as a man not to be entrusted with the presidency.

* Marks was named director of the United States Information Agency in 1965.

Normally, these editorials would not have found their way to congregations across the country until months after publication. The Anti-Campaign operation duplicated them by the hundreds and saw that they got to appropriate church groups throughout the nation in a matter of days.

Another project was more typically in the realm of black politics. If Goldwater were to speak somewhere at six o'clock, one local anti-Goldwater speaker—usually a Democrat but sometimes a Republican—would be scheduled at four o'clock and then another one at eight o'clock. Thus, Goldwater would be bracketed by the opposition. An impression of feverish anti-Goldwater activity would be given on the very day of his appearance.

Another Anti-Campaign ploy was to make generous use of the letters columns of local newspapers. The Anti-Campaign group would ask a Republican businessman known to be backing Johnson to write an anti-Goldwater letter to the editor of his local newspaper on a day calculated to get the letter published just as the Goldwater caravan swept into town. Or, just before Goldwater's arrival, a local Democratic official would be told to plant a letter in the newspaper publicizing Goldwater's position on a major issue, if, as so often was the case, the Goldwater position was anathema to the majority of voters in that city.

This clandestine operation was Johnson's campaign pet and he was kept closely informed of everything the group did. Feldman was the bridge between Johnson and the propagandists and often rushed downstairs to the Oval Office to get the President's reaction before approving a specific plan.

Inherent in the Anti-Campaign operation was the Frontlash, Lyndon Johnson's own contribution to the political vocabulary of 1964. Johnson had examined Ollie Quayle's poll for evidence of the fearful Backlash—Democratic voters, North and South, defecting to Goldwater because of resentment against the Negro Revolution. Instead, he found far more Republican voters defecting to Johnson and promptly dubbed it the Frontlash. Although the Negrophobic character of the Backlash was clear enough, the roots of the Frontlash were not so visible. It seemed to grow partly out of a distrust of Goldwater, partly out of Johnson's skill at forming a consensus. These two elements of Frontlash—hacking away at Goldwater and enlarging the consensus for Johnson—were the major work not only of the Anti-Campaign operation but also of another remarkable element of the sprawling Johnson campaign.

That was the clumsy sounding National Independent Committee for Johnson and Humphrey, announced by the President himself at the White House on September 3, which lay at the heart of his political philosophy of consensus. Weeks in the making, the committee had been put together by James Rowe, chairman of the Citizens for Johnson-Humphrey, and the committee's chairman, Henry H. Fowler, who had resigned as Under Secretary of the Treasury and was practicing law in Washington. The list of members, forty-five strong, read like a Who's Who of Eastern big business, men and titles linked to the Republican party of Thomas E. Dewey and Dwight D. Eisenhower but now cast adrift by the nomination of Barry Goldwater and wondrously attached to the Johnson-Humphrey standard. Henry Ford II of Ford Motors; Marion B. Folsom and Robert Anderson from the Eisenhower Cabinet; Thomas S. Lamont and ex-Republican kingmaker Sidney J. Weinburg of Wall Street. The list, gilt-edged down to the middle initials, comprised as prestigious a collector's item as any Democratic presidential nominee ever carried into a campaign.

In announcing the committee at a ceremony in the Cabinet Room, Johnson spelled out a political philosophy of the Frontlash that made it easier for Republican businessmen to turn their backs on their ancient home and support Johnson for President:

> I did not, I do not, and I shall never seek to be a labor President, or a business President, a President for liberals or a President for conservatives, a President for the North or a President for the South—but only President for all the people.

Once the list of its forty-five sponsors was announced in the White House, the Anti-Campaign group used it to telling effect in working on individual business leaders around the country. In Idaho, the impact of the Independent Committee was probably what swung the state into the Johnson column with less than 51 percent of the vote. There the target was Robert Hansberger, president of the Boise Cascade Corporation whose extensive operations in lumbering, wood products, and sporting goods made it an economic and political power in Idaho. Using the Independent Committee membership list as its main weapon, the Anti-Campaign group persuaded Hansberger to come out for Johnson. His conversion had a pronounced effect on all of Idaho business.

Frontlash politics exploited the staid Republican businessmen's basic fear of Goldwater as an undependable radical politician. It resulted in an unprecedented flood of large contributions to the Johnson campaign, which in combination with Johnson's Texas money opened up financial resources never before available to a Democratic presidential nominee.

For the actual voter, the message of the Frontlash was carried in frightening terms by a series of television and radio commercials prepared by the advertising firm of Doyle Dane Bernbach, new to partisan politics but the hottest thing on Madison Avenue because of its campaigns for Volkswagen and Avis Rent-A-Car. Doyle Dane Bernbach worked on the Frontlash—not to gild Lyndon Johnson—but to terrify the voters with the mere thought of Barry Goldwater in the White House.

Two of the television spots went too far. In one, a hand reached to press a nuclear button and plunge the world into atomic war. In another, a little girl pulled petals from a daisy, and with each petal that fluttered to the ground, a gloom-laden voice recited the countdown for the firing of an intercontinental ballistics missile. On a political fact-finding trip to Cleveland, Larry O'Brien heard so much criticism from Democrats that he recommended killing the daisy spot. His advice was followed and eventually both were taken off the air.* But other commercials from Madison Avenue were played again and again with telling effect against Goldwater. One depicted a Social Security card being ripped in two. It was perfect Frontlash propaganda.

More than any other aspect of the unplanned campaign, the President's role had a peculiarly evolutionary quality. For at Atlantic City, there was no sign he was to conduct much of a campaign at all.

For many weeks before the Atlantic City convention and for several weeks thereafter, a constant stream of advice poured into the White House from Governor John Connally in Austin, Texas. His recommendation was clear. Johnson should sit tight in Washington making periodic use of the television networks to remind the voters that the man behind the big desk in the Oval Office was taking good care of the people's business. But travel in the conventional campaign sense must be reduced to the minimum. Johnson had the election won, said Connally, provided he didn't make mistakes in the campaign, and the odds on that were substantially reduced the more he stayed home. As viewed in Texas, Johnson would win all and lose nothing by running a front-porch campaign of the kind attributed to William McKinley in 1896.

Connally's plan would lift the President above the election battle,

---

* Even though it was soon withdrawn, the daisy commercial made so sharp an impression on the national political consciousness that Republicans later swore it ran throughout the campaign. They credited it, inaccurately, with a major role in defeating Goldwater.

and place him on the highest pedestal in the land—behind his desk in the White House. The picture would be that of a President too concerned about the welfare of his people to take time out for electioneering, too preoccupied with the great affairs of state to shake hands along the barricades. Leave that to Goldwater. Johnson would campaign by *being* President.

Impressed by this strong advice from his Texas friend, Johnson gazed one hot summer day of 1964 out to the Rose Garden, lying just beyond his Oval Office, and remarked: "That's where I'm going to run my campaign from this fall."

The campaign began in an atmosphere approaching chaos. Always secretive about his plans and desperately maintaining his options to make last-minute changes without anyone knowing, the President was silent whenever he was asked—even by aides—to elaborate on his campaign plans. He went to extraordinary lengths to argue that he was not really interested in the campaign, that he was too busy as President to worry about elections. On September 5, at the traditional starting point of campaigns, he told a press conference:

> We have a job to do here and we are going to try to do that first. When, as, and if we can, we will make as many appearances as we think we can without neglecting the interests of the nation. . . . But just where I will be at some certain day in October I can't determine and I don't want to announce because then you have me canceling and adjusting my plans, things of that kind. That makes more of a story than my appearance would make, or maybe what I had to say would make.

It was, then, to be a campaign that started with the President's insistence that it was no campaign at all. For example, two days before he went to Detroit to open the Democratic campaign with the traditional Labor Day appearance at Cadillac Square, Johnson was asked what kind of a political speech he had in mind.

> We never characterize any speech. The President of the United States is not in the business of applying labels and making speculations on matters of this kind. You will have copies of the speech and if you want to indulge in that, it is all right. You can say it is constructive, progressive, prudent, or radical; it is political or nonpolitical; whatever you want to say about it.

Even before the campaign opener in Detroit, Johnson had taken shrouded but clear steps to strip the campaign of one of its most dramatic—but most dangerous—aspects. In 1960, Congress passed a special waiver of Section 315 of the Communications Act, so that Kennedy and Nixon could debate over television without the networks violating the requirement of equal time to all candidates. After the 1960 election, Kennedy said he hoped the presidential candidate debates were here to stay and that he definitely would debate his 1964 opponent. But Kennedy knew that in 1960 the debates probably elected him. He was fast on his feet and a master of television. Having been tested once, and won, Kennedy could afford to take a friendly view of televised debates.

Johnson was in a different contest in 1964. He was so far ahead that he and most Democrats felt debates with Goldwater could only reduce that lead. He was no Kennedy on television, either. Unable to throw his arms about and use the earthy idiom that made The Treatment so magnetic, the televised Johnson came over stiff and wooden. Consequently, to debate Goldwater was both a senseless waste of time and a dangerous exposure. He and all his advisers privately ruled out televised debates early in the game.

But the President would not admit it and thereby give the Republicans and Goldwater campaign ammunition. All through the spring and summer, Congress toyed with the bill to exempt the presidential candidates once again from Section 315 and enable debates to be held. At one press conference after another, the press badgered the President: Would he debate Goldwater? Did he want to debate Goldwater? The President side-stepped. On August 18, after passing both the House and Senate in different forms and after being compromised by a Conference Committee of the two branches, the repeal of Section 315 went to the floor of the Senate and, on direct but private orders from Johnson, was killed. That seemed to be the end of it.

Instead, the idea was revived by the networks. It was discovered that the two candidates could legitimately be paired against each other as a regularly scheduled television news show, without violating Section 315. And so, at his September 5 press conference, the President was asked one last time:

> Mr. President, sir, you said you would withhold a statement on whether you would engage in televised debates until you received the nomination. Will you now engage in debates with Senator Goldwater on a regularly scheduled news program?

The President replied straight-faced:

> I haven't reached any decision on that yet. I haven't said I would withhold the statement. I said we would cross that bridge when we got to it. I haven't reached it yet.

Johnson had reached the debate bridge, and declined to cross it, several months before. There were to be no debates but he would not give Goldwater an opening by saying so.

The successful side-step of a confrontation with Goldwater was skillful politics by Johnson but scarcely a triumphant maneuver, and a triumph of some sort was precisely what Johnson needed in those early days of the campaign. In early September, the presidential mood was not exuberant, but intense and reserved. Just as he had fretted over The Bobby Problem from the moment he entered the White House until Atlantic City, so he now agonized over a new worry: would he be well received by the American voters in his campaign forays, as well received, he wondered, as Jack Kennedy had been received in 1960? Could he, coming from the Texas hill country, exhilarate and thrill the voters as the leader of the Democratic party and candidate for President, or would he be out of place in the mainstream of American politics—in the garment district of Manhattan, or at Detroit's Cadillac Square, or at a traditional party rally at, for example, the airport in Burlington, Vermont, and in a hundred other places far from the Pedernales?

Yet despite these doubts, despite Connally's advice, despite Johnson's wistfulness that summer day when he gazed at the Rose Garden and thought of campaigning from there, it was never in the nature of Lyndon Johnson to abstain from his own presidential campaign.

Whether he himself was aware of this is neither clear nor important. The truth was that nothing could prevent him from being swept up in the excitement of the campaign at some point. And then, when that moment came, he would be exuberantly off, purveying a fundamentalist brand of personal politics based on love, peace, and the brotherhood of man that had no clear precedent in American political history but that would certify him as leader of his party and nation. All that was needed was a catalyst, a glittering triumph that would instill confidence and propel him forward. It was to come late in September in John F. Kennedy's political heartland of New England.

The personal campaign of Lyndon B. Johnson for President began somewhat tentatively on Monday, September 28, in New England—almost a full month after Barry Goldwater started crisscrossing the country in his leased jet. On that long and memorable day, Johnson started at a Brown University convocation in Providence, Rhode Island, in the preponderantly Democratic country of lower New England, worked his way up through Connecticut, and concluded in the upper New England states of Maine, Vermont, and New Hampshire, steadfastly Republican by tradition but highly susceptible now to the Frontlash.

It was certainly not Goldwater Country, but neither was it Johnson Country. Thus, neither the President nor his entourage was prepared for the spontaneous burst of emotion that poured out of the supposedly staid, reserved New Englanders. Both the polls and the instinctive judgment of politicians showed Johnson to be not genuinely popular in his own right, but running far ahead of Goldwater because Goldwater was so unacceptable as President. In the minds of many, Johnson was the lesser of two evils. But not since November 22, 1963, had America cheered anybody. The nation wanted to cheer its President and pent-up emotion spilled over and engulfed Johnson.

At one stop that day, Johnson was so elated that he dragged Frank Cormier, White House correspondent for the Associated Press, to the restraining fence where flushed New Englanders were cheering and reaching out to touch their President. Johnson told Cormier that here was proof the people *did* like him. Write *that* in your story, he told Cormier, so the whole country can know!

The result for Johnson was intoxicating. Millions welcomed him on John Kennedy's home ground and the caution of the previous month evaporated. He was transported by the size and enthusiasm of the crowds. At jammed street corners, his motorcade pushing a hole through masses of people, he repeatedly left his seat, clambered to the roof of his limousine—smashing the radio antenna in the process—and yelled to the throngs through an electric bullhorn. Here was the feel of power, but deeper than that, of being loved and wanted. It perceptibly enlarged Lyndon Johnson in all his dimensions. Standing surrounded by human beings, he towered bigger than life, pulsing with vitality, glowing with assurance as the crowds pressed in. Johnson just took off at those New England stops. Gone was the stilted, confined television presence of Lyndon Johnson; here was the master administering The Treatment en masse. In turn, the enormous crowds were infused by his vigor, by the sheer power of performance, and reacted spontaneously.

His actual message, neither profound nor demagogic, was sheer Great Society consensus. America is *one* family, not North or South, not Republican or Democrat, not white or black. America is love, not hate; reason, not extremism; peace, not nuclear war. The implication was, of course, that Barry Goldwater stood on the opposite side. Here was the embodiment of the Frontlash.

Thus, at the portico of the *Hartford Times* building in Hartford, Connecticut, on September 28, Johnson ignored the words of his army of speech writers and set the tone of the Frontlash campaign in his own clear, unadorned style:

> There is a time for party and there is a place for partisanship. But there are times in the history of a nation when higher values matter more than party, and there are greater issues than partisanship.
>
> All that America is, and all you want America to be is challenged today by those who stand on the fringe. Against such a choice as this, responsible people have only one course of conscience, and that is to choose their country's interest over all other interests. I believe that this is a choice that you will make come this November.

New England ended all pretense of a non-campaign, ended all memory of John Connally's cautious strategy. The President was off and running on a six-week courtship of the American voter, seeking that record landslide and simultaneously shedding his inferiority complex as a national politician, acquired through repeated humiliations in national politics during the 1950s.

The lack of tight planning and organization in his travels had changed not a whit since 1960. Nobody could be sure of his schedule from day to day. Advance men, who prepared for the President's reception in a city long before he actually arrived, became superfluous. They carefully prepared for a Johnson visit to Madison, Wisconsin; the visit was scheduled on several occasions, but it was never made. There were no plans to visit Salt Lake City, and no advance men were dispatched there; to everybody's surprise, that's where Johnson went on October 29.

But if disorganization reflected the campaign of 1960, all else was different in 1964. The confidence that came out of New England on September 28 grew steadily through the campaign. The pattern was the same everywhere: the enthusiastic throng at the airport waiting for the thundering Air Force One to land; handshaking along the fences; the open car through the city streets with the President shouting over his bullhorn, "Y'all come down and hear the speakin'; come on down now to the speakin'"; the "speakin'" itself, with Johnson going on and on, like a country preacher, far longer than political candidates were supposed to speak—an hour, sometimes more. He gave them The Treatment, and he gave it with passion, gusto, humor, solemnity. He shouted—and he whispered. The "speakin'" was a fabulous success. The voters had never heard anything like it before, certainly never in a presidential campaign.

At a hundred-dollar-a-plate dinner in the Cleveland Convention Center the night of October 8, the President all but lost a fifteen-minute prepared speech in extemporaneous rambling that fascinated his audience for over an hour. By now, the image of Barry Goldwater as the warmonger ready to press the button and unleash a nuclear holocaust was complete. These words at Cleveland were the words of no anonymous ghostwriter, but of Lyndon Johnson himself:

> You don't get peace by rattling your rockets. You don't get peace by threatening to drop your bombs. You must have strength, and you must always keep your guard up, but you must always have your hand out and be willing to go anywhere, talk to anybody, listen to anything they have to say, do anything that is honorable, in order to avoid pulling that trigger, mashing that button that will blow up the world [and the President suggestively moved his hand toward an invisible box with the nuclear button].

For all his high success on the campaign trail, however, the President sometimes grew gloomy—not because he feared defeat but because he doubted the depth of the people's affection for him. To two old friends—Senator J. W. Fulbright and Dean Acheson—the President separately and sadly complained in mid-October that, notwithstanding his triumphant campaign tours, too many people seemed to be backing him only because of Goldwater's unacceptability. (This "lesser of two evils" theory had some basis in fact, indicated after the election when the total vote was found to be 1.2 percent less than the 1960 vote as a proportion of the total number of eligibles.)

Johnson asked Fulbright and Acheson what he should do about changing his image. He was told, first, that he was correct in thinking himself not the best-loved President in history; second, that there was nothing in the world he could do about it; and, third, that it did not make the slightest difference because *great* Presidents were often not greatly *loved* Presidents. Lyndon Johnson, whose quest for power had always been laced with an appetite for the public's affection, was not impressed.

These conversations with the President were reported to John Kenneth Galbraith. It was suggested that Galbraith, as an intellectual with a long acquaintance with Johnson, write a political pamphlet aimed at putting the President in a more positive light—and possibly cheering up Johnson a bit. As a result, Galbraith wrote a tract entitled "The Case for Lyndon Johnson," an unemotional, closely reasoned political pamphlet that made one point: Johnson deserved an overwhelming vote for President not because Goldwater was the only other choice but because, quite simply, "no one measures up better in our time."

"It is not enough that we elect President Johnson," wrote Galbraith. "We must elect him with a sense of satisfaction in our opportunity and of warm pride in our man."

From the beginning, the realistic among Barry Goldwater's campaign advisers felt that the one slim hope for a monumental political upset lay in what became known as the morality issue. A vague, unfavorable image of the President—based partly on emotion, partly on his reputation as a Texas wheeler-dealer not unwilling to cut a corner here and there—had taken hold throughout the country. Like all such moods, this one was based on innuendo, coupled with the hard fact of Johnson's fortune, built up while he held public office, and his earlier relationship with Bobby Baker in the Senate years. The polls showed that this mood was prevalent even among some voters who definitely planned to vote for Johnson anyway.

But how to exploit it? A tough, skillfully prepared documentary movie called "Choice" made a subtle effort to connect Johnson with a decline in public morality. But a sharp difference of opinion inside the Goldwater high command kept it off the television screens. There was surreptitious Republican help in some areas in distributing anti-Johnson smear literature, most disreputable of which was A Texan Looks at Lyndon by J. Evetts Haley, a Texas right-wing Democrat. As the campaign grew more bitter, the speeches of Goldwater and lesser Republicans became more explicit in challenging Johnson's character.

But to elevate these fragments into an important campaign issue required a genuine scandal. The Bobby Baker affair happened to be the only scandal at hand, and Republicans hoped and prayed that somehow the revelations of Baker's extracurricular financial deals would implicate the President. The Baker case had been glossed over by the Senate Rules Committee, but Republicans got new hope on September 10 when the Senate, by a vote of 75 to 3, reopened the matter because of new evidence and assigned it for full investigation to the Rules Committee. For a moment, it appeared that the escapades of the bright young man from Pickens, South Carolina, whom Johnson had not seen or spoken to since he became President, might suddenly spring into the headlines again, just on the eve of the presidential election.

Certainly that was the intent of Senator John J. Williams of Delaware, whose persistent sleuthing had uncovered the new evidence sufficient to convince the Senate to reopen the case.* Certainly that was the hope expressed by the Republican minority on the Rules Committee. But the President was in close touch with the Senate on the Baker case through the discreet efforts of Abe Fortas. Thus, having reopened the case on September 10, the Senate on October 13 postponed the investigation until *after* the election. The last question during the campaign asked the President on this subject came on September 9. He answered that he favored "a thorough investigation and study of every indication that any federal law may have been violated." What he meant but didn't say was that it not come during the campaign.

Against this backdrop of Republican frustration, the tragic events revealed on October 14 came like a ray of hope to the Republican National Committee. Here was a bona fide scandal in being, perhaps striking at the heart of personal conduct that was Johnson's weakness. It was the first and only crisis of the campaign for Johnson.

On October 7, Walter Jenkins was arrested—along with an inmate of an old soldiers' home—in the men's room at the YMCA, one block west of the White House on G Street, for "disorderly conduct," a euphemism for inexplicable departure from accepted sexual conduct. Rumors flooded Washington, and the Republican National Committee, quickly notified, helped spread them. Abe Fortas and Clark Clifford vainly tried to kill publication of the news by personally visiting each of the three daily Washington newspapers. But the news could not be suppressed and was transmitted across the country by United Press International on October 14.

Walter Jenkins was no mere employee of the President. For twenty-five years, he had labored faithfully, effectively, and energetically as Johnson's confidential assistant. Alone among all of Johnson's aides, he had stayed and lasted, the faceless, anonymous servant to the end, serving Johnson without question and without ambition. His daughter Beth was Luci Johnson's best friend. Lady Bird Johnson and Marge Jenkins were warm friends. Jenkins had been privy to every Johnson hope and aspiration not only during the long years in the Senate but in the White House as well. He had, in fact, brought on his own destruction by driving himself in the service of Lyndon Johnson eighteen hours a day, seven days a week, until, his body exhausted and his mind stretched taut by overwork, he had simply fallen apart.

On October 15, Mrs. Johnson, heartsick over the tragedy, issued a statement from the White House filled with sympathy for Jenkins and his family. Johnson was campaigning in New York. He said nothing

* Johnson made an unscheduled, last-minute campaign stop in Delaware in a futile effort to beat Williams, who was running for a fourth term in the Senate.

for well over twenty-four hours, despite the strongest advice from both his staff and from Mrs. Johnson herself that he say something to ease the anguish of his friend. But Johnson was torn between two conflicting forces: friendship and the fact the election was less than three weeks away.

For, in those dark hours the evening of October 14, a wave of fear swept through the White House that this could be the happening that would change the course of history. Jenkins had been privy to every piece of classified intelligence in the White House. Was it possible that he had been subjected to blackmail, that the incident of October 7, or perhaps previous incidents, had been exploited by enemies of the United States? Within hours of the disclosure, Republicans were suggesting just that. Goldwater began talking about Johnson's "curious crew" to the roar of approval from the Republican faithful.

Johnson resolved the conflict between friendship and the election by coming down on the side of the election.

He said nothing at all about Jenkins. He did not speak to Jenkins. He did what he had to do as President, instructing Abe Fortas to get Jenkins' resignation. He ordered an immediate investigation by the FBI (resulting in a report by J. Edgar Hoover on October 22 that there was no evidence of any kind that Jenkins had compromised the security of the United States).

Simultaneously, the President commissioned Ollie Quayle to take an emergency public-opinion poll. It indicated the Jenkins case would have no perceptible effect on the election.* Only then, late at night on October 15, the day after the story had broken, did the President finally issue a statement praising Jenkins' twenty-five years of "personal dedication, devotion, and tireless labor" and expressing "deepest compassion" for both him and his family.

And although the Jenkins case would not in any event have had an impact on the election, a torrent of dramatic world news soon drove the sad story from the front pages. One day after the fall of Walter Jenkins, Soviet Premier Nikita Khrushchev was deposed in Moscow (and the British elected a Labor government). Two days after the fall of Walter Jenkins, the Chinese Communists exploded their first nuclear device. (Besides, Americans were preoccupied by a cliff-hanging World Series between the Cardinals and the Yankees.) The fall of Walter Jenkins was ignored. Efforts by Goldwater's staff to re-

---

* A voter sample in three widely separated areas—California, Michigan, and Kentucky—taken by the authors on October 16 and 17 had similar results. One housewife, asked if the Jenkins affair had weakened her support for the Democratic ticket, seemed surprised at the question. "Why should it?" she replied. "I never was going to vote for Jenkins."

vive this personal tragedy as a symbol of decadence in the Johnson Administration and deterioration in American life failed. Having come through a dangerous political crisis with his assets untouched, it was strange indeed when, two weeks later, the President remarked in San Diego that President Eisenhower had also had a problem with sexual deviates. Now Johnson was trying to pyramid his assets, but it was a foolish thing to do. For Eisenhower had solved his White House problem by the simple expedient of not employing the young man in question. More important, by trying to associate Eisenhower with the problem of sexual deviates in government, Johnson was risking the very political recriminations he had successfully avoided for two weeks. But nothing came of it. In the fall of 1964, nothing could help Goldwater, nothing could hurt Johnson.

In Austin, Texas, on election eve, Lyndon Johnson said: ". . . it seems to me tonight . . . that I have spent my whole life getting ready for this moment." On the next day, that moment was sweet for President Johnson. Goldwater carried a mere 60 congressional districts out of 435, running far behind his party. Johnson ran far ahead of his, expanding the Democratic majorities in the Senate by 2 seats and in the House by 37, to a point not exceeded since the 1936 election. He captured slightly over 61 percent of the presidential vote, with a record-breaking 43,126,757 votes, and 486 electoral votes, the highest since Roosevelt's 1936 sweep. Although his plurality and his total popular vote both established new records, they resulted from population growth. Johnson had failed to equal Roosevelt's 63 percent in 1936 and Harding's 64 percent in 1920. Yet, Lyndon Johnson had no cause for unhappiness.

Behind the statistics was a revolution in American politics. The first Southern President since the Civil War captured 90 percent of the Negro vote and lost the Deep South by large margins. Mississippi voted 87 percent for Goldwater; Alabama 70 percent; South Carolina 59 percent; Louisiana 57 percent; and Georgia (which the President and his political aides had thought up to the very end would squeeze into the Democratic column) 54 percent. Outside the South, the Goldwater defeat was staggering. Goldwater beat Johnson in only one non-Southern state—his own state of Arizona, where his margin was embarrassingly close—and carried no congressional districts at all in thirty-two states outside the South. Of the seven non-Southern states in which Goldwater did carry one or more congressional districts, two were Border States and two were Mountain States.

And in his own state of Texas that had been such a source of trouble for thirty years, the divided Democrats were all winners. Johnson ran behind Connally but ahead of Senator Ralph Yarborough. Yarborough, in fact, symbolized the convulsive transformation in the politics of Lyndon Johnson, President, as contrasted with Lyndon Johnson, Texas politician. Having skillfully headed off a primary fight by Joe Kilgore against Yarborough, Johnson now campaigned hard for his old enemy in the last hours of the campaign.

I don't know what is going to happen tomorrow [he said in Houston on November 2] but I know what I'm going to do. I am going to get up early and I am going down to that Johnson City, Texas, courthouse and I am going to put a vote in for Ralph Yarborough and I am not going to do it just because I like him or because he is a friend. I am going to do it because I think that he has loyally and effectively worked for the Democratic program for all the people, and I want to be President of all the people.

On election eve, Johnson went to the LBJ Ranch and waited for that moment "that I have spent my whole life getting ready for."

It had been a chaotic campaign, with schedules canceled without forewarning, with no central management, with no coordination, with the right hand not knowing what the left was doing. Indeed, Johnson had learned little about the management of national politics since 1960.

Yet the campaign was a complete success. With Goldwater on the other side, it could not have been otherwise. But this campaign, which may have changed no more than a handful of votes, changed Lyndon Johnson. He might not be loved in Washington and by the eggheads and the stylish intellectuals, but he had proved to himself that he could be loved and had been accepted by the masses in the North. Acceptance of this solitary fact by Johnson himself—his last unmet goal—was the consummation of his power as a politician.

Late at night on November 3, with the returns piling up, Johnson left his headquarters at the Driskill Hotel in Austin to drive the few blocks to Austin's Civic Center. Now, of all times, was the time to let the tension run off, to relax, to bask in the glow of victory. The radio was on in the presidential limousine. A voice announced that President Lyndon Johnson had left the Driskill and was driving to the Civic Center to make a victory statement. Johnson listened, and his anger rose. He had authorized no announcement.

At the Civic Center, the newly elected President demanded to see Malcolm Kilduff, his assistant press secretary. He turned angrily on

Kilduff. Who let that out? he demanded. I didn't authorize any statement about where I'm going, when, or why. He accused Kilduff of
leaking to the press. Kilduff was innocent, and so pleaded, but the
President kept after him, furious that a premature leak had spoiled his
surprise.

But what had really happened was quite different. The reporters at
the Civic Center, kept in ignorance of the President's plans, had noticed that workmen were installing Johnson's special reading stand, an
elaborate rostrum with built-in Teleprompters, on the stage. Putting
two and two together, they correctly got four and reported that the
President was on his way.

Still later that night, in the high excitement of a victory celebration,
Johnson took pains to apologize to Kilduff for his outburst. Governor
Connally, who was with the President, turned to Kilduff and said:
"Mac, that's the first time in all these years I've ever heard him make
an apology." But November 3, 1964, was the first time Lyndon Johnson had ever been elected President. Now, his power consolidated, he
stood ready to build his Great Society—and a consensus America.

Chapter XXII

★ ★ ★ ★ ★ ★ ★ ★ ★

STOCKPILING ADVERSITY

No man can hold such a concentration of authority without feeling the urge, even though the urge be honest and patriotic, to push it beyond its usual bounds.

—Clinton Rossiter in *The American Presidency*

Shortly after noon on Saturday, March 20, 1965, seven men about to be named to high federal office by Lyndon B. Johnson gathered in the unpretentious dining room of the LBJ Ranch for luncheon with the President. For weeks they had known of their nominations, but they were admonished by the White House not to let a word of it seep out. It was already well known in Washington that press speculation about an unannounced Johnson appointment might change the President's mind. After weeks of worry that a chance word by wife, secretary, or business associate might give birth to the fatal newspaper leak, the seven appointees were secretly flown to Texas on that sunny weekend in March so that the President, flanked by the lucky seven, could break the news to the nation on a televised press conference from the ranch.

Now, just before that press conference, facing the President over the luncheon table, they were about to hear a remarkably revealing description of Lyndon Johnson's consensus. Six were being named to new jobs. The seventh was a progressive Republican from Vermont named Charles B. Ross who was being given a second four-year term on the Federal Power Commission. This was no routine reappointment. The FPC term that President Kennedy gave Ross had expired nearly ten months earlier on June 21, 1964. Although Ross had continued to serve through all those months of uncertainty, his ambiguous status was a source of controversy that had troubled Johnson even before the end of Ross' term. Almost from the first day of his presidency, Johnson had worried about Ross.

More than any other regulatory agency, the FPC dealt with basic industry-versus-consumer pocketbook issues through its regulation of the electric power and natural gas industries. Accordingly, ever since the end of World War II presidential appointments to the commission were the subject of intense behind-the-scenes lobbying and bitter ideological struggles. The majority that controlled the five-member commission throughout the Eisenhower Administration was pro-industry, enough so to postpone carrying out the Supreme Court's *Phillips Petroleum* decision of 1954, which authorized federal regulation of natural gas prices. In his first year in office, President Kennedy radically changed the complexion of the commission with nominations giving it a 3 to 2 majority in favor of the consumer. One member of that majority was Ross, a peppery Yankee lawyer recommended to Kennedy by Senator George Aiken, the influential and sardonic Vermont Republican who had battled the utilities all his public career.

Ross' reappointment to another term in June, 1964, was a foregone conclusion—if Kennedy had lived. But Johnson was another matter. As Vice-President, he had heard the bitter grumbling from friends in the oil and gas industry over Ross' appointment, particularly from Senator Robert Kerr, who complained vociferously to Johnson. Thus, when Johnson entered the White House, the oil and gas lobby had understandable hopes that Ross would be replaced by a pro-industry commissioner, restoring the old Eisenhower balance. The fact that a series of landmark decisions resulting from the *Phillips* decision was about to be settled in 1965 made it all the more urgent to the natural gas industry that Ross not be reappointed. Backing up the oil and gas lobby was Senate Minority Leader Everett M. Dirksen, who privately urged Johnson to name a conservative Chicago railroad lawyer named Carl Bagge. By early spring of 1964, with pressures against Ross intensifying, it seemed unlikely that Ross would be reappointed.

But a vigorous counter-lobby on Ross' behalf was started by Senator Aiken, who enlisted the liberals in Congress and the press. To liberals who were not yet fully convinced by Johnson's performance during the transition, the Ross question transcended the price of natural gas. If Ross were not reappointed, their suspicions would be confirmed that the man in the White House was still the same Lyndon Johnson who in 1950 had led the fight against the reappointment of Leland Olds to the Federal Power Commission.*

Johnson was furious over the pressure on Ross' behalf. Before the 1964 election he advised New Frontiersmen still on the White House staff to warn Ross and his friends to pipe down if they wanted Ross

* See pages 34ff.

reappointed. But in fact, the lobby for Ross had made it close to impossible for Johnson to dump Ross on the eve of the 1964 campaign. So, characteristically, he neither reappointed Ross nor appointed a successor. Ross simply lingered on after his term expired and Johnson waited for some sort of compromise to present itself. It did, late in 1964, with the death of Harold Woodward, a conservative commission member. Johnson immediately perceived the essential elements of a trade. The vacancy could be filled with Dirksen's man Bagge and Ross could be reappointed. Johnson, in short, could name *both* Bagge and Ross, satisfying both Dirksen and the liberals and continuing the 3 to 2 consumer-minded majority.

But the President had no intention of making it that easy for Ross. He left the power commission question unresolved for several months after the election, not once contacting Ross. Johnson made certain Ross knew not only that he was mightily displeased by the lobbying campaign on his behalf, but that he did not fancy members of the power commission being designated either pro-consumer or pro-industry. In effect, the President was rationalizing the conflicting demands upon him from his Texas friends and his liberal supporters by turning to the Great Society consensus for the answer. *His* power commission would be neither pro-industry, as was Eisenhower's, nor pro-consumer, as was Kennedy's, but pro-consensus, as befits a President elected with forty-four out of fifty states.

So it was that on that late March Saturday afternoon in Texas, Lyndon Johnson faced Charley Ross across the luncheon table, relaxed in the total privacy of his ranch house, and discoursed freely on his concept of consensus government.

"As far as I'm concerned," the President began, "every one of you people who are going to be on these regulatory agencies has got to act just like a judge. I get sick and tired of having people tell me that I have got to appoint someone on one of these agencies because they represent one of the interests that is concerned with the operations of the board."

If anyone at the table did not know Johnson was talking about Ross, he dispelled the doubt. "You take Charley Ross here," he said. "All of the liberal groups in the country kept telling me I had to reappoint Charley because he represented the consumer and I had all the conservative groups tell me I should *not* reappoint him because he represented the consumer groups.*

* Although Bagge had been vigorously supported by the conservatives, and was seated at the luncheon table, Johnson directed his remarks primarily to Ross. Curiously, it was Bagge, not Ross, who ran into trouble before the Senate Com-

Johnson gave the impression that Ross' public identification as a consumers' man at one point had marked him for a quick return to Vermont. "But then," Johnson went on, "the Governor up there [Philip Hoff, a Democrat], one of the finest Governors in the United States, told me that he went to school with Charley and practiced with him and he told me that while Charley was a Republican, he was one of the fairest he ever knew and every decision he made, he made because he thought it was the right one, not because it was on behalf of one group or another or because it was good for the Republicans or for the Democrats but because it was the right thing to do." In other words, what changed Johnson's mind, he was implying, was that despite Ross' record as a consumers' man he was also a *consensus* man, and that met the essential LBJ job qualification. He would take not the liberal position but the *right* position.

Continuing his monologue, the President next turned to Samuel Zagoria, a former newspaper reporter who had been the administrative assistant to Senator Clifford Case, the liberal Republican from New Jersey, and who was now being appointed to a vacancy on the National Labor Relations Board in the one big surprise among the seven appointments.*

"I got word," said Johnson, "that the business groups didn't want Sam because he was supposed to be too close to labor, and I had a number of other people call to tell me he would be a good appointment because he was liberal."

But Johnson wanted to make clear that whether Zagoria was or was not a liberal had nothing to do with his appointment: "I knew Sam up on the Hill and I knew his boss, Cliff Case, and I knew that both of them were fair-minded people whose first interest was the future of this country. I was sure that Sam would do what he thought was right whether it happened to be at the same time good for labor or good for business." Then Johnson expounded his philosophy of consensus: "In every instance I've ever seen, what's good for the country turns out, in the long run, to be good for business and labor. That's why we've got this great economy of ours and this great country of ours."

merce Committee—an indication of the deep change in the Commerce Committee and in Washington since the Leland Olds affair fifteen years earlier. The Americans for Democratic Action charged that Bagge had opposed housing desegregation in the Chicago suburbs but was unable to prevent his confirmation.

* In the group beside Ross, Bagge, and Zagoria were John L. Sweeney, chairman of the Federal Development Planning Commission on Appalachia; John G. Adams, member of the Civil Aeronautics Board; Stanley R. Resor, Secretary of the Army; and Howard Woods, Associate Director of the United States Information Agency.

In his consensus government, the President hastened to add, there was to be no public feuding. That was set before the new presidential appointees not as a hope but as an order. He cited as the messy example the public dispute between John Connor, the new Secretary of Commerce, and John Kenneth Galbraith over the international balance of payments problem. "Instead of conducting this debate in a proper manner," said Johnson, speaking like a schoolmaster to wayward pupils, "they ended up wiring telegrams to each other which quickly got printed in the newspapers. Now, how two men with the brains and talent of Jack Connor and Ken Galbraith can end up fighting in public is beyond me."

Next, the President issued a veiled warning to his new appointees to keep their disputes out of the newspapers: "I hope that all of you here today, if you've got anything to say to anybody else in this government that you disagree with, I hope you do it over the telephone. . . . Important people sitting on the outside [are] dying for an opportunity to step in and exaggerate every conflict that is bound to arise when we are trying to decide what policy to use to run this government." Speaking from the experience of more than thirty years in Washington and six administrations, Johnson said: "There's nothing the news people like better than open conflict between members of any President's administration."

Furthermore, said the President, the business of government should be conducted in as much secrecy as possible to facilitate compromise and avoid disputes. "When I was Senate Majority Leader, time after time I tried to talk it out with one of the folks opposing me or opposing what I knew a majority of the Senate wanted to do. The next thing I knew everything I said was on the front page of, first, that fellow's hometown paper and sure enough on the front page of the Washington papers the next day." That was enough to harden positions and make a solution impossible.

"Fortunately," the President added, "there was always enough Senators up there who knew you had to give and take to get a job done and the best way to do the giving and the taking was in the privacy of the Senate chambers, not on the television screens or the front pages."

Again, this injunction for secrecy was aimed squarely at Ross, whom Johnson blamed for leaking stories about his possible removal from the commission. But quite apart from Ross, the President's luncheon monologue on March 20 captured the vital core of the Johnsonian concept of power and its exercise. Symbols and ideological slogans had no part in his administration. They simply reduced his flexibility and aroused counterproductive pressures.

Johnson saw himself at the center of a new "Era of Good Feelings" similar to the period of one-party rule during the Virginia "dynasty" between the two Adamses that reached its culmination in the administration of James Monroe. He regarded his vast majority against Goldwater as a permanent base of support. Partisan, ideological, and factional disputes would give way to serene consensus presided over by Johnson. Members of the Federal Power Commission should be neither pro-industry nor pro-consumer and members of the National Labor Relations Board should be neither pro-union nor pro-employer.

But a conflict between this euphoric vision of American politics and the personality of Lyndon Johnson soon became evident. To achieve truly the new Era of Good Feelings would require a forbearance against the use of power that was basically alien to his nature. Even by itself, Johnson's grand design for the Great Society was likely to open up cracks in the consensus he achieved on Election Day. Thus, the Era of Good Feelings was inherently inconsistent with the Great Society. It was crumbling at the edges at the very moment the President was lecturing his new appointees on March 20. For his insistence that the 89th Congress break all records in the passage of legislation was already straining the Johnson consensus on which the Era of Good Feelings depended.

Arriving in Washington as a New Deal Congressman in 1937, Lyndon B. Johnson was appalled to find Congress in revolt against President Roosevelt because of his ill-conceived effort to pack the Supreme Court. The spectacle of a politically attuned President, just elected in a landslide, being repudiated by Congress because he had pressed his mandate too far never was forgotten by Johnson. To Johnson, moreover, the history of the presidency during the twenty-eight years following Roosevelt's disastrous Court fight had been one of unceasing warfare with the legislative branch in which the White House, while gaining some great victories, suffered all the while from continuous harassment and flanking attack by Congress. No President had escaped such affliction at the hands of Congress. Knowing that as well as he did, Johnson was not apt to underestimate the tenacious power of Congress.

There was, then, immediately after the election, determination by the President not to make Roosevelt's error and squander the great political potential of his landslide over Goldwater by allowing his relations with Congress to deteriorate. The power derived from his election victory, Johnson felt, must be employed judiciously. To a visitor at the LBJ Ranch shortly after the election, Johnson compared that power to a bottle of Bourbon. "If you take it a glass at a time," he said, "it's fine. But if you drink the whole bottle, you have troubles. I plan to take it a sip at a time and enjoy myself." He planned to "take it a sip at a time," but he also planned to pass the Great Society legislative program in the most furious burst of speed since Roosevelt's Hundred Days.

A similar theme was set forth in January, 1965, when the congressional liaison officers of the federal government—the administration's lobbyists whose task was to push the Great Society program through Congress—assembled in the Fish Room at the White House for a private pep talk from the President.

"I have watched the Congress from either the inside or the outside, man and boy, for more than forty years," Johnson began, "and I've never seen a Congress that didn't eventually take the measure of the President it was dealing with." He then took the federal lobbyists on a guided tour of presidential-congressional relations, beginning with the Senate's refusal to ratify Woodrow Wilson's Versailles Treaty and going on to tell how he had watched the Senate investigation of the Teapot Dome scandal "drive Warren Harding to an early grave" and how the Democratic-controlled Senate in 1931–32 "made Herbert Hoover's last two years sheer misery."

He came to Roosevelt's defeat on the Court issue in 1937, only days after he had taken his own seat in the House. "Here was a man who had just been elected by the biggest landslide in history and had the Congress slap him down," Johnson continued. "That poor man sat there in his wheelchair in the White House and just couldn't get around to all the congressional offices."

Now, he came to the present: "I was just elected President by the biggest popular margin in the history of the country, fifteen million votes. Just by the natural way people think and because Barry Goldwater scared hell out of them, I have already lost about two of these fifteen and am probably getting down to thirteen. If I get in any fight with Congress, I will lose another couple of million, and if I have to send any more of our boys into Vietnam, I may be down to eight million by the end of the summer."

Precisely because of this inexorable attrition in his power, Johnson went on, it was necessary to pass the Great Society program *now*, without delay. Between the Great Society program and "one sip at a time," there could be only one choice: the program.

The very existence of that voluminous program was bound to accelerate the decline of presidential power following the election. No

President could ask for so much and hope to maintain totally amicable relations with Congress.

And beyond that was the corruptive quality of presidential power— corruptive because it was a constant temptation for any President to reach too high and too far, as Roosevelt had done in 1937 and as Johnson was to do in 1965, although with infinitely less disastrous results. In taming Congress after Kennedy's death, Lyndon Johnson had already abandoned the caution so essential to run the Senate with the meager power offered by the office of Majority Leader. From his first showdown with Congress over the wheat-to-Russia issue, he had treated Congress with a whip hand that, effective as it was, was reckless by comparison with his former methods.

Now, in 1965, his power as the country's chief legislator was greatly magnified, not merely by his own victory but because the Goldwater debacle had produced the largest Democratic majorities in Congress since 1937. With a net Democratic gain of one seat in the Senate, the 2 to 1 Democratic majority first attained in the 1958 landslide was maintained, 68 to 32. But the impact of the 1964 vote was truly felt in the House, which had been so troublesome for President Kennedy. The Democrats now controlled it 295 to 140, a net gain of thirty-seven seats. With such swollen majorities, anything seemed possible and the specter of Franklin Roosevelt's humiliating defeat in 1937 might well have retreated from Lyndon Johnson's consciousness after that January lecture in the Fish Room.

At the core of Johnson's legislative program were those two liberal measures that had eluded the Democrats throughout the postwar era and could not be attained even in the legislative rush immediately after the assassination: medical care for the aged, financed via the Social Security system, and federal aid to elementary and secondary schools. Even with the huge Democratic majorities of 1965, passage of these two key bills was by no means a certainty, so formidable was the opposition.

Well before the 1964 election, Johnson got to work finding a new approach to the education problem. Without announcement, a presidential task force headed by Dr. John W. Gardner, president of the Carnegie Corporation, was directed by the President to find a new concept of federal aid to break out of the stalemate pattern that had ensured defeat in Congress in past years.* Wilbur Cohen, the Under Secretary of Health, Education, and Welfare, suggested in a flash of

* Gardner later became Johnson's Secretary of Health, Education, and Welfare.

insight that the education program should somehow be blended into the War on Poverty. He tossed his idea on the table: Why not channel the federal aid into low-income school districts? That concept, essentially so simple, was the prelude to a breakthrough of sensational proportions. It was enthusiastically adopted by the task force.

The second great accomplishment of Johnson's Task Force on Education was a scheme to give Catholic schools access to books and educational centers for special instruction under the new program. Here was the solution to the tangled religious puzzle over aid to parochial schools, the rock on which one federal aid bill after another had foundered. Moreover, education aid was now an idea whose time had come in 1965, just as the time had come in 1964 for the New Economics and the Kennedy tax cut. The school aid bill was passed overwhelmingly by the House on March 26 and, under the President's whiplash, was adopted by the Senate on April 9 without a comma changed.

Medicare proved scarcely more difficult. To reflect the increased Democratic majority, the ratio of Democrats to Republicans on the vital House Ways and Means Committee was increased from 15–10 to 17–8. That ended the ten-year fight. Not one to swim upstream against the current, Representative Wilbur Mills, the committee chairman, abruptly dropped his old opposition to Medicare (already crumbling in late 1963) and devised an ingenious substitute package that went beyond the administration's proposal but effectively disarmed the opposition by incorporating parts of a Republican substitute. By the Easter recess, Medicare had slipped easily through the House and was headed for certain passage in the Senate in July.

Education and Medicare were only a part of the torrent of legislation that rolled through Congress. Not since Roosevelt's Hundred Days had the first few weeks of a session accomplished so much. Indeed, Johnson kept one eye on the calendar in his frantic exhortations to the congressional leaders to pass as many bills as possible during his Hundred Days, ending April 13. Just as the Senate had rubber-stamped the House education bill, so now did the House approve without a single change the Senate bill providing special federal aid to the Appalachian states—a bill that Speaker McCormack had declined even to bring to the House floor the previous autumn because he feared it would be overwhelmed. With education and Appalachia bills passed, Johnson could and did make the factual claim on April 8 that his Hundred Days made "a record of major accomplishments without equal or close parallel in the present era."

It was only the beginning. Never had so much of such importance been passed in a single year: a major liberalization of the immigration laws; creation of a Cabinet-level Department of Housing and Urban Development; creation of a new Economic Development Administration (to replace the old Area Redevelopment Administration killed by the congressional revolt of 1963); a major housing bill. For the most part, the immense Democratic majorities placidly and obediently passed each succeeding element of the Great Society program. Occasionally, however, a presidential nudge was needed. At Lawrence O'Brien's request, he telephoned eleven members of the House to switch their votes on a cotton bill.* When Congress was about to give Governors a veto power over poverty projects in their states, Johnson phoned several Democratic Governors, not only changing their minds but persuading them to lobby against the Governors' veto with members of their home-state delegations.

For much of 1965, Congress was a curious study of conformity after decades of semi-rebellion. In the ancient tribunal, where Senators in the caustic, independent mold of Robert Taft and Lyndon Johnson grappled with the man in the White House, there was now a mood that approached slavish timidity and obedience to the merest presidential suggestion. Johnson's performance was mesmerizing Congress and the country watched transfixed. Indeed, the most surprising event of early 1965 on Capitol Hill was not the defeat of a bill that was supposed to pass, but the passage of a bill that nobody thought would even be brought up—the Voting Rights Act of 1965.

Far-reaching though it was in desegregating public accommodations and employment, the 1964 Civil Rights Act soon proved as inadequate as the 1957 and 1960 Acts in guaranteeing the Southern Negro his right to vote. In the deep South, massive resistance by White Supremacist sheriffs and voter registrars had not abated. So it was that in early January, Dr. Martin Luther King, Jr., leader of the Southern civil rights movement, concentrated on Selma, a small town in Alabama, for a campaign of voter registration. Within seven weeks, a bully-boy sheriff named James Clark had jailed two thousand men, women, and children, including Dr. King himself. On February 18, violence erupted when state troopers, summoned by Sheriff Clark, and Clark's own mounted possemen, routed unarmed Negro demonstrators. In the clash, a Negro boy was fatally shot.

When King called for a protest march to the state capital of Mont-

* The President employed typical hyperbole in telling reporters later that he had switched "twenty-one or twenty-two votes" on the cotton bill, giving rise to a rash of presidential arm-twisting stories that angered him. He didn't like being portrayed as an arm-twister, but he had only his own "statistics" to blame.

gomery, fifty miles away, on Sunday, March 17, state troopers ordered the marchers, numbering some seven hundred, to disperse, then attacked them with clubs and tear gas. On March 19, another march to Montgomery, this time with fifteen hundred marchers, including aroused clergymen who poured into Selma from all over the country, was blocked by a phalanx of troopers. That night, the tragedy reached a new climax when James Reeb, a thirty-eight-year-old white Unitarian minister from Boston who had come to Selma for the march, was beaten to death by white toughs. The wrath of the nation welled up against Alabama and its prophet of segregation, Governor George Wallace.

Seldom had such a wave of national indignation rolled across the country. Appalled and angered over the events of Selma, their emotions running deep and hot, Americans staged sympathetic protest marches in dozens of faraway places. For Johnson and his quest for an Era of Good Feelings, Selma was an agonizing wrench, quite apart from his own deep resentment. The President had hoped the 1964 Civil Rights Act would be the last word in such legislation for several years to come. Now it was clear that another civil rights struggle in Congress could not be avoided. The President ordered the Justice Department to draft a voting rights bill providing for federal voting registrars in areas where Negroes had been systematically deprived of the vote—precisely the type of federal intervention he had successfully opposed as Senate Majority Leader in 1960.* But now Johnson was President, and there was no question where he stood.

More pressing than the coming battle over the voting bill were demands by civil rights leaders that he send federal troops to Selma immediately to protect the civil rights workers. Although he had contingency plans to dispatch seven hundred soldiers there at a moment's notice, Johnson quietly advised one delegation of prominent civil rights leaders at the White House that he could not take such a step lightly. But the longer he delayed that decision the more latitude he gave extreme elements in the civil rights movement to make the ridiculous claim that Lyndon Johnson was in league with Wallace and the Alabama segregationists.

This was not Johnson's idea of the Great Society. Lyndon Johnson, even more than John F. Kennedy had been, was out of sympathy with the politics of demonstration. The civil rights workers who wanted so much to march from Selma to Montgomery, he privately mused, would accomplish a great deal more "if they were in Washington, working on their Senators, getting a voting bill passed."

* See page 221.

He was even more upset by the uproar in Washington caused by members of the radical Student Non-Violent Coordinating Committee who staged a sleep-in on the Pennsylvania Avenue sidewalk in front of the White House to protest the President's failure to send troops to Alabama. For a time, Johnson ignored them, then sent White House aides Bill Moyers, Lee White, and Cliff Alexander (a Negro) to talk to the sleep-ins. Although the President would not see them himself, and was uncomfortable about their presence, he would not use his power to remove them or in any way risk a comparison, no matter how farfetched, between himself and Sheriff Clark and Governor Wallace. "A lot of people think I should have just had those kids thrown out, just like that," Johnson remarked later. "But I know how much power I've got. I know I've got four million men under my command."

Selma was hardening into precisely the kind of dispute that Lyndon Johnson abhorred, with no easy solution, when suddenly George Wallace, a relentless publicity seeker, inadvertently came to the rescue with a surprising request to talk things over with the President.

At their White House meeting on March 13, Wallace assured the President he would call up the Alabama National Guard to protect the civil rights marchers, who at long last were to proceed on March 25 on their march to Montgomery under the mandate of a federal court order. Specifically, Wallace told the President that federal intervention to safeguard the march would not be necessary. But Wallace left the President's office and never publicly mentioned his assurance to Johnson. Back in Alabama, he sent Johnson a wire on March 18 flatly contradicting his pledge, asserting that the state of Alabama could *not* protect the marchers and requesting "sufficiently adequate federal civil authorities."

That was all Johnson needed. He set the stage with a statement deploring the need for federal intervention. "It is not a welcome duty for the federal government to ever assume a state government's own responsibility for assuring the protection of citizens in the exercise of their constitutional rights," said Johnson. He immediately federalized the Alabama National Guard and 1,862 guardsmen, as well as regular soldiers and federal marshals, were ordered to guard the route of march from Selma to Montgomery. Johnson was delighted that Wallace's blunder had at the time enabled him to intervene, thereby satisfying the civil rights protesters, and at the same time placed the responsibility squarely on Wallace, the champion of the bitter-end segregationists.

Now, having irrevocably set his course, Johnson began to view the

Selma crisis as a rare opportunity for personal leadership. Despite his misgivings about the Selma-to-Montgomery March, he concerned himself personally with every detail of it. It was Johnson who first noticed that the preliminary plans had made no provision for automobiles to return the marchers to Selma after they reached Montgomery.*

Moreover, he now threw himself with great zest and enthusiasm into the battle for the voting rights bill. He decided to go to Congress personally on March 15 to ask passage of the bill, the first special message on a domestic bill that any President had delivered in person since Harry Truman unsuccessfully asked for powers to break a nationwide railroad strike in 1946. But unlike Truman nineteen years before, Johnson allowed full play to his sense of theater. He went to the House chamber not at the normal hour of noon, when Congress convenes, but at night, when Americans would be home to watch him on television. The speech was both dramatic and evocative, and it was entirely a White House effort not cleared with the Justice Department lawyers. As such, it came closer to the Johnson Treatment than any of his former orations to Congress.

Adopting the "we shall overcome" battle cry of the civil rights movement, he declared:

> Their [the Negroes'] cause must be our cause too. Because it is not just Negroes but really it is all of us who must overcome the crippling legacy of bigotry and injustice. And we shall overcome. . . .
> This great, rich, restless country can offer opportunity and education and hope to all—all black and white, all North and South, sharecropper, and city-dweller. These are the enemies— poverty, ignorance, disease. They are enemies, not our fellow man, not our neighbor, and these enemies, too, poverty, disease, and ignorance, we shall overcome.

Johnson recalled the Mexican-American children he had taught at Cotulla, Texas, thirty-seven years before.

> My students were poor [he continued] and they often came to class without breakfast, hungry, and they knew even in their youth that pain of prejudice. They never seemed to know why people disliked them. But they knew it was so. Because I saw it

---

* The march was conducted without violence. After it was completed, a volunteer white civil rights worker—Mrs. Viola Liuzzo of Detroit—was shot to death by Ku Klux Klan nightriders while driving back to Selma from Montgomery. This murder further deepened public indignation and made all the more probable the passage of a strong voting rights bill.

in their eyes. I often walked home late in the afternoon after the classes were finished, wishing there was more that I could do. . . .

I never thought then in 1928 that I would be standing here in 1965. It never even occurred to me in my fondest dreams that I might have the chance to help the sons and daughters of those students and to help people like them all over the country. But now I do have the chance, and I will let you in on a secret. I mean to use it. . . .

Finally, in his peroration, Johnson explained the kind of President he wanted to be, and in the process came closer than ever before to defining the Great Society.

I do not want to be the President who built empires, or sought grandeur, or extended dominion. I want to be the President who educated young children to the wonders of their world. I want to be the President who helped to feed the hungry and to prepare them to be taxpayers instead of tax-eaters. I want to be the President who helped the poor to find their own way and who protected the right of every citizen to vote in every election. I want to be the President who helped to end hatred among his fellow men and who prompted love among the people of all races and all regions and all parties. I want to be the President who helped to end war among the brothers of this earth.

Although somewhat long, it was by all odds the best, most genuinely moving speech Johnson had made as President. It was the zenith of the first three years of his presidency, and it achieved that elusive rapport with the people that is so vital to any presidency. What started as frustration and irritation both with George Wallace and the Student Non-Violent Coordinating Committee ended in oratorical triumph.

On the next day, a friend complimented the President on his speech and asked who wrote it. Johnson pulled from his desk drawer a photograph showing him and the Mexican-American youngsters at Cotulla and pointed to his former students. "*They* did," Johnson replied.

The voting rights bill was passed by Congress in due course, for little that Lyndon Johnson asked was denied him by the first session of the 89th Congress. *Congressional Quarterly,* the unofficial congressional news service, calculated that Congress approved 68.4 percent of the proposals submitted by Johnson in 1965, the highest percentage since *CQ* began keeping its tabulations in 1954; it compared with the

57.6 percent for Johnson in 1964 and with the 27.2 percent for Kennedy's low point in the congressional revolt of 1963.

Yet, that 68.4 percent was attained at heavy cost. One of Washington's shrewdest lobbyists, watching the Great Society legislation pour out of Congress at an awesome rate, observed that the President was "stockpiling adversity," that the successes were leaving behind them a stock of ill will for the future.

The cost was heavier than it might have been. Caught up in the frenzy of the bill-passing splurge and continuing to ride the momentum, Johnson ignored both his own post-election warnings about the overexercise of power and the retributive power of the Congress against the President. In demanding that the Senate accept the House version of the education bill without changing a comma, and that the House accept intact the Senate version of the Appalachia bill in order to enact both bills within the first Hundred Days of the session, Johnson was inviting widespread criticism that Congress had become a rubber stamp—the kind of criticism to which the pride of Congress responds with anger and intransigence. So intent was the President on passing the Great Society legislation without change that he showed irritation at weekly meetings of his congressional leaders because Wilbut Mills had rewritten his Medicare bill in the House Ways and Means Committee and was getting credit for it in the press. Moreover, the incessant demand for more and more bills right up to the sine die adjournment of Congress on October 23, the seventh straight congressional session to go into the autumn months, was taking its toll.

But what most soured relations between the President and Congress was not a legislative matter at all, but a matter of economy. Boldly determined to save money for Great Society programs by stripping some of the fat out of the pork barrel, the President gave the Veterans Administration authority to close down thirty-two inefficient facilities. On January 12, it was announced that eleven veterans' hospitals, four old soldiers' homes, and seventeen regional offices across the country would be padlocked.

Johnson had unaccountably failed to take into consideration the first rule of life on Capitol Hill. Even the most conservative, economy-minded Congressman will fight unto death the removal of any federal facility in his own district. Less cautious now with the cushion of his immense majorities, Johnson had made no preparations for his reform. Representative Olin (Tiger) Teague, a conservative Texan who headed the House Veterans Affairs Committee, was lost as a potential ally in the hospital fight when Johnson informed him of the hospital closings after the decision had been made. "He *told* me, he didn't *ask* me," Teague complained.

Nor had any attempt been made to prepare Senator Mike Mansfield, the ever-faithful, ever-docile Senate Majority Leader, for the blow. As a result, the January 12 announcement unlocked deep resentment lurking just beneath Mansfield's placid exterior. Furious at the proposed closure of the Veterans Administration hospital at Miles City, Montana, in his home state, Mansfield lashed out on January 13 in an uncharacteristic attack on the economy move as "an appalling, backward, and insensitive act." Testifying before the Senate Labor and Public Welfare Committee on January 22, Mansfield's fury had not abated. He condemned the closings as "heartless" and "outrageous."

Johnson resented Mansfield's public display of anger. At meetings with his congressional leaders, the President repeatedly turned to Mansfield and, embarrassing the other Democratic leaders, mercilessly needled him about his opposition to the hospital closings. But it was not a laughing matter to Mike Mansfield. Tense and white-faced, he sat silent, puffing on his pipe and seething inside.

At the first meeting of congressional leaders after the announcement of the hospital closing, Johnson told Speaker McCormack he planned to go ahead and close the hospitals no matter what Congress said. Speaker McCormack replied quietly that if the President did that, Congress might pass a bill forbidding him to close any hospitals. I'll veto it, said Johnson. Mr. President, McCormack said gently but firmly, I have to caution you that Congress would pass it over your veto. Johnson replied that he had always heard that no President could get along with Congress and now his own Congress was proving it.

Johnson had to retreat. The closings were suspended, and a special advisory committee was appointed to make recommendations. On June 8, following those recommendations, Johnson announced he would close only six of the eleven hospitals, two of the four old soldiers' homes, and nine of the seventeen regional offices. Among those installations reprieved was Mansfield's Miles City hospital. Although Johnson was forced to draw back, his success in closing *any* of the politically protected veterans' installations was a formidable achievement often contemplated but never attempted during eight years of Republican rule under Eisenhower. Yet, the wounds of this battle between President and Congress never quite healed. The President was stockpiling adversity.

By summer, the Era of Good Feelings had evaporated on Capitol Hill. The supposedly docile 89th Congress was displaying an undercurrent of rebellion. The preview of what would come later occurred June 17 on a relatively minor matter—Johnson's proposal that the

Federal Aviation Act be amended to permit a military man, retired Air Force General William McKee, to be named director of the Federal Aviation Agency. A motion to recommit the bill to the Senate Commerce Committee was beaten 35 to 33 in a vote that had more to do with stirrings of anti-Johnson rebellion than with General McKee.

As the long session neared its end, the rebellion came increasingly into the open. Nevertheless, the President insisted on pressing ever more proposals on Congress, proposals which, unlike federal aid to education and Medicare, lacked a long gestation period and for which no consensus had been developed. In his determination to milk the last bit of legislation from his huge majorities, the President was courting defeat.

Defeat came for the first time on September 29 when the House surprisingly rejected a home rule bill for the District of Columbia, 227 to 174, in a direct repudiation of Johnson. Only two days earlier, the President put on an extraordinary exhibition of The Treatment to get the bill discharged from the hostile House District of Columbia Committee and onto the floor for a vote. On an issue of less than transcendent national importance, he implored Congressman after Congressman to sign the discharge petition. They did—but then, rebelliously, they refused to vote for the bill itself two days later.

The final six weeks of the session, with President Johnson recuperating from his gall bladder operation, were unpleasant indeed. On October 12, the Senate refused by a 47 to 45 vote to impose cloture on a filibuster against repealing Section 14(b) of the Taft-Hartley Labor Act, which enabled states to pass "right to work" laws banning compulsory unionism. The President's failure to come through on organized labor's most coveted legislative proposal weakened his tenuous ties with the labor movement.

Two days later, on October 14, the House voted 185 to 162 against appropriating funds for a new program of subsidies to low-income families to help pay their rent. Under heavy presidential pressure, the House had voted 208 to 202 on June 30 to authorize the rent-subsidy program. But like the earlier support for the discharge of the home rule bill, this vote was based on an artificial majority resulting from intense presidential pressure, not conviction.

These autumnal defeats could not detract from Johnson's magnificent triumphs in the 89th Congress and, before that, in the second session of the 88th Congress. Yet, by seeking to stretch his power a notch too far, and ignoring his own advice on how to deal with Congress, he lost his momentum on Capitol Hill and diminished his power there in a way that would be clearer in 1966.

Following the 1964 election, Walter Heller, about to end his long tenure as chairman of the President's Council of Economic Advisers and return to his chair of economics at the University of Minnesota, was quietly promoting an economic plan as daring as the income tax cut. It was now clear that the flowering of the economy, fertilized in large part by the fiscal and psychological impact of the tax reduction, would create ever greater tax revenue. That extra revenue could be used for still further tax reduction, for higher federal spending, or, least likely under Johnson because of its deflationary impact, for reduction of the federal debt. Heller proposed a fourth course: the return of a portion of the tax revenues to state governments, perhaps to be limited to expenditures for education.

Although difficult details remained to be worked out, the Heller Plan offered fascinating vistas. In one stroke, the public sector of the economy could be enriched and the increasingly comatose state governments revived. Moreover, by undercutting the Republican attacks against Democratic centralized government, the Heller Plan would place Johnson side by side with an enlightened concept of states' rights and thereby contribute to the LBJ consensus.

The Heller Plan fascinated Johnson. Consequently, just as Heller had lofted trial balloons for the tax cut early in the Kennedy Administration, he now selectively leaked his tax return scheme throughout Washington. But Heller misjudged his President. The early exposure of the Heller Plan stimulated a debate in and out of print that naturally included some little criticism of the plan. While President Kennedy had welcomed such debate in regard to the tax cut, President Johnson regarded public criticism of any proposal still in the formative stage as not just undesirable but actually destructive.* In Johnson's view, the exposure of the Heller Plan had subjected it to premature attack from pressure groups—most notably, organized labor—which, thought Johnson, mortally wounded it. Peeved at Heller, the President put the Heller Plan in a remote filing cabinet to be forgotten for a long and indefinite period, not because it had an inherent failing but simply because of its exposure.

The fate of the Heller Plan reflected the President's tendency in the weeks and months following the 1964 election to shroud his true

---

* "You are my poker," Kennedy told Heller in encouraging him to float trial balloons. "I want you to poke around with new ideas and see what you come up with."

moves in a pattern of secrecy and sometimes duplicity that might be called Government by Indirection. It was a tendency born not of caution and restraint but of quite opposite causes. Now that he had his own mandate, Johnson simply reverted to form, to the real Lyndon Johnson, shedding the restraints of the transition and re-establishing the politics of indirection that he had used so masterfully in the Senate. But in the Majority Leader's chair, indirection escaped criticism. Now it could not. Thus, Government by Indirection had a discordant result. It filled the hoped-for Era of Good Feelings with needlessly strident overtones.

A clear sign of the President's obsession with indirection came even before the election. Secretary of Commerce Luther Hodges, former Governor of North Carolina and the only member of the Kennedy Cabinet to have supported Johnson for President at Los Angeles in 1960, submitted a letter of resignation on October 30, 1964. It was no mere formality, Hodges informed the President, but a sincere desire to leave public service at age sixty-six. Johnson regretfully accepted the resignation but pleaded with Hodges not to say a word about his resignation before a successor had been found, lest he give the impression that the Cabinet was deserting the President. After the election, Hodges gently inquired if a successor had been found. The President said no and again asked Hodges not to disclose his resignation.

On the morning of December 16, Hodges was summoned at 9:15 A.M. to see the President, with no explanation given. At the White House he was ushered into the Fish Room and introduced to John T. Connor, president of the drug concern of Merck & Company, and a Republican-turned-Democrat who had served on the prestigious National Independent Committee for Johnson and Humphrey during the campaign. Connor, the President told Hodges, was the new Secretary of Commerce. In order to achieve maximum surprise, Johnson neither consulted Hodges nor gave him any warning so that he could prepare his staff in advance. The surprise was just as great for another man present in the Fish Room that morning: Franklin D. Roosevelt, Jr., Under Secretary of Commerce, who had hoped to succeed Hodges in the Cabinet.

Government by Indirection reached a dizzying peak at the LBJ Ranch over Christmas, 1964, when the President engaged the press in long monologues under ground rules providing that his comments could be printed but could not be attributed to him. The President said it would be impossible to keep the federal budget under one hundred billion dollars in the new fiscal year, which was, of course, headlined in all the newspapers. But as it shortly developed, Johnson's budget was again under one hundred billion dollars and the "informed" stories he generated greatly enhanced the wonder of his achievement.

The President told the press quite angrily that he had no intention of naming Marvin Watson, the conservative Democratic party leader in Texas, to the White House staff. In fact, Watson soon became his appointments secretary. The President told the press he did not plan a detailed State of the Union Address for 1965 but would limit himself to a statement of political principles similar to his article, "My Political Philosophy," appearing in the Winter 1958 edition of the *Texas Quarterly* (setting off a mad dash by reporters to get copies).* In fact, Johnson delivered a most detailed State of the Union Address giving the particulars of his voluminous Great Society legislative program.

But the most devious example of Government by Indirection that Christmas season in 1964 was the President's background advice to the press that, to give his administration a distinctive LBJ brand, he was planning drastic changes in the "Little Cabinet"—the number two men in the departments.† Only Cyrus Vance, Deputy Secretary of Defense, and George Ball, Under Secretary of State, would be immune, he said. In fact, Johnson had no such plan, but he did have a hidden motive in saying that he had a plan. He wanted to remove a single member of the Little Cabinet: John Henning, the Under Secretary of Labor. Secretary Wirtz, who by now was one of Johnson's most trusted advisers in the Cabinet, was at odds with Henning and wanted him out. But Henning, a California union leader, was under the ample protective blanket of AFL-CIO President George Meany. Johnson intended to solve this dilemma in the same way that he solved The Bobby Problem in 1964 by eliminating the entire Cabinet from all vice-presidential consideration. By planting the story that almost all members of the Little Cabinet were about to lose their jobs, the ouster of Henning would not be noticed. But the ploy failed. The labor politicians sniffed out the President's design, and pressure from Meany kept Henning in his job.

The fullest use of Government by Indirection in the months immediately following the election concerned not dismissal of high administration officials but their appointment. High-level appointees were

---

* This was the famous pronouncement that began: "I am a free man, an American, a United States Senator, and a Democrat in that order."

† To give an extra twist to the indirection, Johnson declared that any such story—not, of course, attributable to him—should be printed under a Washington dateline even though it had originated in Texas. The *New York Times* refused to play the game and did not run the story, but most newspapers complied.

warned by the White House not to permit premature disclosure before the President decided to announce it, and with good reason. Johnson named Angier Biddle Duke, the State Department's Chief of Protocol, as Ambassador to Spain. But before the announcement, Duke's family in Philadelphia informed the *Philadelphia Bulletin* and a story quickly appeared there in early January. When he heard about it, the President telephoned Secretary of State Dean Rusk, ordering him to withdraw Duke's name. Rusk replied that that would be difficult because the Spanish government had already agreed to Duke's appointment. Never mind the Spanish government, Johnson insisted. He wasn't going to stand for premature announcements. At great length, Rusk persuaded the President not to withdraw Duke's name, but Johnson warned he would not be so amenable if it ever happened again.

Johnson was not at all amiable that spring when his plan for a three-way, high-level personnel shift, involving the Commerce Department and the United Nations, leaked to the press. Lloyd Cutler, a prominent Democrat and Washington attorney who had generously volunteered of his time and skill to promote enforcement and acceptance of the 1964 Civil Rights Act in the South, was to replace Franklin D. Roosevelt, Jr., as Under Secretary of Commerce. Roosevelt was to take Franklin Williams' job as United States Ambassador to the United Nations Economic and Social Council. Williams would transfer to Washington to fill the long-empty deputy directorship of the Peace Corps, unofficially vacated by Bill Moyers on November 22, 1963. It was not surprising that in so complicated a bureaucratic shift quite a few people—including Cutler's fourteen law partners—would have to be notified well in advance of any announcement. Word of the Cutler-for-Roosevelt switch leaked out and was printed in *Newsweek* and the *Washington Post*. Convinced without a shadow of proof that Cutler himself had dropped the word, Johnson canceled the entire complicated personnel shift.

But if that seemed madness, it had its method. By striking hard at alleged transgressors, the President quickly got the message to everyone in his administration that indiscreet officials would not be tolerated. As awareness of this fact seeped deep into the collective subconscious of the federal government, the inevitable reaction was a tendency to clam up. That enhanced the President's personal control over the federal establishment, and enlarged the presidential exercise of power.

But outside the government, the Lloyd Cutler affair frustrated Johnson's efforts to recruit businessmen and lawyers. The recruitment problem was not a new one. Corporation officials and lawyers had heard about long hours, hard demands, and occasional abuse from above, and some of them were reluctant to join the Great Society. On December 5, 1964, in the East Room of the White House, while awarding the Congressional Medal of Honor to Army Captain Roger Donlon for heroism in Vietnam, the President was moved to extemporize:

> There are some men . . . who resist the glamour of gold and come here at great sacrifice to do for freedom in the capital of the free world, what Captain Donlon did for freedom in Vietnam. So very often, nine-to-five hours, Saturday at the country club, profit-sharing and pension trusts all mean so much that the call of country is sometimes answered with a "no."

The recruitment problem did not improve as stories of Johnson the Private Person came out of the White House. Indeed, many high-level officials in Washington were the very same ones Johnson had inherited on November 22, 1963. Although he had long since put his personal stamp on the government, the Cabinet remained for the most part the Kennedy Cabinet—even in its most critical positions.

Dean Rusk as Secretary of State and Robert McNamara as Secretary of Defense were firmly entrenched in Johnson's confidence, and he did not want to change them, but surely he would want his own man to fill the vacancy left by Robert F. Kennedy as Attorney General —the President's lawyer. Nicholas de Belleville Katzenbach, a former Yale and University of Chicago law professor who was Kennedy's Deputy Attorney General, had been serving as Acting Attorney General since Kennedy's resignation but seemed to have small chance to replace him permanently. In Johnson's view, Katzenbach was the wrong kind of Kennedy man—a Bobby Kennedy man, not a Jack Kennedy man.

A half dozen lawyer friends of the President—including his close advisers Clark Clifford and Abe Fortas—were sounded out for the job. One of them advised Johnson that with the Bobby Baker case still pending in the Justice Department, it might be wise to appoint a dispassionate lawyer without an intimate relationship to the President so that no charge of cover-up could be made. Accordingly on January 28,

Katzenbach was named Attorney General after five months as Acting Attorney General.

Johnson's difficulty in putting his own stamp on the Cabinet was underscored in his search for a Secretary of the Treasury, the most important domestic post in the Cabinet. Douglas Dillon, the New York Republican investment banker, informed the President of his intention to resign soon after the 1964 election. By the same token, it was no secret that Johnson wanted as his successor his old friend and adviser, Donald C. Cook, who as a private citizen in 1964 had helped devise Johnson's successful program of voluntary restraint in business investment abroad to reduce the balance of payments deficit.

But ever since serving Johnson full time in his 1951–52 defense preparedness investigation, Cook had turned down one job offer after another from Johnson. Now, to take the Treasury post and return to Washington would both frustrate his wife's desire to remain in New York and deprive his family of financial security by sacrificing lucrative pension benefits as president of the American Electric Power Company. Cook nevertheless might have taken the Treasury job had he not been subjected to a withering pincer from left and right. On the right, conservative bankers attacked him as an easy-money man. On the left, Senate liberals attacked him as a private-power man. What finally tipped the balance was Cook's concern that he might be the target of a Senate fight over confirmation. He firmly informed the President in late February he could not accept.

Thunderstruck, Johnson turned to Kermit Gordon, then preparing to resign as Budget Director to return to academic life with the Brookings Institution. Gordon also declined, fearing that the financial community might not have enough confidence in him. Then began a vast talent hunt for a new Secretary of the Treasury that turned up nobody. Morale at the Treasury, headless now that Dillon was gone, dropped. More serious, however, was the fact that the administration had no chief fiscal officer.

Johnson finally decided he could delay no longer and settled on Henry H. (Joe) Fowler, a veteran of the Truman Administration who had returned to serve ably as Kennedy's Under Secretary of the Treasury before resigning in April, 1964, to practice law in Washington. On Thursday morning, March 22, Fowler was called to the White House without explanation. When he arrived, he was *told* he was going to be Secretary of the Treasury. He quickly accepted.

Later, in private conversation, Johnson claimed Fowler had been his first choice all along and extravagantly praised his missionary work with Congress on the tax cut in 1963 and 1964. "He was there night after night," said Johnson, "plugging away while Doug Dillon was going to tea parties or putting on his white tie and tails." Yet, Fowler was not a presidential intimate as Cook was, nor would he become a strong man of the Cabinet as Cook would have.

As 1965 progressed, the President made a few spectacular appointments, topped by moving Arthur J. Goldberg from the Supreme Court to the United Nations on the death of Adlai Stevenson. Johnson also perfected techniques designed to prevent refusals. When Abe Fortas demurred at Johnson's proposal that he replace Goldberg on the Supreme Court, the President replied that he would make the announcement anyway at a televised press conference and then Fortas could refuse if he so desired. Fortas had very little choice. Lawrence F. O'Brien, who had been trying for months to resign as chief political expert on the White House staff, was called into the President's office in late August and informed he was to be Postmaster General. Even had O'Brien wanted to say no, which he didn't, he had precious little opportunity.

Yet the filling of high-level appointments remained troublesome and frustrating for Johnson. For all his skill in wielding the power of the presidency, he had not quite solved his old problem of Senate days, the problem of recruiting and *keeping* top-grade personnel.

Overshadowing President Johnson's housekeeping problem was the recurring image crisis. Despite the exciting accomplishments of the Great Society and the remarkably high public approval of his presidency, as shown in the polls, these polls continued to reflect the hard truth that Lyndon Johnson was not *liked*. And the politicians privately agreed with the polls.

In an effort to correct this vague mood, White House aide Jack Valenti appeared before the Advertising Federation of America in Boston on July 3, 1965, and delivered a three-thousand-word panegyric on Lyndon Johnson that was to have indignant reverberations. Anxious over the unfavorable press accounts of the President, ex-advertising man Valenti wanted to describe the real Johnson. He talked of "extra glands . . . that give him energy that ordinary men simply don't have"; of a man "not fond of those who continually say yes to him"; of a man who renews his spirit "in the tears and the laughter of the people." Then followed this sentimentalized verdict:

> I sleep each night a little better, a little more confidently because Lyndon Johnson is my President. For I know he lives and thinks and works to make sure that for all America, and indeed

the growing body of the free world, the morning shall always come.

Valenti's speech drew a picture so far removed from the general conception of the President that it set off sarcastic giggles throughout Washington, thereby unwittingly putting the spotlight on the flaws of Lyndon Johnson, the Private Person.* But that was only the culmination of the President's new image problem, just as the Easter joyride in 1964 had climaxed rather than created his public-relations problem that year. Thus, though the President had started the year with buoyant hopes of being a President of all the people and ushering in an historic Era of Good Feelings, an unfavorable image at odds with that goal had become so evident by July that Jack Valenti felt moved in his Boston speech to try to repair it.

In the summer of 1965, Johnson's truly formidable accomplishments in Congress were being overlooked by the fascination of the press with his personality, his foibles, his sudden excesses, the infinite variety of Johnson stories that made their way in a flood out of the White House. The press once again had become mesmerized by the Private Person, and he was being written about with a wealth of uncomplimentary detail and in such a way as to erode his broad base of national support. Johnson's giant idiosyncrasies were dwarfing his giant accomplishments, and he was inadvertently feeding these unflattering typewriters by taking the press on exhausting walks around the White House lawn, and by delivering marathon monologues in his office. Trying to win the press, he was alienating the press, for what they saw was so much bigger than life they could not absorb it.

The image crisis of 1964 had been solved when the Exposure school defeated the Containment school and put the President on view as a Public Person, typified by the genial, kindly President shaking hands with tourists at the White House gates. But by the summer of 1965, the Public Person was familiar—too familiar, perhaps—in every household across the land. Now it was time for the Containment school to take over and, led by Bill Moyers and Lady Bird Johnson, ration both the Private and Public Person.

On July 9, at the private urging of Mrs. Johnson, Moyers was named press secretary to replace George Reedy, who longed to leave the job and needed surgery to correct a painful foot condition. It was a fundamental change, not just of personnel but of basic function. For Moyers, retaining his role as Johnson's policy staff chief, was to be no

* In May, 1966, Valenti was named President of the Motion Picture Association of America at a salary of approximately one hundred and fifty thousand dollars a year.

mere press aide to the President. He would *supplant* the President in dealing with the press. In keeping with the Containment theory, Moyers was determined to interpose himself between Johnson and the press. Johnson, who finally concluded that a beneficial relationship with the Washington press corps was impossible and that close contact tended to breed mutual contempt, was agreeable.

This radical change had immediate benefits. The news accounts of Johnson as a Private Person ceased. He was presented to the country now only as a Public Person, and even then heavily shrouded by Moyers' intercession.

But though the image problem was eased, it was not solved to the degree that it had been in 1964. For in 1965, long before Jack Valenti's speech and Bill Moyers' intercession, Lyndon Johnson had become increasingly confronted with foreign policy crises of such agony that no President dealing with them could maintain the image consistent with an Era of Good Feelings. The growing United States involvement in the Vietnam war was becoming a bloody test of the courage and skill of any President. But before the Vietnam crisis reached its full flower, Johnson had to face a flash crisis in the Caribbean that would indelibly change his presidency.

Chapter XXIII

★★★★★★★★★★

THE DOMINICAN INTERVENTION

[Johnson's] irrelevant rationalizations and often inaccurate reconstruction of events . . . conspired to turn an essentially unman-
ageable and, in some ways, unavoidable crisis in a fundamentally
unstable and crisis-prone Caribbean nation into a crisis of confidence in the President himself.
> —Philip L. Geyelin in *Lyndon B. Johnson
> and the World*

"You can imagine what would have happened," Lyndon Johnson said
privately on May 3, 1965, five days after he had ordered the United
States Marines to land in the Dominican Republic, "if I had not done
so and there was an investigation and the press got hold of that cable."

"That cable" arrived in the White House at 5:14 P.M., Wednesday,
April 28, from W. Tapley Bennett, the United States Ambassador in
Santo Domingo. Bennett had the deeply inbred caution of a career
foreign service officer in a post of utmost sensitivity. He recommended
an immediate landing of the Marines and warned that "American lives
are in danger" ("blood will run in the streets," Johnson was to para-
phrase it later) if the Marines didn't quickly arrive.

It was, by any reasonable standard, the obvious advice to follow,
unanimously given not only by the ambassador but also by his deputy, the three military attachés, the economic attaché—the entire
"country team." When the full country team recommends immediate
emergency action, even so drastic an action as military intervention in
a foreign country, a President is more likely to accept that recommendation than not, particularly a President who, like Lyndon Johnson, is
guided by the consensus.

Yet, this obvious, wholly reasonable decision by Johnson was to subject him to criticism, primarily from the liberals, of an intensity he had

never before experienced in the White House and thereby change the nature of his presidency. In time, the growing United States participation in the ugly Vietnam war was to prove infinitely more damaging to Johnson's support from the liberals.* But in the spring of 1965, when Vietnam had not yet become the all-consuming issue of the day, the dramatic events of Santo Domingo sheared away the left wing of Lyndon Johnson's Great Society consensus. It was the first of a one-two punch—Vietnam being the far more lethal second punch—that was to undermine his high purpose to build a Great Society and that would force him into Great Power politics for which he had little taste.

Not since 1925 when Marines were dispatched to Nicaragua had the United States overtly intervened with military force in the affairs of a Latin country.† The Nicaraguan intervention occurred two years after the United States Marines left the Dominican Republic, following an eight-year occupation ordered by President Woodrow Wilson to restore order after a series of bloody revolutions. The upshot of that long occupation had not been cheerful. In 1930, a young police officer named Raphael Trujillo won a rigged presidential election and established the most efficiently ruthless dictatorship in the hemisphere. After thirty-one years of total power during which he operated the Dominican Republic as a private business, extracting a vast fortune out of its miserable three and one-half million people, the Generalissimo was assassinated on May 30, 1961. A few days later, with the future of the Dominican Republic uncertain and dangerous, President Kennedy remarked that three possibilities were open in "descending order of preference." They were: "a decent democratic regime, a continuation of the Trujillo regime, or a Castro regime. We ought to aim at the first, but we really can't renounce the second until we are sure that we can avoid the third."

What Kennedy was saying was that no American President could tolerate the establishment of a second Communist state in the Caribbean. A totalitarian government of the right was to be avoided if at all possible, but one of the Communist left, with political, military, and economic links to the centers of Communist power in Moscow and Peking, was unthinkable.

* President Johnson's Vietnamese policy is dealt with in detail in Chapter XXIV.
† The Marines were dispatched by President Calvin Coolidge to put down a liberal insurrection and support a conservative for president. They did not leave until 1933, although the Havana Conference of Latin American states in January, 1928, adopted a resolution declaring that "no state has the right to intervene in the internal affairs of another."

For four years, the question never presented itself either to Kennedy or to Johnson in quite that form. But the Dominican Republic was scarcely tranquil. After a series of transitory provisional governments following Trujillo's assassination, the Dominican people on December 20, 1962, elected Juan Bosch as their president. Bosch was a leftist, non-Communist visionary and writer who had spent years as an anti-Trujillo exile. Kennedy dispatched Vice-President Lyndon B. Johnson as his emissary to Santo Domingo for the Bosch inauguration on February 27, 1963, when Johnson and Bosch were photographed in a much-publicized Latin *abrazo*. The "embrace" was followed by higher per capita foreign aid than the United States gave any other country in the world, although reduced from the aid level to the preceding provisional government. Both before and after Bosch was elected, the United States injudiciously talked about making the Dominican Republic the showcase for democracy in the Caribbean, in stark contrast to Castro's totalitarian Cuba.

Actually no infusion of United States dollars could instantly counteract the oppressive weight of thirty-one years of dictatorship. The police and segments of the right-wing military remained corrupt. The far left was noisy and troublesome. And once in office, President Bosch inflexibly refused to take seriously the small but dangerous totalitarian left—comprising both Moscow and Peking Communists and Castroites trained in Cuba. Through his eyes, they were a threat neither to his Dominican Revolutionary Party (PRD) nor to his government. Moreover, Bosch showed a marked ineptitude in dealing with the political generals of the Dominican military, who for so long had been the protectors of the oligarchs. The result was a military coup on September 26, 1963, overthrowing Bosch, who fled to exile in Puerto Rico.

The successor government headed by Donald Reid Cabral, a progressive-minded member of the Dominican oligarchy, attempted on a businesslike basis to build a sound economic and political foundation for the troubled country. But Reid was handicapped by a long cessation of United States aid following the coup, a lack of support from the Dominican masses and politicians, and increasing trouble with the military. His hard-headed reforms were attacked and subverted by special interests on all sides.

By early April, 1965, the Dominican Republic was getting ready to explode. Ambassador Bennett, in a secret telegram to Washington urging an immediate United States pledge of aid for the embattled Reid government, paraphrased the Bible to sound a melodramatic warning:

Little foxes, some of them Red, are chewing at the grapes. It is impossible to guarantee a good harvest in view of the many unfavorable aspects of the local scene. It is, however, fair to say that a diminution of our effort or failure to act will result in a bitter wine.

Bennett wanted a pledge of twenty-five million dollars, but Washington allowed only four million dollars. On April 23, Bennett returned to the United States to spend a few days with his family in Georgia. It was an unfortunate choice of dates, because on Saturday, April 24, with the sudden violence of long-suppressed passion, Dominican civil war burst out in uncontrolled fury. What began as an attempted coup by Boschist Army officers turned into civil war as angry masses poured into the streets of Santo Domingo. It was now clear that Reid had fallen. But who would succeed him? A junta of the regular military, which became known in Washington as the Loyalists? Or the young officers and their supporters in the various leftist parties of the country, called the Rebels, whose announced goal was to restore the overthrown Bosch?

On Monday, April 26, the State Department summoned Bennett to Washington from Georgia to advise him of deep concern over a possible Communist coup. The ambassador was informed of two possible contingencies: a violent upheaval which would leave the country at the mercy of extremists, both left and right; and, more to be feared, a sudden Communist take-over.

Returning to Santo Domingo that evening, Bennett lined up the full force of United States diplomacy on the side of the Loyalist generals. The primary reason was United States belief that the Rebels had quickly been infiltrated by disciplined Communists. In addition, however, the fact that the Rebels had committed themselves to return Bosch to power put Bennett on the side of the Loyalists. The entire United States "country team" in Santo Domingo regarded Bosch's return as little short of catastrophic.

Romulo Betancourt, the brilliant democratic politician who fought and defeated the Communists as President of Venezuela in the 1950s while maintaining the allegiance of the military, said of Bosch during the height of the Dominican revolution: "He is the best short-story writer and the worst politician in the hemisphere, and we should make sure that he keeps on doing what he is good at." Betancourt's judgment of Bosch was not much different from that of Johnson and the State Department but his judgment of the character of the revolution and the wisdom of Johnson's intervention was diametrically opposed.

When Bennett arrived back in Santo Domingo, blood was flowing in the streets and the United States Embassy itself was about to come under fire. At 1:43 P.M., on Wednesday, April 28, he sent the first of three critical cables to Washington:

> . . . while I regret reliance on a military solution for a politi-
> cal crisis engendered by a confused, democratic left, all valid
> elements of which are either in hiding or in asylum as much from
> the extremists in their own camp as from the military forces, the
> plain fact is that while leftist propaganda may fuzz the issue,
> the issue here now is a fight between Castro-type elements and
> those who oppose. I do not wish to be overdramatic but we
> should be clear as to the situation. . . . If the anti-Rebel forces
> lose for lack of heart, we may well be asking in the near future
> for landings of Marines to protect United States citizens and pos-
> sibly for other purposes.

At 3 P.M., Bennett dispatched his second cable to Washington:

> . . . Benoit [Colonel Pedro Bartolome Benoit, a leader of the
> right-wing Loyalist forces] telephoned to ask for twelve hundred
> United States Marines to help restore order. He was given no en-
> couragement. I do not believe the situation justifies it . . . the
> outcome is still in doubt . . . recommend contingency planning
> in case situation should break apart. Logically, the [Loyalist]
> forces should be able to control the situation. But the situation is
> not really very logical and a severe test of nerves is in process.

The reason the "outcome is still in doubt" was that the Loyalist forces had stopped their tanks on a bridge over the Duarte River, leading into the very heart of the rebel bastion, fearful that in the narrow streets of the old city the tanks could be destroyed by Molotov cocktails and other arms of Rebel street fighters. At that point the Loyalists, through lack of nerve, sacrificed the chance for a military victory.

At 5:14 P.M., what the President was later to refer to as "that cable" arrived. Called a "critic" or top-urgent message in diplomatic termi-nology, it was rushed to the White House. It made the following points: the situation "was deteriorating rapidly"; the military forces of the Loyalists were in a hysterical mood and ready to retreat from the Rebel forces; the Loyalists had formally asked for United States mili-tary intervention; American lives were in danger; "if Washington wishes," the landing of the Marines could be explained as essential to protect evacuation of American citizens. Bennett's conclusion: "I rec-ommend immediate landings."

When the "critic" arrived in the White House, Johnson was in the midst of a discussion on Vietnam with Secretary of State Rusk, Secretary of Defense McNamara, Under Secretary of State George Ball, and McGeorge Bundy, his principal White House adviser on National Security. There was not the slightest question what the carefully worded message was saying in between the lines: act now, Mr. President, or you may wake up tomorrow morning and find that the Rebel forces have come under Communist control and that the Dominican Republic is in their hands, the second Red island in the Caribbean.

For Johnson, the master of compromise and architect of persuasion, there now could be no compromise, no persuasion—and no escape. There was only one option: to exercise his power as Commander-in-Chief and send in the Marines. He took that option without flinching and, notably, without even the pretense of calling the congressional leaders to the White House for consultation before issuing the fateful order. Not one of his advisers opposed the decision.

Exactly seventy-six minutes later, the U.S.S. *Boxer*, an aircraft carrier with fifteen hundred Marines aboard, which the President had ordered to patrol off Santo Domingo on April 24 as a "precautionary measure," received the terse presidential order: Land the Marines. The decision that would so change the tone and mood of his presidency, and open a gaping wound in the Johnson consensus, had now been irrevocably made.

No decision in Lyndon Johnson's first seventeen months as President would subject him to such furious criticism. No decision would so expose him to charges of yielding to panic, of trigger-happy, gunboat diplomacy, of despoiling the American image around the world. But in fact, Johnson had precious little choice. Even had he been able to stop the clock, freeze the action in Santo Domingo, and dispatch a high-level mission for an on-the-spot investigation, his decision would have been precisely the same. Johnson did not panic, and was not trigger-happy. If the American image did suffer, that price had to be paid to avoid the catastrophe that his agents in Santo Domingo predicted.

Not only had they predicted catastrophe, they had taken an action on Tuesday, April 27, that all but sealed the decision the President would be compelled to make on the following day. On that afternoon, a delegation of Rebel leaders arrived in confusion and haste at the United States Embassy to plead for Bennett's help in arranging talks with the military. Convinced at that moment that the anti-Bosch Loyalist generals were about to end the revolution with their tank sweep through the heart of the old city, Bennett flatly refused. It was beyond his instructions, he told the Rebel delegation, to offer the good offices of the United States as conciliator in the revolution. Angry and broken in spirit, the Rebel leaders left the embassy, and with their departure the last chance to avoid the slaughter of the weeks ahead ended. For within the next twenty-four hours, the whole complexion of the revolution changed. Now the Rebels were suddenly rejuvenated in a transformation that amazed Western diplomats in Santo Domingo, and the Loyalists were turning tail and running. It was at this point that Bennett, convinced that Communist control of key elements of the Rebel command was responsible for the suddenly changed complexion of the revolution, called for the Marines.

Whether Ambassador Bennett and his "country team" did or did not exaggerate the Communist threat is not the point. In Cuba, the Eisenhower Administration had made the mistake of misjudging Fidel Castro, who masqueraded in the cloak of a reforming democrat and pledged free elections. When Castro dropped his cloak and emerged as a puppet of Moscow his deeds were past undoing. As Kennedy said in 1961, no President could risk a recurrence of the Cuban tragedy.

Thus, the decision to intervene seemed at the time the *only* logical decision and Johnson's choice of it the *only* logical choice. If there was panic in the President's performance during those turbulent days, it showed itself not in the act of intervention but in increasingly erratic behavior *after* the Marines had landed, as Johnson become inordinately concerned with criticism of his action. For having commanded bravely and speedily that Wednesday afternoon in a situation where all maneuver was denied him, he transformed the crisis of revolution in the Dominican Republic into a crisis of credibility in Lyndon Johnson.

It began an hour after the President's fateful command, when congressional leaders arrived at the White House, some in long, black limousines that glided silently through the Southwest Gate of the White House, some in their own cars. The atmosphere of high drama that always attends a sudden summons to the White House was especially marked now. Although the eventual extent of the United States military involvement was known to no one at that hour, including the President, the prospect of Americans fighting in two small countries—Vietnam and the Dominican Republic—halfway around the world from each other, was disturbing, and the meeting in the Cabinet Room was somber.

Johnson informed the congressional leaders that the decision to land the Marines had been taken, but he said nothing of his fear that Communist rule would be the result of no intervention. Instead, he followed the advice in Bennett's third cable and justified the intervention with a single purpose: protection of American lives in Santo Domingo. The President's closest advisers believed he could continue to explain the intervention in these terms without going into the difficult question of charging Communist control. But Senator Everett McKinley Dirksen, the Senate Republican Leader, raised the question—thus opening a dialogue that was to plague Johnson long afterward.

Dirksen told Johnson: "We're behind you one hundred percent. We cannot stand to have another Communist government in the Caribbean." Dirksen then asked Johnson the extent of Communist involvement. Admiral William F. Raborn, just seven hours on the job as the new director of the Central Intelligence Agency, answered with great care. The full extent of that, he said, was not yet known but the CIA was making an exhaustive study at that very moment. He did not want to exaggerate, he said, but it had been established beyond question that at least two known Communist agents, and possibly seven or eight, were in positions of authority in the Rebel camp. Johnson then gave the congressional leaders a preview of the statement he was about to make over television to the American people, explaining why it was necessary to intervene. Many hands had a share in drafting that initial statement, and not one of them thought, in the tension of the moment, to include any reference to the Organization of American States. When Johnson finished his reading of the statement, Senator Mike Mansfield, the Senate Democratic Leader, noted the omission. Agreeing with Mansfield, Johnson turned to Rusk and said: "Dean, that's a good idea, now you make certain it's there. . . ." A paragraph was quickly added to the President's television statement.

Although this omission was rectified in time, another was not, and it gave critics a pretext for complaint. That was the failure of the State Department to alert Johnson to the purely psychological and political expedient of notifying the OAS—not consulting it, because there was no time for that and it would have only led to tendentious and inconclusive debate among the Latins. The OAS was notorious for not acting—for delay, procrastination, and long speeches. Nevertheless, this seemingly minor oversight was a serious error in Johnson's usually meticulous preparations. Although the fault was the State Department's, it was Johnson who got the blame. José Mora, Secretary-General of the OAS, learned of the United States intervention not from the State Department but by coincidence. He was watching television when, at 8:51 P.M. Wednesday night, Johnson went on the air with his statement.

But far more important than the failure to notify Mora was the justification for intervention. As originally drafted at the White House, the President's announcement of the intervention included a vague reference to the danger of a Communist take-over, inserted by Dean Rusk. It simply stated that an additional requirement for the Marines was the need to protect "democratic institutions," a hint that nondemocratic forces, *i.e.*, Communist forces, were contesting for power. Adlai Stevenson demurred. He said that until the President could make a compelling case—that is, until the CIA and the United States Embassy in Santo Domingo could complete their investigation on the scene—it would be a mistake to drag in the Communist angle by indirection. Bill Moyers and Richard Goodwin joined Stevenson, and the President agreed. Rusk's reference to "democratic institutions" was crossed out. Johnson told the American people that night:

> . . . The United States government has been informed by military authorities in the Dominican Republic that American lives are in danger. These authorities are no longer able to guarantee their safety and they reported that the assistance of military personnel is now needed for that purpose. I've ordered the Secretary of Defense to put the necessary American troops ashore in order to give protection to hundreds of Americans who are still in the Dominican Republic and to escort them safely back to this country. . . . Four hundred Marines have already been landed.

Johnson followed up that carefully drafted speech with careful preparation through Thursday, Friday, and Saturday. At the suggestion of Moyers, telephone calls went out from the White House on Friday and Saturday to several liberals prominent in making Latin American policy under President Kennedy: Arthur Schlesinger, Jr., who now was writing his memoir of the Kennedy Administration; Teodoro Moscoso, who had been eased out as head of the Alliance for Progress early during Johnson's presidency; John Bartlow Martin, the magazine writer and Kennedy speech writer who had been Ambassador to Santo Domingo until the coup that toppled Bosch. The opposition to the Dominican intervention was bound to come from the Schlesingers, the Moscosos, and the Martins. It was typical of the Johnsonian technique to try to disarm the potential opposition by taking it into his camp.

Schlesinger agreed to undertake a mission to Costa Rica, a center of the democratic left in Latin America, to explain the Johnson position on the Dominican Republic, but internal problems in Costa Rica forced a cancellation. Moscoso was sent on a tour of Latin American countries with Under Secretary of State Averell Harriman. Most important, Johnson sent Martin to Santo Domingo.

His mission from the President was to "open up contact with the rebels" and keep the President informed. Thus Martin was, in fact, commissioned directly by Johnson to perform one of the main functions of Ambassador Bennett, with possible implications as to the reliability of Bennett's reporting. Assistant Secretary of State Thomas Mann told a White House aide, only half-joking, that Martin's arrival in Santo Domingo would "hurt Tap Bennett's self-confidence"—a view widely held in the State Department. But Bennett's self-confidence was secondary to the President. Johnson's primary purpose in sending Martin to Santo Domingo was to prove to skeptical critics of the intervention that a trained observer with impeccable liberal credentials would uphold the President's decision. Martin did exactly that.

But that was not enough. The flow of adverse criticism from the liberals that Johnson had dreaded and avoided since November 22, 1963, now burst forth. Condemning the United States policy, the *New York Times* editorialized: "Little awareness has been shown by the United States that the Dominican people—not just a handful of Communists—were fighting and dying for social justice and constitutionalism." Walter Lippmann called the Rebels the "legitimatist party" of the Dominican Republic. On-the-spot accounts from Santo Domingo by reporters of the principal Eastern Seaboard newspapers—the *New York Times*, the *New York Herald Tribune*, and the *Washington Post* —were highly favorable to the Rebels and highly critical of the intervention. College professors signed indignant letters and bought space to display them in the Sunday edition of the *New York Times*. The Americans for Democratic Action, stirring echoes from out of the 1950s, condemned Johnson's policy. Harshly critical articles appeared in the liberal journals of opinion such as the *New Leader* and *The New Republic*, and this criticism was strongly reflected in friendly foreign countries, including most of Latin America.

What stirred such a reaction went far beyond the Dominican Republic or even the principle of non-intervention. "Mr. Johnson's tough action is cheered loudest by those who want only strong-man right-wing governments in Latin America," complained *The New Republic* of May 22. Indeed, the Dominican intervention was to many liberals the ugly vindication of all their fears, building since November, 1963, and reinforced by the strong stand in the 1964 Panama crisis, that Lyndon Johnson and Tom Mann were plotting to return Latin American policy to the Eisenhower days or worse, favoring rightist generals and stifling democratic revolution. It was, to these liberals, a dastardly betrayal of John F. Kennedy and his Alliance for Progress.

Moreover, the protest transcended Latin America. The gradual escalation of United States effort in Vietnam had sensitized the liberals and they were ready to explode at the first major grievance that came along. Finally, their honeymoon with Johnson had about run its course. They had lived with consensus long enough and were not only prepared but were eager to make the break with Johnson.

Under these conditions, liberal professors and writers were motivated by their instinctive distrust for any breach of the doctrine of non-intervention, rather than by fact. They believed what they wanted to believe, ignored what they wished to ignore. Thus, Mann became the architect of intervention and the chief villain, although in point of fact he had only a tangential role in the intervention and did not even attend the Wednesday night meeting in the White House before the President's decision. The fact that Communists had taken over strategic posts in the Rebel forces, and that in the chaos of Santo Domingo the American Embassy was being fired on by Rebel troops, was conveniently overlooked by the rising chorus of liberal protest. In this frame of mind, the liberals were in no mood to be convinced by Johnson's efforts at persuasion.

Consequently, the President would have been well advised to suffer the liberal attack—to ignore it and get on with the business. Instead, by Friday afternoon, the President's obsession with criticism had embarked him on the most blatant personal campaign to sell the intervention to the country through the White House press corps that any President in history had ever undertaken. It was this campaign, which centered on but was not restricted to the press, that brought about the crisis of credibility that was to heighten, not lessen, tensions between the President and the liberal politicians and the liberal press—the very political elements that, with great skill, Johnson had made his staunch allies in the preceding seventeen months.

The first in a dizzying whirl of presidential efforts to lobby the press —in walks around the oval drive of the White House, in exhausting monologues in his office, in uncounted telephone calls—came on Thursday, April 29. Even though the country as a whole was solidly behind him, a few lines of criticism were appearing in liberal newspapers and there were sharp protests (including one from Senator Robert F. Kennedy of New York) about his failure to notify the OAS.

In an adventure so delicate and unorthodox as the Dominican intervention, some criticism was inevitable, but the President would not accept that fact. He was resolved not just to stamp out the criticism, but to overwhelm it with his own overpowering personality. By sheer, unsparing, profligate use of his powers of persuasion, he set out to compel the critics to reverse their first quick judgments and force them by his own willpower to come around to his view of the matter. For days he exercised the full power of the presidency to one end: convince the critics and the skeptics that they were wrong and he was right. It was an unprecedented but futile endeavor. He *had* the country with him from the start, and the polls soon proved it. But he began to lose strength by overplaying his hand. Not satisfied with a healthy consensus, he insisted on an absolute consensus, and progressively risked the nation's confidence by appearing uncertain, confused, and on the defensive.

In the process, he was getting into ever deeper water on the justification for intervention.

On Thursday, Johnson was asked in the White House whether concern over a possible Communist take-over had influenced his decision to dispatch the Marines. He bridled and switched the subject. One day later, confidence reasserted itself when he was informed (erroneously, as it turned out) that a cease-fire was about to take effect. When the question of Communist infiltration of Rebel forces came up that day, the President indicated he was indeed concerned, but did not wish to discuss it.

Then, at 7:07 P.M. Friday evening, Johnson went before the television cameras for the second time in three days, and officially underlined the Communist menace for the first time, just four hours after he had said privately that he could not discuss it at all.

> . . . meanwhile [he said] there are signs that people trained outside the Dominican Republic are seeking to gain control. Thus, the legitimate aspirations of the Dominican people and most of their leaders for progress, democracy, and social justice are threatened and so are the principles of the Inter-American system.

That was the precise truth. The next day in Santo Domingo, Martin reported to Johnson on the telephone, then held a press conference and said the same thing more specifically:

> This was originally an attempt to restore Bosch's constitutional government, but I am now convinced after having talked to many people on the Rebel side that this is Communist-dominated, and moderate elements [within the Rebel camp] are themselves aware of this fact.

But the truth was no sure defense for Johnson. Now he had given up the tried and true justification—protecting American lives—and had taken the first step toward a futile struggle to prove Communist penetration of the Rebel camp.

On Sunday, May 2, Johnson was wholly preoccupied with the worsening situation in Santo Domingo. More United States military force, including elements of the crack Eighty-second Airborne Division, was arriving to open a corridor between the opposing forces and protect the initial battalion of Marines from being overwhelmed in the civil war. With a meaningful cease-fire now impossible, Johnson faced the hard prospect of a far larger United States force than seemed likely at the start. He conferred in the White House off and on all day, all but exhausting Cabinet officers and the White House staff, and called in the congressional leaders again that evening. Finally, at 10 P.M., he went to the American people for his third speech in four days, this one a long, rambling talk that was at the same time an emotional appeal for support and an emotional justification of actions already taken.

> . . . I want you to know [the President said] that it is not a light or an easy matter to send our American boys to another country, but I do not think that the American people expect their President to hesitate or to vacillate in the face of danger just because the decision is hard when life is in peril. The revolutionary movement took a tragic turn. Communist leaders, many of them trained in Cuba, seeing a chance to increase disorder, to gain a foothold, joined the revolution. . . . What began as a popular democratic revolution, committed to democracy and social justice, very shortly moved and was taken over and really seized and placed into the hands of a band of Communist conspirators.

Seeking an absolute consensus, Johnson now was undercutting his own position. It would have been more than enough to stand on the modest warning of a *possible* Communist take-over that Johnson had given the American people on Friday, April 30. There was proof of dangerous Communist participation in the revolution, but there was no proof and never would be that Communists had "taken over and really seized" control of the revolution.

It was overkill, beyond the overkill in the Panama crisis of a year earlier when Johnson, responding to his old Senate friends, pulled the rug out from under the careful mediation efforts of the OAS and his own State Department.* The overkill in March, 1964, was a direct result of Johnson's fear that he had *under*reacted to Panamanian toughness, and was endangering his prestige with Congress. The overkill now, in May, 1965, was a direct result of Johnson's worry that he

* See pages 402ff.

had *over*reacted by landing the Marines and was endangering his prestige with the liberals.

But the May 2 speech was vulnerable on other scores. Continuing his campaign to show that the liberals who knew what really was happening in Santo Domingo supported the intervention, the President invoked the name of Romulo Betancourt, beloved of the non-Communist left throughout the hemisphere.

> We are in contact with such distinguished Latin American statesmen [said the President] as Romulo Betancourt. . . . We are seeking their wisdom and their counsel and their advice.

In fact, no top official from either the State Department or the White House had consulted Betancourt. The President was advised to see him that very Sunday, because by chance Betancourt was in Washington. But Johnson did not have time, and instead invited him to the White House the following day. The implication that Betancourt was behind the intervention was, therefore, not only not accurate; it would soon be disproved. Betancourt was later to oppose the intervention publicly, as every Latin American politician opposed it out of respect for the deep-seated Latin fear of military intervention by the Colossus of the North.*

Moreover, an uncharacteristic lack of dignity marked the President's effort that Sunday night. He was fatigued and uncertain of his lines. A mistake in the Teleprompter led him to repeat two paragraphs, to the wonderment of the nation. He referred to himself in the third person as "your President" on three occasions. An unmistakable sign that the President was running scared that night was his reference to his predecessor in the White House. Johnson had rarely invoked the name of John Kennedy since his landslide election victory six months earlier. Now, however, he quoted from a statement made shortly before the assassination by "our beloved John Kennedy" to help justify the intervention. The Sunday night speech damaged Johnson, for the simple reason that he *was* so obviously running scared. He was protesting too much, when there was no reason to protest.

The impulse to overexplain, in an effort to gain his consensus, continued unabated the next day, Monday, May 3, a day on which he spent hours walking the White House driveway with newspaper reporters and talking in his office. Now, the avowed motive for interven-

---

* Although opposing it publicly, Betancourt made a valiant effort on behalf of the United States to explain Johnson's reasoning and justify the intervention from the vantage point of Washington. In fact, Betancourt was skeptical about the degree of Communist penetration of the Rebels.

tion was coming full circle back to its original cause: the protection of American lives.

The "primary" reason for the intervention, Johnson commented on several occasions that day, was to save American lives. There was no particular point, he said testily, at which he became concerned about Communist control of the revolution. But he was highly skeptical about the ability of Juan Bosch to control the radical element in the revolution. Bosch was sincere in wanting to help his people, but he had exhibited far too much naïveté while he was President. Johnson was realistic about Latin reaction to the intervention. He knew on April 28, he said, that if he ordered the Marines in he couldn't live in the hemisphere, and if he didn't, he couldn't live in the United States.

Late that afternoon, the President went to the Washington-Hilton Hotel for an unscheduled speech to the AFL-CIO Building Trades Council, and this time he explained the intervention not as a result of a Communist seizure of power but for "two purposes":

> We want to evacuate our citizens and we want to preserve, to see that a plan is worked out where the people themselves can select their own government, free from any international conspiracy or any dictatorship of any kind.

Johnson was back on firmer ground. It was not that the revolution "was taken over and really seized" by the Communists but that the *threat* of a Communist take-over existed. But by now he had badly confused what never had to be confused. Moreover, in continuing to justify the intervention he permitted an element of self-pity to creep into his speeches.

> No President ever has a problem of doing what is right [he told the AFL-CIO leaders]. I have never known one to occupy this office, and I have worked with five of them, that did not want to do what is right. The big problem is knowing what *is* right. But I knew this, this was no time for indecision, or procrastination, or vacillation. The American people hadn't elected their President to dodge and duck and refuse to face up to the unpleasant. . . . Now I am the most denounced man in the world. All the Communist nations have a regular program on me that runs twenty-four hours a day. Some of the non-Communist nations just kind of practice on me. Occasionally I get touched up here at home in the Senate and House of Representatives. . . .

Yet, still more was to come. In an effort to back up Johnson's hyperbole of Sunday night that the Communists had actually seized the

Rebel movement, the State Department on Tuesday, May 4, released the names of fifty-four "Communist and Castroist" leaders in the Rebel camp, turning the Dominican debate in Washington into a numbers game. Liberals claimed that the list, supplied by the CIA, was exaggerated and smacked of McCarthyism. And in point of fact, the number of Communists was quite irrelevant. In releasing its list, the State Department unwittingly raised more questions than it answered in its attempt to prove that the President had acted in the national interest on April 28.

Returning to Washington in mid-May, John Bartlow Martin put the debate back in perspective. "All doors were closed, except the Communist door. They were the disciplined ones and they were with the revolution. This was more important than the names and card files of Communist agents. Everything had been swept away, the whole political party structure, everything was drowned in this blood bath." But Martin's words were drowned in the political tumult.

Behind the self-pity and the rationalizations that raised more questions than they answered, President Johnson was working valiantly to arrange a cease-fire and install a temporary government in Santo Domingo, taking a concentrated course of instruction in Dominican politics and politicians. But a cease-fire was even more elusive than the unanimous backing the President vainly sought in the United States. The Rebels repeatedly fired at American soldiers from behind the barricades that blocked the exits from the Old City of Santo Domingo. Fighting between the Rebels and United States forces made headlines in the United States, which prompted charges by the liberals that Johnson was wantonly using United States power to liquidate the Rebels, an accusation that was not only false but laden with political danger at home for the President.

On May 19, aided by the United States troops, the right-wing Loyalists seized control of the Rebel radio station and the State Department felt compelled to issue a strong denial that United States troops had orders to attack the Rebels.

That certainly was not Johnson's intention. The next day, in a meeting with his top Dominican strategists, Johnson turned to Mann and said heatedly: "I'm not going down in history as the man responsible for putting another Trujillo in power in the Dominican Republic."

Mann had no more desire than Johnson to install another Trujillo, but there were differences between various presidential advisers on precisely how the United States should use its power on the scene to bring about a political solution. In short, the President was getting conflicting advice, and Lyndon Johnson did not enjoy having to choose between advisers who did not agree on even so difficult a question as a provisional government in a foreign country.

This lack of unanimity, coupled with his preoccupation with growing criticism among the liberal politicians, kept the President in a highly agitated state during the most difficult days of the crisis. His advisers, for instance, could not agree on a single more or less neutral Dominican politician to be backed by the power of the United States as head of a provisional government. The first candidate, sponsored by John Bartlow Martin, was a pugnacious, wily political general named Antonio Imbert, who had received his rank for being the last surviving gunman among the killers of Trujillo. Imbert proved to be far too truculent and ambitious and, after building him up, the United States knocked him down. A substitute was needed, but Johnson's advisers could not agree on whom. Mann was skeptical about dealing with any of the ringleaders in the Rebel camp, but McGeorge Bundy was convinced that without high-level Rebel participation there could be no provisional government.

The President presided over White House meetings that lasted later and later into the night in an effort to unify all his advisers behind a single provisional government. Still, he continued to get different readings on various Dominican politicians from different advisers. Finally, in an unprecedented move which he hoped would resolve the crisis of conflicting advice within his official family, he sent three of his chief aides to Santo Domingo together on May 15. They were Bundy of the White House staff; Mann of the State Department; and Cyrus Vance, the Deputy Secretary of Defense.

The Bundy-Mann-Vance team spent an aggregate of some thirty days in Santo Domingo, working in close harmony, despite the differing viewpoints between Bundy and Mann. But they never did solve one of the most perplexing political puzzles ever to confound the United States in a foreign country. The team returned, mission not accomplished. The job of setting up an acceptable provisional government was not accomplished until months later, on September 3, by the United States Ambassador to the OAS—Ellsworth Bunker, a senior United States diplomat and one of the most patient and proficient emissaries in the business.

Long before then, President Johnson had publicly withdrawn himself from the day-by-day events, although his own persistence and patience behind the scenes were essential to Bunker's success. Johnson spent literally hours examining the credentials of various coalition governments which his agents in the field were desperately trying to establish with the approval of the two warring sides.

On May 13, to the joy of his staff, which had been pressing for just such a withdrawal, the President for the first time since April 28 failed to mention the Dominican Republic in a formal speech (to the American Editorial Cartoonists). Johnson's staff wanted him to leave the public announcements and backgrounding of the press to the routine briefing offices of the State and Defense Departments. For more than two weeks he soft-pedaled the Dominican crisis.

Then, on May 28, in a commencement address to Baylor University in Waco, Texas, the President put a new face on the bloody events of late April. The OAS had by now established its peace-keeping force in the Dominican Republic, the first time in history that the hemispheric nations had ever taken so bold a step. Lining the 17-mile corridor through the city of Santo Domingo and protecting the International Zone were the troops of four nations in addition to the U.S.: Brazil, Paraguay, Costa Rica and Honduras.

Johnson said at Baylor, in a speech that Martin helped draft: "For the first time in history, the Organization of American States has created and sent to the soil of an American nation an international peace-keeping military force. We have learned that we can act decisively and together."

From the defensive, Johnson had gone on the offensive, finding comfort in this precedent set by the OAS. It might seem a small comfort, but in fact that vote by the OAS endorsing a peace force for the Dominican Republic was in its way a major breakthrough for an organization that was hide-bound, slow-moving, and devoted to its precedents. At any rate, it was one small triumph that Johnson in the spring of 1965 could salvage from the Dominican intervention.

The Dominican agony dragged on through the autumn months, sometimes quiet, sometimes violent, as insoluble as it had been in the tormented days of April and May. Lyndon Johnson kept daily watch, but said nothing publicly. Gradually, the prospect of relative political stability, to be followed by a free and democratic election in the spring of 1966, became a strong possibility.

That hopeful prospect was, of course, vital to the Dominicans, but it was scarcely less significant to President Johnson, for the simple reason that the final product of crisis diplomacy is more important than all the events between the beginning and the end. The President's conduct in the Panama blowup raised serious questions, but in the end he not only stabilized a dangerous situation but set his country and Panama on a far more hopeful course. Now in the more severe and explosive Dominican crisis, the President by the spring of 1966 was on the threshold of a conspicuous success, one no optimist would have dreamed possible on April 28, 1965, when thirty-nine years of military non-intervention by the United States in Latin America ended. On June 1, 1966, Juan Bosch was defeated for president in a surprise land-slide victory by Joaquin Balaguer, a moderate rightist. Balaguer's victory and Bosch's acceptance of it opened the door to Dominican stability. It also vindicated Johnson's decision to intervene on April 28, 1965. But even if his decision of April 28 had not finally concluded on a hopeful note, it could not be faulted for that reason.

What was at fault was not the President's intervention but his obsessive preoccupation in the spring and early summer of 1965 with the lack of unanimous support in carrying it out. As one of Johnson's oldest friends and staunchest admirers remarked, an elder statesman who had been through his own share of crises, the President did the job well but spent too much time agonizing over the way he was doing it. As a result, until he perceived his error and stopped making daily statements on the Dominican crisis, he allowed himself rather than the Dominican crisis to become the paramount issue. Hoping to recapture his lost liberal support, his actions instead made him even more suspect to the liberals. Nor would Santo Domingo soon be forgotten as Panama was.

The emotional energies released by the Dominican intervention would persist in United States politics, as Senator J. William Fulbright of Arkansas, the chairman of the Senate Foreign Relations Committee and a loyal ally of Lyndon Johnson, soon made clear in the autumn of 1965. Although restive over the hard anti-Communist line taken by Johnson in Latin America and Southeast Asia, Fulbright had held his peace and maintained cordial relations with the President. But the Dominican intervention proved too much for both him and other foreign policy liberals. Delaying his attack until he was certain it would not further exacerbate conditions in Santo Domingo, Fulbright made a bitter speech on the Senate floor on September 15, 1965, charging that Johnson's decision to intervene had been "based on inadequate information or, in some cases, simply false information." If the policy followed in Santo Domingo were extended throughout the hemisphere, Fulbright continued, it would "make us the enemy of all revolutions and therefore the ally of all the unpopular and corrupt oligarchies of the hemisphere."

Johnson was hurt and indignant. He was angered by the fact that

Fulbright had dined at the White House the evening before he made his speech without mentioning it. With that speech, the old Johnson-Fulbright alliance abruptly ended. Fulbright's open opposition in September, 1965, on the Dominican question, which long since had been swept off the front pages, mattered little. But its other implications were highly significant. Fulbright had been a well-behaved member of the Great Society consensus refraining from any but the mildest criticism of Johnson's Vietnam policy. Now, freed from this restraint by his break over the Dominican Republic, Fulbright was ready to move to an overt break with Johnson on the incomparably more dangerous and important issue of Vietnam.

That was the deeper significance of Johnson's split with the liberals on the Dominican intervention. It sheared off the liberal end of his consensus precisely at the moment he needed it most, when the torment of Vietnam already menaced the Johnson consensus and threatened wholesale erosion of his support.

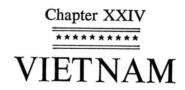
VIETNAM

> We are resisting aggression, and as long as aggressors attack, we shall stay there and resist them—whether we make friends or lose friends.
>
> —Lyndon B. Johnson on April 27, 1965

In late December, 1964, Lyndon Johnson momentarily put aside the unending nightmare of Vietnam and, in a confidential talk one brisk, sunny day on the LBJ Ranch, revealed his inner, optimistic thoughts about foreign policy. Relations with the Soviet Union, the President confided, were less antagonistic than at any time since the end of World War II, and he meant to improve them further. He looked hopefully toward *détente* with the Russians, taking advantage of the warming trend between the West and the Communist states of Eastern Europe.

In Asia, Johnson went on, the United States was on friendly terms with both India and Pakistan. He was enthusiastic about state visits of Pakistan's President Mohammed Ayub Khan, scheduled for April, and of India's Prime Minister Lal Bahadur Shastri, to follow in June. Furthermore, the President continued, the international prestige of the United States had held up exceedingly well during his thirteen months in office. He fished a poll out of his pocket showing that in Canada his administration had a 93 percent popularity rating.

Then, with the exasperated voice of a man discussing an ugly, incurable disease, the President turned to the war in Vietnam. For twenty years, he said, French Indochina and its successor states had been an insoluble problem for the West, and, for the last ten of those twenty years, the United States had been inexorably pulled into its deadly embrace. We're in a mess in Vietnam, the President said, and there's no easy solution, none at all, for the dirty little war ten thousand miles away.

Lyndon Johnson inherited Vietnam from irrevocable decisions made by his predecessors. Dwight Eisenhower started the United States commitment with a letter of October 1, 1954, to Ngo Dinh

Diem, the high-minded but inflexible ruler of the struggling new anti-Communist country of South Vietnam. Unable to contain Ho Chi Minh's Communist Vietminh army, the French had withdrawn from Indochina, which was partitioned into the states of Laos, Cambodia, and Vietnam, with Vietnam divided between a Communist North and an anti-Communist South. President Eisenhower strengthened his commitment to South Vietnam with the Southeast Asia Treaty Organization in 1955, designed as a bulwark against Communist expansion and with an almost imperceptibly widening stream of economic and military aid as Communist Vietcong guerrillas supported by Ho Chi Minh in the North began to threaten the Saigon regime.

John Kennedy built higher on the Eisenhower commitment with a heavy increase in military assistance starting in late 1961, including more United States military "advisers" who fought side by side with South Vietnamese troops against the Vietcong. Now, in December, 1964, it would soon fall to Lyndon Johnson to make momentous decisions that had their roots imbedded in those earlier years, decisions that would commit the largest array of United States military power on the Asian mainland since the Korean War.

In no endeavor of his presidency did Lyndon Johnson display more fortitude than in this one, and in none did he suffer such continuing political misfortune. For on that bright December day on the LBJ Ranch, events were moving rapidly to a climax. The war was being lost to the Vietcong in the hidden spaces of the Vietnamese highlands, in the lush paddies and elongated hamlets of the Mekong Delta, and in the political quagmires of Saigon, where Diem more than a year before had been killed in a military coup and no stable successor government had yet been installed.

Within short weeks of President Johnson's hopeful *tour d'horizon* of foreign policy, United States bombers would be pounding the supply lines in North Vietnam; the visits of Ayub and Shastri would be peremptorily postponed; the United States would be abruptly and rudely criticized on its own soil by Canadian Prime Minister Lester Pearson; *détente* with the Soviet Union would remain a distant dream; and Lyndon Johnson would be on the verge of political conflict that would shred his consensus at home and damage his prestige abroad.

All during the 1964 presidential campaign, Johnson had ridiculed the pugnacious chauvinism of Barry Goldwater's war-hawk policy in Vietnam and contrasted it with his own restraint. "Some . . . are eager to enlarge the conflict," Johnson told the American Bar Association in New York on August 12, 1964.

They call upon us to supply American boys to do the job that Asian boys should do. They ask us to take reckless action which might risk the lives of millions and engulf much of Asia and certainly threaten the peace of the entire world. Moreover, such action would offer no solution at all to the real problem of Vietnam.

Six weeks later the President said "there are those that say you ought to go North [across the 17th parallel into North Vietnam] and drop bombs to try to wipe out the supply lines. . . . We don't want our American boys to do the fighting for Asian boys." And, twelve days before the election: ". . . We are not about to send American boys nine or ten thousand miles away from home to do what Asian boys ought to be doing to protect themselves."

The words were comforting. They held the promise of an easy way out. Against the clamor of the Republican right wing for immediate escalation of the Vietnam war, they were soothing, reassuring. In retrospect, however, they were to read like Franklin Roosevelt's 1940 campaign pledge never to send American boys to fight another war in Europe. The hard fact was that Johnson had simply not had time to educate himself fully on the collapsing state of affairs in South Vietnam. Although he studied all the reports of his advisers and spent hours in briefing sessions with Secretary of State Rusk, Secretary of Defense McNamara, and National Security aide Bundy, he could not immerse himself in the war in Vietnam during the process of adjusting himself to the presidency and campaigning for re-election. His look was inward—to Congress, to the Great Society, to the election—not outward to a still small war in Southeast Asia.

It was simply a matter of the President budgeting his time from November 23, 1963, to Election Day, November 3, 1964. He persuaded Kennedy's policy-makers in foreign affairs and national security to stay on the job, then told them, in effect: You take over, I'm going to have my hands full beating Barry Goldwater.

So, with one conspicuous exception in that pre-election period, Johnson left the war to McNamara and his field commander in Saigon, General William Westmoreland. That exception was the President's prompt reaction to an attack in the Bay of Tonkin, the body of water lying between the Communist Chinese island of Hainan and the mainland of North Vietnam, by North Vietnamese gunboats on the United States destroyer *Maddox* on August 2. It resulted in a swift presidential order to the Navy to double the United States patrol in the Bay of Tonkin, to provide an air cover, and, in the event the August 2 attack was repeated, to retaliate immediately "with the objective not only of driving off the force but of destroying it."

On August 4, North Vietnamese gunboats struck again and the President's order of instant retaliation immediately came into play. Two enemy boats were believed to have been sunk. At 11:36 P.M. on that night, August 4, Johnson went on television to explain what had happened in the Tonkin Bay and to announce that he had ordered a retaliatory air strike against the boat pens along the coast of North Vietnam, one of which was far up near the Chinese border. "Repeated acts of violence must be met not only with alert defense but with positive reply," the President said in his midnight report to the American people. "That reply is being given as I speak to you tonight."

The incident provided Johnson a perfect rationale to exploit presidential power and go to Congress for a special resolution giving him clear congressional authority to use the Armed Forces just about as he wished in the Vietnam war. It was a shrewd political act, shoring up Johnson against the Republican campaign charge that he was "soft on Vietnam." Clothing himself now with an overwhelming congressional mandate to use United States arms as he saw fit, Johnson created the strong impression that the man in the White House could not be taken advantage of by the Communists.

Although rushed through Congress in just two days with a combined Senate-House vote of 502 to 2, the Tonkin Bay Resolution was to become the President's partial justification for far greater United States military involvement in Vietnam based on broader general grounds than the eye-for-an-eye retaliatory concept implicit in the post-Tonkin Bay air attacks.*

With the exception of the Bay of Tonkin and some very secret air operations in Laos against Communist forces which the President personally supervised, not until after the election did Johnson give full attention to the grave affairs in South Vietnam.

He soon learned that, starting in the summer and fall of 1964, organized battalions of North Vietnamese regulars were marching down the Ho Chi Minh trail, running along the eastern border of Laos, into South Vietnam. Moreover, the Vietcong had by now graduated from hit-and-run guerrilla tactics and had recruited what was called its Main Force units, a formidable regular army quite capable of taking the measure of South Vietnamese troops.

In view of these adverse developments, General Maxwell Taylor, the United States Ambassador in Saigon, and Washington experts informed Johnson that the twin pillars of United States policy were be-

---

* The only votes against the Tonkin Bay Resolution were cast by Senators Wayne Morse of Oregon and Ernest Gruening of Alaska, who were outriders of what was to become the Senate's Peace Bloc.

ing undermined in the fall and winter of 1964. These were, first, a reasonably stable government in Saigon to promote the war; second, a reasonable prospect that the Vietnamese forces, with their United States "advisers" now numbering close to twenty thousand men, could slowly roll back the Vietcong. Drastic action would be essential to end the deterioration.

In early February, 1965, five weeks after his hopeful soliloquy on the LBJ Ranch, the President dispatched McGeorge Bundy to Saigon to make an on-the-spot inquiry into the military and political situation, to talk to General Westmoreland and Ambassador Taylor, and report back to him. Long before Bundy left Washington, however, detailed and elaborate plans had been made in the White House to launch United States bombers on missions north of the 17th parallel.

Through the fall of 1964, Air Force generals, along with Secretary McNamara and his staff, had studied aerial reconnaissance photographs, taken by the high-flying U-2 spy planes and other reconnaissance aircraft, which covered almost every inch of North Vietnam. In November and December, President Johnson had pored over these blown-up photographs pinpointing the location of every bridge, railroad, highway, ammunitions depot, barracks, petroleum storage tank, thermal power plant, and other potential targets of military significance north of the 17th parallel.

Laid out on the large Cabinet table in the White House, these amazingly precise photographs gave the President an accurate picture of the entire country, along with informed estimates of how many civilians lived within the blast pattern of bombs of varying sizes, and which targets could be bombed without human habitation feeling the effect of the explosion. Elaborate analyses were made of the extent of civilian casualties if certain targets were struck—enough information to enable targets to be chosen with careful discrimination.

Ambassador Taylor, the uniformed military, and probably a majority of the President's civilian National Security advisers wanted more than just the pinpointing of targets in the White House Situation Room. By December, it was clear that the Vietcong was winning the war, and speculation—inaccurate speculation—began to spread that Johnson was about to pull out of Vietnam. Thus, the President's advisers were pressing him for immediate bombing in the North, both for military and political reasons; that is, both to make it more difficult for Ho Chi Minh to provide assistance to the Vietcong and to show both him and Saigon that the United States was in Vietnam to stay.

But no decision to bomb had been made by the President. There was in Johnson's mind, rather, a strong hunch that he would never have to order bombs dropped on North Vietnam. Ever leery of advice from the military, Johnson was acutely aware of the danger of Chinese intervention in the war. He knew, too, that "going North" would immediately endanger his consensus at home, and his highest interest was not the still small, though ugly guerrilla war in South Vietnam, but the Great Society legislative program. The President's caution brought a cold chill to advisers in the Pentagon and State Department who foresaw a dreary chain of events: the crumbling of the Saigon government, South Vietnam eventually being sucked into the Communist orbit, and Communist subversion or influence spreading into all of Southeast Asia and from there to the Philippines. They were not at all certain that Johnson would send bombers north of the 17th parallel to abort this chilling scenario.

But all speculation became academic on February 7, when the United States Air Force barracks at Pleiku, in the Vietnamese highlands, were attacked by mortar fire and hand grenades from a Vietcong raiding party. Eight Americans were killed and 126 wounded. Against the backdrop of dangerously declining morale in the Saigon government, Johnson showed the same toughness and swift reaction to the Pleiku raid that he had displayed six months earlier in the Bay of Tonkin.

McGeorge Bundy, on his mission to Saigon at the time of the Pleiku raid, joined Ambassador Taylor and General Westmoreland in recommending instant retaliation in telephone talks with the President from the communications headquarters in Saigon. With McNamara and the Pentagon generals making the same recommendations in Washington, the President personally selected the first targets from hundreds of choices clearly marked on the large-scale map of North Vietnam pasted together, section by section, from the reconnaissance photographs.

The bombers streamed North, and, from that moment, the war that had been impersonal, distant, and secondary became for Lyndon Johnson the consuming passion of his presidency. It became, more than any war in the twentieth century for any other President, Johnson's personal war; a war he had not started and could not end, a war that broke his consensus, alienated the liberal wing of his party, and threatened to undermine his higher purposes; a war fought without major allies, without front lines, and without the comfortable and easy goal of total victory that glorified other wars.

The purposes of the bombing were, primarily, to bolster confidence and morale in Saigon and, secondarily, to make it more costly for Ho Chi Minh to send his legions South to help the Vietcong. As evidence that the United States and its newly elected President were indeed committed to the war and willing to make higher sacrifices to continue it, the bombing program (called Rolling Thunder by its secret code name) was an obvious success in its primary purpose. It stopped an alarming decline of morale in the South. And in Bangkok, the capital of Thailand, anxious Thai officials who knew they were next on the list of targets to be subverted by Communist China, regarded Rolling Thunder as impressive evidence that the United States meant to stay in Vietnam and would not abandon the Southeast Asia salient. The same attitude was reflected in other anti-Communist capitals of Southeast Asia.

But in its secondary purpose, to turn back the invaders from the North, Rolling Thunder was but a paper barricade across the Ho Chi Minh trail. The supplies poured South partly by trucks moving at night, mostly on the backs of Vietnamese coolies. As quickly as a strategic bridge was knocked out by American bombing, a pontoon by-pass was thrown over the river. Thousands of Vietnamese soldiers and civilians were taken off their regular jobs and put to work repairing the damage. The civilian economy of North Vietnam suffered, but war supplies continued to pour South.

In the White House one day about two weeks after President Johnson sent the first flight of bombers North, the President talked with friends about the war. The morale in Saigon, he observed, was improved, but the political situation was still precarious. A new bloodless coup had just installed another in the succession of post-Diem governments, although Taylor thought he could work with the new group. Johnson emphasized how much he wanted to bring the enemy to the negotiating table, but only if the chance of a peaceful settlement were better than fifty-fifty. To negotiate and fail, he feared, would be worse than not to negotiate at all.

As for the United Nations, a route to possible settlement that the liberals now were pressing on him, that route seemed hopeless for the simple fact that neither Communist China nor North Vietnam were members. The Soviet Union would be compelled to act in their interest, and undoubtedly would make it impossible for the UN to do anything. Summing up that day in late February, President Johnson struck a note of somber realism: "We've got a bear by the tail." Nor was there any way either to let go or to kill the bear.

Long before Rolling Thunder carried the United States bombers north of the 17th parallel, the Senate's leading advocates of a soft line in foreign policy—the doves—were attacking the President's policy in Vietnam. Senator Wayne Morse, who had long since called the war "McNamara's War," and Senator Ernest Gruening frequently popped up on the Senate floor to pontificate against Johnson. Their basic complaint was twofold: the President had failed, they claimed, to press for negotiations with North Vietnam and had refused to offer the Vietcong a seat at the peace conference even if negotiations could be arranged.

But with the onset of Rolling Thunder, criticism in the Senate jumped far beyond Senate mavericks such as Morse and Gruening. More stable Senate liberals—George McGovern of South Dakota and Frank Church of Idaho from the Midwest and West, regions where the tradition of isolationism was by no means dead—began publicly to question the President's basic policy in Vietnam. McGovern and Church both made speeches on February 17 calling on the President to work harder for negotiations. They did not condemn the bombing in the North, but by itself, they said, it would have little impact on negotiations. The President must state publicly that negotiations were at the heart of his policy, and must continue to restate it.

Soon thereafter, misgivings about the Johnson policy were voiced publicly by other liberal Democratic Senators from the Midwest—Eugene McCarthy of Minnesota, Gaylord Nelson of Wisconsin, Stephen Young of Ohio. Other Democrats, including the chairman of the Foreign Relations Committee, J. W. Fulbright, and Joseph Clark were most disturbed by the bombing policy but somewhat unhappily withheld public criticism for the time being.

The Senate only reflected the larger political spectrum. Although previous concern over Washington's support of Saigon had been pretty much limited to the far left, now it spread into the volatile, vital liberal wing of the Democratic party.

All this could not be ignored by Johnson as he had ignored Morse and Gruening. The President sent McGeorge Bundy, just back from his mission to Vietnam, to Vice-President Humphrey's office in the Capitol for a private talk with the five critical Midwestern Senators—McGovern, Church, McCarthy, Young, and Nelson. And Johnson himself, to stem the rising protest, held elaborate briefing sessions in the White House for small groups of Senators and Representatives, at which the Vietnam high command—Rusk, McNamara, the CIA's Raborn, and, of course, the President himself—briefed with maps and charts, followed by questions and answers. In these evening meetings, Johnson was superlative, exerting his charm and persuasion and attempting through The Treatment to limit his critics to the minimum possible number. Presidential lobbying was not restricted to Congress. Outside groups representing business, labor, and other economic sectors were hustled in and out of the White House to hear the President explain and justify the war ten thousand miles away.

But in addition to these more or less formal sessions, Johnson took special pains with responsible critics. One day soon after the bombing started, he talked to visitors in his office for an hour and a half about the restraint and patience he was showing in operation Rolling Thunder. He was no LeMay, he said, referring to General Curtis LeMay, who had retired as Air Force Chief of Staff on February 2, 1965.* A story was then going around Washington that LeMay, a former bomber pilot himself, in an off-guard moment had offered a special prescription for ending the war. "We ought to nuke the Chinks," LeMay was reported to have told a high State Department official. Johnson had no intention of "nuking the Chinks"—that is, dropping nuclear weapons on Communist China.

In fact, the President had presided over top-secret sessions in the Cabinet Room of the White House that "war-gamed" the probable results of a preemptive strike against China's nuclear installations to prevent China from becoming a full-fledged nuclear power and radically changing the world balance of power. Invariably, preemptive attack was decisively rejected. Johnson told his liberal critics that far from being a LeMay, he was painstakingly, perhaps inordinately, cautious about possible Chinese reaction to the United States bombing of North Vietnam. Johnson was fortunate that among his generals in the Pentagon was not a single one with the Man-on-Horseback characteristics of a Douglas MacArthur, an Arthur Radford, or a Curtis LeMay, not a single one powerful enough to slip propaganda to the political opposition in Congress and court a public dispute with the civilian authorities in the Pentagon—or the President.

Still, Johnson could and did complain to liberals and others in the confines of the White House about private urgings by his bomber gen-

* Johnson's regard for LeMay was not enhanced when during the final budget review at the LBJ Ranch in December, 1964, the famed bomber pilot was caught in an embarrassing error. LeMay was complaining that one requested appropriation item for the Air Force had been omitted from the budget, but McNamara interrupted to point out, correctly, that the item actually was in the budget. With his bias against the military, Johnson relished the story and told it often.

erals to expand the air war. "I won't let those Air Force generals bomb the smallest outhouse north of the 17th parallel without checking with me," he said. "The generals," he went on derisively, "know only two words—spend and bomb." But he, the President, was running this war, not the generals.

To illustrate his caution, he showed critics the map of North Vietnam and pointed out the targets he had approved for attack, and to the many more targets he had disapproved. As for Communist China, he was watching for every possible sign of reaction. Employing a vivid sexual analogy, the President explained to friends and critics one day that the slow escalation of the air war in the North and the increasing pressure on Ho Chi Minh was seduction, not rape. If China should suddenly react to slow escalation, as a woman might react to attempted seduction, by threatening to retaliate (a slap in the face, to continue the metaphor), the United States would have plenty of time to ease off the bombing. On the other hand, if the United States were to unleash an all-out, total assault on the North—rape rather than seduction—there could be no turning back, and Chinese reaction might be instant and total. Johnson's language left nothing to the imagination and shocked those who heard it. It made an unforgettable image. The United States was engaged in a period of testing against Ho Chi Minh, but the exercise was seduction, not rape.

Despite his full use of the presidential power to influence, Johnson could not stop the critics. To the contrary, condemnation of the bombing in the North spread quickly to university campuses where the anti-Vietnam war "teach-ins" suddenly took hold, to peace groups, and to zealous idealists in the civil rights movement. It spread, too, to foreign countries, where anti-U.S. demonstrations—often Communist inspired —took on a fiercer aspect. And foreign statesmen began openly to criticize the President of the United States.

This rising criticism from abroad played a part in the postponement of the Ayub and Shastri visits. In early spring, Johnson blew up over the intemperate anti-U.S. mood developing in the governments of Pakistan and India. The Pakistani foreign minister, Z. A. Bhutto, was outspokenly critical.* In New Delhi, neutralist Indian politicians were flailing the United States. Equally important to Johnson, the foreign aid debate would be in full swing just as the two foreign leaders came to Washington. Unless they supported America's effort in Vietnam, a forlorn hope, their presence would exacerbate that debate and make his problems with Congress more difficult. Johnson did not rel-

---

* It will be remembered that Bhutto and Johnson had a nasty encounter after the Kennedy funeral on November 25, 1963. See page 384.

ish the thought of them sniping at his policy on "Meet the Press" and "Face the Nation."

Accordingly, the obvious move, thought the President, was to postpone the two visits to a more propitious time. Although a sound idea, the dual postponement was quickly condemned not only in Rawalpindi and New Delhi but also in Washington. The fault lay not in the postponement but in the execution.

Ayub's visit was scheduled for April and Shastri's for June. The Pakistani President was to be notified of his postponement first by Walter P. McConaghey, the United States Ambassador to Pakistan. If Ayub took the postponement as a personal affront, the State Department informed him, the ambassador could play on the mutual hatred between Hindu India and Moslem Pakistan (which, before the year was over, was to erupt in open warfare on the Indian Subcontinent). McConaghey, in short, was authorized to tell Ayub the Shastri visit to Washington was also being postponed. But when McConaghey so informed the Pakistani government on a confidential basis, the news was gleefully leaked. Thus, Shastri read about the postponement of his own trip in the newspapers before he heard it from United States official sources.

Nevertheless, the President's decision made sense. The Ayub and Shastri visits at the height of the congressional session would only have caused Johnson political trouble at home. There was already more than enough of that.

For days before President Johnson's speech on April 7, 1965, at Johns Hopkins University in Baltimore, the Peace Bloc, in and out of Congress, had been pressing him to make a major, public statement welcoming negotiations. For days, the President pointed out that he had many times made it clear that he would do anything and go anywhere in the interests of peace. It was, he said, *Hanoi* that would not talk peace, *Hanoi* that was subverting South Vietnam, *Hanoi* that was making it possible for the war to continue by funneling supplies and manpower over the Ho Chi Minh trail. Washington was not to blame. But Johnson, seldom bound by his own arguments, decided a few days before the speech to add an appeal for "unconditional discussions."

The Johns Hopkins speech began with the now familiar defense of the United States engagement in Vietnam as necessary to prevent "total conquest" of South Vietnam by Communism—"part of a wider pattern of aggressive purposes"—and to honor "a national pledge to help South Vietnam defend its independence." Johnson then came to the words he hoped would satisfy the principal demand of the doves:

> We will never be second in the search for . . . a peaceful settlement in Vietnam. There may be many ways to this kind of peace: in discussion or negotiations with the governments concerned; in large groups or in small ones; in the reaffirmation of old agreements or their strengthening with new ones. We have stated this position over and over to friend and foe alike. And we remain ready with this purpose for *unconditional discussions.*[*]

Next, Johnson put a brighter face on his Vietnam policy by pledging the United States to "a billion-dollar investment" for economic development of Southeast Asia, including development of the Mekong River, running throughout southern Asia, "on a scale to dwarf even our TVA." Johnson put a new, hopeful, and positive aspect on United States involvement in Southeast Asia, painting the picture of a peaceful five-nation area—North and South Vietnam, Laos, Cambodia, and Thailand—cooperating in internationally financed development.

For days before going to Baltimore, Johnson gave private previews of his speech to leading critics of his Vietnam policy, including columnist Walter Lippmann, an early and enthusiastic supporter of Johnson as President who was now disillusioned over Vietnam. Lippmann read the speech in the White House while the President sat in a raised chair posing for a sculptor. The speech was highly satisfying to Lippmann as well as other critics.

One group of visitors to whom the President gave a preview was a dozen or so leading members of the Americans for Democratic Action, holding its annual convention in Washington in early April. On Friday, April 2, Johnson invited the liberal organization's leaders to come to the Cabinet Room and talk about his Vietnam policy, which most ADA members by now opposed. He sat them down, and then proceeded to read the just-completed Johns Hopkins speech. He read quickly over the part explaining why "we must fight." When he got to the sections about "unconditional discussions" and the Mekong River program he slowed down, reciting carefully and letting the impact of each word—words that were music to the ears of the ADA—sink in.

After reading the speech, Johnson asked for questions. During the question period, one of his visitors passed a written question to John Roche, ADA national chairman, who was asking the questions. Roche read his question: Shouldn't the United States go to the United Nations and seek a solution there? Why didn't the President do that?

[*] Emphasis is added,

Johnson answered that the UN wasn't interested. Roche then crumpled up the note and tossed it in a Cabinet Room wastebasket.

The ADA leaders had been allotted fifteen minutes with the President, but he kept them there for an hour and a half. When they left, the National Security Council was standing in the hall waiting for one of its regular sessions with Johnson. The ADA filed out, the NSC filed in, and when these policy-makers were seated at the Cabinet table, the President reached into the wastebasket, retrieved Roche's crumpled note, read the question, and ridiculed the ADA for being so stupid as to ask it.* Reports of the President's conduct got right back to the ADA and largely vitiated the excellent impression Johnson had made on them. He had wanted to persuade them to be patient with his Vietnam policy, and he had succeeded. But when they discovered he had ridiculed them behind their backs, they naturally suspected his sincerity.

As one critic after another was brought into the White House to preview the Johns Hopkins speech, the President became more and more excited about it. But one critical detail remained.

To manage this grandiose economic program, which would draw its major support from a new Asian Bank which was not yet established, the President needed somebody of stature. On April 7, the very day the speech was to be given, a presidential aide came up with the right name: Eugene Black. Georgia-born Eugene Black was a rare combination. He ranked at the top of the Eastern Seaboard foreign policy Establishment, a tall, urbane banker with a delightful sense of humor who had been president of the World Bank and a moving force on boards and commissions appointed by many Presidents to study such diverse subjects as foreign aid and the supersonic transport plane. Further, he was a figure of high prominence in international finance who knew the European bankers by their first names, a born politician who had open lines to both Democrats and Republicans.

Black it had to be, and President Johnson, in a whirlwind performance reminiscent of his recruitment of Chief Justice Earl Warren for the commission to investigate the assassination, set out to capture Black. There wasn't much time. The Johns Hopkins speech was only a few hours away and Johnson wanted Black in the White House the following afternoon to introduce him with appropriate formality to the Cabinet and to the press.

* Ironically, Roche, unofficial aide and adviser to Vice-President Humphrey, later became a staunch defender of Johnson's strong position in Vietnam and leader of the ADA minority faction supporting the President.

VIETNAM

543

McGeorge Bundy put the telephone call in to the Chase Manhattan Bank, of which Black was a director, and reached the President's target in the bank's private dining room, where Black was lunching with Henry Ford II to discuss various matters dealing with the Ford Foundation. Bundy came directly to the point. The President, he said, was about to announce a major new Asian development program and he wanted Black to run it. Black said no, not a chance. He was already on several government boards, his job was in New York, and he was overloaded. Bundy persisted. So did Black. Bundy said, "Here's someone who wants to talk to you."

The President came on the line. Just a minute, just a minute, he told Black, who still resisted. Johnson said he wanted Black to hear something about his plans for developing the Mekong River. He then proceeded to read Black his entire Johns Hopkins speech. Lunch got cold. Overwhelmed, Black realized the President wouldn't take no for an answer. Besides, Ford, listening to one end of the conversation, quickly caught the drift of the talk and whispered to Black that he could not turn down the President. Black yielded.

Now, having made his conquest, the President was all business. He wanted Black to be at the White House at 5 P.M. the following day, April 8, to discuss the plan with the Cabinet. Black had a committee meeting in New York at 3 P.M. the following day that he couldn't cancel. "Mr. President, I'll try to fly down on the four o'clock shuttle, but I don't see how I can make it." Nonsense, said the President. He would send Air Force One to New York to fly Black to Washington.

At a few minutes after five the next afternoon, Black was met at Andrews Air Force Base outside Washington and whisked to the White House. The Cabinet waited. So did the President. So did key members of the White House staff. When Black entered, everyone rose. The President introduced Black, sat back in his chair, and said that Black would now explain the Asian development plan!

Having only heard the barest outline of the plan twenty-four hours earlier, Black asked questions instead of giving answers. The President was in a cheerful, optimistic mood. His Johns Hopkins speech had been extremely well received the previous evening and he had managed, in that brief twenty-four-hour period, to change the emphasis of the crisis in Vietnam from war to hopeful prospects of economic reconstruction. He told his Cabinet that Black was to have the Cabinet's total assistance in planning and running the new program, the heart of which would be United States participation in the Asian Bank. After two hours of discussion, the President called in the press, and introduced Black.

He was playing master of ceremonies and loving it. Having marshaled all the ingredients of a major initiative almost overnight, he was expansive and ingratiating. A reporter noted that, in his Johns Hopkins speech, he had said "a special team of outstanding, patriotic, distinguished Americans" would help him set up the economic development plan. Who were they? The President pointed to Black and said: "That's my distinguished group right there." The team was never named.

Johnson's economic initiative was a bold recasting of the United States involvement in Southeast Asia. In choosing Black as his personal agent, the President at one blow assured the support of Congress, which regarded Black not as a spendthrift economic dreamer but as a hard-headed banker who would insist on tight planning and high fiscal standards for whatever program might emerge. Furthermore, the President also saw to it that the initiative for the Asian Bank seemed to come from the Asian nations, not from the West. Thus, he instructed Adlai Stevenson at the United Nations to sound out Secretary General U Thant, a Burmese, on how the Asian nations would react to America's participation in the projected Bank. Thant was enthusiastic.

The entire enterprise was planned with that delicate, distinctive Johnson touch that used to distinguish his successful operations in the Senate. No source of possible complaint was overlooked, no source of possible strength untapped. The selection of Black was inspired, and although he hardly knew what had hit him on the day he first met with the President and the Cabinet, Black pulled the loose reins into his own hands and the project moved ahead. On June 1, the President asked Congress for eighty-nine million dollars as an initial fund for social and economic programs. That fall, the founding meeting of the Asian Bank was held in Bangkok. In early 1966, Congress approved United States participation without a quiver of the tendentious debate that normally would accompany a departure of that magnitude.

But for all these successes, there was a haphazard pattern about the Johns Hopkins speech that was disturbing and that would mark future policy initiatives in the President's desperate search for a solution to Vietnam. The decision to insert the appeal for "unconditional discussions" was a last-minute concession to the Peace Bloc that amazed those who had seen the earlier version of the speech. Johnson's intention to entrust the economic program to a "team" was suddenly forgotten with his last-minute acquisition of Black, and never mentioned again. The very concept of a vast economic development program for an area in the midst of war, even though it put a hopeful and humanitarian cast on United States involvement in Southeast Asia, seemed unrealistic.

And, although just after the speech an exuberant Johnson was convinced that he had won over most of his critics, the truth was something else. In fact, his own reaction to the speech exceeded any realistic prospects it truly held, either for negotiating with the Communists or for a lasting improvement in his standing with the Peace Bloc.

No single problem ever faced by Lyndon Johnson so frustrated his exercise of power or eluded his search for solution as the snake pit of Vietnam.

In his long struggle to survive in Texas politics, Johnson had successfully contrived one temporary expedient after another to balance off the Democratic party's liberal and conservative factions. As Majority Leader in the Senate, if he could not solve a political problem outright, he managed to tunnel under or around it with makeshift solutions. In these Senate struggles, Johnson was dealing with flexible politicians. Richard Russell could be counted on to make a vital concession on a Senate bill that required some give from the conservatives. Hubert Humphrey could be counted on to trim his sails on a bill that needed a concession from the liberals.

Now, however, the President was dealing not only with political forces he could not manipulate but forces whose inner strength and convictions he did not know. Johnson had often said that "a man's judgment is as good as his information," but in dealing with Vietnam he was compelled to listen to conflicting advice from experts that was based not on hard information but on speculation. Thus, J. William Fulbright could argue that Ho Chi Minh would be no more likely to surrender under the bombing of his country than would the United States if it were attacked, and Dean Rusk could argue with equal force that the presence of United States bombers over North Vietnam would be bound to break down the confidence of his people in Ho Chi Minh and eventually force him to the bargaining table. Moreover, there were no Dick Russells or Hubert Humphreys in Southeast Asia. Nor could he lock up Ho Chi Minh with the Prime Minister of South Vietnam in the White House Cabinet Room, as he had the railroad presidents and the rail union leaders, knock their heads together and instruct them to reach a compromise, any compromise, that he would then adopt as his own.

There was, in short, no way of applying to Vietnam the masterful Johnsonian political techniques that had rescued Johnson from so many other political crises.

Thus, when the Johns Hopkins speech neither brought the Communists to the negotiating table nor stilled the Peace Bloc, Johnson voiced his frustrations to intimates in the White House. These frustrations were galling him even before the Johns Hopkins speech failed to silence his critics. If he had not retaliated to the attack on Pleiku in early February, he said one afternoon a week before going to Baltimore, he would have been impeached. How could the United States sit back quietly and accept the atrocities that were being staged by the Vietcong? The American Embassy in Saigon had been bombed by a suicide squad on March 30, and, with emotion, the President described how American girls, secretaries in the embassy, had been killed and maimed in the attack. And yet, he went on, the Peace Bloc made no mention of this outrage but was now insisting that he stop the bombing of the North! He could hardly claim to be the Commander-in-Chief, he said, if he didn't strike back. Of course, most Americans wanted a political settlement of the war. So did he. In fact, Johnson continued, he was "the ringleader of that crowd." But the Stop-the-Bombing crusaders ought to understand that he, the President, would not handcuff American soldiers and airmen while the Vietcong attacks continued.

Johnson was angry, and justifiably so, about the speech in Philadelphia on April 2 by Prime Minister Lester Pearson of Canada. Pearson had called the White House from Ottawa and asked whether he could see the President informally on April 3, the day after his speech in Philadelphia, and the President had graciously invited him to lunch at Camp David, the presidential retreat in the Catoctin Mountains of Maryland. Pearson sent a copy of his speech to the White House, but it arrived only hours before it was delivered. Pearson, who had won the Nobel Peace Prize as Canada's Minister of External Affairs, sought to bring peace to Vietnam by suggesting gratuitously at Philadelphia that President Johnson ought to order a "pause" in bombing North Vietnam.

At Camp David, Johnson made no effort to conceal his indignation. This was precisely what he had sought to avoid by washing out the Ayub and Shastri visits. Johnson snapped at McGeorge Bundy, complaining that it was Bundy's recommendation that he invite Pearson to Camp David (though, in fact, Bundy fully shared the President's irritation with the Canadian leader). When Pearson arrived for lunch, the President displayed his displeasure by spending much of the time on the telephone, while Pearson sat cooling his heels. He let Pearson know he had transgressed. A foreign visitor simply didn't invite himself to lunch with the President and then instruct him how to run his business in a public speech the night before.

Pearson's call for a bombing pause was particularly obnoxious to

Johnson because the pause had become the battle slogan of the anti-Vietnam movement. Students had picketed the President's ranch in Texas, demanding a cessation of bombing. A massive teach-in had been scheduled for May 15 in Washington, with academicians who wanted withdrawal of American influence from the Asian mainland, ready to demand as a first step an immediate end of the bombing. Pressure for a pause was building up, too, in Congress among liberal Democrats.

Irritated though he was by this pressure, Johnson handled it with his familiar technique of disarming his critics by accepting their suggestions. Just as his Johns Hopkins speech in early April surprisingly accepted the Peace Bloc's call for "unconditional discussions," Johnson in early May accepted the advice he had been rejecting. Without announcement of any kind, American bombers suddenly ceased their pinpoint attacks on May 13. For six days no bomb dropped. And for six days, just as Johnson's critics had been told, there was no change in the political climate. On May 19, bombing resumed. The pause was over, and the attacks from the liberal critics resumed.

Clearly, the long evolution of Johnson's course on Vietnam was nearing a decisive stage. All through the 1964 presidential campaign he had preached severely limited United States participation in the war. In February, he had ordered retaliatory bombing. But that soon became not just a means to retaliate for specific Communist acts of aggression in the South but an end in itself. In April, his Johns Hopkins bid for negotiations had not the slightest answering echo in Hanoi. In May, his pause in the bombing of the North again had no response from Ho Chi Minh. As a difficult, frustrating spring gave way to summer, the President was running out of options, which by now had been gradually and ominously reduced to just two: maintain the status quo, which meant slowly losing the war, or order a massive increase in American ground forces to turn the tide. After all the scarcely perceptible increases in the United States commitment to Vietnam, Lyndon Johnson was face to face with the political nightmare of sending American troops to fight in an Asian land war. Yet, that was the only real option left, the dispatch of tens of thousands of United States troops to take over a major share of the ground action in the South. It was a course both dangerous and courageous, but it had become essential in the long pursuit of the United States objective to enable South Vietnam to choose its own future without having it imposed by the North.

As he approached this crucial decision, the President became progressively more immersed in the details of the war. Gone were the
days of the 1964 campaign when Johnson could afford the luxury of
leaving the war to his agents. Gone were the delay and procrastination that marked the immediate post-election period, when the President waited for three months to order the initial bombing of the
North. Probably that delay had not greatly affected the course of the
war. But a delay now on the question of ground troops might well
mean Communist victory in Vietnam.

After the attack on Pleiku in early February, it was necessary to
land small contingents of United States Marines as security forces in
the Danang area and eventually elsewhere to protect major American
installations. That was step two in the three-stage operation, beginning on February 7 with the first bombing sorties, that transformed
the fiction of American "advisers" to the fact of an outright American
fighting role.

The third step, the dispatch of combat troops not for security but
for offensive actions, was by far the most significant. On July 21, the
President started the last week of intensive studies leading up to this
grave decision. He had sent McNamara to Saigon on July 14 to learn
exactly what General Westmoreland and the Marine Corps Commander, General Lewis Walt, needed in the way of reinforcements to
deal with the rapidly increasing North Vietnamese infiltration. McNamara returned to Washington with a strong recommendation: within
a year, the United States force should be quadrupled from the seventy
thousand troops already there. Initial reinforcements, to be sent as
soon as possible, should number about fifty thousand.

That was indeed a vast increase, not merely in the size but in the
nature of the American commitment to Vietnam. But coming from
McNamara, the formal recommendation carried special weight with
Johnson. Although the Peace Bloc had picked up Wayne Morse's lead
to brand McNamara as the arch warmonger, the truth was far different. McNamara, the President remarked privately one day in April,
was more professor than industrialist, more intellectual than militarist.
Hell, Johnson continued, he's not even among the top three hawks in
my administration. The President ranked McNamara behind Dean
Rusk, McGeorge Bundy, and Lyndon Johnson himself.

Even with McNamara's influence, none of the President's key advisers and policy-makers gathered around the Cabinet table those
long, hot days in late July viewed Johnson's decision on the McNamara recommendations as an open-and-shut case. Johnson never had
been more authoritative, more restrained, or more in control of the

debate than he was during that fateful week. He skillfully resolved the issue around the Cabinet table by shrewd questioning without stating flatly his own decision.

The questions he asked at the Cabinet table were fundamental: What are the risks in raising the level of the American military participation? What is the proof, or if no proof, what are the indications that it will work? If it doesn't work, what will have to follow this first step? Are we absolutely sure that the South Vietnamese cannot do the job themselves?

The answer to all these questions pointed to Johnson's only possible decision: unhappy though the prospect was, American troops had to take over a major combat function of the war. The decision was a declaration of intent to *win* the war, not just to prevent losing it.

But the further problem around the Cabinet table was how to raise the extra troops, whether through the draft or a call-up of the reserves. And here the debate was intense. It was the same question that had confronted Kennedy in the Berlin crisis of 1961. Was it necessary, and if not necessary, was it advisable to call up the reserves? The generals argued that it was. Although McNamara declined to veto the military, he made it clear to the President that he was personally skeptical about a reserve call-up. In Pentagon jargon, McNamara's unpublicized position was described as a "non-veto."

The pros and cons of a reserve call-up were debated around the Cabinet table off and on for a full week, starting Wednesday, July 21. Johnson was personally involved in more than fifty hours of meetings that week. As the meetings progressed, he increasingly shared McNamara's skepticism about calling up the reserves unless necessary to preserve America's global military position in the face of the drain-off caused by Vietnam. Johnson did not believe Kennedy's call-up of the reserves in 1961 had been wise. Moreover, he was afraid that a call-up would exacerbate his problems in Congress, now moving into the last couple of months of the session, and delay important legislation. Finally, the last thing the President wanted was to stir up any more emotional resistance to the war in the United States, or to provoke the Soviet Union into retaliation, either political or military, against what the Kremlin might regard as a calculated provocation. When the generals at last conceded that massive reinforcements for Vietnam could be raised without a reserve call-up, the President's mind was made up.*

* An interesting sidelight to these vitally important sessions the last week of July is the fact that some of the most astute members of the White House press corps incorrectly suspected that they were a mere charade. Some wrote in their

But in deciding against a reserve call-up, Johnson sacrificed a valuable psychological tool and inadvertently dulled the cutting edge of the basic decision to *win* the war, and not just prevent losing it. A reserve call-up would have shocked the American people, just as Kennedy's Berlin call-up in 1961 had shocked them, into a deeper appreciation of the crisis. More important, a call-up of the reserves would have notified the Soviet Union that the United States, after months of pussyfooting and equivocation, really meant business in Vietnam. Far from provoking a rash reaction in Moscow as Johnson feared, it might well have galvanized Moscow into throwing its weight behind peace negotiations.

But Johnson's decision not to summon the reserves reflected the truth: he still sought a middle position, a gray area, still hoping for peaceful settlement and careful not to look the whole warrior. He was acting as he acted in the Senate, refusing to make an all-out commitment to one side or the other, keeping all paths open. But this was not the Senate, and the contesting forces now were not Dick Russell on one side and Hubert Humphrey on the other. This was war, but the President was emphasizing peace; this was guns, but the President was still talking guns *and* butter. Thus did he pass up an opportunity to mobilize the American people, deciding it would not be wise to arouse a martial patriotism in the land.

Vice-President Humphrey, who had been valiantly but unsuccessfully seeking to soften criticism of the Vietnam policy among his liberal friends, was caught short by Johnson's decision to understate the crisis when he announced the fateful jump in troop commitments. On Tuesday evening, July 27, the night before Johnson's speech to the nation revealing the President's decision, Humphrey was in Minneapolis making the major address at the annual Governors' Conference. Humphrey's speech had been cleared by proper officials in the State Department and White House, but the President himself had not read it. In that speech, Humphrey made an emotional appeal to the flag and said the impending presidential announcement would bring to tens of thousands of American homes the grief and anguish of war in quest of preserving freedom. It was a speech not in keeping with the President's policy of playing down his decision.

Early that very evening, Johnson called congressional leaders of both parties to the White House for an advance look at what he was

---

newspapers that the decision to send more troops to Vietnam, probably accompanied by a call-up of the reserves, had already been made, and that Johnson was merely going through the motions of these long sessions in the Cabinet Room for public consumption. The contrary was the truth.

going to say the next day. Assembled in the Cabinet Room were the most powerful leaders of the United States—with one exception. Vice-President Humphrey had already gone to Minneapolis. The President appealed to the congressional leaders for their support and spoke of the importance of a bipartisan front on Vietnam. Then he reached into his pocket and extracted a news-ticker story based on Humphrey's speech, which had not yet been delivered but which had been given to the press in advance. Johnson read Humphrey's rather emotional words and then administered a cutting rebuke to his Vice-President for departing from the official line. It lasted only a moment or two, but this thoughtless insult to the Vice-President in the presence of the White House staff, the Cabinet, and the congressional hierarchy made a chilling impression on those who heard it. Meanwhile, Humphrey was taking a telephone call from the White House. When he went before the Governors, the offending language had been deleted from his text.

The Tuesday night session at the White House had yet another surprise. Johnson normally held the floor at these briefing sessions, and then at the end asked for questions. This time, however, Senator Mike Mansfield broke precedent. He pulled from his pocket a three-page typed statement and read it in full. For a decade, Mansfield had become more and more skeptical about United States commitments to South Vietnam's changing governments, but as Senate Majority Leader he had suppressed his own criticism out of loyalty to the administration. On this day in the privacy of the Cabinet Room, however, he read to the President his carefully prepared dissent. While promising Johnson to stand behind him *publicly* on the large reinforcements to be sent to Vietnam, Mansfield made clear he was privately opposed to it and just about everything else the United States had done in Vietnam since Diem's murder, particularly the bombing in the North. Johnson was not pleased by the interruption. "Well, Mike," the President asked the Majority Leader, "what would *you* do?" Mansfield had no reply. But his statement was a sure signal of the liberal reaction to Johnson's decision.

The President's nationally televised message to the country the next day, July 28, was low-keyed and undramatic—purposely scheduled in midday, not in the evening when, as Johnson knew better than anyone, the television audience would have been much greater. The timing of the speech, the decision not to call up the reserves, and the subdued tone all added up to the loss of another opportunity to galvanize the American people and arouse their support for the war. But cautious though it was, the July 28 television appearance was still the

President's most effective declaration of American war aims up to that point.

Specifically, he announced an immediate, initial dispatch of fifty thousand men, including the famous First Cavalry Division (Air Mobile) to Vietnam. But beyond that, the President used the occasion to try once again to explain why the United States was in Vietnam. He began:

> Not long ago I received a letter from a woman in the Midwest. She wrote: "Dear Mr. President, in my humble way I am writing to you about . . . Vietnam. I have a son who is now in Vietnam. My husband served in World War II. Our country was at war but now, this time, it is something that I don't understand. Why?"

Johnson answered that poignant question as follows:

> Most of the non-Communist nations of Asia cannot, by themselves and alone, resist the growing might and grasping ambition of Asian Communism. Our power, therefore, is a vital shield. If we are driven from the field in Vietnam, then no nation can ever again have the same confidence in American promise or in American protection. In each land the forces of independence would be considerably weakened. And an Asia so threatened by Communist domination would imperil the security of the United States itself. . . .
>
> Moreover, we are in Vietnam to fulfill one of the most solemn pledges of the American nation. Three Presidents—President Eisenhower, President Kennedy, and your present President— over eleven years have committed themselves and have promised to help defend this small and valiant nation. . . . We cannot now dishonor our word or abandon our commitment.

Johnson's harshest critics scarcely heard him. Within minutes after the President finished speaking, Wayne Morse was on the Senate floor charging that the President had no authority to send troops without a declaration of war, and that therefore, "if American boys are killed in an undeclared war, it is murder." Grumbling over the dispatch of troops came from a good share of the Democratic side of the aisle in the Senate. A group of young Democratic House members were privately pushing a scheme to keep American troops penned up in enclaves, barring them from combat with the Vietcong.

For the moment, Johnson skillfully deflected attention from this Democratic criticism. Accounts of the highly confidential Tuesday night meeting at the White House, including Mansfield's reading of his manifesto, had leaked to the press. At the private request of the

White House staff, a reporter asked Johnson at an informal news conference at the LBJ Ranch on August 1 about the Mansfield report. Primed for the question, Johnson fingered Representative Gerald Ford of Michigan as the source of the news leak—without actually mentioning him by name. Seven months earlier Ford had ousted Charles Halleck as House Republican Leader. "That was the result of a man who broke my confidence and . . . distorted it," said Johnson, implicitly referring to Ford as "an inexperienced man, or a new one, or a bitter partisan." Ford hotly denied the President's implication the next day, and public attention was skillfully, if temporarily, transferred from the embarrassing criticism by Mansfield to a noisy partisan free-for-all with Ford.

By the time the First Cavalry had been assigned to Vietnam, the President was making clear to his top advisers that he was determined to settle the Vietnam question, and settle it quickly, in one of two ways: negotiations or military victory. He meant to pursue both courses simultaneously. As his captain on the negotiating front, the President assigned Arthur Goldberg, his peripatetic new Ambassador to the United Nations. But while cutting a broad swath at the UN, Goldberg's diplomatic overtures were no more successful than earlier United States efforts to bring the Communists to the negotiating table. Thus, the major personal effort by Johnson in the summer of 1965, and his principal hope, was necessarily on the military front. Almost every night for five months after July 28, Johnson stayed up past midnight to learn the results of major engagements between American forces and the Vietcong, how many United States planes had been shot down and whether "my boys" had been rescued.

The bombing program in the North had now become routine, but still Johnson personally supervised the choice of targets. Each week, McNamara formally asked the Joint Chiefs of Staff for a bombing plan for the ensuing seven days. The Joint Chiefs of Staff passed the request to the Commander-in-Chief, Pacific. The targets were laid out, described, and located, with an estimate of the number of sorties required, and the program returned to the Joint Chiefs in Washington, thence to McNamara and his deputy, Cyrus Vance, and then to the President. The President approved, disapproved, or changed the schedule, and the order to proceed went back to Saigon via the Joint Chiefs. The wonder of it, as the President commented to his advisers, was that from scratch in February, 1965, the bombing level was gradually escalated to some five thousand sorties a month one year later without intervention of any kind from Communist China, and with a bare minimum of civilian casualties in the North. It was one of the most exactingly supervised military operations in American history.

With increased operations in the North and the steady escalation of the ground war in the South through participation of American troops, there were favorable signs. The casualty rate among the Vietcong and North Vietnamese regulars continued to climb. So did the rate of Communist defectors, who reported shattered morale in the Vietcong base areas, now under heavy air attack from the B-52 superbombers. But the bombing program obviously was not reducing the infiltration of regular battalions from the North. And the improvement on the battlegrounds of the South, though significant and necessary, was far from conclusive. Clearly, the military victory the President wanted so badly was almost as distant in November as it had been in July. Although there was now no chance of *defeat* on the battlefield, as there had been early in the year, there was little chance of *victory* either, and the enemy still showed not the slightest interest in negotiations.

Early in November, the President received the first tentative proposal for a second bombing pause in the North. Oddly, it came not from the State Department but from the Defense Department, and it had the solidly responsible backing of Robert McNamara. For seven months, the bombs had dropped on North Vietnam, and it was this more than any other feature of the war that was making enemies for the President among the politicians, no longer limited just to the liberals. If the bombing were costing Ho Chi Minh so much that he would be forced to the conference table rather than absorb more punishment, then, of course, it should be continued. But it obviously was not.

In November, 1965, after long discussions with his staff, McNamara decided that instead of continuing the drip-drip-drip treatment the United States should try a sudden switch in tactics. If the daily pounding from the air was having not the slightest noticeable effect on Ho Chi Minh, perhaps breaking the pattern of bombing would break the pattern of intransigence in Hanoi and Peking. In early November, a long memorandum by McNamara suggesting this possibility, with a proposed Christmastime target date, was sent to the President. A second memorandum by McNamara, still more detailed, was drafted toward the end of that month and also went to the President's desk.

In the White House, McGeorge Bundy was skeptical. In the State Department, Dean Rusk at first opposed the idea. The President kept his own counsel. The first memo he read only hastily if at all. The sec-

ond he studied carefully, and for an interesting reason. A rash of headlines appeared in mid-November charging that the United States in
1964 had cavalierly rebuffed a peace effort by U Thant, Secretary
General of the United Nations. The news of Thant's aborted effort
came out in a *Look* article posthumously quoting Adlai Stevenson's
regret over the rebuff to Thant. Although every high official in the
Johnson Administration flatly denied the import of Stevenson's alleged criticism, the President was angered and embarrassed by stories
painting him as uninterested in peace. Always worried about his
image, he suddenly saw a tangible political motive for accepting
the McNamara arguments for a Christmas bombing pause. Just as his
"unconditional discussions" speech in April was a direct response to
his critics, so was he now deeply influenced by the bad publicity that
resulted from the Adlai Stevenson interview.

In December, during discussions at the LBJ Ranch, Johnson finally
agreed to go ahead with the pause. And once he made the decision, he
became the most enthusiastic exponent of the idea of a new pause and
quickly used it as the foundation block for what was to become the
most elaborate, most heavily publicized peace probe in the nation's
history. If we're going to have the pause, Johnson told his aides, let's
do it right!

Thus, on December 24 the cessation of bombing in the North was
announced for an indefinite period whose length no one could have
predicted in advance. Johnson was personally managing every detail of his peace offensive. On December 29, on notice of only a few
hours, he dispatched his emissaries around the world to talk peace,
stage-managing the leading actors and their itineraries himself with
just enough secrecy to give the whole enterprise the aura of international intrigue. This was the kind of theater that Johnson gloried in. With foreign heads of government part of his cast and the
whole world watching the drama unfold, the great peace offensive
of 1965 was a thrilling challenge, activated by the full power of the
presidency.

One by one, his special ambassadors were propelled to the four corners of the globe in special presidential jets: Averell Harriman to
Warsaw, the Middle East, and on around the world; Arthur Goldberg
to the Vatican; McGeorge Bundy to Canada; Thomas Mann to Mexico—all bearing the urgent message to the statesmen of the world that
the President of the United States wanted them to help in making
the bombing pause the prelude to negotiations and peace in Vietnam.

This was drama with the distinctive Johnson touch, as the Democratic Convention in Atlantic City bore that imprint, written, di-

rected, and produced by Lyndon Johnson. And for all its frenetic quality, it was a critical success, even if it didn't change Hanoi's mind. Because now, in one grand gesture, Johnson had convinced the skep- tics that his offer for "unconditional discussions" indeed was valid. He had seized the initiative, and his rating in the world's capitals as a man genuinely in search of peace would remain high in future months.

But in its primary purpose, the great peace offensive was as much a failure as the earlier bombing pause in May. When it became appar- ent that North Vietnam would not respond, the President had no op- tion but to order the bombing resumed. Although the private White House odds on success of the December-January pause had never been more than one chance in seven that Ho Chi Minh could be per- suaded to talk, failure came hard to Lyndon Johnson. For days he agonized over the question of when to end the pause, and he took pains to make the country aware of his agony through leaked stories to the press. Calling the congressional leaders to the White House to discuss the question of resuming the bombing, he read several para- graphs from Bruce Catton's *Never Call Retreat* depicting Abraham Lincoln's lonely agony during the Civil War.*

On January 31, 1966, having first ordered the State Department to send elaborate instructions to all American ambassadors, the Presi- dent reluctantly ordered the bombing to resume after a thirty-nine- day pause. The secret instructions to the ambassadors described ex- actly how to explain the President's position on the resumption to the governments involved. These instructions reviewed the ambitious, far- flung peace probe and detailed the lack of response from Hanoi and Peking. By contrast to its hopeful, exuberant beginning, the end of this experiment was sad and wearying for Lyndon Johnson, still recu- perating from his October 8 gall bladder operation. The end of the long pause was one more demonstration of Johnson's fierce desire to take the dispute to the negotiating table—and one more failure. The vicious cycle continued and peace seemed as distant as it ever had. Now, the President faced another session of Congress and a spirit of revolt quite absent the previous two years.

* Although Johnson told the congressional leaders he had been comforting him- self at night by reading the famous Civil War historian, the very copy of the book he held in his hand had been sent to him only that day, with the pertinent passage marked, by a Senator who wanted the President to know he had his sym- pathy. The Senator was Robert F. Kennedy.

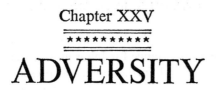

Chapter XXV

ADVERSITY

Well-rested and strengthened by pulse-feeling back home, the Congress returns to Washington far less docile and far more doubtful than when it left. . . .

—*Time*, January 14, 1966

Seldom had a Washington secret been so closely held on a matter not affecting the national security. When Lyndon Johnson drove up Pennsylvania Avenue the evening of Wednesday, January 12, 1966, to address a joint session of Congress, only four other people in the government knew that his State of the Union Address would propose a constitutional amendment to change the term of House members from two years to four years.

The President was bound and determined to keep it a complete surprise—or else! He warned Attorney General Nicholas de B. Katzenbach, who both drafted the constitutional amendment and would be in charge of guiding it through Congress, to maintain perfect security. If word leaked into the newspapers ahead of time, Johnson warned Katzenbach, he would drop the proposal from his speech and from his program.

Returning to the White House immediately after the speech, Johnson hurried to the wire-service tickers to examine the congressional reaction to his address. To his dismay, he quickly discovered that the four-year House term was under attack from a powerful figure: Representative Emanuel Celler of New York, chairman of the House Judiciary Committee which had life-and-death power over all proposed changes in the Constitution. Mightily annoyed by Celler's opposition, the President telephoned Katzenbach at home late at night. Why didn't you do your homework? he demanded of Katzenbach. Why didn't you bring Manny Celler into camp? Katzenbach patiently replied that the President's insistence on secrecy foreclosed all advance lobbying and this very foreclosure contributed to Celler's opposition. Irritated over not receiving advance notification, Celler felt no compunction about expressing his genuine opposition. His was the first of a fatal series of attacks on the four-year term.

The success or failure of the four-year-term proposal was, in itself, a matter of no great importance for Johnson. But the fact that the proposal was made at all and, furthermore, was presented with absolutely no advance preparation reflected what was wrong with Lyndon Johnson's third State of the Union Address.

When it became clear the previous summer that the first session of the 89th Congress would pass just about everything of significance in the Great Society program, the President wisely contemplated a minimal program for the second session. He spoke hopefully of adjournment by the Fourth of July—the earliest since 1953—so that happy and contented Democratic legislators, taking a spectacular record with them, could have the whole summer and autumn to campaign for the 1966 congressional election. Lawrence O'Brien, now Postmaster General but still Johnson's chief lobbyist, vigorously agreed that with little to be gained and much to be lost by a long 1966 session, it would be best to hurry Congress home with a truncated second session.

But the elaborate machinery set up by Johnson in 1964—the task forces, the White House memoranda, the legislative studies, the expert consultants—could not be stopped just by the press of a button. Like the sorcerer's apprentice, their output continued long after the master willed it otherwise. The flow of legislative proposals from the departments soon overwhelmed the White House. Importuned by Cabinet officers unwilling to see the pet proposals of their departments put aside for a whole year, White House staffers took the course of least resistance and crowded all the new ideas into the State of the Union Message. After all (so they rationalized) it can't *hurt*. Against his better judgment, Larry O'Brien acquiesced. More important, so did the President.

Consequently, the 1966 State of the Union Message was a throwback, in both length and heterogeneity, to the kind not seen since the 1950s, before President Eisenhower wisely switched from dreary catalogues of specific legislative requests to concise statements of general policy. For fifty minutes, Johnson droned on, mercifully faster than his usual leisurely pace, reciting legislative wants that the second session of the 89th Congress would need all year to satisfy, and then some.

The four-year term for House members was only the first unwelcome surprise.* Out flowed one new proposal after another as his con-

---

* The first reaction to the four-year plan was spontaneous cheering and applause from House members, delighted by the prospect of running for office half as often. By the time the President finished his address, however, many had started to nurse misgivings over political implications of the four-year term, fearing it would increase presidential power.

gressional audience gaped: removal of trade barriers with the Eastern European Communist bloc; a rebuilding program for urban slums; new ambitious anti-water and anti-air pollution programs; reform of the federal prison system; a new civil rights bill (the third in three years) including a federal prohibition against discrimination in both the sale and rental of housing; a Cabinet-level Department of Transportation; new community development districts for rural areas; a federal anti-crime program; a highway safety act; safeguards to protect the consumer; reorganization of the executive branch of the federal government; construction of a supersonic transport plane; revision of federal-state-city relationships; reform of laws governing contributions for political campaigns.

There was also unfinished business from the first session. Johnson asked Congress to complete it: repeal of Section 14(b) of the Taft-Hartley Labor Act; home rule for the District of Columbia; rent supplements for low-income families; a new Teacher Corps to help schooling in the city slums.

All this came as a shock to those who had expected partial suspension of the Great Society to finance the war in Vietnam. The former Senator from Texas, who in 1950 had rapped Harry Truman for seeking both guns *and* butter, was now doing precisely the same thing. He told the joint session:

> There are men who cry out: We must sacrifice. Let us rather ask them: whom will they sacrifice? Will they sacrifice the children who seek learning—the sick who need care—the families who dwell in squalor now brightened by hope of a home? Will they sacrifice opportunity for the distressed—the beauty of our land—the hope of the poor?
>
> Time may require further sacrifices. If so, we will make them. But we will not heed those who will wring it from the hopes of the unfortunate in a land of plenty. I believe we can continue the Great Society while we fight in Vietnam.

The guns and butter decision was also clearly evident in the President's record high budget estimate of 112.8 billion dollars for the fiscal year. Nor was there an income tax increase to finance this spending. Instead, the President rigged up a patchwork fiscal program of accelerated tax collections providing windfall collections on a one-year basis only, together with restoration of some of the excise taxes repealed only the previous summer. He was not asking for wartime sacrifice.

Indeed, his State of the Union Address was thirty-six minutes old before he began his exposition on Vietnam ("Tonight the cup of peril

is full in Vietnam," he began).* Hard talk about Vietnam was what
Congress and the nation had expected. But after the President recited
the liturgy of new Great Society proposals, the Congress and, presumably, the television audience, were anesthetized. The appeal for support on Vietnam came out flat and uninspiring. On this, his fifth
appearance as President before a joint session of Congress, Lyndon
Johnson had failed for the first time to evoke a sympathetic response.

The failure was more than artistic. That weighty list of Great Society proposals was a dead burden about the President's neck that he
had to carry through 1966. Most of his new proposals were too unfamiliar and too controversial for passage by what was now a far from
docile Congress. Furthermore, that long impassable list of bills kept
Congress in session months after Johnson would have wished it gone.
The 89th Congress, which started life as a well-oiled bill-passing machine would soon become unproductive, quarrelsome, and impatient
to second-guess the President about Vietnam. Within weeks, it was
clear that Johnson's third State of the Union Address was, particularly in comparison with the earlier two, a major blunder.

To say that the President took the course of least resistance by em-
bracing rather than resisting the avalanche of recommendations
spawned by his own legislative-drafting machinery is not enough to
explain the miscalculation. There was some conscious manipulation
by Johnson in his desire to minimize public uproar over Vietnam. By
prefacing his somber exposition of the Vietnam crisis with a laundry
list of legislative goals, he distracted the critics in the growing congressional Peace Bloc. But Johnson's espousal of the Great Society
was basically sincere. A nation where water and air would be free of
pollution, where city slums would be rebuilt, where highways would
be safer, where the federal bureaucracy would be more efficient—this
was the Great Society. Thus all these bills were worth proposing and
worth passing, Vietnam or no Vietnam. The fact that their proposal
might not be expedient or their passage might not be possible became
secondary to the President. In a sense, Johnson for the first time was
sublimating techniques (the effective use of power) to ideology (the
desire to become the President who changed the face of American society).

Here, too, was the corruptive quality of presidential power at work,
an example of the belief that there are few if any limitations on what a

---

* Despite the delay, this constituted the first full exposition of the Vietnam
question by Johnson in an appearance before a joint session of Congress. In his
1964 State of the Union Message, he had mentioned Vietnam only twice in passing. In his 1965 message, he had devoted only one hundred and twenty-six words
to Vietnam.

President can do. Mesmerized by his historic and prodigious legislative harvests of 1964 and 1965, Johnson made an uncharacteristic overestimate of what Congress would accept in 1966. He failed to appreciate the incipient rebellion on Capitol Hill in the late stages of the 1965 session when, after swallowing the landmark proposals of the Great Society, Congress choked on such relatively small measures as home rule for the District of Columbia and rent supplements.*

One extenuating circumstance partially explained Johnson's lapse in judgment. On October 8, 1965, his gall bladder and a ureter stone were removed in surgery at Bethesda Naval Hospital. Despite the cheery official bulletins about the President's condition, this operation was no frolic for a man of fifty-seven. Bone-tired and in constant pain following surgery, Johnson resisted efforts of his staff to impose the full burdens of the presidency on him even before he left Bethesda. When one presidential assistant handed him a complicated memorandum calling for a detailed response, the President replied by scrawling on it with his felt-tip pen in inch-high letters: "I'M SICK." Even after he left Bethesda, through the rest of 1965 and into the early weeks of 1966, the pain and fatigue continued to make it a period of unaccustomed low vitality and low activity for Johnson.

In such a weakened state, he could not be expected to maintain the efficient intelligence operation so vital to the Johnson System in the majority leadership days and continued into the presidential period. Without seeing and talking to members of Congress, he could not catch the ugly mood of growing revolt. Indeed, his very absence from the center of activity during the last three months of 1965 encouraged that mood. Members of Congress did not see the President either in intimate sessions in the Oval Office or in mass meetings in the East Room. The Johnson Treatment, so vital a part of the Johnson presidency, was dismantled during the President's long convalescence.

Thus, having misread the mood of Congress and having asked for far more than he could get, Johnson found himself, by virtue of his convalescence, unable to make the careful advance preparations for his overambitious program. For a politician of Johnson's innate caution, that was heresy. The fatal failure to notify Representative Celler about the four-year term for House members was symptomatic of 1966. Legislators first learned about new proposals over which their committees would have life-and-death power while sitting in the House chamber and hearing the President's address the night of January 12.

More important, however, was a basic decision stitched all through

* See page 500.

the State of the Union Address. In continuing to subordinate Vietnam to the Great Society in his message, Johnson was refusing to issue a clear and compelling call to his countrymen to stand up straight beside him. Implicit in that refusal was his continuing conviction that the more dangerous threat to him lay not in peace-minded doves but in war-courting hawks. He deliberately eschewed stirring up national fervor with an emotional appeal to the colors.

But it was Vietnam, still Vietnam, that remained the core of all of his problems. If that "dirty little" war ten thousand miles away would only disappear, all of the President's lesser afflictions—the revolt in Congress, the disappearing consensus, the curious joylessness pervading his administration—would shrink. But Vietnam would not go away. Rather, it became the awful adversity in Lyndon Johnson's presidency, the bone in his throat.

When a constituent of importance visited Senator Vance Hartke of Indiana in 1959 and 1960, he would often be escorted to Lyndon Johnson's Taj Mahal in the Capitol. No matter how busy the mighty Majority Leader might be, he would take time to usher the visitor into the splendid inner office with the thick, soft carpet, and exchange a word or two. Johnson also found time in the early evenings for highballs and political talk with the freshman Senator from Indiana. In short, Vance Hartke was a member of the Johnson Network. Eclipsed by the famous Governors and Congressmen elected to the Senate in the big Democratic Class of '58, the former Mayor of Evansville, Indiana, was an ideal candidate for the Majority Leader's cluster of satellites. Through Johnson, he found the sources of power in the Senate of the United States.

The relationship strengthened through the barren years of the vice-presidency and into Johnson's early presidency. But after the 1964 election, the President found fewer minutes to spend with his old Senate friends. Even Richard Russell was not so frequently consulted, and not so often invited to the White House. As Hartke saw less and less of the President, he began to pursue a more independent course. In the summer of 1965, Hartke took his first public stand in opposition to Johnson by leading the fight against General William F. McKee to head the Federal Aviation Agency.* Nor was Hartke's standing at the White House enhanced when Eliot Janeway, the New York financier, became his political patron. Janeway's old relationship with Johnson had long since cooled, and Johnson resented his intimacy with Hartke.

* See pages 499–500.

But Johnson did not really take offense until Hartke openly opposed him on the issue of Vietnam, the issue that had become the vital test of who was friend and who was foe of Lyndon Johnson. Through the 1965 session, Hartke had not been an identifiable member of the Senate's tiny Peace Bloc. But sometime before the 1966 session convened, his opposition matured. He concluded the increasing United States involvement was wrong, could lead to general war and—on this point, Hartke was most emphatic—would mean Democratic disaster in the 1966 congressional elections. When the second session of the 89th Congress convened, Hartke was ready for rebellion.

So were other Democratic Senators. The cloakrooms hummed with complaints and criticism over the President's Vietnam policy. What had started in 1964 with the two-man opposition of Wayne Morse and Ernest Gruening and then grew to a half dozen or more in 1965, now had mushroomed to perhaps half the sixty-six Democratic Senators in 1966. But there was no leadership, no cohesion, and little willingness to take an exposed position against the President.

The revolt was not joined until January 27 when Hartke, at least temporarily, supplied that leadership. He drafted a peremptory letter to Johnson urging him not to end the pause in the bombing of North Vietnam, talked fourteen other Senators into signing it, and then released it publicly. Signing the letter were familiar critics from the Peace Bloc, but now they were joined by new names not clearly aligned in the Vietnam debate—including Senator Eugene McCarthy of Minnesota, a serious prospect to become Johnson's Vice-President just eighteen months before. The outright opposition of the Hartkes and the McCarthys dramatized the harsh political fact that Johnson's problems had assumed a new and far more ominous dimension.

The President replied to the Hartke group with a curt, two-paragraph note. It was little more than an acknowledgment, and it wounded senatorial feelings, always tender, by referring to a longer, more complete response that Johnson had sent a group of House members who also had written him on Vietnam, but in much friendlier fashion than Hartke. Four days later, on January 31, Johnson ordered the resumption of bombing.

Actually, the fifteen names on the Hartke letter were no more than perhaps half the total number of Democratic Senators opposed to resumption of the bombing. Missing from the list, for example, was Majority Leader Mike Mansfield, who was finding it increasingly difficult to harmonize his loyalty to the President with his desire for a soft line on Vietnam and now made no secret of his opposition to ending the pause.

Also opposed to the renewed bombing but absent from the Hartke list was Senator J. W. Fulbright, who had moved into open conflict with the President since their rupture over the Dominican intervention. Fulbright, the Rhodes scholar who had always insisted that his Foreign Relations Committee operate soberly and somberly *in camera*, had cast aside his scruples and was preparing a televised inquiry into Vietnam in the Caucus Room of the Old Senate Office Building— scene of so many investigative extravaganzas.

The change in technique reflected a basic, even momentous change in goals and constitutional philosophy. Ever conscious of the President's constitutional prerogative to make foreign policy, Fulbright was now launching a naked congressional attempt to force a change in Johnson's Vietnam policy by putting that policy on public trial. In short, he intended to go over the President's head to the people. One of Fulbright's committee members said privately that if the investigation undermined the country's confidence in its President, that was a small price to pay for changing American policy in Vietnam. Clearly, feeling was running deep in the greatly expanded Peace Bloc.

There was a time in his majority leadership, or perhaps early in his presidency, when Johnson would have tried to conciliate his old friends—Fulbright, Mansfield, and Hartke—and make them Johnson men again. But Johnson's pattern had changed. Now he ignored his old allies of the past who had gone astray. Instead, he set out to find new friends. That was a conscious exercise of the power of the presidency, but it created pockets of deep resentment in the Senate. The old friends felt aggrieved, and aggrieved friends make bitter enemies.

Fulbright, who in the early weeks of the Johnson presidency had sat upstairs in the White House with Dean Acheson, Clark Clifford, and Tom Mann and gaily edited the President's speech to the United Nations, was no longer welcome at the White House—for either intimate visits or formal occasions. Johnson privately described Mansfield as a combination of Jeanette Rankin and Burton K. Wheeler, one famed as a pacifist, the other as an isolationist, from Mansfield's home state of Montana—an unfriendly characterization that quickly threaded its way through the Washington gossip mill back to the Majority Leader.

But while Fulbright and Mansfield had been former allies, Hartke was a protégé and received the full measure of presidential anger. When another Democratic Senator delivered a speech about Vietnam, Johnson telephoned to congratulate him on a constructive suggestion, and gratuitously remarked that he was "not like that obscenity Hartke." Later, when Hartke took a group of Indiana party workers on a tour of the White House, the President made it his business not to greet them and, through Bill Moyers, publicly referred to Hartke as "obstreperous." Presidential resentment of Hartke extended to the Department of Agriculture, which refused to reappoint Hartke's men to the agricultural stabilization committees in Indiana. All this was part of the exercise of power. Making an example of Hartke might be a warning to others.

Significantly, in the only direct effort Johnson made to change the mind of those who signed the Hartke letter, he used a third person, General Maxwell Taylor, rather than himself. Taylor, the distinguished soldier-diplomat, had returned from his tour as Ambassador to Saigon and was part-time consultant to the President. Johnson sent him to Capitol Hill to explain Vietnam policy to two signatories of the Hartke letter, Senators McCarthy and Gaylord Nelson of Wisconsin. They were not moved. The revolt on Vietnam was not so easily quelled, and Johnson instinctively sensed that fact. And so instead of trying to convert the Peace Bloc, he set about building a new Johnson Network of younger Senators who would support him on Vietnam: Gale McGee of Wyoming (who would soon become the President's leading spokesman on the Foreign Relations Committee), Birch Bayh of Indiana, and Fred Harris of Oklahoma. They replaced the Hartkes, Fulbrights, and Mansfields at informal suppers at the White House.

So did Senator Paul Douglas of Illinois, whose crusading liberalism had so often been mocked and foiled by Majority Leader Johnson. Douglas, a hard-line anti-Communist, had suddenly become a friend in need for President Johnson. He backed him on Vietnam, and did so at the cost of some of his liberal supporters in an election year. Douglas became a guest at the LBJ Ranch as the President recuperated from his gall bladder operation and was told by Johnson his election to a fourth term in the Senate was the most important political necessity of 1966. Having lost his old allies, Johnson embraced an old enemy.

If the Peace Bloc could not be conciliated, the President was limited in his response to the growing revolt on Capitol Hill. Fearing popular demand for overescalation of the Vietnamese conflict resulting in the apocalyptic possibility of general war with China, he still shied away from patriotic appeals to the people. Instead, what Johnson sought was a new masterstroke on the order of his Johns Hopkins speech of a year earlier, some fresh initiative to still, at least for a while, his liberal critics. Johnson had coupled his January 31 announcement of resumed bombing with a declaration that the United States would seek a United Nations debate on the Vietnam question, long a demand of the Peace Bloc. But by early 1966, taking Vietnam to the UN was too little, too late. Besides, as Johnson's advisers had said all along, Vietnam quickly sank into the miasma of UN parliamentary intricacies. Clearly, something more was needed for Johnson to regain the initiative at home on Vietnam.

On Friday, February 4, a member of McGeorge Bundy's "Little State Department" in the basement of the White House decided things were slow enough for the first time in many days to permit him to go outside for lunch in a restaurant. He returned an hour later to find the usually imperturbable Bundy in a dither. "Where in the world have you been?" Bundy exclaimed. He had good reason to be excited. The President had suddenly decided to leave the very next day for a face-to-face meeting in Honolulu with Air Vice Marshal Nguyen Cao Ky, the flashy thirty-three-year-old aviator who had become Premier in the military government holding forth in Saigon. Lyndon Johnson had decided on his masterstroke to recapture the initiative in the political battling over Vietnam.

The idea for Honolulu was not a new one but had been brewing at the White House for several months. Howard Jones, former Ambassador to Indonesia and now Chancellor of the East-West Center at the University of Hawaii, had strongly advocated a novel proposal: an all-Asia summit meeting in Hawaii. Both McGeorge Bundy and Dean Rusk liked it and Johnson himself was enthusiastic. But after the President's gall bladder operation in October, other projects of greater priority superseded Honolulu and the plan languished. Now, on February 4, with Fulbright's nationally televised hearings in progress, the President resurrected it for immediate use to regain the spotlight. Indeed, Fulbright's hearings on Friday afternoon were interrupted on the television screen by the President's announcement of the sudden trip.

The White House staff quickly decided that the time was far too short to work out Jones' original plan for an all-Asia conference, but the President and high Cabinet officials would go to Honolulu to meet the top officials in the Saigon regime, including Marshal Ky. Equally important, Johnson would meet General Westmoreland, the United States military commander.

The theme of the Honolulu conference was to be the peaceful reconstruction of South Vietnam, first, because Johnson deeply believed in it, and second, because it should improve the President's position in the political debate at home. To emphasize the importance of reconstruction as apart from the United States military operations, the President took along two Cabinet members far removed from the military and all other aspects of national security—John Gardner of Health, Education, and Welfare and Orville Freeman of Agriculture. These two were to proceed to Vietnam itself for a quick study of conditions there.

On that Friday afternoon before the presidential party left Washington, it was decided that a mere communiqué at the end of the Johnson-Ky meeting would be prosaic. A full-fledged "Declaration of Honolulu" was needed, pledging the reconstruction of South Vietnam, but time was short. As Air Force One streaked across the continent and then the Pacific on Saturday, Lyndon Johnson's first transoceanic flight as President, Bundy and his staff hurriedly began preparation of the Declaration of Honolulu.

By the time Johnson and Ky had finished their cordial though scarcely momentous talks on Tuesday, February 8, it was ready to be issued. Most important were its nonmilitary provisions, pledging the Saigon government to "the eradication of social injustice," to "a true social revolution," and to "a modern society in which every man . . . has respect and dignity." For its part, the United States pledged "special support to the work of the people of that country to build even while they fight."

Beyond the rhetoric were some solid accomplishments. Just as Lincoln conferred with his generals in their tents from time to time, so did Bundy want Johnson to meet Westmoreland. Their encounter was cordial, and the President went away with a better appreciation of that remarkable military man. Moreover, Johnson was able to lay down the law to Ky, as no ambassador in Saigon could, making him understand that the United States was insisting that Saigon start a social and economic revolution and start at once. For good measure, Vice-President Humphrey was dispatched to Saigon as soon as the Honolulu conference had ended.

But reminiscent of Johnson's sudden unveiling of the Mekong River development plan in the Johns Hopkins speech a year earlier, the Honolulu conference had a haphazard, impromptu quality. Furthermore, in the Honolulu meeting were seeds of impending trouble. For example, in the haste of organizing the trip on February 5, it was decided that an invitation issued at that late date to Prime Minister Harold Holt of Australia would be considered an affront. In fact, Holt, who had taken a grave political risk in sending a contingent of troops to Vietnam in the first dispatch of conscript soldiers to a foreign war in Australia's history, was hurt that he was not invited.

But a more fundamental hazard was that the hastily planned conference would upset the delicate alignment of South Vietnamese politics in a way that could have calamitous results which would not be certain for weeks to come.

Nor did Honolulu achieve Johnson's purpose of drawing attention away from the Peace Bloc. The transparent effort to steal the headlines from the Fulbright hearings received almost as much attention, all of it adverse, as did the substance of the conference itself. When the Foreign Relations Committee hearings resumed on February 11, Fulbright snapped testily that the Honolulu conference had so hardened the American commitment to the Saigon government that it posed "a further obstacle to a negotiated settlement" with the Vietcong. The conference was soon forgotten in the United States, and the nation's television watchers fixed their attention on the historic Senate Caucus Room.

Johnson's worries that the hearings would generate a national tide of sentiment against continuing the war proved groundless. His two spokesmen, Dean Rusk and Maxwell Taylor, handled Fulbright with skill. But seated in the rear of the Caucus Room was a serious-faced young man with a shock of bushy chestnut hair: Senator Robert F. Kennedy of New York, next to Johnson himself the most intriguing political figure in the nation.

From the moment of his election to the Senate in 1964, Bobby Kennedy became the hope for the future to New Frontiersmen who counted the days to a Kennedy restoration. Kennedy had no desire to break openly with Johnson and lead a government-in-exile. But he did regard himself as preserver of John F. Kennedy's mystique and, a critic by nature, he began through 1965 to take issue here and there with Lyndon Johnson's presidency, particularly his foreign policy. He was less than happy with the Dominican intervention. By calling for greater efforts to halt the threatened proliferation of nuclear weapons, he implied Johnson was not doing enough in the field of disarmament. Prior to and during a South American trip late in 1965, he left an impression that it was he who was adhering to the true meaning of his brother's Alliance for Progress and that the *Alianza* was being subtly debased by Johnson.

On the central issue of Vietnam, he similarly held views critical of Johnson but kept them to himself. Kennedy stayed aloof from the Peace Bloc in the Senate. Although his key foreign policy aide was in intimate and sympathetic contact with its plans, Kennedy declined to attend meetings of the bloc. Declining also an invitation to sign the Hartke letter attacking the resumption of bombing, Kennedy instead issued a statement that was equivocal as to whether the bombing should have been resumed, but that suggested bombing in the North would never win the war ("If we regard bombing as the answer to Vietnam, we are headed straight for disaster," he said). Kennedy's uncharacteristic reticence resulted from his refusal to split the Democratic party and, indeed, the entire nation, into Johnson and Kennedy wings over so critical an issue as Vietnam.

Yet, Bobby Kennedy was no man to keep quiet indefinitely on the great issue of the day. Sitting in on the Fulbright hearings brought him to the erroneous conclusion, which was to seem naïve in hindsight, that he could make a constructive suggestion which, even though a sharp departure from Johnson's Vietnam policy, would not lead to a personal split with Johnson. In fact, however, his suggestion became a *cause célèbre* and the split with the administration he had carefully sought to avoid was immediate.

Kennedy did not appreciate the significance of what he was about to say. In private conversation with his aides before his press conference on Saturday, February 19, he was skeptical whether his statement would arouse much interest. The proposal he was about to make had already been made by Eugene McCarthy, without attracting a single headline. At that press conference, Kennedy took pains to spell out that he rejected United States withdrawal from Vietnam as "impossible for this country." But the heart of his statement was this: "We must reveal enough of our intentions to Hanoi to eliminate any reasonable fear that we ask them to talk only to demand surrender." That means, he went on, granting the Vietcong "a share of the power and responsibility" under a new coalition government in Saigon.

Unintentional though it was, here was the long-expected public break. McGeorge Bundy and Under Secretary of State George Ball in Washington and the Vice-President on his Far Eastern tour immediately attacked Kennedy's position (Humphrey compared Vietcong in the Saigon government to "putting foxes in the hen house"). A Democratic party already split into warring camps on the transcendent issue of Vietnam now was in danger of becoming split into Johnson and Kennedy factions. Democrats from one end of the country to the other were picking sides, though faintly understanding the substance of the Washington debate that was to rage in the coming weeks over the desirability of a coalition government in Saigon. Kennedy's Vietnam stand put still another crack in what used to be Johnson's consensus, subtly diminishing a major source of his strength. Thus did one press conference by Kennedy limit Johnson's power at a time of maximum adversity.

Lyndon Johnson was regaining his full physical vigor. Once again, The Treatment was being administered—to intimate groups around his desk, to large groups in the East Room. Every member of Congress was invited to the East Room in two shifts, on February 24 and 25, nominally to hear Vice-President Humphrey report on his trip to the Far East. But it was the President who popped up to field the questions in his old-time bantering form.

At one session, Johnson commented that Senator Stephen Young of Ohio, a particularly vocal member of the Peace Bloc, had remarked publicly that he wouldn't sleep well so long as Dean Rusk was Secretary of State. "I went to the drugstore last night," the President told his congressional audience, "to buy Steve Young some sleeping pills, because Dean Rusk is going to be Secretary of State for a long, long time, and Steve ought to be sleeping nights."

Still, the President believed his real danger came not from the doves but from the hawks. At every session in the East Room, he explained —in graphic, earthy terms—the need for restraint in confronting Communist power in Asia. Always he talked of a confrontation not between the United States and China, but between *Lyndon Johnson* and China. "I don't want China to spit in my eye, and I don't want to spit in China's eye," he would say.

Johnson was looking ahead to the vote on the supplemental appropriations bill providing another 4.8 billion dollars for the military, and so was the Peace Bloc. The doves now reckoned that perhaps thirty Democratic Senators were in some degree of opposition to Johnson's Vietnam policy. If that many could actually be recorded, they believed, it might even change the policy. Moreover, they were now claiming Bobby Kennedy as one of their own for the first time. His bridges to the administration temporarily burned, Kennedy attended his first closed-door session with the Peace Bloc on Saturday, February 26, one week to the day after his statement proposing a coalition government in Saigon, and argued against any showdown vote on the floor of the Senate.

That session was, like all the others, lacking in any consensus. The doves could find no answer to the problem they had been puzzling over since the first of the year. What kind of issue could be brought forth on the floor of the Senate to produce the maximum votes? Senators shied away from an actual cut in military appropriations with a shooting war in progress. Richard Russell almost solved the Peace

Bloc's problem when he introduced an amendment reaffirming Johnson's authority to use American military power in Vietnam, a resolution that almost certainly would have drawn a score or more Senators in opposition. But after a call from the President, Russell dropped the amendment. Johnson wanted no showdown either.

All that remained was a narrow amendment by Wayne Morse that would repeal the August, 1964, Tonkin Bay Resolution, which Fulbright and others deeply resented as one of the basic sources of power claimed by Johnson for growing American participation in the war. That vote on March 2 was 92 to 5, with Fulbright severing all ties with Johnson to join the five dissenters. Johnson had weathered the worst of the anti-Vietnam rebellion in the Senate. On the next day, March 3, McNamara increased the United States troop commitment another thirty thousand to two hundred and thirty-five thousand.

Just one month later, the President confronted an unwelcome legacy of the Honolulu conference. Returning from Hawaii with the embrace of Johnson still fresh, Ky had wildly brandished his new power by removing General Nguyen Chanh Thi, a semiautonomous warlord and a favorite of the Buddhist politicians, from command of the First Corps in the northern part of South Vietnam. That was the signal for the Buddhist leaders to set in motion rioting against Ky in Hue, Danang, and eventually in the capital of Saigon, much of it with a strongly anti-American flavor. Until a stopgap political solution could be worked out, the war came to a virtual standstill.

Even if Ky had not fired Thi, the Buddhist revolt would have come sooner or later. But the fact remains that the confidence instilled in Ky by Johnson emboldened him to move against Thi and thereby set in motion the dangerous chain of events.

Even though it was irrational to blame the instability of Vietnamese political institutions on the Hawaii conference, every anti-American slogan shouted in the streets of Saigon, meant that support for the President's policy at home was fading. Members of Congress returning from the Easter recess from every part of the country told the same story. Everywhere, voters were asking why it was that they and their sons should die for a people who apparently did not want to be helped. Johnson's consensus was shrinking at an ever more rapid pace.

As the insoluble problem of Vietnam agonized Washington and the nation, the list of new Great Society proposals that the President had submitted on January 12 seemed lifeless in Congress through the winter and spring. Repeal of Taft-Hartley's Section 14(b) failed. The four-year term for House members was given up for dead. Lesser proposals were not even considered.

Nor was Vietnam the only source of trouble for the Great Society consensus. Organized labor, angered at Johnson's efforts to fight inflation by controlling wage increases and his inability to repeal Section 14(b), threatened to break its ties with the Democratic party. After Johnson's successful roll-back of attempted price increases in aluminum, copper, and steel late in 1965 through full use of government power, the unprecedented support that business had given Johnson declined in both size and intensity.

The President's relations with Democratic party leaders across the country were chilly. Never fully at home with national Democratic politics, the President in his preoccupation over Vietnam had turned control over the Democratic National Committee to his appointments secretary and confidential assistant, Marvin Watson. A conservative Texan with less understanding of national politics than Johnson, Watson promptly dismantled the apparatus of the National Committee to save a few thousand dollars.

And with Johnson's popularity ebbing, Democratic Congressmen, fearing a Republican resurgence in November, 1966, rejected close identification with him.

But these were manageable problems of limited dimension. All of them could have been coped with by the master of power in the White House had it not been for Vietnam. Vietnam was the malignant cancer of the Great Society, somber and oppressive. It infected all else in 1966—a bloody, insoluble dilemma that did not lend itself to the brilliant weapons of power developed by Lyndon Johnson during thirty-five years in politics.

Thus, on May 13, 1966, at the National Guard Armory in Washington, Johnson unsheathed one of those weapons—the sharp saber of sarcasm—as he addressed a $100-a-plate Democratic fund-raising dinner. Twenty seats down the head table from the President was J. W. Fulbright, now the uncrowned leader of the Peace Bloc. Fulbright was becoming increasingly biting and immoderate in his attacks on the "arrogance of power" displayed by Johnson and the United States in Vietnam.

The President began by saying that he was "glad to be here among so many friends—and some members of the Foreign Relations Committee." Embarrassed laughter. "You can say one thing about those [Foreign Relations Committee] hearings," said the President, "but I don't think this is the place to say it." More embarrassment. In a party so deeply split, the sarcasm was resented. Nor was there enthusiasm for the President's summons to all Democratic candidates that night to campaign on a policy of supporting his stand in Vietnam. It was, on the whole, a sour night for both Lyndon Johnson and his party, and it reflected how useless Johnson's old and tested political weapons were in dealing with the great crisis of Vietnam.

Throughout his long climb upward, Johnson's posture had always been deliberately and necessarily flexible. There was, first, his shifting constituency in Texas. Representing the barren hill country of poor farmers and small-town merchants still impoverished by the Depression, Johnson was Franklin Roosevelt's young protégé, a New Deal stalwart. Then, seeking the larger constituency of all of Texas—including the new Texas of oil and big money—Johnson became a labor-baiting, Southern-style freshman Senator. And in the Senate, Johnson survived in two worlds: that of Senate Majority Leader, a national party spokesman, and that of a Texan who was never quite sure of survival in his home base. And finally, the emancipation from that Texas constituency to become Vice-President, free now at last to be as liberal as necessary for his national constituency. Up that long and tortuous path, his flexibility of ideology was essential to maximize his power.

He had magnified those pitifully small prerogatives of the Majority Leader's office and made that office, while he held it, one of the mightiest in the land. Once in the White House, he had further stretched and refined to new dimensions the powers of an office inherently more powerful than any in the world.

For the most part, the power of Lyndon Johnson had been well used for public purpose. His Senate had censured Joe McCarthy, passed the first civil rights act since Reconstruction and subdued a brief but concentrated assault on the Supreme Court by the reactionaries. His presidency had welded together a national consensus at an hour of strife and sorrow, tamed the Congress to produce a vast outpouring of legislation, and presided over an unprecedented economic prosperity.

But Vietnam was none of these. Here Johnson's flexibility, which had enabled him so long to endure and grow, was of no avail. It was, perhaps, a liability. Wayne Morse could draw from his rigid ideology the certitude that the United States *must* withdraw from Vietnam. Richard Russell could conclude from his own set of principles that the United States *must* increase its use of armed power to win the war or withdraw. But for Johnson, the pragmatist and the compromiser, there were no axioms and no certitudes. He could not call upon the nation to wage holy war—nor withdraw from the holocaust. Torn between the need to hold the line against Communist aggression and fear of a general war, he had no complete answer. Perhaps that would turn out to be best for the nation. But the ideological flexibility that had always served him so well before, that had allowed him to move from one political milieu to another, and that had brought him to the presidency, could bring no great triumph now. Even his diplomatic breakthrough in the Dominican Republic produced no outburst of applause. Much to the consternation of Johnson's inner circle, only silence came from arch-critic Fulbright.

As the summer of 1966 began, United States forces were scoring consistent military successes against both the Vietcong and North Vietnamese regulars. Moreover, free elections in South Vietnam had been scheduled with at least some hope for political stability. But the Gallup Poll in June showed Johnson's popularity at only 46 percent, the lowest since Harry Truman.

Never was there an unhappier warrior than the Commander-in-Chief in mid-1966. For the future and shape of Lyndon Baines Johnson's presidency rested with events singularly intransigent, taking place 10,000 miles away in a war that month after month refused to respond to the mastery and exercise of presidential power.

SOURCE NOTES

Our basic sources for information not contained in the public record were, first, our own experience as reporters in Washington; and second, more than two hundred special interviews with political figures and government officials who were either participants in or observers of the events described. The information derived from both our day-to-day reporting and from these special interviews was obtained on a confidential basis. Therefore, we cannot disclose the source of the original information contained in this book.

The purpose of these notes is extremely limited. It is to attribute information not obtained by us from primary sources or contained in the public record but derived from secondary sources. Such sources were of only limited value in researching Johnson's Senate period and of even less value in our study of the presidential period.

CHAPTER II

Pp. 11–12: The Garner incident is from Michael C. Janeway, "Lyndon Johnson and the Rise of Conservatism in Texas" (Unpublished thesis. Harvard University, 1962).

Pp. 22–23: The origin and growth of Johnson's television interests is taken from articles by Louis M. Kohlmeier in the *Wall Street Journal* of March 23 and 24, 1964.

CHAPTER IV

Pp. 56–57: The account of the Johnson-Humphrey conversation is based in part on Winthrop Griffith, *Humphrey: A Candid Biography* (New York: William Morrow, 1965), pp. 213–214.

CHAPTER VI

P. 105: "a good deal more attractive"—Arthur M. Schlesinger, Jr., *A Thousand Days: John F. Kennedy in the White House* (Boston: Houghton Mifflin, 1965), p. 11.

Pp. 116–117: The analysis of Johnson's stop-and-go tactics in 1959 is from Austin P. Sullivan, Jr., "Lyndon Johnson and the Senate Majority Leadership" (Unpublished thesis. Princeton University, 1964).

CHAPTER VII

P. 132: "in my purpose of protecting"—Dwight D. Eisenhower, *Waging Peace* (Garden City, N. Y.: Doubleday, 1965), p. 156.

P. 133 fn.: "a blow"—*ibid.*, p. 158.

P. 137: "any labor skate"—Douglass Cater, "How the Senate Passed the Civil Rights Bill," *The Reporter* (September 5, 1957).

P. 139: "I can get Ervin"—Eisenhower, *op. cit.*, p. 161.

CHAPTER VIII

P. 144: "Naturally, we don't know yet"—*Newsweek* (December 6, 1954).

P. 155 ftn.: "lost opportunities"—Richard Neuberger, "Making a Scapegoat of Lyndon Johnson," *New Republic* (July 4, 1955).

CHAPTER IX

P. 169: "made the weekly meetings"—Sherman Adams, *Firsthand Report: The Story of the Eisenhower Administration* (New York: Harper, 1961), p. 26.

P. 169: "always reacted impulsively"—Eisenhower, *op. cit.*, p. 384.

P. 169: "skill in legislative maneuver"—Eisenhower, *op. cit.*, p. 11.

P. 174: "The existing vacuum"—*ibid.*, p. 178.

P. 175: "You know you are as welcome"—*ibid.*, p. 179.

P. 179: "After all, there are times"—Adams, *op. cit.*, p. 282.

P. 182: "that gummed up the sapworks"—*ibid.*, p. 367.

P. 188: "irresponsible diminution"—Eisenhower, *op. cit.*, p. 138.

CHAPTER X

P. 205: "Every sort of foolish proposal"—*ibid.*, p. 385.

P. 213: "It should not have taken the Senate"— *ibid.*, p. 392.

P. 214–15: The Dodd incident is from Sullivan, *op. cit.*

P. 222: "a somewhat awkward attempt."—Eisenhower, *op. cit.*, p. 557.

CHAPTER XI

P. 236: "It's the Governor's decision"—Ralph G. Martin, *Ballots & Bandwagons* (Chicago, New York, San Francisco: Rand McNally, 1964), p. 400.

P. 238: "I talked to Lyndon"—*ibid.*, p. 411.

P. 240: The Bean incident is from Larry L. King, "Growing Up with Lyndon B. Johnson" (Unpublished ms., 1966).

CHAPTER XIII

Pp. 275–76: The Sorensen-Baker conversation is referred to in Theodore Sorensen, *Kennedy* (Harper & Row, 1965), p. 165. Further details were supplied by Sorensen during his October 3, 1965, appearance on "Meet the Press."

P. 283: "A large group of Southern Governors"—J. Oliver Hall, "The Behavior of the Michigan Delegation to the Democratic National Convention on the Nomination of Lyndon B. Johnson for Vice President" (Unpublished ms., 1963).

P. 284: "Jack wants Lyndon" and other Michigan comments—*ibid.*

P. 284: "the prerogative of the nominee"—*ibid.*

P. 285: "That's all right, Bobby's been out of touch"—Memorandum by Philip Graham published as appendix to Theodore White, *The Making of the President, 1964* (New York: Atheneum, 1965).

CHAPTER XVI

P. 344: The Busby incident is from Stewart Alsop, "Johnson Takes Over: The Untold Story," *The Saturday Evening Post* (February 15, 1964).

CHAPTER XVIII

P. 384: The Bhutto incident is from Philip L. Geyelin, *Lyndon B. Johnson and the World* (New York: Frederick A. Praeger, 1966), p. 3.

P. 385–86: The de Gaulle-Alphand incident is from *ibid.*, p. 4.

CHAPTER XXIII

P. 511: "a decent democratic reg'me"—Schlesinger, *op. cit.*, p. 769.

INDEX

ABOUT THE AUTHORS

ROWLAND EVANS was graduated from Kent School and attended Yale until the outbreak of World War II, when he joined the Marines and served in the Solomons. His first newspaper job was with the Philadelphia *Bulletin.* He moved to the Associated Press Washington Bureau in 1945, and was assigned to cover the U. S. Senate in 1953. Two years later he transferred to the New York *Herald Tribune* Washington Bureau, where he covered politics and Congress. On the foreign scene he traveled extensively in Eastern Europe, the Soviet Union and the Far East, writing for the *Herald Tribune* and various magazines. On May 15, 1963, Mr. Evans joined with Robert Novak in writing a daily Washington column, "Inside Report," nationally syndicated by the Publishers Newspaper Syndicate. Writing by himself and in collaboration with Mr. Novak, Rowland Evans' work has appeared in the *Saturday Evening Post, Harper's Magazine, The Reporter,* the *New Republic* and other national magazines.

ROBERT NOVAK was graduated from the Joliet, Illinois, Township High School and the University of Illinois. His first newspaper job was as a reporter for the Joliet *Herald-News* in 1948. He later worked for the Champaign-Urbana *Courier* before Korean War service as an Army lieutenant. Following his discharge from the service, he joined the staff of the Associated Press in Omaha, Nebraska, in 1954. He was later transferred to Indianapolis, to cover the statehouse and politics. In 1957, the AP transferred him to Washington, where he helped cover Capitol Hill. He joined the Washington Bureau of the *Wall Street Journal* in 1958 as Senate correspondent and political reporter, becoming chief Congressional correspondent for the *Journal* in 1961. As a *Journal* reporter, he traveled from coast to coast in covering the national political campaigns of 1958, 1960 and 1962. In May, 1963, Mr. Novak teamed with Rowland Evans to write the syndicated political column, "Inside Report." He is the author of *The Agony of the G.O.P. 1964* and his writings, both alone and in collaboration with Evans, have appeared in many national magazines.